NSEN

r

FEMINISTS DESPITE THEMSELVES

Feminists Despite Themselves:

Women in Ukrainian Community Life, 1884–1939

by
Martha Bohachevsky-Chomiak

Canadian Institute of Ukrainian Studies
University of Alberta
Edmonton   **1988**

Copyright © 1988   **Canadian Institute of Ukrainian Studies**
University of Alberta
Edmonton, Alberta, Canada

Canadian Cataloguing in Publication Data
Bohachevsky-Chomiak, Martha.
Feminists despite themselves.
Includes index.
ISBN 920862-57-8
1. Feminism - Ukraine.   2. Women's rights - Ukraine.
I. Canadian Institute of Ukrainian Studies.   II. Title.
HQ1664.U4B65 1988.   305.4'2'094771   C88-091068-2

Cover design: Tanya Krawciw

Distributed by   University of Toronto Press
5201 Dufferin St.
Downsview, Ontario
Canada M3H 5T8

DEDICATION

To my mother, Rostyslava Nychay Bohachevsky, and in her person to the women of the Ukrainian National Women's League of America who served as a link between the values of the old country and the opportunities offered by the new. Their work has made possible our own.

Contents

Terminological note

Historically Ukrainians have also referred to themselves as Ruthenians, a Latinized form of *Rusyn*, which derived from the medieval state of Rus'. The designation, which had important political repercussions in nineteenth-century Western Ukraine, is mentioned only where appropriate. For our purposes, Ukrainians and Ruthenians are the same people.

Another thorny issue is the translation of the term *narodnyi*, which can be rendered either as "people's" or "national." However, there is a specific term in Ukrainian for the latter (*natsionalnyi*), and the use of the term *narodnia* during the revolutionary period of 1917–21 inclines me to translate *Ukrainska Narodnia Respublika* as Ukrainian People's Republic (UNR). Yet even in émigré circles, the popular appellation *narodnia* rather than the specifically national *natsionalna* continued to be used when referring to the nation.

Finally, for the sake of simplicity, the name of the major Western Ukrainian territory, Halychyna, has been Latinized as Galicia, and Peremyshl is referred to by its current form, Przemysl.

List of Abbreviations

I have used the modified Library of Congress transliteration system.

AAN Archiwum Akt Nowych, Warsaw

AGAD Archiwum Akt Dawnych, Warsaw

AGKB Archiwum Grecko-Katolickiego Biskupstwa, Przemyśl

CPWU Communist Party of Western Ukraine

EU *Entsyklopediia Ukrainoznavstva*

ICW International Council of Women

LNV Literaturno-naukovyi visnyk

NTSh Naukove Tovarystvo im. Shevchenka

ODIA Oblasnyi Derzhavnyi Istorychnyi Arkhiv, Lviv

OUN Organization of Ukrainian Nationalists

RSDLP Russian Social Democratic Labour Party

RUP Revolutionary Ukrainian Party

TsDIA Tsentralnyi Derzhavnyi Istorychnyi Arkhiv, Kiev and Lviv

TsGIA Tsentralnyi Gosudarstvennyi Istoricheskii Arkhiv, Moscow

TsGALI Tsentralnyi Gosudarstvennyi Arkhiv Literatury, Moscow

TsGAOR Tsentralnyi Gosudarstvennyi Arkhiv Oktiabrskoi Revoliutsii, Moscow

UID Ukrainskyi Instytut dlia Divchat, Przemyśl

UNDO Ukrainian National Democratic Alliance

UNR Ukrainian People's Republic

URE *Ukrainska Radianska Entsyklopediia*

URSP Ukrainian Radical Socialist Party

URSR Ukrainian Soviet Socialist Republic

USDLP Ukrainian Social Democratic Labour Party

USRP Ukrainian Social Revolutionary Party

USSR Union of Soviet Socialist Republics

UVAN   Ukrainian Academy of Arts and Sciences in the U.S., New York
VSE   *Vistnyk Stanyslavivskoi Eparkhii*
WAP   Wojewódzkie Archiwum Panstwowe, Przemyśl
WUNR   Western Ukrainian National Republic

Preface

Throughout the years, many persons and institutions helped me on this book. Credit is due first and foremost to the Ukrainian National Women's League of America and its president, Mrs. Iwanna Rozhankowsky, who supported me financially and emotionally through the research and writing. The approbation I have received from these women, individually and during large conferences, strengthened my will to work. The World Federation of Ukrainian Women's Organizations provided the first stipend for this study, and Mrs. Lydia Burachynska convinced me to take it on. She realized, even if I naively had not, that the history of the women's movement in Ukraine could not be written in the projected year, but that once I became aware of the topic my own interest in it would grow.

Manoly Lupul, the former Director of the Canadian Institute of Ukrainian Studies at the University of Alberta; Bohdan Krawchenko, its present director; and John-Paul Himka, assistant professor of history at this same university, offered generous support, effective criticism and open commitment to the project. In its early stages they arranged for a series of lectures throughout Canada at which I saw tangible proof that the resonance my research elicited was not limited to women of Ukrainian origin. The Harvard Ukrainian Research Institute, especially Omeljan Pritsak and Frank Sysyn, readily provided a sounding board for some of the ideas developed here. Peter Potichnyj of McMaster University and Jaroslaw Pelenski of the University of Iowa included the women's dimension in the conferences they organized on Ukrainian relations with Jews, Russians and Germans. Karen Offen of the Center for Research on Women at Stanford University, Edith Couturier of the National Endowment for the Humanities, and Lynn Stoner of Arizona State University offered helpful suggestions and friendly encouragement on the development of the structural framework for this study.

In addition to the generous financial support I received from the Ukrainian National Women's League of America and from the Canadian Institute of Ukrainian Studies for this work, I have been a grateful recipient of the Founders' Fellowship of the American Association of University Women, as well as of grants from the Fulbright programme and from the International Research and Exchanges Board (IREX), which supported my work in the archives of Poland, Ukraine and Russia.

A number of persons have died since this book was written whose support I valued and whose memory I would like to invoke here. My father, Daniel Bohachevsky, who always encouraged me in my studies, read a draft of the manuscript. Although he never quite reconciled himself to the absolute importance of this particular book, he helped me with materials, suggestions and even some deciphering of manuscripts. Oleksander Zhorliakevych, my guide in Przemyśl, introduced me to Nusia Nementowska, the daughter of the poet Uliana Kravchenko. The materials she shared with me augmented useful hours of reminiscences.

Many persons shared the materials in their possession or their memories of the various aspects of the Ukrainian women's movement. I would like to thank them all, especially Olha Kuzmovych, Uliana Starosolska Liubovych, Antonina Horokhovych, Stefania Vitoshynska-Devosser, Daria Vytanovych, Lidia Hladka, Liubov Drazhevska and, last but not least, my mother, Rostyslava Nychay Bohachevsky. Iaroslav Dashkevych was helpful in orienting me in Lviv, especially in the University library, around the sources in nineteenth-century history. I would also like to acknowledge the good will shown to me and to my children by the many persons who made our first stay in Poland pleasant, and my subsequent trips there and to the Soviet Union both productive and enjoyable.

The staffs of the following archives and libraries were helpful and I thank them for their assistance. In the USA these are: the New York Public Library, especially Liubov Abramiuk Wolynec and Svitliana Lutska Andrushkiv; the Columbia University Library; the Harvard University Widener Library, especially Yaryna Turko Bodrok; the Harvard Ukrainian Research Institute Library, especially Edward Kasinec; the Library of Congress, especially Basil Nadraga. In Ukraine: the University Library, Kiev; the University Library, Lviv; the Library of the Lesia Ukrainka Museum; and libraries at all archives. In Austria: the Nationalbibliothek in Vienna. In Poland, the National Library in Warsaw; the Library of the University of Warsaw; the Jagellonian University Library; the Sejm Library in Warsaw; and the Przemyśl City Library. In Czechoslovakia, the Karolinum and its efficient staff were most helpful.

Ania Savage, a loyal friend, selflessly edited the first drafts of this manuscript; David Marples and Myroslav Yurkevich of the Canadian Institute of Ukrainian Studies edited the later drafts. Olha Bilyk did a superb typing job; Peter Matilainen had to input the draft and its variants because of technical incompatibilities; George Liber helped with the chapter on Soviet women. Manhattanville College, through the years, has provided an environment conducive to the growth of its faculty and helped integrate my new research interest in women with my teaching. Johns Hopkins University provided amenable surroundings and interested students during the proofing of the manuscript. Mari-Lesia Krawciw and Dora Chomiak helped with the index.

Finally, I would like to thank my family for their support of this project. My children grew up with the completion of this book, and my husband learned more about the women's movement than he needed to know. My mother took more than her share of household duties, and my thanks to her are expressed in the dedication.

Naturally, all this support did not shield me from the drawbacks and errors in the book, for which I alone bear responsibility.

Martha Bohachevsky-Chomiak
McLean, Virginia

Introduction

The story of Ukrainian women is interesting in itself and as an example of how women in non-sovereign nations assume a visible role in their community. The second part is by no means obvious.

When I began researching the topic, almost a decade ago, I did not realize the intrinsic interest of the Ukrainian women's movement or the theoretical contribution to women's studies and the analysis of feminism the study could make. Frankly, I expected to find a small feminist and an even smaller socialist movement of marginal importance which, while it would contribute to the knowledge of the history of the area, would do little to deepen our understanding of how women's organizations, as contrasted to those composed primarily of men, functioned. I was not really interested in theoretical issues of women's studies. Trained in intellectual and political history as a historian of Eastern Europe, I was wary of theoretical models superimposed on past events. I was especially suspicious of theory that could shade into ideology. Although I followed developments in women's and social history, and read the new literature on family and local history, I did so not to contribute to their development but to keep up with the new currents.

As I probed into my topic, however, an organizational and theoretical framework emerged from the historical data I collected simply because I could not fit the Ukrainian women into the existing patterns of women's organizations. A closer study of the Ukrainian women's movements led me to conclude that I was dealing with a phenomenon different from other European women's movements on which I had thought that the Ukrainians had patterned their organizations. I was interested in how the women perceived themselves, not in how others saw them, so I drew my information from the women themselves. I used ethnography, folk arts and literature for the impact they had upon the women's movement, but I have tried to recreate the overall picture of the women from sources other than the perception of women in literature or through folklore. Here I ran into the first major difficulties.

Although Ukrainian women produced some interesting feminist thinkers and writers, the impact of their theoretical work was very limited. Often their most interesting ideas remained without resonance. At times, these women themselves even denied being feminists. Yet their attempts at creating women's organizations and setting a practical agenda for them generally took root. This contradiction was puzzling, while the denial proved to be one of the most intriguing and pervasive issues in the emergence of women in public life. The phenomenon could be discerned throughout the nineteenth century; it continued to surface as recently as July 1985 at the deliberations held in conjunction with the UN World Conference to Review and Appraise the Achievements of the United Nations Decade for Women at Nairobi, Kenya. There many of the participants argued that they were not feminists, and that their concerns were not limited to women's issues. Their primary interest, they often maintained, was "more important than mere feminism." Yet these same persons, like the Ukrainian women on whom I had been focusing my research, enthusiastically supported an active role for women in society. In Nairobi that role was clearly stated in the final document. "Many delegations considered that one of the main achievements of the Decade was the recognition of the essential role of women in development."[1]

The issue in Nairobi was the same one I confronted when studying Ukrainian women. It centred in the perception and articulation of women's roles in their communities, in the definition of feminism as practiced by women, not as defined by those who wrote about it, favourably or critically. Why the Ukrainians? I studied the Ukrainian women to cast light on a limited segment of the history of women, and in the Ukrainian case the female experience could readily be isolated. Of all the nationalities in the vast area between Russia proper and Germany, the Ukrainians were among the most heterogenous in terms of internal politics and regimes under which they lived. There were also significant differences among them in geography, social and religious make-up and even specific historical experience. The area was subjected to a variety of colonial pressures which contributed to its national heterogeneity and complex class structure. In the nineteenth century Ukrainians experienced a national renaissance, but in the twentieth they were not successful in maintaining an independent state. Yet, despite an ostensible lack of interest in women's issues, the Ukrainian women developed between 1884 and 1939 effective women's organizations in all states in which they found themselves——the Russian Empire, the Austrian Empire, Poland, Romania, Czechoslovakia, Austria, Germany, the United States, Canada and, in a different manner, the Soviet Union. There were striking underlying similarities in the organizations of Ukrainian women, regardless of their location. All these organizations except the Soviet one rejected Marxist socialism as a means of women's liberation and most of their members denied being feminists. Their program reflected the specific needs of the society in which the women found themselves, and none of the organizations developed an ideology, or even coherent theoretical precepts for their actions.

Their reaction to feminism was similar to that of the women in Nairobi: they did not see their concerns as part of the feminist agenda but as an integral part of the community. They did not subject this difference to the scrutiny it deserved. Like other practitioners of community feminism they failed to systematize their activities into a coherent conceptual framework. In other words, they did not develop an ideology. Their views constituted a variant of feminism but were not readily identifiable as such, either to them or, for that matter, to those who wrote about them. I was as unprepared to see in operation a version of feminism, which I call pragmatic or community feminism, as its own practitioners have been and continue for the most part to be unwilling to articulate it.

Nationalism was one of the most popular ideologies in the nineteenth century. Women, if educated and well read, were as likely to subordinate their aspirations to the cause of the nation as were socialist women to set aside their needs until the emancipation of the workers. While the relationship between socialism and feminism has been scrutinized, the tight connections between nationalism and feminism have been overlooked. Both posit an entity——the nation or women——whose collective rights have been questioned. Both nationalists and feminists battled a political and social system that relegated them to a subordinate position. Both groups considered their cause just and liberating to the individual and beneficial for the group. Neither (we are referring here to nationalism proper, not to chauvinism or integral nationalism) intended harm to any other individual or group. On the contrary, both groups considered themselves to be working for the benefit of the whole community. Both the women and the subordinate nationalities experienced the same drawbacks: lack of an institutional base, inability to formulate an ideology that would be free of charges of exclusiveness and pettiness. Even the means available to both for the spread of their ideas were limited to education and literature.

Yet these similarities were not apparent either to feminists or to nationalists. Nationalism, unlike socialism, did not co-opt the cause of women's rights and women's liberation into its programmes. Feminism, in turn, failed to provide an integrating ideology or symbolism which would combine national and women's liberation.[2] It failed to produce symbols which would fire the imagination and inspire action in the same fashion that nationalism did, and in a sense continues to do. In Eastern Europe, and specifically on Ukrainian territories, the feminist issues of the nineteenth century, the vote and equal rights, were goals for the whole community and not exclusively for women. National liberation overshadowed the cause of women's liberation. The nation provided the heroes; the plight of the people justified the cause. Women contributed to the struggle, but remained peripheral in its identification. In Ukrainian both land and Ukraine are feminine, and a female figure generally represents both. Even the term for Fatherland is of feminine gender, yet these are niceties that the Ukrainians had not yet explored. While the symbol of the nation might have been a female, its values and identity remained male preserves.

The distinction between the masculine and the feminine is not simply a biological one. Its ramifications are determined by socio-cultural traditions and philosophical or religious convictions. In terms of power, reality can differ from theory as far as gender is concerned as much as it does in any other relationship. For women of non-sovereign nationalities, however, power is not the issue at all. Frustration in the quest for justice might eventually drive them to violence, but not for the sake of power as such. Hence, the discussion of the women's issue in Ukraine in terms of power is meaningless.

Liberation is meaningful as a vision, an ideology, a call to action. Modern liberating philosophies, most of them stemming from the Enlightenment, failed to consider women's reproductive and nurturing functions, and hence either subsumed women's liberation within the definitions determined to be universal ones or considered women to be not only potentially equal to males but in all respects identical to them. It was generally presumed that once women were freed from the shackles of law and custom, they would replicate the nobler versions of existing societies. Elements of a specifically female vision that would go beyond existing ideologies of change and existing social structures could be gleaned at times from the writings of individual thinkers. But a systematic analysis, with essential attendant conceptual restructuring of theory and practice underlying the perception of gender relations, is a genuinely con-temporary phenomenon. It is, moreover, very much the product of Western societies. Even theories which are most critical of Western development are conceptually grounded in Western traditions of thought.[3]

The society which forms the backdrop of the subject of this book lay in great measure outside the philosophical framework that shaped modern Western Europe. Its Orthodox Church, as will be seen from subsequent discussion, became an arm of the state; its Catholic part was not known for fostering philosophical inquiry. In short, the society which we will study did not have a tradition of self-perception or of analytical inquiry which, according to some of the Western feminists, forms the basis of the women's movement.[4]

Does that mean that there is no women's movement outside the Western framework or that the activities of women in these areas are less significant or less compelling? On the contrary, it offers yet another illustration that women's participation in society is not a matter of this or that ideology, but rather an integral facet of the past that might not readily fall into the conventional Western framework. My goal, in this book, is to begin making Ukrainian women visible not merely as an oppressed group but as a valid subject of study. The study might have some relevance to women's organizations in other emergent societies, but its immmediate significance lies in the fact that it helps us understand the past.

The activities of women in Ukraine draw attention to a community-oriented self-help women's movement which differed from political movements, from Western feminism and from the Russian women's movement. Even branches of Russian Imperial women's organizations were significantly modified on Ukrainian territory. One can speak of feminist regionalism or, better yet, of a pragmatic feminism whose major characteristics were a stress on self-help, co-operation among socio-economic classes and sometimes among the nationalities inhabiting the area, lack of interest in the theoretical discussion of the women's question, a practical bent in women's activities, avoidance of ideology, but in the final analysis, subordination of women's goals to those of the nation or the prevalent ideology.

The grass-roots approach, stressing the functioning of small groups, turned out to be the best way to study the women's movements in Ukraine, and provided an equally important focal point for Ukrainian history. By shifting the focus from politics and ideology to community endeavours, stereotypical perceptions of Ukrainian history were frequently altered. Hence the dual complementary thrust of this book——women's history and the history of Ukrainians. Women, even if subordinate, remained part of their society, and must be studied within its context. Yet the manner in which history and society impinges upon the story of the women is concrete and specific and must be studied individually. Theory can inform and frame the presentation, but it cannot replace the historical specificity.

My interpretation of the history of Ukraine, because of my stress upon women and because of the sources I use, often differs from the interpretations of other historians. My sources also account for the disproportionate detail on Western Ukrainian as compared to the Eastern Ukrainian women's movements. Because of different political and social circumstances, the Western Ukrainians were in a position to develop and articulate their community base more openly and fully than did the Eastern Ukrainians. Yet, were I to focus solely upon the Western Ukrainian women's movement to the exclusion of the Eastern Ukrainian women, I would do the women a disservice: whatever the objective reality, the organized women of Western Ukraine looked toward the East as the centre of their country, and whatever the political circumstances in Eastern Ukraine, women there also tried to organize for community action. Indeed, it was the similarity of approach of all the organizations in which Ukrainian women participated that made me see a pattern in them.

My task was all the more difficult because there is no comprehensive study of the social or political history of Ukraine, either of the Ukrainians or of the many national minorities that inhabited the area. I had to uncover information about the existence of women's organizations and trace the women involved in them while frequently having to establish the whole context of Ukrainian social history. As I was literally digging my way through various archives, most not readily accessible or catalogued to facilitate work on the topic, my colleagues in women's studies were developing sophisticated modes of analysis of the role of gender in history and politics and of the work of women in volunteer organizations. Much of that work informed my thinking as I read about women in areas that had been subjected to keener analysis than Ukrainian history has been. Yet for all the probing analyses of language, of the topic, even of the deconstruction of the usage of the language, the story of Ukrainian women as it emerged from the jig-saw puzzle of my research did not fit into the rapidly growing framework of women's studies.

Except for women who functioned in political organizations, both conservative and radical, women in Ukraine, compared to Western European and Russian women, showed little interest in traditional ladies' causes. Among these would be the struggle against prostitution; promotion of conventional philanthropy; and public discussion of women's equality, including the right of women to the franchise and to education. Instead, organizations in Ukraine tended to focus on concrete activities, which were self-help rather than philanthropic. More research will have to be done before definitive generalizations can be made. On the basis of my work, however, I can suggest that the thrust of women's work in Ukraine was more in the direction of the projects that characterize the activities of women under colonial regimes than of those of women in established European states.

Ukrainian women provide a good case study within which to look at this type of feminism, since it was a group of Ukrainian women outside the USSR that organized one of the largest (per capita) women's organizations in inter-war Europe and that effectively mobilized peasant women, especially for social action. Neither socialism nor feminism were motivating factors for these women. Other issues were more important for several reasons. First of all, the context within which the Ukrainian women functioned was one of development, not of sexual liberation. The goal of these women was not so much to free themselves from the strictures and conventions of their own society (although that played a part for some of them) as to become active members of their own community. They sought to expand the role of women within existing institutions, making women part of a broader liberation struggle. They did not focus either upon the rights of women or on their independence, but rather upon the importance of women and the need to expand opportunities for them. They stressed the special role of women in society and made opportunity, rather than equality, their goal.

A number of factors contributed to the distinctive development of Ukrainian women. One can speculate that while for the Europeans and the Russians the family was seen as an extension of state power, for the Ukrainians (as for some other subject nationalities) the function of the family was perceived as the preservation of cultural autonomy of the nation against the encroachment of the state. The Ukrainian women sought to use the family as an enclave against the state since they saw the family and, by extension, the immediate community as sources of strength and protection from which to launch the conquest of the broader society. There was no initial reason to oppose the family. It was only with the growth of the organized women's movement and with the increased urbanization of society that the constricting nature of the household became evident to most women. The frontier mentality and the absence of Tatar-induced seclusion influenced the position of women in Ukraine markedly. Their development further differed from that of the Russian women because the *Domostroi,* that major family manual of the Russians of the early modern period which mandated the subordination of the women through corporal chastisement sanctified by religious precepts, does not seem to have been used widely in Ukraine. These considerations created a different environment for women in Ukraine than for those in Russia.

Secondly, women's organizations in Ukraine were the outgrowth of community initiatives addressed to remedy not the second-rate status of women in society but the major needs of that society. Eliminating social ills——slavery, drunkenness, illiteracy, economic dislocation or inequality——has frequently been the initial goal of women's organizations. Even the welfare of children and the functioning of the family, although generally viewed as an aspect of the women's issue by historians, were really social issues, not solely the concerns of women. But they came to be identified as women's concerns, and thus the circularity developed: women addressed the needs left unattended by society, and society considered those needs to define women's issues. Failure to change the position of women contributed to the perpetuation of the very needs that women's concerns highlighted. When the women in Nairobi argued that development was a critical factor in determining the position of women, they were asserting the type of feminism we are attempting to discuss. They were addressing the issue of women as part of society and perforce dependent upon it.

Thirdly, the work of Ukrainian women's organizations differed from the philanthropic activities of the early feminists in that it was directed not toward offering help to the needy but toward developing effective self-help organizations. Despite some influence of liberal feminist and socialist organizations, which will be discussed in the course of the narrative, the women's organizations in Ukraine differed from both in significant ways. They were characterized by a lack of interest in the theory of liberation, by very little discussion of sex, by stress upon community affairs and not upon women's position in them. Most significantly, they adapted to existing institutions and mores and did not challenge society, highlighting the importance of the family, of housekeeping by women, of the economic and socializing role of the mother.

Finally, these women maintained their political independence and integrity and did not become adjuncts of political parties. As will be amply demonstrated in later dicussion, these women stressed the autonomy of the individual, and especially of the woman, and could not in any manner be part of the later right-radical movements.

Why did Ukrainian women not define the type of women's organization they were developing? Because the educated middle-class Ukrainian women who were most likely to write on these issues saw themselves as functioning within a European context and looked toward concepts developed in Western Europe to articulate their views. They failed to note that they did not share the Western European middle-class ideal of mothering and domesticity. They also failed to realize, just as the European thinkers failed to do, that the universality claimed by Western Europeans in their world-view was less comprehensive than they presumed. Grounded in a rural, pre-industrial society, the Ukrainian women had no problems with identity. The realm of the private flowed into that of the public, since the public was the readily identifiable community and not the abstract state or political forces. The latter were the enemy, not the immediate community. Increased educational and social opportunities made the Ukrainian women less likely to recognize differences between the organizations they developed and those that emerged in Western Europe, because the education the

women received socialized them into existing cultural values and prevented
them from analyzing what was peculiar to their experience.

The formative years of modern Ukrainian political parties coincided
chronologically with the discussion of the woman question, which in Western
Europe was generally posed either within the internationalist-socialist
framework or in the national context. Ukrainians did not discuss the women's
issue. But Ukrainian women, once they developed their community-oriented
women's organizations, became politically active in their society. As soon as
they became a visible force in the society, opposition to them became more
open. That forced the women to articulate a feminist agenda. Interest in
feminism among these women developed as a result of their activism; feminism
was not its initial motivating force.

An analysis of the Ukrainian women's movement suggests that by
socializing women into more active involvement, women's community
organizations create conditions in which women's concerns become
highlighted. These concerns are a genuine part of the overall women's
movement and must be studied as such. In short: for the women's movement to
be understood, its unarticulated motivational underpinnings and presuppositions
must be addressed. Social history alone would not suffice, even if all the data
were available to us. We must resort to more traditional approaches of
intellectual history and educated conjecture to help us recreate the untold story
of women.

Although the archival base for my studies has been more extensive than I
had initially thought possible, there are a number of glaring gaps in it. I could
not gain access to the unpublished materials of the leading Ukrainian feminists
of the nineteenth century, especially of Kobrynska and Pchilka. The archives of
the Women's Union, which had its headquarters in Lviv between 1919 and
1939, seem to have been lost.

Information on Soviet Ukrainian women has been limited mostly to
published sources. In that part of the book I have avoided the discussion of
women's issues within the entire Soviet context, since this has been done by
others. Rather, I stress the peculiarities of the situation facing Soviet Ukrainian
women, often drawing upon Soviet sources. We must keep in mind, however,
that some of the crucial materials about the 1920s and 1930s perished with the
victims of the various waves of terror.

The bibliography is limited to items most directly relevant to this study of
Ukrainian women. Considerations of space prevented the inclusion of all the
pertinent literature from the growing field of women's studies from which I
profited.

Naturally, this first comprehensive book about Ukrainian women cannot
make any claims to completeness. I tried to tell as much of the story as I could
reconstruct. My stress on the participation of women in community life made
me concentrate more upon the so-called upper-class women than upon the daily
life of the peasants. I make no pretense to writing a social history, an analysis
of gender relations or a history of family life in Ukraine or to using a statistical

data base, which could not be very reliable, given the sources available. I focus on Ukrainian women, since they constitute the majority population in Ukraine. The story of non-Ukrainian women in Ukraine must await another opportunity.

I have tried to outline the contours of women's activities in Ukraine and to place them within a historical and political setting. My hope is that others will be stimulated enough by this story to pursue related topics, dig into social, family and regional history, as well as into cliometrics, elaborate on the story I have begun to tell, and alter the very contours of my design to make room for a fuller picture.

Part I.

Ukrainian Women in the Russian Empire

1.
Historical Background

While the French revolutionaries raised the standards of liberty, fraternity and equality at the end of the eighteenth century, Ukraine lost the last vestiges of its ancient autonomy. Within a few decades, however, the modern Ukrainian democratic movement began to develop, stressing human rights as its historical goal: liberation was the slogan of all Ukrainian activists. The study of the history of Ukrainian women has always played a secondary role within this context. Like other disenfranchised, colonized and oppressed groups, Ukrainians have, to some extent, lost their history. In the second half of the nineteenth century, Ukrainian scholars' perception of events in their country became strangely ahistorical. They frequently overlooked the significance of specifically Ukrainian developments. Most of the upper classes of Ukraine had become either Polonized or Russified at a time when both Poland and Russia were not national states but multinational empires. As modern Ukrainian national consciousness crystallized, Ukrainian historians tended to identify the cause of Ukraine with the peasants. Ukraine's agriculture-based economy and its foreign-owned industry strengthened that approach.

This ahistoricism, also a characteristic of scholars of emerging nations, had a detrimental effect upon women's self-perception and on the study of women's history. Among the few brief works on the Ukrainian women's movement, we come across several that stress the similarity between Ukrainian and Russian women. For instance, Pavlo Hrabovsky, a progressive Ukrainian activist and author, wrote in the Ukrainian newspaper *Narod* (People), which appeared in 1884 in the Ukrainian territories under the Austrian Empire: "The Ukrainian women walk alongside the Muscovite women, since history has bound them together, thus we perceive no difference between one and the other."[1] Zinaida Mirna, a patriotic Ukrainian activist and a member of a government that unsuccessfully fought the Bolsheviks in 1919, expressed similar views as late as 1937:

The women's movement in Ukraine cannot be separated from the overall Russian women's movement, since for more than two hundred years Ukraine, conquered under Muscovite rule, had to live a common life with Russia, and all political, economic and cultural events [of the Russian Empire] were reflected in the life of Ukraine.[2]

Yet, when studying the historical development of Ukrainian women and women's organizations in Ukraine, one is struck by the differences rather than the similarities between the Ukrainian and Russian movements. Hence the anomaly: the perception of historical development has been different from the reality, to the detriment of Ukrainians.

Finally, the predilection of populist Ukrainian historiography for the oppressed masses and the loss of the Ukrainian upper class to the imperial nobility affected the study of Ukrainian history, including the history of Ukrainian women. The heterogeneity of the Ukrainian movement was overshadowed by a stress on the communality of the national experience. Conservative, organic tendencies were overlooked. In turn, the study of Ukrainian history was discouraged in the Russian Empire. For example, in 1906, Oleksandra Efimenko, a Russian by nationality and a specialist in Ukrainian history by choice, was nonetheless accused of "national subjectivism."[3]

Within the Russian Empire, Ukraine constituted an internal colony. Ukrainian resources were exploited not for the welfare of the area, but for the growth of the empire. The communications system was oriented toward the imperial political centre, not toward Ukraine. Schools were neglected. Agriculture was labour-intensive and backward. The territory was settled by Russian and Polish colonizers who saw Ukraine, at best, as a charming region of the great empire. Even among anti-government groups, overt pro-Ukrainian feelings were viewed as both suspect and of limited use.

The first scholars to study the history of the women also studied the minorities in the empire. In 1847, the historian and ethnographer Mykola Kostomarov drafted an emotional appeal identifying the cause of Ukraine with universal ideas of brotherhood and justice. Arrested and exiled, he returned to formulate an analysis of the separate development of Ukraine and Russia. Soon afterward, he wrote a study of the social history of Russian women. Danylo Mordovtsev, who popularized the Cossack period of Ukrainian history among the Russians, also wrote a book on Russian women.[4]

A number of facets of Ukrainian social history have a direct bearing upon the modern women's question. Mykhailo Hrushevsky, on the basis of the research done by Mykola Ziber, Mykola Chernyshiv, Volodymyr Okhrymovych and especially Fedir Vovk, posited the existence not only of a matriarchy in prehistoric times, but also of communal and trial marriages.[5] Oleksandra Efimenko's studies on the latter bear out this thesis.[6] Trial marriages appear to have persisted among Ukrainian peasants well into the nineteenth century. In her discussion of the role of women in Ukrainian history, Nataliia Polonska-Vasylenko stressed that until the mid-seventeenth century the nature of the marriage ceremony was significantly different from the marital vows used in later Orthodox and Catholic services. Polonska maintained that the vows exchanged by the couple, the crucial part of the ceremony, were the same for both partners: "I take you as my helper." The phrase that became the woman's vows——"I pledge you love, faith, consideration and obedience in marriage"——only appeared in church books after 1646. One of the first steps taken by the new Russian rulers of Ukraine was the replacement of Ukrainian church books containing the traditional marriage ceremonial with Russian versions emphasizing the woman's obedience to her husband. The old version, however, must have been deeply ingrained in Ukrainian consciousness. It resurfaced in Volyn in the 1920s, when the fall of the tsarist government removed the major prop of the Russian Orthodox Church.[7]

The right of women to dispose of their dowry and other wealth had its origins in the Kievan state between the tenth and the thirteenth centuries, at which time there were women rulers. Even after the fall of Kiev in 1240, despite subsequent Tatar invasions and cataclysmic political changes throughout Eastern Europe, women retained their right to own property and money. They could also sue, appear in court and testify. Women not only administered local areas, but also participated in battle. The Tatar practice of secluding women had no impact on Ukraine: their rights to their possessions and persons are duly documented in the Lithuanian Statute.

Repeated Tatar incursions that continued into the seventeenth century, the instability of the Polish Commonwealth and the Cossack state, which became sovereign in 1648, and the settling of the steppe lands ensured that Ukrainian women were as free as any frontier women. The constant struggle with the Tatars and Turks provided the raw material for sagas and songs, some of which, written by women, carried female spirit into modern times.[8] The tumultuous life of Ukrainian gentry women in the Polish Commonwealth was described by Orest Levytsky in such popular studies as "Hanna Montovt," serialized in the newspaper *Dilo* (Deed) in 1888. Hanna Chykalenko Keller, a Scottish-educated activist from a rich Ukrainian family, wrote in 1920 in her still halting English:

It is probably in the [fifteenth through the seventeenth] centuries that we must look for the origins of the relative independence of the Ukrainian women in the following epochs. The upper Ukrainian classes as well as the common Cossacks led a warlike existence defending the frontiers against foreign invasion. Women were often obliged to follow their husbands in their expeditions, even to partake in the battles. Fighting at the side of the men for the defense of their country, the Ukrainian woman of this time displayed great energy and great strength of character. In her husband's absence, she was accustomed to rely on herself, on her own initiative. She took part in the political life, in the seatings of the Diets, and public assemblies, she was admitted to law courts. The religious movements of the time have found passionate partisans among Ukrainian women, who studied religious doctrines, founded monasteries, schools, hotels, actively collaborated in the spreading of instruction and charity, took part in ecclesiastical communities that played so great a role in the struggle for national independence.[9]

In 1654 the Ukrainian Cossacks, in conflict with the Poles and Tatars, sought the protection of the distant Muscovite Tsar, the only Orthodox Christian monarch in the world. In contrast to the Russians, Ukrainian women had never known the Oriental seclusion imposed on the Russian women under Tatar rule. The partition of Ukraine in 1667 between Muscovy (the Russian Empire was not proclaimed until 1721) and the Polish Commonwealth accentuated the difference between the two nationalities.

Modern Ukrainian history possesses several distinctive features. First, there is the Ukrainian tradition of independence. Rooted in the countryside, it was strengthened by the individualism of frontier life in far-flung settlements and homesteads. The village commune (*mir*), characteristic of the Russian peasantry, never became popular among Ukrainians. Further, the tradition of individualism survived Russia's reintroduction of serfdom into East Ukrainian territories in the eighteenth century. The absorption of the Cossack elite into the imperial Russian bureaucracy involved the enserfment of the Ukrainian peasant population, but initially Russian rule had little impact on the women of the Cossack elite and even less upon the peasants.

A vast network of Cossack families covered the countryside. Family ties were reinforced by extended family relationships such as formalized god-parenthood and arranged marriages, which persisted into the twentieth century. For example, Andrii Livytsky, cut off by his father, received food, lodging and money from other relatives. Sought by the police, he was able to hide himself, his wife and two children for over a year by visiting various relatives, many of whom were in government service. They formed a closed world in which an outsider rarely felt at ease.[10]

Upper-class Cossack women enjoyed a comfortable existence. They had money, security in the family estates and a personal independence that extended into marital relationships. Husbands and wives often had separate residences and were together only during holidays. The growing interest of some women in education, job opportunities and political affairs was a frequent cause of family discord. Most women, however, lived a more conventional life.

Ukrainian lands were incorporated gradually into the Russian Empire by the end of the eighteenth century owing to a process of centralization that was supported by sections of Ukrainian society. Some Cossack leaders received gentry status, while serfdom was reintroduced in Ukraine during the reign of the same Catherine II who assured Voltaire of her enlightened views. Serfdom in Ukraine was generally the onerous corvée, which involved mandatory labour in the fields and could not be exchanged for payment to the lord, although that was often levied as well. The heavy burden of work took its toll on the life expectancy of Ukrainian women.[11]

Enserfed until 1861, Ukrainian peasant women, like their husbands, performed compulsory feudal services on manorial land, which left them with little time to attend to their personal plots. The Ukrainian peasant women were subject to the highest mortality rates in Europe. Although in constant danger of being taken into the service of the brutal overseers of the manor house, who were particularly inhumane when administering estates of absentee landlords, the peasants, generally, were considered a lesser breed and thus avoided cultural and linguistic Polonization or Russification. The gentry, on the other hand, were obliged to accept the dominant culture and language of the empire.

Catherine actively fostered intermarriage between the Russian nobility and nobles of the Polish Commonwealth, acquired through conquest and partition between 1772 and 1795. This resulted in some blurring of national identities among the upper classes, although the process took longer among women. For the peasants, however, there was no such fusion. The Russians were foreigners——be they nobles who took over the peasant lands, or newly arrived seasonal labourers, or odd tradesmen or peasants who filtered into their midst. In the late 1870s, the rich and talented Poltava-born painter Mariia Bashkirtsev, wrote in her narcissistic journal that Russian peasants who entered her native village were objects of derision and were treated as total strangers by nobles and peasants alike.[12]

Even the village's Orthodox clergy, a major Russifying force, produced Ukrainian activists. The impact of humanism, idealism and patriotism was stronger in Ukrainian seminaries than in the Russian parts of the empire, reflecting Western influence on the Polish Commonwealth. Unlike Russians, Ukrainian nobles willingly entered the priesthood. Women in clerical families evinced a desire "to get close to the peasants and not to pretend that the wife of the priest is superior to the rest of the women in the village."[13] The peasants, moreover, preserved an oral tradition of the Cossack past. Women composed many songs that entered the folk repertoire of the male wandering minstrels (*kobzari*).

Many women of the upper classes continued to share the politics of the males in the family. For example, women in the Orlyk family followed their husbands in support of Mazepa's ill-fated bid to establish a Ukrainian Cossack state in the early eighteenth century.

Other Ukrainian women actively aided the careers of their husbands and families. For instance, the mother of the last Hetman of Ukraine, Natalka Rozumykha, was a Ukrainian peasant woman who built her own village house in 1742. Three years later she had an elaborate church built in Kozeltsi, and signed herself Countess Nataliia Rozumovska. One of her sons became Hetman through the influence of another who was the lover of the Empress Elizabeth. One of her grandsons, exemplifying the integration of the family into the imperial structure, rose high in the Russian bureaucracy.[14] Imperial Russia granted the status of nobility as a means of undermining Cossack cohesion. At the same time the government pacified the Russian gentry by holding periodic inquests into the question of those of non-noble status entering government service.[15] Some women petitioned for noble status for their sons.

But even after the incorporation of Ukraine into the empire, direct contact with the Russians was limited. As a result, life changed less for the Ukrainian woman on the *khutir* (the individual homestead characteristic of Ukraine) than for her husband, who was drawn into civilian or military imperial service.[16]

Russia's growth into an empire, her participation in the Napoleonic Wars, her partitioning of Poland and the incorporation of Right-Bank Ukraine into the empire, placed her indisputably in the ranks of the leading European powers. In 1825, the Russian nobility, drawn to French rationalism and German idealism, made an unsuccessful bid to create a constitutional monarchy in Russia. Although centred in the military, and largely devoid of a national component, the most successful actions of the Decembrists, as those officers were known, were carried out on Ukrainian territory. Many of the activists were drawn from old Cossack officer families now serving the imperial cause.[17] The failure of the Decembrists led to the further growth of autocratic tsarism.

The reforms of Alexander II in the early 1860s were a direct result of the Crimean War, which illustrated the weakness of the state. Foremost among them were the abolition of serfdom, the creation of limited local assemblies (the *zemstva*), some decentralization of education, and a thorough reform of the courts and the military. For the Ukrainian peasants the abolition of serfdom was of great symbolic significance, but landlords retained most of the land, and the peasants still required permission from the police and the village assembly before they could leave the village. Peasants throughout the empire were subject to indemnity payments. In Ukraine, the establishment of a communal *mir* structure to serve as a link between the peasants and the government disrupted traditional society. Above all, land hunger characterized the life of peasants in grain-rich Ukraine.

The awakening of a nation and the role of women

Throughout the nineteenth century, criticism and opposition to the tsarist government grew. As the Cossack state became assimilated into the Russian Empire, Ukrainians began to forge new forms of self-expression. In this process, they followed the example of the Poles, who were trying to remove the same Russian authority to which Ukrainians had succumbed a century earlier (as a result of conflict with these same Poles). The Poles raised issues of universal validity; they developed their literature, and a political ideology formulated by organizations on Ukrainian territory.

In the early nineteenth century, an influential Pole, Stanisław Konarski, decided that a network of women might convey new ideas to the peasants, and serve as messengers among the conspirators.[18] At this time, some of the Polonized gentry rediscovered their Ukrainian roots in the countryside. Folk ornament, handicrafts, weaving and embroidery——predominantly products made by women——became the symbols of Ukrainian identity in the nineteenth century. Other gentry of Ukrainian origin still considered themselves Russian, but treasured elaborate Ukrainian peasant costumes of regions from which their families had originated, and in which some still lived. Thus they remained attached to the customs and folklore of Ukraine without accepting the more liberal political ideology of progressive Ukrainians. Sometimes a symbiosis of imperial Russian and particularist Ukrainian identity occurred. Nikolai Gogol, the Ukrainian-born "father of the Russian short story," transformed the Ukrainian tales told by his mother and nanny into Russian classics. His relatives were active in the Ukrainian *zemstva*.[19]

The person who did most to transform the old traditions of freedom into new symbols of liberation was a former serf who had been condemned by the tsar to penal military service in Central Asia. Taras Shevchenko became the bard and symbol of the new Ukrainian national consciousness. He found friendship and support in the Volkonsky family, which was related to the Rozumovskys, the last hetmans of Ukraine, and had property near Poltava, in the Ukrainian heartland. The son of the Decembrist Volkonsky had been raised near Poltava by his paternal uncle. The gentry who visited the household knew Ukrainian songs, were advocates of progress and legality, and memorized Shevchenko's poetry.[20] In his poetry Shevchenko bemoaned the fate of Ukrainian serfs, especially the women, for whom he predicted a bright and free future. He spoke for the downtrodden and reminded the whole nation of its Cossack past and the freedoms it had enjoyed.

Writing by women was encouraged by the Ukrainian intelligentsia, and female literary careers were facilitated by the popularity of poetry, much of it patterned on well known folksongs. There was no feminist literature in the Ukrainian territories of the Russian Empire, although many literary works raised the issue of women. The thrust of Ukrainian writing lay in the portrayal of the plight of the individual and oppressed people. The writers themselves, who came from both peasantry and nobility, were people of modest means. But the difficulties they had encountered with censorship and the police strengthened their fighting spirit. Women writers, operating in an agricultural society in which the role of women was crucial, had little need to develop theories about women's concerns.

Literature, the first public arena accessible to women, was used to present new ideas, enunciate programmes of public action, and serve as a forum. The portrayal of the lot of women, however, served not to elicit pity but rather to highlight and try to rectify their situation.

The first modern influential woman writer among Ukrainians was Marko Vovchok——Mariia Vilinska Markovych Zhuchenko (1834–1907). Born of a Russified family, she married an activist of the national revival movement, Opanas Markovych. As a member of the short-lived but significant Cyrillo-Methodian Brotherhood, uncovered by the police in 1847, Markovych had been exiled to the town in which Vilinska lived. Marriage to the gentle and unassuming Markovych ensured Vilinska's lifelong conversion to Ukrainian identity, although the marriage did not last. Vovchok's personal life was stormy, but this had a beneficial effect upon her writing. She spent part of it in Western Europe, and supported herself and her son by her writing and translations of Ukrainian, French and Russian texts.

Vovchok often wrote about women, although not about feminist issues directly. Her heroines were Ukrainian peasant women, victimized but vigorous. She drew on history and contemporary life. Her *Marusia*, about a bold young girl, was very popular even in Western Europe. According to a Russian feminist, Vovchok "was probably the first writer to use literature to fight the vestiges of serfdom."[21] Shevchenko saw her as his heir, while the Russian writer Turgenev learned Ukrainian for the sole purpose of translating her stories into Russian. But none of these influential friends dominated this proud and independent woman.

The first Ukrainian women writers came from old Cossack families. They followed in the footsteps of the women philanthropists, but instead of dispensing money to the churches, schools, artists or the poor, they donated their talents to the Ukrainian cause. The Russian regime and even the liberal Russian elite opposed Ukrainian culture. They feared the strength of the Ukrainian national reawakening, its vitality and its support among the peasants. In 1876, by the notorious Ems Ukase, the Russian government banned the publication of all Ukrainian-language works. But the vast majority of peasants needed no books to carry on their age-old traditions.[22] Ukrainian writers, however, sought alternate means of publication, which involved a more open role in the political life of the nation and encouraged them to seek closer contacts with Ukrainians in the Austrian Empire.

Among the most important writers in Ukraine was Oleksandra Bilozerska-Kulish (1828–1911), who wrote under the pseudonym Hanna Barvinok. Borys Hrinchenko, a Ukrainian writer and educator, dubbed her "the poet of woman's fate."[23] Hrinchenko's wife, Mariia Gladilina (1863–1928), a Russian by origin, became a Ukrainian activist through teaching in a Ukrainian village, and wrote under the pseudonym Mariia Zahirna. Liudmyla Berezyna Vasylevska (1861–1927), who chose as her pseudonym the poetic Dniprova Chaika ("Seagull of the Dnieper"), was a priest's daughter who became one of the first proponents of symbolism in Ukrainian literature. Valeria O'Connor Vilinska (1867–1930) and Natalena Dunin-Borkovska Koroleva (1888–1967) also chose to identify themselves with the cause of the people among whom they lived. Oleksandra Sudovshchyk Kosach (1867–1924), writing as Hrytsko Hryhorenko, did not declare publicly the tension between her Russian origin and her Ukrainian marriage and writing, but noted it in her diary.[24] The writings of Liubov Ianovska (1861–1941) reflected her enthusiastic public activity in Ukrainian organizations. The poet Khrystia Alchevska (1882–1932?) was also dedicated to the Ukrainian cause. The writer Nataliia Romanovych-Tkachenko (1884–1933) actively fostered closer contacts with Galicia.

The greatest Ukrainian woman writer was Lesia Ukrainka——Oleksandra Kosach-Kvitka (1871–1913). In childhood she was stricken by tuberculosis of the bones, but through her idealism and rational approach to life, she overcame the depression that accompanied the disease. She grew up surrounded by independent women, did not have children, and felt that the second-rate status of women was a result of their reluctance to break with convention. Yet she sewed, embroidered, took care of her younger sisters, and interrupted her jam-making to work on a play or a poem. At public meetings she would knit quietly until asked to speak. She exhibited this deference to others in public life: in 1905 it was Ukrainka who performed the tedious task of drafting by-laws for new organizations.[25]

In her writing, however, she portrayed strong individualistic characters. Of particular and immediate significance was her 1910 drama, *Boiarynia* (The Noblewoman). Set in the seventeenth century, it deals with a Ukrainian woman who marries a Russian and is confronted with the Oriental subordination of Russian women of the pre-Petrine era.

The work of Lesia Ukrainka's mother, Olha Drahomanov Kosach (1849–1930), who wrote under the pseudonym Olena Pchilka, was important for the development of the Ukrainian women's movement. Pchilka was energetic, resolute and determined, and actively involved in all aspects of Ukrainian cultural and political life. A firm advocate of national rights, she fostered closer co-operation among Ukrainians in both the Russian and Austrian Empires. She came to realize through personal experience that as the Russians discriminated against Ukrainians, so Ukrainian males tended to be patronizing toward females. Her daughter, Lesia, a "second-generation feminist," took equality of the sexes for granted because Pchilka practiced it.

Many Eastern Ukrainian women writers were poets who strengthened village ties by patterning much of their work on folksong lyrics. While Lesia Ukrainka's ability placed her above others, Pchilka, with her Jane Austen-type heroines, was not popular with literary critics. In fact, women writers who moved beyond populist writing ran the risk of being labelled elitist by Ukrainian literary critics such as Serhii Efremov. Pchilka's self-assessment of her contribution to Ukrainian literature combined her writing and her public activity:

> I am no follower of Vovchok and her contemporaries. I have stepped upon new ground——although it would be more appropriate to say that I have only trod on *fresh soil* in the same Ukrainian field of literature, of life. [My heroes] are drawn from life, but I do not choose the same types of heroines as Vovchok, Kulish or even Shevchenko (those gentle lovers, sisters, wives). [Rather] I portray the figure of the woman patriot.[26]

She decried social pressures to use Russian as a language that enhanced upward mobility, and shielded her children from this pressure: "Although no one really told us 'reject your own,' 'don't use your language,' it was nevertheless taken for granted. In public, and when there were guests, we had to speak Russian."[27]

The trend was reversed for the next generation, who grew up in consciously Ukrainian families. Hanna Chykalenko-Keller spent a happy childhood in a family that was closer to its servants than to the Russian-speaking neighbouring gentry.[28]

Pchilka perceived the Russian government's policy in Ukraine as "flattening out," or "equalization"——*vyrivniannia*. It was similar to the more recent Nazi-German policy of *Gleichschaltung*, i.e., the abolition of all distinctive characteristics. The Russian government was confident enough in the success of its Russification policy to support an initial collection of Ukrainian ethnographic materials. In the first half of the nineteenth century, scholars transcribed Ukrainian songs, aphorisms and folktales, and described customs and modes of dress in an attempt to preserve some legacy of an ostensibly dying culture. "The dying culture" proved to be food for the living. It was adaptable to new literary trends and relevant to democratic political ideas. All Ukrainian activists were involved in ethnographic activities. Women were particularly attracted to that type of work, since their ties with the village were often stronger than those of the men. Pchilka published the first book on the Ukrainian ornament in 1876, the year of the Ems Ukase. By this date, however, the government felt so threatened by the "dying culture" that the book had to be published in Russian. It was as if the nation, made mute by a government decree, had found a new voice in the nonverbal folk motifs. Pchilka's work in the preservation of folk art was continued well into the twentieth century, while her daughter Ukrainka was among the first to make wax recordings of Volhynian folksongs. The formation of choirs, which popularized and systematized the songs, was by then a cultural and social undertaking.

One result of Ukrainian ethnographic and literary activity was the creation of a Ukrainian theatre. Before the establishment of a Ukrainian state in 1918, drama depended upon the efforts of the community. Frequently harassed or even banned by the government, the theatre groups of Sadovsky, Karpenko-Kary and Starytsky functioned on the verge of bankruptcy. Nevertheless, as Shevchenko's poetry was taken up by society ladies, so the Ukrainian theatre took even Russian critics by storm. As late as 1907, the Russian critic Aleksandr Suvorin published in St. Petersburg an elaborately illustrated collection of his glowing reviews of various Ukrainian plays, albeit under the derogatory title, *Khokhly i khokhlushki*, which was analogous to the American usage of *niggers* or *darkies* to refer to blacks.

The theatre played the role of a secular church in the development of Ukrainian public culture. The first Ukrainian theatrical group was founded in Kiev at the same time that Mykhailo Drahomanov began his political activity and Mykola Lysenko his work in Ukrainian music and drama. Theatrical productions by local amateur groups mobilized Ukrainian communities. Many activists, male and female, began their careers by participating in amateur dramatic presentations. For the women the theatre offered new roles in its presentations and in the life-style of its actresses. That it was a community- rather than government-sponsored effort strengthened the independence and self-reliance of Ukrainian women.[29]

The significance of the theatre for Ukrainians is illustrated by the twenty-fifth anniversary of the career of Mariia Adasovska, who under the stage name of Zankovetska was the undisputed star of prerevolutionary Ukrainian theatre. She had turned down offers to join the Russian Imperial Theatre, contenting herself with the meagre material rewards of the Ukrainian troupe. A civic committee, which included Nataliia Doroshenko, Mariia Starytska, Borys Hrinchenko and Mykola Lysenko, prepared a programme in her honour that, in the words of a Russian newspaper, "turned the festive gathering into a major celebration."[30] For many Ukrainians, Zankovetska was "the incarnation of Ukraine."[31] The readings of the congratulatory telegrams alone lasted over two hours. The crowd, too large for the hall, spilled into the street. The police were taken aback by the size of the gathering and began to make arrests.[32] In their eyes, it reflected the growth of the Ukrainian movement[33] and their apparent failure to deal with it. Almost a year after the celebration, the Kiev police chief was still reporting on the matter to the Governor-General: "The demonstrative character of the evening was not caused by the reading of the congratulatory addresses, which in themselves did not have seditious overtones, but rather by the very special tone of the celebration of Zankovetska, which it was both impossible to foresee and impossible to prevent."[34]

Toward the end of the nineteenth century, therefore, Ukrainians were developing viable links among all strata of Ukrainian society, and creating symbols, mythologies, political and social ideologies in keeping with the people's needs.[35] Articulate women participated in this process, which drew its strength from the Ukrainian village.

The elemental force of Ukrainianism——the *stykhiia*——made it possible for Ukrainians in Eastern Ukraine to accept readily the internationalism concomitant with socialism and communism. They were more willing than the Western Ukrainians, who lived in the heterogeneous Austrian Empire, to consider nationalism of secondary importance to overall reforms. The Ukrainian cause and that of human emancipation were one and the same in their eyes. Although Russian was the official language of the empire, Ukrainians from the little Zbruch River, which marked the border with Austria, to the mighty Don River in the East, constituted the overwhelming majority of the population of Ukraine. In the villages and settlements, their national identity was neither challenged nor threatened. But their human rights and the articulation of their nationality were severely limited. The issue, therefore, was how to harness the force of the village to limit the power of the Russian tsar. Education, enlightenment, the spread of consciousness concerning the tyranny being exercised over the peasants seemed to be the major tasks facing articulate Ukrainians at the end of the nineteenth century. Women shared this burden. Like their menfolk, they did not look to the past for their justification: emancipation and justice were their mottoes, democracy their strength.

2.
Women and Education

Ukraine had a tradition of community-supported schools, which lingered even after the incorporation of Ukrainian lands into the Russian Empire and the closing of many schools. Whenever they could, Ukrainians tried to establish Ukrainian-language schools that would serve the needs of their communities. Literacy for the peasant masses was implicit in all Ukrainian political programmes. Discussion of the education of women became secondary to the quest for a native school.

The imperial government was ambivalent toward the creation and expansion of a network of schools. Schools would help provide an educated secular bureaucracy to run the expanding government. But education also constituted a challenge to the government by nurturing a secular intelligentsia, hence the imperial government allocated it only limited funds.

Ukrainians were at the forefront of attempts to establish schools and an educational system in both Ukrainian lands and the empire generally. Ukrainian scholars set up schools in the Russian capitals——first in Moscow, then in St. Petersburg. But most worked in their native lands. During the 1750s, more than 300 schools were established in Chernihiv province alone as a result of local pressure.[1] Local initiative also lay behind the creation of the University of Kharkiv in 1805 and St. Vladimir University in Kiev in 1835.

The sensitivity of the Ukrainian population to educational needs was partly a result of the presence of Poles. Since the Counter-Reformation, the Poles had waged a vigorous campaign against the Orthodox Church, relying heavily on Jesuit-run schools. Before their annexation to the Russian Empire, Ukrainians founded their own schools, of which the Kievan Mohyla Academy was the most significant. Women, along with men, donated funds for the schools. Convent schools, which moulded upper-class Polish girls into domesticity, patriotism and loyalty to the Catholic church, were established in Right-Bank Ukraine. Incorporation of those territories into the Russian Empire brought the spread of Polish and Catholic influence.

The push for higher education for women in the empire came in the 1850s and 60s, together with demands to abolish serfdom, introduce a parliamentary system, reform the judiciary, and establish some local autonomy. In Ukrainian territories, the Kharkiv, Poltava and Rivne educational districts wanted to create women's high schools alongside regular high schools in order to prepare women to enter the universities. In other areas, Ukrainians sought the creation of more elementary schools.[2]

Ukrainian women struggled for educational opportunities at all levels: the right to secondary education, admission to universities, and the establishment of schools to combat illiteracy among the peasants. Their difficulties were compounded because the official language of the schools was Russian, which Ukrainian children did not understand.[3] As pointed out earlier, Olena Pchilka refused to send her children to school because she did not want them speaking Russian. Secondary schools for girls run by the government were established in Kharkiv in 1812, Poltava in 1817, Odessa in 1828, Kerch in 1835 and finally in Kiev itself in 1838. Various private schools followed, but were also obliged to teach in Russian.

The Institute of Young Ladies of the Nobility in Kiev ranked second only to the prestigious Smolny Institute for Girls in St. Petersburg, founded by Catherine II.[4] Natalena Laserda y Medina Coeli Dunin-Borkovska Koroleva spent a year there in 1906–7, following study at the Mesdames of the Sacred Heart in Provence. She was taken aback less by the low academic standard in the Kievan Institute than by the pettiness of the regulations, the bitterness of the women personnel and the lack of enthusiasm among the students. Male teachers and clergy showed a greater tolerance, and were more attuned to the needs of the girls. At the Kievan Institute Ukrainian teachers, among them the composer Lysenko, tried subtly to provide Ukrainian students with at least a minimal understanding of Ukrainian history and culture. Mariia Livytska's similar experiences at a less refined school in Kiev were characteristic for Ukrainian activist women; secondary education in the mandatory Russian did little to provide the young women with a sense of self-worth.[5]

Education for women was intertwined with political issues. In Russia, in addition to the conservatives' usual argument concerning the dangers of education for gentle female natures, was the radicals' view that higher education was a luxury for the few who exploited the many. The radicals exhorted youngsters to pay their debt to society by foregoing their own higher education and by working among and educating the peasants instead. Along with the desire for education among women came their involvement in various community education programmes.

Higher education became a volatile issue from the 1860s until 1905. Students expelled for making political proclamations became involved in political and, at times, terrorist activities. In the 1860s the government permitted universities some autonomy, but student demonstrations continued. A restrictive system introduced in 1884 also failed to pacify the students. The government began to question the feasibility of higher education for the lower classes and to assume a link between education and revolutionary activity. Consequently, it had misgivings about the concept of higher education for

women, and refused women admission to universities, fearing that they would
become revolutionaries. Separate university-level courses for women were
organized in 1869, first in St. Petersburg, later in Moscow. University faculty
taught the higher women's courses, which duplicated the regular introductory
programme. At different times, certain subjects, spanning the gamut from
philosophy to chemistry, were restricted as being especially conducive to
revolutionary activity. Petitions in the 1860s from Kiev, Kharkiv and Odessa to
establish women's higher courses were not granted until the 1880s.

Kievan women attended the public lectures held frequently in that city and,
following the creation of higher women's courses in the Russian capitals, tried
to develop coordinated programmes in Kiev. The initiative came from the
liberal middle-aged women, who enjoyed secure positions in society through
their class or by marriage. Many came from old Ukrainian families with
traditions of philanthropic and cultural work. They were aided by moderate and
cautious liberal academics among Kievan men who also feared their children's
involvement in revolutionary activity.

The moving force behind the courses was Ievdokiia Gogotska, wife of a
university professor. That in itself made the authorities wary, since they had
accused Gogotska, the publisher of *Kievskii telegraf* (1874–6), of both
Ukrainophile and revolutionary tendencies.[6] The courses finally commenced in
1879 with high enrollment, even though the women got no academic credit for
them and paid fees that were beyond the means of many.[7] Indeed, gaining the
qualifications to earn financial independence was one goal of women in
demanding a full university programme instead of the planned two-year one,
which the government initially wanted to limit to only one year. After the
assassination of the Tsar in March 1881 the courses were closed for four years.
This suspension stimulated the creation of the first Ukrainian women's
organization. In 1883, on the initiative of Olena Dobrohaieva, women students
started a study circle which became a women's organization in the following
year. As the organization was never officially sanctioned, its members soon
dispersed into other types of activity.

The Kievan courses attracted women who would achieve much in later life:
Nadezhda Sokolovskaia (the future Bolshevik leader), Mariia Starytska (the
actress, socialist and finally victim of the Bolsheviks), Olha Khoruzhynska
(who was soon to marry Franko and participate in public work in Galicia),
Iryna Antonovych, Anna Berenshtam, Zinaida Tulub, Dariia Shevchenko,
Neoniliia Chyzhevska, Liudmyla Kistiakovska, and many others. Some women
expelled from the Moscow and St. Petersburg courses for political activity were
permitted to continue their studies in Kiev. They contributed to the
popularization of radical ideologies, or at least gave the police such an
impression. Women's courses were founded in Kharkiv in 1878, and in Odessa
shortly afterward.

The police mistrusted them, although politically most women students were
moderate and craved education for self-betterment, a career and financial
independence.[8] Like the faculty in Kiev, female students argued repeatedly for

the incorporation of the women's courses into the regular university curriculum. Many Ukrainian women found it easier to gain permission to study at the women's courses in Moscow and St. Petersburg, despite the distance and the need to acquire police permission for the change of residency.

Among the gains of the 1905 Russian Revolution were university autonomy and the opening of private higher schools. There were even attempts to establish private universities. In Ukraine, Olena Pchilka continually urged the Ukrainian upper classes to raise the funds necessary for the creation of "people's universities in Ukraine."[9] Sofiia Simirenko donated money and property in Kiev for a Ukrainian-language university to be named in honour of her husband, the industrialist V.F. Simirenko.[10]

Some exceptional Ukrainian women pursued scholarly interests. Sofiia Kovalevska (née Korvin-Krukovska, 1850–91), born in the Poltava region, was the first modern female mathematician to teach at a university (Stockholm). Pelahiia Bartosh Lytvyn (1833–1904) was evidently the first Ukrainian woman to collect samples of embroidery systematically. Hanna Berlo (1859–1942) was a teacher who wrote a number of historical studies.[11]

Like the men, Ukrainian women were freer to pursue scholarly interests in Moscow and St. Petersburg than in Kiev. Varvara Adriianova-Peretts and Sofiia Shchehlova, students at the Kiev courses and scholars of early Rus' literature, were harassed by police and moved to St. Petersburg. Oleksandra Stavrovetska Efimenko (1848–1918) took the nationality of her Ukrainian husband and produced several influential works on the social history of Ukraine. She moved from Kharkiv to Moscow, where she taught at the Bestuzhev Women's Higher Courses. In 1910, she became the first woman in the empire to receive an honorary doctorate in history from the University of Kharkiv. Five years earlier, at the XIII Archeological Congress in Katerynoslav, she had led a protest of 190 participants against discrimination of Ukrainians.[12]

A few women became university assistant professors before the October Revolution, such as Nataliia Polonska, who joined the University of Kiev in 1916. After the revolution more women entered the scholarly community following the various reorganizations of the universities. Ukrainophile circles encouraged women's scholarly ventures insofar as they did not interfere with maternal and connubial duties.[13] Students without such obligations joined organizations founded by male students. Of particular significance for the crystallization of political and national views were the student groups in Moscow and St. Petersburg founded by Ukrainians, in which the women participated on an equal basis with men.[14]

The need for higher education for women was overshadowed by the illiteracy which pervaded the empire. The literacy rate in Ukraine was only slightly above the empire average where at the turn of the century only 32 per cent could read. In 1897 in Ukraine 40 per cent of men under 50 years of age could read; of those over 50 only 20 per cent were literate. Illiteracy among women was three times higher than among men, a ratio in which Ukraine mirrored the empire.[15] The abolition of serfdom did not improve matters. The government had to support programmes of effective compulsory education. Professor P.V. Pirogov, the supervisor (*popechitel*) of the Kievan educational districts, proposed in October 1859 the creation of Sunday schools staffed by volunteers to promote literacy among peasants and workers. The proposal was successfully carried out and the Sunday schools were later merged with the primary schools that were ostensibly under *zemstvo* jurisdiction. As with other expressions of private initiative, the government viewed the schools with mistrust or hostility.[16]

Work among the peasants demonstrated a need for the improved pedagogical methods. The government forced peasants to learn to read and write in Russian, to them an incomprehensible language. That they somehow managed reflected the dedication and ingenuity of many women who constituted a large proportion of the teachers.

Two imperial reforms sought by Ukrainians were an expansion of the networks of primary education and the opening of the clerical estate to men other than the sons of clerics. The shortage of schools compelled various community groups to create their own programmes to promote literacy. In turn, the granting of permission for children of the clergy to enter secular schools and professions increased the size of the intelligentsia and raised its national consciousness. In many Ukrainian provinces most teachers were children of clergy, since teaching was the profession most accessible to them.[17] Ukraine, with its tradition of community schools, was quick to produce village teachers. Women were especially drawn to that work.[18] The government, perturbed, banned the use of the native language in schools soon after the Sunday-school and adult-literacy effort began: all programmes had to be taught in Russian.

Educational, especially popular and cultural, work among the peasants and workers provided an outlet for the intelligentsia,[19] and was considered by Ukrainians a patriotic endeavour. But there was some debate about the propriety of Ukrainian participation in Russian-language Sunday schools. Borys Hrinchenko and Olena Pchilka, especially, opposed this course, although the former remained active in the pedagogical field.

Even the Russians became painfully aware of the difficulties of teaching peasants to read in a non-native language. But the government feared that efforts to eradicate illiteracy would encourage the spread of either revolutionary or Ukrainophile propaganda. The linguistic issue soon became a political one. Public use of the Ukrainian language became a major issue for Ukrainians in Russia. In 1905, Ukrainians demanded education in their native language at all levels. After 1905, they repeatedly raised the question in the Duma. Conscious Ukrainianism became widespread among high-school students, especially among young women.[20]

By the end of the nineteenth century there emerged a striking confluence of the Sunday-school movement, Ukrainian aspirations, and a more prominent role for women in public life. Its explanation begins, as is frequently the case in modern Ukrainian history, with Taras Shevchenko. In the last years of his life, Shevchenko became interested in programmes of education for the common people. He drafted textbooks suitable for use by the peasants, and helped to write and publish the successful primer, *Bukvar iuzhnorusskii*, which appeared in 1861, the year of his death, and the year that saw the abolition of serfdom.[21]

The first Sunday schools were established in the Kiev area at the initiative of a Kiev-Kharkiv secret society that had been in close contact with Shevchenko. In 1862, of the 331 Sunday schools in the Russian Empire, 111 were in Ukraine.[22] The most prominent woman in the Sunday school movement was Khrystyna D. Alchevska,[23] who epitomized the many currents in Ukrainian life before 1914. Through the Society of Sunday Schools in Kharkiv, which she founded and led for more than half a century, Alchevska developed an effective method of teaching adults through use of regular literary works rather than mere spelling books. Her work gained imperial and international recognition: in 1889 she represented teachers of adults in the Russian Empire at the Paris Exhibition. In 1904 her work was singled out at the International Women's Congress in Berlin.[24]

The city of Kharkiv was the location of the Ukrainian cultural renaissance, the groundwork of which had been laid in the early 1800s.[25] Between 1850 and 1870, the city doubled its population through rapid industrialization. Alchevska reflected the dynamism of the new city. She was raised in Russia by Russified Ukrainian parents. As a young girl she was influenced by both Shevchenko and Herzen. She married a Ukrainian who became a successful businessman. Of her three children, one became a promising poet, another an opera singer. Alchevska was drawn to work among the poor women, workers and peasants, with whom she found genuine rapport. She was one of the first practitioners of community festivals in honour of cultural leaders. At these concerts and ceremonies the girls and women wore the costumes of their region and performed folksongs as well as some artistic work. Alchevska, like a number of upper class women, wore the peasant costume as a symbol of their dedication to the people's cause. Alchevska's school was the first public building to erect a statue of Shevchenko, and sought to acquire that poet's name.[26]

Alchevska not only pioneered successful methods for teaching adults, but also effectively adapted folk culture to city life to help peasants who were moving into cities adjust better. Her use of Ukrainian folk art offset the alien nature of the Russian language for many of her pupils. Her programme served as a model for other schools. Yet the ties of the peasant to the village remained unbroken: the peasant returned when the factories were idle or to perform seasonal work at the farm. In the villages, if there were schools or libraries, the peasants were confronted by Russification.[27]

For Ukrainians in the Russian Empire, the quest for women's education at all levels was inextricably tied to the use of the Ukrainian language. Here also the goals of feminism went hand in hand with the needs of the people and of the nation.

3.
Ukrainian Women in Political Life

Emergent Ukrainianism in Eastern Ukraine in the nineteenth century was based upon the ideals of equality, freedom and progress. The main validity of the cluster of ideas that made up Ukrainian nationalism lay in its connection with the common people; its democratic character. Ukrainian nationalism lacked both a specific ideology and a party, and Ukrainians did not stress historical continuity despite some use of terms and symbols of the Cossack age. Rather, they based their arguments for cultural and eventually political autonomy on ideas of universal democracy and justice.[1]

Political parties became legal in the Russian Empire only after the 1905 Revolution; prior to that political ideas and strategies were developed in informal groups and structured clandestine organizations. Since Ukrainians were the object of particular discrimination by the Russian government, they added the struggle for national rights to all other desiderata for change in the Empire. They participated in all the political movements in the empire, and despite severe limitations, organized their own societies, publishing ventures, economic co-operatives and clandestine parties.

The need for secrecy, unwarranted persecution, lack of political education and political experience, and a lack of support even from so-called progressive Russian parties all help to account for the underdevelopment of Ukrainian political activity before 1914. Eastern Ukrainians wanted territorial autonomy. Only gradually did the idea of national independence begin to emerge. "The Ukrainian national movement as formulated in the late nineteenth and early twentieth centuries...had been a protest movement, struggling not so much for political power within the framework of existing institutions as against national oppression."[2]

Adherents of the Ukrainian movement, including those who stressed national as well as social and political liberation, united in seeking human rights and freedom in the Russian Empire. All Ukrainians, from the radicals to the most moderate, wanted somehow to convince the Russians of the justice of Ukrainian claims.

They had tried to assert their rights not only in the face of tsarist autocracy, but also against the opposition or apathy of Russians of all political persuasions. Most national minorities in Ukraine, such as the Jews, opted for the Russian rather than the Ukrainian political variant. Yet the Ukrainian national movement did not succumb to extremism, chauvinism or exclusiveness, nor did it compromise its liberal character.

For Ukrainians, feminism could not become a political goal. The injustice of the suppression of Ukrainian culture as a whole superseded the pain of traditional discrimination against women. Many Ukrainians aspired to the same goals as Western European women who worked toward emancipation: autonomy, freedom of conscience, the right of choice in work and education, economic independence, civic participation, the right to vote, and abolition of discriminatory measures.

Women did not formulate any specific aspects of Ukrainian political or cultural programmes, but since Ukrainianism was an organic rather than systematic development and women were less interested in political issues than men, they were more likely to take a practical course than male-dominated parties. Some political activists in the Russian Empire belittled the women's approach as "petty deed" politics when compared to the ostensibly comprehensive programmes of reform or revolution put forward by the the political parties.

In theory, the role of women in Ukrainian opposition movements was equal to that of men. While they wrote and theorized less than men, they participated actively in Ukrainian developments. The identification of the Ukrainian cause with the people, its persecution by the government and the indifference and hostility with which it was viewed by the Russians made conscious Ukrainians progressive, even somewhat revolutionary in rhetoric. The abolition of serfdom and other reforms of the 1860s in the empire made possible some community organization. But the popularity of the Ukrainian movement caught the Russian government by surprise. Police reports emphasized a new word: Ukrainophile. Being pro-Ukrainian was seen as being implicitly anti-Russian and revolutionary. The persecuted Ukrainians became politically more active. To the suggestion that she cease her political activities and concentrate on literature, Lesia Ukrainka replied: "I cannot stop seeing the totally enslaved Ukraine, so I cannot give up [political activity]. Were I to do so I would have to reject my poetry, my most intimate expression, for to utter and write it while avoiding the actions it exhorts would be shameful."[3] As the Ukrainian national movement developed, it attracted more and more women.

The work of women was an important, if not always a recognized, part of the "communities" (*hromady*), the cultural and political organizations created in the 1860s and 70s. Their membership was fluid and they functioned under tsarist surveillance. They espoused a liberal political programme, rejecting violence and placing great hope on the enlightenment and education of the masses. The most influential hromada, the one in Kiev, was essentially an old-boy network that functioned from the 1870s until 1917. Although it barred women in the style of the Cossack *Sich*, many meetings were held under the guise of social functions in which women were involved, despite Cossack traditions.[4] The Hromada sent Mykhailo Drahomanov, a liberal federalist, to Western Europe to facilitate publication of Ukrainian works, establish links with Russian liberals, especially in the *zemstva*, and make closer contacts with Ukrainians in the Austrian Empire. Olha Hortynska, a Chernihiv student living in Geneva, who used the code name "Miss," served as a clandestine liaison between Kiev and Drahomanov.[5] Ielysaveta Myloradovych Skoropadska was another activist operating in the Poltava Hromada during the 1860s. The first major Ukrainophile newspaper in Kiev, *Kievskii telegraf*, appeared in 1874 largely through the efforts of Ievdokiia Gogotska.

Activist families intermarried and perpetuated the movement. Women frequently ran technical operations, evidently with more success than the men. Political activities mingled with various social and cultural needs. Olena Pchilka smuggled fiction and apolitical poems for publication in the first women's almanac in Galicia. Other young women reportedly brought pistols from Galicia, hidden in their elaborate hairstyles. Hiding clandestine leaflets in baby cribs was common. Sometimes Ukrainian girls married merely to be free of legal parental authority and embark on their studies unhindered. Chykalenko, in his unpublished memoirs of 1882–5, recounted one case in which the couple fell in love during the wedding ceremony but were too ashamed of their emotions to admit them during their casual meetings after the agreed separation. The man particularly did not wish to appear to be taking advantage of his legal rights. Ukrainianism played a role in the selection of a partner. Chykalenko noted in March 1911, that the writer Vynnychenko was marrying a Jewish girl who had promised to learn Ukrainian and raise their children in that language. The couple remained childless.

Populism in the Russian Empire began as a series of overlapping movements and organizations in the 1870s, culminating in the creation of the Social Revolutionary Party in 1903. Populists stressed individual action, working in small groups and using dramatic actions to try to jolt the peasants into mass protest and revolution. From its inception populism gravitated between two poles——peaceful propaganda work among the peasantry and terrorism. The populists hoped to ease the Russian Empire into socialism without the intervening phase of industrial capitalism. Such an ideology was particularly attractive to Ukrainians.

Alchevska contributed the first printed political statement by a woman in the oppositionary press of the entire Empire in Herzen's London-based *Kolokol* (The Bell) in 1863. She appealed to Russians to support the Polish uprising against the tsar, signing herself Ukrainka.[6]

Large-scale populist activity began after Tsar Alexander II, fearing the spread of revolutionary propaganda, ordered all Russian students in Europe to return home. Herzen, writing from abroad, exhorted the student youth——now devoid of occupation——to go to the people to spread the democratic cause. The trek to the people began in the summer of 1874. But the students soon discovered that the countryside was not exclusively Russian. The "Grandmother of the Revolution," Ekaterina Breshko-Breshkovskaia, for example, who at the age of sixteen was among the first to don peasant costume and go to the village, soon realized that the peasants did not understand her refined Russian. Ukrainians among whom she began her revolutionary pilgrimage naturally responded more readily to their native language than to the unfamiliar Russian.

Ardent youths of both sexes preached the gospel of collectivism and revolution to the peasants. To the populists, all evil in the Russian Empire was embodied in the tsarist bureaucracy; all the good in the peasant and the Russian commune. First they dealt with the "evil" through petitions. When these failed, they resorted to terrorist actions against the tsar and bureaucracy. Some revolutionaries committed suicide to call attention to the atrocities of the system. A conflict ensued between the young revolutionaries and the plodding all-male Okhrana or Third Section, the imperial secret police. The police kept detailed files on literally thousands of suspects and employed agents to shadow them and a staff to interpret the data. Women played a crucial and highly visible role on all levels of revolutionary activity. There were no women in the police or among the investigators. Nor are there known cases of female double agents.[7]

The Okhrana immediately connected populism and Ukrainianism. At the first sign of "Ukrainophilism," the Okhrana doubled its security.

The sacrifices of women in the populist movement encouraged others to look beyond domestic concerns. Although these women perceived no link with the Ukrainian girls who had fought the Turks and Tatars, they served nonetheless as role models of selfless martyrdom.

It was a descendant of the last hetman of Ukraine, Sofiia Perovskaia (1853–81), who pointed the direction in which the fatal bomb was to be hurled at Alexander II in March 1881. Before the assassination she was an organizer in Kharkiv. Her close collaborator, Andrii Zheliabov, a Ukrainian, argued that tsarism had to be destroyed before the national question could be addressed. M.O. Vitrova, another Ukrainian woman, immolated herself in 1886 as a protest against police brutality.

The Kovalevsky family is a poignant example of the work of the populists. Mariia Vorontsova Kovalevska (1849–89), born in Katerynoslav, was active in the populist group in Kiev. While her husband supported peaceful work within the Ukrainian movement, she advocated armed actions against the regime. Following her arrest and exile to Siberia in 1879, her husband Mykola visited her in a classic reversal of roles. Upon returning from exile, Kovalevsky was barred from work because he was married to a terrorist. His most radical actions, however, were drafting petitions, donating money to Ukrainian causes, and working with Ukrainian groups. Mariia, highly strung, emotional, torn between revolutionary activities and the child she had to abandon, unable to bear the rigours of the hard labour, went mad. Recovering after treatment, she returned to hard labour. In 1889 she and several other women committed suicide to protest brutality against prisoners.[8]

In 1898 populists were challenged by the founding of a Marxist party. Marxism attracted many among the intelligentsia of the empire. At the founding Congress of the Russian Social Democratic Party (RSDP) in Minsk, of the nine delegates present, four represented organizations from Ukrainian territories. The party remained small in numbers, as it represented the vanguard of the proletariat; its role was to lead the workers, not necessarily to represent them.

Among the first Ukrainian Marxists was Anna Kuliscioff, an activist in the Italian Social Democratic Movement since 1878 who paid no attention to the nationality issue. Along with Turati she was elected a delegate to the Brussels Congress of the Socialist International in 1903.[9]

The Russian interpretation of Marxism implicitly sanctioned the unity of the Empire. Russian communist nationality policy was not formulated until Lenin had spent some time in the Austrian Empire and realized the ideological importance of the recognition of the principle of national self-determination, and even the right of secession for the most progressive element of the proletariat. The party subsequently posited the proletariat's ties with Russia; breaking such ties was construed as joining the bourgeoisie.

Marx foresaw the transformation of great empires into workers' states and consigned the smaller East European nations wedged between the Russian and German colossi to the dust-heap of history. Nevertheless, the links between Marxism and nationalism have remained central to Eastern Europe, a measure of Marxism's ability to tolerate diversity. For Ukrainian women, these links were to prove more crucial than those between Marxism and feminism.

Ostensibly a minor movement, communism, at first, did not seem threatening to Ukrainians. Before the Revolution of 1917 social democracy and Marxism were seen not as Russian but as international movements that would help Ukrainians overcome their isolation from Europe and enhance progressive ideas. Drahomanov's democratic brand of socialism helped make this ideology palatable. The Western Ukrainian social-democratic movement disseminated Ukrainian-language publications in the Russian Empire, thereby linking the ideas of social democracy with those of national liberation. The Russian police were suspicious of Ukrainian-language materials circulating in the empire that originated in Galicia. There, as we shall see, discussion of socialism led naturally to discussion of the position of women. In Russia, on the other hand, the women's issue was discussed in an international rather than a specifically Ukrainian context. More important, the quest for basic rights was the most rudimentary issue confronting Ukrainians in the Russian Empire. Even within the international and Russian Social Democratic movements, Ukrainians had to struggle to assert their national identity. It is within the latter context that the destiny of modern Ukraine was shaped.

The first Ukrainian political parties, like those of the Russians, began to emerge at the turn of the century with the formation of the Revolutionary Ukrainian Party (RUP), the Ukrainian Radical Democratic Party (URDP), the Ukrainian Social Democratic Labour Party (USDLP). Meanwhile the Ukrainian deputies in the Duma (the representative assembly established in 1906) founded the Society of Ukrainian Progressives (TUP), from which developed the Socialist Federalist party in March 1917.

Women joined these parties, but played only a minor role in formulating their programmes. The parties provided men with a legitimate forum for ideological discussions and led to a splintering of Ukrainian activists.

Women's cultural work, however, did have political repercussions. Khrystyna Alchevska (1843–1920), the promoter of adult education, is not considered a political activist, but she raised the consciousness of the hundreds of women she prepared for political and community work. Her older contemporary, Ielysaveta Skoropadska Myloradovych (1830–90), had continued public-spirited philanthropic work, helping to fund the publications of the Shevchenko Scientific Society in Galicia. The latter stimulated Ukrainian scholarship and popularized the Ukrainian cause. Lesser-known benefactresses of the Ukrainian movement were Sofiia Albrant Simirenko, the wife of the Kievan industrialist, who supported Ukrainian causes; Kateryna Skarzhynska, a rich landowner who founded a museum of ethnography, and Mariia Trebynska, who not only financed theatre troupes, but also helped organize them.

Olena Pchilka (1849–1930) is the least-known female activist of pre-revolutionary Ukraine. Her literary talents paled beside those of her daughter, Lesia Ukrainka, while her brother, Mykhailo Drahomanov, belittled her public activity. Drahomanov, who shaped the views of the 1917 generation, promoted equal rights for women, encouraged and prepared his daughter for higher education, and used his wife's help in his own work. But he also insisted that the mother should take care of the children. He complained that Pchilka's public activity had a detrimental effect on her children and was not averse to her receiving police attention if it would prevent her activities and bring her home.[10] Drahomanov underestimated the intelligence of the woman who educated her children at home lest they become Russified in government-run schools, translating literary classics into Ukrainian and developing a Great Books programme for them. Pchilka was also the first woman to publish a book on Ukrainian ethnographic ornaments. Drahomanov objected to the type of literature that Pchilka wrote, such as her conscious creation of new words. But she was proud of her art: "I am forging new words," she wrote.[11]

Pchilka was one of five delegates who petitioned the ministry of interior for permission to publish in Ukrainian at the end of 1904.[12] Her uncompromising stand was unpopular among Kiev's Ukrainian youth, which considered a guarantee of national rights unnecessary pedantry: "We were repelled by the directness of her accusations and by her curt behaviour toward all persons she felt did not possess proper nationalist convictions.... We considered her a chauvinist in the fullest sense of the term."[13]

Olena Pchilka was critical of the sacred heroes of the Russian intelligentsia. In her self-published journal that appeared (with interruptions) between 1905 and 1914, she complained about the "personal hostility of Belinsky [the father of Russian radical literary criticism] and later Russian writers toward Ukrainian literature."[14] Nor did she endear herself to Ukrainians when she pointed out that many Jews, as residents of Ukraine, supported the Russian colonizers. Moreover, in a series of articles that Pchilka published in 1908, Pchilka asserted that Jews in Ukraine not only exploited Ukrainians economically, but actively opposed Ukrainian national and cultural strivings. The majority of the Ukrainian intelligentsia was pro-Jewish and resented Pchilka's handling of the issue. They felt that eventually the Jews would recognize the justice of the Ukrainian cause.

Pchilka predicted——earlier than most Ukrainians——that Russian opponents of the tsarist regime would not necessarily support the non-Russian nationalities. In her own journal and in the few publications that granted her a forum she documented case after case of Russian radicals' and liberals' hostility to Ukrainians. She reminded her readers that not a single Russian had protested the closing of the Ukrainian Enlightenment Society in Kiev, Chernihiv and other cities. Most Russian liberals, Pchilka felt, were totally ignorant of their closest Slavic kin, the Ukrainians.[15] Her support for the rights of Poles in Ukraine was also unpopular among her compatriots. When the government closed the Polish society *Oświata* (Enlightenment), on the grounds that Polish-language schools threatened the interests of the local population, she countered that "those Ukrainians who yearn for the expansion of the rights of their own language would have no objections to such schools."[16] She was also less critical of the Austrian Empire than most others, noting in July 1912, that although there were few Ukrainian deputies in the Austrian parliament, the situation in the Russian Empire was much worse.

Pchilka preceded Mykola Mikhnovsky, an early modern proponent of Ukrainian political independence, in her contention that the success of the venture lay solely in the hands of Ukrainians: no outside help would be forthcoming. She persisted in her uncompromising stand after the 1917 Revolution, courageously criticizing the Bolsheviks. Few attended her funeral in 1930.

The ideologue of Ukrainian integral nationalism, Dmytro Dontsov, wrote in 1931 that "Olena Pchilka will occupy a leading place in the history of active Ukrainians."[17] Ukrainian nationalists in the 1930s did not single her out: it is Mikhnovsky who still enjoys the status of father of modern nationalism.[18] Pchilka is remembered mainly as the mother of Lesia Ukrainka.

The daughters, real and spiritual, of the so-called Ukrainophiles and activists of the hromada became even more involved as new spheres of activity opened up. Ukrainian patriots came from families with such names as Lindfors, Berenshtam, O'Connor, Gladilin, and Sudovshchik. They joined the Chykalenkos, the Starytskys, the Lysenkos, the Livytskys, the Levytskys, the Ianovskys, the Hrinchenkos and countless others in erecting the Ukrainian national movement. Many shared the broad ideology of the social-democratic movement. Some, like Sofiia Lindfors Rusova (1857–1940) and Mariia Gladilina Hrinchenko (who wrote as Zahirna, 1863–1928), were teachers by profession.

Most Ukrainian activists were under police surveillance by virtue of their nationality. Contrary to some analyses, many members of the gentry were involved in the Ukrainian movement. Oleksander Rusov, Sofiia's husband, was dismissed from his teaching position in 1876 because of his work at the *Kievskii telegraf* and his friendship with Countess Sofia Panina, the sister of the Petrunkevych brothers, who are well known as Russian liberals but not remembered for their Ukrainian origins. Rusov later lost his position in the statistical bureau of the Chernihiv *zemstvo* on the suspicion that he had organized a Ukrainian society in Kharkiv. But the Okhrana agents reported that "Rusov seems milder than his wife. His wife——now she is a hopeless woman, incapable of reforming herself. She definitely is a terrorist who encourages the most extreme views in young people."[19]

Neither in theory nor in practice were the Rusovs terrorists. But nineteen-year-old Sofiia did arrange for the publication in Prague and importing into the Russian Empire of an uncensored complete version of Shevchenko's *Kobzar* (The Minstrel). Subsequently, Rusova was fully occupied with teaching and the preparation of textbooks, but the Okhrana kept imputing terrorist activities to the determined diminutive teacher.[20]

In their correspondence, Sofiia Rusova and Olha Skadkovska, a member of the Social Democratic Party, discussed new German books on social and economic issues. The Rusovs rented their house to Anna Ruban, who was suspected of trafficking in proscribed literature from the Austrian Empire. The police found it especially disturbing that the Rusovs and friends (among whom were Volodymyr Antonovych, Volodymyr Naumenko, Elisei Trehubov, the marshal of the nobility in Poltava, and Mykola Koval) ''become acquainted with students, on whom they exercise a particularly strong impact.''[21]

The Kosaches, Pchilka, the Starytskys and Lysenkos were neighbours in Kiev. The women helped and encouraged one another, becoming involved in both clandestine and legal actions.

In the *zemstvo* movement Ukrainians developed a network of co-operatives that grew dramatically after 1905 and in which many women participated.[22] Although Pchilka complained that the co-operative organization did not reflect the composition of the Ukrainian rank and file, the whole co-operative movement in Ukraine nevertheless assisted the Ukrainian cause. Drahomanov had sought a unified moderate opposition, with headquarters in Geneva. His sister and other women travelled to Galicia and helped to bring about the publication of works banned in the Russian Empire.

Closer contacts between Eastern Ukrainians and Galicians provided further opportunities for publication and other activity. The famine of 1890, which was more acute than previous ones, also acted as a uniting force in the Ukrainian community, as did the cholera epidemics and the relief efforts they necessitated.

A highlight of the Ukrainian national movement was the unveiling of the monument to the writer Ivan Kotliarevsky in Poltava on 30 August 1903. The celebrations were called under the guise of "special meetings of the Poltava city duma" chaired by Trehubov, an old friend of the Kosach family and the Rusovs. Ukrainians throughout the Russian Empire and delegations from the Austrian Empire made their way to Poltava. Upon arrival they discovered that the minister of interior, von Plehve, had specifically banned the public use of Ukrainian at the festivities. The first reaction, supported by students from the RUP, was to stage a protest demonstration. But eventually it was decided that it would be wiser not to give the authorities a pretext to cancel the whole affair. Instead, the unveiling ceremony took place in a moving silence.

That evening, at a formal gathering in the presence of the mayor, two keynote addresses were delivered in Russian by the historian Oleksandra Efimenko and the writer Ivan Steshenko. Ukrainians from Galicia and Bukovyna who did not have to comply with Russian ordinances and knew no Russian gave speeches in Ukrainian to enthusiastic applause.

The second part of the programme consisted of formal greetings from various organizations. The first speaker was Olha Andriievska of the Chernihiv Literary Theatrical Society. She spoke so quietly that only after several sentences did the mayor realize she was speaking in Ukrainian. He then interrupted her. The other participants and the audience left in protest.[23]

This was the largest single Ukrainian gathering that had yet been held in the Russian Empire, and it provided a manifestation of national power that took Ukrainians themselves by surprise. The ranks of Ukrainian activists were being augmented by younger people who were not satisfied with small-scale actions and did not join in local activities. Instead they launched bolder ventures: some tried publishing; others formed new political parties made up of local activists. Their discussions centred on the issue of national identity, not on work among the people. Among both the Social Democrats and the Social Revolutionaries, the two major revolutionary groupings in the empire, more people recognized the importance of using the local language. The RUP had links with the Social Revolutionaries. For instance, Kateryna Gaudentsova-Lyss used the publications of the Kiev and Chernihiv branches of the RUP in her work for the Social Revolutionaries. Olha D. Kseshynska, who had close contacts with the Chernihiv peasants, used Ukrainian brochures in her work, while Vera A. Cherkesova used Ukrainian publications to proselytize Kharkiv workers.[24] Oleksandra Sudovshchyk Kosach, who returned to Kiev in 1904 after an absence of a few years, was surprised by the rapid growth and pervasive influence of the Ukrainian movement.[25]

Rising national consciousness was not the only issue confronting women, however. The political activity of Mariia Tkachenko Livytska emphasizes the significance of the continuing need to define priorities. While still in high school Livytska became an advocate of social reform. Her future husband, Andrii, and his sister gradually convinced her that reform could succeed only by taking into account the national aspirations of the local population. Livytska and Andrii became a political couple in the best revolutionary tradition. Andrii proposed to Mariia from a prison cell. They both joined the Revolutionary Ukrainian Party at its founding in Kiev. Mariia worked in the Women's

Hromada in order to enhance the party's influence on the older generation of women. The Livytskys' apartment was used for political meetings, to hide the writer Volodymyr Vynnychenko before he left the country, and to store various political leaflets.

Although poor, Mariia never questioned the need for help and maintained a nanny for the children (one born in 1902, the other in 1907). Like Rusova or Starytska Cherniakhivska (1868–1941) or Liubov Ianovska (1861–1941), the younger generation of women also combined dedication to the cause with family life. But as their political activities developed, conflicts emerged over personal and political issues. Livytska openly discussed clashes with her husband over child-rearing, especially on political and national emphases.

The revolutionary movement engendered a reactionary, anti-Semitic and anti-Ukrainian backlash, especially between 1903 and 1907. To defend themselves, local leaders created defence leagues. In Lubni, where the Livytskys now lived, the RUP moderates, who co-operated closely with the Social Democrats, formed a coalition committee with the Jewish Bund and Poale Zion and thereby prevented a pogrom. The local police even thought that Lubni was the centre of a revolutionary republic and arrested local Ukrainian leaders.

The Livytskys were actively involved in both the Social Democratic Party (SDP) and the RUP. Nastia Hrinchenko, the daughter of the writer and an SDP activist, visited them frequently. Livytska led a workers' group with Volodymyr Stepaniuk, alias Ovksentii Lola, an ardent Leninist sympathizer, in Lubni. When the coalition committee was organized, she naturally presumed that she would play an active role, but her husband "forbade me, as a woman, to take part in the self-defence of the city."[26] Even after her husband was arrested she declined to chair the committee, maintaining that it was not seemly for a woman to occupy such a visible position.

The Revolution of 1905 was actually a series of crises, interspersed with pogroms and with the formation of various political parties. After the October Manifesto of 1905, the parties became legal and were eventually centralized. The development of a party structure and programme resulted in a decline in the participation of women.

Early in 1905, RUP activists formed a separate Ukrainian Social Democratic Party. In an attempt to undermine this new grouping and in response to pressure from Ukrainians within the all-Russian Marxist movement, a group of Marxists known as the Spilka (Union) was founded in Ukraine at Lenin's behest as an autonomous part of the RSDLP. In contrast to the Russian party, which was dominated by intellectuals, the Spilka attracted a substantial number of workers and peasants. It also attracted women: Nastia Hrinchenko remained a member until its dissolution, while Genia-Leia Kirnos, a midwife, offered the use of her address for Spilka purposes. Gilda Vulson served as liaison between the Spilka and Chernihiv. Among the original adherents were Mariia Vynohradova, a Ukrainian political activist, and Sarah Shatz, a Jewish activist. Soviet works stress that the goal of the Spilka was to encourage the proletariat of Ukraine to join an all-Russian rather than a Ukrainian separatist organization.[27]

Like subsequent Ukrainian socialist organizations, this group was accused of nationalism. Both the day-to-day work in the local language and the popularity of the Spilka made the central party wary. Therefore, it moulded the Spilka as an organization to co-ordinate peasant membership for the Social Democratic movement in the Empire. But it was short-lived, liquidated by the police a year after its formation as "the major disseminator of the revolutionary propaganda in the villages and the centre of the activities of the revolutionaries."[28]

The Spilka tried to attract all Ukrainians with social-democratic sympathies; it regarded Lesia Ukrainka and her sister Olha Kosach Kryvyniuk as members, and Liudmyla Drahomanova as a candidate for one of its posts. But supporters of Lenin's concept of a centralized party, such as Evgeniia Bosh, a Jewish woman from Ukraine, never considered Ukraine anything but a territorial entity. The same can be said about Rosalia Zalkind, the daughter of a Kiev merchant who served loyally, under the pseudonym Zemliachka, as the disseminator of Lenin's journal, *Iskra* (The Spark). Yet the police always referred to the Spilka as the "Ukrainian Social Democratic Workers' Party Spilka," and had severe problems translating confiscated materials "in the Galician dialect."[29]

The Spilka was used by the police as a pretext to close the Ukrainian Kievan newspaper *Hromadskyi holos* (Community Voice), edited by Borys Hrinchenko, whose daughter Nastia was a member of the Spilka.[30] Its demand for autonomous status within the Russian Social Democratic Labour Party, like that of the Bund, was rejected——the first of many rejections the Ukrainians were to receive from their ostensible allies. The Party dissolved the Spilka.

The Social Democrats were the only political party to support women's liberation formally and to organize activities to promote this cause. But they made no attempt to link women's liberation with nationalism. Women active in the social-democratic movement had no interest in Ukrainian problems.[31] The lack of support for Ukrainian demands on the part of the Russian Social Democratic Labour Party was not obvious to most Ukrainians, who still trusted both the small splinter Bolshevik party and the Russian opposition parties.

Among the gains of the revolutionary years was a limited representative assembly——the Duma. Women, however, remained disenfranchised. The Ukrainians acquired the right to publish in their native language, as well as to establish community organizations and political parties. The largest Ukrainian party in the Duma was the URDP, whose policies were liberal. An offshoot of the URDP was the Society of Ukrainian Progressives (TUP), which included Hrushevsky, Chykalenko and Iefremov, and demanded autonomy for Ukraine. Its female followers worked in the women's organization in Kiev, and elsewhere in the empire.

But the period of liberalization in the Russian Empire was short-lived. Ukrainian organizations suffered particularly during the repression that followed: many were closed, and publication of works in Ukrainian severely curtailed.[32] Ukrainian women worked in the *zemstva*, which they considered a forum where the nationality issue could be raised successfully.[33] Tsarist hostility toward Ukrainian organizations was expected; more surprising was that of so-called liberal and radical Russians. The Russian intelligentsia at the turn of the century was experiencing an intellectual and moral crisis, which entailed a re-evaluation of their views on revolution, materialism, their relationship to the church and the national minorities. The Ukrainian intelligentsia, closer to the village, was less affected by such matters.

Discussion of nationality focused on the Jewish question in the empire and rarely took the non-Russian nationalities into consideration. The original Pale of Settlement of the Jews was limited to Ukrainian, Lithuanian and Belorussian territories. Some Jews co-operated with Ukrainian radicals, including women, in organizational and political work, but the majority identified themselves with the Russians and were indifferent to the Ukrainians' search for identity. Others set up specifically Jewish organizations, and Jewish nationalism developed among students in some Ukrainian cities.[34]

Russian liberals were more responsive to Jewish than to Ukrainian demands. After Jewish students complained in 1915 that the Russians did not understand "our human suffering," within a month, both the Constitutional Liberals and the Social Democrat Mensheviks called public meetings to discuss the position of the Jews in the Empire.[35] Ukrainian issues, on the other hand, were rarely raised in the Russian press. In the 1880s, when one of the foremost Russian philosophers, Vladimir Solovev, wrote a series of articles on the nationality issue, Oleksandra Efimenko responded on behalf of the Ukrainians,[36] but such occasions were rare. After 1905, when Ukrainians were allowed their own press, discussion on the nationality question became heated, especially in the years preceding the First World War. In the Moscow journal *Ukrainskaia zhizn* (Ukrainian Life), Mykhailo Hrushevsky asked Russian progressives to support openly the rights of the Ukrainians, without success. On the contrary, in 1911, the Club of Russian Nationalists in Kiev denounced Ukrainianism as the most dangerous movement threatening the empire. Also in this year, the police felt obliged to report on a paper delivered in Ukrainian by Mykola Hladky, at a meeting of the Hromada at the home of the Petrovskys, on the innocuous topic of "the flora and fauna of the world."[37]

In 1913 the Romanovs celebrated the three-hundredth anniversary of their accession to the throne of Moscow, but there were serious indications of imminent change.[38] Authority was breaking down; there was increasing peasant and worker unrest, and mounting political opposition.[39] On the other hand, revolutionary terrorism seemed under control, and the Russian intelligentsia was becoming more patriotic.

By the outbreak of the First World War, Ukrainian women were participating in public life, but no major debate had taken place among the activists on the subject of women's rights. Women activists accepted male assurances that feminist concerns would be satisfied by the Ukrainian national movement, just as they believed that the social revolution would resolve women's issues.

These were the Ukrainian feminists in the most noble meaning of the term. They considered the task of Ukrainian feminism to be work with the people and for the people, work for the realization of our national ideals, for the liberation of our people, work for which the woman must give as much energy as the man, and in which she must be an equal partner with her life's comrade.[40]

Most women worked quietly but were proud of their achievements. Pchilka printed with pride a letter from a peasant taught by Alchevska who had migrated to Siberia in search of a better life, in which progressive and Ukrainian patriotic sentiments were merged.

4.
Women's Organizations in Ukraine

The work of one generation of women was a stepping-stone for the next. The suspension of the Women's Higher Courses in Kiev in 1881 spurred younger women, led by Olena Dobrohaeva, to organize a study circle of their own three years later. Simultaneously, Galician women established their first women's society. Thus, 1884 saw the start of an organized women's movement on both sides of the Zbruch.

The Kiev circle existed for more than a year. It enabled women to study topics that helped them understand conditions in Ukraine. They discussed writers not on the curriculum of Russian universities, including Mykhailo Drahomanov, who conceived the idea of fusing liberal socialism and federalism.[1] The study circles provided women with an entry into public life. Ukrainian activists were popular: M.M. Kovalevsky, for example, drew women into political discussion groups, and suggested readings. Sofiia Lindfors Rusova, Mariia Berenshtam Kistiakovska, Vira Vovk-Karachevska and Vira Bordychevska——all of whom were to become prominent in the Ukrainian women's movement——participated in these discussions.

In other cities, especially Moscow and St. Petersburg, where there were large groups of Ukrainian students, women participated in student clubs supported by Ukrainians in the community. In St. Petersburg, for example, a rich Ukrainian noblewoman provided financial aid.[2] In Kharkiv and Katerynoslav (now Dnipropetrovsk) students organized themselves according to nationality and Ukrainians were very active.[3]

The aims of the students' and women's groups coincided: to study subjects proscribed by the regime, to foster national consciousness, and to prepare for community work. The students helped popularize Ukrainian culture by setting up libraries and holding concerts and theatrical performances. Women were not only accepted as equals in these groups, but also elected officers.[4] Since in theory women were accepted as equals of men, feminism was not their main concern. Only after marriage and childbearing did the full ramifications of their second-rate status become evident. Of more obvious concern to them was the oppressed condition of Ukraine and their lack of civil rights.

The colonial status of Ukraine was reflected in her cities, which had lost their Ukrainian character before industrialization. During the latter period there was an influx of Ukrainian peasants to urban factories. Although the major cities had philanthropic women's societies, these were the preserve of the Russified upper class. The Ladies' Branch of the Kievan Society for the Welfare of the Slavs, for example, expressed interest in Slavs outside the Russian Empire, whom it considered Russian, but completely disregarded the existence of Ukrainians.[5]

Kievan women who espoused moderate political views tried repeatedly to organize a women's club, only to be prevented by the police. On 12 May 1895, Liudmyla A. Tarnovska, the wife of the politically moderate Ukrainian philanthropist, requested permission from the governor of Kiev on behalf of fourteen women for regular meetings "to spend free time in comfort, pleasure and usefulness, and to see to the material and spiritual needs of the women." The governor was amenable, but the police delayed permission, probably because they identified some of the women as "Ukrainophiles." No formal answer was given until 1910, by which time the women had developed other forms of activity.[6]

Many Ukrainian women joined and helped create societies which provided a framework through which aid, information and skills could be channelled to needy women and children. Such organizations generally ran literacy schools, cafeterias, day-care facilities and orphanages. This work was sometimes connected with community organizations, sometimes with political parties. Usually it was an *ad hoc* effort, since the Russian police was wary of a community effort and was reluctant to register organizations. The exact number of such ventures is uncertain, but they ran into the hundreds.

Not only organizations but all fund-raising activities, especially lotteries and concerts, required police permission. Hence, a wide-scale women's operation became possible only after the 1905 Revolution eased the regulations governing associations.

Two important associations founded by Ukrainian women were the Hospice for the Children of the Working Class, which was established in the 1870s in Kiev and survived until the First World War,[7] and the Kievan Association of Mutual Aid for Working Women. The latter was established in the same city in 1906 "to help ameliorate the material and moral condition of its members." It was tied loosely to similar organizations in the empire. Although its founders were of diverse nationalities——Countess Plater, Oleksandra Sudovshchyk Kosach, V.P. Prykhodko and L.S. Shcherbacheva——these women worked harmoniously. They operated a day-care centre, legal aid services and commercial courses.[8] In Kharkiv, where another branch of the same society was composed of Ukrainians, Russians and Jews, it ran a number of philanthropic and educational establishments, summer camps for needy children and a service for various emergencies. It was also instrumental in opening the first co-educational gymnasium in the city.[9]

In 1900 or early 1901, Ukrainian women whose husbands were active in the Old Hromada in Kiev decided to establish a Women's (Zhinocha) Hromada. Since Ukrainian organizations were still banned, the group met under the pretext of tea drinking, usually in the home of the Chykalenkos. Despite being a generous patron of Ukrainian causes, and a loving and supporting father of daughter Hanna, Ievhen Chykalenko was set in his ways and cannot be considered a promoter of women's causes. But he did not prevent women from organizing, although he had several disagreements with the younger women in the group. The elder Mrs. Chykalenko, Mariia Viktorivna, acted as a conciliator.

The founders of the Women's Hromada included, in addition to the Chykalenkos, Mariia Kistiakovska-Tymchenko, the wife of another activist; the wife of the influential librarian of the journal *Kievskaia Starina* (Kievan Antiquity), Mariia Stepanenko; the Lysenko sisters, Katria, Halia and Mariana; and Liudmyla Starytska Cherniakhivska. Isydora Kosach, Lesia Ukrainka's youngest sister, and Dariia Romanova, the writer, also participated in the society, along with the writer and teacher Mariia Zahirna Hrinchenko, and the activist Mariia Hozhenko Matiushenko. Other regular participants included Liubov Shulhyna and Ievheniia Shcherbakivska-Krychevska.

Some younger women in such groups yearned for more overt political and social work, but remained members to take advantage of the opportunities offered.[10] The Zhinocha Hromada had close contacts with both the RUP and the Student Hromada. The young Livytska, who was interested primarily in social revolution, scorned the group's goals: raising children as Ukrainians and popularizing Ukrainian literature. She remained in the Hromada under pressure from her husband and her more radical colleagues, but had harsh words for the Hromada in her memoirs. In addition to drinking tea——or at least preparing the table in case the police arrived——the women wrote book reviews on Ukrainian topics and participated in Ukrainian functions. They worked among the peasants, encouraging the girls to attend secondary schools, discussing political subjects with them and showing them how to disseminate political literature. They also set up libraries in villages, tried to promote adult literacy and to establish child-care centres.

Kharkiv was an emergent metropolis. As late as 1907, Russian women from Moscow found the richness of life in Kharkiv "rather extraordinary for a provincial town." In 1905, the Society for Literacy (*Obshchestvo gramotnosti*) made plans to publish a Ukrainian-language social-democratic newspaper in Kharkiv. The police, on the other hand, noted the ties of the Kharkiv women activists with the Social Revolutionary party.[11] The women in Kharkiv were anxious to make contact with other women's organizations, particularly in the international sphere. The Kharkiv Society of Mutual Aid for Working Women, for example, sent a delegate to the Berlin Congress of the International Council of Women in 1904. Kharkiv did not, however, become the centre of the Ukrainian women's movement. Instead, the Kiev Hromada, a community-oriented body, served as the model for other Ukrainian women's organizations. By 1916 there were eighteen branches of the Hromada.[12]

Ukrainian women wrote little about the women's hromady, perhaps because they felt uncomfortable in a women's organization that was not identified openly with the needs of the workers. Hanna Chykalenko stressed in her memoirs that the society was not feminist in make-up, while Lesia Ukrainka argued that women's organizations and feminism were passé. As the moderate Ukrainian movement increasingly refrained from open activity, it turned to other ideologies, such as liberalism and socialism, which did not consider feminist concerns important. Consequently, Ukrainian women did not regard themselves as feminists, and for the most part ignored the issue.

They did, however, grasp instinctively the opportunities women's organizations offered. As contacts with Galicia increased, Ukrainian women in the Russian Empire became more aware of the subordinate position of women in the so-called liberal societies. Women became more active, began to recognize the more subtle aspects of sexism, and joined women's groups more readily. In addition, women's organizations provided yet another forum for Ukrainians.

One of the early activities of women's clubs was combating prostitution. The Russian Society for the Protection of Women, founded in 1900 and affiliated with a main office in London, had branches in Kiev and Odessa. In St. Petersburg the organization was run by members of the nobility. The provincial branches of the imperial organization developed work along a pattern different from that of their European counterparts. The Kiev branch was composed of members of the intelligentsia dedicated to helping the poor. It was characterized by national heterogeneity and responsiveness to national and social issues. For some years it was led by Dr. V.G. Klachkina, a Russian, whose daughter became an active Ukrainian patriot after living and working among Ukrainians. Its leadership reflected its diverse ethnic makeup. Two Jewish women, Rozalia I. Margolina and Sofia A. Sats, were frequently on the board, as was the Kuban Ukrainian Zinaida Mirna.

The organization held weekly meetings, but its major activity was helping the poor. It maintained a cheap dormitory for women and subsidized a cafeteria. It ran an employment agency, a free legal clinic and a literacy school. It raised a large portion of its funds from its sewing school. The working-class orientation of the Society was underlined when it moved its headquarters from a fashionable central location on Fundukleevskaia to the working-class district near the present-day hotel Lybed. It had an active membership of about 200 persons and a sound financial base. In June 1913 the Kiev Office of the Ministry of Internal Affairs turned down the Society's request to hold a fund-raising lottery on the grounds that it did not need additional funds.

Of more concern to the police than fund-raising was the use made of the money. The sewing school, which charged two rubles a month for tuition, was a money-making proposition for both students and the teachers. It inspired the women to hold sewing workshops for working women, as well as other activities: reading and discussion classes, pattern making, concerts, choral singing and various social events.[13] Sometimes well known artists agreed to perform at the concerts.

The Society tried to establish a separate Jewish Women's Section, but the Jewish working-class women rejected attempts to attract them, and with a few exceptions avoided organizations with an implicitly Ukrainian coloration.[14]

The 1905 Revolution brought the Ukrainians two major gains: acknowledgement of the Ukrainian language, albeit without formal recognition of its use, and the lifting of restrictions on Ukrainian organizations. Ukrainians concentrated on societies that could serve political and national purposes. Every conscious Ukrainian was drawn into some aspect of this activity. Lesia Ukrainka complained that she spent an entire week drawing up by-laws for new societies, "a literary genre that is not my métier." But it was worthwhile, she continued:

> We live as if we were persons in a romantic novel surrounded by contrasts, antitheses, impossibilities, tragedies, comedies, tragicomedies, chaos and among these some heroic scenes and figures, as if from a [classic] ancient drama. No one knows what will happen tomorrow; few remember what happened yesterday. There are moments when you lose the sense of reality: then you lose the feeling that you are living in a revolution.[15]

Feminist demands, even the acknowledgement of women's equality, found few adherents in Kiev. In her memoirs, Oleksandra Sudovshchyk Kosach recounted bitterly a meeting in Kiev in 1904:

> Our intelligentsia was elated, moved, triumphant and naive. Some embraced, kissed one another, and lauded one other for drawing up a constitution.... They did not say a word about women. When I tried to add [the principle of the equality of sexes] to the others in the future democratic constitution, I was told that that it was implicit in the other rights.[16]

The most important organizations developed by Ukrainians after 1905 were the Enlightenment Societies (or Prosvitas) and the co-operatives. Women were extremely active in both. Women's sections were established in Prosvita, patterned on the Western Slavic community organizations founded in the mid-nineteenth century. The native intelligentsia worked with the peasants in community-based volunteer programmes. Their goal was to enhance the economic, intellectual and social well-being of the peasants and to fulfill community needs ignored by the government.

In Eastern Ukraine the Prosvitas frequently developed literacy schools or programmes for adults. They sprang up spontaneously during the 1905 Revolution from Hrubeshiv, the little town near Kholm, all the way to distant towns in which some Ukrainians lived, such as Tomsk and Baku.[17] Their further development was enhanced by a law of 27 March 1907 that sanctioned private educational societies and legalized cultural functions, concerts and amateur performances without specific police permission. This law owed much to Russian liberals, who had argued that educational programs would prevent further revolutionary upheavals and would prepare the masses for a democratic system of government. Since the government lacked funds for new educational programmes, it acquiesced to private initiatives.[18]

Russian liberals, however, did not anticipate the sudden growth of organizations of non-Russian makeup and goals. For example, the Zhytomyr (Volhynia) Ukrainian Prosvita, a member organization of the All-Imperial Russian League of Enlightenment, sought "the enlightenment of the Ukrainian people in its native tongue."[19] It was connected closely to the local Volhynia Society for Literacy, founded in 1901. Ukrainians in other areas also took advantage of the umbrella organization to further their nationalist goals. In Katerynoslav those who had founded the Gogol Literary Society four years earlier now tried to establish a Prosvita. Women were active participants in these societies.

The police surmised correctly that the public educational associations would be a front for nationalist activity. For example, the Poles, a minority on Ukrainian territories with a tradition of community action, established organizations dealing with all aspects of cultural, religious and social life. The police and the government, however, did not consider these a threat to the social order. On the other hand, according to the Special Section of the Police, all Ukrainian patriots engaged almost exclusively in revolutionary activity, had links with the Social Democrats and Social Revolutionaries and, above all, were in league with those Galician Ukrainians who openly supported a break between Ukraine and Russia.[20] In reality, the Ukrainian Prosvita effectively linked the Ukrainian intelligentsia and Ukrainian peasants. The police, observing university faculty, professionals and ordinary workers identifying themselves with Prosvita, foresaw the establishment of a network of potentially subversive organizations.[21]

Many Ukrainian women who participated in the Prosvitas had a police record. The police noted that the most active members of Prosvita were Mariia [Zahirna] Hrinchenko and the Kosach sisters, all associated with the Social Democrats.[22] Even when Lesia Ukrainka petitioned the ministry of interior for permission to open the Kiev Prosvita Library, she was turned down because of her political views.[23] Often the police moved against the Prosvitas from their inception: they considered the Nizhyn Prosvita leftist-dominated, and closed the Kozelets organization for revolutionary activity. The Odessa Prosvita was viewed as a front for the Social Revolutionaries.[24]

The Prosvitas were populist-oriented. Women were prominent in programmes to set up libraries and health centres, and to hold public lectures. The Chernihiv Prosvita, for example, included Vera Deish Kotsiubynska, F.S. Levytska and Olga D. Kalynovska, all of whom were banished from the city in September 1908[25] by the police, who also dissolved the Prosvita. In Poltava, the local governor witheld approval from the Prosvita, fearing that it would heighten the national consciousness of Ukrainians and endanger the Russian state.[26]

Ukrainians of both sexes expended much energy in trying to keep the moderate Prosvitas from being closed by the government. In Konotop the Prosvita ingeniously affiliated itself with the Lviv organization in an attempt to prevent its dissolution.[27]

The police repressed as many organizations of Ukrainian coloration as they could. The Co-operative Kiev Coffee Shop, run by women, was alleged to be part of the Ukrainian national movement because the police accused Elena P. Horska, one of its directors, of being a revolutionary who was raising her children in a non-Russian atmosphere, popularizing social-democratic literature, and attempting to obtain a gun permit. They were also perturbed that Pavlyk, the moderate Galician socialist, mentioned Horska's name in a letter.[28]

Despite persecution, the Prosvitas served as nuclei for other Ukrainian organizations. The co-operative movement and the cultural activities of Ukrainians expanded. The Prosvita in Zaporizhzia produced more than forty plays between 1906 and 1908. Exhibits of agricultural and industrial achievements popularized the activities of the Ukrainian clubs.[29] Local branches of all-Russian organizations staged Ukrainian-language productions: Starytsky's *Ostannia nich* (Last Night, 1908), for instance was sponsored by the Kievan workers' branch of the Literary Society.[30] Between 1905 and 1917 "Ukrainian women took part in civic activities, in educational and scientific enterprises, in artistic productions...in all aspects which dealt with the most important tasks of our life."[31]

Historians have overlooked completely the participation of Ukrainian women in the all-Russian feminist movement for two main reasons. First, the Russian feminist movement was weak. Second, it was identified politically with the Russian liberal movement. The Russian liberals did not openly espouse either national autonomy or women's equality. Sometimes they maintained that women's equality was a basic political right, but never reached a consensus on the nationality issue. They considered both issues divisive, since they allegedly weakened the all-important struggle against absolutism throughout the empire.

The Russian liberal women who founded the Union of Equality for Women (*Soiuz Ravnoupravleniia Zhenshchin*) in 1905 quickly became accustomed to political and public work. While some Russian liberals viewed the Union as an extension of the party, the women on the central board supported openly the principle of national autonomy, in recognition of the demands of its members. The Union branch in Kiev made little headway, proving incapable of rivalling the established popularity of the Society for the Defence of Women. An inaugural meeting, moreover, was run by males, and its resolutions reflected a liberal programme rather than feminist concerns.[32] In contrast, the branch in Kharkiv concentrated on feminist concerns and co-opted the women who had sent representatives to the International Council of Women at the Berlin Congress in 1904. Also, with the co-operation of the Society of Mutual Aid for

Working Women, it organized advanced academic courses for women. Its activists were followers of the Social Democratic and Social Revolutionary parties rather than of the liberals.[33] More than 100 women joined the Odessa branch, and branches were established in other cities. Soon, however, a disagreement emerged between the local branches and the centre.

The Union of Equality for Women was a moderate political organization that sought legal equality for women. Efimenko tried to use existing legislation to assert the rights of women. The women also demanded equality of educational opportunity and favoured equal land allotments for both sexes. But local branches of the Union had diverse interests.[34] Some supported nationality rights. That issue emerged at the Union's first Congress on 6–9 May 1905, which was attended by over 300 delegates. It took place a few weeks before the *zemstvo* congress that divided the Russian liberals.

The women assembled in the revolutionary atmosphere of the time. The Russian feminists were, nevertheless, genuinely taken aback by the demand for national autonomy put forward by the Ukrainian, Jewish, Polish, Belorussian and Lithuanian women. These women, representing local branches, declared that they would not join the All-Imperial Union unless it supported national autonomy and recognized the right of all nationalities to cultural and national self-determination. The Russian women considered the demand for nationality rights extraneous, illicit, divisive and ill-timed. They were surprised that "for the oppressed nationalities the issue of national freedom was the most pressing one."

The non-Russian women presented a compelling case and the congress, with only four abstentions and no opposition, "acknowledged the right of the different nationalities which are part of Russia to political autonomy and national self-determination."[35] The Lithuanian and Ukrainian delegates stressed the connection between "liberation of women and the autonomy of the native land,"[36] a connection that was not obvious to all. At the Third Congress of the Union, held from 8 to 12 October 1905, Lithuanian, Polish and Ukrainian women demanded the federation of Russia. After a debate, the congress agreed that "the liberation of women is inseparably tied to the attainment of autonomy for their native land (*rodnoi krai*) and its liberation from the yoke of Russification."[37] This was a concession on the part of Russian liberals. Moreover, the organizational statute ratified by the Union provided for a large measure of branch autonomy.

Shared feminist goals, however, were not enough to break down national animosities, even if Russian feminists, snubbed by their male colleagues over the suffrage question, considered their views on the nationality issue to be politically sophisticated. "This question had barely emerged in Russian society, and our association was one of the first to solve it in a positive fashion," the association president boasted.[38] But the solution proved difficult, and debate among its members in the branches was even more bitter than at the congresses. Russian women outside the capital showed little inclination to co-operate with Ukrainian and other non-Russian women. Polish women, who comprised a minority in the Ukrainian countryside, began to establish their own organizations at a more rapid rate.[39]

The situation in Poltava typified the broader picture. The Russian women withdrew from the Poltava branch upon the adoption of the following addition to the programme:

> The Ukrainian women, in addition to the general and painful aspects of the women's issue, recognized the difficult circumstances which stem from the oppression of the Ukrainian nation. The woman of Ukraine, being part of a nation of many millions that is deprived of political rights, which for generations has been forced to subject itself to a centralized government, could not but experience upon herself all the consequences of the spiritual subjection of the whole nation. Language, the sole means of expression of thought, could be used only privately from the time of the Pereiaslav Treaty, when Ukraine lost its independence. Ukrainian works could not be published in their own land. Elementary schools, which used to be of a high calibre in Ukraine, were slowly reduced to such a level that they lost all their national and community characteristics (*natsionalno-hromadski prykmety*). The denationalization of Ukrainian women who went through the Russian school was the inevitable consequence of a political system that had as its aim the separation of the educated part of society from the rest of the nation. Such a situation greatly harmed the national public cause——the upbringing of the younger generation. Ukrainian women considered it their prime duty to take a stand on this point.
>
> Ukrainian women added their own demands to the platform——that an autonomous-federative structure be introduced into the government, based upon the ethnic territorial principle, and that decentralization in the administrative structure of the government also be implemented; that elections be held on the basis of universal, direct, equal and secret suffrage with no distinctions according to sex or nationality. Moreover, all persons residing in Ukraine, without regard for gender or nationality, must enjoy the same equal rights, with the guarantee of all the customary freedoms.[40]

The language of the resolution, which was probably drafted by Pchilka, was striking. Eleven years later, during the 1918 Revolution, the Universals issued by the Ukrainian Central Rada were much more placatory in their espousal of self-determination and, ultimately, independence.[41]

Pchilka's determined stand on the nationality issue was not recorded by Ukrainian men, and Ukrainian activists generally felt uncomfortable with overt feminist activity. Feminism, as we recall, tended to be identified with liberalism, whereas Ukrainian political activists adhered to radical rhetoric. Although tension between Ukrainian women and men was kept below the surface, the older generation of Ukrainian activists such as Efremov, Hrushevsky and Chykalenko felt uncomfortable with assertive women. The younger generation, on the other hand, shared Lesia Ukrainka's view that feminism was irrelevant to the "liberation of the masses." Feminism itself generated little open discussion. Even Ivan Nechui-Levytsky's novel about feminism failed to stimulate interest. *Nad Chornym morem* (On the Coast of the Black Sea), published in 1889, is one of the least known novels of the popular writer.

Ukrainian women demonstrated the political acumen and ability to make use of the limited chan,.els available. They showed clarity of thinking in their dealings with all-Russian women's organizations. With Ukrainian men, however, they were more deferential, and failed duly to record their own achievements.[42]

While Ukrainian women readily participated in community work, the feminist platform did not interest them.[43] Even Pchilka's advocacy of feminist organizations was based less on intrinsic need than on the needs of all Ukrainians. Pchilka focused on the need for a Ukrainian women's organization in March 1908,[44] following the publication of the first issue of the progressive women's newspaper in Galicia on the first of that month. She argued that the Ukrainian women must organize themselves before the convocation of a women's congress in St. Petersburg. This appeal was signed by M.D.——Mykola Dmytriiev, Pchilka's close collaborator from Poltava and his wife, Anna Dmytriieva——because Pchilka was unpopular within the Ukrainian community. It argued that Ukrainian women must participate effectively in the women's congress to be able to assure, first of all, a reform of women's education. Ukrainian women were not taught anything about their own country, nor were they even taught their own language. How could they be good mothers and raise nationally conscious children? "It is up to the educated, conscious women, who understand well the needs of their country...to assess our strength, to delineate the needs of our nation, of our land...and to articulate those needs...."[45]

The organization never materialized, and by the end of the year Pchilka was arguing for separate Ukrainian women's organizations:

> Should women's organizations be founded in Ukraine, with a separate women's agenda, it would be desirable that these not be sections of a Russian [women's] union, but Ukrainian organizations, because in an all-Russian union these sections would either drown or not be able to serve effectively the most immediate needs of the Ukrainian women.[46]

Although a Ukrainian women's organization was not established, the Kiev Ukrainian Women's Hromada acted as an organization for the Ukrainian branches of the Union.

Ukrainian women activists continued to assert the concerns of national groups. For example, Ianovska, the writer from Kiev, delivered a paper on "The Position of the Peasant Woman in Ukraine" at the Women's Congress in St. Petersburg in 1908, and Pchilka's "The Tasks of Ukrainian Women" was also read.[47] Pchilka continued to monitor women's concerns: difficulties encountered by women lawyers, prostitution, and developments in women's higher education. Ukrainian women continued to be active in women's organizations: Anna Dmytriieva, the Union delegate from Poltava, represented the interests of Ukrainian women in Moscow.[48] But specifically feminist concerns remained subordinate to political and national rights, and Russian feminism was itself weak.

The limited political rights attained by Ukrainian women in 1905 were tenuous. Even as the gains were being celebrated, gangs of hooligans, abetted by the local police, acted to "Save Russia, beat the Jews" and keep the country safe from non-Russians. Some women's organizations, such as the Kharkiv Branch of the Union for the Defence of Women, stressed the need for defence against the Black Hundreds, as the most notorious group was known. The episode in Lubni noted earlier, in which the Ukrainian and Jewish communities mounted a joint successful defence, was not an isolated case.

Like the pogroms against the Jews, the pogrom against the Ukrainian cultural movement was brutal. Its perpetrators came not only from among known reactionaries, but from all segments of Russian society. The attack was open, though not always dramatic. Sometimes it was masked as community action, for example, the removal of Ukrainian books from libraries.[49] The hostility of progressive Russians toward the Ukrainian movement was also marked by a malicious passivity. They offered no protest at the closing of the Prosvitas.[50] On other occasions, that hostility took an active form. At a conference of activists in the All-Russian Movement for Peoples' Universities held early, in 1908, at which Sofiia Rusova spoke on reawakening national consciousness among Ukrainians, the chairman resigned rather than vote on resolutions about "the right of each nationality to education in its own language." [51]

Alongside increasing reactionary activities, there was a return to officially tolerated activities. The Ukrainian women, like their Russian counterparts, gained acceptance into schools, participated in politics and even held minor offices at the local level.[52] More and more women entered the work force as labourers, operators and clerks in the telephone and telegraph offices, and at the post office. Educated women were expected to have interests outside the home, and Ukrainian women considered it their duty to be involved in community-oriented activities.[53]

The years immediately preceding the First World War saw a growth of national consciousness among Ukrainians. In turn, opposition mounted from Russian settlers: women students at a Kiev high school, for example, were forbidden to wear for a school play the fashionable embroidered peasant costumes. The still-born Russian feminist party had little interest in the nationality issue.[54]

Despite these drawbacks, Ukrainian women in the Russian Empire developed women's organizations and participated in an organized fashion in community life. The war and the concomitant dislocations severely tested the achievements of their work.

Part II.

Ukrainian Women in the Austrian Empire

5.
Priests, Wives and Daughters

Western Ukraine includes the former medieval state of Halych (Galicia), Bukovyna, and other areas. In the tenth century the whole territory had been an outpost of ancient Rus' and over the next five centuries it manifested many of the traits characteristic of Eastern Europe. Unlike Muscovy, which developed into a monolithic empire, East European states were marked by political instability, frequent border changes, nationally mixed populations and social strife. These conditions made for an active political role for women in Ukraine.

After Kiev fell to the Tatars in 1240, some of its princes opted to stay in the relatively safer north. For Ukrainians, the centre of political gravity shifted westward to Halych, whose lands, although temporarily prey to the Tatars, were not integrated into the Mongol Empire. The struggle with the Tatars, described in ballads as a time "when our land was ploughed not by ploughs but by sabres," took place within the Western modes of development. Ukrainian lands entered into a political union with Lithuania, and subsequently into the heterogeneous Polish-Lithuanian Commonwealth.

The latter was dominated by the gentry class that comprised about 10 per cent of the population, institutionalized serfdom, and encouraged both Polish expansion eastward and the Polonization of the Ukrainian and Lithuanian gentry. It circumscribed the powers of its elected monarchs and limited severely the standing army, so that the king relied on the gentry for the defence of the country. The gentry's reluctance to undertake this task allowed it to be taken over by the Cossacks, who fled serfdom and fought the Tatars and Turks. They defended Orthodoxy, because of the Polish Commonwealth's identification with Catholicism. To counteract Jesuit schools, Ukrainians formed their own lay brotherhoods, schools and monasteries. Lively religious polemics developed. In 1596, at the Union of Brest, some leading Ukrainian clerics accepted union with Rome while preserving complete church autonomy and structure, Eastern traditions and a married clergy. Most Ukrainians remained Orthodox.

In 1667 Ukraine was partitioned between Russia and Poland along the Dnieper. This led to the gradual demise of the Cossack state. The Ukrainian Orthodox Church was incorporated into the Russian Orthodox Church, which was completely subordinate to the government. In Western Ukraine the Ukrainian Greek-Catholic (Uniate) Church became the focal point of Ukrainian life. In the nineteenth century Ukrainian clerics initiated a national cultural revival, created the first community organizations and laid the groundwork for the development of a Ukrainian intelligentsia. The Western Ukrainian women's movement originated in this milieu.

Polish-Ukrainian antagonism persisted after the partition of Poland in 1772 between Austria, Prussia and Russia. The Austrians combined traditional Ukrainian Galician lands with Polish-inhabited territories around Cracow into a province called Galicia, thus giving a historical name to an artificially unified entity. Galicia became the empire's easternmost province, bordering on the Russian Empire. Catholicism was the state religion of the Austrian Habsburgs and the Catholic Poles gained the upper hand in the provinces, controlling both the administration and educational policies.

Galician Ukrainian women of clerical families limited themselves to the virtues of home and hearth, their church, and raising children. Accounts of Galician history have done little to explain how, immediately after the First World War, this milieu gave rise to the Ukrainian Women's Union (Soiuz Ukrainok), a large organization with more than 50,000 members, led for the most part by the daughters and wives of priests. But a close examination explains why such a development occurred.

The Uniate Church of Galicia prided itself on being a bridge between the Christians of the East and West, while in reality it did not have close contact with either. Instead, it developed certain peculiarities of its own because of attacks from both Poles and Russians. This church's insularity, which limited its horizon, nevertheless became a source of strength. For Ukrainians, whose elite stratum had become linguistically and culturally Polonized, the priests and their families constituted an intelligentsia. The higher clergy, the unmarried bishops and the abbots of prestigious monasteries had some access to the upper echelons of Austrian society, sat *ex officio* in the legislature and had contacts with government leaders, but in the second half of the nineteenth century the standard of living of the higher Ukrainian clergy gradually declined. The parish clergy, even in larger towns and richer parishes, were hampered by their rite and their language from enjoying the perquisites of their status.

Uniate parishes were poorer than their Roman Catholic counterparts; the fees and contributions received from the peasants were smaller; and the gentry intervened more frequently in the lives of Uniate priests. The Uniate priest, therefore, was definitely the underdog of Polish society, and there were cases of priests and their sons participating in and even leading armed expeditions against the Polish gentry. Before the Austrian government regulated the parishes, the landlords, who were either Polish or Polonized, often victimized the Ukrainian Catholic priest. Even after Austrian rule was established, the local Polish administration actively supported the creation of Roman Catholic parishes in ethnically mixed territories as well as in territories settled largely by Ukrainians.

Reaction to the expansionist policies of the Polish Roman Catholic Church in the sixteenth and seventeenth centuries, combined with the growth of Ukrainian nationalism in the nineteenth century, reduced Polish influence over the Ukrainian clergy, which began to identify its interests with those of the peasants. The latter, in view of the relative poverty of Ukrainian priests, did not adopt the class antagonism of their Russian counterparts.[1]

Joseph II, who travelled to the lands acquired by his mother in 1772, saw the Ukrainian clergy as potential teachers, administrators and physicians, and provided new schools for them. But the Ukrainian clergy, oriented toward the people rather than the state, helped define a modern Ukrainian national ideal. The recruits it nurtured for the secular intelligentsia were later to challenge Austria.

Modern nationalism, the use of vernacular, and new forms of community organization developed from the clergy. Mohylnytsky, Shashkevych and Ustiianovych, who together with Holovatsky and Vahylevych are considered the fathers of Western Ukrainian nationalism, were priests. Modern political ideas spread among seminarians and led to clashes with the Poles in the cities, revealing the ephemeral nature of the "brotherhood" the Poles had propagated among nationalities. In 1848 the priests took advantage of the Polish revolution to wrest concessions from the Austrian government.

Some sons of priests entered lay professions, marking a difficult break with family tradition. For instance, in 1861 at the University of Lviv two young students justified their transfer from theology to another department while retaining their scholarship stipend:

We plan the transfer not in self-interest——for who can deny that the position of the priest is among the best in status as well as in income? Especially now [the Poles were preparing another armed uprising in Russia and hoping that it would spread into Austria] if we take the present mood into consideration it is probably one of the safest ones. But we are planning to take this step from pure love for our nationality so that it might be represented also in other professions.[2]

Rather than become government functionaries, the role envisaged for them by Joseph II, the Ukrainian priests viewed themselves as community leaders. While some enjoyed an affluent way of life, a significant number were genuinely concerned with cultural and social issues. They sought Ukrainian-language education, more schools, and economic aid to alleviate poverty in the villages.

Women played a significant role in the clerical milieu. Some were interested in spiritual issues and well versed in ritual and religious practice. A few knew canon law and were consulted informally by the priests. In the absence of boys, girls were even asked to serve at mass on weekdays.

But most wives of priests were fully occupied with church upkeep and household tasks. While the parish priest attended to the spiritual and material needs of the parish, his wife not only administered her household, looked after the education of her children, and supervised the servants——she had at least one——but carried out many household tasks herself. She was also expected to take care of the villagers, the sick, the pregnant, and the needy. Few women lived up to expectations, and others never relished their public role. Yet clerical women seemed even closer to the village women than clerics were to the men. They had grown up among them, participated in the same rituals and shared the same fears. This bond formed the basis for the women's organizations of the inter-war period.

Conventional morality was the norm in the clerical families. The Uniate Church in Galicia stressed the usual precepts of marriage: the wife's obedience to her husband, and the love of the latter toward the wife. To the average parish priest, it was more important that his daughter make a good marriage than that she be educated. There were, however, significant exceptions: the Reverend Ivan Ozarkevych, who insisted upon travel for his daughter, and the Reverend Amvrosii Krushelnytsky, who helped Solomiia achieve world renown in opera by enabling her to train her voice.

Some wives practiced birth control, which was not widely condemned by the Uniate Church. According to interviewees, birth control had become an acceptable practice among educated women within the clergy by the twentieth century. The priests resisted the introduction of celibacy vehemently, and, until the Second World War, effectively.[3]

Clerical women showed a tendency less toward promiscuity than to excessive religiosity. Natalia Ozarkevych-Kobrynska, a major pioneer of the women's movement, aided by her father and brothers, tried to channel her zeal into what she felt were more productive areas than contemplative religious fervour. Many unmarried, separated and widowed women from the clerical milieu devoted themselves to the needs of the church. In contrast to the Protestant parson's wife, who directed her efforts toward religious charities, the Uniate woman was more concerned with the maintenance and appearance of the church than with organized philanthropy.[4]

Church aesthetics had social and national significance as well as importance for women's organizations. Beautification of churches provided a legitimate *raison d'être* for a women's organization, since no man could criticize such activities without attacking the church itself. For the wives of priests, the church constituted an extension of their homes. The elaborate decor of the Eastern churches provided the backdrop for their belief in the physical presence of God. A beautiful church in the parish could also enhance the priest's career. On their visits, the bishops held the priest's wife and daughters responsible for the maintenance of the church.

The church provided visible evidence of a distinct Ukrainian nationality. Ukrainian church architecture differed from that of the Roman Catholic Church in a number of important respects: the Ukrainian church had an iconostasis, a floor-to-ceiling screen of icons separating the nave from the altar, significant variation in layout and in the use of building materials. There developed a drive to rid the Ukrainian churches of statues, pulpits and the use of flowers, which were considered vestiges of Polish Latinism. Clerical women led peasant women in making folk-motif embroidery for church use. Such embroidery became identified with the Ukrainian rite as opposed to the more elaborate silk stitching of earlier centuries. The women embroidered vestments, cloths that were draped above the icons, tablecloths for the altar and banners to be carried during processions.

In Uniate church rituals, since there were no organs as in the Latin rite, the entire congregations chanted the responses to the priest; Uniates used Old Church Slavonic, a language the people could understand, and over time, folk elements were incorporated into the ritual. The Uniate service encompassed the farming seasons. The priest blessed the fields, the harvest food, and the waters on Epiphany. At the marriage ceremony, he offered prayers for the woman's fertility and after she had given birth he prayed to cleanse her of impurity.

The interaction between the priest and the people transmuted folk customs into religious worship. The church took into account the popular beliefs of the period. Prayer for Ukraine was incorporated into church services, and public functions invariably began with a church service and procession.

There are numerous examples of clerical-community contacts. Clerical families, like the old Cossack ones in Eastern Ukraine, were interrelated by blood and marriage. The men also made lasting friendships in seminaries. As for families, the traditional Ukrainian country hospitality——"the guest enters the house; God enters the house"——was practiced at the slightest pretext. Marriages, holidays, and feast days, especially of the parish patron saint, were occasions for festivities that often lasted several days. Peasant houses were offered as sleeping quarters for guests who could not be accommodated in the parsonage, and students hiking through the countryside during the summer were welcome at each parsonage. Peasant boys in the seminaries spent summers at the homes of friends whose fathers were priests, enabling them to marry into the clergy.

Although income levels among clerical families varied, few enjoyed a high standard of living. By nationalizing the churches the Austrian government reduced the priest's dependence on the Polonized lord of the manor and on peasant contributions, thereby strengthening the priests' independence.

Priesthood was not always a secure position. While a priest retained his priesthood in perpetuity, he was frequently transferred to another parish. The case of the Reverend Teodosii Shchavinsky, an undistinguished priest from a poor peasant family, was not unusual. His first parish was a poor mountain village and his second scarcely better. Attempting to gain better parishes, he moved four times within seven years at his own cost. Finally he died of pneumonia in 1883. His widow, Honorata, was thereafter obliged to live with her parents so that the children could attend school. She supplemented her meagre pension of 180 zlotys by sewing and embroidery.[5] Young priests in particular received the less desirable parishes.

During the reign of Joseph II, mutual aid societies were established to allay poverty among families of the clergy. The Institute of Widows and Children of the Clergy, for example, was an insurance society supported by levies on the clerics to provide pensions for widows and orphans of the clergy. The institute performed two functions: it helped raise the standard of living of widows by providing some financial security and created a structure that the clergy could use to develop an insurance association.

At first, the local clergy were reluctant to join the institutes, fearing that the latter would antagonize the Polish landlords. They were created only after pressure from higher church officials, backed by the Vienna government of the post-1848 period. The institutes, based on the diocese and run by elected priests, functioned within the framework of general Austrian organizations. But while their concerns were financial, their politics reflected the growing awareness in the clergy of the effectiveness of community action and self-help societies. The institutes helped break even further the clergy's economic dependence upon the Polish landlords and thus helped the church to articulate independent aspirations. They served as a prototype for community organizations of Western Ukrainians in the latter half of the nineteenth century.[6] Despite the institutes, many widows and orphans of priests remained poverty-stricken. The Statute of the Society of Lviv, published in 1848, stated that "the Greek Catholic clergy are so poorly remunerated that even with the most careful management and supervision of the household, the priest can rarely leave anything for his widow and his orphans."[7]

The financial dilemma of the clergy was exacerbated by an increase in the life expectancy of the priests and a decline in infant mortality. In a letter dated 24 June 1866 to the Przemyśl commission studying revisions to the statutes of the Przemyśl Institute, the Reverend Petro Kolpakevych argued for modifications that would ameliorate the difficult conditions of aged clergymen, which for him meant those over 40 years of age.[8] Thirty years later, a committee in Przemyśl composed of secular intelligentsia, clerics and an industrialist also complained that the financial remuneration of the clergy was inadequate.[9]

Discussion of the financial condition of the clergy led to the establishment of schools for girls and the creation of women's organizations. The issue of sexual equality was evident in the institutes. The 1884 revisions of the Lviv institutes, drafted by Ivan Kobrynsky, a relative of Nataliia's husband, abolished the differences in the stipends paid to boys and girls:

Orphans——without regard to sex——both boys and girls equally...if not other-wise disqualified, are to receive a pension until they are 18 years of age.... Orphans of both sexes are entitled to their pensions even if they receive other scholarships, if they meet the necessary qualifications of age and moral behaviour, provided they adhere to their holy Greek Catholic faith and their Ukrainian nationality.[10]

The church also exerted some social control in battling alcoholism, a serious scourge not only of the village, but also to nationality relations in Western Ukraine. Before the abolition of serfdom, the production and sale of alcohol was one of the landlord's major sources of revenue. Each peasant had to buy a quota of liquor through the local tavern, which was usually run by a Jewish steward of the absentee landlord. The tavern-keeper also had ready cash to lend to the peasants at high interest rates. Peasant consumption of alcohol was thus in the interest of both landlord and tavern-keeper. Only toward the end of the nineteenth century did the state abolish the exclusive right of the nobility to produce and sell liquor, but the peasants had to pay a heavy indemnity for the abrogation of "right to propination" and the law itself was not enforced.

The Temperance Brotherhoods, founded in the 1830s, were initially male organizations. Alcoholism was considered a male problem, and cases of alcoholism among peasant and clerical women were generally overlooked. To help increase the Brotherhoods' influence over the peasants, women were drawn into the battle for sobriety. The temperance movement outgrew the confines of church brotherhoods to become one of the major public movements among Ukrainians both in the Austrian Empire and in inter-war Poland. A number of women played a prominent role in it.

The temperance movement brought into light the extent of poverty, ignorance and despair of the Ukrainian peasants. Although an imperial decree had mandated some village schools, most peasants remained illiterate. As late as the 1890s, only the Russian Empire among the European states ranked below Austria in illiteracy and infant mortality, the major indicators of poverty.

The Austrian government had pursued advancement for Ukrainians in Galicia more vigorously after 1848, but the policy proved to be short-lived. By the 1860s, it became clear that social change in Galicia would require action from Ukrainians themselves.

The cream of the Ukrainian clergy had been sent to Vienna to special schools founded for them by Emperor Joseph II. These seminarians established contacts with other students, particularly Czechs, who were facing similar hurdles. As was the case with Ukrainians, their culture was being reduced to a second-rate folk curiosity. Rights to their lands were challenged by a better educated, more advanced and richer colonizer who claimed ownership of the territories. The Ukrainian secular intelligentsia also established close contacts with the Czechs, participated in the first international Slavic gathering in Prague in 1848 and corresponded with Czech intellectuals. These links, which were facilitated by the Czechs' service in the Galician bureaucracy, increased the clerics' responsibility to the village and to the Ukrainian people. The consensus among them was that "our rite is connected irrevocably with our nationality."[11]

The introduction of schools into the villages and the democratization of the educational system in the second half of the nineteenth century made possible some minimal upward mobility for peasant children. The teaching of German in the high schools brought Ukrainians closer to European currents of thought.

The Galician Ukrainian intelligentsia emerging from the clerical mileiu, augmented by students of peasant origin, was attracted to socialist ideology, albeit of a less revolutionary and rigid nature than its Eastern Ukrainian counterpart.

The Galicians debated whether to call themselves Ruthenians or Ukrainians, while a few argued for association with the Poles. Some Galician Ukrainian clerical families insisted upon a vague notion of common Rus' spirituality, while others identified themselves with the Russian tsar. By the end of the century the latter had split into two groups: the conservatives and the Russophiles (*moskvofily*). The conservatives were essentially opposed to modern trends, while the Russophiles tried to maintain links with the sole Eastern Orthodox sovereign, the Tsar of all the Russias.

The vast majority of Ukrainians in Austria opted for a Ukrainophile cultural orientation, involving the use of the vernacular, the same Cyrillic script as the one used in Eastern Ukraine and adherence to a democratic form of nationalism. Political parties, which emerged at the turn of the century, were not as revolutionary as the Ukrainian organizations in the Russian Empire. The community organizations, reflecting a mixture of ideological commitment and pragmatic need, organized the peasants and formed the basis of Ukrainian public life in the western lands. To date, they have not been fully studied by historians.

Many of the community organizations were conceived and developed by priests and gradually were supplemented by laymen. Their growth was intertwined with ideological discussions in which the participation of women was both limited and undocumented. While Galician Ukrainian males (in the manner of the intelligentsia) took minutes of every meeting and expounded on the significance of their proclamations, women (with typical middle-class deference) failed to put themselves into the broader picture. Women were expected to participate in the daily and auxiliary work of community organizations without acknowledgement. As the cultural needs of the community increased, women began to play a wider role in community action.

The largest and most important of the Ukrainian societies was Prosvita (Enlightenment). Based on a Czech model, it was founded in 1868 by the Reverend Stepan Kachala. Its mission, embodied in its name, was to spread enlightenment through community self-help programmes, and to attain community self-sufficiency. Although founded by a priest, and often run by priests in the first decades, Prosvita was never a clerical organization like the Institutes of the Widows and Orphans. Before long, teachers and lawyers challenged the predominance of the Uniate clerics in Ukrainian political life. Prosvita became a battleground as the clergy's concept of politics gave way gradually to the newly emergent political parties. Prosvitas developed throughout Galicia, making the population more aware of the importance of community institutions, political action, organization and national cohesion. The Prosvita began its work modestly, with public readings of books and newspapers, discussions and amateur theatrical performances. In 1871 Ivanna Osterman was the first woman to be officially admitted to the Prosvita, and women took an active part in all undertakings.[12] Since village resources were limited, all literate persons helped set up libraries, develop programmes, organize literacy courses, arrange or give lectures, and prepare concerts.[13]

The women's question was becoming more prevalent at this time. A year after the first Prosvita was founded, in 1869, Harriet Taylor and John Stuart Mill published *On the Subjection of Women*. In 1870, the first Austrian women's petition of rights was drawn up in Vienna. Two years later, the Austrian government made it mandatory for all girls in the empire to have a minimum of three years of schooling. Further, the variants of democratic socialism that pervaded Galicia strengthened the notion of equality for all people inherent in interpretations of Christianity, popular philosophy and the Polish democratic revolutionary movements. Ukrainians also felt the dawn of a new, more promising age.

Most Western Ukrainian women in the 1870s were not adventurous enough to strike out on their own, although a few "demonstrated the proper understanding of our national cause and went hand in hand with our brothers, husbands and fathers in the cause of national renaissance, to help draw openly and fearlessly the downtrodden mother Rus'...to progress."[14] These women were so isolated that today we cannot even identify them.

Most literate Western Ukrainian women had been brought up as genteel ladies and taught to abhor brashness, self-assertion and self-aggrandizement. They were deferential toward the church. Life had accustomed them to be followers and not leaders. Few women wrote about themselves or about other women other than as reflections in a male mirror.

The first separate women's organization with a formal statute and structure was the Obshchestvo ruskykh dam (the Society of Ruthenian Ladies). It was established on 14 December 1878 as a direct result of social differences between the parishioners of the Assumption Church in Lviv. The Russophile faction of the Galician clergy began losing ground at the Cathedral of St. George in Lviv. This faction rallied around the Assumption Church, popularly known as the Ruska Church, and connected with the Stavropygian Brotherhood. Dmytro Bilenky, a parishioner at the Assumption Church, in an attempt to increase Sunday donations, decided to ask "Society Ladies" to pass the collection plate one Sunday. The resulting dramatic increase in donations prompted the ladies to create a formal organization for themselves. However, this action offended the local townswomen who had usually passed the collection plate and resented this infringement on their traditional privileges. The "ladies," in turn, "decided not to grieve their sisters——the townswomen——at all. And since the townswomen had called their sisters of the intelligentsia *rus'ki damy* (Ruthenian ladies), the latter decided to reorganize the sisterhood at the church into a Society of Ruthenian Ladies."[15]

Although connected with the Assumption Church, the Society functioned within the social sphere. It sponsored many fund-raisers: lotteries, raffles, dances and socials. It organized public lectures on various topics and established its own welfare and scholarship fund.[16] From its inception, the Society became a battleground not only between the two classes of women, but between the whole conservative Russophile faction and the liberal forces. "It is difficult," wrote a male reporter from the influential Ukrainian Galician newspaper *Pravda* a few days after the founding of the Society, "to understand why Ruthenian women necessarily must be called ladies and not women...and why the proposed activities of the Society have so little in common with the true needs of women, so removed from social issues, so lacking in reality (*malo-zhyznennym*)."[17]

The pro-Ukrainian women showed great tolerance toward the Russophile camp, postponing discussion of the by-laws for almost a year. Finally, unable to come to terms with the Russophiles, many of them withdrew from the Society. However, attempts to keep the women united continued. The Society even donated money to the Basilian school and dormitory for girls, and according to Kobrynska "it attracted the flower of Ukrainian society in Lviv."[18] The failure to dissuade the Society from its conservative leanings permitted it to remain a small bastion of conservative and pro-Russian forces until the outbreak of the Second World War in 1939. Its influence outside Lviv was minimal. Outside Lviv, as a contemporary noted, "Ukrainian women, with few exceptions, were wholeheartedly dedicated to the Ruthenian nation and not ashamed of their native language either in private or in public. Their patriotism was genuine, heartfelt, dignified and honourable."[19]

These women, coming from clerical families, discussed neither women's rights or emancipation, nor were they interested in the woman issue. They did not challenge the males; initially they did not even demand equality. In their view, life was a series of interlocking pieces: feminism, nationalism, socialism and modernity. While West European women strove for emancipation from the strictures of society, Ukrainian women concentrated on expanding the role of women in society. The most successful women's organizations embraced a pragmatic outlook and did not become openly embroiled in political discussion or theoretical analyses. Individual women, however, who were becoming better educated, began to broaden their horizons.

6.
Women's Education and Society's Aspirations

The organic nature of Ukrainian feminism was evident in the education of women within the Austrian Empire. Galician Ukrainians recognized the need for education on all levels, but faced an uneducated peasant mass, and the need to create an intelligentsia, which took up most of their energies. There was little discussion about the type of education or upbringing the young women were to receive. Femininity was regarded not in its own right, but within the context of literature, the peasant class or ethnicity. Articles promoting better women's education in the Galician Ukrainian press couched their arguments in terms of national and economic needs.

Discussion about the need for women's education emerged in the 1870s in the Polish press and filtered down to Polish women's magazines, which were also read by Ukrainian women. A Ukrainian attempt at publishing a conservative women's magazine——Severyn Shukhevych's *Lada*——to advise women how to be dutiful wives and good mothers failed miserably in 1853. It was written in an incomprehensible style and failed to draw the Ukrainian women away from Polish magazines.

The first schools for girls in Galicia were Polish convent finishing schools which Ukrainians avoided because they inculcated Polish patriotism. Among the Greek Catholic orders, only the Basilian nuns kept schools open for girls, one in Iavoriv and the other in Slovita. They offered education beyond the primary level to a small number of Ukrainian girls.

No Ukrainian private schools for girls were founded until the 1880s. The "pension" schools for girls in Galician cities arose on the initiative of German-speaking or Polish women. One of the Lviv schools was "attended by many girls from the Romanian aristocracy, Polish women from the nobility and bourgeoisie, and many Armenians."[1] Russian suppression of Polish uprisings in 1830 and 1863, with the resulting confiscation of Polish estates and arrest of Polish noblemen, forced the Polish women in the Russian Empire to seek an education in order to provide a living for families of prisoners. The Polish women's plight enhanced the expansion of educational opportunities for all women in Galicia.

Hitherto, Western Ukrainian women had acquired their meagre education in their own homes. Ukrainian Galician women did not demonstrate an active quest for knowledge for its own sake. In fact, the women's main argument for opening schools for them was that secondary and higher education would make women better and more patriotic mothers. Discussion in the Ukrainian press stressed the conventional notion that women's education should be patterned more on the "heart" than on science and reason. Other articles warned of excessive religiosity, superstition and irrational fears that might be instilled in young women through faulty education.

For Ukrainians, the crucial issue was not the education of women, but rather the education of teachers and the promotion of Ukrainian culture through more Ukrainian courses at the university. Once Austria consolidated its hold on Galicia in the 1800s, the Ukrainian clergy tried to introduce Ukrainian-language teaching for Ukrainian children. A major demand in 1848 was the expansion of Ukrainian schools. In 1867, the education department in Austria was decentralized and local schools were placed under the supervision of the provincial school boards. In Galicia the school board was controlled by the Poles, who complained about Vienna's discrimination against the province. Ukrainians, in turn, protested that the Polish-run school board was channelling the few funds available to Polish-speaking western Galicia, thus depriving Ukrainian schools of their share. The Poles opposed the creation of Ukrainian schools, and instead promoted bilingual, rather than exclusively Ukrainian, schools. Ukrainians reacted by creating a Committee for the Defence of Ukrainian Education.

All Ukrainian parties tried to point out to the peasants the benefits of education.[2] Since post-elementary schools were located in towns, dormitories had to be maintained for the peasant children.

In 1887, the National Council (Narodna Rada) of Ukrainians prepared a "petition of rights" to the ministry of education and to the *Reichsrat*. It pointed out that while the Poles in Galicia had 28 gymnasia for 8,900 Polish and Jewish male pupils, the Ukrainians, for their potential 2,000 pupils, had only one gymnasium. The situation at teacher-training high schools (seminaria) was similar. Although there were 1,376 primary Ukrainian-language schools, there was no Ukrainian language seminarium. The Poles, on the other hand, had five seminaria for the graduates of their 1,212 schools. The remaining four seminaria were theoretically bilingual, but in fact Ukrainian was rarely used. As for women, "not a single Ukrainian woman has the possibility of being a teacher of Ukrainian only; the teaching of the Ukrainian language as a high-school subject is not systematized; and there are only four chairs with Ukrainian as the language of instruction at Lviv University."[3]

The school board, which appointed the village teachers, frequently sent Polish teachers into Ukrainian villages. Moreover, it seems that it sent the less desirable teachers to Eastern Galicia.[4] For Ukrainians, teaching was still a male profession, even into the twentieth century. Women who entered it experienced the dual drawback of national discrimination and sexual harassment. Nevertheless, after the 1880s, an increasing number of Ukrainian women became teachers.

Their life was difficult. Until the end of the century women teachers had to remain single. Most women taught at village elementary schools isolated from their peers. Eastern Galician villages had a high illiteracy rate, even by Austrian standards. Illiteracy was higher among girls than boys. A law of 1872, which stipulated that all girls in the empire must have at least three years of education, was not enforced. Many girls who attended school forgot how to read from lack of practice. Some Galician peasants reasoned that boys ought to be literate in order to communicate after being drafted, but since girls remained at home they had no use for such skills. Only as more young women left the villages to work as seasonal labourers or domestics did the peasants realize the advantages of education for girls. An analogous situation has occurred in contemporary third-world countries, in which the issue is not so much peasant opposition to education as access to a way of life in which reading and writing are useful.[5]

The poverty of the Ukrainian countryside, the changing economic conditions in Galicia and the inclusion of handicrafts into the school curriculum contributed to the creation of practical schools and courses for women. But while the government perceived the need to equip women with marketable skills, it was slow to organize these schools and, moreover, used Polish as the language of instruction. The language barrier, rather than an antipathy toward learning, kept most Ukrainian peasant women away from these schools.[6]

Ukrainians therefore turned to self-help organizations, using as their model the Czech school of handicrafts for women founded in Celowa in 1868.[7] Women were at the forefront in organizing trade schools for women in both the villages and cities. Czajecka, an impartial observer and author of a detailed study on the subject, concluded:

> Despite the lack of funds, we have to stress the lively development and the broad impact of [the Ukrainian community-run trade schools]. Compared to similar Polish organizations, the dynamic activity of the Ukrainians no doubt stemmed from the lack of government support of women's schools for Ukrainians.[8]

Many of these courses for women remain unknown because of their temporary nature and lack of documentation. For instance, a group of girls home for a vacation might sponsor courses on sewing, literacy or cooking. Later, older women would only vaguely recollect this activity. Some schools and courses were noted in newspapers. Such courses had an impact on students and organizers by increasing self-confidence, a sense of national cohesion, and the need of women's organizations.

A model for Ukrainian community trade schools was the co-operative Trud (Labour) for girls over thirteen years of age founded by the Ruthenian Women's Club in 1901. It was largely community-financed, although it received a small government subsidy. The school taught sewing, design, basic nutrition and some academic topics (all the girls were graduates of the four-year elementary school). It found jobs for its graduates and lobbied for more trade schools for women. *Trud* helped subsidize the cafeteria and dormitory that the Ruthenian Club also organized. Similar schools were organized in other cities. Individual parishes of the Ukrainian Catholic Church sponsored trade schools and co-operatives for women.

There were also less ambitious ventures. Evheniia Iaroshynska, the noted Bukovynian writer and teacher, for instance, spent a winter in Silesia studying modern looms in order to teach the peasants a more lucrative method of producing handicrafts.[9] As a young teacher in a Galician village, Kateryna Trembitska accepted a loom and some money from a Polish noblewoman in Horodok who had a rug-weaving shop. Trembitska taught the girls to operate the loom, and the children earned three to four *rynski* a week after school. (The monthly average wage of a village teacher at the time ranged from 25 to 50 *rynski*). The experience was so successful that Trembitska enlisted the help of the semi-official League of Economic Aid (*Liga Pomocy Przemysłowej*) and expanded the operation to include button-making. She also encouraged the girls to embroider and sold their work for them.

The need for community dormitories, already evident in the 1870s, became more urgent with the growth of schools and peasant realization that education was productive. Women's organizations established dormitories for girls and boys, as well as for day domestics.[10] For women attending intermediate schools, the dormitory helped them establish friends throughout the province by bringing women of different classes and areas together, and strengthening national feeling and women's consciousness.

Girls' dormitories, a necessary adjunct to all convent schools, became essential for secondary schools founded by Ukrainians. They became a bone of contention between the conservatives and the liberals. Although the arguments were bitter, they did not lead to the dissolution of any dormitories. Again, the women showed greater tolerance than the men. In Lviv, in the 1880s and 90s the conservative Society of Ruthenian Ladies supported the girls' dormitory which was run by the Basilian nuns and was identified with growing nationalist feeling. They even gave scholarship money to Konstantyna Malytska, who was to become a major writer of children's patriotic literature. The conservative Russophile faction only began collecting funds to create a dormitory for their young women after the turn of the century.[11] More threatening to Ukrainians was Polish opposition to their dormitory building. In Kolomyia, for example, the Poles prevented construction of a dormitory funded by the bequest of Mykhailo Bilous for several years.[12]

As a result of the lack of training facilities there was a shortage of teachers in Galicia.[13] The first teacher-training secondary schools (seminaria) for women were established in 1871, in Lviv and Przemyśl (Cracow followed suit), but Western Galicia quickly outstripped Eastern Galicia in the number and quality of schools. The language of instruction was Polish, but Ukrainian was also taught, because legally (although not in practice) graduates had to pass government examinations in both Polish and Ukrainian to be certified to teach. Ukrainian teachers in Lviv and Przemyśl schools nurtured both effective teachers and active Ukrainian community workers.[14] Omelian Partytsky, the editor of *Zoria* (The Star), encouraged Uliana Kravchenko to write in Ukrainian. Katria Hrynevych, the writer, began reading the Ukrainian press while in school in the 1870s.

In contrast to the Poles, Ukrainians welcomed the influx of women into the teaching profession.[15] The first generation of Ukrainian women teachers, Emiliia Nychai, Uliana Kravchenko, Kateryna Trembitska, Olha Bohachevska, and Konstantyna Malytska served as models of patriotic dedication. Teaching in Galicia was an underpaid profession which attracted both Polish and Ukrainian patriots. When the Pedagogical Society of Galicia (totalling 1,800 members, of whom about half were Ukrainians) began to publish chauvinistic Polish booklets, the Ukrainians formed their own Ukrainian Pedagogical Society in 1881. Unlike its Polish counterpart, it encouraged women to join and was one of the first community organizations to elect a woman to its executive board——Varvara Lishchynska served as treasurer in 1897.[16]

To combat discrimination by the school board and to alleviate their weak economic position, Ukrainian teachers organized a Mutual Aid Society of Galician and Bukovynian Male and Female Teachers in 1905. This Society published a journal, collected information about Ukrainian schools, promoted close ties between parents and school, and set up day-care centres.[17] Attempts to co-operate with similar Polish organizations, such as the *Towarzystwo Szkół Ludowych,* were unsuccessful. Nevertheless, symbiosis between the Ukrainians and Poles was enforced on women studying in the bilingual seminaries. When the Seminary in Przemyśl celebrated its twenty-fifth anniversary, the festive programme and cantata were in both Polish and Ukrainian, and the girls recited poems "To the Polish Girls" and to "Mother Rus'."[18]

Ukrainian teachers considered the Pedagogical Society a modernized Prosvita. They expected non-teachers to join, and soon changed its name to the popular Native School (*Ridna Shkola*). The teachers also created a few women's branches of the Pedagogical Society outside Lviv. The Pedagogical Society in Lviv, in co-operation with the Ruthenian Women's Club, established about ten private schools and dormitories mainly for Ukrainian peasants. The Institute of St. Olha, opened in 1899, was run by Maria Biletska and Hermina Shukhevych. It offered residence for girls studying at various schools in Lviv, half of whom were of peasant origin, and supplemented their cultural and recreational activity. The Society opened an intermediary school for women in Lviv and an experimental primary school at which the girls carried out student teaching. The latter served as a model for other schools and took over Volodymyr Shukhevych's magazine for children, *Dzvinok* (The Bell), which became successful after 1903 when Konstantyna Malytska became its editor.[19]

Meanwhile, other private and public schools, responding to Ukrainian pressure and government requirements, introduced the Ukrainian language. In

1900, for example, the Cracow seminary introduced Ukrainian so that Polish teachers would qualify to teach in Ukrainian regions. Yet Polish patriotic literature enabled some girls to discover their Ukrainian heritage at bilingual or Polish institutions.

While some Polish noblewomen such as Dzieduszyńska, writing in the 1870s and 1880s in Lviv, argued publicly and in print against education for women, Ukrainian women were among the first in the empire to petition for entry into public secondary schools and universities. In the 1890s and early 1900s Polish and Ukrainian women co-operated in demanding public high schools for girls. Kobrynska, the Ruthenian Women's Club and the young socialist women initiated petitions, held rallies and used other forms of public protest to press for educational opportunities for women, including open entry to government-run gymnasia. In 1890, Ukrainian women were among the first to petition for access to universities for qualified women, and, to qualify them, for the establishment of at least one women's high school in Galicia.

Ukrainian petitions to the Reichstag demanding higher education for women were presented in 1890 and 1891. In 1893 Ivan Ozarkevych again raised the issue of a women's gymnasium in Galicia. That year, the Polish Galician women, spearheaded by the Women's Reading Club (*Czytelnia dla Kobiet*), which was supported by Ukrainian and Jewish women, presented a petition for higher education for women.[20]

The Poles identified the general striving for Ukrainian schools with nationalism, and their opposition to Ukrainian schools only led the Ukrainians to make education a major political goal. In 1899, during the parliamentary discussions, Bishop Chekhovych pointed out that of 690 students in women's seminaries, only 86 were Uniate Catholics. Ozarkevych worked tirelessly for the creation of Ukrainian seminaries. The Reverend Teodor Bohachevsky, a deputy to the Galician Sejm, whose sister was a teacher, argued that the shortage of Ukrainian women teachers contravened the ordinances about mandatory teaching in the native languages.[21]

The first fully Ukrainian gymnasium for boys was established only in 1874, although it had been sanctioned seven years earlier. By 1905, only five additional Ukrainian-language gymnasia had been founded. In contrast, forty-seven Polish-language high schools were established over the same period.

Language was only one issue in the debate over secondary schools. The gymnasium itself, with its seven years of classical Greek and eight years of Latin, in addition to compulsory German, was under attack. By 1900, there was pressure to introduce the so-called *real*-gymnasium, replacing some classical subjects with physics, chemistry, other natural sciences and more modern languages. Both types of schools (the latter was introduced in Austria only in the 1900s) prepared pupils for the aggregate examination, the *matura*, which made possible entry into a university.

Women's schools in Galicia did not prepare for the *matura* examination, nor did the instruction include Greek and Latin. To enter a university (outside

Austria), women had to take the *matura* examination privately. The first to do so in Galicia was a Ukrainian, Sofiia Okunevska, in 1885. Subsequently, she became the first Austrian woman to earn a medical degree (in Zurich and Cracow, in 1894 and 1900 respectively), and also the first woman in Galicia to practice medicine.[22]

The feasibility of a classical education for women was much debated by Austrians. Conservatives were concerned that women in Eastern Europe would become nihilists and even assassins, like their Russian counterparts. Among the Poles, the National Democratic group and the conservative faction also opposed higher education for women. Ukrainian radicals——who championed equality for women——considered higher education for women a frivolous whim, while the conservatives believed that it threatened the traditional family.[23]

The Austrian government made temporary compromises. In 1895, the first authorized intermediate schools for girls were called not gymnasia, but *lycées*. Their programme, developed by the minister of religion and education, Dr. Hartel, was devised to preserve *das ewig Weibliche* of its pupils. Although it laid less stress upon Latin and Greek, and incorporated the handicrafts beloved of German pedagogues, the *lycée* curriculum resembled that of the gymnasium. Existing girls' schools immediately restructured themselves as *lycées*, with the right to grant the *matura* examination.

The pressure for gymnasia for girls continued and led to the opening of the first girls' gymnasium in Cracow in 1896. A number of *lycées* then restructured their programmes into a gymnasium curriculum. Most of the pressure for high-school education came from middle-class women. For Ukrainian women, the two most important gymnasia were those in Przemyśl and Lviv. Public high schools for girls were authorized in December 1900, but government funds for them were limited.

A look at the ethnic make-up of the students in the classical gymnasia reveals the tremendous increase in the number of Jewish girls, mostly from the merchant class and the professions. In contrast, the numbers of Ukrainian women rose more slowly, which seems to confirm the adage that urban women were more anxious than those from the countryside to pursue a higher education.[24] Compared to Armenian, Jewish and Polish girls, few Ukrainian women sought higher education, which was partly a consequence of the lingering effects of serfdom upon Ukrainians.

But the situation was changing among Ukrainian women. Many studied independently, others audited classes at local high schools. In 1910 the Austrian ministry of education issued an ordinance to limit the number of auditors:

Private students can attend public high schools as auditors only in towns where there are no women's *lycées*, no higher women's school and no women's seminarium. The number of auditors cannot exceed 5 per cent of the total students in each class. If there are fewer than 20 pupils in a class, only one female auditor is permitted.[25]

Ukrainian and Polish women were able to hold four or five joint demonstrations in the 1890s, focusing on the right to vote and entry into university, but the quest for higher education for women in Western Ukraine was subsumed into a struggle between the Poles and Ukrainians over the language to be used at the University of Lviv.

The patriotic feelings of the Poles in the Austrian monarchy were strengthened by the influx of Polish students from the Russian Empire, where they had begun a boycott of universities for discrimination against the Poles. Polish women from the Russian Empire were admitted into Galician universities along with the males in 1898. They awakened the Galician Polish women's interest in politics, helped organize national conferences of Polish women, and encouraged them to press for entry into the universities.

Sexual and national lines crossed. Some Jewish students and a few Poles supported the Ukrainian demand for wider use of their native language at the university.[26] Another small group of Polish students opposed actively the demand of the women to attend university. By the turn of the century Austrian women were permitted as auditors, and in a year were allowed to attend. Once there, however, both women and men became more aware not of sexual inequality, but rather of the nationality struggle, the most visible issue confronting Poles and Ukrainians.

Once matriculated, Ukrainian women students at the university joined Ukrainian student organizations, and some were elected to executive boards of the Ukrainian Student Union, Academic Community, and the *Sich*, the patriotic organization of physical fitness. Evidently there was a need for women's organizations, and in mid-December 1910, Ukrainian women students at Lviv University established a women's branch of the Student Union. The twenty members met almost every Sunday to hear lectures and to discuss current affairs. On 2 July 1912, they met with the Jewish counterpart society (*Związek Słuchaczek Żydówek*) to discuss the representation of women in the student body.[27] Since many of the university and high-school faculty were, in the measured understatement of Olena Stepaniv, "not among the ardent supporters of the women's cause,"[28] the classroom discussion made the students more aware of the woman issue.

The demand for a Ukrainian University in Lviv,[29] voiced by Ukrainian students at a rally in Lviv on 13 July 1899, became the political goal of the Ukrainians in parliament. Ukrainian women at the University of Lviv went beyond this demand, initiating in 1912 a national emergency fund for use in a "national-liberation" struggle, demonstrating their immersion into university political life, with its atmosphere of charged patriotism.

For the vast majority of Ukrainian women, however, university education was unattainable. Women from the clerical milieu were limited to schools in Lviv or Przemyśl (see the appendix to this chapter). By the outbreak of the First World War, daughters of the Ukrainian Galician elite generally received secondary education, although few reached the *matura*. Even fewer Western Ukrainian women attended universities, yet even the fifty women university graduates before the war was a significant number. While peasant women usually received a third-grade education at best, attitudes were beginning to change. Women's expectations were rising and many more women would seek a higher education after the First World War.

Appendix 1: The Ukrainian Girls' Institute in Przemyśl

The Ukrainian Girls' Institute in Przemyśl offers a rare glimpse into the workings of the Ukrainian urban middle class.

Przemyśl was a city of restrained practicality. Nestled in a valley of the winding San River, at the entrance to the Carpathian Mountains, this medieval city was 250 kilometres from the Russian border. Yet the Austrian military strategists wanted to make it an impregnable fortress. (History justified this decision. In the First World War, Przemyśl was subjected to a long and bitter siege, while in the Second World War, between 1939 and 1941, the San divided the Nazi and Soviet camps.)

For Ukrainians, Przemyśl was a citadel of Ukrainian culture, situated 60 kilometres west of Lviv, on the road to Cracow. The Uniate bishopric maintained a seminary there. The Ukrainian community was composed of solid burghers who did not identify with the modern Ukrainian political parties, but nonetheless, along with the priests, considered themselves ardent Ukrainian patriots. By the 1880s, the women, through formal or informal ladies' auxiliaries, had become actively involved in community work, although a Society of Ruthenian Women emerged only in 1897. It carried out low-profile community work, and was linked closely with the church.

Ukrainians in Przemyśl felt keenly the need of a Ukrainian school for girls. They complained that the existing schools——the Teacher Training Seminary and the Benedictine Convent School for Young Ladies——were militantly anti-Ukrainian. The girls were punished for speaking Ukrainian or Yiddish, and were being subjected to anti-Ukrainian propaganda. The Ukrainians demanded a special fact-finding commission to investigate these institutions.[30]

Having used institutions to attend to community needs, Ukrainians in Przemyśl realized the importance of educating women for the Ukrainian cause. The repeated difficulties with the local school board and the growing intransigence of the Polish authorities toward the teaching of Ukrainian subjects in public and private schools rendered private Ukrainian schools an increasingly attractive proposition. One consequence was the impressive Ukrainian secondary school for girls in Przemyśl. The buildings, which remain in use today as a Polish music school, were built to rigorous specifications and were among the first in the empire to use central heating. The building of the school, however, was a slow and arduous process.

Initially, the Ukrainians planned a boarding institute for girls attending public schools, but after a decade of bitter conflict with the school board, they decided on a private school under Ukrainian control (the board would not permit a Ukrainian public school). The institute was the brainchild of the Reverend Lev Kordasevych, a prominent priest.

> This ardent patriot, pondering the reasons why Ukrainian society had so many shortcomings, came to the conclusion that one of the most important causes was the lack of higher education among the women of the Ukrainian intelligentsia that prevented the development of strong patriotic spirit, which can be imbued by a deeper knowledge of the native language and our own history.[31]

Early in the 1870s he started donating money and collecting small sums to establish an institute for Ukrainian girls. In 1875 he turned over 1,000 złoty to the Institute of Widows and Orphans to administer until more money was raised, although the Institute would not commit itself to the project.

Bishops Konstantyn Chekhovych and Hryhor Shashkevych became ardent supporters of the project, as did many clerics and members of the lay intelligentsia. The Reverend Zakhar Podliashevsky, for example, donated all the money he won at a state lottery in 1884, while Bishop Hryhor Shashkevych invested money in land, which he later sold at cost to the society. With these unexpected windfalls, the *peremyshliaky* decided to build not only a dormitory but a school for girls and, by 1887, 60,000 złoty had been set aside for that purpose. The shrewd citizens of Przemyśl delayed construction until the building costs, pushed sky-high by the fortifications, dropped.

The building committee was composed almost exclusively of men, divided evenly between clergy and lay persons. Women, however, made up a quarter of the membership of the Society for the Ukrainian Institute for Girls, founded in 1888 and reorganized two years later. Mariia Hrushevska, one of the first Ukrainian women teachers, wife of the historian Mykhailo Hrushevsky and daughter of a Lviv cleric, was elected to the building committee.[32] The Society was founded to promote the education of the Ukrainian girls of Przemyśl and the vicinity. A board, elected annually, supervised the building and the administration of the institute and school. By 1901, more than 70 of the Society's 200 members were women.

The cornerstone was laid on 7 October 1893. The Board closely supervised the building's construction, and Bishop Chekhovych, whose palatial residence and chancery were nearby, made about four hundred visits to the site during construction. Ukrainians took particular pride in the institute, and kept careful and detailed records. It was a grand three-storey structure (a third wing was added in 1900), with a one-thousand-book library, a tennis court, playing fields, gardens, modern laboratories and, after 1910, electricity.

The Society——whose membership fluctuated between 300 and 350——took an active interest in the running of the Institute. Besides electing the Board, or Directorate, it met weekly to review plans for expansion, financing, borrowing, the layout of the rooms, the hiring of staff and salaries. The institute was established as a *lycée* in 1901, but soon became a full-scale gymnasium, holding its first whole class *matura* in May 1909. It was also affiliated with the teacher-training seminary in Przemyśl.[33]

While generally successful, the institute was not without its problems. There was disagreement with the Society over the teaching of Ukrainian. Some insisted on a non-phonetic old-fashioned orthography. The vernacular took preference only after Mariia Pryima, the director of the Institute, brought the case to a general meeting on 29 June 1899. The feasibility of day-students was also reviewed periodically, because the Society feared that they might introduce a "non-Ruthenian spirit." There were also difficulties with parents, some of whom were sceptical about a Ukrainian school in the first place.[34] Others sent their daughters to the Institute but did not want them to study Ukrainian. The board, in a move supported by the general meeting, "categorically rejected any exemption from the study of Ukrainian...[girls] who do not wish to study it should leave the institute."[35]

The Society served as a debating forum between the conservative and the democratic Ukrainian camps. The conservatives, outnumbered and out-argued, frequently resorted to diversionary tactics. Reverend Nesterovych, for example, insisted on having membership lists checked, fearful that the democrats were packing meetings with their supporters. The conservatives were concerned about modernist trends. Thus on 6 June 1901, the Reverend Dr. Iosyf Cherliunchakevych insisted that the by-laws be amended so that the girls would receive not "moral upbringing" but "religious-moral upbringing." Hryhor Tsehlynsky, the official director of the institute, also wanted to change the description of the girls' upbringing from the old term *umyslovyi* (intellectual) to *dukhovnyi* (spiritual). Neither motion was accepted. By 1902, the polemics were so bitter that the Society threatened to sue four priests for slander.[36] The conservatives sought to undermine the institute by witholding dues or tuition fees for their daughters,[37] and the conservative newspaper *Halychanyn* (The Galician) was taken to court by the institute for slanderous articles.[38]

The Poles were irked by the institute's palatial grandeur, which added another major Ukrainian building to the silhouette of the city. Reverend Falat, the Polish director of the Seminary, publicly ridiculed the institute and the Shevchenko celebration held there in 1901, but apologized to Ukrainians when threatened with a court action.[39]

Despite its problems, the institute grew into an important Ukrainian cultural centre. Among those who lectured to the students were the historian Mykhailo Hrushevsky; Volodymyr Kotsovsky, who spoke on literature, and Volodymyr Shukhevych, whose lecture on photography drew the largest number of young women in the audience.[40] The impressive auditorium served as a setting for ambitious student programmes, as well as for visiting artists.

Enrollment at the institute increased steadily from an initial 23 students in 1893 to more than 250. Unlike the secular and religious Polish-language schools, in which there was a substantial increase in the number of Jewish girls, the student body in Przemyśl was homogeneously Ukrainian Catholic. The girls were predominantly daughters of priests, with a smaller number from families of the intelligentsia.[41]

The programme reflected the interests of the parents and the demands of the school board: religion, Ukrainian, Polish, German and French languages and literatures were stressed. Native speakers were hired for conversational practice. The courses on world history were supplemented with others in Ukrainian history. The girls studied some pedagogy and hygiene, music and drawing, handicrafts, and physical education. By the turn of the century, the programme for those working toward the *matura* also included physics, biology, chemistry, Latin and Greek. Caretakers and kitchen and cleaning helpers were hired, but the girls took turns serving meals. Only close female relatives could stay in the guest rooms. All other visits were closely supervised and special permission was required to leave the school.

Most students came from Galicia and Bukovyna, with a few from Silesia. The girls' parents supported higher education. Thus the Reverend Karanovych, at the graduation of one of his daughters in 1909, made an impassioned plea for the graduates to enter the universities.[42] The arguments in favour of education for women had more to do with national considerations than with emancipation. Matkivsky even totally ignored the female aspect when he spoke of the glories of the institute, its magnificent buildings, and the feelings that enveloped him as he stood in its palatial auditorium:

> You are in a national fortress, which the beleaguered but invincible people built through widows' small donations.... A tear of hope, joy and faith in the future glistens in your eye.... From this fortress warriors will emerge...who by their relentless, quiet, ant-like labours will bring new strength, might and freedom to sacred Mother-Rus'.[43]

The patriotic theme stressed activism and determination. On 1 June 1897, at a concert in honour of the institute's patron, Bishop Chekhovych, Ievheniia Tsehlynska reconciled religion, good upbringing and a will to act: "Not only do we want to be pious, studious and good girls, we want above all to be pious, studious and good Ruthenians. We want to be those Ruthenian Spartan women who are able at all times to defend our sacred faith, our native language, and our violated freedom."[44] To Tsehlynska, national freedom took precedence over sexual equality. Having received an education above the elementary level, she realized that new opportunities were opening for her generation.

These patriotic comments were not mere rhetoric, since they enhanced the self-confidence of the entire Ukrainian people. Polish primacy could only be challenged from a position of strength and only through centres such as the institute could Ukrainian potential be realized.

Although few students at the institute were of peasant origin, the girls were repeatedly reminded of their duties to the largely peasant nation. At the 1909 graduation ceremonies Bishop Chekhovych told the students "how they could further enlighten their younger village colleagues and thus, while still very young, serve their nation."[45]

The institute survived the First World War, and continued to expand under the Polish state to keep pace with the growing needs of women. In 1939, it announced the opening of the Women's Business School (Torhovelnyi Zhinochyi Litsei), a two-year programme that recognized "the need for a new business management school, since quite a few girls were already working in Ukrainian-run businesses, both in the co-operative and private sectors, and often went on to establish their own businesses."[46]

Appendix 2: The Gymnasium of St. Basil in Lviv

Of special importance to Galician women, and especially to those in Lviv, was the opening of the first women's Ukrainian gymnasium (as opposed to a *lycée*) in 1906. Developed from the School for Girls run by the Basilian Sisters between 1881 and 1888, it was attended by the Ukrainian elite of Lviv. At this same school Uliana Kravchenko had shocked parents and teachers in 1885 by teaching in the vernacular orthography. Nevertheless, the Basilian Academy soon became a centre for the patriotic education of Galician Ukrainian women. In the 1890s, and particularly after 1902, when the Poles opened the first private gymnasium for girls in Lviv, Ukrainians became better organized, and eventually established a Ukrainian-language gymnasium in Lviv.

Compared to Przemyśl, the community effort was belated and mundane. There were several reasons for this. First, the girls' gymnasium was but one of many community endeavours in Lviv. Second, while the women's gymnasium was urgently needed, Ukrainian radicals perceived it as an elitist institution of limited use to the common people. They identified themselves more readily with the primary and trade schools and dormitories being organized by the Ukrainian Pedagogical Society. Third, the clergy as a group was not involved actively in the Basilian nuns' project.

The Ruthenian Women's Club was behind the plans for restructuring the Academy of St. Basil into a full-scale gymnasium. In 1906, a special committee was organized by Dr. Spyrydon Karkhut, director of the Ukrainian Gymnasium in Lviv. Its secretary, Dr. Ostap Makarushka, was married to the secretary of the Ruthenian Women's Club. Metropolitan Sheptytsky immediately offered his help, and is widely considered the real founder of the gymnasium. He became its patron, major benefactor and a father-figure for generations of Ukrainian students.[47]

The nuns who ran the school taught only from grades three through eight.[48] Most of the faculty of the boys' gymnasium agreed to teach the girls, giving the school a good image. The women did not challenge male supremacy in either academic or community matters, and by 1908, when the school opened as a full gymnasium, the public was amenable to the concept of secondary education for women. The majority of the 200 students at the Gymnasium of St. Basil were daughters of the clergy. Lviv was considered the ideal place for a young woman of breeding and dedication to be educated.

The school exposed the girls not only to humanistic education and a rational defence of patriotism, but also to the concentrated experience of dormitory living. The girls developed skills they later applied in community organizations. Before the outbreak of the First World War, some organized girl scout groups. These communal experiences strengthened the girls' desire to be of service to the nation through education and community work.

7.
Kobrynska's Feminist Socialism

Nataliia Ozarkevych Kobrynska was the first outspoken theoretician of feminist thought among Ukrainians and the first to organize secular Ukrainian women's associations. Her conception of the woman issue was shaped by liberalism, socialism and a first-hand knowledge of the economic situation in her native Galicia. Within a socialist framework Kobrynska juxtaposed theoretical analysis with a pragmatic approach to the problems confronting Ukrainian women in Galicia. She tried to balance feminism and socialism. She thus concluded that, although economic and political changes such as those predicated by socialism were necessary for progress, women themselves must work to bring about these changes and must create a philosophical framework for them. Kobrynska was one of the first women in Europe to advocate the fusion of feminism with socialism.[1]

Kobrynska is considered the founder of the women's movement in Ukraine. Yet her conjunction of feminism and socialism was unpalatable to Ukrainian men and rejected by most Ukrainian women. As a result her theoretical views have not received due attention. Some of her writings are still unavailable. Socialists downplay her feminism, while authors of studies on Ukrainian women have overlooked much of her socialist analysis and bolder ideas. This chapter, while sketching Kobrynska's life, will focus on her views and her attempts to organize women during the 1880s. Chapter 8 examines the activities of Ukrainian women over the following three decades, noting Kobrynska's role in these events.

Kobrynska was born on 8 June 1851[2] in the Carpathian village of Belelulia, into a family of Ukrainian Catholic priests. Her parents, Ivan Ozarkevych and Teofiliia Okunevska, came from a segment of the clergy that had devoted itself to secular aspects of Galician life while remaining practicing believers. In 1848, Kobrynska's grandfather Ivan introduced modern Ukrainian theatre into Galicia and co-operated in the publication of the first Ukrainian newspaper, *Zoria Halytska* (The Galician Star). Her father (1826–1903) was a community activist who successfully combined sacerdotal and parliamentary duties. In 1893 he led a 220-member Ukrainian-Galician delegation to Emperor Franz Josef. He revised some by-laws of the Institutes of Widows and Orphans, and lobbied actively for equal education for women. Kobrynska's mother came from an established clerical family, which showed great deference to the maternal grandmother, leading the young Kobrynska to believe that all women enjoyed high status in society.

The oldest of five children, Nataliia was close to her father, who went out of his way to defend her views even before Count Kazimierz Badeni, governor of Galicia in 1890. Badeni once commented ironically that Kobrynska was "a free spirit." But Ozarkevych vehemently defended his daughter as being so intelligent and knowledgeable that some men were uncomfortable in her presence. So certain was Kobrynska of her father's support that after his death, she would recall in moments of deep dejection his vibrant call, "Don't lose heart."[3] The Reverend Ozarkevych personally supervised his daughter's education after her three younger brothers went off to the gymnasium (the gymnasia were not open to girls).

Kobrynska's family lived in the picturesque Kolomyia-Sniatyn-Kosiv area of the Carpathian mountains. The mountains and the customs of the Hutsuls made surprisingly little impact upon Kobrynska. Her writings show scant regard for nature. Even toward the end of her life, when she turned to symbolism, her subject was the emotional life of humans rather than the transcendent beauty of nature. She was a voracious reader. During her adolescence she was for a time deeply religious, and in fact she remained a Catholic all her life, but interpreted the faith in her own way.[4]

The family led an active social life, yet Kobrynska did not regard it as unusual. She noted that she could obtain copies of Buckle, Büchner, Haeckel and Darwin at the home of another priest, omitting to mention that these authors, stalwarts of positivism, were on the Vatican's index of forbidden books. Through her brothers, who went to schools in Chernivtsi (the German-language gymnasium) and in Lviv (the Ukrainian gymnasium), she met the young members of the Ukrainian intelligentsia. Her brothers also introduced her to the works of some Russian writers: Chernyshevsky, the prophet of Russian populist positivism; Belinsky, the patron saint of the Russian radical intelligentsia; Dobroliubov, an influential literary critic who stressed the positive aspects of revolutionary life; as well as "Turgenev and our own Gogol."[5] But she stressed her originality, not the influences upon her. In a letter to Pavlyk on 28 November 1888, she repeated what she had earlier written to Ivan Franko, a literary and political giant in Ukrainian matters, "I reached my own ideas by my own efforts, without the help of men, through my own life and especially through my own experiences."[6]

The lively social encounters of the summer months at her parents' home played an important role in Kobrynska's development. The parsonage was visited by family and friends, older students making trips into the mountains to collect folksongs, and seminarians in search of wives. The house was bustling with both young and well-established people who brought new ideas and new books. Kobrynska took an active part in these debates.

During these encounters she met Teofil Kobrynsky, a sensitive and artistic seminarian, whom she married in the summer of 1871. His first gift to her was the collected works of both Gogol and Turgenev. Intellectual pursuits were an integral aspect of this almost ideal marriage, and Kobrynsky encouraged his wife as her father had done.[7] Through him, she came to know works of Renan, Lassalle, Marx and Engels. As she espoused socialism and internationalism, the two pillars of her upbringing, God and country, tumbled down. Thus, Kobrynska experienced the traditional crisis of the modern intelligentsia, as her description makes clear:

> I suffered when I understood the positivists. Their works destroyed not only my religious convictions but also my views on life and the social system surrounding me.... I felt that I was losing ground and the most acute spiritual struggle completely unnerved me.[8]

Her husband, about whom Kobrynska, always reticent about personal matters, wrote only that he was always "a frank confidant,"[9] had a remarkable ability to adapt new ideas to the existing social and religious system. His understanding and support during his wife's crisis indicates that he may have undergone a similar experience.

The works of Ivan Franko, the son of a Galician blacksmith, both a Ukrainian patriot and a professed socialist, persuaded Kobrynska that in order to help the international proletariat Ukrainians must first work among Ukrainian peasants, nurturing in them an awareness of their national identity and human worth. Henceforth, for Kobrynska, the issues of nationalism and socialism became intertwined.

At this point Kobrynska confronted the woman issue. When she and her husband moved to a small town, she noted the unproductive character of women's work; how much time they wasted on trifles. She tried to reorganize her household, but ran into opposition from the servants, and her concept of a co-operative of households to divide housekeeping duties scandalized the ladies in the small provincial town. This reaction convinced Kobrynska that it was necessary to introduce Ukrainian women to the idea of emancipation for women. Kobrynsky evidently concurred, and together the couple planned to translate J.S. Mill's *On the Subjection of Women*.

Both Kobrynska and her husband became feminists. They decided not to have children so that Kobrynska could dedicate herself to the cause of women. But on 14 March 1882 Kobrynsky died of tuberculosis. Kobrynska plunged into such despair that she refused even to read. To allay her misery, her father took her to Vienna, where Ukrainian activists encouraged her both to write and to organize women into a potent force to promote social progress.

In 1878, the Austrians and the Polish Galician administration had staged a trial of several Ukrainian socialists, including Ivan Franko, Mykhailo Pavlyk, his sister Anna (whose work will be discussed later), and Ostap Terletsky, a graduate student in Vienna (who also used the pseudonym Ivan Zanevych). The trial destroyed Franko's academic career and personal life, but served to popularize the views of the Ukrainian socialists and reaffirm their convictions. Ukrainian youth often fervently expounded radical ideas, but rarely put them into practice.

Kobrynska, however, was taken aback by the supercilious attitude of the radicals toward the rest of Galician Ukrainian society, which they dismissed as hopeless and reactionary.

> I dislike their shock tactics. The works I had been reading made the case first and foremost for toleration, while our reformers' scare tactics manifested intolerance. Their application of such tactics to family relations hurt me most. Parents were seen by their own children as exploiters of the nation. Yet these same children demanded an education at whatever cost. Our women were considered one degenerate mass, more ignorant than the peasant men...but all their personal wealth was to be confiscated for the benefit of the other sex.[10]

Kobrynska was as level-headed in her adherence to socialism as she was in her practice of Catholicism. She found a kindred soul in Ostap Terletsky, a historian and a socialist implicated in the Lviv trial, who was an activist in the Ukrainian Student Society (Sich) in Vienna. The Society, founded in 1868, served as a forum for the discussion of new ideas, and it was here that Terletsky encouraged Kobrynska to express her feminist views. She did so in her first story, "Madame Shumynska," later called "The Spirit of the Times," which Terletsky read without disclosing its author at a meeting of the Sich at the end of 1883. It was an immediate success, as Kobrynska, sitting in her usual corner, noted. Kobrynska used the story to advocate a change in the social position of women, yet she also revealed a rare sensitivity to the opposition to that change. A few months later she wrote "For a Piece of Bread," a short story that became a favourite among Ukrainian women.[11]

Almost overnight Kobrynska had become an established writer in the prevailing realistic style. She found a convivial group of people who encouraged her ambition. Terletsky, Franko, Mykhailo Pavlyk and a whole generation of young Ukrainian patriotic socialists in Galicia shared her views and initially gave her support. She reconciled herself to the loss of her husband, but continued to wear black. The colour accentuated her tall, slim figure and set off her dark eyes and hair against an ivory complexion, giving her an aristocratic bearing.

Kobrynska could have continued writing within the radical milieu, but she felt a stronger duty toward women. She was determined that women could only change their fate through their own effective organization. Kobrynska remained a feminist until death, and resented the unpopularity of militant feminism among Ukrainian women. Duchyminska, a young writer who met Kobrynska after the turn of the century, was taken aback by the passion of the older woman's convictions: "I had gone to see an author, but came back a convinced feminist myself."[12]

Kobrynska brought a new perspective to Galician politics by linking the fate of all women: peasants, "upper classes," and "oppressed classes." She argued that women's needs could only be met in a socially progressive state, that social and political issues were linked, and she criticized Polish women for sidestepping the social question. She quipped that women of her class, despite their social pretensions——and especially widows of priests——"are the proletariat of Galicia."[13]

Kobrynska valued political liberalism, pragmatism and pluralism and used various means to organize women. In August 1884 at a political rally in Kolomyia, at which the student Vasyl Poliansky spoke on the rights of women, Kobrynska drew together some young women, especially Emiliia Nychai, a teacher, Uliana Kravchenko, a poet, and the Pavlyk sisters, peasant activists of socialist persuasion, and convinced them of the need to organize women. She also cultivated society dowagers such as Ivanna Osterman. Although those women came from different social classes and political camps, all became convinced of the need for a secular, apolitical women's organization that would popularize the benefits of education and modernization.

On Kobrynska's initiative, the women held their first public meeting and set up the first society in Stanyslaviv rather than in Lviv itself. There were several reasons for this. Stanyslaviv had a proportionately larger Ukrainian population than Lviv and, unlike Lviv, did not have an already existing women's society. The Lviv Society of Ruthenian Ladies had gravitated toward the Russophile-conservative camp. Kobrynska wanted neither a political confrontation among Ukrainians nor an identification of the new women's organization with any of the political camps (the conservative Russophiles, the liberal *narodovtsi* (populists), or the radicals). A radical herself, Kobrynska realized that open identification with the radical cause would make it harder to attract all women.

There was strong support for the creation of the women's society in Stanyslaviv, with the enthusiasts ranging from older women to the teenager Olena Simenovych-Kysilevska.[14] Ninety-five women founded the Society of Ruthenian Women. The initial meeting was held on 7 October 1884, only four years after the first general public rally of Ukrainians.

Franko was very helpful. He wrote advertisements and articles in *Dilo*, the major progressive Ukrainian newspaper in Galicia, founded in Lviv in 1880. He publicized the first organizational meeting of the women in Stanyslaviv and the newspaper also published the proposed by-laws of the organization. After the Austrian government approved them they were published as a brochure for use by women in other towns.[15]

Initially, the Stanyslaviv group called itself the Society of Ruthenian Women and held its first public session on 8 December 1884. The meeting was attended by about 100 women from various parts of Western Ukraine, while representatives of the intelligentsia and the clergy followed the proceedings from an adjoining room. The women felt that the men's presence would make some women uncomfortable about speaking out. The secular nature of the undertaking was underlined by having no religious service to initiate proceedings. The major speaker, Kobrynska, outlined the Society's aims, and later published her comments in the Ukrainian women's almanac.[16]

Kobrynska argued that in the absence of formal schooling, literature was the best means "of popularizing new ideas developed by humanity."[17] She perceived clearly the role of the village clergy and their families in transmitting new ideas to all segments of female society in Galician Ukraine. Women, she felt, had to be made aware of the peasants' needs and of how to help the peasants help themselves. The Society's aim was to advise women of literature that would enable the "individual woman to free herself from the bustle and chaos created by opposing points of view" and inform her about the political situation while creating a broader reading public.[18] Kobrynska stressed the political importance of literature for women:

> Women, who are excluded from general public affairs [zahalnykh i publychnykh sprav], who do not enjoy any power which might have some influence upon current events, [who] have no opportunity to express their views on the everyday needs of their life, should all the more look toward literature and use it to reflect these needs and demands.[19]

The Ukrainian populists used literature in the same way. But while the populists were oriented toward the illiterate or semi-literate peasants, Kobrynska sought to reform society by changing perceptions and modes of thinking among its leaders. She argued that violent change (revolution) would not bring genuine change for women. Real change had to be more deeply rooted. Although a radical, Kobrynska was willing to work patiently to create a climate capable of changing the patriarchal system. She thought she could mediate between the outspoken radicals, such as Franko, whom she valued highly, and the women who feared radical rhetoric.

At first, the Stanyslaviv Society tried to establish a journal or newspaper. The main candidate for editor was Franko, who considered the venture a welcome opportunity for progressive Ukrainianism in Galicia and shared Kobrynska's hopes. To most women, however, Franko was a dangerous radical. Thus he was rejected and the inexperienced women were obliged to abandon this idea. Instead, they agreed to publish an almanac composed exclusively of women's contributions.[20]

Franko published an extended report of the Stanyslaviv proceedings, as well as Kobrynska's opening remarks.[21] He also wrote a poem of greetings to the Society. In it, a genius——obviously a male——pushes a woman off her pedestal, then endows her with a loving heart and a passionate mind, thus making her his equal.[22] The poem proved to be a prophetic allegory of the subsequent relationship between the women and progressive Ukrainian men.

Kobrynska took it for granted that men would support women in their common cause.[23]

The women were organizing at a time of changing political configurations in Galicia. Their fear of the radicals was well grounded. The popularity of the village Prosvita provided a basis for political parties. Organized, run and supported by the clergy, it created a secular means of making the peasants aware of the political, social and economic situation in Galicia. In the 1870s, the Habsburgs secured the good will of the Polish gentry by granting them autonomy in Galicia. The latter then increased their discriminatory policies against Ukrainians, which strengthened both the Russophile movement and the overall political involvement of Ukrainians.

At the same time the Russian government sporadically fostered Slavic liberation movements in the Ottoman Empire and, by implication, in Austria. Ukrainians from Hungary and Galicia were encouraged to emigrate to Russia with promises of lucrative positions and with money channelled into conservative Galician Ukrainian societies. The pro-Russians gained further exposure after the trial of Olha Hrabar in 1882 for alleged anti-Austrian activities.[24] The tense situation in the Balkans, which at times even led to the severing of Austro-Russian relations, made both empires more aware of the impact of their internal policies on their foreign policy.

The drift toward terrorism within the populist movement in the Tsarist Empire and the active participation of women in it made Galician women apprehensive of the new trends. They identified socialism with terrorism, atheism, the disintegration of the family and runaway children. Accordingly, they condoned the repression of the socialist movement in Galicia in 1878 that resulted in the temporary arrest of Franko, Pavlyk and others.

The Ukrainian Galician radicals, on the other hand, resented Kobrynska's gradualist approach toward social and political policies and took issue with her feminism. Their insistence upon class antagonism and their gratuitous talk of free love antagonized moderates and was particularly shocking to women. (Kobrynska specifically opposed "free love" on the grounds that, in condition of poverty and inequality, it would become yet another method of exploiting women.) The radicals were, however, more radical in rhetoric than in deed, and used the women's issue to assert their radicalism. Pavlyk, for example, developed the free-love doctrine for its own sake, regardless of the effect upon the party or himself. He and his colleagues criticized Kobrynska's writings for both content and style. After the publication of *Pershyi vinok* (The First Wreath) in 1887, in which she developed her feminist views, she received little active help from the Ukrainian intelligentsia.

Kobrynska ran the Stanyslaviv Society from her village. The announcement of the almanac, soliciting manuscripts and money, was published in *Dilo* in September 1885. To Kobrynska, the almanac had three main goals: to serve as a literary aid to women, to foster their self-confidence, and, by publishing works of Ukrainian women from the Russian Empire, to stress the solidarity of Ukrainian women.

The women were being pulled in three directions. Kobrynska wanted to focus on women's issues and organizations. The dowagers, supported by the men in their immediate environment, gravitated toward the familiar church-related activity. Some younger women, encouraged by the socialists, argued that feminist concerns reflected exclusively bourgeois strivings. They focused instead on the pressing needs of the people as formulated in conventional radical populism.

In 1885 the Pedagogical Society in Stanyslaviv, run by Ukrainian radicals, suggested that Kobrynska's group sponsor a school for women, or at least build a dormitory for needy female pupils. The latter idea was backed by Emiliia Nychai, who had been a close supporter of Kobrynska. In March 1886, Nychai was elected chairperson of the Stanyslaviv Women's Society. For her part, Kobrynska tried to keep the focus on womens' affairs. She asked the editor of *Dilo* "to hold off with the pedagogical projects for Stanyslaviv until I successfully put together...the women's almanac."[25] She resented the divisive role of the political groups among the women, which weakened the Society.

Meanwhile, the fund-raising committee for the women's publication, headed by Sofiia Buchynska, had collected a sizeable amount of money with which Kobrynska wanted to launch a whole series. She solicited the active cooperation of Olena Pchilka and Hanna Barvinok, and through them obtained assurances that Ukrainian women east of the Dnieper would send material to Galicia. Nychai, meanwhile, kept raising the issue of a dormitory to house the children of the peasants who, lacking village schools, had to study in the city. Kobrynska, considering herself to be of the same political camp as Franko, Pavlyk, and the other radicals, resented such subversion of a carefully planned strategy. She hit on another compromise. The Society would defray some of the publishing costs of Omelian Ohonovsky's history of Ukrainian literature in Galicia. Since it would be used as a textbook, it would be of direct and immediate benefit to the people. Part of the money collected for the almanac was used for that purpose. But publication of the almanac now needed Olena Pchilka's subsidy. It was finally published in Lviv in 1887.

Pchilka insisted that the publication be called *Pershyi vinok* (The First Wreath), rather than Kobrynska's more prosaic "Women's Almanac." The women, who had first worried about a shortage of material, were faced with a surfeit. They immediately planned a "Second Wreath," which was to include Kravchenko's memoirs and a short story by Kobylianska that had been omitted from the first publication.[26] While Pchilka and Kobrynska in effect edited the material, Franko described himself as the real editor. In fact, the published correspondence between Franko and Kobrynska suggests a joint operation.[27] It seems evident that the almanac was the product of Ukrainian women. It had all the strengths and weaknesses of a collective work with contributors from different political, geographical and generational groups. It was well received, but not all the copies were sold. Almost ten years after its first appearance it was still possible to purchase the almanac.[28]

Pershyi vinok contained poems and prose by Ukrainian women, ethnographic materials, and articles on the woman question by Kobrynska. The literary contributions frequently depicted the fate of the poor and the women, and exhorted readers to live in the "new way," a phrase coined in a poem by Uliana Kravchenko. Sofiia Okunevska's ethnographic study on the subservient position of the women in the folk ritual bridal songs illustrated the lowly position of peasant women in society.

Kobrynska analyzed the woman issue from a historical perspective, illustrating her points with quotations from Western European literature on the woman issue and describing women's position in various countries. In a separate article on Ukrainian women in Western Ukraine, Kobrynska depicted the poverty and squalor of both peasant life and that of matrons of the Ukrainian clergy. She complained that progressive ideas came late to Galicia, while "dark and retrogressive ones found their way rapidly and found great resonance."

Kobrynska attributed the limitation of women's role to home and motherhood to Polish aristocratic influences. In contrast, she connected the emancipation of the Ukrainian nation with active support of emancipated Ukrainian women. As an example of how the treatment of women impinged directly on the fate of the nation she pointed out that Ukrainian men claimed they could not afford to send girls to school, thus giving priority to the education of boys. These same young men upon graduation tended to marry Polish women, on the grounds that Ukrainians were not suitably educated. Hence, the number of Ukrainian families declined. Kobrynska also publicized the positive achievements of women who entered teaching and business.

Favourable reaction to the almanac encouraged Kobrynska. She spent the summer of 1887 in her native mountains with Sofiia Okunevska, who had just become the first woman medical doctor in Galicia. In the autumn, Kobrynska accompanied Okunevska to Switzerland. There, she established contact with women activists from Western Europe and Austria. Subsequently she also travelled to the Russian Empire.

For almost a decade Kobrynska tried to popularize the idea of the organization of women for self-improvement and fuller participation in the life of the community. She developed her views on women in articles included in the additional three volumes of Galician Ukrainian women's writings that she edited. She published *Nasha dolia* (Our Fate) in 1893, 1895 and 1896 with her own funds. To clarify her position, Kobrynska engaged in frank discussions on Galician politics, but these did little to further her popularity.

In addition to political difficulties, Kobrynska's public work was complicated by her personal life. She did not remarry. Her poise, striking beauty, elegance, erudition and stately bearing, even in a peasant costume, kept people at a distance. She was generally addressed by the formal "Madame." Pavlyk, a proud peasant's son, oblivious of his short round frame, apparently fell in love with Kobrynska. He wanted to free her from the tedium of small-town life, proposing marriage and an apartment in Lviv or Kolomyia.

When Kobrynska declined, Pavlyk felt that she had spurned him because she could not transcend her class to marry a peasant; that Kobrynska was not a genuine socialist. In fact, there was some truth to this. Kobrynska accepted socialism not as a way of life, but for the scientific, political and social insights it offered. Pavlyk, on the other hand, was a passionate adherent of the radical ethos. For him it was an identity, a symbol and a cause. He could not conceive that a woman would find him unattractive and that the rejection might reflect on his personality. Franko tried unsuccessfully to act as a mediator, but Pavlyk never missed an opportunity to criticize Kobrynska and goaded others to do likewise.[29] Kobrynska's response was to place more stress on the progressive elements in her views than she might otherwise have done.

Kobrynska saw the woman's issue as basically an economic question. She argued in 1887 that the woman's active contribution to the economy was a necessity. Lower-class women were already contributing to the family income, while the privileged position of the middle-class woman was steadily declining. A downturn in the economy contributed to a reduction in the number of marriages and increased the number of single women who had to fend for themselves.[30]

Criticisms directed at her personally made Kobrynska aware of the tension generated by the women's question in socialist thought. She disagreed with doctrinaire radicalism and socialism on two grounds. First, within the Galician context, she stressed practical and expedient action rather than ideology.[31] Second, within the broader theoretical framework of socialism, she denied that feminism could be considered a bourgeois phenomenon.[32] She argued with Klara Zetkin, stating that even among socialists and within socialism, women must struggle for their rights. Men would not dispense with their attitude of superiority toward women simply because economic and social conditions changed.[33] Progressive political parties, Kobrynska pointed out, were as male-dominated as the conservative ones. Men would have to be persuaded of the need to educate their daughters along with their sons. Kobrynska further noted that the workers only supported the women under pressure. Thus in Essen, in 1894, miners voted for an eight-hour working day but did not support women's right to work. Kobrynska commented that "It would be more realistic for women workers, while admitting that the victory of the workers will also be their victory, to ensure their own rights and not become dependent upon the grace of men."[34]

The socialists differentiated between a "bourgeois" and a "workers'" women's movement. Kobrynska, on the other hand, saw the woman's issue as a social rather than a class phenomenon. Its main characteristic, in her view, was the conviction that women's equality was essential for progress of the whole society. In "that great conglomerate, Austria," she saw the women's movement playing a role similar role to that of the students in the revolution of 1848. Kobrynska pointed out that social revolutions such as the one in Austria could take on different guises that did not fit the conventional revolutionary mould. These changes would be even more cataclysmic than those of 1848, and could not be predetermined.

Repeatedly, Kobrynska argued that the needs of women could only be fulfilled in a socially progressive state and that feminist, social, political and economic issues were interrelated.[35] She examined in detail the self-help organizations of American and British women. At the same time Kobrynska realized that most Ukrainian women did not yet understand her views, and thus she favoured a gradualist approach, especially to socialist issues.

In 1889 the Galician Social Democratic Party refused to sanction a separate women's section. It also rejected Ukrainian demands for an autonomous Ukrainian party within the framework of the Galician group. Thus when Ukrainians formed their own Radical Party in 1890, Kobrynska considered that women should be given organizational status within that party.

Kobrynska was a firm advocate of universal suffrage, which became a key issue for Ukrainians after Badeni was appointed governor. But she went beyond politics in her reform plans and maintained that feminist concerns would have to be raised even after the most far-reaching social and political changes occurred: "Some women activists appear rather naive: they assure proletarian women that the bourgeois right to vote will be of benefit only to men...while the proletarian men, when they acquire the right to vote, will keep in mind their [woman] helpers and will guarantee them their political rights."[36] While convinced that only a socialist restructuring of society would assure equality, she argued nevertheless that even that was not enough for women. Her basic point was that men must be made to see not only the justice but the necessity for women's equality. Underlying philosophical constructs would have to be changed in achieving this end. She was, in fact, arguing for a feminist philosophy that went beyond existing structures which made no provision for women. "It is a pity that the age-old slavery of women is etched like a scar in the concepts of men. Therefore women must struggle not only against the social order, which keeps them in slavery, but also against the concepts articulated by men."[37] Changes in the perception of women would not come about without basic changes in the perception of society itself, of philosophy, of power. Kobrynska never spelled out her views on the development of a feminist philosophy, nor did she have the means or environment in which to do so, but she certainly realized the need for conscious change in that direction.

Some change in the status of women, Kobrynska said, would arise automatically because of the economic changes in the country: industrialization, increased employment of women outside the home and urbanization.[38] The mother would no longer be able to combine working in the home and the fields with caring for small children and family. In fact, Kobrynska argued that women had been burdened with this dual role to the detriment of their own welfare and the well-being of their children.

Kobrynska was one of the earliest proponents of child-care centres, both as a practical answer to family needs and as a precursor of the co-operative/communal social order of the future. Since neither the Austrian government nor the Polish administration would support day-care centres,

Kobrynska advocated community-sponsored associations. No special teachers were needed. The children would simply receive the practical care that women had been giving them for centuries. Kobrynska did suggest, however, that both a peasant and an intelligentsia woman work in each day-care centre, because she felt that peasant women were sometimes too severe with children. Kobrynska laid out the *raison d'être* of the centres as follows:

> In our primitive conditions, day-care centres not only aid working women by caring for their children while they work in the fields, but also educate the children. Moreover, most of our neighbours strive, by any means, to destroy the Ruthenians as a nationality (*vynarodovlennia*). One of the ways they carry this out is by...putting young children into their day-care centres. It seems superfluous today to explain that the enforced use of a foreign language hinders the enlightenment of the masses.... By establishing their own day-care centres our women can stand at the very centre of the struggle against denationalization of the masses. By preserving the language of the common people the women can best serve the cause of universal enlightenment.[39]

Kobrynska appended a model statute for day-care centre organizations to the first volume of *Nasha dolia* in 1893, but only at the turn of the century did Ukrainians establish a Society for Day-Care Centres. Kobrynska was one of its founders and the keynote speaker at the opening ceremonies.[40] The first centres were founded in the cities. Few villages were able to sustain a full day-care centre before the First World War. But public discussion, the creation of the Society for Day-Care Centres, and sporadic efforts to establish them accustomed Ukrainians to the concept.

Few women accepted Kobrynska's justification for the day-care projects. She argued, partly to placate the radicals, that the bourgeois family was disintegrating, and that the day-care centres were the kernels of the new society, which would be based on communal principles.[41] One such principle concerned nutrition. The peasants were ignorant about nutrition and, when women worked in the fields, the family went without hot food for days. Kobrynska proposed the preparation of meals at a central kitchen in the village to ensure better nutrition for the family and an easier life for the overworked mother. The communal kitchen never caught on, but Kobrynska repeated the idea periodically.

In addition to the conservatives and radicals, the liberal-national camp also opposed Kobrynska's ideas. In a typical article entitled "Rodyna" (Family), published on 1 and 29 August 1893, *Dilo* attacked Kobrynska, accusing her of wanting to destroy the family. Women's efforts to gain admission to universities, for example, were also considered an attack upon the nation, since for many the family was the heart of the nation, the woman the keeper of the national identity and the transmitter of patriotism. To offset that charge, Kobrynska argued that educated women made better mothers.[42]

While praise for *Pershyi vinok* encouraged women to continue their literary efforts, *Nasha dolia* (Our Fate), which delved into politics, drew fire from leading Galician periodicals. The Ukrainian Galician men who had praised the achievements of Polish, Jewish and Russian women, and even Ukrainian women in the Russian Empire, went out of their way to criticize Galician women.

The first volume of *Nasha dolia* appeared in 1893 as the first volume of the Women's Library Series, not as a women's almanac. Kobrynska was its publisher and editor. Hanna Barvinok sent a story for the first collection, which included the statute for a model society of day-care centres. In addition to Kobrynska's analysis of the women's movement in Galicia, the volume included a speech by Ievheniia Iaroshynska, a writer and teacher, contributions by peasant women, an article on women's cottage industries, and a section on the women's movement throughout the world. Among the few scattered poems were contributions by Rakhylia Korn, a close friend of Uliana Kravchenko who wrote poetry in Yiddish. Poems by Jewish authors, in Ukrainian translations, were included in each volume of the almanac.

The second volume, which Kobrynska published two years later in Lviv, also served as a vehicle for her views. To emphasize the women's interest in West European cultural matters, she published reviews of Zola's *Lourdes*, Knut Hamsun's *Neue Erde* and *Alltagsfrauen*, and Strindberg's *Die Beichte eines Thoren*. In the third volume, which appeared in 1896, Kobrynska continued to stress the relationship between socialism and feminism. Her goal was to convince the Radical Party that her work contributed to the general development of the Ukrainian people.

The radicals took care not to antagonize women.[43] Pavlyk refused to publish Mykola Hankevych's *About Women's Slavery in its Historical Development*, which portrayed monogamy as a major cause of the subjection of women, because it would have shocked women unnecessarily.[44] This suggests that the party was interested in organizing women. Kobrynska considered herself the obvious choice to direct such work.

There was considerable discussion of the question whether the women should publish another almanac or concentrate on a simple newspaper for the peasant masses. Franko, Pavlyk and other radicals opted for the latter course. Kobrynska, however, in a letter to Iaroshynska after the Stryi rally, discussed the collection of materials for a second almanac. Around this time Lesia Ukrainka was writing to Franko about *Druhyi vinok*.[45]

Kobrynska's support for another almanac did not indicate, as her critics would have us believe, that she was adamantly opposed to a women's newspaper and to working with the broader masses. On the contrary, at the October 1891 meeting of the Radical Party, Kobrynska requested a regular column in the new party organ, *Narod*. Pavlyk, who received the request, bypassed Kobrynska and asked Olesia Bazhanska (who eventually married Lonhyn Ozarkevych, Kobrynska's brother) to edit the paper. At the same time Pavlyk also asked Olena Pchilka for support and ideas. Pchilka, like

Kobrynska, could not see why the radical men considered the almanac and a women's newspaper mutually exclusive. Bazhanska refused to edit the newspaper without Kobrynska's participation. Thus the matter was tabled.

Kobrynska's rebuttals were considered a result of pique. She responded in measured tones:

> Why, if the polemics of men can be called the defence of truth, the heroic achievement in the field of civilization, cannot the polemics of women be of equal importance? Why is the answer of women to their male critics simply considered a quarrel, anger, attack, inability to distinguish individual matters from those of public significance?

She perceived the attacks upon herself as an example of ingrained male prejudice, symptomatic of the broader problems of society:

> Trivia ceases being trivia when we take into consideration the blind faith of our women in male authority and the tragic economic dependence of women upon men. Certainly, anyone familiar with the situation of our women will recognize the full force of ill will of these seemingly casual words and comments.[46]

Although the unrelenting criticism hurt Kobrynska, she was resilient. "Weakness and despair," she wrote, "are the worst enemies of humanity, be they called pessimism or religion or resignation."[47]

By the beginning of the 1890s, Kobrynska's pioneer work began to bear fruit. Galician Ukrainian women had begun to organize their own societies, even if the model was not to Kobrynska's liking. Kobrynska even persuaded some of them to publish newspapers that produced feminist writers. Ukrainian women became involved in co-operative concerns with Polish and Jewish women. Kobrynska cultivated women from other nationalities within the empire, especially the Czechs. Her publications included selections of poetry by Jewish women, and she herself offered a sensitive portrayal of young Jewish girls. She published works by Adelheid Popp, editor of the Viennese *Arbeiterinnenzeitung*, and by Anna Perl, a women's activist in Austria.

Kobrynska showed remarkable courage in publicizing her views. Despite rebuffs, failures and her own resentment, she withdrew from public life only in her late sixties. Because of her interest in the woman's question and feminism in all its aspects, some historians of Ukraine——like her contemporaries——have dismissed Kobrynska as of marginal significance or even irrelevant in modern Ukrainian history. Only through the survival of the organized Ukrainian women's movement has her memory been kept alive.[48]

Kobrynska neither made Ukrainian women conscious feminists nor convinced them that it was as *women* that they lacked status in the community. Ukrainian women were more aware of national discrimination than that against them as a sex. But Kobrynska had successfully encouraged women to become involved in community life. She helped them move toward a pragmatic feminism. The organizations, the day-care centres and community action all oriented women toward feminism. It remained an undeveloped but well ingrained part of women's consciousness at the close of the nineteenth century.

8.
Widening Circles of Community Involvement

The Western Ukrainian women, like women in other parts of the world, lacked an ideology. The birth of "pragmatic feminism" was slow and unplanned, its existence unrecognized, its ideology unarticulated. Kobrynska's fusion of feminism with moderate socialism lacked support. Staid society matrons clustered in philanthropic or religious women's organizations and engaged in relief activities, but avoided anything that might be construed as radical politics. Younger women devoted to the radical cause, on the other hand, would not admit the relevance of feminism. For Ukrainian women generally, women's liberation was less important than national emancipation. The slow progress of industrialization in Galicia protracted the traditional role of women within the family.

For Ukrainians in the Austrian Empire, the most immediate aims were access to education and the right to vote. Both goals were part of the struggle for national rights rather than for sexual equality.

Voting in Galicia was indirect, favoured the propertied and was riddled by local abuses. Vigilantes often attacked the electors in broad daylight under the eyes of the police and confiscated their voting cards. Consequently, electors from the villages developed a strategy of going to town escorted by priests and surrounded by hefty youths. They marched to the polls singing the Habsburg anthem, carrying religious banners and pictures of the emperor. An attack on such a procession——in an attempt to prevent Ukrainians from voting——was thus an insult to both God and the Crown. Other ruses had to be developed to evade new attempts to stymie the right to vote repeatedly devised by local authorities. Consequently, Ukrainians demanded the complete overhaul of the indirect voting procedure and its replacement by direct, universal and secret ballot. They did not however, accept the request of some women that women should be included in the category of "universal."

Educational reform was also aimed at the expansion of educational opportunity for all Ukrainians and did not focus on women. The administration and Polish students openly opposed the extension of Ukrainian-language instruction at the University of Lviv. Ukrainian students held demonstrations, and the violent reaction of the police led to the death of a Ukrainian student in 1911.

Another factor had a direct bearing upon women's issues. The demand for land was forcing Ukrainian peasants to emigrate either as migrant workers to Western Europe or as immigrant labourers to the United States and Canada. This was seen as a means of earning money to acquire more land in Galicia. The peasants who emigrated kept their ties with their village, sent money to relatives, information and requests for priests.[1] Emigration increased the contacts of the Ukrainian intelligentsia, clerical and secular, with other nationalities. Travel and correspondence soon began to encompass women and thus contributed to increased pressure for education for women.

The principal achievements in community affairs by Western Ukrainian women during the 1880s were: (1) the reorganization of the Assumption Sisterhood in Lviv as the Society of Ruthenian Ladies in 1878–9; (2) the public meeting and the founding of the Society of Ruthenian Women in Stanyslaviv in 1884; and (3) the publication of the Women's Almanac in 1887. Besides group action, individual women, such as Anna and Paraskeviia Pavlyk, began political agitation among the peasants. As a result, Anna Pavlyk was arrested for the first time in 1880 and charged with spreading revolutionary propaganda. In 1882 a woman at the opposite end of the political spectrum——Olha Hrabar——was arrested for spreading Russophile views. Concurrently more works appeared in print by Western Ukrainian women, including Uliana Kravchenko's book of poetry, *Prima vera*, in 1885.

Interest in women's organizations increased during the 1890s along three main lines. Kobrynska developed her theories of socialist feminism; the socialists tried to establish a socialist women's movement without a feminist component; and futile attempts were made to unite Ukrainian, Polish and Jewish women in their demands for educational reform and suffrage.

In the spring of 1890 Czech women petitioned the Vienna government for the right to attend universities. Kobrynska immediately collected signatures from Ukrainian women in Galicia and asked Olha Kobylianska, a budding Bukovynian writer, "to...collect signatures, naturally in Ukrainian,... from the Bukovynian women."[2] Kobrynska had to act quickly, because the parliamentary session was expected to be a short one. Her father took the petition to Vienna on 1 May 1890, and its text was also printed in *Dilo*.

The petition has been described erroneously as simply a demand from the women for entry into the universities (the second such attempt made in Austria). In fact, the text bears the unmistakable stamp of Kobrynska and goes beyond the entry of women into the university: "The woman's question is with-out any doubt the most important movement in our century. While other issues relate to some one part of society, this movement touches half of the whole human race." An impassioned feminist manifesto followed:

The present social system differentiates between man and woman on all levels of spiritual and economic life. Conflicting...interests in community and private life make it possible for the men who control the public realm to overlook even the most justified wishes and needs of women.

This Galician woman advised the august Austrian Imperial Reichstag that there would be no improvement in either the social or the political system until women, who were totally dependent upon men, became truly independent. Work outside the home, she continued, was being forced upon women of all classes by economic realities. As a result the family, the core of society, was endangered, not by women working outside the home but by their lack of preparation for the task.

Kobrynska then turned to finance and its relationship to the woman issue:

When we study the budgets of nations we see that governments appropriate millions for the army, yet put only a minute sum into the pensions of widows and orphans. We keep being told that the family constitutes the basis of society, yet the family is identified with only one breadwinner. [Once he dies, or becomes incapacitated] no attention is paid to the needs of the family. It is then up to the woman alone to maintain the family.

Her argument for educational equality continuted in a singularly radical fashion:

We are not asking for a dole——that we leave for the cripples and beggars——we only want access to work in the open market, since as long as competition underlies the preservation of life, it would be most unjust to exclude half the people capable of participating in this competition. All who have reached maturity have the right to demand the work they are capable of performing.

Kobrynska argued that American women had proved all women capable of professional work. "No lawgiver," she warned, "can restrain a person from exercising his natural talents and needs.... Women have proved that they are capable of reaching the same level as men; no government should stand in their way." Finally, she struck a patriotic note: "In almost all large European states, with Austria as the glaring exception, women are admitted to university studies. This is an anomaly, [given Austria's] constitutional structure."[3]

After these preliminaries "the undersigned respectfully submitted" the following petition:

The Reichsrat should grant women legal admission to the universities and, since secondary schools are a prerequisite to university admission, the government should establish at least one gymnasium for women in Galicia.

Ozarkevych had the petition read into the record of the Reichstag.

Karolina Svétla, Louisa Celákova and Anežka Mákovska, Czech women leaders who had also been among the first to demand better educational opportunities for women, complimented the Ukrainian women. The German Austrian women followed suit. The Ukrainian petition was read at a meeting of the Viennese Society for the Extension of Women's Education, and commended at a rally held on 14 December 1890 in Lviv.[4] The Polish press, however, in referring to the petition, neglected to mention that its initiators were Ukrainian women.

The Ukrainian political parties did not discuss the women's petition, pleading more pressing matters. In 1890 the major national populist party had embarked on a period of co-operation with the Austrian Polish administration on a promise of extended rights to Ukrainians, the so-called "new era."[5] In October 1890, the Ukrainian (Ruthenian) Social Democratic Party reaffirmed that women's and workers' demands were identical and that specifically women's issues were therefore a bourgeois whim. The socialists decided that individual proselytizing, as carried out by Mykhailo Pavlyk's sister Anna among the peasants, was the most suitable political activity for women.[6]

Kobrynska again tried to prove that women needed separate organizations to achieve genuine equality. She received support from some Czechs. František Rehoř, a Czech ethnographer, organized an elaborate exposition of Slavic artifacts as part of the 1891 International Exhibition in Prague. Rehoř corresponded with the leading Ukrainian activists, including Kobrynska, Hermina Shukhevych, and a young teacher and writer from Bukovyna, Ievheniia Iaroshynska. When he invited the Ukrainian Lviv choir Boian to Prague in the summer of 1891, the Ukrainian women activists came along. The Czech women's movement offered visible proof that women's organization raised the cultural and economic level of the whole nation. Kobrynska befriended Vilma Sokolová, the editor of Zensky listy, the major Czech women's journal. On her return to Galicia, Kobrynska wrote about the trip in Zoria. Dilo published a photograph of the Ukrainian women in their colourful costumes.[7]

That same summer, Kobrynska, aided by Iaroshynska, organized a rally in the mountain city of Stryi to support Ukrainian political efforts. The success of the rally seemed to ensure women's organized participation in the emerging Radical Party. No feminist constituencies were set up, but Kobrynska was elected a spokesperson for Galicia, and Iaroshynska for Bukovyna.

Much of the rally was spent discussing Kobrynska's two pet projects——day-care centres and communal kitchens. Although the rally was attended by forty women, which was more than the thirty men who founded the Radical party a month later, Kobrynska complained about the low attendance.[8] The rally received very scant coverage in the Ukrainian press, and the Polish press ignored it.

The rally renewed the petition to further higher education for women, noting that the government itself had advertised the need for a woman physician in Bosnia (Moslem women there could not be treated by a man). The resolution, drafted by Kobrynska and Iaroshynska, called on all women of Galicia and Bukovyna, regardless of nationality or religion, to support educational equality for women.[9]

In 1892, the Polish women in the Galician Social Democratic party made an unsuccessful attempt to form a women's organization within the party. The failure led to a brief interlude of co-operation between Polish and Ukrainian socialist women in Galicia. In this seminal time it seemed that feminism might assuage the nationality conflicts that pervaded all aspects of Galician life.

Despite a boycott by some Polish groups, Poles and Ukrainians organized a joint rally of socialist women in Lviv on 10 April 1892 in which more than 200 women participated. Felicja Nossig-Próchnikowa presided at the meeting, Jadwiga Czajkowska served as secretary and Kobrynska spoke for the Ukrainians in support of both higher education for women and Ukrainian-language schools in rural districts. The attempt at Polish-Ukrainian co-operation faltered on this issue: Polish women felt that their support of Ukrainian language schools would be construed as a lack of Polish patriotism. Kobrynska, on the other hand, was wary of "hiding Ukrainians behind the crinoline of the old Polish state (*Rzeczpospolita*)."[10]

The failure of even such a limited attempt at co-operation demonstrated to Ukrainian women the need for self-reliance. Both town and peasant women supported Ukrainian women's societies with self-help programmes that included reading, cooking and sewing, and recreational activities such as choral singing and dramatic presentations. Children's talent shows developed from day-care centres. These outlets were similar to the church-related societies, not threatening to the males, and well within the boundaries of non-political community work.

Women's organizations combined economic and cultural concerns almost unconsciously. The most important new organization was the Ruthenian Women's Club, founded in Lviv in 1893.[11] Modelled on British ladies' clubs,[12] it was composed of socially prominent women who did not share Kobrynska's enthusiasm for feminist issues. Yet Kobrynska was its first speaker, and she emphasized the importance of heterogeneity in the women's movement.[13] Hermina Shukhevych, and two of Kobrynska's associates, Olha Franko and Iryna (Orysia) Harasymovych, were the active organizers of the club.

The Club pursued a more limited goal than the provincial circles:

> The initiative to form a Ruthenian Women's Club came from a small circle of women who, noting the passive role of women in society (*zhyttiu tovaryskim*), decided to create a centre for intellectual life. This would rejuvenate the intellectual life of Ukrainian women, strengthen and elevate their national spirit and activate their social life.... To achieve their goals, the women decided to establish a library, subscribe to periodicals, organize lectures, meetings and

discussions, and host parties, dances and amateur theatrical productions.[14]

More ambitious interests soon became evident. Orysia Harasymovych began a campaign to collect funds to erect a monument to Shevchenko. More important, the women decided to establish a co-operative workshop to make and sell garments and yard goods, which would hone the marketable skills of peasant women. The Trud co-operative, established in 1901, became a model for other institutions, offering a two-year course and providing a dormitory for students. Girls with a completed four-year elementary education were taught dress design, pattern making, and sewing as a business skill, and the co-operative sold the clothes they made. The profits received financed courses in book-keeping, grooming and conduct, and hygiene, as well as socials, concerts and lectures. Two years after its founding, the school had more than 100 students. The Shevchenko Scientific Society donated Ukrainian-language books for the library.[15]

The Club in Lviv also responded to Kobrynska's repeated pleas for day-care centres. In 1899, it helped create the Society for Day-Care Centres (Ruska Okhronka). In 1902, with a membership of more than 100, the club set up a subsidized cafeteria (Desheva Kukhnia) for students and workers in Lviv. It also initiated a programme for the preservation and popularization of folk art. In preparation for the Galician provincial exhibit in 1894, it co-operated with moderate Polish women's organizations in raising funds and collecting artifacts. The club published a book on the Ukrainian folk ornaments that won a major prize from the Exhibit Commission.[16] Hrushevsky's review of the three volumes of Kobrynska's work in *Literaturno-naukovyi vistnyk*[17] provided the women's movement with publicity. The two Ukrainian women's organizations in Lviv stimulated the creation of similar clubs in other cities.

The Women's Community in Berezhany ran a very successful library.[18] In Kolomyia, a Women's Circle, founded in 1893, established a library, organized lectures and concerts and developed a home economics self-help programme. More than fifty women met weekly in Horodenka to devise ways to make cottage industries more productive. In Sambir a co-operative vestment-making venture, primarily employing widows and orphans of priests, operated at a profit. With some support from men like Vasyl Nahirny and Illia Kokorudz (who founded the network of co-operatives which soon encompassed Western Ukraine), women's co-operatives and schools became an integral part of Western Ukrainian society.

The growth of women's organizations was further facilitated by the opening of new schools, the campaign for reform of the suffrage, increased Ukrainian political activity, and the growth of industrialization and the strike movement.[19] Ukrainians were becoming more militant. Younger women were affected by events such as the boycott in 1901 and 1902 by Ukrainian students of the university as part of a tactic to create a Ukrainian university.

The women's societies, especially the Ruthenian Women's Club of Lviv, were too mundane to attract young women. Daughters of club members, bolstered by young women from both Eastern and Western Ukraine attending school in Lviv, decided to organize their own circle to protest the club's policy of excluding young women from speaking publicly. Many of the girls had grown up together, and were of similar background and education. Most wanted to reform society and create a better life for Ukrainians. Their youthful enthusiasm, ebullience and impetuousness were refreshing and brought hope to the staid fathers of society and the aging radicals.

Led by Natalka Budzynovska and Dariia Shukhevych (the daughter of Hermina, later Starosolska), the women organized the Circle of Ukrainian Girls. They were supported by the Student Academic Community (Akademichna Hromada) and the older generation of political radicals. Unlike Kobrynska, who had difficulties publicizing women's activities, the Circle of Ukrainian Girls, located in Lviv itself, made the news easily. *Moloda Ukraina* (Young Ukraine), the monthly journal of Ukrainian youth that appeared between 1900 and 1902, immediately ran a story about the Circle and published its appeal. When a satirical journal ridiculed the Circle, *Dilo* at once published its rebuttal.[20]

Youth became the qualification for effective work. The term "girls" in Ukrainian had a different connotation from the American notion of girls meeting for bridge on Wednesdays and lunch on Fridays. In Galicia the term *panna* was used to refer to refined young ladies. *Divchyna*——girl——was very colloquial and, according to one organizer of the circle, "for the beginning of the century plainly revolutionary."[21]

The initial activities of the Circle carried an aura of modernity even though its plans and programme did not go beyond those of the women in the 1880s. The "girls" referred to one another as "Comrade" (Tovaryshka) which for Ukrainians was a reversion to the Cossack past and a denial of class distinctions, and saw themselves as part of the progressive movement.

> Comrade Budzynovska [the president] explained the rationale for the creation of a separate society for Ukrainian girls that focused on self-education, on the awakening of interest in public life, and on preparing for that work. She noted that the circle ought to lead our women into public life as active individuals. It should arm them with [weapons] necessary to fulfill the duties of a social being, an essential cog in the national machine.[22]

In the first decade of the twentieth century, following socialist directives, the young women worked in the literacy schools of the Pedagogical Society and began organizing townswomen and domestics.[23] But it was only with the co-operation of older women that a Society for the Care of Servants and Working Women was founded in 1903. Eventually, a subsidized cafeteria was established, also largely through the efforts of the Women's Club.[24] In emergencies, the two groups worked jointly to set up public kitchens.[25]

With the recklessness of youth, the members of the Girls' Circle saw themselves as founders of an authentic women's movement:

> This was the beginning of community work, the first step toward the intellectual uplifting of the Ukrainian women.... Here we girls ought to break finally with the vicious circle of eternal complaints about the subjection of women and the empty demands of women's rights; first, we ought to try to fulfill our duties using all the means at our disposal, all the means that should have been used long ago.[26]

Ignoring the previous accomplishments of Ukrainian women, the group avoided discussion of women's rights, stressing their own willingness to sacrifice themselves for society, especially for the peasants: "We girls...recognize the sorry state of the vast majority of our women, especially of the peasants, and we are willing and ready to help them, because we feel a burning need for this aid and understand its importance."[27] The Girls' Circle called on its "sisters"——a common term in the romantic politics of the Slavs of this period, without feminist overtones——to establish similar societies in other cities.

But they also realized "how difficult it [is] to fulfill our duties consciously and effectively, hence we consider it crucial to [first] prepare ourselves, to arm ourselves for this work, which means that *we must all strive toward our own enlightenment.*"[28] Like the radical populists, they meant to go to the peasant women to "organize them, to raise their consciousness through lectures and serious discussions and by setting up libraries."[29]

The veterans of the women's movement have left no record of their reaction to the rhetorical naivete of the Girls' Circle that enchanted Ukrainian politicians and cultural activists. Hankevych, Franko, Lutsky and other luminaries were among those asked by the Circle to deliver lectures; Kobrynska was not. But Kobrynska was above being rebuffed——she tried to establish contact with the young women whom she considered her spiritual followers, even though they refused to acknowledge her influence. She tried to show that feminism must be an integral part of their progressive social views and suggested joint actions. She hoped that they would publish a women's newspaper. In 1904, soon after the death of her parents, Kobrynska even moved to Lviv in order to spur on possible cooperation. But she found little support, and within a few months, finally dejected and depressed, she returned to Bolekhiv. The Girls' Circle, influenced by male rhetoric and oblivious of its kinship with Kobrynska's views, rejected her overture and mistrusted her. The young women considered feminism too restrictive. At a rally in Stanyslaviv in 1902, even Konstantyna Malytska, a teacher and writer, and the first woman to edit a Galician children's magazine, on whom Kobrynska pinned great hopes, pointed out that:

> We are not proposing women's separatism, since we do not consider that to be natural. We are not trying to lead women along separate paths, but we are going along new roads in order to make it easier for everyone to walk. We understand

emancipation to be the community work of women and men, the joint spiritual life of both sexes of our national organism.[30]

Malytska's rhetorical devices shed light on the self-perception of the younger generation. Malytska acknowledged Kobrynska's achievements, but faulted her inability to establish a centralized women's organization. Malytska went on to argue that women should establish a centralized society, similar to that of the Jesuits, whose members would go where they were most needed. She dramatized the issue: it was up to the women whether the nation itself would exist. She praised the women's social activities; the day-care centres, the literacy schools, the societies for servant girls, cottage industries, and the like. These, she concluded, were "women's issues," a term that "must exist, exists and will manifest itself constantly in varied forms, so we cannot close our eyes to it."[31] Malytska did not seem troubled by the contradiction of denying the significance of feminism and yet supporting women's issues. In fact, the typical position of Ukrainian women was to practice pragmatic feminism while renouncing the feminist label.

On 12 February 1904, the Girls' Circle organized a rally in Lviv which adopted the following resolution:

We agree with the premise that the only task of a women's organization is the enlightenment of Ukrainian women in their struggle against exploitation and oppression. We realize that the implementation of this liberation in our [present] social system, which permits the exploitation of one class by another, of one person by another, is impossible. We see no other allies in this struggle but the mass of oppressed worker-proletarians, both in villages and in cities. The meeting therefore ratifies and proclaims that we will fight in the name of the new social order for the liberation not only of women but of all suppressed groups of society.[32]

Thirty years later, on the eve of the Bolshevik take-over of Galicia, one of the participants in the rally recalled only that it passed a resolution for equal rights.[33] That perception was fairly typical. The Girls' Circle reflected the duality of revolutionary rhetoric and practical politics so characteristic of Ukrainian radicalism. The women of the circle considered the rally of 1904 an initiative for effective political action. They were proud that their counterparts from Eastern Ukraine, especially Nastia Hrinchenko, who upon her return to the Russian Empire had joined the Social Democratic Party, participated in the planning and execution of the rally.

The Girls' Circle was not monolithic. Some members wanted it to defend the interests of women teachers and to drop all social gatherings and dances. They approached Ievheniia Iaroshynska and suggested that she take over the presidency of the circle. The Bukovynian teacher and writer replied:

[I] would gladly take on this function, but only on the condition that all the members pledge to attend meetings and lectures, and agree to take on enlightenment work [in the villages]. For I do not want to be the chairperson in name only. I would like to raise the society to a European level, making it prestigious so that we could be proud of its achievement.[34]

Iaroshynska even considered establishing another society, considering "the girls" too frivolous.[35]

The euphoria of listening to the leading representatives of the Ukrainian movement and of obtaining press coverage did not last long, nor did the title "girls." On 14 October 1905, the circle formally changed its name to the Circle of Ukrainian Women (Kruzhok Ukrainok) and amended its statute to make possible the founding of local branches in other cities.

Members of the circle, along with Polish and other Ukrainian women, participated in a series of suffrage rallies, but there was little interest in forming a united women's front. The Polish and Ukrainian Social Democratic and Radical Parties, for their part, agreed that women's suffrage was not a worthy issue. In an article in *Dilo*, Kobrynska again stressed the need for a women's programme. She pointed out that the Ukrainian women's movement had shown greater awareness and better organization than the Polish movement. She also argued that "the woman issue cannot be enclosed in narrow political...terms...and goes beyond the relations of male and female working class. It encompasses cultural, public and political rights, as well as any other area of possible discrimination against women."[36] Kobrynska maintained that unlike the Poles, whose awareness of the need for liberation matured gradually, Ukrainians recognized its importance at once in the decade of the 1880s that marked the rise of Ukrainian political awareness. "It was through this simple historical juxtaposition that Ukrainian women understood they had to speak for themselves."[37]

With the active support of both the Socialist Party and the students, the Lviv Women's Circle began to publish a journal in March 1908. They hoped it would rally Galician women and that it would bring the women of Eastern Ukraine closer to the Galicians. The journal——*Meta* (Aim)——appeared every two weeks between March and December 1908. Its editor was Dariia Shukhevych Starosolska, the daughter of one of the founders of the Ruthenian Women's Club. Starosolska's collaborators were Olena Okhrymovych Zalizniak and Iryna Sichynska. Its progressive nature was stressed by its subtitle, "the organ of progressive Ukrainian women." But its credo reflected the feminist strivings its young proponents were not yet willing to articulate.[38]

Meta had the support of several Ukrainian writers. Foremost among them were Vasyl Stefanyk, who captured the tragedy and the beauty of peasant life; Bohdan Lepky, who preserved the romance in history and poetry; and Ostap Lutsky, the apostle of modernism among Western Ukrainian poets. The Galician women had the active co-operation of Eastern Ukrainians such as

Mariia Zahirna and the younger Khrystyna Alchevska. The Eastern Ukrainian writer and bandurist Hnat Khotkevych contributed to the journal, as did Katria Hrynevych, an author of historical fiction. *Meta* included articles on Turkish women, British women, and on the types of women portrayed in the works of Nekrasov, the Russian realist beloved by the revolutionaries. Some of Klara Zetkin's pronouncements on women were published in the journal, along with translations of Tolstoi, a review of Masaryk's book on women, and a synopsis of popular books by Lily Braun, *The Work of Women* and *Household Management*. The young Ivan Krypiakevych, later to emerge as a major Ukrainian historian, wrote an article on the active role of women in Ukrainian history. There was even an obituary on Korneliia Tymiakivna, who died in Kosiv at the age of twenty-one, after an active career in the Social Democratic Party and the Prosvita. But there was no mention of Kobrynska, nor of the earlier attempts of Galician feminists to create both a women's organization and a women's press.

Meta gave extended coverage to the *cause célèbre* of Ukrainians in 1908——Myroslav Sichynsky's assassination of the Galician Governor, Count Andrzej Potocki. Sichynsky, a young student, became a Ukrainian martyr for killing the governor, who condoned electoral abuses. Sichynsky had joined the ranks of those populists and anarchists in the Russian Empire who demonstrated their zeal for a cause by assassinating public figures. At his trial (which preceded his escape to Norway and later to the United States), Sichynsky declared his willingness to "sacrifice his life for his people." In a series of articles in *Meta*, Konstantyna Malytska, the bespectacled ascetic teacher, even likened Sichynsky's exploit to the sacrifice of Christ. After describing the elaborate pomp of the Austrian courtroom in Lviv, Malytska observed "the dwarfed silver Cross of the Lord...and I saw...the Lord approach this youth, lay his good pale hands upon his full head of hair and say: 'Son, you loved much and suffered much, your transgressions are forgiven.' "[39]

Despite their politics and their stress on supporting peasants, women in the circle failed to achieve *de facto* equality even within the milieu of progressive men. By the end of 1908, they realized the need to collaborate with other women to create a more powerful organization. The Meta group, the Circle of Ukrainian Women and the Ruthenian Club agreed to create a central women's organization and a central press. As a compromise between a feminist journal for the intelligentsia and a mass-circulation paper, the women decided to publish a journal aimed at the intelligentsia, with periodic publications for peasants and the townswomen. In suspending publication, *Meta* announced that a women's journal would soon reappear "as the organ of a new organization of women. Under an expanded committee and with the broader participation of women it will be able to fulfill its tasks better."[40]

On 26 December 1908 the Ruthenian Women's Club and the Ukrainian Circle of Women held a congress of representatives of various Ukrainian women's organizations in Lviv. It was chaired by Olena Sichynska, the mother of Potocki's assassin. The congress debated the benefits of a centralized as opposed to a loosely structured federation. The former was supported by the Lviv women, such as Malytska and Sichynska, but most of the provincial groups preferred the latter. The disagreement was masked under the guise of whether the organization should be called Zhinocha Hromada (Women's Community, Society), the central alternative, or Soiuz Ukrainok (Union of Ukrainian Women), the loosely federated structure.[41]

The women adjourned without reaching a final decision but agreed to meet again within a year. Although that meeting was poorly attended by women outside Lviv, the Lviv women used the forum to combine the Ruthenian Women's Club and the Circle of Ukrainian Women into a Ukrainian Women's Community (Zhinocha Hromada).

In its eight years of existence in Lviv, from 1909 to 1917, the group organized public lectures, founded a dormitory for girls, and ran subsidized cafeterias and emergency kitchens. It continued to expand the work of the women's co-operative Trud, set up branch organizations, and popularized the Society of Domestics. It also attracted young women students.

But the women did not reactivate either a newspaper or journal, because they could not decide on the type of publication they wanted. The Student Community, which published a booklet commemorating Shevchenko in 1912, pressured *Dilo* to permit Olena Simenovych-Kysilevska (the youngest participant in the first women's rally in Stanyslaviv in 1884) to edit a weekly women's supplement, *Zhinoche Dilo*. Malytska's editing of the children's journal, *Dzvinok* (1903–09), was also considered a female achievement, since her successor was also a woman writer, Katria Hrynevych (1909–11). In 1912, Kobrynska began her last effort to establish a series for women (*Zhinocha Knyha*). She published a translation of a patriotic novel by the prolific Czech writer, Karolina Svetla, and scheduled Maeterlinck's *Bluebeard* as the next publication. Future authors were to include Bergson and Ibsen. These were a far cry from Bebel's *Woman and Socialism*, which she had hoped to publish in Ukrainian ten or fifteen years earlier. Two volumes in this series appeared before the outbreak of the First World War.

Combined activities of Poles and Ukrainians continued sporadically. In 1910, the women sent a joint deputation to the Galician Sejm to press for suffrage. They were met by Governor Badeni and about thirty deputies. Among the Ukrainian participants were Mariia Biletska, the teacher and activist from Lviv, Ievheniia Verhanovych, another society lady, and the peasant Ohronikova, whose first name has not been preserved. The women were peaceful, but the Ukrainian Radical Party leader, the fiery peasant orator Semen Vityk, led a march through the streets of the city, drawing a crowd which sang the *Marseillaise*. The government used that the demonstration as proof that all women's organizations were merely a front for revolutionaries.[42]

But women were less interested in revolution than in patriotism, which became an important theme of all their organizations. The stress on the family, self-sacrifice, and the importance of defending national tradition fit into the ethos of progressive nationalism. Polish women's organizations, especially the financially secure *Liga Kobiet Polskich*,[43] became adjuncts of political parties. Ukrainian women's organizations, however, preserved their autonomy.

The Ukrainian Catholic Church accommodated itself to the increasing public role of women. In 1911, women were permitted to teach catechism, and priests willingly helped to certify women teachers for the catechization of children in the villages. Later the Przemyśl diocese popularized the work of Cardinal Innitzer and Dr. Berta Pichl on the need for education of women, mainly because it needed an aware laity.[44]

When the church became concerned with the pre-school education of children, the Sisters Servant of the Immaculate Conception established nursery schools and day-care centres. They were supported even by those who had earlier opposed day care. Kobrynska again offered her frank comments:

> When the first calls for the creation of day-care centres were made by the Sisters Servant, the women's projects raised at the rallies were not opposed; instead rumours began to spread that the day-care centres proposed by the women were in principle different from those of the Sisters, that they were allegedly stimulated by anti-religious considerations. That this is not the case can be seen in the day-care centres run by nuns, since the majority of Ukrainian women are, I think, no less religious and religiously informed than the professed nuns.[45]

The need for day care was obvious, so the church became involved in it just as it had earlier encouraged self-help and cultural societies. Priests continued to be active in all these organizations. Brotherhood-type societies were founded for workers, including working women, who were mainly domestics.

In Sambir, for example, the Society of the Blessed Virgin Mary of the Immaculate Conception for Domestics was founded in 1909. Its draft statute was written in an unschooled primitive hand, but its goals were both practical and ambitious. It was to provide a hostel for working girls, or for those between jobs. It planned a literacy school, a library, aid for the unemployed and medical care. It was organized in circles of twelve young women who formed the immediate support group. The entrance fee was one crown, with a monthly assessment of 10 *groschen* for candles. The Society helped the girls to "lead a moral life...by encouraging frequent communion, use of the library, and by praying to the Blessed Virgin, especially in times of temptation." A provision for prayer to St. Joseph, the patron Saint of the workers, had been dropped. The members were exhorted to avoid bad company, "aimless wandering through the city, and too early an acquaintance with members of the opposite sex."[46] The parish priest provided guidance by leading religious practices. In reality, the pastor also administered the funds. Among the activities of the Society was the decoration of the altar dedicated to the Virgin. Yet this society, like other groups, also introduced the girls to budgeting and money management. Every member was encouraged to have a savings account in the credit union. Essentially, the Society helped country girls adjust to city life through the organization they had known in the village——the Ukrainian Catholic Church.

In the village, where the church had always been a social centre, some priests established separate religious societies for young girls which often served the same function as clubs did. In 1897, in the village of Tustanovychi, near Drohobych, the local priest, Reverend Ivan Demykevych, mentioned the society in his parish while discussing the change of rite of a woman.[47]

Socialism, modernism and secularism challenged the primacy of the church. Attacks on obscurantist clericalism, however, should not blind us to the continued peculiar symbiosis of religion and politically and socially progressive programmes. Denunciations of priests by parishioners——which were always investigated by the higher echelons of the hierarchy——show that some parishioners were more conservative than the pastor. Reverend Emiliian Konstantynovych, who was at school with Franko, wrote an indignant reply to the Diocesan Consistory in 1897 when questioned about the propriety of his having hosted Franko, an avowed socialist and unbeliever. Would the bishop, wrote the priest, have preferred that he turn Franko away from his door, thereby ruining relations with the village?[48]

The Ukrainian Catholic Church tried to extend its influence over the urban intelligentsia. The pronounced views of Pope Leo XIII were that the church should promote humane and socially progressive policies. Now that it no longer monopolized Ukrainian cultural and community life, the Uniate Church had to show the relevance of religion to modern life. Like other Catholic churches, the Ukrainian church moved toward the creation of prayer groups, retreats for the laity and spiritual rather than community functions. The men were uncomfortable with these changes and societies founded for men were frequently taken over by women.

Retreats for Catholic women, however, did not receive much support from the Ukrainian Catholic clergy. According to Kobrynska's acerbic comment, the priests found it more convenient to have women around to prepare meals and carry out other household chores than to have them secluded in contemplation.[49]

Prayer societies were more successful in attracting women than men. The most popular prayer society was the Sodality of the Blessed Virgin, which became exclusively a women's group, although in some of the larger societies there were male directors. The sodalities in the cities were composed of Galician society ladies——wives of priests, richer townsmen, journalists, lawyers and the like. The first Ladies' Marian Sodality was founded in Lviv in 1904, and other branches followed. Depending upon the parish, the sodality engaged in philanthropy and self-betterment activities. The Lviv Sodality, chaired by Olha Barvinska Bachynska, organized in 1908 a society of domestics and a fresh-air fund for the urban poor.[50] The sodalities usually ran some kind of trade school, dormitories or cafeterias for needy students and pupils, and supervised the beautification of churches. Frequently, members established a library, prayed together, marched in processions, and each month one of them had to prepare and deliver a talk at the chapter meeting on some current aspect of life and religion. For many women, this was their introduction to public speaking; for some, even to research. Attempts to organize young women along these lines did not make much progress until the 1920s.

The Catholic women fused the concept of nation and church. In an attempt to encourage Ukrainian women to attend the Eucharistic Congress of 1912 in Rome, they proclaimed: "we are the daughters of a nation that has always been characterized by an ardent faith and dedication to our Holy Church."[51] The pressure for women's community involvement even penetrated the conservative Russophile groups. In Kolomyia, the latter ran a sewing school for women, but did not feel very secure in the project. Men played an active role in both the women's society and in the administration of the school. The ambitious "Mirny Trud,"[52] organized by the Society of Women of Pokuttia under the patronage of the Immaculate Conception in 1910, did not show much life.

As problems of economic backwardness, land shortage, and exploitative industrialization continued to plague the Ukrainian population of Galicia, economic self-help organizations such as the Village Farmer (Silskyi Hospodar) (1899) were created. These groups stimulated the co-operative movement in the villages, which was supported but not controlled by the priests. The Reverends Toma Dutkevych and Stepan Onyshkevych were among its founders. Prosvita, without abandoning its cultural functions, moved into the economic sector and women took an active part in this new sphere.

On 2 February 1909, Prosvita, in honour of its fortieth anniversary, held the first Ukrainian Enlightenment-Economic Congress in Lviv. Seventy-two women participated, six of whom presented papers. Among the women in attendance was a radical Polish teacher from Warsaw, Irena Kosmowska, and a Jewish medical student from Lviv, Rachel Schneiderson.[53]

In addition to community involvement, more women were entering the labour market, including the difficult entry into the professions. The first public institution to hire a Ukrainian women was a bank in Stryi, where Olha Tyshynska Bachynska became an accountant in 1897. She worked so effectively that by 1911 she had become a member of the executive board.[54]

Self-employed women did better. The most successful were Klymentyna Avdykovych Hlynska, who parlayed a recipe for candy into the first Ukrainian-owned factory in Galicia, Fortuna. Olha Levytska founded a chemical factory in Lviv. But these were individual achievements. Most women, if they sought employment, did so in teaching, sewing, housekeeping, i.e., working for others.

Throughout the pre-war years, Galician women continued to press for progress, for suffrage, equality, women's publications, schools and day-care centres. They organized rallies, held meetings and published articles. Ukrainian public activity in Galicia brought them inevitably face to face with the pervasive issue of nationalism. The Poles, favoured by the Austrian government, were better organized and richer. They resented the aspirations of Ukrainians in territories claimed by the Poles, but in which they constituted an unquestioned minority. As colonizers, they were resented by Ukrainians, but at the same time, unconsciously emulated. The Poles were deeply patriotic, ostensibly self-reliant, and ready to make sacrifices for an independent Poland. The concept of a politically independent Ukraine was not articulated until the turn of the century, and was slow to gain acceptance. It was propagated by young people, and women were among the first to espouse ideals of Ukrainian sovereignty.

Galicia and Bukovyna, lying on the rim of the Austrian Empire, closely watched the growing tension between the Austrian and Russian empires over control of the Balkan lands. The Balkan states broke away from the disintegrating Turkish Empire and used each international crisis to improve their situation. Ukrainian patriots decided to pursue similar tactics.

The political leadership of the Ukrainian Galician parties, composed entirely of males, held a secret meeting on 7 December 1912 and concluded that "all of Ukrainian society *unanimously and decidedly will support Austria against the Russian Empire, which is the greatest enemy of Ukraine.*" There were no women among the "most prominent activists of *all Ukrainian parties in Galicia.*"[55]

But there were activist women in Lviv who considered themselves politically experienced, including Konstantyna Malytska, Mariia Biletska, Olimpiia Luchakivska and Ievheniia Verhanovska. They forced their way into the secret meeting over the protest of Volodymyr Bachynsky, who would not allow them to participate in discussions for fear that they would undermine the "serious businesslike character of the proceedings."[56] Deeply resentful, the women decided to act on their own.[57]

A week later, on 14 December 1912, they called a secret women's meeting attended by representatives of women's organizations and by some students. The moving forces were Olena Stepaniv, who had been particularly outspoken about the duty of women to work alongside men for the emancipation of the country, Olena Zalizniak and Konstantyna Malytska. The meeting was chaired by Olena Sichynska. The women took issue with the men's unqualified support of Austria and their lack of a constructive strategy in case of war. The women concluded that public opinion should be steered away from simple Austrophilism, that appropriate articles analyzing various aspects of the international situation should be placed in the Ukrainian press, and contingency plans should at least be discussed. The women also proposed the establishment of a national emergency fund, and arranged courses in first aid. Their resolutions were outspokenly patriotic:

> Ukrainian women, realizing the gravity of the moment, initiate a fund for the defence of the Ukrainian cause, should a conflict arise on our territories. Were this conflict to break out now, the need for the fund would be all the more pressing. However, should an international conference succeed in working out a peaceful resolution of the current crisis, so much the better for us. That will give us time to raise more money. When the crisis breaks we must be prepared to meet it morally and physically.

Heed our call: *raise money* for the defence of *Ukraine* in this auspicious time! [In a paraphrase of Franko's poem:] Let those in whom the centuries-old bondage has not broken the spirit, "in whose veins blood still races, whom hope still entrances, whom struggle still excites"——let those place their offering upon the national altar. Today our dreams, our struggles, and our wishes should fuse into one torch whose bright light will illuminate the path of liberation.[58]

The women expressed their support of Austria, but only on condition Austrian interests did not run counter to those of Ukraine.

The women's resolution was not well publicized, since the men were resentful of what they considered an intrusion into their concerns and feared possible reprisals. The women, however, were supported by patriotic students. "It is sad, but our women proved more dignified and honourable than our notables and youth in general," commented a sympathetic student.[59] The women themselves considered the meeting a momentous step, a foray into real politics and into genuine risk-taking.

On the eve of the First World War, the Ukrainian women of Galicia had established their right to take part in public activity for the common welfare. There was an unstated consensus among the clergy, the patriotic moderates, the nationally progressive socialists and the more prominent peasants that the nation could not afford to ignore the dedicated work of half of its population. The question was, how should the women be involved?

9.
Olha Kobylianska in Literature: Feminism as the Road to Autonomy

The Eastern Europeans of the nineteenth century considered literature a matter for public concern as well as private endeavour. Its importance lay not only in its intrinsic value, but also in its impact upon society. Writers were often protagonists of new ideas and writing a means for social mobility. Fiction went hand in hand with social commentary, essays and poetry. Vernacular literature was an integral part of the articulation of national goals. The author generally practiced some profession, such as the priesthood, teaching, law, or journalism. Although literature rarely provided a comfortable living, by strengthening the writers' sense of communality with the people it provided psychological benefit to its practitioners.

In the first half of the nineteenth century, women participated in the discussions on language and the relationship between the Poles and the Western Ukrainians which took place in the drawing rooms of the nobility and the clergy. The standard of living not only of the nobility but of many families of the Ukrainian clergy was higher in the 1840s than in the 1880s, so women had more leisure time earlier in that century. As the discussion shifted into print, very few women, either on the Polish or the Ukrainian side, took part in the polemics.

Nevertheless, there is some documentation of the public activity of women in the nationality issue, which erupted in the aftermath of the events of 1848–9. For example, in Berezhany, where discussions were both heated and well documented, there is an extant brochure written by Elzbieta z Zdrowieckich Felzenberg, addressed to the Polish National, Council in which she stresses her Ukrainian heritage and alludes to the heteronational structure of historical Poland. Reacting to charges imputing her lack of patriotism, she counters: "And what is so strange, or evil or undignified about the fact that I am Ruthenian and proclaim myself to be such? My mother Danilovych [sic] comes from an old Ruthenian family. Her father, Pilecki [sic], was even a practicing Uniate. Their family, the Zdrowieckis, are from Ukraine, and now you want me to be [exclusively] Polish?"[1] But the more democratic the Ukrainian national movement became, the less frequently such voices were raised in Galicia, since the Poles openly stressed the Polishness of the area, not its multi-national character.

In contrast to Eastern Ukrainian women, Galician women were in no position to publish or even to write literary works. True, a poem by the unidentified K.P., dedicated to the abolition of serfdom in 1848, was popularized, but generally, the young ladies of Galicia did not consider literature as a field of public activity. Rather, the women viewed writing as they viewed their water colours——as an object of beauty, strictly for private enjoyment. Few considered publishing their verses. The lack of Ukrainian-language schools for girls pushed the women toward Polish, Russian and German literature. From these literatures, especially the Polish, they read about the virtues of domesticity and patriotism. Such writing subsequently undermined the influence of Polish culture among Ukrainians.[2]

Western Ukrainian ladies gradually became consumers of both Eastern and Western vernacular Ukrainian literature, which contained stories that were romantic, patriotic, and compassionate toward the peasants. Sometimes, there were portraits of women surmounting their misfortunes, but more frequently the literature reflected male perceptions. This literature had a minimal effect on moulding Western Ukrainian women's consciousness, and a need for effective literature became obvious. Kobrynska expended much energy on making what she considered proper literary works available to Ukrainian women in Galicia and encouraging women to write.

Franko's publication of his ethnographic study on "Women's Slavery as reflected in Ukrainian folksongs" in 1883 legitimized the woman issue as one of national and social concern and as a suitable literary topic. It also gave Kobrynska the courage to send him her first literary work. But Franko did not delve into specifically feminist or women's issues in his fiction. In contrast, Pavlyk's "Rebenshchukova Tetiana" defended the principle of free love. He refused to modify the text and willingly spent six months in jail upholding the principle he equated with true socialism and women's emancipation. Kobrynska's theoretical disagreements with the Ukrainian socialists spilled over into literature. She argued that free love was simply another means of control by the male, especially in societies where women were economically dependent on men. She also maintained, realistically, that Western Ukrainian women had more pressing matters on their minds than free love and romance.

In addition to Kobrynska, the works of Uliana Kravchenko and Olha Kobylianska had a direct and powerful impact on the consciousness of Ukrainian women and their organizational success after 1919. Franko had been grooming his early love, Olha Roshkevych, to be the first Western Ukrainian woman writer, but the disintegration of their relationship ended her literary career. Instead, it was Uliana Kravchenko Nementovska (1861–1947)——born Julia Schneider——who became the first Galician woman to publish a collection of poems, *Prima vera*, in 1885. She later became the poet laureate of the women's movement, as well as a versatile Catholic poet.

For our purposes, Kravchenko is important not only because she was the first woman in Galicia to publish a book, but also because she was one of the first and most articulate women teachers in the province. Unlike Kobrynska, for whom autobiographical information is scanty, and who was concerned with public activity, Kravchenko first considered writing her memoirs at the age of eleven, and did so ten years later.[3] Kravchenko was almost morbidly self-centred and wrote at length about her feelings. Her life was a surrealist composition of seemingly unrelated developments, a dream robbed of its dream-like quality in the harsh sunlight. Here we shall only mention her importance in the women's movement, in which she was both a pioneer and a bard; a tormented creature whose poetry was a spirited call to action; a religious mystic who married a sensual dandy; a fervent Ukrainian patriot who married a Pole and whose son was killed by Ukrainians in an apparent case of mistaken identity.

Kravchenko came from a family of German colonizers who married into the Ukrainian clerical milieu. She herself was raised in Lviv by a Ukrainian uncle, and attended one of the two teacher-training seminaries in Galicia. While still a student there, she decided to dedicate herself to the cause of the Ukrainian people. The decision was a conscious one, and meant the loss of good job prospects as well as attractive suitors. As a result of Polish discriminatory policies, upon graduation in 1881 she was assigned to a school in a remote mountain village near the area where Kobrynska had spent her childhood. There she began her service to the people as both teacher and writer. The villages in which Kravchenko held her first two positions were particularly poor and isolated, and the scenes of peasant life she painted were especially grim.[4] The village greeted her with reserve, while the Polish educational administration regarded her with open hostility.

Kravchenko was the most persistent, the most prolific, and the most dynamic of the young Western Ukrainian women writers. Her poetry, now dated, enjoyed tremendous popularity in Western Ukraine. Kravchenko's impact upon generations of Western Ukrainian women transcended the level of her writing. She served as an important link between the Ukrainian democratic movement and the women's movement. As a teacher who married and had children, she became a role model for younger women.

Even more important than Kravchenko in terms of literary impact and talent was Olha Kobylianska, a friend of Kobrynska and of Lesia Ukrainka. Kobylianska survived until the end of the Second World War and concentrated on longer works of fiction. She came from a picturesque, mountainous part of Bukovyna between Galicia, Carpathian Ukraine, and Romania. Its vibrantly colourful, even gaudy embroidery reflected its cultural mixture of Ukrainians, Romanians, gypsies, Germans and Jews. Against that background, picture the gaunt figure of Olha Kobylianska: dark hair pulled back, large serious eyes, solemn expression and dress almost invariably black. Kobylianska wrote the first and most consistently feminist novel in Ukrainian literature, *Tsarivna* (The Princess), published in 1896. Her numerous other works, which appeared in

Ukrainian, German and Polish, also incorporated her particular brand of feminism.

The largest city in Bukovyna was Chernivtsi, the centre of Ukrainian community life. Most Bukovynian Ukrainians were Orthodox by religion; others were Uniates. Culturally, they identified themselves with the Ukrainian Galicians, and there was little friction between the two groups. Socially and politically the Ukrainian situation in Bukovyna was similar to that of the Galician Ukrainians, except for the larger number of linguistically Germanized Ukrainian functionaries of the Austrian government in Bukovyna. Germanization——oriented toward Austria rather than Germany——was a greater threat than Romanianization before 1919, although Romanian nationalism was visibly growing.

Kobylianska was the daughter of an Austrian official. Her mother, of German-Polish background, became a Uniate upon marriage. Information about the language spoken at home, and the culture with which the parents identified themselves, is contradictory. Kobylianska published her first short stories in German, and only after she became friendly with Sofiia Okunevska and Nataliia Kobrynska did she begin writing in Ukrainian,[5] despite the fact that both Kobrynska and Franko rejected the stories she sent to *Pershyi vinok* in 1887. Kobylianska's close personal friendship with the younger Lesia Ukrainka also had an important influence on her writing. Kobylianska became a conscious feminist in the 1890s, when she was trying to make a name for herself in literature.

Kobylianska lived in a small town, but frequently came to Chernivtsi, where a church-related women's organization, the Myrrh-bringers (Myronosytsi), had been founded in 1886 and survived until 1940. A philanthropic organization identified with conservative Ukrainians, its members sought an active community role and in the 1890s began setting up day-care centres. In 1890, Kobrynska asked Kobylianska to collect signatures for her petition for higher education for women and to contact German and Romanian women's organizations. It was probably in this context that Kobylianska met the Ukrainian women of Chernivtsi, including an important acquaintance, Mariia Matkivska.[6]

Through Matkivska, Kobylianska met women who were interested in creating a secular women's organization. She also learned of another Bukovynian writer, the young and spirited teacher, Ievhenia Iaroshynska (1868–1904). Iaroshynska was, in every respect, the opposite of Kobylianska. She was short, stout, with reddish-brown hair, and liked to dress in colourful peasant costumes. Frank, ebullient and aggressive, she relished a fight with the conservative Ukrainian establishment. She deliberately chose controversial topics for her writing; she maintained excellent relations with Pavlyk, and wanted to organize the progressive women, especially her fellow teachers. Her exuberance belied the heart condition which was to kill her before she reached the age of thirty.

Kobylianska realized how easily she and Iaroshynska could have become German rather than Ukrainian writers. Also perturbed by the inroads of Romanian culture into Ukrainian life, she participated actively in the founding of the Society of Ruthenian Women (Obshchestvo Ruskykh Zhenshchyn) in Chernivtsi in 1894. She felt that the Society might become a magnet for the Ukrainians of Bukovyna. She explained to Iaroshynska that:

> Although the by-laws of the Society are written in the old-fashioned dialect (*iazychiie*), this society will unite the two camps for purely practical purposes. I am a true Ukrainian (*chysta ukrainka*) and want all Ukrainian women to join it, for while we are making a tremendous rumpus (*hamoru*) about phonetics and dead letters, the Romanians are drawing the Bukovynian Ukrainian girls to their side.[7]

Kobylianska concurred with Iaroshynska that Mariia Matkivska showed an inclination toward the conservatives, but argued that she also "was an exceptionally tolerant woman and ardent patriot." This contrasted with the narrow outlook of some Ukrainian patriots, who failed to perceive the benefits that the Society could bring to the whole community. Iaroshynska herself did not attend Society meetings because she did not much like the "ladies." The Ukrainian journal *Bukovyna* insinuated that the Society was receiving Russian funds and should not be supported by Ukrainians. Kobylianska was indignant, since the Society planned to teach Ukrainian history to young people who could not study it in Bukovyna, in addition to sewing and teaching courses for women, but all the self-styled defenders of the fatherland could see were:

> rubles...they really cannot see anything else, any other possible motivation, no good faith...and they really are afraid of Moscow, here in Chernivtsi, where our young women are being Germanized, Romanianized and Polonized.... Anyway, suppose we were getting even Chinese funds, our "soft" patriots should not lose sight of the fact that the money still would not go to Romanian children but to Ukrainian ones.[8]

For several years Kobylianska worked in the Society, supporting Matkivska and the moderates in an attempt to expand its effective role in the community. She tried to broaden its membership by attracting young women. Ultimately, like Kobrynska, she failed in that endeavour. In Chernivtsi, as in Lviv, the younger women followed the lead of the progressive intelligentsia in rejecting feminist concerns. This played into the hands of the conservatives, who tried to keep the Society within the traditional church-related activity.

At the turn of the century, young Bukovynian women manifested their independence by organizing a Circle of Ukrainian Girls in Chernivtsi. Its initiator was Nataliia Popovych, the daughter of the school inspector who had persuaded Iaroshynska to write in Ukrainian rather than in German. The "Girls," like their counterparts in Lviv, engaged in gratuitous radicalism, anti-clericalism and revolutionary posturing. Ignorant of their history, they followed the lead of the male intelligentsia in crediting Omelian Popovych with the initiation of the women's movement in Bukovyna. They sponsored lectures by prominent males, as well as social functions and trips to the villages to enlighten the peasants. With the help of the Sich Student Society of Chernivtsi they set up a library and planned to publish a book on folk ornaments.[9]

In 1906, the Circle of Girls renamed itself a Women's Community (Hromada), and established branches outside the city, although the Society continued to exist. The joint women's front sought by Kobylianska did not develop until the First World War. Kobylianska limited herself to literary themes. She became intimate with Lesia Ukrainka——"someone white" (*khtos bilesenkyi*)——as she dubbed her endearingly in their correspondence. Lesia Ukrainka's dismissal of feminism reinforced Kobylianska's decision to withdraw from women's societies. Earlier Kobylianska had developed an interest in Osyp Makovei, a writer two years her junior who visited and corresponded with her. She tried to reassure him that she was not a feminist and that he should not feel threatened by her, but to no avail. Instinctively sensing her superior talent, he married a more passive woman.

Kobylianska never married and lived on a tight budget. Sometimes, she seemed to hide her poverty under a facade of radicalism. Her popularity and fame as a writer grew, and she became one of the most widely read Ukrainian authors. Young modernist writers, especially Vasyl Stefanyk, became close to her.[10] Critics, such as Serhii Efremov, a literary scholar in Eastern Ukraine, considered her elitist. Others would later attack her for symbolist trends, or give their own interpretations of her feminism. Kobylianska rarely engaged in debate, preferring to let her work speak for her.

In fact, she spoke to generations of Ukrainian women, despite her disclaimer of feminism. In 1928, on the occasion of the fortieth anniversary of Kobylianska's writing career, a visibly emotional Sofiia Rusova thanked her "for discovering the beauty of the female soul, of leading humanity to this mystery which is accessible to only the few most talented writers.... Your works drew women from drudging slavery (*pobutova nevolia*)...and created an authentic revolution in human lives."[11]

Kobylianska understood feminism primarily in terms of individual autonomy. Her own formal schooling had ended at the fourth grade. Thereafter, she read voraciously, largely in German. She familiarized herself with all the classics of positivism and developed a sympathy for the downtrodden. She began writing early, but felt writing was a form of self-aggrandizement not seemly for young ladies.[12] Her frustration at stifling the demands of that talent led her to conclude: "When nature created woman, it did not ask: Is this person a man or a woman, so that I might endow it with the appropriate characteristics? No! Nature only said——Here you are! Now live."[13]

How should one live? Kobylianska answered that question most directly in *Tsarivna*. The novel is feminist in that it deals with a woman in search of autonomy. Yet its underlying issue is the discovery of how people can learn to come to grips with themselves. Because many of the obstacles facing the heroine were caused by her womanhood, few men have viewed this novel as one concerned with individual emancipation and not only women's liberation. An exception was Mykyta Shapoval, a young Eastern Ukrainian activist, who between 1906 and 1914 helped found the journal *Khata* (House), a vehicle for literary modernism. Shapoval considered Kobylianska's *Tsarivna* a model for the attainment of personal autonomy.[14]

The book portrays *Tsarivna*, an orphan raised in a materialistic family, who first strives for personal autonomy rather than independence. True independence, she declares, is possible only for those who know themselves; the others are simply headstrong. She also refuses to renounce love and accept a financially comfortable but loveless marriage. Particularly interesting in the novel is the fact that the heroine, Natalka, while admitting to her sexual passion, refuses to identify it with love. Without denying her physical attraction to a man who likes her and even shares her social and ideological predilections, Natalka feels that she is not yet ready for real love. She needs time to know herself, a fact that the man is unable to comprehend. Natalka takes a job as a companion to an elderly, intelligent, well-travelled woman, who helps her to grow intellectually and emotionally.

The attainment of autonomy is a painful, conscious, and long-drawn-out process. Natalka has to work hard for her happiness through physical labour, mental exertion and emotional suffering. The ending, though happy, is unconventional. Natalka marries a non-Ukrainian who helps humanity quietly, without making speeches or joining a particular party.[15] The secondary characters in the novel serve as types in Kobylianska's analysis of society, whereas only the two major protagonists achieve the potential available to all.

Kobylianska's novel was written in the style of Chernyshevsky's *What Is To Be Done*, which, according to Pavlyk, was one of the most popular novels in Galicia before the turn of the century. Chernyshevsky's novel is concerned with social action rather than psychological complexity of character. For Kobylianska, the liberation of women had to be an individual effort. She stressed the importance of hard work, of overcoming melancholy, depression, and moods of hopelessness and dejection. Compatible male company, especially reciprocated love, was a pleasurable part of the denouement, but neither central nor necessary for autonomy or happiness. The novel stressed the support of women of various ages and interests for the heroine. But Kobylianska also showed that patriarchy could not survive without the duplicity of marriages arranged by greedy, cunning and limited females who meet their match in equally limited, conceited and lustful males. The victim herself was neither innocent nor passive: she embraced the convenient match willingly.

After writing *Tsarivna*, Kobylianska decided she had exhausted the specifically feminist theme, which was transmuted into a discussion of the general human condition, especially the relationship between love, reason and God. The heroine of the popular *V nediliu rano zillia kopala* (She Gathered Herbs on Sunday Morning) had little control over passion when she killed her faithless lover. One senses that the less educated her heroines were, the closer they were to nature, but that nature and romance themselves were far from ennobling, since neither promoted individual autonomy.

Kobylianska kept up her search for truth, authenticity and new forms of expression. As such, she remained a defender of women's rights. Like Kobrynska, she remained a solitary personality; unlike Kobrynska, she became a symbol in her own lifetime. The Western Ukrainian women's organizations considered her the greatest living Ukrainian woman author and treated her accordingly. Kobylianska's novels of the inter-war period explored the relations between individuals and society, as well as society's manipulation of them. *Apostol cherni* (The Apostle of the Commoners), for example, touched on the manipulation of a community.

By viewing feminism as a striving toward individualism and self-esteem, Kobylianska strengthened the pragmatic bent of Ukrainian women, creating role models for them. Women, she demonstrated, could better themselves and their societies without compromising their own human dignity and their cherished beliefs in the sanctity of love, family and, implicitly, God.

Part III.

The National-Liberation Struggle

10.
Sisters Across the Zbruch

There were many differences between Ukrainian women of the East and Western Ukrainian lands. There were also significant similarities, not recognized or discussed, since such a discussion would have necessitated an ideological leap of which neither women nor their better-educated and more experienced brothers were capable at the time. On both sides of the little river Zbruch, which for almost two centuries divided the Eastern and Western Ukrainians, women carried out practical work, denigrated its importance, failed to integrate it into the broader context of social and cultural activity, stressed its limits rather than its potential, and did not write much about it. In other words, they deferred to men.

The establishment of formal political parties narrowed the ideological outlook of the intelligentsia. The creation of formal, albeit clandestine, organizations tended to exclude the women. Since women could not vote, legal political parties perforce excluded them from positions of power. Concurrently, women's organizations in all areas of Ukraine tended to be devoid of many characteristics of the intelligentsia, even though their members were well educated.

Both West and Eastern Ukrainian men dwelled on the weakness of the Ukrainian national movement, the difficulties they encountered in their work, and how their own personal superior dedication, intelligence and skill enabled them to overcome the otherwise insurmountable obstacles facing them. One has a feeling of reading a secular variant of medieval accounts of conversion——the sins of the prospective saints have to be presented in as dark a light as possible in order to illuminate the miracle of the conversion itself. And yet only the unprecedented measures of terror in its Stalinist and other forms could suppress the nation's vitality. Accounts of recent Ukrainian history tend to offer variants, either positive or negative, of a similar process. The approaches vary, stressing either the national ideal or the revolutionary potential of the international proletariat. But the underlying manner of presentation remains the same, and stereotypes often persist.

One such stereotype has been the identification of the Eastern Ukrainian intelligentsia with the progressive movement. Its corollary was to stress the conservative nature of the Western Ukrainian intelligentsia, especially the clerical families. This stereotype, reinforced by contemporary accounts and presented as political analysis, has obscured the organic nature of the modern Ukrainian national movement in Eastern Ukraine, as well as the genuinely progressive characteristics of the Galician society. Thus, the distinguished and otherwise careful historian, Nataliia Polonska-Vasylenko, makes the unlikely claim that the initiative to organize women in Galicia came from Drahomanov and from Pchilka. It seemed inconceivable to Polonska that a Western Ukrainian Catholic woman of the clerical milieu could be progressive enough to hit upon the idea herself.[1]

The Ukrainian communities within the Austrian and Russian Empires functioned under different handicaps. Although ostensibly both empires were monarchies connected with state religions, and both served as agents of social and political change, there were essential differences. While the tsarist state persisted until 1905 in denying the very existence of Ukrainians as a separate ethnic and linguistic entity and in banning political parties, the Austrian Kaisers experimented with administrative-parliamentary systems and with balancing the nationalities in their empire.

The Russian Empire produced a Russian intelligentsia single-mindedly opposed to the tsarist system, but not to the boundaries to which the tsars had expanded their realm. The Austrian intelligentsia, like the Austrian government, was unclear about its priorities. Ukrainians in the Austrian Empire had more political and cultural freedom, and Ukrainians from the Russian Empire bitterly criticized Western Ukrainians for not making full use of their opportunities. Galicians were impressed by the vastness of Eastern Ukraine, the homogeneity of its peasant population, the immediacy of its Cossack past, and——less tangibly——its romantic image in literature. But they were disappointed to find out that Eastern Ukrainian city streets reverberated with Russian and Yiddish chatter. The closer the two groups of Ukrainian men became, the louder became the grumblings of each about the habits and eccentricities of the other. Yet that was not the case with women.

Ukrainian women in the Russian Empire enjoyed certain advantages over their Western counterparts. They had a stronger tradition of independence as women. They had at least a legal right to dispose of their money, and a number of them had both the money and the sense of independence that went with it. Certainly, these advantages were limited by custom and by a debilitating political system, against which some women struggled with great ingenuity. But peasant women were less affected by Russification and other factors than their urban counterparts.

Active contacts between Ukrainians on both sides of the Zbruch developed after the reforms of the 1860s in both empires. In the early nineteenth century, the Russian scholar Pogodin had "discovered" Galicia when a broken cart axle forced him to spend a few days in Lviv. Thus began the active courting by the

Russians of the conservative Ukrainian faction in Galicia. The Russophile faction received financial support from both the Austrian government, which banked on its conservatism——although at times it persecuted the faction for its pro-Russian sentiment——and from the tsarist Empire. Some prominent Galician scholars, among them Iakiv Holovatsky, an original member of the Ruthenian Triad, emigrated to the Russian Empire, but had little impact on either Russian or Ukrainian society.

Up to the outbreak of the First World War, a few Russophile families continued to send their daughters to finishing schools for young ladies, or at least for visits to the Russian Empire. Once there, the peculiar language of the Russophiles——neither Russian nor Ukrainian——prevented their getting to know either the Ukrainians or the Russians. The Russophile women who settled in or visited Ukraine did not even make an impact upon the Ladies' Benevolent Societies, whose function was to aid the Slavs not under Russian rule. Only when the Russian Empire invaded Galicia during the war did Russian society discover the "Russian" character of the Western Ukrainian lands. After the revolution, some sought refuge there and in the Carpathian valleys. Around 1920, the influence of Russian culture produced a variant of Russian-oriented communism quite distinct from that of other social-democratic parties.[2] As yet, this question has not been researched by Western scholars.

Relations between the Western and Eastern Ukrainians were also coloured by the Polish presence in Right-Bank Ukraine. In 1863, as mentioned earlier, "Ukrainka"——probably the young Khrystyna D. Alchevska——was calling for Russian support of the Polish uprising against tsarism. Herzen, in whose journal the exhortation was published, lost much of his popularity in Russia because of his favourable view of the Poles. Ukrainians in Galicia sometimes saw the limitations of Russian liberalism more clearly than did their Eastern confreres:

These "liberals" from Moscow are Muscovite centralists who, although they oppose the regime, nevertheless see eye to eye with it when it comes to the principle of the Russification of Rus' (*omoskalennia Rusi*). I don't see much moral value in such liberals; it is a pity that they pride themselves on being Slavophiles *par excellence* not only in Muscovy (*Moskovshchyni*), but in all of Russia (*Rossii*).... Better they should call themselves centralizers of Slavdom, then they would be rightfully proud, for they have no equals in the whole world——not even among the Viennese centralists.[3]

The Kiev Hromada, we recall, had been composed partly of Polonized gentry returning to the Ukrainian fold. It was the Hromada that actively fostered links with Western Ukrainians. Drahomanov established contacts with promising young Ukrainian Galicians through both publishing and politics. His characterization of the Galician Ukrainian psyche and mores, particularly his views on women, became the norm for generations of the progressive

Ukrainian, especially Western Ukrainian, intelligentsia.

Drahomanov, a social-liberal, was shocked by the "petit-bourgeois philistinism" which he considered deeply rooted in "Galician society." Galician women did not appear alone on the streets, never entertained callers unless they were chaperoned, and never took hotel rooms alone. Drahomanov mocked these quaint customs, for which he held men more responsible than women. But ironically, Drahomanov dismissed women's issues because of his ingrained and unconscious sense of male superiority. This made it easier for Galician Ukrainian males to criticize unconventional women. Drahomanov was very much a traditional *intelligent* in his view of women: they could have equality as defined by the male society. We recall his critical attitude toward his own sister who, nevertheless, did not hesitate to leave her small children for months at a time to help her brother when he needed her.

Ukrainian women in the Russian Empire were accepted as writers within the Ukrainian community. Western Ukrainian women had a more difficult time overcoming their lack of schooling and different socialization to gain acceptance into the intelligentsia. For example, Fedir Vovk, the ethnologist, recalled how his wife, the niece of Volodymyr Antonovych, shocked Galician Ukrainians in 1876 by advocating sexual equality, amicable separation if the marriage failed, and civil marriages for divorced people. Vovk insisted that these matters were no longer even debatable issues among Eastern Ukrainian activists. Western Ukrainian males, Vovk continued, still literally screamed at women's rights and divorce, considering that it was unnatural and destructive to all that was sacred in society, and that women had to follow their husbands wholeheartedly in all matters. Yet this same Vovk saw divorce as part of the "woman question," not as a social issue.[4]

Visits by Eastern Ukrainian women to Galicia slowly helped to ease this restrictive attitude. In 1872, Olena Pchilka visited Galicia; daughters and wives of Ukrainian activists came to see Lviv and its surroundings; students hiked in the Carpathians, and in 1885, Olena Dobrohaeva and Katria Melnyk, student activists from Kiev, joined the excursion. By the end of the decade these personal contacts had become more frequent. The wealthier Galician Ukrainian families sent their daughters to visit Eastern Ukraine, and Eastern Ukrainians sent their children to study in Lviv.[5]

Yet the differences in the position of women in the two societies and the failure of the progressive Ukrainian male intelligentsia to support feminist strivings precluded full participation of Western Ukrainian women in Ukrainian life. In Eastern Ukraine we have seen that, at least in theory, women's equality was accepted——provided they did their duty as mothers and wives. In Western Ukraine, even though a network of Ukrainian community organizations already existed, women had a much more difficult time being accepted as equals in their own society. The long-term consequence was the development of women's organizations independent of male tutelage.

Feminists on both sides of the Zbruch, supported by a few moderate male political activists, did not easily find a common language. They were few in number and restricted by Ukrainian male radicals, who used the alleged equality and undisputed activism of Eastern Ukrainian women as a model for their Western counterparts. At the same time, Eastern Ukrainian women unconsciously strengthened the traditional deference of Galician women to the "superior" wisdom and experience of men. By blocking women's organizations within the progressive, especially socialist configuration, the men——for whatever motives——prevented a genuine discussion of the issues raised by Kobrynska within the Galician context.

Mariia Bashkirtsev, the daughter of the Poltava Marshal of the Nobility who took part in Ukrainian amateur theatrical productions, left her father's beloved Ukraine (and the tsarist Empire) in search of freedom of creativity. On trips home and in meeting compatriots abroad, she was reassured that she had made the right decision. In 1878 in France, meeting with childhood friends from Ukraine and listening to their accounts of life in the empire, she wrote in her diary:

> Unhappy land! There was a time when I accused myself of cowardice for not wanting to live there! But is it possible at all? The socialists there are brutal thugs who kill and rob; the government is stupid and all-powerful. Both these ghastly forces struggle with each other, while all who are reasonable and honourable are pulverized between them.[6]

Bashkirtsev was five years Kobrynska's junior and died in the year that Kobrynska convened the women's meeting. She was one of the few Ukrainians who foresaw the danger that radicalism would become a mirror image of the excesses of the tsarist regime. Since she was not regarded as one of the intelligentsia, Bashkirtsev was never invited to Galicia. One can only wonder what kind of political and social analysis would have emerged from a meeting between Kobrynska and Bashkirtsev.

Since co-operation between the intelligentsia of the two parts of the Ukrainian nation was difficult, the first collective publication of Ukrainian women was a significant event that transcended purely women's concerns. The idea of publishing a women's almanac originated with Kobrynska, and all the publications that she edited were all-Ukrainian in scope.

Initially Kobrynska had sought a sustained publication for women, and Franko, during his misunderstanding with the publishers of *Zoria* (Star——a popular Western Ukrainian journal), even suggested that he would edit the women's newspaper. But the women, understandably, were not ready to accept a newspaper edited by a socialist whom the males spurned. Accounts, however, have depicted the women as unappreciative of Franko's willingness to work for them, while Franko's difficulties with men who shared his views tend to be overlooked.

Pershyi vinok appeared in Lviv in 1887 under the joint editorship of Nataliia Kobrynska and Olena Pchilka. Franko's assistance was extensive enough for him to claim actual editorial functions.[7] The years between 1884 and 1887 also marked the most energetic efforts of the Ukrainian intelligentsia to publish a joint newspaper or magazine of Eastern and Western Ukrainians. Franko, Drahomanov and Pavlyk were directly involved in planning the enterprise, which never materialized. They hoped that the Stanyslaviv Women's Society, which had been founded in 1884, would provide them with support they were unable to muster elsewhere. Kobrynska tried to convince the Stanyslaviv women that it would be in their best interest "to join a newspaper which would inform us about the work and the struggles of the current wave of women in other countries."[8] The women, however, remained wary of the undertaking their husbands feared.

The Stanyslaviv Society board nevertheless approved the outline of the almanac as prepared by Franko and Kobrynska. The board suggested Kobrynska seek Franko's advice privately so as not to antagonize the more conservative members of the Society. Franko had suggested that Drahomanov's work be included in the project, but Kobrynska refused categorically, since that would not have been approved by the executive board. The few published letters of Kobrynska's correspondence with Franko during these two years——between the decision to publish the Almanac in 1885 and its publication in 1887——show an openly insecure Kobrynska whose deference to and praise of Franko bordered on obsequiousness. Strangely enough, the decision to limit contributions to the almanac to women was not Kobrynska's, but that of the executive board of the Society.[9] Kobrynska wanted to include a translation of an article by the German economist Hans Schell on the education of women for professional work, as well as a small sample of John Stuart Mill's writing. The women, however, insisted on keeping the entire almanac exclusively a women's undertaking, a decision which Kobrynska later defended wholeheartedly.

While the women mounted a full-scale campaign to collect funds for the almanac, Franko did not even keep Kobrynska apprised of his own activities. Once, after informing him of the decision on the almanac, she chided the poet for not visiting them when he was in the area:

> We were very sorry to find out that you and Konysky stayed two more days in Bolekhiv (Kobrynska's home town), and we did not even know that. I realize we are not very good company (*shcho u nas ne veselo, to ia sama znaiu*), but father had wanted to see Konysky again, and I wanted to know more about what prompted you to rejoin *Zoria*. I must confess that I was deeply hurt by your return [to *Zoria*], but after further deliberation, I agree with your move.[10]

Although the almanac was already being undermined by both radical and conservative forces, Kobrynska was willing to share her meagre resources for the journal with Franko. He, in turn, offered her materials, but never any money.[11] As Kobrynska despaired of ever seeing the almanac in print, Pchilka moved in with her energy and funds.

Pchilka saw the Zbruch not as a boundary but as another thread linking Eastern Ukraine to European culture. She and her brother Drahomanov shared the conviction that Ukraine must be brought out of its culturally isolated existence and exposed to new currents of thought. Pchilka was especially insistent upon making the vernacular language a suitable vehicle for expressing sophisticated views. She rejected the notion that the democratic character of Ukrainian be preserved by limiting it to peasant speech. She, in her own words, "forged the language, forged new words in Ukrainian," and insisted that the almanac be printed in the modern vernacular Ukrainian orthography.[12]

Pchilka was impressed by the achievements of Galician Ukrainians and readily sent her own works, those of her daughter, and her future daughter-in-law for publication there. Lesia Ukrainka made her literary debut in *Zoria*. Rather than criticize Galicia, Pchilka joined those who were inspired by it. Such sentiments were stated most openly by Oleksander Konysky, the poet and literary scholar, whom Franko accompanied to Bolekhiv in 1885. A year earlier Konysky had written:

> The everyday life of Ruthenians in Galicia (*Rusyny*) rekindles the spirit and gives us strength to work [among us, Eastern Ukrainians]. For one thing (*bachte*), there is a women's society in Stanyslaviv; then Shukhevych is considering publishing a magazine for children...[I have great hopes] that this guiding light will resurrect our nation and our trampled, demolished world.... I know that beyond the Zbruch our light is shining and that it will not be extinguished by any dark fortress (*nichni tverdi*).[13]

On 1 October 1885, Kobrynska wrote to Pchilka asking for her co-operation as well as that of other Ukrainian women "who have been wielding the pen longer and with greater skill than we have."[14] Pchilka agreed readily and enthusiastically because she had a very high assessment of Galician potential. This can best be seen in a letter written to a Galician some years after the publication of *Pershyi vinok*:

> The situation...within the Ukrainian Galician intelligentsia is not bad.... We are worse off as far as the knowledge of the Ukrainian language is concerned.... I know that when someone from Galicia finds himself in [Eastern Ukrainian] company, we feel ashamed simply because we cannot converse as easily in the Ruthenian-Ukrainian language as your countryman (*vash brat*)——it is obvious you use it in everyday life, so that your language is even more beautiful than ours. At times I noticed that some of us are quiet, translating mentally what we want to say from Russian into Ukrainian, and in general groping for the right word...while your countrymen go on and on——it is a joy to listen! The same with writing——just compare how much better your correspondence is than ours. So you have no reason to complain of your Galician intelligentsia! May God grant that we speak and write as well as you.[15]

Pchilka was well known in Western Ukraine, even among the children. A twelve-year-old girl picked up *Pershyi vinok*, simply because she recognized the name of Olena Pchilka from the book on folk ornaments she used.[16] Pchilka's willingness to collaborate with Kobrynska and to act as co-editor of the almanac greatly raised its prestige. While the men were still negotiating for some joint venture,

> in this publication Ukrainian women of all classes ignored political boundaries, held out their hands to one another and combined their efforts in the first wreath of women's liberation, which laid the firm and basic [*sic*] foundation of women's emancipation in Galicia.[17]

Franko, as promised, supervised the publication of the almanac and checked the final proofs.

There were disagreements as to what material should be included. The plan Kobrynska had outlined to Pchilka envisaged (1) the inclusion of works of fiction, (2) a "scholarly part, on...the women's question and women's education in the civilized world," and (3) a third part which would include biographies and bibliographies of women, articles on folk art, women's work, customs, household management and the like. Kobrynska worried about a lack of material; Pchilka wanted a thick volume. It turned out that there was too much material, and the third part was omitted completely. Franko insisted on the exclusion of a short story by Kobylianska, and all three agreed that the contributions of Ievheniia Bokhenska, Ievheniia Tanchakivska, Iefrozyna Vitoshynska and Olha Bohachevska should be rejected as inadequate. A short story by Anna Pavlyk was excluded because its sharp presentation of social conflict might have served as a pretext for censoring the whole almanac. For the first time, Uliana Kravchenko, the erstwhile Julia Schneider, signed her work with her pen-name. Sydora Navrotska (later Paliiv), Mykhailyna Roshkevych (later Ivanets), Klymentyna Popovych (later Boiarska), and Olha (Khoruzhynska) Franko appeared in print in the *Wreath*.[18]

Sofiia Okunevska published a short study of urban life and a study of "Family Slavery of Women in Wedding Songs and Customs." Pchilka cut considerably her major contribution, a novelette entitled "Tovaryshky" (Friends) and dropped the projected biography of Hanna Barvinok. Kravchenko's memoirs about teaching in a small village were left for publication in what was to have been *Druhyi vinok*, in which Lesia Ukrainka's poetry and Kobylianska's prose were to have been included.[19] Anna Pavlyk and her sister Kateryna Dovbenchuk contributed materials from Carpathian life. Among the Galician contributors were also Olha Levytska, Olesia Bazhanska and Olena Hrytsai. In addition to a short story, Kobrynska wrote a piece about the Stanyslaviv Society, an article on the women's movement in general, and another on the position of middle-class women in particular.

The Eastern Ukrainian women, accepted as writers in their own land, now found a publishing outlet. The publication also showed the potential of women's writing and of joint publications by Western and Eastern Ukrainians. Representing Eastern Ukrainians, in addition to Pchilka and Lesia Ukrainka, were Liudmyla Vasylenko (Dniprova Chaika, 1861–1927) and Liudmyla Starytska-Cherniakhivska. Rejecting Pchilka's veto, Kobrynska insisted on the inclusion of two stories by Hanna Barvinok, who supported Kobrynska in subsequent publications. Hanna Barvinok, Kulish's wife, was known for her stories about peasant women. Pchilka purposely tried to write about other classes in Ukrainian society.

Kobrynska wrote the introduction to the almanac, while Pchilka wrote a brief poem noting that this was the first collective women's undertaking in which many novices had participated. Critics should not be too harsh, she pleaded; the women were like violets that are noticed only in a cluster.

In response, the men received the women's almanac favourably. Drahomanov, however, while not overly critical, felt that Ukrainian women really had nothing to say on the women's issue. He saw women's inequality simply as a result of their faulty education, which, he argued, should be combated by the same means as laziness and drunkedness. He did not think that Pchilka's smuggling of her "Tovaryshky" for publication was a good idea, because "the story did not tell the truth about reality."[20] This one sentence, characterizing Pchilka's sensitive description of modern young Ukrainian women studying abroad and returning to Ukraine to practice medicine, succeeding both in career and in happy marriages, illustrated Drahomanov's superior tone vis-à-vis women. Was he saying that sensitive and successful heroines did not exist, or was he trying to avoid the combination?

In the 1880s and early 90s, when modern political parties were emerging, there were attempts at co-operation between the socialists and other reformers among Ukrainians and Poles of both empires. Franko tried writing on Polish themes. He also corresponded with Eliza Orzeszkowa, a Polish realist feminist writer, whom he informed of new literary developments. He mentioned Kobrynska's writings, but gave no details of her work with women. Both Franko and Orzeszkowa complained about their respective narrow-minded co-patriots. Orzeszkowa further lamented about the lack of intellectual interests among Polish women. She was preparing an anthology of Ukrainian literature in Polish but did not express any interest in Ukrainian women as such, although on occasion she was attracted to the Polish feminist movement.[21]

Although not always smooth, the personal relationships between Western and Eastern Ukrainians became more profound. The secular Western Ukrainian intelligentsia, attempting to live up to the standards of Eastern Ukrainian radicalism, became even more critical of its own society and of its leadership, especially of the clergy. This approach alienated the more moderate segments of Galician society, exacerbated feelings of negativism toward conditions in Galicia, and encouraged an unstated deference toward the politics of Eastern Ukrainians. It became particularly open in the treatment of women and the whole issue of the women's movement. Western Ukrainian males criticized the backwardness of their women, dismissed the women's movement, and rejected the co-operation of qualified women.

Kobrynska tried to maintain very friendly relations with Franko and his wife, and with Pavlyk, whose productivity she admired.[22] She expected to be included in any Ukrainian journals or newspapers published in Austria that they planned. Her interest and involvement in politics, her publicistic writing, and her experience in public life made her——as she wrote openly to Franko——a natural candidate for active collaboration in the radicals' newspapers. Yet, when an opportunity arose, Franko asked Olesia Bazhanska to edit the projected women's supplement to *Narod* and Olena Pchilka to write an editorial, bypassing Kobrynska (Bazhanska, soon to marry one of Kobrynska's brothers, declined the offer.) Nothing came of the women's supplement in any case.

At this time Lesia Ukrainka was writing about the projected *Druhyi vinok*. Drahomanov, however, unhappy with "the women's separatism," argued that a women's press and a women's journal were unnecessary. Galician radicals, meanwhile, tried to follow the Eastern Ukrainian radicals' lead in effective revolutionary work among the peasants. They gloried in the work Anna Pavlyk was doing, convening groups of peasant women and arguing the need for change. Interestingly, Lesia Ukrainka, critical of precisely such populist tactics in Eastern Ukraine, judged Galicia to be ripe for them.[23] She did not share Kobrynska's feminism. She wrote to her uncle that:

> I agree with your view on a women's journal. We are not thinking exclusively in terms of a women's journal, and certainly not a journal in Kobrynska's style. As far as I am concerned, I cannot see what else can be said on the woman issue...the only thing that is not boring, perhaps, is when women's lives are described, and female psychology is discussed in good taste with talent, and even then, this separatism is slightly humorous. I wrote to Kobrynska explaining this, and she probably took it as a major insult, for she has not written to us since. She suggested that I work on topics such as the "role of women in the Ukrainian national renaissance." I do not even know how to go about starting on this subject. She suggested even stranger topics, but there is no point in mentioning them.[24]

The stereotype of the Western Ukrainian woman was so deeply ingrained that even Lesia Ukrainka, certainly one of the most perceptive commentators on the Ukrainian scene, did not see through it. She realized that the social strictures were more confining for the Galician than for East European women, but she saw no reason to establish women's organizations. Instead, she felt that customs ought to change and women should adjust to the change. Her own experience with Galician men, however, exasperated her to such a degree that she would become angry about an incident that had occurred eight years earlier.

In the early 1890s, when the plans for some sort of publication, women's or intelligentsia's, were being discussed, Lesia Ukrainka recalled meeting with a group of rather progressive Galician students in Vienna in the Sich society:

> I remember how angry I was about a confusion of concepts: women's equality and free love, which so baffled the *Sich* members. They're obsessed by it! Even Mr. Pavlyk, the most "eastern-Ukrainized" of the Galicians, is confused by it. That is the reason why the Galicians who came to Ukraine looking for a wife became the justifiable butt of jokes. We choose hats the way they chose wives! And it wasn't your average fellow who came, only the real progressives. Phew! I don't even want to talk about it....[25]

Yet she could not understand Kobrynska's exasperation.

In 1893, with the help of Ievheniia Iaroshynska and Hanna Barvinok, Kobrynska published the first volume of *Nasha dolia*, her women's almanac. She included material on the day-care centres, a speech by the peasant Anna Hrymaliuk, and information about the achievements of women in the Russian Empire, which credited them with greater sucess than was warranted. Hanna Barvinok's literary contribution, entitled "Pravnuchka baby bortsia" ("Great-grandmother Fighter's Grandchild") narrated by a naive, but cunning, strong peasant woman, was a tale about the times when women were stronger than men. Kobrynska published two other editions of the almanac in 1895 and 1896. In all three she developed her views on socialism and the woman question. Except for the aged Hanna Barvinok, she failed to obtain the support of Eastern Ukrainian women. Criticism of Kobrynska's work continued. Lesia Ukrainka found the lead article in the second volume interesting, but did not comment on it publicly, nor did other women, while the men dissected its every flaw.

On both sides of the Zbruch, Ukrainian society remained sexist in different ways. Eastern Ukrainian women made fun of women's gatherings, while participating in them nevertheless.[26] The anti-feminist undercurrent among the intelligentsia was unnoticed because contacts between the two parts of the nation focused on patriotism. The Russian police identified Galicia as the centre of the Ukrainian movement. The Austrians also watched both suspicious foreigners and their possible contacts with Austrian Ukrainian socialists. Konysky's daughter, Ievheniia, was shadowed on her visit in the summer of 1884, since both she and her father had met with Franko and the Pavlyk sisters. She had also met the Okunevsky family. Five years later, a Ukrainian student, Serhii Degen, and his sisters, Nataliia and Mariia, as well as Bohdan Kistiakovsky, were detained by the Austrians while visiting the Carpathians. Franko and Pavlyk were arrested, and Kobrynska was under suspicion.[27] Such experiences strengthened patriotic feelings and camaraderie.

The Galician struggle for more Ukrainian-language schools and for more use of Ukrainian at the university facilitated closer contacts among the youth. In

1898–9, it led to the convocation of all-Ukrainian student congresses. The willingness of Eastern Ukrainians to finance Ukrainian scholarship in Galicia was another important factor in the maintenance of closer ties. Ielysaveta Skoropadska Myloradovych was the major donor to the Shevchenko Society in Lviv, the surrogate Academy of Sciences which many Eastern Ukrainian scholars supported. Very few women, even in the twentieth century, penetrated this influential organization, which showed no particular interest in women's education, but was involved in expanding scholarship on Ukrainian subjects.

The appointment of Hrushevsky to the new chair of East European history at Lviv University in 1894 to teach courses in Ukrainian was a significant victory for Ukrainians. An increasing number of Eastern Ukrainian women came to Lviv to study after the turn of the century. In 1904, a special summer course in Ukrainian studies was organized in Lviv, primarily for Eastern Ukrainian students. The young women who remained to study at the University of Lviv, among them Nastia Hrinchenko and Katria Lozenko, became active in the Circle of Ukrainian Girls. In 1908, Ukrainian women from both sides of the Zbruch published *Meta*. In 1911, Kobrynska again tried to launch a women's library, publishing quality translations of literary works. Pchilka supported her fully in *Ridnyi krai*.[28]

Several factors led Eastern and Western Ukrainians toward greater political co-operation: (1) the establishment of the Revolutionary Ukrainian Party and its links with the Galicians, as well as with the Jewish Bund; (2) the involvement of more Galicians in helping revolutionaries get to Western Europe; and (3) the crackdown on the Revolutionary Ukrainian Party in 1903–4 by the tsarist government, after which many of its members moved to Galicia.[29] The liberalization which followed the Revolution of 1905 in the tsarist Empire, and the limited permission to publish in Ukrainian or about Ukrainian subjects, enabled Eastern Ukrainians to write about the achievements of Western Ukrainians. In 1907, Hrushevsky noted that "the renewed struggle for a Ukrainian university in Galicia...will force Ukrainians in Russia to raise analogous demands."[30] Rusova wrote periodically on educational developments in Galicia, and in 1915 Petliura's *Ukrainskaia zhizn* included a series of her articles on the Ukrainian organizations in Austria.

Cultural contacts, in which women participated, also increased. In 1881, the Tobilevych theatre troupe visited Galicia, and in 1904–5 Sadovsky and later Zankovetska were able to come. But attempts to get Solomiia Krushelnytska, the renowned soprano from Galicia, to perform in Kiev were stymied by the Russian police.

By attending functions in the Russian Empire, and speaking Ukrainian, Galician Ukrainians greatly bolstered the morale of Eastern Ukrainians who could not use the language publicly. Kobrynska and Kobylianska used the XII Archeological Congress of 1899 as a pretext for visiting Eastern Ukraine. The participation of Ukrainians from Galicia and Bukovyna at the unveiling, in 1903, of the Kotliarevsky monument in Poltava was also significant.

Contact with Eastern Ukrainian women helped change the tone of Ukrainian Galician society significantly.[31] The notion that feminism was a bourgeois whim, widely held in Eastern Ukraine, was readily shared by Galician progressives and prevented the establishment of a united women's organization. But contact with other Ukrainian women frequently led younger females to a heightened realization of the need for community action. The call, again, was not for liberation of the individual, but of the people. Nationalism and patriotism, not feminism, were becoming the most frequently used terms in women's vocabulary.

11.
The National-Liberation Struggle

The changes for Ukrainian women between 1914 and 1922 were cataclysmic. Wars and revolutions were followed by new governments, military occupations, guerrilla warfare, banditry and epidemics. Ukrainian territories bore a major brunt of the First World War and the ensuing Russian, Polish and Ukrainian wars.

The Russian imperial armies occupied Galicia twice during the war. Each occupation was marked by enforced relocation of populations. German and Austrian armies occupied parts of Eastern Ukraine. Ukrainians served in the armies of both sides, a circumstance not lost upon contemporaries. One of Kobrynska's last stories ("Brothers") was an impressionistic tale of two Ukrainians——one in the Austrian army, the other in the Russian——dropping their bayonets to embrace, only to be killed from behind by soldiers of their own armies.

Between the overthrow of tsarism in February, 1917, and the creation of the Union of Soviet Socialist Republics, of which the Ukrainian SSR was a constituent part, on 30 December 1922, governments in Kiev changed at least five times. In addition, other parts of Ukraine were occupied by anarchist and tsarist forces fighting in the area, and numerous private bands staked claims to various parts of Ukraine. Throughout the land there was unprecedented carnage.

Women were largely submerged in the formation of a new society. Between 1914 and 1922, they were thrust into conditions over which they had no control. Compared to war and diplomacy, the problems facing women seemed minor——food, shelter, care——but were concrete. While women's tasks in society expanded, and the difference in the functions of the sexes became blurred, the actual separation between the sexes was striking. In a wrenching disjointed sketch, written in February 1917, Olha Kobylianska divided war-torn humanity not into warring countries, but into "the island of the men" and the "island of the women, children, and geriatrics." The men fought for their ideals while the women tried to feed the children, till the land, and save life itself.[1]

The dual role of women——nurturers of the family and members of the work force——that emerged during the war became characteristic of Soviet Ukrainian women. Women took up untraditional functions, culminating in military service. During the war women replaced men in the fields, offices and factories. They had to cope with disintegrating economies and collapsing societies. The breakdown of traditional work roles gave women a sense of independence, and helped to convince them that they could manage alone. The feeling was similar to that of a peasant woman in charge of her household in pre-industrialized societies during the absence of her husband. Yet the women knew that they were not the ones determining the type of society in which they were destined to live.

Women's goals in the post-war aftermath transcended women's liberation. For Russians, the central events of the period were social and political, but for Ukrainians, as for other Eastern Europeans, the primary considerations were national. The difference between the Western and Eastern Ukrainian women during the war and the revolutions were differences in degree. Proportionately more Western than Eastern Ukrainian women served in the military. Western Ukrainians felt they owed some allegiance to Austria. Austria had recognized the existence of Ukrainians, funded schools, textbooks, and supported community organizations. When the war broke out, Austrians, yielding to Ukrainian pressure, organized a small Ukrainian military detachment. Eastern Ukrainian women, on the other hand, reflecting the pacifist bias of even the moderate Ukrainian intelligentsia, downgraded the importance of the military. Few thought it would be necessary to wage an armed struggle for Ukraine. Even had they not been pacifists, there was little reason for Ukrainians to support tsarist Russia. A number of Eastern Ukrainian émigrés saw the war as an opportunity to wrest independence for Ukraine and established an Alliance for the Liberation of Ukraine, with headquarters in Vienna. The Russian government used the Alliance as additional evidence to discredit Ukrainians.

The Alliance, however, represented no threat to the Russians, and did not capture the imagination of the majority of Ukrainians, most of whom supported the Russian Empire. Two future leaders of the Ukrainian state, for instance, manifested their loyalty to Russia openly. Hrushevsky, the historian and future president of the first revolutionary government in Ukraine, although married to a Western Ukrainian woman, returned to Kiev from his university chair in Lviv. Petliura, who would emerge as the military leader of the third Ukrainian government (having overthrown the second one), stressed in an editorial in the newspaper *Ukrainskaia zhizn* on New Year's Day 1915 the close co-operation of the Ukrainian and Russian intelligentsia. Nevertheless, the Russian government used the war as a pretext for clamping down on Ukrainians in the interest of state security.

The Russian intelligentsia had also disregarded the aspirations of non-Russians for decades preceding the war. Only the growing strength of the non-Russian intelligentsia, coupled with the outrageous anti-Semitic pogroms, forced the Russians to address nationality issues. Throughout the war, the

Russian intelligentsia's spirited discussion of the nationality issue demonstrated the growing patriotism of the Russians rather than an understanding of the grievances of the non-Russians. The Russian government perceived the intelligentsia's slight interest in the "Ukrainian question" as a potential problem, even though Ukrainians tried to demonstrate their loyalty.[2] For Russian women, nationalism was not an issue of primary importance, despite initially favourable reactions of Russian feminists to the aspirations of non-Russian women. The war made many Russian women, like Russian men, more patriotic.[3]

The growth of international tension preceding the outbreak of the First World War made public functions for all Ukrainians extremely difficult. Eastern Ukrainian activists were not only placed under police surveillance, but were frequently deported to Russian areas of the empire. Most Ukrainian-language publications were closed down.[4] War hysteria led the government to see Ukrainians as potential Austrian spies. Priests or teachers speaking Ukrainian in Ukrainian villages were placed under surveillance. The fact that "Russian agents [russkie agenty]...[functioned] in Galicia" made the government suspect that the Austrians had Ukrainians spying for the Habsburgs.[5] The police dragnet drew in some very improbable targets——a Zinaida Mykolaivna Sulynych was detained in conjunction with preparations for the centennial of Shevchenko's birth, which the police feared might trigger mass demonstrations.

The war proved that the government alone could not care for refugees and the wounded, nor could it meet the necessary increase in economic production. Civilians were drawn into relief work. Special organizations were authorized to co-ordinate the war effort and relief activities, the most important of which, the Alliance of Zemstvos and City Councils (Zemgor), played a significant role in the Russian Revolution. This type of work accustomed the population of the empire to organized activity, and strengthened its self-confidence.

The police had always monitored those involved in most Ukrainian-oriented organizations, and Ukrainians were subjected to special surveillance. Institutions connected with the military, such as hospitals and first-aid stations,were particularly careful about whom they hired.[6] Ukrainians had a difficult time obtaining responsible positions, since the government and the police carefully screened all relief workers. Nevertheless, Ukrainian women carried out significant work in welfare organizations and hospitals. They helped the needy and the wounded, and assisted Galician deportees.[7]

The war shifted the focus of the welfare organizations. Programmes among workers, such as literacy and cultural affairs, were replaced by hospital work, nursing and care of refugees and deportees. Members of welfare societies and schools under the patronage of the dowager Empress Maria donned nurses' uniforms, prepared bandages and cared for the wounded. A special society, bearing the name of the daughter of the Tsar, Tatiana, was established solely to care for the wounded. Since much of the fighting was taking place on Ukrainian territory, a Society for the Organization of Aid to the Population of

South Russia which Suffered from the Warfare was created, with headquarters in Kiev. Although the membership was not limited to women, they were its most active participants.

Deportations of Ukrainians were a result of the Russian government's attempt to destroy the Ukrainian movement in Galicia, which Russia occupied in 1915. Prominent Ukrainian leaders, among them the Primate of the Ukrainian Catholic Church, Metropolitan Andrei Sheptytsky, were deported to the Russian hinterland. Konstantyna Malytska, the writer, teacher and women's activist, was also arrested and exiled to Siberia after a four-month imprisonment. The vast majority of deported Galicians were peasants, bewildered and driven out of their homes wearing their summer clothes. They were dispersed throughout the Empire, but many were transported to Siberia and left to fend for themselves. Some were Russophiles, attracted to the same mythical White Tsar who was being discovered by the Russian intelligentsia, as well as by the alleged riches of the empire. The group also included a sprinkling of love-struck women lured by the promises of dashing soldiers. The Galicians, uninitiated in the demi-monde of the Russian police, did not know how to resort to the bribery customary in the empire to alleviate their plight.

The work of Eastern Ukrainian women in the Society to Help the Victims of the War ameliorated the lot of the refugees and deportees. The women helped provide clothes and food, set up shelters, especially for children, and organized some family reunification centres. Maria Ishunina (1878–1920) served as Secretary of the Kievan Committee, in which Nataliia Doroshenko-Savchenko, Liubov Shulhyna, her daughter Nadiia, and Liudmyla Starytska-Cherniakhivska were very active. Cherniakhivska tracked down Ukrainian deportees, and raised additional private funds that enabled some of them to travel in greater comfort, although under escort, on their forced journey to Siberia. She also ran a programme to send books and newspapers to deported Ukrainians.

The writer Nataliia Romanovych-Tkachenko attempted to set up shelters for orphans throughout Ukrainian territories. She and other women tried to unite Ukrainian children with their families. Buildings of cultural organizations were turned into hospitals: the Kievan Women's Club, for example, functioned as the *zemstvo*-run hospital.[8] Ukrainian women in other cities of Ukraine and the empire also threw themselves into the war-relief efforts. On the initiative of Ukrainian women in St. Petersburg, a Ukrainian section was created in the War Hospital in 1915 to help Ukrainian soldiers write letters home and obtain Ukrainian publications. The Ukrainian Women's Circle in the capital existed more or less openly. Among its most active participants were Elizaveta B. Zhuk, N.A. Mohylianska, O.F. Tuhan-Baranovska, N.V. Enhel, A.V. Alekseeva, V.K. Troshchyna and Ia.P. Zaiello.[9] These efforts, however, were hampered by a lack of funds and police harassment, as well as by a growing opposition to Ukrainians on the part of non-Ukrainian women.[10]

As the war continued and food shortages became more acute, the fertile lands of Ukraine attracted more and more Russians. In a process greatly accelerated after both Russian revolutions, Russians with and without property flocked to Ukraine, particularly to Kiev. Simultaneously, Poles and Jews, fleeing the devastation of the Russo-German conflagration, left the countryside for the major cities. Housing, food and sanitary conditions, which had never been adequate, became deplorable in the cities. War rationing exacerbated the shortages, led to greater corruption, and served as a pretext for more police control.[11] The influx of Russians, Poles and Jews into the already heterogenous Ukrainian cities complicated the urban situation.[12]

Throughout the war, women in Ukrainian cities co-operated in their work, which increasingly took on an economic dimension. Feminists were among the first to note that the dramatic influx of women into the work force resulted in a drastic decline in women's pay. The Union of Equality for Women, in planning its congresses, began to focus on the economic needs of women. Women's sections emerged within professional societies in the first years of the war. Socialists continued their support of some types of women's activity. In October 1915, Anna I. Dobrokhvatova, a Menshevik, suggested the convocation of an All-Imperial Congress of Women's Organizations. Olga V. Pilatskaia, a Bolshevik who was to become Moscow's representative in Ukrainian women's organizations in the 1920s, co-operated with Dobrokhvatova. The Congress, held from 27 to 29 December 1915, dealt primarily with relief for war victims and did not address the needs of non-Russians.[13]

The Social Democrats picked up on the revolutionary potential of women and non-Russians, and used International Women's Day (8 March) as a special means of increasing the awareness of women. In a leaflet distributed in Ukrainian areas, especially in Katerynoslav, the Social Democrats attacked the Russian government for the duplicity of its nationality policy: "the war is [ostensibly] fought for the liberation of peoples...[but once Russia] sent its police into "liberated" Galicia, it abrogated its autonomy, suppressed Poland, the Caucasus, Little Russia, encouraged the Poles to attack the Russians and organized pogroms against the Jews."[14]

Despite Allied pressure on Russia to continue fighting, and despite the growing patriotism of the Russian intelligentsia, the war became unpopular in the empire. In Ukraine, the peasants' attachment to the land made absence from home all the more painful. Although the Cossack system had been abolished more than a hundred years earlier, Ukrainian peasants yearned for control over the land they tilled. When the Tsar abdicated in February 1917, in fact, Ukraine reverted to its older landholding systems.[15]

One of the immediate catalysts of the Tsar's abdication was the women's demonstration for bread in Petrograd. The creation of the Provisional Government was a spontaneous change, and its policies were unclear. While the Provisional Government seemed to mark a radical break with the tsarist regime, reversion to tsarism remained a possibility. This explains the repeated and continued willingness of Ukrainians to work with any opponents of the tsar.

The Ukrainian Revolution of February 1917 was also spontaneous, neither planned, orchestrated, nor led from above. It was a mass movement played out on different levels, interacting and at times opposed to one another. For Ukrainians, the revolution marked a political and social upheaval. Unlike the Russian Revolution, it was also a period of national revival. It coincided with foreign intervention——Russian, in the form of tsarist or White forces, and Soviet, masquerading as international Bolshevism, but in essence directed against even Ukrainian communism. In make-up, the whole revolution was peasant-oriented: bands of anarchists controlled certain territories, setting up "little republics," some of which were headed by women. In general, women were very active in the villages, but their role remains to be studied in detail.

The Bolsheviks were but a tiny wave in the swelling revolutionary sea, potentially the most responsive of the Russians to Ukrainian needs. Because of their final victory, there is a tendency to see them as an organized, centralized, coherent and relentless force, forging ahead with their preplanned course. That was not the case in Ukraine. The initial failure of the Bolsheviks in Ukraine was so dismal that the party had to revise its ideology and organize an expeditionary force to conquer that land.

The Ukrainian intelligentsia, divided and harassed by the police, was incapable of assessing the situation realistically. (Neither was the Russian intelligentsia.) In their memoirs of this period, Ukrainians have complained of the low level of national consciousness among the peasants, their illiteracy and lack of culture. They saw salvation only in the wholesale acceptance of their own political and social solutions. Yet at the first opportunity, these illiterate peasants flocked to meetings and congresses to make their social and national demands known. Members of the Ukrainian intelligentsia worked in the countryside, setting up schools and helping to organize co-operatives. Many memoirs contain an inherent contradiction: if the Ukrainian movement were as weak as they maintained, why was Ukrainianism so strong, able to conduct protracted warfare with the Bolsheviks and the Whites; why the radical changes in Bolshevik policies toward Ukrainians; why the stress on Ukrainization in the 1920s among the hardened international communists? In this respect the Bolsheviks assessed the situation more realistically than the Ukrainians. While pursuing their other goals, the Bolsheviks realized the strength of the national feeling prevalent in the Ukrainian countryside.

The elation that followed the overthrow of the Romanovs has been captured by Nataliia Romanovych-Tkachenko in her brief memoir on "the first days of freedom": the endless debates on freedom and autonomy, the chaos, the singing of patriotic Ukrainian songs, including Franko's "The time has passed to serve the Pole and bend the knee to the Muscovite."[16] Ukrainians supplemented revolutionary demands with calls for local autonomy and cultural rights. Frequently, they used existing organizations, such as the *zemstvo*, the co-operative or the Prosvita, if the branch had survived the war. Other local Ukrainian organizations sprang up, especially political committees in smaller towns. Co-operatives were revitalized and took on more community functions.

In Kiev, the first centre of organized Ukrainian life in 1917 was the Women's Club, which had been turned into a *zemstvo*-run hospital. It became a meeting place for Ukrainian activists, *zemstvo* workers, co-operative organizers, and for priests who were groping toward autocephaly, i.e., making the Ukrainian Orthodox Church independent from Moscow. The official representative body of Kiev, the Rada (Council), was formed on 13 March. Women's participation was taken for granted, since women had been active in political life. On 16 March 1917, the first Ukrainian military detachments, partly formed by Galician POW's, marched down the main street of Kiev waving Ukraine's blue and gold colours. Within two days the first Ukrainian-language co-educational high school was opened in Kiev, followed by the opening of more than one hundred Ukrainian-language schools in that city. The City Council (*Duma*) voted to use Ukrainian in its deliberations.

On 19 March Ukrainians held a parade on the wide main streets of Kiev, which swelled into a grandiose demonstration of Ukrainian strength. Although the political aspirations of Ukrainians were modest at the time, there was no doubt of their visible presence and growing importance in the city. Many Russian and Russified Jewish women in the Kiev Women's Society, which had functioned as an umbrella organization during the war, objected to the participation of their members in this demonstration and to the active involvement of Ukrainian women in Ukrainian organizations. They could not reconcile themselves to Ukrainian aspirations, and forced Ukrainian women to resign from the Women's Society. Russian feminists, particularly those living in non-Russian areas, had become quite chauvinistic during the war.[17]

Yet there were also women, in Kiev and elsewhere, who chose a territorial rather than a historical or ethnic approach to national self-determination. Mariia Zarchii, an ardent Ukrainian feminist active in the early 1920s, was of Jewish origin, as were a number of other Ukrainian women activists. The Ukrainian People's Republic, as the state represented by the Rada was known, was one of the first East European states to proclaim laws guaranteeing the rights of national minorities and to co-opt representatives of minority parties, especially Jews, into the state machinery.[18]

The Rada, reflecting its democratic and pacifist bias, held local elections, convened numerous well attended congresses and negotiated fruitlessly with the Provisional Government for recognition of the rights of non-Russian nationalities. Ukrainians wanted to preserve a liberal Russian regime, and were friendly toward the Provisional Government. The Russian liberals, however, were loath to accept political rights for any of the so-called minorities, including women. Ukrainians, who were among the first to attempt to create a liberal-democratic state, could neither comprehend nor accept that rejection.[19] Events in Ukraine took their own course, and the Provisional Government soon became irrelevant. Ukrainian organizations and political parties blossomed, and Ukrainians from other parts of the empire hastened to Ukraine, especially to Kiev. Members of the Women's Circle from Petrograd who had engaged in demonstrations in the imperial capital welcomed the hostage Metropolitan

Sheptytsky and organized popular concerts. The circle moved almost en masse to Kiev.[20] By the end of March, the Kievan women had created a Women's Union (Zhinochyi Soiuz), which participated actively in the political life of the future capital of Ukraine and published a journal, *Zhinochyi visnyk* (Women's Messenger). Women were active in all political parties. When the Ukrainian Social Revolutionary Party was established as an entity separate from the Russian one, Halyna Chyzhevska became the secretary of its Central Committee.[21]

During the municipal council elections, which were held early in April, voting was considered a manifestation of the revolutionary national spirit. Thus no one questioned the right of women to vote. One of the women even noted that what mattered "were not the formalities but the elemental force of the people."[22]

The first Ukrainian National Congress, held in Kiev between 6 and 9 April 1917, was composed of representatives of various parts of Ukraine and of Ukrainians living outside Ukraine. Many of the delegates were peasants and soldiers. It was proposed that Hrushevsky be elected president by acclamation, but he insisted on proper voting by secret ballot.

The practical side of the congress caused some problems. The peasant delegates refused to stay in hotels, which were overcrowded, nor would they eat in restaurants, which made them uncomfortable. However, Starytska-Cherniakhivska, with the help of Mariia Hrushevska, Oksana Steshenko and Valeriia O'Connor-Vilinska, arranged private lodgings and board for the delegates.

The Congress elected a 115-person Ukrainian Central Rada, which included at least eleven women. An executive council, the so-called Small Rada, was created from the larger body. The women among its twenty members were: Valeriia O'Connor-Vilinska, representing the Socialist-Federalist Ukrainian Party (which was very moderate in its views), the most conservative of the Ukrainian parties; Zinaida Mirna, a direct descendant of the Cossacks who settled in the Kuban after the destruction of the *Sich*; and Liudmyla Starytska-Cherniakhivska, the Ukrainian activist and writer.

Other women in the Rada, whose membership fluctuated, were the educator and political activist Sofiia Lindfors Rusova (who represented one of the Kievan cultural organizations); Valentyna Nychaivska, the official representative of the Women's Union; Olimpiia Pashchenko, one of the delegates from the Teachers' Union; and Sofiia Liubynska, who represented the Ukrainians in Saratov.[23]

The Rada developed its administration and established contacts with local committees that had replaced government institutions. It continued its formal friendly relations with the Provisional Government, but at the same time worked out its own legislation. As the scope of the Rada's activities increased, specialists were brought in and women's effective participation declined. Women, in fact, moved willingly into areas where they felt more comfortable, namely, welfare and education. Mirna headed the committee which integrated welfare and relief functions; Rusova worked in the ministry of education, and Valentyna Radzymovska, a biologist, worked in the ministry of health.[24]

Throughout 1917, groups of Ukrainians held various congresses of peasants, teachers, workers, soldiers and activists of the co-operative movement. In addition to participating in all types of community work, women created or reactivated women's organizations. They affiliated themselves with the Women's Union in Kiev. Together, the women held a number of meetings culminating in a women's congress in Kiev between 27 and 29 September 1917. The return of Eastern and Western Ukrainian prisoners from Siberia, the freeing of political prisoners, and the disintegration of the despised *Okhrana* elated most Ukrainians. Some formal measure of autonomy was taken for granted by the Eastern Ukrainian intelligentsia, who, because of their ideology——progressive, peaceful, optimistic——could not conceive that force might be used against their democratic national movement. When the freed Western Ukrainian POW's organized a military regiment and argued that the Rada should move quickly to form a Ukrainian army, the Rada leadership rejected this "sensible suggestion of the practical Galicians,"[25] fearing no threat from the left.

The Rada issued laws assuring the minorities of their rights and tried to remain in close contact with the Provisional Government. Indeed, Ukrainians continued to deplore the unwillingness of the national minorities, especially the Jews, Poles and Germans to co-operate with the Rada, despite repeated assurances of nationality rights.[26] In contrast, Moscow remained adamantly opposed to Ukraine's autonomy. The Bolsheviks, who overthrew the Provisional Government in October 1917, also refused to recognize the Rada.[27]

The Rada, lest it be accused of stabbing Russian democracy in the back, cautiously proclaimed the complete independence of Ukraine only on 22 January 1918. Ukrainians' primary interest, for men and women alike, was the land question. Ukrainian peasants, with their traditional individualism and homesteads in the steppe, were even more deeply attached to their land than their Russian counterparts. The Rada devised a plan for the socialization of the land in which women played an active role.

Women's rights were enshrined in the Constitution of the Ukrainian People's Republic (UNR), proclaimed on 29 April 1918: "[The] statutory, civil and political legality of a citizen of the Ukrainian People's Republic begins at the age of twenty. The law of the UNR does not recognize any difference in the rights and duties of men and women."[28] The formulation of women's equality extended to all aspects of life, including military service.[29]

At the time the Constitution of the Ukrainian People's Republic was ratified, the Bolsheviks were preparing to invade Ukraine. Ousted from Kiev, the Ukrainian government had signed a separate peace with Austria and Germany in early February 1918. The Treaty of Brest-Litovsk, supported by Lenin, officially recognized Ukraine's status as a sovereign nation.[30] This clause was not forced on Russia by the Germans, as some interpretations maintain. Soviet Russia was simply in no position to hold on to Ukraine. It achieved inroads into

Ukraine only with the creation of a rival *Ukrainian* government in Kharkiv, and a war against the Rada.

Ukrainians feared a conservative reaction and a return to traditional Russian rule. Consequently, the Rada was afraid to create agencies that might abuse their authority and serve as vehicles to bring back the Russian conservatives. German and Austrian troops, meanwhile, had occupied large territories of Ukraine, which they perceived as a source of food for both their armies and populations. The peasants resented this encroachment on their land, and the Rada was neither willing nor able to enforce the requisitions of grain.

There was an influx of Russian refugees into Kiev as the Bolshevik invasion and the food shortages made life difficult in the north. The small Bolshevik groups in Ukrainian cities played on the fears of a conservative takeover and tried to direct discontented mobs against the Rada. The Bolsheviks were also adroit at using women to create and exploit disturbances. Memoirists have cited the exploits of some women called Sokolovsky——both related and unrelated. In Kiev, Sonia Sokolovska, the daughter of a local judge, was effective in helping spread anti-Rada sentiments. In nearby Radomyshl, a Sofiia Sokolovska joined the Bolsheviks, while her sister Mariia, an ardent supporter of Ukrainian independence, headed a Ukrainian armed detachment against the invading Bolsheviks when its previous commander, her brother, was killed.

The Rada withstood the first onslaught of the Bolsheviks, but refused to meet German demands for grain. The Germans then supported the Ukrainian conservatives and Pavlo Skoropadsky became Hetman of Ukraine. The Hetmanate, which lasted until mid-November 1918, marked a conservative period in the Ukrainian Revolution. It was characterized by German intervention and increased attempts of both Russian conservatives and radicals to use Ukraine as a springboard to re-establish a Russia to their liking. During this time, some conservative Russified families, including Skoropadsky's, returned to conscious Ukrainianism.[31]

Generally, the progressive Ukrainian intelligentsia regarded the Hetman as an outsider. He had been, after all, a tsarist general who did not share their ethos. This opposition to both the Hetman and the regime he personified cut across national lines. Skoropadsky reorganized his army unit in March 1917 as the First Ukrainian Corps, with some 30,000 men, but the Rada's distrust of him grew, especially after the Congress of Ukrainian Free Cossacks elected him honorary commander (*pochesnyi otaman*) in October 1917. He was closely connected to the conservative Ukrainian landholders, and helped conservative Russian émigrés come to Ukraine. To the Ukrainian intelligentsia he seemed a potential Napoleon.

Accordingly, most progressive Ukrainians refused to co-operate with the new regime and continued to place their hopes in the revolutionary proclivities of the Ukrainian masses, the goodwill of the Allies, and the alleged democratic sentiments of the Russian revolutionaries. Hrushevsky, who had withdrawn from political activity, apparently advised the young Nadia Surovtseva to fan anti-Hetman sentiments among Ukrainian peasants. Liudmyla

Starytska-Cherniakhivska was one of the few members of the Executive Board of the Rada who had urged co-operation with the Hetman regime, so that Skoropadsky would not have to rely exclusively upon the Russians. Reflecting the pragmatic approach of women activists, she later commented ironically that "the Socialist-Federalists [the most moderate Ukrainian party in the Rada] were afraid to sully their socialist virginity" by this co-operation.[32]

The Hetman regime was under German pressure to enforce the requisition of grain, and under growing Russian (and, through them, Allied) pressure to merge itself into a unified Russia and fight the Germans. The stronger the Bolsheviks became in Russia, the greater the pressure upon Ukraine to serve as the saviour of the former empire. The Hetman himself, however, was becoming painfully aware of the needs of his homeland. He continued the Rada's policy of establishing and supporting Ukrainian schools, the university in Kiev and other institutions, culminating in the creation of the Academy of Arts and Sciences, which still exists today. The Ukrainian intelligentsia, which dealt with the German and Austrian troops, was impressed by the Germans' familiarity with Ukrainian matters, in contrast to the ignorance of the Russian radicals, including the Bolsheviks.[33]

The Hetmanate, faced with a variety of pressing issues, did not establish any policy toward women, but its grain requisitions turned all peasants against the regime. While there were no women in the small circle that plotted and executed the overthrow of the Hetman in mid-November 1918, women had participated in the more widely based Ukrainian People's Union and had been as perturbed as the men by some of the Hetman's policies. In a popular movement, spearheaded by Ukrainian army units and the Battalion of Galician Ukrainians under Ievhen Konovalets, Ukrainians re-entered Kiev, proclaimed the Ukrainian People's Republic, and, within a few months, its fusion with the Western Ukrainian Republic.

Eventually headed by Petliura, this government, also known as the Directory of the Ukrainian People's Republic, attempted throughout the early 1920s to preserve the progressive traditions of the UNR and to stem the tide of the Bolsheviks. The task was difficult, because the Allies did not recognize the Directory and considered it communist. The Allies enforced a blockade of Ukraine which denied it badly needed medical supplies. The outbreak of a typhus epidemic, combined with dysentery and other scourges of warfare, devastated Ukrainian forces.

The role of women in this particular phase of Ukrainian history was determined by two factors: war and epidemics. The Directory from its inception was a government threatened from all sides. It proved to be a well-intentioned but weak government that was held responsible for atrocities it had tried to prevent. The revolution had brought hope and euphoria. The overthrow of the Hetman and the alacrity with which the democratic republic had been re-established reaffirmed that hope. But the future brought repeated disillusionment. Women's issues were, at best, a factor of minor significance, although the functions of women themselves became wider.[34]

Ukraine also became a theatre of the Russian Civil War. The White Russian forces, aided by the Allies, were trying to reach the "heartland" through "South Russia." The Bolsheviks, who occupied Kiev in January 1919, were immediately pushed out, and tried to reconquer Ukraine from the north and east. Initially, the Ukrainians "did not consider the Bolsheviks dangerous," and disregarded the danger posed by them as opposed to the potential strength of the Whites.[35]

During the 1920s, the economy collapsed, governments changed, and the social fabric disintegrated. The line between army service and guerrilla action depended on one's political convictions: the heroes on one side were the villains on the other. Fighting women do not fit into any particular pattern. Some led armed or guerrilla detachments, sometimes under pseudonyms——Swallow, Seagull, She-Eagle and the like. Ukrainian women fought on all sides of the struggle——nationalist, communist, anarchist, and in the independent detachments that frequently determined the outcome of a battle and even the war. Only Russified Ukrainians would have supported the Whites, and they would have opposed the very concept of an independent Ukraine. Bolshevik women, such as Evgeniia Bosh, Olga Sokolovskaia, Olga Pilatskaia, and Alexandra Kollontai, who at some point had Ukrainian appointments, acted as members of the centralized Communist Party and did not take part in the bitter nationality debates that surfaced in the Russian Social Democratic Labour Party. Information on Ukrainians who were connected with or accused of "national communism" is generally incomplete, particularly that on women. For instance, Sofiia Sokolovska, a patriotic Ukrainian who joined the communists, was elected leader of the Chernihiv Revolutionary Committee, and averted a mass murder of Ukrainian men in February 1919. (As they were retreating from Kiev between 18 and 28 February, the Bolsheviks shot about 5,000 Ukrainian men; apparently the same fate was in store for the residents of Chernihiv.) Sokolovska herself vanished shortly thereafter, apparently killed by the Red Army.

The more desperate the Ukrainian situation became, the more the women took an active part in the military activities, especially guerrilla warfare. Perhaps the most famous Eastern Ukrainian women engaged in the struggle with the Bolsheviks were Vira Babenko and Mariia Tarasenko. The first served as a major liaison for the Petliura government-in-exile, which was preparing for a mass uprising against the Soviets (1921). One of Petliura's close aides, however, was a Soviet agent. Babenko was picked up and died at the hands of the Cheka, as her father had done a year earlier. The same fate awaited Tarasenko, who served as a courier for over two years. She was executed with her whole family on 27 August 1923.[36]

The women portrayed in literary works of the time were generally strong and likeable. Mykola Khvylovy's "Puss in Boots" fictionalized the socialist-communist version of an endearing but determined woman. Halyna Zhurba also wrote a period drama about a resolute heroine and a weak man. In contrast, in *Dni Turbinykh* (Days of the Turbin Family), the Russian writer Mikhail Bulgakov presented bored groups of Russian women in Kiev who found the whole revolution simply tedious.[37]

Ukrainian women in the Ukrainian People's Republic recognized the importance of women's organizations both to co-ordinate women's activities in Ukraine and to gain a window on Europe through the international women's movement. Working with the men in the Rada and later by themselves, these women experienced at first hand the limitations of "legal equality." The Women's Union and women's rallies in Kiev had demonstrated the interest in a women's organization. As the Directory shuffled from city to city, trying to find a military and diplomatic buttress for itself, the women formally re-established the Women's Union. They made contact with the Galician Women's Union, and early in August 1919, on the initiative of Blanka Baranova, Ivanna Odryna and Mariia (Pisetska) Strutynska, they met in Kamianets-Podilskyi, then the headquarters of the UNR, to announce the creation of the Union of Ukrainian Women (Soiuz Ukrainok), which overlapped with the Western Ukrainian Women's Union. In its public pronouncements, the Union often referred to itself as the Ukrainian National Council of Women.[38]

Initially, the Union, influenced by feminist philanthropy, ran a convalescent home for soldiers recuperating from the typhus epidemic. The organization was equally concerned with community affairs and with organizing women. It comprised five sections: one for medical and another for relief services for soldiers (headed by Mariia Iurynets and Oksana Biretska); an economic section headed by Olena Odryna (her husband's ministerial post in the UNR gave that section particular status); a cultural section under Rusova and Starytska-Cherniakhivska; and an art section under Mariia Hrinchenko. Since participation of all citizens was assured, these women did not see the need for a separate political section. The concerns of women were, in any case, community-oriented.

But even in times of acute and prolonged crisis old prejudices against women flourished. In 1919 and 1920, the women complained about it to the government sporadically. After the collapse of the UNR——it became an organization of exiles——the issue was dropped, and the women again deferred to the national cause.

The position of the UNR was further complicated by the government of the Western Ukrainian People's Republic. In brief, Western Ukraine formally joined the UNR to proclaim a sovereign unified Ukraine, but to retain all possible international options, it was agreed that the Western Ukrainians would maintain a separate administration and government. They had a separate army, which had been one of the best in Eastern Europe before its decimation by the typhus epidemic and the French-equipped Polish soldiers. The Galicians hoped to benefit from the Wilsonian doctrine of self-determination. The Directory, meanwhile, was willing to enter into an alliance with Poland and give up Ukrainian claims to Galicia in return for Polish support in unseating the Bolsheviks in 1920. By 1923, however, Ukrainians had lost on all fronts: the Allies sanctioned Polish rule in Galicia and the final Ukrainian attempt at an uprising against the Bolsheviks failed.

The collapse of the UNR was a result of several factors: superior Bolshevik arms and propaganda, inadequate Ukrainian medical facilities, lack of military aid to Ukrainians, and extremely effective Bolshevik penetration of the Petliura camp.

During these years of chaos, the Women's Union considered its work of prime importance to the whole nation. Women presumed that they would naturally play a part in shaping the new society, based upon justice and equality. Because their male colleagues had themselves experienced discrimination and inequality, the women expected to be treated as equals. Thus, when they were excluded from important political consultation within the Ukrainian camp, they gave the men the benefit of the doubt: "Was that due to the opposition of men, the leaders of our government, or perhaps because of the maelstrom which raged on the three fronts of Ukraine, or maybe the whole issue was not important to them? Be that as it may, Ukrainian women did not raise their demands so as not to exacerbate the situation."[39]

A letter Petliura wrote to the Union of Ukrainian Women excusing himself from attending a function of the "young society" was symptomatic of the intelligentsia's patronizing tone toward women. Petliura wrote:

> I thank you sincerely for the invitation, but unfortunately I will not be able to attend your evening of the Young Society, *Soiuz Ukrainok*.... Together with the beloved Society, I, too, am celebrating the birth of the Women's Union——citizens who were awaited by our entire society with palpitating hope. The whole past of Ukrainian women...beginning with that glorious period when the Ukrainian mother readied her sons to seek a [better] fate for the Native Land, and ending with the last tumultuous hour, when she herself had to stand on the barricades of the revolution...has demonstrated that the Ukrainian woman stood together with the warriors and the martyrs.
>
> Therefore, now she has to answer the question: "Will there be freedom or not?" But the past is the guarantee of the present. The Ukrainian woman has already said to herself, "There will," and leaving the comfortable shelter of her home she turns to civic activity.
>
> Good luck to her, and let the better genii of the native land swaddle the crib of the newborn 'Union.' Glory to Ukrainian women![40]

The health threat to Ukraine was as grave as the political one, and even more pressing. The unabated warfare, the lack of trained medical personnel and hospitals, the absence of disinfectants, "the continual requisitions of food by enemy troops, the difficulties in tilling the soil because of fighting, the unsuccessful harvest of last summer, all these have brought to the population extreme misery and famine and made it more difficult for the weak and malnourished to resist epidemics."[41] In order to obtain badly needed medical supplies, the Ukrainian women appealed to the "Women of the Whole World," explaining that the UNR was not a communist state and should be offered the very limited aid for which it asked.[42]

Western and Eastern Ukrainian women co-operated even as the relationship between the two governments-in-exile deteriorated. In November 1919, Olena Fedak Sheparovych, Sofiia Volska-Murska and Nadiia Surovtseva delivered a memorandum on the Galician issue to the American and British correspondents stationed in Vienna. Fedak was a Galician women's activist married to one of the organizers of the Western Ukrainian takeover on 1 November 1918 and better acquainted with the Ukrainian situation than the average Galician woman. Not only had she visited Eastern Ukraine before the War, but her husband, a specialist in radio-technology, had monitored Russian activities for Austrian military intelligence. Murska, although from Eastern Ukraine, was a Catholic and Surovtseva a radical.[43]

The women, ardent supporters of a democratic system in Ukraine, tried to popularize Ukraine's cause in Europe through the major women's networks, as well as through the Red Cross. They arranged for a Red Cross fact-finding mission to visit Ukrainian prisoners of war in Poland, and were instrumental in setting up another Red Cross mission from Vienna to Ukraine. The mission to Poland was composed of Ukrainian women from Galicia. A similar group of Polish women travelled in the Ukrainian-held territories to observe the condition of the Polish POW's.

Iaroslav Okunevsky, a relative of Kobrynska, organized four doctors, one businessman, one cook, seven disinfectant specialists and ten registered nurses to accompany him to Ukrainian battlefields. He felt that the Allies favoured a federalist Eastern Europe and that a *modus vivendi* among Ukrainians, Russians and Poles would be worked out partly as a result of Allied pressure.[44]

The popularity of the Ukrainian cause had proved even to the most obdurate Bolsheviks the need to make concessions to the nationality principle. Even the proponents of complete internationalism (such as Evgeniia Bosh from Katerynoslav), realized the importance of patriotism.

As in the nationality issue, so in the woman question, the Bolsheviks maximized the potential women offered. Many Ukrainian women, even at the height of the struggle with the Russian Bolsheviks, were not blind to the pro-woman policies of the Communist Party.

This is precisely the area where, as much as one might oppose the regime, we have to admit its achievements. Woman, in so far as she is not basically hostile to the Bolshevik regime, has full power, access to all functions, institutions.... Lunacharsky pointed out that the woman of the intelligentsia was the first to break with the sabotage and boycott [of the Bolsheviks] and approach the difficult task of enlightening the dark masses.... Although in her heart she might oppose communism, as do the majority of the intelligentsia, she is conscious that schools, theatres, children's centres, if they exist under this or that power, always lead to the final goal: nobility of the soul of humanity.[45]

As the UNR moved westward, the Poles penetrated Galicia. The Bukovynians found themselves in a greatly expanded Romania, while the Transcarpathians were ruled not by the oppressive Hungarians, but the rather by the benevolent Czechs and Slovaks. The Eastern Ukrainians lost their bid for a democratic Ukraine to the communists. Psychologically, the loss may have been more bearable because the Russians had been equally unsuccessful in creating a democratic Russia.

The existence of a sovereign Ukraine, however brief and chaotic, strengthened the feeling of solidarity among Ukrainian women. The experiences of women in all parts of Ukraine were quite similar. Generally, women had expected equality along with justice. They found neither, but emerged from these setbacks even more ready to organize effective women's groups.

The attitudes of Western Ukrainian men toward women "in the momentous struggle" of the war and liberation were frequently contradictory. On the one hand, in song, literature and rhetoric, they gloried in the women who had joined the army and fought for a free Ukraine. On the other, they were as reluctant to accept the participation of women in public affairs as they had been before the war. For Western Ukrainian women, the war and the liberation struggle brought suffering, heroism, and a realization of the need for a women's organization. The war forced even the most sheltered of women into some type of public activity and into contact with a hostile environment. The shock of war was compounded for the Galicians when the Austrians set up concentration camps, to which they deported those suspected of pro-Russian sentiments. The mass arrest and deportation of Ukrainian civilians by the occupying Russian forces brought the war even closer to women. Young Western Ukrainian women who had tried to be politically active before the war had also joined the physical-fitness organizations whose goal had been to prepare the youth to serve the nation. The few young women in these organizations, mainly students and members of the intelligentsia, demonstrated their courage by enlisting in the army.

Compared to the Poles, Ukrainians had been slow to organize paramilitary organizations before the war. There were two reasons behind such tardiness. First, the Polish-controlled local Galician administration, which had sanctioned Polish paramilitary formations, refused to permit Ukrainian ones. Second, Ukrainians themselves were not convinced of the need for such groups. Nevertheless, in early 1914, some young persons managed, without official recognition, to reorganize a part of the Sich fitness society into what "they themselves considered to be a revolutionary army," the Ukrainian Sich Riflemen (Ukrainski Sichovi Striltsi), which included "a place for women." Drawing on Cossack military usage, Roman Dashkevych became the commander (*koshovyi*), Ivan Chaikivsky, his deputy (*osaul*), and Ievhen Banakh his secretary, while Olena Stepaniv, apparently with no opposition, became the quartermaster (*oboznyi*). Of the original 300 Striltsi, 33 were women, and they formed a separate unit (*cheta*). The women were composed of university and high-school students and a few skilled workers and artisans, but no peasants.[46]

Within two months, when the Austrian government agreed to the creation of the Striltsi as a paramilitary group, the participation of women became a moot issue. Although the women's group continued, it could not enlist *en masse* when war began. Its leader, Stepaniv, through the personal intervention of Ivan Chmola, joined the Striltsi to fight the Russians. The young, strikingly beautiful and photogenic Olena Stepaniv was the first woman in the Austrian Empire to enlist in the army, a fact widely publicized in the Austrian press. She was soon followed by Sofiia Halechko, Handzia Dmyterko and others from the Ukrainian women's contingent. All served in the Ukrainian Austrian forces and participated in combat.[47]

The women became heroic figures, duly eulogized on commemorative occasions, but there is little information about their functions. They may have made the men feel uncomfortable, while they themselves forsook feminist concerns for patriotic ideals. Iryna Shmigelska Klymkevych, a Western Ukrainian woman who fought in the Eastern Ukrainian guerrilla detachments, worked on a book about women in the forces, but not even her notes are extant. She did compile a list of about forty Western Ukrainian women who took part in the armed Ukrainian formations. Among them are a few Austrians, one woman with a Jewish name——Savyna Tsukenberg——and two nuns of the Basilian order. Experience led Stepaniv to change her mind about the wisdom of women bearing arms; Halechko drowned tragically at a young age——it was rumoured to be a suicide.

Stefaniła Vitoshynska Devosser, whose military service was not spectacular, offered one of the most candid accounts of young women volunteering for military service in the beleaguered Western Ukrainian People's Republic, proclaimed on 1 November 1918 in Lviv. Devosser attended a teacher-training school in Stanyslaviv run by the nuns of the Order of St. Basil:

> Female agitators (*agitatorky*) came to the school and with their fiery oratory encouraged us to come to the defence of the threatened fatherland. The girls from the High School and Teacher-Training School volunteered, my sister and I among them. Women who worked in Ukrainian institutions, in military headquarters as secretaries, as telephone operators, in hospitals, and those who took part in the actions of the first days of November now gave themselves up to fate. Sixteen-, eighteen-, twenty-year-old girls, of their own free will, became involved in a game (*rozhra*) which they considered their duty.... Our amazement was great when we did not see a single one of the agitators at the [recruitment] centre.

Male feelings toward the women volunteers were ambivalent. The Zaliznyi Zahin (Iron Detachment), a little known Western Ukrainian unit which had separate women's sections, was disbanded after the women, who had participated in the fighting near Zhmerynka, complained of discrimination by the Ukrainian soldiers.[48] Many women served in the administrative and medical units: in the office, as nurses in hospitals and on the front, and in the kitchens. This type of work was considered more suited for the women than actual combat.

The women's impact in the war lay in the fact that they resurrected the image of women bearing arms in the defence of the fatherland, the dedicated warrior-woman. But most women, motivated by the same patriotic feelings, chose more conventional ways to help their country that did not undermine the "traditional" role of women. They established committees, set up emergency lodgings, collected and prepared food, and cared for Ukrainian soldiers.

The Ukrainian Women's Committee in Vienna was especially effective and visible. The Austrian capital became a major Ukrainian centre during the war, since it was the initial headquarters of the Union for the Liberation of Ukraine, which supplemented the relatively large community of Ukrainians living in and around the capital. During the war, Ukrainians organized a Ukrainian-language secondary school that also offered co-operative training courses attended by women. Among the first 146 graduates, however, only five were women: four were Ukrainian and one was Jewish.[49]

Women who worked in the Vienna Ukrainian Women's Committee were later instrumental in creating a co-ordinated network of women's organizations in Western Ukraine. Olha Tsipanovska, Olena Kysilevska, Olena Fedak Sheparovych, Stefa Budzynovska, the Kulchytsky sisters, Olha Levytska Basarab and many others were, at some point, members of the committee. The committee itself was initiated by Olena Levytska, the wife of a member of parliament, Ievhen Levytsky, with the help of a Ukrainian Catholic pastor, the Reverend Zhuk. Another cleric, the Reverend Lytsyniak, initially served as secretary-treasurer, while Levytska and Kabarovska were president and secretary, respectively. The committee's first major activity was to search for Ukrainian soldiers in hospitals. It soon extended its scope to include care for Ukrainian prisoners of war throughout the empire.

Galicia remained a battleground for most of the war. There were serious shortages of food, medicine and medical care. Thus women became involved in relief work, both for the local population and for POWs and refugees. But they also had to defend their homes and possessions. As peasant opposition to the war grew, more women took action against abusive officials. To cite one graphic example: in June 1918, in the village of Hiicha, in the Rava-Ruska area which borders on Belorussia, a group of 100 peasant women and a few men stormed the home of the Austrian official to retrieve a grindstone that he had confiscated from one of the women. The leaders of this action were Sofiia Derkach, 22, single; Nastia Fediuk, 33, married; Mariia Trush, 21, single; Mariia Pylyp, 21, single; Mariia Pistun, 19, single. All were arrested and sentenced to between three weeks and three months of incarceration.[50]

Ukrainians in Galicia had the chance to assert political power in October 1918, when the Austro-Hungarian Empire approached collapse. Ukrainian political leaders hoped for an orderly transition in which Ukrainians would receive their territories and rights. However, a number of young military officers decided to act to prevent power from falling into the hands of the Poles. Hence, Ukrainians took possession of Lviv at dawn on 1 November. Other cities followed suit. Those cities in which Ukrainians hesitated to take power, arguing that Austria was still legally sovereign, fell to the Poles.

The "Action of November First" became a heroic symbol for Ukrainian Galicians, and a few women were directly involved. Olena Sheparovych, who had experience in managing welfare functions in Vienna, was brought in by her husband to help the soldiers.[51] Olha and Halia Onatsky, sisters from Eastern Ukraine, steadfastly manned the telephone and telegraph exchanges throughout the first weeks of fighting in Lviv, since there were no other women to relieve them.[52] The men engineering the takeover did not seek women's help, however. In contrast, Polish women were actively engaged in winning back Lviv. In one incident, Polish women smuggled weapons stored in the Czytelnia Akademicka past gullible Ukrainian patrols who did not suspect that women would be smuggling arms.[53]

Before any enactment of legislation, an arduous, block by block, city by city, village by village, war with the Poles ensued. At the same time, Ukrainians, Eastern and Western alike, were engaged in fighting with both White Russian troops and the Bolsheviks. The "fourth front" was the typhus epidemic, in which women and men died in equal numbers. The gruesome finale to these macabre years was a deadly flu epidemic.

Through military and diplomatic means, the young Ukrainian Republic struggled for survival. Soldiers and refugees swarmed in areas where control by any army or government was tenuous. Western Ukrainians, as an adjunct of their government, organized a Civic Committee (Horozhanskyi Komitet) to address the needs of the population. Women established a Women's Section which took over the welfare activities, care for the wounded, and functioned as a Red Cross. The Lviv Women's Union had a number of affiliated sections in other towns and carried on regular business during the war years. Even as Lviv fell under Polish control, Ukrainian women set up their own newspaper *Nasha meta* (Our Aim) and announced in no uncertain terms that they were in charge of the wounded: "Be it generally known that no one may visit the wounded and interned Ukrainians without prior approval of the Women's Section of the Civic Committee."[54]

In other Galician cities the situation was similar. Frequently, women and clergy were the only able-bodied persons left in the towns and villages. Where the women's organizations did not exist, or had suspended their activities, the priest galvanized the women not only into relief work, but also into creating an organization which would make that work more efficient.[55]

The useful, indeed essential nature of the work, the willingness of women to avoid the limelight, and the need for all available bodies finally reconciled Western Ukrainian males to the importance of women's involvement outside the house. In Polish-occupied Lviv, Sheparovych and Kosevych personally intervened with General Sikorski on behalf of the Ukrainian Civic Committee to grant Ukrainian women permission to visit wounded Ukrainian soldiers. A few women served as interpreters for the many foreign representatives who visited Galicia; Sheparovych recalled a group of Italians trying to negotiate shares in Galician oil concerns in 1918.

The Women's Section of the Civic Committee not only organized emergency care, but under the most adverse conditions of warfare, occupation and rampant disease, it set up hospitals, clinics, orphanages and missing persons' bureaus. It also trained nurses and day-care personnel; ran literacy and sewing schools; and employment offices. In fact, it hardly qualified as a women's organization in anything but name, "since [its] aims were not women's goals but purely philanthropic [community] activity."[56]

One of the most effective actions of the women came in January and February 1919. An exchange mission between Ukrainian and Polish women, under the auspices of the Red Cross, visited prisoner-of-war camps. The Ukrainian women involved were Dariia Starosolska (Hermina Shukhevych's daughter), Olena Kosevych and Sofiia Oleskiv.[57] Between 23 January and 11 February, the women visited Dąbie, near Cracow, where about 2,600 Ukrainian soldiers were interned by the Poles; Wadowice, also near Cracow, with 2,700 internees; and Pykulychi near Przemyśl, which was more a mass grave than a camp.[58] But the pleas of the women, of Ukrainian society, and even of the Polish Socialist Party were of no avail. By the end of the year conditions in the camps had worsened. When the Hoover Commission visited the area it designated two women, Mariia Burachynska (the wife of the director of the Ukrainian Community Hospital) and Sofiia Tsehelska, as responsible for distributing aid.[59]

The Poles, gaining the upper hand in Galicia, blockaded shipments of medical supplies and arrested Ukrainian civilians, both women and men. Dariia Harasymovych, Sofiia Moisevych, Mariia Kravtsiv, Mariia and Iaroslava Konrad and Mariia Chyzh, all young students, were among the first in Lviv to be arrested, in 1919. Prominent women activists were held as hostages. In Przemyśl, for instance, the Kulchytsky sisters, Olha Tsipanovska and Mrs. Stakhura were deported. Sofiia Oleskiv was arrested because "she seemed suspicious" when she visited some relatives in Bolekhiv, although her intention was merely to bring some food back to Lviv.[60]

Ukrainians considered their defeat a temporary setback. Women retaliated against Polish rule by organizing open protest meetings, and by trying to rebuild many of the pre-war Ukrainian cultural organizations.[61]

The Poles and the Soviets signed a peace treaty at Riga in March 1921, and the Allies mandated Galicia to the Poles in 1923. But Ukrainians did not view the treaties as an unmitigated defeat, and laid claim to the areas in which they lived.

An unexpected result of the liberation struggle was a burst of feminist consciousness and thinking, although this trend quickly subsided in the ensuing reconstruction period. Milena Rudnytska, in an article on the first anniversary of the 1 November 1918 takeover, criticized women from personal experience for not being more active and the Ukrainian community for being too restrictive. She gave a painfully graphic description of innumerable Ukrainian women in Lviv who had offered their services, only to be shunted to the kitchen. Even the latter was administered by a male who could have been better deployed at the front. Rudnytska was arrested on 22 November by Polish female legionnaires who had performed important intelligence and police-keeping tasks. Rudnytska——who became prominent in the women's movement——bitterly accused Ukrainian women of indolence during the liberation, and charged that Ukrainian society opposed the effective use of women's talents.

> We cannot whitewash before the coming generations the charge of immaturity and indolence which can with some justice be levelled at women in the tragic days of November.... But women have expiated this by the work we performed and have been performing this past year. The whole welfare effort, which alone is possible in times of foreign invasion, has been taken over by Ukrainian women: physical and spiritual care over the families of our soldiers, of all the innocent victims of destruction——in a word, the main work of the Civic Committee rests in the hands of the women.... We hope that the work thus begun will not be in vain and that when the time comes the Ukrainian woman will fulfill her duty to her country and her native land as best she can.[62]

A serious obstacle to the unification of the Western Ukrainian women was the continued ambivalence of the socialists toward the women's organization. We recall that the women's attempts to organize in 1908 had faltered because conventional women did not support the rhetoric of the young socialist women in *Meta*. In March 1919, buttressed by contacts with the self-styled Eastern Ukrainian socialist women, Dariia Starosolska again began editing a women's newspaper in Lviv, *Nasha meta*. This paper, published by a committee of socialist women, appeared from February to December 1919, with a gap between the end of March and early August, when Polish authorities suspended its publication. The women kept their constituency informed on the activities of the Ukrainian government, especially of the Western part, which, after its ouster from Lviv, made its headquarters in Stanyslaviv. Milena Rudnytska, an articulate supporter of Konovalets and of unity among Ukrainians, questioned why there were no women in the Rada in Stanyslaviv or among the fifty delegates to the Kievan Workers Congress.[63]

Later in 1919, women experienced not only the defeat of the Ukrainian cause, but also discrimination from their own colleagues. They were forced to confront the issues of *sexual* inequality that Kobrynska had raised thirty years earlier. The treatment of Ukrainian women by their own colleagues led them to study the fate of women's equality in other parts of Europe. They observed reluctantly that "not only here, but in other nations which profess political equality [for women] there is a significant weakening of the women's movement."[64]

Grudgingly, the Ukrainian socialist women began to articulate a feminist stand: "Although we clearly take a position which does not separate the women's question from those dealing with other human issues, we nevertheless consider it necessary...to devote much attention to it."[65] They still argued that there was a communality of interests between women and workers. Yet, as Kobrynska had suggested earlier (but without acknowledging her), they now maintained that Ukrainian women, even "intelligentsia" and society women, were the real proletariat of the country.[66] The articles in *Nasha meta* reflected the shifting focus from plain socialism to socialism with a feminist coloration. Articles on peasants and workers stressed the double burden of the women and the need to go beyond conventional slogans of equality to practical implementation. Articles on education, the upbringing of children, and the relief efforts reflected recognition of "the tragic conflict of the woman as a mother and citizen, [torn] between a profession and marriage."[67]

Aggressive Bolshevik policies in Ukraine and the growing visibility of the Bolshevik secret police made the women wary of the Soviet model for socialist equality. In fact, the tone of *Nasha meta* became increasingly anti-Soviet, because the Bolsheviks

> want to push the programme, and force is always bad.... As far as the nationalities are concerned, the Bolsheviks are as hostile to Ukrainians as the previous Russian bourgeois governments were. We understand their need for food, [but] we do not understand their reliance on force.... We fought against the tsarist regime, we toppled the lackey Skoropadsky.... We will give food to the Muscovite workers and labourers, but we must resist force.[68]

The decisive impetus for the organization of Ukrainian women into a single society came after Ukraine lost its bid for independence. The defeats revealed not the futility of their struggle, but the need to redouble efforts for the cause. The gaining of national independence, they were convinced, would be a gradual process, dependent upon the proper mix of pressure, consciousness and timing. One phase of their struggle had ended, another was beginning.

Part IV.

Western Ukrainian Women Between the Wars

150

12.
Organizing the Union

The Poles, integrating a nation for the first time in over a century, saw the minorities as a Trojan horse of foreign intervention. The Polish administration rescinded many of the political and cultural gains Western Ukrainians had wrested from the Austrian government and tried to make this *Rusin* population Polish. The Ukrainians in Galicia, on the other hand, resolved to be masters in their own land. Young women, especially, yearned to carry out constructive work for Ukraine. The performance of women during the liberation struggle——in the military, in the relief efforts, as well as in organizing tasks of daily survival——bolstered their self-confidence. Ukrainian women had been jailed, taken hostage and even killed by Russians, Poles, Romanians and Hungarians during the war. Moreover, male leadership had proved inadequate. Now women showed a greater willingness to join women's organizations. There was a renewed move toward the united women's organization discussed at the first women's rally in Galicia in 1884.

Throughout the 1920s, Soviet Ukraine arduously promoted the national potential within the Soviet context, although the "siren call" of "mother Ukraine" made no inroads among the peasants. While impressed by the successes of women within the communist state, the Western Ukrainian women's organization was also free of the lure of "Sovietophilism," as the attraction to Soviet Ukraine among the Western Ukrainian intelligentsia was dubbed in Galicia. The attitude of Western Ukrainians toward Soviet Ukraine remained as ambivalent as it had been toward Ukraine in the Russian Empire: attraction to the land but revulsion toward the system by which it was governed. The terror of the 1930s reduced drastically the residual attraction of communism among Western Ukrainian women and Ukrainian émigrés.

The general dissociation from socialism among the Western Ukrainian intelligentsia made women's organizations and even feminism more acceptable. Other factors contributed: Ukrainian women had experienced sexism at first hand from Ukrainian political parties, and they had maintained their families single-handedly throughout the war. Moreover, the women began to feel family-career tension as urbanization increased. Finally, they saw that women's organizations, and by implication feminism, opened a window to the outside world.

The most significant women's organization to emerge after the First World War in Western Ukraine was the Union of Ukrainian Women (Soiuz Ukrainok). Technically, the Union was a continuation of the Union of Ukrainian Women established in May 1917. Its growth followed years of deliberation among the various societies of Ukrainian women. It fused women's clubs, ladies' philanthropic societies, war-relief committees and the clubs of erstwhile young socialist women.[1]

As the appreciation of self-reliance and self-help grew, Ukrainian women convened a Women's Congress in Lviv on 22–23 December 1921. The initiative came not from the staid ladies of the Women's Union in Lviv, but from the Hanna Barvinok Women's Circle at the Ukrainian Pedagogical Society School. Konstantyna Malytska, capitalizing on her deserved reputation as a teacher and a writer, as well as on the Siberian exile from which she had triumphantly returned a year earlier, headed the organizational committee. It was composed of Sofiia Volska Murska (whose mother had helped found the Union of Ukrainian Catholics in Kiev in 1917), Olha Korenets, the mother of three daughters and a writer and teacher, Milena Rudnytska, a mathematics teacher, Olena Sichynska, the mother of Potocki's assassin, Olena Stepaniv, a geography teacher and war veteran, and Olena Fedak Sheparovych, a community activist. The Congress was announced in the progressive *Vpered* (Forward), the only Ukrainian newspaper then appearing in Lviv. The women stressed that the tradition of women's organizations was extremely important for women's solidarity and the national cause.[2]

The post-war women were more independent than their predecessors; they needed no mentors and and no guidance. Those who were not yet used to public work and public speaking learned quickly and readily from other women. A few of the leaders came from families that valued the education of women, and a number were professional women. These women did not operate in their husbands' shadows, and many were completely independent. The war, the collapse of the economy, and Polish harassment had seriously undermined the patriarchal attitudes in the family. There was no public derision of this congress, as with previous gatherings of women.

Milena Rudnytska, whose mother was a Jewish merchant's daughter and whose father had been a public official in Berezhany, although not typical of Ukrainian women, rapidly emerged as their major spokesperson. Disciplined, rational, coolly realistic, highly educated (she had almost completed a doctorate), she was thoroughly politicized. A naturally gifted speaker, she cultivated this talent. Her willingness to learn, to take on public functions, and her capacity for sustained work set her apart from the typical Western Ukrainian woman. Rudnytska resembled Kobrynska in her conviction that reason and hard work were the steps to women's equality. She could not understand self-pity. The death of her father, to whom she was deeply attached, when she was ten; the break-up of her marriage, after which her brothers remained friendly with her husband; her responsibility for the upbringing of her son; all these factors forced Rudnytska to be self-reliant. She was an astute politician who enjoyed power without being overbearing. Both she and Olena Stepaniv raised their children in a society that did not recognize broken marriages (Rudnytska's son was born in 1919; Stepaniv's in 1926). Both women intially hyphenated their names——Rudnytska-Lysiak and Stepaniv-Dashkevych——but eventually dropped their married surnames.

Olena Sheparovych was socially more prominent than Rudnytska. The family was wealthy, Sheparovych had German and French governesses, studied at Lviv and Berlin universities, travelled widely and spoke the major European languages fluently. Her father, a lawyer, had been an important public figure. Her brother, a war veteran, had attempted to assassinate Piłsudski in 1922. Olena had spent 1919–20 in the "Quadrangle of Death" in Ukraine. Her husband, Lev, a radio specialist, had helped engineer the November take-over in Lviv. He was active in the UNR, and worked subsequently in Boryslav, Berlin and finally in 1924 in Lviv for Siemens. He was politically astute and supported his wife's activities, during which hired helpers took care of their daughter.[3]

None of the women organizing the Congress identified herself readily with the socialist camp. But Dariia Shukhevych-Starosolska, the erstwhile favourite of the Galician radicals, and her colleagues now willingly joined the women's movement. They not only realized that it was a *women's*, not a *socialist* liberation movement; they promoted the change of emphasis. Yet they had neither time nor inclination to engage in feminist analyses. They felt that ideological bickering, although feminism played no part in it, had contributed to the collapse of the independent Ukrainian state. Kobrynska, who had died in January 1920, now became their heroine.

The original plan called for a two-day congress to be opened by Rudnytska's presentation on "Woman in Civic Life" and a discussion of women's press and education. One evening was to be dedicated to Kobrynska, with a theatre gala to be held on the other.[4]

Braving the severe winter and unsettled political conditions, 312 official delegates from various women's organizations in Galicia, Volhynia, Vienna, Prague, Berlin, Warsaw and Bukovyna (now part of Romania) attended the Congress. Olena Stepaniv read out greetings from Ukrainian Transcarpathian women, who were now living in a region of Czechoslovakia, and nineteen other messages of support. Representatives of sixteen organizations, from Prosvita in Lviv to Ivanna Blazhkevych's dynamic Women's Circle in the village of Denysiv, delivered personal greetings to the Congress. In attendance also were sixty individual women (not representing organizations) from the outskirts of Lviv. A few days before the convocation of the congress, the Women's Union agreed to sponsor it.

The mood of the congress was one of patriotic dedication. The consensus supported a broadly based women's organization which reflected the interests of women as a *whole* and not of any particular faction, a view expounded earlier by Rudnytska in Starosolska's *Nasha meta*:

> Women's organizations in all states, and especially in such a primitive (*pervisna*), inexperienced (*nevyroblena*), and undifferentiated society as ours, should not have any political colouring. Each one of us should...belong to an existing political party which suits us; the women's organization will link all women regardless of their class or party affiliation, because our women's interest is the same for all of us.[5]

The make-up of the honorary board reflected the all-Ukrainian character of the Congress: Olha Kobylianska, whose *Tsarivna* remained popular and whose later works evidenced a search for new levels of consciousness; Sofiia Rusova, who arrived in Lviv a day after the Congress after making a dramatic escape from the Bolshevik state; Liudmyla Starytska-Cherniakhivska, the veteran of Eastern Ukrainian organizations and literature; and Olena Sichynska. Only the last, however, was actually present at the head table.[6]

Sichynska, the mother of Myroslav Sichynsky, was the first speaker. Her very appearance heightened the sense of expectation, of creative tension, and the novel notion——for many women——that they constituted an important force. Most of the women could sympathize with Sichynska. She was a mother; many viewed her son's assassination of Potocki in 1908 as an act of heroism rather than terrorism. Malytska was elected chairperson, with Sofiia Volska-Murska, the Catholic from Eastern Ukraine and Olha Tsipanovska, a women's activist, as vice-chairpersons. The secretaries were Klymentyna Kulchytska, Sofiia Savytska and Anna Iezerska.

Rudnytska, to frequent applause, exhorted the women to effective participation in political life through a political organization. The Polish policeman present at the deliberations voiced a few objections. Toward the end of her talk Rudnystka proposed the following resolution:

> Ukrainian women consider the fundamental immutable political ideal of the Ukrainian nation an independent, sovereign, democratic (*narodopravna*) Ukrainian state with its capital in Kiev.
>
> Ukrainian women consider that the only conceivable course to attain that ideal is the *de facto* liberation of Ukrainian life in all its manifestations.
>
> Ukrainian women resolve to play a most active part in civic life for this purpose and will support the activities and strivings of our national leadership.[7]

The mention of Kiev led the policeman to disperse the women, and to prevent Malytska, the writer Hrynevych, and Dariia Starosolska from speaking. The memorial meeting in Kobrynska's honour could not be held until two months later.

Instead of the planned commemorative festivities, the delegates held a clandestine meeting. They decided to publish a brochure in honour of Kobrynska——*Pershomu ukrainskomu bortsevi za prava zhinky* (To the First Ukrainian Warrior for the Rights of Women)——which was issued in Lviv in 1922. Among their eight resolutions was a plea to the international community for greater understanding of Ukrainian political aspirations. Finally, they established a united women's society, "a federated union of women's organizations," which was to encompass all Ukrainian women outside the Ukrainian SSR. But the Polish government legalized only the existence of the Women's Union in Galicia, and blocked the formation of even a joint Galician-Volhynian Union.[8]

During its almost twenty years of existence, the Union played a significant role in the social, economic and political life of Ukrainians in Galicia and outside it.[9] The single most striking characteristic of the Union was its predominantly peasant membership. Women of other classes——mainly intelligentsia and some townswomen——formed the rank and file of the town organizations, and led some of the regional ones, but the majority of the membership was peasant. Observers were continually struck by the harmony among the classes, especially in view of the visible signs of class differentiation, educational level, patterns of speech, dress and behaviour. In an era of growing intolerance, political differentiation, and ideological incompatibility, the women maintained a democratic, open organization which opposed, clearly and articulately, all authoritarian and totalitarian ideologies. Although some women were motivated by feminist concerns, an overt declaration of feminism was made only in the mid-1930s, when the organization had achieved mass membership. [10]

The Union was successful because its activities addressed the needs of its membership. The fact that Ukrainians in Galicia were mostly peasants ensured that the activists were close to the village. The sense of perpetual crisis contributed to the generational and class co-operation among women. Wives of priests, with the support of their husbands, frequently initiated the women's organization in the villages. Elderly women of the clerical milieu also added their support. At times the outgrowth of the war-relief efforts served as a nucleus for the women's society. Other women activists filtered into the women's movement from the women's clubs, the anti-alcohol and the Prosvita societies. A significant number were teachers from the community and public schools.

The pervasiveness of nationality issues at this time has led commentators to forget that for Ukrainians, and especially for peasant women, participation in the Ukrainian national movement provided economic and other advantages. For the women activists, work in the women's movement was a form of patriotic duty; for the peasants, the issue was one of subsistence. In the first stages, the organization of women went hand in hand with the organization of peasant co-operatives. To a degree greater than in other non-socialist states, the Polish government in the inter-war years controlled both industry and economy.[11] Poland was a poor country. The area had been ravaged by the war; the protectionist empires were no longer in existence; much foreign capital had been withdrawn. The Polish government, concerned with national security, had few funds for relief, welfare and modernization of agriculture. What funds there were, moreover, were not channelled into Ukrainian concerns, but rather into efforts to settle these areas with Polish colonizers and into programmes intended to Polonize Ukrainians. Poles, especially at the local level, tried to make conditions for Ukrainians as difficult as possible. Even the pre-war safety valves for Ukrainians——emigration and seasonal labour——were cut off by the economic crises in Western Europe and the strict immigration quotas imposed in the United States. Those who had emigrated to Canada and the United States sent some aid, but it amounted only to a fraction of what overseas Poles were sending home.

Community action, therefore, was the sole means of support for Ukrainians. The co-operative movement, begun in the Austrian Empire, was unified through the Central Ukrainian Co-operative Union in 1921. Its aim was to make Ukrainians in Poland less dependent upon non-Ukrainian merchants. By eliminating the middleman, Ukrainians tried to channel profits back to the peasant. The co-operative supplied the peasants with manufactured items and bought goods from them. The slogan "Buy from your own" was not only patriotic; for the peasants it made eminent economic sense.[12]

The co-operative required the active collaboration of women. The products which Ukrainians in Galicia exported, mainly eggs and butter, fell into the women's household preserve. Housewives could sell either to the Co-operative Union or to the private entrepreneur. It was in the co-operative's interest, therefore, that the peasant women be aware of belonging to an entity larger than the village. Moreover, the village was the natural consumer for the co-operative, which could not compete with the established stores in towns. An activist of the co-operative movement grudgingly conceded this fact in his memoirs:

> Since [dairy production] is the domain of the woman, the co-operative had to become interested in women's organizations. Hence, it helped build up women's organizations and even initiated the creation of women's associations either in the circles of the Women's Union or in the women's sections of the Village Farmer (Silskyi Hospodar). Such co-operation helped in the work of the women's organization and at the same time brought the women closer to the co-operative movement.[13]

Thus, the men encouraged women to organize. But as the Union began to grow, the men viewed it with some apprehension, and by the mid-1930s tension developed between the Union and the co-operative movement.

The Union systematized the economic aspect of women's activities. Factories and stores owned and managed by individual women were supported by the Women's Union, and the owners and managers were its members. The organic link between economic development and the women's movement in Western Ukraine was evident in the 1923 reorganization (a year after its creation) of the Business Section of the Union into a self-governing women's co-operative, Ukrainian National Art (Narodne Mystetstvo). Its aim was to foster folk arts and cottage industries, especially in the infertile mountains. It created a market for the products of rustic art at a price favourable to the peasant mountaineers, and was probably one of the first conscious efforts to preserve traditional folk motifs and artifacts by adapting them to modern lifestyles. The Women's Co-operative published a lavishly illustrated monthly, *Nova khata* (The New Home), edited first by Mariia Derkach and subsequently by Lidiia Burachynska. It featured fashionable styles using traditional embroidery, and household interiors which combined indigenous rugs, wood carvings and textile products in a distinctly modern setting. The monthly was aided by Mother Severyna Paryllie, O.S.B.M., a Jewish woman who became a Catholic nun and was one of the most popular teachers at the Basilian Academy for Girls. Her pioneering efforts in the collection and preservation of folk costumes were emulated by Ukrainians all over the world. It became fashionable in the inter-war years for educated Ukrainian women to wear embroidered blouses and dresses, and to decorate their homes in a distinctly "Ukrainian" style. The Union even sponsored contests for the most original decoration or dress incorporating modern elements and folk designs.

The elevation of folk art to high fashion reflected a spontaneous attempt to maintain the village as "home" even for the rapidly growing secular intelligentsia: an atavistic drive toward idealized rural simplicity. There was also an element of national pride. Ukrainians had not produced millionaires or world-renowned scholars, musicians or dancers. But Ukrainians did produce a folk art that met with universal appreciation. Much of that art——in embroidery and batik Easter egg decoration——had been produced and preserved by women. Most women, however, deferring to the patriotic cause, failed to draw any feminist conclusions from this national service.

By 1934 the Union gave each of its branches an economic/co-operative section, and delegated a member of the village circle to take care of co-operative concerns. The latter continued to play a major role in the organization of women, and the work of the two movements overlapped. Through co-operative activities the Union participated in the work of the International Women's Co-operative Guild.[14]

Membership in Ukrainian organizations intermeshed. Women active in community organizations spontaneously formed circles affiliated with the Women's Union. Secondly, since the local police authorities did not readily permit the establishment of a new organization, women worked in branches of already existing societies. These had money and clubrooms, and thus were attractive to women. Although the local societies had a variety of names, their programmes were similar. During the 1920s, when the strength of the movement was not clear, men voiced little opposition to women's organizing; that would come in the next decade.[15]

The women organized themselves, drawing on men for advice and specifics of the law. Women were the speakers, organizers and officers of the circle. Frequently, women from adjoining villages met to help one another in the tehnicalities of organization. For instance, on 20 September 1922 (after the harvest), about 150 women, formally representing over thirty villages, held a closed meeting to develop strategies for refining organizational efforts in Pokuttia.[16]

The work of the Union was carried out on three levels: the local circle, the branch organization and the central executive board. The branch organizations, located in the towns, served as centres of activity for the intelligentsia women and as co-ordinators of village circles in the area. Branch activists made frequent trips to the villages, organized courses and lectures, and helped plan and carry out the work of the local circles.

The impact of the women's work was feminist; its justification was patriotic. Dislocations caused by the war necessitated the greater involvement of women in the everyday struggle for survival. The Union was successful because it proved that purposeful activity of the female half of the population could increase the standard of living of Ukrainian peasants. In turn, successful contacts with the peasants encouraged the intelligentsia. The Ukrainian intelligentsia in the Polish lands, as well as in other areas of Eastern and Western Europe, was never alienated from the people and during the inter-war years it threw itself wholeheartedly into community work.

The Women's Union functioned best at the grass-roots level. The activists at the branch level, and the intelligentsia——teachers, workers in the co-operative movement, wives of priests, lawyers and doctors——wanted to work "specifically in the women's sector." They made a conscious, sustained and successful effort to include as many women as they could in their work. But their memoirs stress the difficulties they encountered: the more difficult the community work, the greater its importance. The village circles mushroomed quickly, for the peasants saw the very practical benefits provided by the Union.

The organization's programme reflected the needs of its membership. The lack of political education among the women created an organization geared to pragmatic activity and not wracked by the sterile ideological discussions so characteristic of Eastern European life. The women catered to the needs of the movement. Except for the grand slogans of "God and Country" and "Sovereign Ukraine," which reflected the aspirations of all conscious Ukrainians, the women did not develop——especially in the first decade of the organization——a plan or a programme of action. As noted, the Union's major successes lay in the sphere of economics.

It is possible to reconstruct the women' work in detail from the press, some correspondence, and the few memoirs of the period. Little of the actual Union archive is extant, however. An invaluable service in this respect was performed by Olena Kysilevska, who had been the youngest participant in the Stanyslaviv rally of 1884.[17] She had committed herself to feminism from the age of six, when she discovered the injustice of the disenfranchisement of women. Married to a lawyer who was very much involved in Kolomyia's community life, she joined him in a small, part-time publishing house funded by two Simenovych brothers who later migrated to the United States and to Canada. Iuliian Kysilevsky encouraged and helped his wife found and edit a bi-monthly journal written specifically for the Ukrainian peasant women, which popularized the work of the Union. Kysilevska herself was on the Union's executive board, and headed the Organizational Section for a decade, living in a small, non-industrialized, mountainous and very picturesque town. She adopted a common-sense approach to all problems, strongly influenced by her brother in America, who extolled the "pull yourself up by your own bootstraps" philosophy of the new continent.

With the full backing of the Women's Circle in Kolomyia, whose most active members included Mariia Melnyk, Olena Vytvytska, Mariia Kichurova, Nataliia Chaikivska, Nataliia Shypailo, and Mariia Tymkevych, Kysilevska published *Zhinocha dolia* (Women's Fate) from her home. The first issue appeared in 1924, with Kysilevska as editor-in-chief, aided by the young Milia Dorotska, a local peasant, and Mariia Stavnycha.[18] Kysilevska stated that the main purpose of her journal was "to enable the peasant women to profit from equality and to...stand alongside the men in the struggle for our civil rights."[19]

For her peasant audience——for which she also edited, from 1932, an even more accessible supplement, *Zhinocha volia* (Women's Will)——she argued for feminism with no embellishments as a matter of survival. She confirmed for the peasants that immigration from Galicia for seasonal labour to Western Europe or to the New World was no longer an option. The only means of peasant subsistence was more intensive and rational farming. This could not be done by men alone; the active participation of women was crucial. Education, both formal and through community self-help efforts, a greater community role for women, and the more effective participation of women in the political life of the country were obvious preconditions for the modernization of the Ukrainian village. A women's organization was necessary to provide the peasant women with the information they needed for both rational housekeeping and an effective public role.

The modest beginnings of the organization of the women's group in the village in 1926 are evident from the advice offered by Kysilevska. She described how to get the women together, where to meet, how to conduct a meeting and set up an agenda. She discussed the officers to be elected and their functions. She suggested a division of labour and of interests: one member would report on developments in housekeeping, others would examine poultry operations, gardening, dairy production, farming, health care, child-rearing and baby care. One person should be elected to advise on educational matters and to serve as a liaison with other Ukrainian organizations. Ten years later, in a paper delivered at a conference of the Union on 15 December 1936 on the methods of organizing village women, Mariia Melnyk still referred to the work performed by the Union as pioneering.[20]

Kysilevska's journal, in which most of the women activists participated, was clearly and simply written, avoided rhetoric and bombast, dealt with manageable subjects and offered practical and detailed advice. The basic needs of women in the post-war years remained much the same as before the war. Reports on the activities of the circles show that the peasant women wanted day-care facilities; health clinics, even if staffed only by a volunteer trained to recognize rudimentary symptoms; home-economics courses; and dissemination of information on feminine hygiene, farming, gardening and child care. The journal, and the work of the Union, repeatedly met these requests. Rarely can one observe the process of modernization on such an elementary grass-roots level. We witness the inculcation of a work ethic, self-confidence and self-reliance. While Ukrainian men of the 1920s and 30s wrote studies on the relationship between the Ukrainian national character and the unhappy history of Ukraine, women saw the root of so-called peasant apathy in poverty, hunger, disease and lack of control over one's life. They sought to remedy the situation wherever they could. The major women activists in Western Ukraine were still of that generation which had to struggle for university-level education, and were better able than most to develop the sense of self-reliance in other women.

Each issue of the journal offered practical instructions on running the farm and household——what to plant, what to clear, what to throw out, what to use. Through the journal, the Union waged a continual campaign to vary the diet of the peasants and to introduce them to nutritious but not yet utilized vegetables and meats (among them veal and mutton). Exotic vegetables such as zucchini were introduced, their nutritional value discussed, and instructions given for planting, growing and cooking. Recipes for a variety of casserole dishes were given to stretch the nutritional value of what little protein was available. There were repeated warnings not to overcook vegetables. Within the first year of its appearance, the journal offered pointers on how to save fuel by building an insulated box in which cereals could finish cooking in their own steam. Another suggestion was to place the pot under a mattress, or rather, since few peasants had mattresses, under several pillows. Useful information was given to the peasant on how to make a flour paste to cover a dirt floor, how to care for babies, and how to use available natural fertilizers. In addition to regular articles on health care, there were instructions on the preparation and use of medicinal herbs.

Peasant women readily attended and even set up cooking courses, hiring and maintaining a teacher, and at times buying utensils as a group. They were interested both in varying their own diet and in teaching themselves marketable skills. A woman who could cook and bake fancy fare was much in demand in the countryside, and even more in the towns. Sewing courses also became very popular toward the end of the decade.

Kysilevska not only offered enlightened advice herself, but also allotted space in the journal for columns by her brother from the United States. He and other American immigrants tried to break the pretentiousness of Galician society. The column of advice from the New World, "like American newspapers," stressed self-reliance, small beginnings, ingenuity and willingness to take on menial work regardless of one's status as the keys to success.[21] Repeatedly the column emphasized more rational household management and the sharing of household duties among family members, including boys. It was aimed "at the young housewives [and] girls, in whom we place our entire hope, since the mothers are set in their ways in running the household."[22]

The Union exhorted women to join as many community organizations as possible——the day-care centres run privately or by other organizations, the Prosvita, the co-operative, the Community School, theatrical groups, gymnastic societies such as the old Sokil (Falcon) or the newer Luh (Meadow), and youth groups such as the scouting organization, Plast. The presence of women, argued the female activists, would have a beneficial effect upon the work of these societies. "Women will bring order to the meeting halls and even make dances more refined——and there is nothing wrong with holding a dance after work, but it must be a nice, cultured affair, as is customary among educated people."[23]

The effective participation of women in international women's organizations, which is discussed in Part V of this book, the creation of affiliated women's organizations in the United States and in Canada, and the recognition of the role of women in Ukrainian politics bolstered the self-confidence of the Galician women. Polish political pressures on Ukrainians, like Russian pressure on Poles a century earlier, led Ukrainians to cluster in both legal and illegal community organizations. The Women's Union stressed legal activity and open community action: separate women's circles or, if the police refused permission, sections of Prosvita or the Co-operative exclusively for women. Many joined the co-operative movement, which had interests similar to those of the women.[24] At rallies held throughout Ukrainian Galicia, women's links to co-operative and Prosvita work were stressed, although women constituted only 13 to 15 per cent of co-operative membership, and even fewer in the central governing board. By the end of the decade, tension had developed between the women and the co-operatives.

By the end of the 1920s women had the clout to pressure organizations such as Prosvita to take positive action to meet women's needs. In Berezhany, for example, the women pushed the local Prosvita into organizing a rally to discuss women's concerns. More than 600 women, of whom 427 were formal delegates from neighbouring villages, gathered at the local theatre. The main speakers were women from the opposite sides of the political spectrum——the radical Ivanna Blazhkevych and Mariia Bachynska Dontsova, the wife of the chief ideologist of the right-wing nationalist movement.[25]

Kysilevska looked at politics as follows: women must learn to exercise their political rights, for no one else would pass legislation on their behalf. If women had run society in the first place, she asked rhetorically, would there have been so many encumbrances on the family and its finances? "There are many economic, educational and welfare issues which the woman-housekeeper, the woman-mother, the woman-sister or daughter understands better than the man."[26]

The organization of the peasant women's circle reflected women's interconnecting interests with the broader society. Initially, the women chose an executive. Then they added persons in certain key areas, such as gardening, poultry-raising, dairy production and farming. To these were added persons who would perform the same service in health care, child-rearing and education. Before long, the co-operative had an official liaison person to keep in touch with other Ukrainian community organizations. By these means women were also drawn into political activity, and by the end of the decade began to participate in mass demonstrations of village women.

The leaders of the Union, on the branch and executive board levels, were generally young, in their mid-twenties and thirties. They were members of the intelligentsia, in the Western Ukrainian sense, by occupation or by marriage. Most had completed some type of secondary education, either teacher training or a gymnasium, but few had a university degree. They came from families that were active in the community, or even on the provincial political level. Eventually, the most active women in the Union became active in politics on the national level.

Branch activities reflected the concerns of middle-class women, cultural and organizational, rather than economic work. The branches organized sewing and cooking courses of about three months' duration for women from the villages and towns. While the participants wished to learn marketable skills, the organizers saw these undertakings in cultural terms. Many of the participants were young girls who, because of the land shortage, would have to work as domestics, at least until they earned some money for a dowry or to set up housekeeping. Service in a Polish or Polonized Jewish family for such a young woman could lead her to identify herself with the Poles, who dominated urban culture. The courses, in addition to teaching the girls marketable skills, introduced them to Ukrainian society and culture. The larger branches maintained dormitories for participants: the major women's schools, as in Lviv and Przemyśl, rented out dormitory space for them. Job referral services and clubs for domestics developed from these courses.

The branch organization elected officers responsible for liaison with the village. Many found personal contact with the Co-operative useful, and by 1934, the Central Executive Board agreed on the appointment of a special representative for each branch of the Co-operative.[27]

It was difficult for Ukrainian women to make inroads into the urban ranks. Retail trade was still largely in the hands of the Jewish population. Although Jewish merchants often found it useful to know Ukrainian for business transactions, they frequently identified themselves with the Poles. As Polish industry remained underdeveloped, there was little peasant influx into the towns. The few Ukrainian burghers were not eager to have the women join a Women's Union. Nevertheless, some progress was made through energetic individuals. If these were removed, however, the circle tended to disintegrate.[28]

Women's societies, as well as societies with primarily female membership, or which were concerned with women's issues, such as the Society for

Day-Care Centres, the Committee for the Defence of Political Prisoners and the Medical Advice Clinic in Lviv reported regularly to the Women's Union. The most significant among them were the Society for the Care of Children and Youth, and the Day-Care Society founded in Lviv before the First World War, which expanded its activity in the inter-war period. It administered a Fresh Air programme, gave supplementary food handouts, and provided financial aid to youth groups. The generous financial support of Metropolitan Sheptytsky aided the functioning of the Lviv Mothers' Clinic (Poradnia Materei), which was connected with the Ukrainian Hospital (Narodna Lichnytsia). Medical personnel and medical students were aided by volunteers——mostly Lviv women such as Mariia Perfetska, Mariia Voevidka and Irena Fedusevych. Other women's societies, among them the Marian Sodality and the Hanna Barvinok Circle, were constituent parts of the Union.[29]

The central executive board of the Union was elected annually by delegates from branch organizations at a convention held in Lviv. The village circles participated by electing their representatives to the branch organization. Usually, women elected a five-member board which then appointed a president, two vice-presidents, a secretary and a treasurer. At the same time, an unspecified number of women were elected to serve on boards. In the 1920s there were eleven boards: organizational, cultural-educational, folk art, youth, village activities, and household affairs, economic and co-operative concerns, finances, public health, liaison with Ukrainian women's organizations outside Galicia, and international relations.

A group of women activists formed the nucleus of the Union leadership during its twenty-year existence. While it did not exclude the socialists or the nationalists, the Union tended to attract moderates. Like most women's organizations, a large part of its membership was composed of married women. Attempts to organize teenagers, both in the villages and towns, were not suc-cessful. Most Union activists and members led conventional lives. A number of the prominent women, however, were either separated or divorced (depending on the local law),[30] giving ammunition to anti-feminist arguments. The Union gave special attention to women prominent in their fields. Kobylianska received periodic acclamation, but not the financial and medical aid she badly needed. Uliana Kravchenko, retired in Przemyśl from her teaching career, became the poet laureate of women. She wrote the Union anthem (for which Anton Rudnytsky, Milena's younger brother, composed the music) and poems for var-ious occasions. Katria Hrynevych, whose historical novels provided Ukrainian women with positive role models, was drawn to the work of the Union's Executive Board. New talent was not only encouraged but sought out. Work on the local level accustomed women to the public forum.

The first president of the Union was Mariia Biletska, the long-time principal of the Ukrainian Girls' School in Lviv. In 1922–3 it was led by Malytska, a writer and a pedagogue. Then Olena Fedak Sheparovych, the sister of the man who attempted to assassinate Piłsudski in 1922, led the Union for the next two years. Her first treasurer was Olha Levytska Basarab, who had organized aid to the wounded in Vienna during the war. In February 1924, she was arrested by the Polish police on suspicion of belonging to a political terrorist group and brutally killed. The death, at first covered up by the Poles, was later presented as a suicide, but the exhumation of her body proved otherwise. Her martyr's death endowed her life of simple patriotic dedication——so characteristic of Ukrainian women——with an aura that inspired the activities of the women and the Union. Another activist, who led the Union in 1927, was Mariia Bachynska Dontsova. Her marriage to the nationalist ideologue Dmytro Dontsov cut short her leadership, and in 1928, Milena Rudnytska was elected president, remaining at her post for the next ten years.

In December 1928, the Union decided to vote as a group for the President, and separately for all members of the executive board. The election of Rudnytska, their first choice, had momentous consequences. Rudnytska was re-elected president each year until the disintegration of the Union in 1939; she also tried unsuccessfully to rejuvenate it in the emigration after the Second World War. Without doubt, Rudnytska was one of the most prominent Ukrainian women of modern times. She made significant contributions to the social and political life of the community in the 1920s and 30s and was a pillar of the Ukrainian women's movement. Certainly the Union was neither exclusively her achievement nor her sole accomplishment. Her life, after all, was similar to that of thousands of other Union women. But she provided the movement with a voice and with leadership, bringing it out of the women's sphere into the political and international arena. As a leader, Rudnytska was energetic, effective, an excellent organizer and a persuasive speaker and politician, who represented Ukrainians well in the Polish parliament and on the international forum. Her personal prestige grew with that of the organization she represented.

The rapid growth of the Union necessitated a restructuring of its central organizations in 1928. Instead of the eleven committees, which proved to be too unwieldy, four central sections were formed——educational, organizational, social and business. The latter initially worked closely with the Co-operative Association and fostered the creation and growth of women's co-operatives. The organizational section co-ordinated the formation of new sections and branches, while the educational category developed study programmes, ran teacher-training courses, and supervised the preparation and dissemination of materials, texts, lecture notes and discussion topics. Its interests ranged from history to cross-stitch embroidery, from economic co-operatives to weaving, and it represented women of villages and towns.[31]

The make-up of the new executive board illustrated the continuity of the organization. Sheparovych was the first vice-president, Anna Palii the recording secretary; Kysilevska and Olha Paliiv, respectively, chaired and recorded the organizational section; Kysilevska was also the chairperson of the press section; Iryna Vytkovytska and Mariia Mudryk, long-standing members of the executive, headed the new economic section. Dr. Sofiia Parfanovych, an anti-alcohol activist, and Evheniia Tyshynska, who was prominent in the lay

Catholic movement, headed the educational section. Dr. Dariia Dzerovych, who had moved back to Lviv from Vienna, headed international relations, while Mariia Koltuniuk chaired the social affairs section. A sub-committee was responsible for the village home-economics courses. That same year, the election of Kysilevska to the Senate and Rudnytska to the Polish parliament further enhanced the prestige of the Union.

The members of the Union considered their work an important civic and social duty rather than a club or charitable activity, and easily dismissed occasional taunts. Although they frequently engaged in "auxiliary" activities such as preparing refreshments or holding fund-raising lotteries, this sort of work was considered peripheral. The Union was an integral part of Ukrainian society and its work affected the life of the community economically, politically and socially. Above all, it developed a role model for women that went beyond the confines of the home. By expanding the woman's sphere of interest and stressing self-improvement, the Union affected the entire Ukrainian society. The ideal was not that of the housewife, but that of the politically aware woman who had become an active citizen. Even while the Ukrainian middle class——intelligentsia in the Western Ukrainian sense——was developing, the bourgeois ideal of domesticity never took root in Western Ukraine.

These same activities made women increasingly aware of feminist concerns. Sensitivity to overt and covert discrimination was felt mainly by those women working in the male domain. Such concerns eluded the rank-and-file members of the Union, for whom economic and national concerns (the two being tantamount to politics) remained of prime importance. Sexual equality achieved after the war in some legal and educational areas hindered the development of feminist consciousness. Also, political harassment and continuing economic crises made feminist concerns seem secondary to the interests that fell broadly under the label of nationalism. Women, like men, were drawn into the whirlpool of national antagonisms that permeated political life in Galicia.

Next to home economics, education was of primary concern to women. Throughout the 1920s, the struggle for the preservation of Ukrainian-language schools on the elementary and secondary levels, and the creation of a Ukrainian university, which the Poles had promised, were major issues in Ukrainian political life. Priests, and by extension their wives; teachers, many of them women; students and their parents were drawn directly into the fray. Education touched the lives of the entire Ukrainian population in Poland and also directly contributed to the involvement of women in public issues.

Before 1914, the struggle for educational opportunity for women had been a goal for politically aware Ukrainians; in the Polish Republic the issue became one of nationality rather than sex. Education provided the only means of social mobility and affected every family. The elementary school, in which religion continued to be a compulsory subject, was integrally connected with community concerns. Women were directly involved, because their children were subjected to daily harassment by Polish teachers and through a Polish curriculum. Even the characterization of the native language in documents and in the census as the "mother tongue" stressed the community role of the mother.[32]

The importance of pre-school education and day care for children had been established by the first generation of women activists. Setting up day-care centres, play groups, kindergartens, and time sharing for the care of children were an integral part of the women's work. The Union arranged for cultural events for and by the children, as well as for the popularization of children's literature and theatre. It engaged in these activities at all levels——village, branch and the central executive. The greater the involvement of the women in the co-operative movement, the more glaring was the need for child care. The more aggressive the attempts of, say, the Polish nuns to establish day-care centres in the Ukrainian villages, the more active the Ukrainian women, nuns and lay women alike, became in joining forces to set up Ukrainian day-care centres.

In the words of one writer, "from the first years of [Polish] independence the gradual curtailment of Ukrainian schools in favour of Polish ones was very much in evidence."[33] Ukrainians had established Prosvita in 1868 and the Ukrainian Pedagogical Society (which subsequently became the Native School, Ridna Shkola) in 1881 mainly to foster the education of their own people. Ridna Shkola attempted to co-ordinate Ukrainian private schools, and in 1920 all of them (except the Przemyśl Institute for Girls, the Basilian-run schools, and those run by the Redemptorist order) voluntarily placed themselves under its jurisdiction.[34] The closing of government-run Ukrainian-language schools, and the establishment of bilingual schools, generated the growth of Ukrainian private schools. Many Ukrainian children, however, were forced to attend Polish schools, even when there were no Poles in the village. The enforced use of a foreign language accelerated the political awareness of children's mothers and prompted them to join Ukrainian community associations such as the Women's Union that tried to alleviate the situation.

The Polish government also shut down secondary schools with Ukrainian as the language of instruction, and increased teaching in Polish. Secondary schools became tinderboxes for ethnic confrontation. Polish policies, introducing compulsory participation of teenagers in public celebrations honouring Polish heroes in an attempt to forge new Polish patriots, backfired. The closing of the Ukrainian scouting organization, Plast, and the encouragement of student pogroms of Ukrainians also rankled the impressionable Ukrainian youth, who were frequently provoked into demonstrations. Such tactics strengthened the trend to subordinate all other issues to that of nationality. Young women, therefore, were not likely to develop feminist concerns *per se*.

As a reaction to Polish repression and to the growth of clandestine organizations among Ukrainian youth, mothers more readily involved themselves in the politics of the Union. The traditional gravitation of women in the legislature toward educational and social concerns meant that Kysilevska and Rudnytska, after their election in 1928, were at the forefront of the defence of Ukrainian youth. On behalf of the entire Ukrainian community, they spoke out against the closing of Ukrainian-language schools and the discrimination against Ukrainian organizations.

The Union and the teachers, especially women, co-operated. Embattled on all fronts, secondary schools for girls became bastions of the national spirit. Mother Severyna Paryllie, who continued teaching at Lviv and collecting folk costumes, stressed the connection between the social, economic, ethnographic and pedagogical activities of the students and faculty.[35]

The social welfare of the children was another aspect of the Union's work. Branch sections of the Union organized supplementary kitchens, fresh-air funds and emergency care for needy students. Cooking and sewing courses were so popular that in many towns they came to be held on a regular basis, and dormitories and other facilities were established for the girls. The economic depression that followed the inflation of the early 1920s, and the decision of the Ukrainian schools to dismiss female teachers before males, as well as to cut the salaries of married women, stimulated some feminist discussion. But its greatest impact was to increase the popularity of trade education for women. The Union urged unemployed teachers to supplement their education with practical skills and with village co-operative work. By the beginning of the 1930s, trade and technical education gained many adherents among previously wary parents. Trade and technical courses became increasingly institutionalized,[36] and the union branches tried to establish trade schools and systematize those run on an irregular basis.

In discussing a suitable career for women, Mariia Krushelnytska, whose family emigrated to the Soviet Union only to perish there, stated: "Every career is suitable for women, once the old tradition is finally broken."[37] The Polish government, intent upon Polonizing the village as well as Ukrainians, was reluctant to permit the opening of trade schools for Ukrainian girls. But after several years, the Basilian nuns were permitted finally to open a three-year trade school in Lviv in mid-1929.[38]

Ukrainian interest in pre-school education encouraged the Ukrainian Basilian nuns and particularly the Sisters Servant of Mary, to open new schools. The latter order of nuns did not require as high a dowry as the former, and had more candidates than it could handle. These nuns opened new houses in Uhniv in 1927, Zhuravnytsi in 1928 and Bircha in 1929. The nuns also attended the special training courses that were required to run day-care centres and the Union worked with them in running the day-care programme.[39]

The Union was also involved in programmes of continuing education. These were not the systematized courses of today's adult education, but rather series of lectures, discussions, and readings on subjects of interest to women or within the competence of the available speakers. Self-education was a major plank of the Union programme, as was the fostering of self-motivation and individual growth.

Work with children, either in the centres run by the Union or in helping other schools, constituted the most popular activity of the Union. Children's recreational, cultural and sporting activities included theatricals, outings, concerts, and masquerade or theme parties that stimulated the children's imagination. High-school students home for holidays were very much involved in preparing theatricals in which children were major participants.

The Union had no direct involvement in the quest for a Ukrainian university, a major concern of the Ukrainian community in the 1920s. Since the Poles showed little inclination to carry out their promise to establish such a university, the issue was again a national one. Women participated equally with the men in all phases of the struggle, including its most dramatic aspect——the functioning of the Clandestine University in Lviv between 1922 and 1925. "We, the young students of the Clandestine University, did not think about feminism, but only deliberated on the [means] by which we could best withstand persecution by the Poles."[40] The nationality issue was so pervasive that it overshadowed the social one.

The Women's Union opposed the growing tendency toward anti-intellectualism, but the nurturing of an intellectual elite was not its forte. A large part of the Union's leadership, while fully supporting educational and career opportunities for women, did not consider the quest for a university education or a scholarly career to be women's main objectives. The creation of a Ukrainian Association of University Women in October 1924 was viewed with great skepticism by most of the women, and with ridicule by the male establishment. Even the prestige of Olena Stepaniv Dashkevych, who was elected its president, did not remedy the situation. The impetus toward the creation of the Association (its Ukrainian name was Tovarystvo Zhinok z Vyshchoiu Osvitoiu) came from Olena Zalizniak, who saw the opportunities for international lobbying. There was some interlocking membership in the Union and the Association——Zalizniak, Rudnytska, Mariia and Sofiia Fedak, Olha Mryts, Olena Sheparovych. There were, nevertheless, cases of open hostility between the two organizations, and the general problems of Galicia overrode the interests of the Association.[41]

Throughout the 1920s, as the economic and political prospects of Ukrainians in Poland became increasingly bleak, Soviet Ukraine was seen by many as a new entity which, given proper guidance and pressure, could well serve the Ukrainian cause. Unsettled conditions in the Soviet Union, its ostensible break with the centralized Russian Empire, its apparent compliance with the national aspirations of Ukrainians by the creation of a separate, albeit federated Ukrainian Republic, its pursuit of Ukrainization, and its renunciation of war communism and espousal of the New Economic Policy seemed to justify such a purpose. Despite the return of an openly disillusioned Vynnychenko from the Soviet Union in 1922——Vynnychenko, more than other Ukrainian intellectuals, wanted to believe in the good will of the Soviets——pro-Soviet Ukrainian sentiments grew in Galicia throughout the 1920s. They were fostered actively by the Kharkiv government and by the Soviet Ukrainian consulate in Lviv, headed by Iurii Lapchynsky. Polish persecution of Ukrainians, the economic crises, and especially the inability of Ukrainian intellectuals and artists to obtain gainful employment further strengthened pro-Soviet sentiments.[42]

Fewer women than men succumbed to the Sovietophile tendency, although mothers and wives generally emigrated with their men. For one thing, many women were passionately attached to their native area and felt they were needed at home. Secondly, the women were either singularly level-headed in their assessment of Soviet Ukraine or politically unaware. At a time when Lapchynsky was the invited guest at many Galician Ukrainian functions (as late as 1929 he was a guest of honour at the Annual General Meeting of Prosvita), the Women's Union, at its meeting in 1928,

> proclaimed a boycott of the pro-Soviet press and those activists who kept one foot in the national camp and the other in the communist world...these resolutions brought many complications and unpleasantness to the Lviv Central Office. But the Ukrainian women did not abandon their position and eventually were able to note with satisfaction the increased strength of the anti-Bolshevik front.[43]

Although peasants did not emigrate to the USSR, communist propaganda made inroads into the Western Ukrainian village. It was effective on the north-eastern frontier, as indicated in contemporary Soviet scholarship.

The political differences that characterized Ukrainian society were reflected within the Union, although no formal split occurred within it. The most crucial elections in the Union were held on the eve of the general elections in Poland in 1928. The contenders were Malytska, Rudnytska, Pavlykovska and Zalizniak. The Poles opposed Malytska's election. A writer and pedagogue, she did not enjoy administrative work, and withdrew her candidacy. Iryna Makukh Pavlykovska and Olena Okhrymovych Zalizniak leaned toward the nationalists and toward the subordination of women's issues to national concerns. Pelenska and Mudrykova, the former connected with Narodne mystetstvo, the latter with a lifetime of activity in the women's movement, were also candidates for the presidency.[44] At the same time, there was open disagreement over the Union's relations with the clandestine nationalist movement, which in January 1929 became the Organization of Ukrainian Nationalists (OUN), to be discussed below. Suffice it to say here that Konovalets, the founder of the Ukrainian Military Organization (UVO), did not see eye-to-eye with the whole programme of the OUN, although the OUN claimed to be a direct descendant of the UVO. Konovalets, married to a sister of Olena Sheparovych, was a close acquaintance of Rudnytska. Politically, Rudnytska leaned toward democratic liberalism, and she staunchly defended the autonomy of the women's movement.

Rudnytska's election underlined the position the women had taken a year earlier——the Union would remain a supra-party organization that encouraged its members to use all legal channels for political work. It would not, as an organization, participate in the work of "nationalist parties" (*v natsionalistychnykh partiiakh*). If any of its members chose to engage in that work, they were not to wear the insignia of the Women's Union.[45]

Local authorities in Lviv were perturbed by the growth of the women's organization. The campaign against the Ukrainian women took a strange turn. Each year in February, on the Sunday closest to the date of the murder of Olha Basarab, the Union held a solemn memorial service.

On 17 February 1929, however, after the service in the Church of the Transfiguration (built in the 1890s with Ukrainian community funds), three women, authorized by Senator Cherkavsky on behalf of the Committee to Aid Political Prisoners, held a collection outside the church. None of the women was a member of the Union. All three were detained by the police but released the same day. The following day, however, they were rearrested at work and charged with defrauding the institutions at which they worked, Tsentrosoiuz and Silskyi Hospodar. Despite attestation to the contrary by their employers, the women were imprisoned for a few days with common prisoners and brought to trial. The court dismissed the charges.[46]

The affair would have been dismissed as a petty farce, but the Lviv City Starostvo (city council) used the women's arrest as a pretext to suspend the Women's Union on 18 March 1929. The Union's books and monies were impounded. The Lviv Women's Union received the following document from the local officials addressed to the executive board of the Union "at the hands of Madame Member of Parliament, Milena Rudnytska":

> Inquests undertaken by administrative and court authorities have proved that on 17 February 1929, members of the Ukrainian Women's Union, on the occasion of the memorial service for the soul of Olha Basarab organized by the Union at the Church of the Transfiguration, carried out an illegal collection of funds and a demonstrative sale of ribbons ostensibly on behalf of the Committee of Aid to Political Prisoners. As a result of this, the Union overstepped its statutory bounds by taking part in actions of a sharply political nature. Hence, taking note of the above, the Lviv City Starostvo, on the basis of paragraph 25, article 2, of the Statute of 15 November 1867, number 134 Dpp (*sic*), is suspending the activity of the Women's Union as of today. This decision can be contested within fourteen days, beginning with the day after its delivery at the office of the Province in Lviv, through the city office. Contesting the decision does not empower non-compliance with it. Signed, Gr. Starostva Kliots.[47]

Such a flagrantly ridiculous charge, made when the Sejm was in session, only provided publicity for the Ukrainian Women's Union. Rudnytska immediately raised the dissolution of the Union as an urgent matter in the Sejm debates. She characterized the Union

> as a feminist organization which has as its aim the civic enlightenment of Ukrainian women and the raising of their educational level as well as their economic welfare. It has a number of branches in cities, and a whole series of

peasant circles; it maintains day-care centres, organizes home-economics and general courses for peasants. Its activity did not and does not have a political character.[48]

The Sejm supported Rudnytska's arguments that the women in question were not members of the Union, and, moreover, that even if they had been, they had not engaged in any illegal activity. Rudnytska also pointed out that even if individual members of a society had engaged in political activity, there was no legal basis for dissolving the whole society. The suspension of the Union made the front pages of the Ukrainian press, and buoyed the visibility and importance of the women and the Union. The Union emerged triumphant, and the suspension was lifted within weeks.[49] Thus, it entered its second decade of existence as a recognized and established force in the Ukrainian community.

13.
Toward a Democratic Union

The high point of the Ukrainian women's movement outside the Soviet Union was attained on 23 and 24 June 1934. More than 10,000 women convened in Stanyslaviv (now Ivano-Frankivsk) to mark the fiftieth anniversary of the first women's rally in Western Ukraine. It was a magnificent, orderly and moving demonstration of unity and strength. The mass participation of peasant women, the well planned and effectively executed programme, the dignified manner in which the women refused to let themselves be provoked into petty demonstrations (which might have been used as a pretext to disband the congress, as in 1921), underscored the maturity of the organization, the vision of its leadership and the responsiveness of the rank and file.

In the five years since the first suspension of the Union in Lviv in 1929, and its triumphant reinstatement, its membership had more than doubled. Circles were established in most Galician villages and related organizations sprung up in Volhynia and other Ukrainian areas. Ukrainian women became more visible in the co-operative movement and in the economic life of the country in general. But despite the co-operative activity, Ukrainians were slow to move into commercial ventures. For years, the only Ukrainian-owned factory was the candy-making concern founded by Klymentyna Hlynska-Avdykovych. The only Ukrainian-owned lingerie-making co-operative in Eastern Galicia was the Ukrainian Women's Bazaar in Kolomyia. The first Ukrainian-owned factory for sweaters and hose was founded in Lviv only in 1928 by a woman, Olha Melnyk.[1]

The co-operatives flourished, often through a successful *spiritus movens*. Ivanna Blazhkevych, from the village of Denysiv, continued the activities she had begun earlier among the peasant women, and reported in 1931 that the Denysiv women were organizing a co-operative.[2] Courses organized for or by women also prospered. The number of exclusively women's co-operatives increased, and in 1927 a congress of women's co-operatives was held in Lviv.[3] The principle of co-operation as a method of organization swept the Ukrainian community: the Society of Widows of Priests in Lviv regrouped itself as a co-operative, Dolia (Fate). A society to care for Ukrainian Catholic domestics based on the co-operative principle, Buduchnist (Future), was also founded in Lviv.

Western Ukraine had never fully recovered from the war. Its industrial base was non-existent, and it received only minimal aid from the government and from Ukrainians abroad. The post-war inflation, followed by the depression, were heightened by natural disasters such as the flood of 1927, which hit the Ukrainian villages in the foothills of the Carpathian Mountains. Women were the worst hit. In the 1920s, women and youngsters received up to 40 per cent less wages than men for their labour. The only career opportunities for Ukrainian peasant women were as domestics, yet in the inter-war years the number of Ukrainian households that could employ domestics declined drastically, compelling these young women to work for Poles.[4] Land hunger was widespread; there was a food shortage, a lack of schools, and no jobs. The co-operative tried to ease the predicament. Dedicated volunteers, such as Blazhkevych or Kysilevska, were replaced by trained co-operative activists——among them Dr. Kharytia Kononenko, the daughter of émigrés from Eastern Ukraine, a graduate of Czech schools; and Neonila Selezinka, a dynamic women's and co-operative activist. These women were effective organizers who combined zeal with training.

Ukrainian men initially paid little attention to the work of the women. When they did notice the strength of the women's movement, they sought to dissipate it by creating women's sections within male institutions. The women met this attack by becoming even better organized.

Piłsudski's coup in 1926 did not ameliorate the Ukrainians' position in Poland. Whatever one's analysis of Piłsudski's policies, the position of the national minorities became worse under the strongman and his successors than it had been under the democratic regime. Piłsudski and his camp were, however, popular among the outspoken Polish women. The spirit of dedication and the glorification of service to the nation in the performance of one's duties permeated the largely middle-class Polish women's organizations.

As various Ukrainian attempts to make compromises with the Poles failed, the popularity of extreme Ukrainian nationalism increased, particularly among the youth. Protest actions against the government escalated, especially in schools and in the countryside. Reflecting the continued land hunger of the peasants and their resentment of the large estates that still dominated Galician agriculture, the OUN initiated a series of sabotage actions in 1930. It began by burning bales of wheat and hay harvested on the large estates. The OUN was also accused of burning 62 houses, 67 taverns, 112 mills and 78 other buildings. It robbed a post office and attempted to disrupt communications, and one man was killed.

The government decided that immediate, drastic action was required. The ensuing "pacification" took the form of a pogrom of Ukrainian leaders through-out Eastern Galicia. Priests, peasants, activists, teachers, women, and some children fell victim to Polish repression in September and October 1930. The peasants were forced to feed the army and police units used against them.

Ukrainian shops were looted, and community meeting rooms vandalized. Ivanna Blazhkevych, despised by the Poles because she was of mixed Ukrainian-Polish parentage, was brutally beaten during the terror. In fact, the government admitted to 1,800 beatings. A considerable number of the victims were women.[5]

The pacification drew women further into public activity. It offered visible and dramatic proof of the vulnerability of the village and the crucial need for organization. The Union network penetrated deeper into the Ukrainian villages, which perturbed the Polish authorities, who made great efforts to build up Polish organizations in Eastern Galicia. In turn, the clandestine OUN, which most openly voiced an intransigent position vis-à-vis Poland, placed its hopes on voluntarism, self-reliance and nationalism. It viewed the woman as a helpmate and potential mother. A nationalist ideologue, Dmytro Dontsov, stressed amorality and complete dedication to the cause. OUN members engaged in acts of terrorism directed against the Poles, and later against Ukrainian political opponents. The ideology generated a popular momentum that swept the area at a time of bleak economic outlook, political repression and national discrimination.

The leadership of the Women's Union opposed many tenets of the OUN, but an increasing number of its members became either active OUN members or supporters. Yet, amid growing internal dissension among Ukrainians, the Union managed to preserve, expand and strengthen itself. Then a myth originated that the Union was an adjunct of the Ukrainian National Democratic Union (UNDO). UNDO emerged from an understanding between a number of Ukrainian political parties in 1925 and became a major legal Ukrainian political configuration in Galicia. Its platform was moderate, liberal, democratic and pro-agrarian. It opposed the continuation of the war effort——i.e., the terrorist activities of the OUN——against the Poles and sought to defend Ukrainians by all available legal means. It was by far the single most popular party among Ukrainians and combined some notable political talent. It was the largest Ukrainian political party in the election of 1928, and included Milena Rudnytska in its ranks.

Economics played a major role in the emergence of women. The war and inflation, as much as a quest for equality, had pushed women into the labour force. Despite the women's past patriotic work, Ukrainian men turned against the interests of working women, urging that men, especially heads of households, be given jobs in preference to women, and that women be first to be dismissed. The annual meeting of the Women's Union held in Lviv on 4 and 5 December 1931 in the large hall of the Besida, in addition to its regular programme, also addressed the needs of professional women. Among its resolutions, it defended women's right to work, which was being severely curtailed by their own professional associations.[6] What made this resolution extraordinary was its adoption by the entire general meeting of an organization largely composed of non-professional women dependent upon the earnings of men.

In the early 1930s, the Soviet Union dropped its Ukrainization policy and pursued forcible collectivization in the Ukrainian village. In making requisitions of grain, the Soviets stripped Ukrainian villages of food and blocked access to towns. Between 4 and 7 million Ukrainians in the Soviet Union starved to death. In the autumn of 1932, news of the famine reached Galicia. As the situation worsened in the following year, the annual meeting of the Union on 9 May 1933 was held in the shadow of the famine. The Union passed a resolution stressing the importance of the organized women's movement for the whole of Ukrainian society:

> The difficult and grave moment which the Ukrainian Nation is now experiencing makes it imperative that Ukrainian women work energetically in all aspects of civic life. Important tasks face the women's organization. Hence the Union demands full consolidation of women's forces, their unity and the strengthening of internal discipline in our organization.
>
> Firmly convinced of the great role which befalls the Ukrainian woman in the struggle of the Nation and in the creation of national culture, the general meeting empowers the Board to stand guard over the rights which belong to the Ukrainian woman in her own community.[7]

A nation as embattled as Ukraine needed symbolic acts to assert its existence and power. There was some talk in the Ukrainian community of holding a congress composed of non-Soviet Ukrainians. The women, who had not been invited to the initial planning sessions, decided to hold a grandiose congress of their own to mark the fiftieth anniversary of the 1884 Stanyslaviv rally and to demonstrate the strength of the Women's Union despite attacks against it.

The women stressed the historical continuity of the movement. They singled out the aged Ivanna Sembratovych-Osterman, who had aided Kobrynska in collecting funds for the first women's publications. They featured the living contributors to *Pershyi vinok*——Sydora Navrotska-Paliiv, Klymentyna Popovych-Boiarska, Olha Roshkevych-Ozarkevych (Franko's first love) and Mykhailyna Roshkevych-Ivanets. Boiarska was bitter; she had sacrificed her literary talents to support her family and was living proof of the pitfalls of that compromise.[8]

The honorary committee was composed of women activists: Mariia Biletska, Olha Kobylianska, Uliana Kravchenko, Sofiia Rusova, and Hermina Shukhevych. The official purpose of the congress was stated in patriotic terms:

> The congress will chart the role of the woman in the struggle of the nation. It will underscore our vast responsibility before the nation; our responsibility as citizens and as mothers of new generations. At the same time, it will serve to remind our entire community that to be able to fulfill her great tasks the Ukrainian woman must enjoy complete equality in all aspects of life, as well as the opportunity to be able to influence its development.[9]

Although Lviv had better facilities, the congress was held in Stanyslaviv to maintain historical continuity. The preparatory committee was chaired by Mariia Makarushka, with Mariia Biliak as vice-president, while Olena Sheparovych and Ielysaveta Kruk shared the secretarial duties. Iryna Bonkovska was the chief financial officer. The programme committee was chaired by the determined Olena Zalizniak, and press and public relations by Kysilevska, who was aided by the youthful Lidiia Burachynska, the editor of *Nova khata*. Special publications were in the purview of Mariia Strutynska, the writer. Local arrangements were handled by Sofiia Olesnytska, a Union activist from Stanyslaviv, and Amaliia Rubel, chairperson of the Stanyslaviv Union branch. Much of the co-ordination fell to Olena Sheparovych.

Particular emphasis was placed upon the area in which most Ukrainian women could make a direct contribution to the national culture: the creation, collection and preservation of folk art. In addition to song and dance, Ukrainians were well known abroad for their colourful embroidery and textiles, and their exquisite Easter eggs. These art forms were very much the products of women's hands and would, for later generations, come to symbolize the Ukrainian ethos. After Olena Pchilka published her book on folk ornament, the women had fostered expansion of folk arts, which became virtually an integral part of the truly Ukrainian home. Professionals headed the effort. Olena Kulchytska, the painter and graphic designer, was in charge of the Art Section; while Iryna Gurgula, an employee at the National Museum of Ukrainian Folk Arts in Lviv, co-ordinated the collection of folk art. Work on handicrafts and folk art promoted the unity of the women and engendered in them a feeling of pride in their work.[10]

The women stressed the historical roots of the women's movement in Ukraine and its integral connection with Ukrainian society rather than foreign influences. In December 1933, questionnaires were sent to branches and circles, asking for detailed information on their founding and work. The women collected photographs, and invited the elderly to write at least brief recollections of earlier events.

The preparations for the congress were meticulous, and the event was well publicized. It represented all Ukrainian women's groups outside the Soviet Union, including those of the American continent. Mary Sheepshanks, of the Women's International League for Peace and Freedom, was an invited speaker. The Congress was a rally of the national spirit and of women's solidarity. In an attempt to limit the number of women attending the Congress, the Poles at the last minute cancelled the reduced-fare train tickets upon which many Ukrainian women had counted to get to Stanyslaviv. Some women ran short of funds and returned in tears from the train stations. Iryna Makukh Pavlykovska, a political activist and the daughter of a renowned peasant political figure, declared defiantly at the congress:

"No one can stop us; we will pay the full fare; if they won't let us into the trains, we will come by horse-drawn wagons; if they stop the wagons, we will come on foot! Nothing will stop us! Is that not so, sisters?"——and thousands of voices answered her——YES! YES![11]

Unlike the first rally of the women in 1884, the proceedings began with a religious service.[12] Thus, the golden anniversary of the Ukrainian women's movement in Western Ukraine began with a moving memorial service in honour of past activists and included an outdoor high mass celebrated by Khomyshyn's aide (the Bishop himself was too controversial a figure to appear personally). Outdoor religious celebrations were particularly festive and, at that time, not very common. They heightened the importance of the occasion.

The four-day congress programme reflected the interests of the women, and drew them closer together as a group. The memory of Kobrynska figured prominently in the festivities. Maria Strutynska spoke about her; and Kysilevska published a very lengthy memoir about Kobrynska written by Olha Duchyminska.

The slogan of the first day was "Our Past and Our Tasks." Zinaida Mirna, formerly of Kiev and Kamianets-Podilskyi, spoke on the historical development of Eastern Ukraine and focused on the position of women and children in Soviet Ukraine. Anna Kurylo from Detroit described the work of women in the United States. Mariia Livytska, the wife of the president-in-exile of the Ukrainian 'People's Republic, analyzed the participation of women in the political life of the emigration. Hanna Chykalenko Keller, in observing West European developments, pointed out the tortuous relationship between feminism and conventional democracy. Olena Zakhariasevych delivered what seems to have been an uncontroversial speech on women and religion. Mariia Melnyk spoke on young people in the women's movement. A youth representative, Oksana Lemekha, was barred from reading a nationalistic political statement, as it might have served as a pretext for the police to disband the congress. Some young women present shuffled their feet in displeasure. "But most of the participants realized that there was more to be gained by having the Congress run its fully planned course than by having it closed. Therefore, they controlled themselves."[13]

Sunday, the second day of the congress, was the highlight. It began with a mass dedicated to the "Peasant Women." More than 2,500 peasant women, from teenagers to grandmothers, participated in the mass and march, which was to have been held in an open field beyond town. The police, however, feared that it might incite a riot. The parade, therefore, was held in the narrow confines of the old town. The containment of this colourful procession——since most of the women wore some type of folk costume——only made it more impressive, and it was viewed by a crowd of over 6,000.

Mrs. Sheepshanks delivered her greeting in English; she was answered in her native language by Marta Olesnytska-Rudnytska, to the thunderous applause of the women to whom the English words connoted international support. Rudnytska, Kysilevska, Chykalenko, Rusova and Pavlykovska spoke at the rally. Bahrynivska spoke on behalf of the Volhynian women; Mariia Stankova from Zakarpattia was seconded by an effective peasant speaker from Iasynnia, Mariia Klempushova. Mrs. Horbacheva represented the Polissian marshlands and Hanka Romanchych represented Canada. Dr. Teofil Okunevsky, Kobrynska's cousin, appears to have been the only man to address the Congress.

The remaining two days were spent discussing education, cultural heritage, economy and health. Dr. Sofiia Parfanovych, who at that time headed the Temperance Union, led the discussion on health, including public welfare and physical education. Alcohol and tobacco were government monopolies, and the Temperance Union, known as Renewal (Vidrodzhennia), which opposed both, had patriotic overtones. Rusova and Kysilevska handled educational matters, while Biliak and Gurgula concentrated on art and folklore. Olha Kishchynska, Neonila Selezinka and Kharytia Kononenko addressed the problems of the economy and the co-operative movement.

The Congress ended with a working session on the organizational aspects of the Union, with Rudnytska as the major speaker. Its main decision was to establish a world organization to encompass all Ukrainian women outside the Soviet Union, which was eventually founded in 1937. The women also decided to publish a newspaper, called simply *Zhinka* (Woman).

The resolutions of the congress, adopted on its final day, provided a comprehensive statement of the political, economic and national position of Ukrainian women. Having deplored the international situation and noted that the position of Ukrainians under the Soviet system was precarious, the women announced that the Ukrainian community in Poland and in other non-Soviet states

considers the splintering of society and the decline in public morality extremely harmful to the Ukrainian nation. We women abhor the unethical methods of political struggle and the waste of national energy on internal bickering.... We demand that all Ukrainian parties introduce measures which will promote civic peace, abolish party strife, tone down press polemics and subordinate their party interests to the general welfare of the nation.[14]

The women recognized the importance of the churches, and called for religious toleration. They stressed the key role of the Ukrainian peasant women, and the active participation of women in Ukrainian community affairs. They continued ostensibly to support the fusion of feminism, motherhood and nation, but defined the role of the mother in public as well as private terms. The resolution on the "bases of Ukrainian feminism" followed that on "Morality, Family and Motherhood."

The Congress asserts that the family is the social and biological unit of the national organism, in which the soul and the future of the nation are forged. For this very reason the Ukrainian Women's Congress desires the healing of family life, the raising of the dignity of the woman-mother and the assurance of equal rights for mothers as well as fathers. [But] valuing very highly the vocation of woman as mother, the Ukrainian Women's Congress goes on record against the contention that motherhood is the sole vocation for the woman in society and the sole measure of her worth as a person.

Concerning the *Zhinka* newspaper, a few months after the Congress, on 26 October 1934, the women set up a Women's Publishing Co-operative in Lviv which was affiliated with the Union, but was kept separate for legal purposes.[15] A decade earlier, we recall, Kysilevska had inaugurated her *Zhinocha dolia*, an echo of Kobrynska's *Nasha dolia*. The circulation of *Zhinocha dolia* was 2,500 monthly, which compared favourably with the 4,600 circulation of *Dilo*, the only Ukrainian daily in Galicia. Although Kysilevska and the Kolomyia group carried a formal column of News from the Women's Union, it did not fully reflect the work of the Union.

The rationale for *Zhinka* was provided in a letter sent to potential collaborators.

As you probably know, the Ukrainian Women's Congress, which met in June 1934, decided there was a real need for a women's journal to develop an ideology and to consolidate women's forces. Fulfilling this resolution, the Executive Board of the Union created a women's publishing co-operative, Union of Ukrainian Women, in Lviv, which will publish the women's journal beginning 1 January 1935.

The journal, *Zhinka* (Woman), appearing bi-weekly, will cover all issues that interest the modern woman as a citizen, mother and housewife. It will comment on current affairs in our society from the point of view of the woman-citizen, presenting them in line with the ideology of the Ukrainian women's movement.

In addition to articles on public matters (political, feminist, cultural, educational, pedagogical, housekeeping, etc.), we will also include literary works and articles dealing with the arts (representational, folk arts, music, theatre, cinema). We will also report on the activities of organized Ukrainian women and chronicle the international women's movement. Finally we will devote some space to the running of the household, daily life, physical culture (hygiene, sport, cosmetics), interior design, fashion, etc. The journal will have a format similar to *Dilo*, will be printed on good-quality paper and will be illustrated.

Based on the above plan it is obvious that our paper cannot be considered competitive with existing women's publications. This is particularly true of *Zhinocha dolia*; we want to stress that its editor and owner, Senator Kysilevska, is co-operating fully with us as a member of the Central Executive Committee of the Union.

The editorial committee will be composed of Milena Rudnytska, Mariia Strutynska, Irena Gurgula and Olena Sheparovych.

We request your co-operation, Madame, in this publishing venture. We are particularly concerned about the tone of the journal. We do not want it to have a separate Galician tint but would like it to represent all Ukrainian lands and therefore have a well-rounded Ukrainian and supra-party character.

Regrettably, in the first months of publication we shall not be able to pay for articles. We trust, nevertheless, that you will not reject our plea and count on your collaboration in publishing your work. Articles for the first issue must be received by 10 December. Please include illustrations for your article (or information where such could be located).[16]

Zhinka appeared as a bi-monthly from January 1935 until the outbreak of the Second World War. For a brief time, in 1938, when the Union was suspended by the Polish authorities, it appeared as *Hromadianka* (Citizen). It was edited by Sheparovych, with Rudnytska's close collaboration. It carried news about the Union, information on women, some literary works, and much discussion of current events. Occasionally, blank spots in the columns attested to materials confiscated by the censors. The newspaper had strong support and generated much interest.

To continue the momentum of the Congress and to strengthen the links between the peasant women and the Union, the women developed programmes called "peasant women's festivities." These were mini-congresses which drew women from neighbouring areas for a day of joint demonstrations, singing and discussion. The programme was planned well in advance. Each village circle learned to perform a series of choreographed exercises and each participant prepared a special, usually embroidered blouse or scarf for the occasion. At first five or more villages converged, later the group increased in size. Finally, the women of the entire area (*povit*) would get together for exercises, marches, dances, singing and speeches. Preparations for these impressive programmes were long and arduous, "since it was necessary to convince the women that the aim of the ceremonies was not to teach them to march, but to enable them to manifest their [strength], to interest them in public work and to bring together all the women of the area." Open-air masses lent them an even greater solemnity.[17] Thousands of women took part in these events. By 1936, some peasant women were preparing the festivities themselves, with only minor help from the intelligentsia.[18]

After the Congress of 1934, the growth of the Union continued, despite escalating attacks from parts of the Ukrainian community and from the Poles, who feared its mass character. Although the Volhynian Ukrainian women were prevented by the government from attending the annual meeting on 18 and 19 March 1935, 109 Union delegates from other territories attended the congress.[19] Representatives of the affiliated organizations also took a formal part in the proceedings. Foremost among them were the Marian Sodality, the Day-Care Society, the Co-operatives of Domestics, the Women's Student Group, the Society of Aid to Widows and Orphans of Priests, and the newly founded Women's Gymnastic Society, Strila (Arrow), which had replaced the scout organization (Plast) suspended by the government. All the major community organizations sent representatives.

The Union took to formulating special slogans (*udarni hasla*) for its annual activity. In 1935 it tried to improve the welfare of the peasant women and raise the level of their agricultural expertise. It redoubled efforts to train village instructors, and attempted to co-ordinate the work of the Union and the co-operative in the village. Union leaders urged the Co-operative to convene another congress of the women's co-operatives.[20]

This type of work continued until the outbreak of the Second World War, although the Union was now in competition with the nationalists for the peasants' loyalty. By 1937, the Union was placing greater emphasis on the growth of civic and national consciousness among women, as well as on unity.[21]

Appendix

The Obshchestvo Ruskykh Dam (Society of Ruthenian Women) was the oldest Ukrainian women's organization in Galicia still in existence in the inter-war years. Originally founded in 1878, it was suspended by the Austrian government at the outbreak of the First World War. Reinstated in 1920, it remained small and drew its membership from the dwindling Russophiles in Lviv, reinforced by contacts with conservative Russian émigrés. Its attempts to expand into the villages were desultory and ineffective. In the summer of 1930, Mariia Martyniuk, from the village of Tadane, near Kaminka Strumilova, wrote to Emiliia Ianovytska, the society's president, suggesting that a branch be organized in her village. The statute of the Society did not envisage branches, and Martyniuk's pleas fell on deaf ears.[22] Late in 1930 the society helped set up a small co-operative (Khoziaika), which, despite governmental help, did not prosper. Oleksander Perfetsky, a student from Sambir, suggested that the Society's name "not be used at all in Galicia's conversational language," since it carried political overtones and was bad for business.[23]

The Society also failed to attract students to its sewing courses. It used the term "Russian" rather than Ruthenian, which further undermined its position. The Lviv women held fund-raising dances to help fund the Russian Casino's literary evenings for youth, but this only advertised its Russian orientation. The Society of Ruthenian Women was one of the Russophile groups that sponsored the annual "Day of Russian Culture," which usually ran a deficit.[24] Within an organization called the Russian School, these groups sought to develop a programme in Russian studies.

With a membership that was small and frequently tardy in paying its dues, the Society was always short of funds, frequently in debt, and desperate for members. It solicited help from émigrés and was on the lookout for prospective inheritances.[25] It failed to attract young people. By exerting pressure on members to use Russian, instead of the "iazychiie" the old Russophiles used, it antagonized some clientele.

The major undertaking of the Society in the inter-war years was the running of a dormitory for young women who attended high schools or training courses in Lviv. Before the war, the dormitory sometimes housed more than 100 students, but when it reopened in 1923, fewer than forty women lived there. The dormitory, run mainly by volunteers, received regular subsidies from the government after 1926. Nonetheless, it too was frequently in debt. It not only had trouble recruiting residents, but often could not collect fees.[26]

The dormitory was intended for conservative Russophile girls who spoke Polish and a version of old Ukrainian, but in 1930 Russian was introduced as the language for the premises. The girls were obliged to study Russian twice a week in classes held at the dormitory. Proposed Russian culture courses, however, were not held.[27]

The dormitory was run strictly, and the life of the students was carefully regimented. They could be tutored only by a fellow dormitory mate or by their own sisters or brothers. They could go to the theatre only in the company of the headmistress. They could visit their relatives only with the permission of their parents and only if they were fetched and delivered on the same day, as no overnight visits were permitted. The girls were "strictly forbidden to stand in front of windows, or to look out of the windows in the study or in the bedrooms."[28]

The Society deplored the changes in the life and politics of Galicia, occasionally denouncing the modern Ukrainian movement. The women continued to use the old Ukrainian orthography, and some knew Russian. But they eschewed all politics and contacts with other women's organizations. The Society was an anachronism supported by men as a matter of principle and because the government subsidized the dormitory. No one took this society seriously except Charewiczowa, who complained in her book *"Ukraiński" ruch kobiecy* that Ukrainian women activists overlooked the Ladies' Society when they discussed the women's movement in Ukraine.

The Ukrainian Society of Women with a Higher Education

The Ukrainian Society of Women with a Higher Education was the Ukrainian version of the Association of University Women. It was founded in Lviv on 18 October 1924 at the initiative of Olena Okhrymovych Zalizniak and Hanna Chykalenko Keller, both graduates of West European universities. A record of the Society's activities until 1928 is extant and reveals that several subsequent meetings of the executive board and the membership were to be held after 6 May 1928, the date of the last recorded gathering of the board, to dissolve the Society. According to its by-laws, the Society could dissolve itself by a two-thirds majority vote at an annual general meeting.

The Society's main goal was to provide Ukrainians with yet another window to the outside world through the International Association of University Women. But the local Lviv provincial administration of the government (*starostvo*) insisted that the by-laws delete all references to contacts with foreign organizations. Nevertheless the women kept up such contacts and tried to institutionalize them. The Society tried to unite all Ukrainian women with a post-secondary education in order to promote their professional and scholarly interests. It planned an information service, a job-referral bureau and a scholarship fund.

Present at the founding meeting of the Society were Dr. Teodoziia Tuna-Nadraga, Iryna Lezhohubska, Dr. Dariia Lezhohubska, Dr. Olena Stepaniv, Mariia Hromnytska, Olha Mryts, Milena Rudnytska, Solomiia Okhrymovych, and Mariia and Sofiia Fedak. Dariia Lezhobuska was the chairperson and Stepaniv-Dashkevych was elected the first president, a position she was to hold several times. Other participants included Stefaniia Danylovych Senyk, Stefaniia Nadraga, Anna Kobrynska, Mariia Luchakivska-Stelmakhiv, Sofiia Dolozhytska, Dariia Bonfrivska, Nataliia Chaikivska, Irena Horliankevych, Irena Lahodynska, Nadiia Shulhyn Ishchuk, Eleonora Zaleska, Mariia Turianska Kuzmych, Dr. Oleksandra Lindfors, Dr. Nataliia Polotniuk Prystai and Dr. Oleksandra Polotniuk. As an association of professional women, the Society grouped all Ukrainian women and was free from regional tensions.[29]

Another major function of the Society was to organize public lectures. In this, it was aided by the efforts of the Ukrainian community to promote a Ukrainian university. By 1924 the Clandestine University had disintegrated, but the interest continued. The Mohyla Society and the Shevchenko Scientific Society sponsored prestigious talks, and the women followed suit, but found it difficult to attract a sizeable audience. The Society also helped publish works in Ukrainian serials: for example, Omelchenko's article on social services for youth in Czechoslovakia was published in *Literaturno-naukovyi vistnyk*. It sought to draw women from outside to its centre in Lviv. Society members tried to develop correspondence with women in Europe and the Americas.

To maintain women's unity, the Society became part of the Women's Union. Many of its most active members were also very active in the Union——Olena Sheparovych, Evstakhiia Tyshynska, Katria Hrynevych, Milena Rudnytska and others. Sofiia Okunevska Morachevska, the first woman in Galicia to hold a *matura* certificate and a medical degree, became a member on 30 March 1925, a year before her premature death. Tyshynska organized a circle of the Society in Przemyśl, and another evidently existed in Stryi. Some of the lectures, such as that by Omelchenko on career choices, were sponsored jointly with the journal *Nova khata*.

But the relationship between the Society and the Union had become increasingly strained by 1926. By its very nature, the Society was elitist. It had only forty members and seventy prospective members. The Union rank and file regarded the Society's members as snobs who kept themselves apart because of their higher education. There were personality clashes, especially between

Stepaniv-Dashkevych and Rudnytska, both regular members of the Society's executive board. Stepaniv was the first chairperson of the Society; Rudnytska was elected to the chair in 1928, but resigned because the burdens of the Union and politics were too much for her.

Tension erupted at a public debate on 27 March 1927, at which Valentyna Zavadska was elected to chair the Society. Zavadska was an outspoken feminist who had even advanced the possibility of female priests. She criticized the hostile attitude of the Galician community and of the Women's Union in particular toward the Society. Stepaniv-Dashkevych supported Zavadska's charge and noted that the Women's Union had not censured those of its members who had made personal attacks on the Society. Rudnytska pointed out that the attacks indeed had been personal and that as an institution, the Women's Union had always been proud of the Society's affiliation with the Union.[30]

At the general meeting held on 1 April 1928, Dontsova, the president of the Women's Union, and a member of the Society in good standing, argued for closer co-operation between the two bodies. The Society's main concern, however, was no longer the Union, but rather, as Dr. Dariia Lezhohubska, a Society founder, put it, "the disregard of [intellectual achievement] by the public that paralyzed our activity. We should not permit that sort of thing to affect us, but should rather turn our attention to the students."[31]

The Society had to face a growing anti-intellectual current in the Ukrainian community. Numerically, it was too weak and its members lacked the stature to be able to forestall this overall trend. Its members were forced to leave Lviv for personal or work considerations. And although the Society continually sought affiliation with the international organization, its hopes were not realized. For a number of years, the Society tried to help its colleagues in need, collected funds, and granted a few small scholarships. But the base of its operations was much too small. Meanwhile, in the 1930s, the Women's Union openly defended the rights of working women, thus standing up for Society members. The Society still kept the list of educational and scholarship opportunities for women, and remained in touch with professional women, but lost its role in Ukrainian life.

On the basis of the Society's lectures, the charge of egotistical self-absorption was unfounded. Tyshynska spoke frequently, both in Lviv and Przemyśl, on such topics as "The Influence of Women on Politics and Culture in the History of Mankind," "Education of Women and Cultural Progress," and "Women's Education and Religion." The topics of other speakers ranged from American Indians to the historical position of Ukrainian women. Both contemporary and historical subjects intrigued these women. Parkhanovych-Bulandova spoke on the women of Ancient Greece, Okhrymovych on the International School in Denmark, and Hrynevych on contemporary Ukrainian women. A number of prominent Ukrainians also spoke under the aegis of the Society. Male participants, among them Volodymyr Kalynovych, spoke on topics as diverse as the interests of children and new theories about the origins of Rus', Dr. Ivan Beley spoke about mental illness, and Dr. Vasyl Shchurat on the

Masonic Order and Ukrainian literature. Some of the lectures attracted over one hundred listeners.

In general, however, Galicia did not foster intellectual achievements among Ukrainian women. The economic situation worsened, and opportunities for advancement for Ukrainians were further hampered by growing Polish repression. Professional women, the most likely candidates for membership in the Society, could find employment only by leaving Galicia. Other young women gravitated toward practical work, either in the Union or in the openly anti-intellectual Right.

The Ukrainian chapter of the Association of University Women never formally affiliated itself with the International Society, because Ukrainians did not have an independent state which could host such a society. It seems to have disintegrated by 1929.

14.
Feminism: The Road to Autonomy

In the inter-war years, it became almost *de rigueur* for the educated to identify themselves with some ideology. The more acute the economic and political crises, the greater the attraction to ideological thinking. Young people, stifled economically and politically and unable to visualize a true democracy, were especially drawn to ideological politics. Hence, in Western Ukraine, moderate parties were often viewed by their critics as spineless. Some of these attitudes influenced women.

The Women's Union in Galicia and elsewhere was able to expand precisely because it avoided espousing the theoretical feminism that some Western Ukrainian women had attempted earlier. It was pragmatic and avoided theoretical debate. Unlike earlier feminists, especially those within the socialist framework, Union activists did not challenge existing Ukrainian social and political institutions. Rather, they sought to expand the role and importance of the woman working within the traditional framework.

The Stanyslaviv Congress in 1934, the new women's publications, the growing popularity of fascism and authoritarianism, as well as a renewed interest by the Catholic Church in social matters generated some debate on the role of women. Ukrainian women writing on feminist topics did so within the ideological framework of middle-class European gentility, and viewed themselves in West European terms. The world they lived in, however, was a pre-industrial society and lacked bourgeois amenities. In reality (but unconsciously), Ukrainian women were trying to transplant the pre-industrial women into a more modern setting.

They tried to validate the autonomous status of woman by using familiar terminology and concepts. They avoided characterizing themselves as feminists. In Ukrainian, that term has always had a slightly offensive connotation. In the Soviet Union feminism is linked to anti-Soviet liberalism; outside the USSR, it is suspect because of its incipient radicalism.

The Western Ukrainian male intelligentsia shared the sexual prejudices of the central Europeans. As a social class, it was only beginning to filter into city life. For many, life in a non-extended nuclear family, with the husband working outside the home, was a novelty. Men slowly accustomed themselves to having women work in community organizations, but they would not share in household duties. A woman was needed in the house. Dinner was taken around noon, and consisted of three courses. Some men had time for a brief nap, and returned home for coffee in mid-afternoon. Between the wars, the economy was in a perpetual state of crisis and did not promote change.

In the inter-war period purely feminist issues came up occasionally in talks, newspaper and journal articles, and daily experiences. For the most part women avoided confrontation. Sometimes, in feminist writings, we detect a note of exasperation with people's unwillingness to accept feminism:

> As we understand it, and as it is understood by all literate persons, feminism is nothing but the conscious participation of women in the creation of a national culture, especially the participation of women in the building of a state.[1]

Ukrainian women turned to historical rather than feminist writing. As nationalities were asserting their rights, it was natural for the women to refer to the past. Of course, the success of the Women's Union offered its own validation, but there was nothing historically Ukrainian about it. It pointed not to the spread of feminism, but to the wisdom of the pragmatic approach to the issues of interest to women. The times and conditions militated against the development of feminist theory. Yet the Union did represent a variant of feminism. Unfortunately, even Union activists, let alone the rank and file, were either unable or unwilling to make that connection and saw their work solely in terms of community service and national dedication. They, of course, considered themselves to be part of the world community of women, and were involved in the international women's movement. But their circumstances were not conducive to the development of consciously articulated international feminism.

One of the international organizations to which the Ukrainian women belonged was pacifist. Yet as representatives of a nation without its own government, it was virtually impossible for Ukrainians to renounce war in theory. War was one means of establishing an independent state. Hanna Chykalenko Keller wrote openly to Lady Aberdeen and Emily Balch, of the International Women's League for Peace and Freedom, on the propriety of Ukrainians' joining a pacifist organization. She argued that Ukrainian women did not espouse war *per se*, nor were they planning one, but, coming from a dependent and politically divided nationality, they could not reject war completely. The fact that the major women's international organizations, especially the International Council of Women, were based on the principle of state, not nation, brought home to Ukrainian women the importance of state sovereignty. Some potential conflict seemed inevitable. Western Ukrainian women were surrounded by nations whose women seemed better organized, more dedicated and more patriotic than they. That perception——certainly true as far as the Soviets and the Poles were concerned——influenced much of the inter-war thinking of Ukrainian activists.

Olena Sheparovych, who had never joined a rightist organization, reflected the prevailing mythology:

> This is not the time for Ukrainian women to think about peace, to believe in beautiful but questionable slogans of "universal peace and freedom," since our neighbours' women for years have been preparing for war. Before our very eyes whole cadres of women engage in military drill and study all aspects of military art. Women's organizations help them, as does the whole society, government...and educators.
>
> For Ukrainian women the main task must be first and foremost work for the liberation of our nation, which should create, within the circumstances in which we function, its own (*svoieridnyi*) unique feminism.[2]

Mariia Bachynska-Dontsova saw international co-operation of women in a highly original light, which was surprising in view of the rightist radicalism of her husband. Dontsova, avoiding the taboo word "feminism," argued that by their very make-up and innate interests women were social creatures to a far greater degree than men. They "were innately driven to civic work for the common good." She saw women of the world, united in their goal of equal rights, searching for means to break out of the stifling "mould of social drones that had been fashioned for them by men, and re-creating themselves as citizens." Dontsova considered conventional politics corrupt, dirty and demeaning. She had a loftier vision: philanthropic work, which she felt to be traditionally women's work, would be elevated into a higher form of civic work and would replace politics. She explained:

> [We] must realize that we do not have to adapt to the old social order (*suspilnyi lad*), but must become the generator of new life, bringing into it new values where the slogan will not be *homo homini lupus est*, but "humans come to the support of each human."

Dontsova's feminist views, however, were lost in the broader issue of conventional politics versus the new rightist movement championed by her husband. The Union chose the former; as a result, Dontsova became estranged from her husband, as well as from the Union.[3]

Ukrainians idealized Western Europe. They were also dazzled by the achievements of the Anglo-American feminist movement. They looked to the West for an elaboration of feminist concerns and felt it incumbent upon themselves to discuss issues already pursued by the advanced West. Although they were interested in women's movements in other parts of the world, they lacked an intimate knowledge of the Anglo-American feminist experience. Yet isolation had its benefits. Since the average Galician Ukrainian woman activist had little contact with the outside world, she was forced to develop her own pragmatic and effective feminism that came to characterize the Union as a whole. By avoiding feminist ideology, the Union forestalled some of the incipient male criticism of women.

The most striking aspect of feminist writing in the inter-war years in Western Ukraine was the emphasis placed on women's responsibilities in their expanded roles. This enhanced the position of women by stressing their contribution to the national cause. It also phrased the woman issue in terms readily understood by men and by the intelligentsia. Female activists exhibited a missionary fervour in their zeal to bring modernity to Ukrainian women. Rudnytska was especially outspoken on the responsibility of women to change their own status. She urged women to overcome their Philistinism, their laziness, their——her favourite word——indolence, to grasp the rights which belonged to them. Stress on women's responsibility to themselves and to society reflected a transference of the Protestant work ethic to the women's movement. Like the early formulators of European feminism, Ukrainian women placed their hopes upon self-reliance and responsibility within the community.

Ukrainian women activists showed practicality and a common-sense approach to the issues at hand. This was their forte. They foreshadowed a similar approach by women in unindustrialized countries in the second half of the twentieth century. In taking this path, however, the Ukrainian Women's Union failed to perceive its own achievement. Rather, its members thought in terms of their contribution to the community and to the nation. This line was similar to that of the early socialists, especially Kobrynska, on the contributions that women——when liberated and conscious——could make to the cause of universal liberation. Olena Sheparovych put it succinctly:.

> The Ukrainian women must above all understand and remember that this new spirit of the times which has brought women of the whole world victory in equal rights has also placed upon them duties which are in no way lesser than the rights and that need to be fulfilled consciously and rigorously. If we women approach our tasks from the same angle as these duties, as equal citizens and as mothers raising future generations; if all our women in all walks of life work hand in hand with men for the highest national ideals, then all women's issues will be solved in our particular circumstances.[4]

Within this framework, women activists stressed the autonomy of women and the social significance of family life. But this was not to be limited by the organic conception of community life and the sacred function of the mother, a myth of the mother doing nothing but caring for and producing babies. The growth of the women's movement and feminist interest aroused fear among some men. Labelling feminism the first step to atheistic communism was an effective verbal thrust at the dinner table, even if it lost its force in print. In this

Ukrainian men reflected male counterparts elsewhere who used tradition, religion and a version of fundamentalism to defend the nation from the threat of feminism.

The new right focused on the patriotic role of women, her higher calling, purity, and intuitive grasp of sacrifice. The Union consistently opposed such tactics, which were designed to subordinate women. But as integral nationalism became increasingly attractive to both young men and women, the Women's Union found itself repeatedly defending its own version of feminist nationalism against patriotic fundamentalism. Consequently, there was greater stress upon the life-giving creative powers of women as mothers than would normally have been the case.

A number of specific characteristics of the Ukrainian feminist movement became more pronounced during the inter-war years. The women, for the most part, were successful in asserting their rights. By the mid-1930s the only challenge from opponents of women's rights was a version of the "separate but equal" roles of the sexes. The role of women in the economy, however, cut into the growing polemics on the functions of women in the family. Participation of women in the labour force was a particularly moot issue for western Ukrainians during the economic crisis of the 1930s, which left many men without jobs.

The feminists stressed motherhood but maintained that good mothering went beyond the confines of the home and mere domesticity. They felt that the mother must realize the importance of society and raise her children as social beings, not as hermits. They did not challenge motherhood, but expanded its role. Motherhood, family nurturing and service to "Mother Ukraine" seemed a triune hypostasis of love of country, family and God. At the same time, however, the women stressed autonomy and self-reliance as the ideal of the "new type of woman." This woman was the product of the specific conditions of the area, although she considered herself closer to her more advanced Western counterpart than was actually the case.

Equality for Ukrainian men and women was one of struggle, not opportunity. Ukrainians in inter-war Poland and Romania were deprived of basic rights. Education in Ukrainian was severely circumscribed, access to higher education limited, economic opportunities virtually non-existent, and the policies of the two governments openly discriminatory toward the nationality, not toward gender. In the effort to combat discrimination, national rather than gender issues were more likely to be raised by Ukrainian women.

In 1919, Rudnytska wrote a number of articles on the tragic conflict between motherhood and career. She did not return to that subject because the problem became one of fitting motherhood into other work. In the lead article for the first issue of *Zhinka* (1 January 1935), Rudnytska pinpointed the particularly difficult problem of the relationship of the Western Ukrainian woman to the nation. She argued that women had to strive consciously and effectively to become full participants in the task of "national consolidation":

We believe the attributes of female spirit, the attributes of the *mother*, freed from the narrow confines of the family, transposed into the public domain and subordinated to the service of the whole, must fulfill an important mission for humanity.... How will you [Ukrainian woman] be able to ward off the fatigue and apathy which creep into our society? How can you make others strong in spirit when you yourself are weak and broken?

While affirming the values of traditional family life and service to the nation, Rudnytska and other feminists stressed the equally sacred task of the woman to educate herself, to better herself, to combat "spiritual laziness...in order to have some impact on the social process."[5]

The argument for equality of women arose not as a defence of individualism, but within a conception of the role of the woman as a public person. "Women who place their health, and frequently their life on the altar of their destiny——motherhood——should participate in the life of the society which they, as mothers, engendered,"[6] wrote one passionate feminist in 1929. It was this aspect of women's rights, so fully compatible with tradition, religion and nationalism, that reflected the autonomous role of the women in pre-industrial societies and sought to continue and expand it in the modern world. As the work of the society, nation or state expanded, demands upon the women become greater. Rudnytska, in a didactic and rather pompous manner, stated in January 1935:

We will demand from you [Ukrainian woman] great creative effort and much self-confidence, dedication and sacrifices for you to be able to fulfill your role. We will jog your conscience, chide you for your mistakes, strengthen you, give you purpose and clarify your place in the striving of the Nation.[7]

The average Western Ukrainian male would have found "the new type of woman" much more threatening had her emergence not been overshadowed by cataclysmic political, economic and social changes. Ukrainian women differed from West European women in their participation in the war-ravaged economy. Warfare lasted longer in this area than in the West, and reconstruction was hampered by unresolved political issues. In the 1920s, therefore, the pressures of domesticity were not as confining in Western Ukraine as in Western Europe; if anything, they were challenging and consuming.

Men perceived the women's movement as dangerous to women themselves. The discussion was unsophisticated and unoriginal. Ukrainian women wrote articles to alleviate male fears "about the loss of traditional femininity."[8] They assured their husbands that the issue did not reside in "a boy-type haircut, but in a person who is fully aware of her moral and economic worth." At first, they assured their menfolk that women did not want to compete but to co-operate with them. By the 1930s women were arguing that feminism was not egotistical, but beneficial to the whole community.[9] Generally these arguments were presented in short articles occasioned by some specific event. Sometimes, however, especially late in the 1930s, these polemics generated discussion among women. The women also recruited men to write articles on the advantages of the "new woman." For example, some men stressed the importance of exercise, or extolled the attractiveness of an educated woman, and declared how such new women would make men happier and society better.

The economic backwardness of Western Ukraine was considered a more pressing issue than the allocation of roles in child-rearing and housekeeping. Certainly the Czechs, with whom Western Ukrainian women were in contact, had demonstrated that time-saving rational housekeeping was possible. Ukrainian women who lived in Czechoslovakia, especially the educated Eastern Ukrainian émigrés, kept Galician women informed of the strides the Czechs had made in scientific housekeeping. Zinaida Mirna, the descendant of the Cossacks, was so impressed by these achievements that she wrote about housekeeping as a career.[10] The Ukrainian standard of living in Poland fell during the 1930s. A number of Ukrainian families that had been able to afford household help now made do without domestics. This changed some of the thinking about the running of a household.

Ukrainian activists stressed practical ways to alleviate the burden of housekeeping. They also continued the articles on grooming, personal time for the mother, and the importance of the mother's keeping up her cultural activities, not sacrificing herself totally for her children. The mothers's company was considered more important than a new dress for her daughter.

There was also a sexual aspect to the discussion. In the 1930s, the women's press, especially *Zhinocha dolia* and the advice column of Dr. Sofiia Parfanovych, performed an inestimable, albeit limited, service in bringing rudimentary sex education and gynaecology to the village. Discussion of sexually related illnesses and sexual dysfunctions occurred with lesser frequency. Some men and some self-styled Catholic women attacked the Union because of "the decline of standards," "eroticism," and "free love," which they associated with feminism. Given the reticence on sexual matters in Eastern Europe, one rarely came across anything more than a vicious innuendo, a malicious half-truth, some titillating news to feed the provincial gossips of both sexes.[11]

There was little sex education; little new on the subject was published in Ukrainian in the inter-war years. The articles in the women's press dealt with health-related issues and tried in particular to break the peasant's reliance on folk medicine, gypsies and charlatans. There was no public discussion of birth control and little about abortion, which was always condemned for ethical and national reasons. But, a number of articles did appear exhorting women to take care of their bodies, to prevent needless mutilation and to see a doctor if an abortion was needed.[12] The women realized that the main problem was poverty and the concomitant ignorance. In 1932, for example, *Zhinocha volia* urged Women's Union circles in the village to purchase a fever thermometer for village use.

Women wrote about the distinction between love and eroticism, on the implications of the entire cultural crisis, and on women's need to be in step with modernity. They also discussed the generation gap. The young novelist Iryna Vilde, in her books and in articles written specifically for the women's press, touched on issues of sexual morality and on the generational conflict reflected in politics. In one article, Vilde discussed the generation gap between mothers and daughters, and advocated more understanding toward aging grandmothers. She also presumed that only a quarter of children born were actually wanted. In a departure from the usual interpretation, she also argued that it was necessary to educate young women to perceive the young men they met not only as beaux and potential husbands, but also as valuable citizens.[13]

Over time, a different life-style emerged, freer, more open, less-traditional, more mobile. But it would be an error to assume that sexual and personal emancipation was central to either men or women. The new woman, like emancipation, was accepted by some women, but the concept meant mainly a responsible, self-reliant person.

Women activists fostered the growth of specifically women's co-operatives as well as co-operatives in general. In February 1932, Ievheniia Verbytska, using Owen as proof, argued that the co-operative movement antedated the founding of the Women's Union, and the women activists considered both types of work complementary. Ivanna Blazhkevych is a case in point. She organized one of the first women's co-operative rallies in Zboriv in 1926. Kysilevska, also, helped establish co-operatives among the mountain Hutsul women. The Union realized the importance of this work, and Neonila Selezinka served as a liaison with the Co-operative. Kharytia Kononenko was hired as a full-time organizer of the co-operatives, but a disagreement with Rudnytska strained her relationship with the Union.[14] To help peasant women aspire to a better life, the Union expanded its programme of training village organizers.

In 1934–5, when the level of unemployment was at its highest in Western Ukraine, women were the first to lose their jobs. As noted above, the Ukrainian Pedagogical Society voted to terminate jobs of women whose husbands were employed. To many, the needs of the family came first; abstract justice and equal opportunity were not important. The economic crisis was so severe that Iryna Paarova, who chaired the Union branch in Iavoriv, wanted to suspend future Union circles because there was no prospect of economic help for the village.[15]

The Union protested what it considered the violation of the right to work. In 1931, it established a standing committee of the executive board to deal specifically with the interests and needs of working women. At the same time, it condemned the Ukrainian Association of Private Office Workers for its preferential treatment of male heads of households, as well as the Native School Society for its decision to reduce the salaries of married women by 25 per cent.[16] Rudnytska complained that "under the guise of war on unemployment and preservation of the family, it is male egotism which triumphs, which solves the issue of the right of women to work——one of the basic rights of each individual——only from the point of view of his own interests."[17] The depression, however, enabled men to argue against the employment of women with impunity, on the grounds of patriotism and the preservation of the family.

The energy and activity women exhibited in the Union, the co-operative movement and the anti-alcohol campaign sparked an atavistic fear in some Ukrainian men. To stress the male domination of the co-operative movement, the Co-operative delegated a man to represent Ukrainians at the Lviv Farmers' Assembly section on home economics. He was the only man amid women delegates.[18] The attempt to wrest the whole co-operative movement from the Women's Union was another stage in the attempt to control women and to block the growth of their political and economic independence. Kononenko, in her work with the women's co-operative, pointed out that the success of the economic co-operative in the village rested very much on the peasant woman, since "only when the housewife realized the important role her daily toil played in the economy would it be rebuilt."[19]

The prolonged economic crisis and the disastrous harvests of 1933–4 went hand in hand with the growth of the Ukrainian and Polish nationalist organizations. These organizations, in theory, glorified the "traditional" role of the woman, primarily as mother and nurturer. In practice, however, with their stress on sacrifice and dedication, they drew an increasing number of young women into direct political and even terrorist activity. For many young Ukrainian women, the politics and policies of the Women's Union were too pedestrian, too limited and too confining to justify their joining it. These young women, like the women socialists of the turn of the century, presumed either equality of the sexes or natural differences, and were not concerned about individual autonomy. Impressionable, raised on Polish and Ukrainian romantic patriotic literature, which they read at school and home respectively, these young women readily joined the OUN or participated in its demonstrations and terrorist acts.

The Union broadened further the definition of motherhood. Indeed, the most significant ideological contributions of Western Ukrainian women to feminist thought were their views on motherhood, which did not limit the autonomy of women; on nationalism, which they defined in universalist, humanistic and democratic terms; and on totalitarian control, which they opposed wholeheartedly. Against the increasing defence of the family, Ukrainian feminists raised the equally insistent slogan of intelligent motherhood and its broader social significance.

Many women described their actions in terms of patriotism and duty. The men, in turn, supported symbolic actions to strengthen the position of the mother. For example, *Dilo* wrote on 5 May 1929 about the introduction of a new holiday——Mother's Day, which was supported by the whole community and approved by the major community organizations. The Polish government, however, perceived Mother's Day as another manifestation of Ukrainian nationalism.

Motherhood in the inter-war years was very much a career, both for the peasant and the intelligentsia women. The household had to be managed; help, if any, had to be trained and supervised. The daily routine included three hot meals and two smaller repasts. Although Kysilevska wrote about accustoming boys to household duties, very few men carried out household tasks. Proper upbringing of the children, efficient household management, and some self-improvement were realistic career goals for the vast majority of Ukrainian women. The Union helped to modernize a traditional structure without attacking it directly.

A favourite criticism of feminists was the view that the liberated female would jeopardize the existence of the family. The Union went out of its way to demonstrate that historically feminism had strengthened the family, the welfare of the child and the security of the mother. As an organization functioning in a society composed of single or extended families, the Women's Union stressed the benefits society would derive from genuinely intelligent mothering. Using contemporary terminology, the feminists insisted that the major beneficiary in the whole process would be the nation.

Chykalenko-Keller, who did not experience fully the restrictions of feminine life in Western Ukraine, stressed the importance of national consciousness rather than the achievements of women:

> The Ukrainian women's movement is and always has been deeply national, as it must be in a nation which is not sovereign. Comparing the women's movements in Western and Central Europe, I have come to the conclusion that our tasks are not exactly the same as those of the women of independent, modernized states (*derzhavni, vysokokulturni*), rich in cultural achievements and political experience. The Ukrainian women's organizations must bring the Ukrainian women not only feminist slogans, but must also unite them and raise their national consciousness.[20]

As a resident of Western Europe, Keller perceived limitations in those Western democracies that the Ukrainian feminists tended to idealize. "Democratic, liberal principles, although in theory favourable to women's emancipation, by no means guarantee it in practice," she warned her Western Ukrainian colleagues. She reminded them that Swiss women still laboured under an antiquated sexist regime, whereas the Turkish authoritarian state had promoted the emancipation of women.

Western Ukrainian women did not focus on theoretical problems of West European feminism. For them the West represented the land of progress and individual rights. The individual within society remained the central concern of the women. Their emphasis on self-reliance enabled some of them to avoid the growing totalitarian movements. The stronger the attack upon organized Ukrainian women, the greater was their emphasis on the importance of the individual and of society as a community of individuals. Mariia Strutynska cited Jacques Maritain in arguing that it was crucial for the individual to develop somewhat apart from the community, in order to strengthen that community.[21]

Confronted by Bolshevism on the one hand, and Polish chauvinism and fascism on the other, Rudnytska realized that Ukrainian society's political polarization was part of a world-wide trend. Ukrainian women recognized, Rudnytska maintained, that their own society was also inundated by "festering sores," by persons who fought Bolshevism with Bolshevik methods. They saw Germany and Italy as a warning, not as an example. On the other hand, the situation of women in the Soviet Union was hardly ideal. Wedged between two equally unpalatable forces, many Ukrainian women felt that a democratic regime was best suited to their interests.

Rudnytska even developed a messianic conception of the function of women in their own society: to convince men of the benefits of genuine democracy. Conceding that the emancipation of Ukrainian women was stymied by unhealthy political authoritarianism, Rudnytska nevertheless was "firmly convinced that women were destined to endow culture with the values of their spirit; that they were to bring to public life her [woman's] understanding of good, justice and beauty."[22] In modern terminology, therefore, Rudnytska saw in what is sometimes referred to as androgyny the moral and political resuscitation of humanity. Male-formulated ideologies had led to repeated wars, terrorism and totalitarianism. Europe was undergoing a cultural crisis; it offered little hope for Ukrainian women, and certainly no role models. For Rudnytska this only demonstrated the need for self-reliance, and for an acknowledgement that the weakness and inaction of women were partly a result of the failures of women themselves:

> Although women are not directly responsible for the condition in which our society finds itself, women are nevertheless indirectly responsible, because they have failed, through their weakness and lack of organization...to prevent distintegration and disorder, which is so destructive to the national organism.[23]

Hence, Rudnytska maintained that women must regenerate their own society. But she did not draw the conclusion that feminists must co-operate on an international basis for the reconstruction of humanity. At the time there was nothing to warrant that contention even as a remote possibility. She did nevertheless insist on expanding whatever international co-operation of women existed.

The emphasis upon the responsible individual, on political moderation, tolerance and compromise as the norms of civilized behaviour continued to dominate the thinking of the Ukrainian women activists. They defended these principles to the very end. But increasingly, the principles themselves had to be defended, not only their relevance to women.

15.
Challenges to the Union

Economic, ideological and religious forces challenged the "new woman" emerging in Western Ukraine in the 1930s. Difficulties in finding jobs predisposed some women and most men to think in terms of one-income families, not equal opportunity for both sexes. The co-operative movement, the Pedagogical Society and the Native School Society, all of which had supported equal opportunity for women during the 1920s, began to stress the need to preserve the traditional Ukrainian family in the 1930s.

Women activists of the moderate left who had readily worked in the Women's Union lost hope in the effectiveness of concerted Ukrainian pressure on the Polish authorities. Instead, they sought to create an organization of progressive women as an adjunct to political parties. Although the move did not seriously undermine the strength of the Women's Union, it violated women's solidarity.

The growth of integral nationalism, with its stress upon the child-bearing functions of the woman, was the most serious threat to the autonomy of the Women's Union. Women's striving for sexual equality was depicted as petty egotism. Young women, steeped in the consciousness of duty and patriotic self-sacrifice, took the benefits of sexual equality for granted, and were drawn to clandestine political work.

Intertwined with these concepts was a religious-traditional argument on the true manifestations of femininity. Although the Catholic Church itself did not challenge the Ukrainian Women's Union, the Catholic secular intelligentsia——often men who were the first in their families to break the sacerdotal tradition——mounted a number of campaigns against the "new woman." The church never supported and was often hostile toward integral nationalism, yet some clergy gravitated toward that orientation, as did their wives and daughters. Thus, there was some overlapping in the Catholic and nationalist arguments. The lay Catholic intelligentsia's portrayal of the ideal devout mother performing her God-given biological functions in the warmth of the family was similar to the nationalists' picture of the self-sacrificing mother. The growth of the Women's Union coincided with the secularization of the

Ukrainian intelligentsia as well as with the dramatic influx of children of non-clerics into the Uniate clergy. The reasons for the latter were practical: the ailing economy and Polish educational policies rendered the Uniate Church the primary means of social mobility for Western Ukrainians. Entrance to universities, investment capital and work opportunities, on the other hand, were restricted.

Throughout the inter-war period the Ukrainian Catholic Church remained a symbol of Galician society. Although the clergy no longer had the monopoly on Ukrainian representation in the public sphere, the secularization of Ukrainian society did not diminish the powers of the church. On the contrary, it diversified the forces that sought to channel the public activities of the church. The priest remained an organizer of political, social and cultural activity, which many priests viewed as the extension of their sacerdotal functions. He became thoroughly involved in community issues. The church's prestige was also enhanced by its leader, Metropolitan Andrei Sheptytsky.

In the early post-war years the church was sometimes the only local institution for Ukrainians. Official church publications, the diocesan "Messengers," published both government regulations and instructions to the clergy on dealing with civil and ecclesiastical authorities.[1] The effects of war and the gradual return of prisoners of war from Russian and Polish camps placed the clergy at the forefront of the reconstruction effort. Priests often recruited their wives and other women to help them re-establish societies, reactivate clubs, and rebuild churches, schools, community halls and parsonages. Relief committees, largely composed of women, were sometimes organized by priests, who also encouraged the establishment of Women's Union chapters. The sociological make-up of Galicia made the priest's wife the motivating force in the organization of women's groups in the larger villages or towns.

Sheptytsky vigorously supported Ukrainian community ventures. He was particularly generous to the Society for the Care of Children and Youth, and it was largely through his donations that the Mothers' Clinic was able to function in Lviv. He also encouraged the revitalization of monastic orders and was instrumental in the spread of the Order of the Sisters Servant of Mary Immaculate, which, since it required a lower dowry than the Basilian Sisters, attracted village girls.[2] The Sisters Servant, continuing the pre-1914 tradition, expanded their network of community-aided nursery schools with the active support of the local circles of the Women's Union.[3]

As the ties between the church and the national movement widened, the ritual of prayer, the power of group singing, and the continued use of processions became essential attributes of Ukrainian public life. Most important public functions began with a Mass or a memorial service. Frequently, meetings started with a prayer. Even non-practicing and lapsed Catholics, as well as the Orthodox, the free-thinking and the few Protestants participated in these ceremonies. Processions were very much a part of public celebrations and all civic and religious organizations took part in them, carrying their standards and banners and wearing distinctive garb. In the early 1920s, the government outlawed the carrying of wreaths made of thorns in either funeral or commemorative processions or marches. Consequently it became an honour for young Ukrainians, especially women, to carry a thorn wreath masked by streamers and flowers in order to test their threshold of pain and manifest their patriotism.

Since priests preached publicly, they were particularly vulnerable to local police, who might detect seditious undertones in their sermons. The authorities were especially vigilant in the case of priests active in Prosvita. The parish priest was usually among the first victims of the "pacification" campaign of 1930.

The war and inter-war period exacerbated the difficulties of married clergy. The dire material position of clerics with large families was a factor drawing attention to the perennial issue of celibacy for priests.[4] This issue was much discussed by the Ukrainian church and intelligentsia during the inter-war years. It did not, however, provoke much discussion of the role of women, since at stake was survival and not discussion of such seemingly far-fetched ideas as female priests.

In the late 1920s, the Vatican developed a programme of "Catholic Action" to organize the laity into groups that would offer a positive social and economic goal as an alternative to fascism. For Ukrainian women——and eventually, for the Ukrainian clergy——Catholic Action proved a mixed blessing. It enabled the laity, especially men from clerical families, to use the authority of the church in pursuing their own interpretations of Christian politics and social action, which were not always congruent with those of the church hierarchy. Whereas the Ukrainian Catholic Church did not theorize over the woman question, Catholic Action by nature encouraged theoretical analyses and debates. The return to Catholicism of a number of prominent Ukrainian public figures who had previously renounced the faith strengthened the penchant for ideological discussions of religion. The Vatican stressed the Kingship of Christ (the Feast of Christ the King was instituted in 1928), activism and social relevance——items which particularly suited the Ukrainian Galician population.

The Catholic Action Institute, established in Lviv in 1931, envisaged itself as a supervisory organization over all existing lay organizations, although this claim was resented by the Catholic milieu, especially the traditional lay brotherhoods. In the first years of Catholic Action, priests viewed the new organization as an auxiliary to help them motivate Catholics. "Being a pastor is not an idle theory that entails distancing oneself from the people and their demands," wrote the Reverend Onufrii Orsky, a professor at the Ukrainian Theological Institute in Przemyśl. He advocated an ideology that would enable a more equitable distribution of wealth and a less oppressive system of government. Predictably, Catholic Action attacked liberalism for its connection with atheism and materialism. Less predictably, Ukrainian theoreticians of Catholic Action also decried "economic liberalism, which created capitalism,

which is the major cause of our social problems."[5] Their socio-economic ideal
was based upon co-operation:

> Socio-economic issues are closely tied to religion and morality.... In a system
> rooted only in the notion of equality, class struggles would indeed cease, but the
> clenched fists of hatred would remain. To normalize the situation we need the
> co-operation of all levels of society. We need the palms of all people raised and
> joined together. This can be done by love.[6]

Some clergy and the lay intelligentsia tried repeatedly to organize a Catholic
political party, but could not agree on a course of action. The Polish authorities
feared even greater clerical involvement in political work and would not give
approval. A Ukrainian People's (*Narodnia*) Party, in which some women
participated, was founded in Lviv in 1930 through the efforts of Bishop
Khomyshyn and Osyp Nazaruk, but its influence was limited to the Stanyslaviv
area, and it never became a major political force among Ukrainians.[7]

Meanwhile, Bishop Khomyshyn, who had pushed the trend toward celibate
clergy, issued an episcopal letter in 1931 which criticized both the excesses of
the Polish government and Ukrainian terrorist acts. Many Ukrainians felt that
the letter was ill-timed, since it followed so closely after the "pacification."[8]
Resentment against Khomyshyn and other bishops prompted more lay
involvement in Catholic organizations. Catholic Action became particularly
outspoken under the leadership of Dr. Mariian Dzerovych, who was helped by
Volodymyr Kuzmovych, the editor of a newly established Catholic paper in
Lviv, *Meta*. Dzerovych tried to turn Catholic Action into a potent political
movement.[9]

As part of its centralization campaign, Catholic Action established a
Women's Section in 1934. Dr. Dariia Dzerovych, Antonina Konrad, Evstakhiia
Tyshynska and Stefaniia Figol were among its organizers. Its task was to
co-ordinate the work of all Ukrainian Catholic women's societies. Some men
also hoped that it would induce the Women's Union to pursue an openly
Catholic course. At the same time they wanted to undermine the political
independence of the Union. *Meta* published a women's page devoted to morally
uplifting topics of particular interest to women. The Women's Section
organized lectures dealing primarily with the upbringing of children, ethics and
education. Although Catholic Action did not lessen the popularity of the
Women's Union, some of its members provoked a number of unpleasant
incidents in the women's organizations.

While Catholic Action in Ukraine never developed specific views on
women, it stressed the maternal role as their primary function. The men tended
to idealize the so-called traditional values for women. They also identified
feminism with atheism, and with destruction of the family and the moral fibre
of the country. They tended to lump rationalism, socialism, liberalism and
capitalism together.

The secular male intelligentsia seemed less comfortable with the whole woman issue than the clerics. In the inter-war years, there was withdrawal from the Old Testament type of acceptance of sex as natural and life-procreating to a more modern prudery among secularized intelligentsia. There were also conservative males who saw in women an unbridled destructive anarchy with sexual overtones threatening the life-bearing male seed, not to mention the salvation of the eternal male soul. But the view that women should be limited to the roles of mother and housewife carried little conviction.

Women, as we have seen, were traditionally involved in the work of the parish. Girls sometimes substituted for absent altar boys at weekday masses. Some articles in Catholic journals reminded their readers of the active role of women in the early apostolic church and the importance of women as active helpers of the clergy; others stressed the separation of functions.[10] As the position of women in society improved, however, so did the role of women within church-related organizations.

A number of church-related relief societies founded during the inter-war years included activist women. The Ukrainian Committee to Aid the Unemployed and the Poor,[11] set up under the patronage of Metropolitan Sheptytsky, carried out secular work. It included Olena Sheparovych, Olha Bachynska, Evstakhiia Tyshynska, activists of the Women's Union, and Nataliia Dzerovych, whose relations with the Union were often strained. Also, of the three representatives from the Co-operative, two, Sofiia Rakovska and Mariia Kordynska, were women.[12]

During this decade, the feminization of lay societies founded to promote piety also continued. The most widespread were the Marian Sodalities which, in their Ukrainian variant, were invariably women's organizations. Originally founded in Lviv in 1904, they spread to virtually every parish in the late 1920s and drew heavily on young people. On 16 October 1935, in an attempt to establish an all-encompassing Catholic Women's Union, the Marian Sodality directed specifically at the Ukrainian female intelligentsia was founded in Lviv under the spiritual guidance of the Reverend Iakym Senkivsky, OSBM. The activity of the Sodalities centred on popularizing monthly communion (at the time this was rare for Eastern Catholics, who were attuned to yearly Eucharist for the laity), joint prayer and work with youth.[13] Some sodalities also engaged in philanthropy. One of their important functions was the public manifestation of faith at processions or special congresses. Organized public demonstrations, including religious processions, proved so effective and uplifting that the Ukrainian Catholic Church began to sponsor such events. Catholic Poland could hardly forbid religious gatherings. The more moderate Poles, moreover, hoped that the influence of the clerics would strengthen Ukrainian moderates and contribute to their acceptance of Polish rule.[14] The fact that the large Ukrainian religious demonstrations were boycotted by the OUN underscored this contention.

The success of the Marian Congress of Youth in 1927 showed that young Ukrainians were willing to attend religious gatherings. In line with the Vatican directive to celebrate the kingship of Christ, public religious celebrations were held in parishes and in larger districts. Marian celebrations also expanded from local to regional devotional manifestations. A major demonstration was held in Lviv in 1933 under the slogan "Ukrainian Youth for Christ." Although boycotted by the nationalists, it was nevertheless extremely effective. This was also true of the 1938 celebrations marking the anniversary of the acceptance of Christianity by Volodymyr of Kiev in 988.[15] But these events failed to stem the nationalist tide. Even though Ukrainian bishops and many of the upper clergy opposed the openly terroristic acts of the OUN, local pastors and their wives increasingly sympathized with the OUN, whose theories of totalitarian exclusiveness exploited rather than supported the church.[16]

The founding of Catholic Action, the attempts to create a Catholic political party and increased social involvement whetted the appetite of the lay Ukrainian Catholic intelligentsia. Some found the independence of the Women's Union annoying, and sought to limit its influence. They were particularly opposed to the convocation of the Stanyslaviv Congress in 1934 and tried to denigrate individual women and women's organizations in general. This attitude continued after the congress. Between 1933 and 1936, with the complicity of women in Catholic Action, attempts were made either to create a rival comprehensive Ukrainian Catholic women's organization or to graft a Catholic label on the Women's Union.[17]

At a time when the women wanted to manifest their solidarity, this campaign against the Women's Union was particularly destructive, since it was supported by some Eastern Ukrainian émigré groups. Sofiia Rusova made a tactful intervention that helped to calm matters. Older women, especially wives of priests, were also effective in preventing a rift, while a similar role was also played by men such as Osyp Nazaruk, a peasant's son and former radical, who edited the influential Catholic newspaper *Nova zoria* (New Star) in Stanyslaviv. He arranged for Rudnytska to meet with Bishop Khomyshyn on the eve of the congress to arrange for an official mass.[18]

Nazaruk delivered a highly publicized lecture in Lviv on "Woman and Society" on 13 April 1934.[19] It was followed by an equally publicized discussion. Nazaruk, who agreed politically with the conservative political thinker Viacheslav Lypynsky, developed different views on women. Rudnytska, who befriended him despite political differences, considered him one of the few male feminists in Galicia. Late in life Rudnytska reminisced:

Nazaruk was an ardent feminist not in the usual meaning of the term, that women ought to have equal rights, but in a deeper sense. He maintained that in their very make-up they are superior to men, that they constitute a more valuable, a more positive part of humanity. Therefore, he ascribed to women an important role in the life of society. He particularly valued Ukrainian peasant women for their wisdom, deep religiosity and high ethical standards. He shared the ideology of the Ukrainian women's movement as it was developed and implemented by the Ukrainian Women's Union, particularly supporting the thesis that women ought to become an autonomous element in national life, and not follow men's party interests.... [Although] all Lviv made fun of his theories...he maintained that women, because of their stronger personalities, reflected national characteristics more clearly than men.[20]

Nazaruk predicted that a public discussion of the issues would demonstrate the ridiculous nature of the attacks. The other speaker was to have been Volodymyr Kuzmovych, editor of *Meta* and author of some of the major polemics on the Union and on Rudnytska. In protest the Executive Board of the Women's Union voted against Rudnytska's attending the discussion and offering a formal reply, whereupon Kuzmovych withdrew as a speaker.

Nazaruk addressed his arguments to the conservatives——laymen, many of whom had broken with tradition by not following their fathers into the priesthood, and clerics cut off from the village while serving in diocesan offices. Defending the equality of women, Nazaruk also argued that only an intelligent woman, well versed in community matters, was capable of raising the morally healthy family that was the foundation of a stable, democratic state. Women who were ignorant of public affairs contributed to the rise of totalitarian movements, warned Nazaruk, an evil far worse than radicalism or atheism. Passivity irked him most. "While ardent atheist women could at some point become genuinely religious ones, apathetic klutzes (*kliotsy*) will be of no benefit to the church, or the Bolshevik revolution, or the nation, or the family, or any organization or movement."[21] Nazaruk lashed out at the lingering reluctance of Ukrainians to press for higher education for women. The mistaken notion that women do not need education would doom Ukrainian society to even greater backwardness, he complained. Only the socialization of women could bring about a healthy and flourishing Ukrainian society.

The ensuing discussion demonstrated that the aspirations of Catholic women and those of the male laity were not always the same. The Reverend Mykola Konrad, a venerable Lviv cleric, argued predictably that equality of women with men was impossible because "women have different abilities than men.... Even Christ Himself did not admit women to equality in the church." But the proto-abbot of the Basilians, the Reverend Stepan Reshetylo, shifted immediately to the contributions women had made to the church, defending the women's movement and its social work.

Two women activists of Catholic Action——Evheniia Tyshynska, a teacher who was also a Union activist, and Mariia Ianovych, also a teacher——questioned relations between the church and women. Ianovych criticized the church for not supporting women's equality, especially when compared to the intensity with which the radicals campaigned for that equality. Tyshynska, an advocate of the religious mission of Ukrainian women, argued that Catholic women could make a singular contribution to the church through the lay apostolate, but were receiving little help from the church. Echoing Nazaruk, Tyshynska also maintained that "religious apathy is the great crime of the day."[22]

She wanted to restructure the Women's Union on the basis of religious education, which she considered the cornerstone of all social activity. She developed her views in a series of articles in the quarterly *Katolytska aktsiia* (Catholic Action), but her organizational plans failed completely. A spinster, she lacked both authority and appeal to younger women. Her argument was ineffective and her ideals unclear. She sought a workers' Christianity, but had not herself grasped the concept. Instead, she used pious terminology and resorted to traditional symbols of the suffering Christ, which, in a predominantly Catholic area, appeared trite. Tyshynska's insistence on a lay apostolate for women, their active participation in worship and a more open ecclesiastical structure made both the Catholic lay intelligentsia and the clergy uncomfortable.

Dzerovych and Kuzmovych, threatened by the independence of the "new woman," tried to polarize the women's movement, imputing atheism, immorality, destruction of family and nation to the Women's Union leaders. They hoped to destroy the power base of the Women's Union by creating a rival Ukrainian Catholic Women's Union or by subordinating the Women's Union to the Marian Society, which, founded in 1904, claimed seniority over the women's movement. At the end of the Nazaruk discussion, Dzerovych accused the Women's Union of irresponsibility and unwillingness to talk about women's issues:

> The General Institute of Catholic Action is the ideological centre of Catholic organization. There can be no aspect of [public] life which would not be discussed and pondered over at this forum. A widely publicized discussion between the two currents among our women is being carried on in the Ukrainian press. The General Institute of Catholic Action also invited women of the other camp to this discussion, but they did not come. Empty seats attest to whether these women are right or not. I think that if they felt they were right, they would have come to defend their views. I thank all those who were kind enough to take part in this discussion and proclaim the meeting adjourned.

This speech was too much for the few members of the Women's Union who attended the discussions unofficially. Iryna Makukh Pavlykovska, the daughter of a fiery peasant political leader, the wife of a Senator, a vice-president of the Women's Union, and an impassioned orator herself, could not remain silent. With growing pathos she spoke for more than half an hour to a supportive audience that showed no intention of disbanding, despite the late hour.

Later, Pavlykovska and Rudnytska had a political rift that continued after the Second World War, when Pavlykovska, in the emigration, helped to establish a rival organization to that envisaged by Rudnytska. Nazaruk's précis of Pavlykovska's remarks is worth quoting in full:

In the first place, I would like to make it clear that I am appearing loyally in support of the president of the Women's Union, for it was her that Chairman Dzerovych had in mind when he referred to the women of the other camp who did not come to defend their views tonight. I am supporting her fully, despite the fact that, as some of you know, we frequently do not see eye to eye in some Union matters. She, and others like her, did not come to this discussion because they objected to the extremely strident polemical tone taken by Kuzmovych in *Meta*, and Kuzmovych was one of the scheduled speakers. [At this point Kuzmovych called out, asking whether he could make that objection public.] You can publicize whatever you wish!

I would like to ask Chairman Dzerovych why, while constantly repeating that 98 per cent of the membership of the Women's Union is Catholic, it is necessary to create another organization opposing it? [Dzerovych interjected here, "Not in opposition!" while Kuzmovych called out, "It has existed from way back!" Pavlykovska continued:]

What sort of an organization is it then? Why reactivate it at this time? Why did we not know anything of its existence previously?

The creation of a Catholic Women's Organization will lead to a splintering of the women's movement. The radical women will organize their own society, and the powerful Women's Union which brought together women of all persuasions and which you yourself point out to be predominantly Catholic will be broken. I ask you, why do you not try to elect a governing board of the Union which suits you? Well, why cannot those 98 per cent of Catholic women do that? Why do you have to create another organization which will in turn stimulate the creation of yet other organizations, which will by no means be Catholic! It will mean the splintering of the women's movement![23]

The obvious answer to this argument was that the Catholic women members of the Union were quite satisfied, and saw no reason to create another organization. But the lay intelligentsia still tried to pin a Catholic label on the Women's Union in an attempt somehow to control it, even if only formally. In 1935, as a political disagreement arose among moderate Ukrainians, Rudnytska broke with her party's conciliatory policies toward the Polish government. Kysilevska was being wooed actively by the Village Farmer.

In 1933–4, the Union updated its by-laws, a cumbersome process made even more tedious by various government stipulations. The statute required governmental approval and subsequent changes would entail repeating the procedure.

The Annual Meeting of the Women's Union was held in Lviv on 18 and 19 March 1935, at a time when Rudnytska's conflict with UNDO was already under way. The major item on the agenda was the ratification of the Statute, which had just been approved by the government. The Catholic intelligentsia, especially Dzerovych, stepped up its campaign against alleged free-thinking in the Union. Yet more women attended the 1935 meeting than that of 1933. The intervening Congress of 1934 and press coverage of the Union only heightened women's interest in it.

Mrs. Dzerovych tried to block the passage of the by-laws. Mariia Ianovych, from the Women's Section of Catholic Action and the Marian Society, made a formal proposal to amend the Statute by adding that the work and ideology of the Women's Union were based on Christian principles. In the ensuing discussion, Ianovych admitted that the idea for the amendment was her husband's and that, moreover, she herself was not a member of the Women's Union. Rudnytska cut short the debate by pointing out that the Statute was an internal matter of the Union, the result of long hours of work and negotiations with the government. Its present form reflected the best interests of the Union, it had been duly ratified and there was no reason it should be changed. Kysilevska supported Rudnytska's statement, which was met by "loud, prolonged applause from the whole auditorium."[24]

Attempts to introduce specific by-laws expressing the Union's adherence to Christian principles kept cropping up in the press and in some discussions. Allegations that practicing Catholics were being purged from the Union prompted wives of priests and others to defend the Union. In Przemyśl, the home of Tyshynska, women protested Dzerovych's methods. Tyshynska herself returned to the Union.[25]

The whole so-called "religious debate" was part of an increasingly hostile attitude toward the independence of the Women's Union in Galicia in the atmosphere of extreme nationalism and growing conservatism. Sofiia Parfanovych, the writer and physician who has headed the anti-alcohol society Vidrodzhennia since 1929, was eased out of her position, since her elementary discussions of hygiene, health, and sex education were considered dangerous to the young by self-styled defenders of morality. Arguing that the organization could not be headed by persons whose "Christian-national outlook" was not evident, a group of Vidrozhennia members began a whisper campaign that led Parfanovych not to run for re-election.[26]

After the communists broke away from the Socialist Party, left-wing women in Galicia felt comfortable in the Women's Union. Many of these activists joined the Union. Anna Pavlyk's insistence that all feminist concerns were irrelevant to community and society cost her all her influence, even in her home district.[27] There were two factors behind this. The rhetoric of the left was now badly compromised by Soviet excesses. Second, the Union's pragmatic approach to the economic difficulties facing the village women was more relevant to them than any Marxist analysis. The Women's Union opened up its ranks to all "parochial" women's organizations, which, its leaders argued, demonstrated the women's development and growth.

Veterans of the pre-First World War socialist movement were undecided about working in women's organizations. But their most active members had already seen that village women functioned most effectively in their own organization, unencumbered by the hostile or patronizing attitudes of men. Ivanna Blazhkevych, a tireless organizer in the village of Denysiv, encouraged women to become active in all phases of community affairs. She believed that women were an integral part of the national political renaissance. Blazhkevych, a teacher who lost her two daughters in tragic circumstances, developed close ties with the poet-teacher Kravchenko and the writer Kobylianska. She was active in Union programmes, but as a socialist she was uncomfortable in a women's organization that did not even pay lip-service to progressive ideology. In 1927 she argued that women's organizations must try to eliminate sexual discrimination. She stressed that in the face of Polonization, women and the family must become the bastions of the nation, like the Polish family under the tsars. She even conceded the primacy of the political over the economic struggle in Poland.[28] She ran consistently on the progressive ticket of the Radical Party, opposed the liberal coalition and maintained that women should enter existing political parties only as equal members. She used her party's newspaper, *Hromadskyi holos*, to defend the Women's Union against various criticisms. As a member of the Union, she not only worked with, but also appeared in the same public forum as her political opponents, the nationalist Dontsova and the liberal Rudnytska. Although *Hromadskyi holos* published some ironic accounts of the work of women, it rarely attacked women directly in the 1920s.[29]

Rumblings about a break of this "united front" swelled by the end of the 1920s as the Union grew in strength. The formation of UNDO in 1926, and the OUN in 1929, led the left-of-centre groups to activate all their forces. The Ukrainian Radical Socialist Party attempted to continue the blend of socialism and nationalism that had been its trademark before the First World War. Like other parties, it stressed both its vision of the future and its ties with the past. The party leaders increasingly felt that the Women's Union, especially with Rudnytska's UNDO affiliation and anti-Soviet proclivities, did not suitably reflect the tradition of the Pavlyk women. Women active in UNDO held leading positions in the Women's Union. Wives and daughters of priests——those rhetorical class enemies of the left——also remained Union activists.

In 1931, radical women, aided by the Ukrainian Radical Socialist Party (URSP), founded the Women's Community (Zhinocha hromada) "as an addition to the...party"[30] in an attempt to maximize the strength of both radicals and women. It reformed itself as the Union of Working Women, and received the necessary legal approval from the Polish government in 1936. Its membership was just under 8,000 women, composed mostly of peasants, but also of some factory workers. It supported all political undertakings of the URSP and engaged in activities similar to those of the Women's Union. Initially, it published a page in *Holos*, but by 1936 it had its own bi-weekly, *Zhinochyi holos* (Women's Voice). The paper was well edited, with the same combination of political and practical information that characterized *Zhinocha dolia* and other women's publications. It was mildly anti-clerical and openly pro-Jewish. Accounts of Jewish and Ukrainian co-operation were frequently featured,[31] as were descriptions of Polish anti-Semitism.

The Union of Working Women was headed by Ivanna Blazhkevych. Her secretary was Franka Stakhova, the wife of one of the party leaders, and its vice-presidents were Nastia Mykytchuk and Liuba Muryn. Among its most active members were Dariia Babiuk and Anna Hohol. Emigré women from Ukraine, among them Liubov Margolina Hansen and Liubov Zalevska, supported the group financially. A large part of the group's funding came from women in the United States and Canada, who, working in the sweatshops or on the prairies, came to realize the importance of political action and union membership. In Volhynia, the Union of Working Women organized a women's section connected with the Volhynian People's Universities.

The organizational structure and range of activities of the Union of Working Women were similar to those of the Women's Union. Membership sometimes overlapped. The Union of Working Women recognized the significant radical anniversary dates and generally tried to keep the radical tradition alive. It published poetry in line with its goals, organized demonstrations, commemorative celebrations and the increasingly popular rhythmic exercises to uplifting, patriotic songs.

Its goal was "to aid the cultural-education and civic-social development and upbringing of Ukrainian working women." This it proposed to achieve by organizing cultural, educational and self-improvement programmes to strengthen the individual dignity and raise the civic-social consciousness (*hromadsko-suspilnoi svidomosty*) of its members. The organization tried to foster trade education, hold public lectures and presentations, conduct other cultural programmes and set up bookstores, libraries and reading rooms. It planned to establish courses for the illiterate, especially young people who were denied an education, and tutorial services; it encouraged shelters, subsidized cafeterias, day-care centres and kindergartens, and summer and day camps. Lastly it offered free employment referral services and free legal aid clinics and established local and regional organizations.[32] Essentially, these goals mirrored those of the Prosvita societies and the Women's Union.

The term "working women" was used as a class and ideological label, not to denote employment status. The Radical Party, ideologically, could not have a feminist adjunct. Any of its women's adjunct organizations would *ipso facto* be considered organizations of working women. Also the needs of working women, either inside or outside the household, were not even mentioned in the goals of Hromada, the Union of Working Women. It was simply a public organization in which women participated. The possible reasons for expulsion were non-payment of dues for a year, or immoral or dishonourable behaviour. Not a word was said about equal rights, emancipation, or sexual discrimination.

The Women's Union saw Hromada as a political organization, co-operated with it whenever possible, and did not consider membership in both organizations to be conflicting. "Hromada was headed and led for the most part by women engaged in the political movement," Franka Stakhova reminisced. "It had greater success in expressing its consciousness of the national and administrative process under the Polish occupation regime than it did in developing social or economic policy."[33] As a political organization, it drew its constituency from women, but did not analyze their specific needs.

In the 1930s the Women's Union articulated openly feminist concerns, while Hromada reasserted its radical position on women. It accused the Union of bourgeois-feminist bias and disregard for the peasant women's interests. By the end of the decade relations between the Union and the Hromada had become tense.[34]

This tension was further exacerbated by the co-ordinated push of the Village Farmer Co-operative, Silskyi hospodar, into the villages. The Village Farmer was a community agency with which the Women's Union had for the most part co-operated and which, in 1935, had again pledged co-operation formally. But in 1935-6 it started to organize women's sections, and its economic resources were considerably larger than those of the Union. It employed more than 150 permanent staff, boasted 160,000 members by the 1930s and had many volunteers. It was supported by the Polish government, or at least had been instructed by the government to expand and create special circles for women. The Poles, as noted, had a similar organization, the Circle of Rural Housewives, to help the women modernize farming, but it was never very effective in Ukrainian territories.

A year earlier, in 1935, the Women's Union, under the guidance of Milena Rudnytska, had refused to pursue another attempt at accommodation with the Polish government. Rudnytska was barred from running in the election, which was boycotted by the women. This show of women's independence, which will be discussed in the next chapter, was yet another reason for the government to try to restrict the activities of the Women's Union. The concerted move into the villages by the co-operative cut deeply into the work of the Union.

First, the "section of village housewives," founded in 1936 (which lasted until 1939), was headed by Kysilevska herself. Pavlykovska, who had defended Rudnytska against the Catholic would-be attackers, became the vice-chairperson. Kharytia Kononenko, on whom the Women's Union had placed hopes for the continued expansion of economic activity in the villages, was drawn to the co-operative. In an uncharacteristic over-reaction Rudnytska asked her to resign from the Union. The women's section also threw its considerable resources into training peasant boys and girls. The schools and courses were under the direct supervision of the moving force of the Co-operative, Ievhen Khraplyvy. By 1938, they had organized more than 13,000 boys and 4,800 girls.[35]

Both the Co-operative and the Village Farmer had initially supported the Women's Union, realizing its potential strength. It was this very strength that they had found disturbing in the 1930s. Earlier some women activists had complained about the secondary role of women in the leadership of the co-operative movement. The uncompromising stand of the women toward the Poles was also resented both by Ukrainian merchants and by the Co-operative.[36] Women were more likely to insist that Ukrainian be used in advertising, a sensitive issue especially for the merchants in Lviv. The Women's Union, moreover, tended to stress co-operative ventures rather than to foster actively the spirit of free enterprise.

A stormy Union meeting of 3 April 1936 discussed its relationship to the Co-operative and——more by implication than discussion——to the ultra-nationalist politics of the OUN. The rhetoric of the Union became even more patriotic. In its resolutions, the Union stated that as the sole representative of "the strivings and the interests of the national (*natsionalnoho*) Ukrainian women...it must take a stand on the most important issues of our national life and influence the direction they take in accordance with the Highest National Ideal to which Ukrainian women were stalwartly loyal." The Union had argued repeatedly that as a women's organization it alone represented all women, and that any other women's organization represented only special-interest groups.

But that was not how many men and the growing number of *engagé* women saw the issue. The Union felt the shift of the Co-operative most strongly. Although Kysilevska remained a member of the Union and even of its board, relations between her and the board elected at the 1936 meeting were strained.[37] The consensus of the meeting was to try to salvage both the autonomy of the Women's Union and the spirit of co-operation with the Village Farmer.

> The general meeting affirms that the most effective form of women's organization in the villages is that of establishing independent circles of the Women's Union, and therefore considers the creation of other women's organizations or women's sections affiliated with general national organizations inimical to national strength.

In the economic part of the document, they pleaded that "only the harmonious co-operation of the Women's Union and the Village Farmer can yield positive results in the agrarian-enterprise sector among women. It is with deep sorrow, therefore, that we note that the Village Farmer has not adhered to the agreement which the two organizations drew up last year." In an attempt at compromise, the Union urged its members to continue to popularize the ideas of co-operation and to urge women to join the co-operatives. But it also told its members "to demand that the Co-operative use part of the profit to buy machines that would aid in the women's household work and would be shared by them."[38]

However, the compromise failed, paralyzing much of the village work. A few months before Germany and the Soviet Union invaded Poland, Kysilevska suggested that the Women's Union withdraw from all economic activity. The Women's Union was indignant: to abandon village women and other Ukrainian women at this critical time would be perfidious (the Union had been temporarily disbanded by the police in 1938). The fact that the Polish authorities had categorized women's organizations by class——dividing the peasants and the intelligentsia——did not mean that Ukrainians should follow in Polish footsteps, commented the *Zhinka* editorial wryly.[39]

The anti-Women's Union backlash continued. Various segments of the Ukrainian community periodically accused the Union of either wanting to monopolize the whole women's movement or of failing to consolidate all women. The Union, in its press and public statements, declared that the men lacked any sense of unity or consolidation themselves, and were responsible for the discord among women.

Despite the attacks, the Women's Union was able to maintain a sense of unity and integrity even through this difficult political period. On the basis of a programme of pragmatic feminism, it had in its first decade successfully united Ukrainian women. They became a political, economic and social force in the Ukrainian community. Partly because of the growth in their power, and partly because the idea of independent women's organizations was inherently threatening to the men, the Women's Union itself was attacked. As a result of these attacks it was compelled to articulate its feminist views more clearly than the women of the 1920s had been willing to do.

16.
Women as a Political Force

Political activity is gender-free. Males, however, have more experience and traditionally politics has been a male preserve. The entry of women into politics through the vote or demonstrations coincided with the democratization of the political process. In addition to equality in the legal sphere, certain other issues were of particular interest to women: they included family legislation, abortion, divorce, health, education, welfare and disarmament, which were also central to the well-being of the entire society. Since women, to a greater degree than men, confront the minutiae of daily existence and family life, these minutiae become the primary concerns of women deflecting interest in feminism as such. Ukrainian women outside the Soviet Union in the inter-war years also often identified women's concerns with issues of social welfare and family legislation.

Ukrainian women for the most part still did not think in ideological terms, because they were too uninformed to do so. Consequently, they were more tolerant and practical-minded than men. The Ukrainian women's movement outside the USSR preserved its united front during the inter-war years, albeit with increasing difficulty. The expansion of educational opportunities and the sphere of women's activity, however, led to greater political awareness.

The difficulties in creating one Ukrainian women's organization with a single political course can be reduced to one still pertinent question: at what point does legal and social equality attain the level at which women can reach their full autonomy and potential? As in other nations that promulgated legal equality of the sexes, there emerged in Ukraine of the 1930s a variant of the current anti-ERA cry: Enough! We women have achieved all the equality we ever wanted! We wish no more.

Western Ukrainians were socially conservative. Most of them opposed the leftist ideology perceived by the progressive intelligentsia in the West as a defence against fascism. Communism in the Soviet Union had a more direct bearing upon Ukrainian women than Western fascism. The relentless suppression of national communism, the first signs of "communism with a human face," the famine and the purges were seen as signs of Russian perfidy.

The average Western Ukrainian identified communism with Russia, which made communism doubly anathema. Soviet promotion of equality for women also made it easier to identify women's striving for genuine autonomy as the first step toward godless communism. Anti-feminism, anti-communism and anti-Russian feelings reinforced the growing attraction of integral nationalism during the 1930s among the younger generation of Ukrainian women. To them, the very word "feminism" was hateful and threatening, even though Ukrainian feminist thought stressed the centrality of motherhood.[1]

Women on the political scene

Since Ukrainians constituted the most compact and best organized political minority in Poland, it was predominantly on Ukrainian inhabited territory in Galicia and Volhynia that Ukrainian women's organizations developed and flourished. And it was here that Ukrainians, both men and women, played an active role.

Ukrainians elected women as deputies to the Polish Sejm in 1922 and 1928. The record was less glorious in subsequent elections. In 1922 Levchanivska was elected from Volhynia, while Rudnytska was elected from Galicia in 1928. That same year Kysilevska was elected to the Senate. The latter two women played an important political role that was only marginally determined by their sex. Blazhkevych, Stakhova, Mirna, Rusova and Pavlykovska continued to be an integral part of the radical movement. Sheparovych looked after women's interests in UNDO and was on the Executive of that party from 1929 to 1933. Baranova and Dontsova joined women's auxiliaries of male parties, which were also highly visible. The women members of parliament used that forum not only to raise and defend "women's issues," but also to help Ukrainian women's organizations. Rudnytska successfully protested the dissolution of the Women's Union in 1929, while Kysilevska, who headed the Union's organizational section, used her free rail-travel privilege to help set up new Union circles. Like other Ukrainian women activists, Rudnytska combined politics with work among women. Sheparovych, as editor of *Zhinka*, was frequently brought to court on censorship charges, and used the legal help of Lev Hankevych, with whom she had worked on various community projects since the Civic Committee in Lviv in 1919.

The most consistent Ukrainian feminists, particularly Rudnytska and Mirna argued for the complete integration of women into the political process. They saw the role of women's organizations as the promotion of the causes of women *qua* women. Other women in the Women's Union, however, felt that women's auxiliaries——or rather parallel women's sections of political parties——were an effective means of political activity. The section versus integration issue became one of the major disagreements among women activists and a manipulative tool for political parties. It continued throughout

the late twenties, broke out sporadically in the thirties and erupted with full
force in the forties among the émigrés.

The political climate in Poland

The relationship between Ukrainian women, Ukrainian political parties and the
Polish regime was complex. Characteristically for a colonized nation,
nationalism impinged directly upon the conception of women's rights. The fate
of the inter-war Polish republic has been told elsewhere and Polish writers have
acknowledged that state's short-sighted treatment of Ukrainians. Ukrainian
resistance to Polish rule was not dissimilar to the resistance the Poles themselves exhibited toward Russian rule in the nineteenth century. The replacement
of the Austrian carrot-and-stick policy with heavy-handed Polish reliance on
the latter galvanized Ukrainian society into community action and political
opposition. The Ukrainian community in inter-war Poland

> was characterized by an élan, an enthusiasm, a rare example of the triumph of
> spiritual strength of a nation which only directed its efforts toward a life free of
> the force of the occupying power.
>
> Disillusioned in international justice, taught by bitter experience that
> self-determination was an empty phrase for a defeated nation,
> Ukrainians...worked with indefatigable energy.... Using the few available legal
> opportunities, valiantly overcoming the chicaneries of the Polish police and the
> obstacles placed in its path, the nation threw itself into building Ukrainian
> organizations with remarkable success.[2]

Ukrainian women contributed significantly to this communal effort. In the
1920s a major goal of Ukrainian political activity had been to obtain schools
with Ukrainian as the language of instruction. Many of the women activists
were teachers; many more were volunteers in pre-school and out-of-school
cultural-enrichment programmes that rendered these women invaluable "in the
struggle for the soul of the Ukrainian child."[3] All three Ukrainian women
deputies were especially active in the legislation and discussions dealing with
education.

The Polish government had no consistent policy toward national minorities
within its borders. Moderate Poles wanted to work out an equitable *modus
vivendi* with the minorities, which made up about one-third of the country's
population. But the moderates lacked both a clear goal and government support.
They were opposed mainly by those Poles who lived in closest proximity with
a given national minority, especially the Ukrainians. In fact the Polish
moderates pursued aspirations rather than policies. These were based upon
reason and moderation, and met with a sympathetic response among moderate

Participants in the Ukrainian studies course organized by Mykhailo Hrushevsky and Ivan Franko for students from Eastern Ukraine (Lviv, summer 1904). Seated in foreground, left to right: Marusia Dvernytska, Viktoriia Chykalenko, Ariiadna Drahomaniv-Trush, Ivan Trush.

First row, left to right: Participant from E. Ukraine (perhaps Radetsky), Tyt Revakovych, Ivan Bryk, Mykola Hankevych, Fedir Vovk, Mykhailo Hrushevsky, Ivan Franko, Mariia Hrushevska, Volodymyr Hnatiuk.

Second row: Volodymyr Doroshenko, Mariia Pidlisetska-Mudrak, Hanna Chykalenko-Keller, Katria Lozenko-Holitsynska, Andriievska, Mariia Lypa, Ivan Lypa, Unknown participant, Vasyl Paneiko, Unknown participant, Harmatii.

Third row: Iurii Lavrivsky, Ievhen Holitsynsky, Iuliian Bachynsky, Maryna Krushelnytska-Drozdovska, Dymtro Doroshenko, Iaroslav Hrushkevych, Levko Chykalenko, Mariia Derkach, Stepan Dolnytsky, Artym Khomyk, K. Rostkovych.

Fourth row: Unknown participant, Oleksander Skoropys-Ioltukhovsky, Demko Rozov, Dariia Shukhevych-Starosolska, Volodymyr Zahaikevych, Teklia Iermi-Bodnar, Mykhailo Mochulsky.

ПЕРШОМУ
УКРАЇНСЬКОМУ БОРЦЕВИ
ЗА ПРАВА ЖІНКИ

Title page of commemorative pamphlet about Nataliia Kobrynska, published by Women's Union in Lviv, 1921.

Zinaida Mirna

Anna Zhukova

Courtesy of Uliana Starosolsky
Dariia Shukhevych-Starosolska

Olha Kobylianska

Olena Stepaniv

Ukrainian delegation at International Women's Congress in Rome, 1923. Left to right: Lu. Zelenevska, Mlada Lypovetska, Sofiia Rusova, Nina Onatska.

Ukrainian delegation at the International Women's Congress in Vienna, 11 July 1921. First row, left to right: Milena Rudnytska, Oksana Khrapko-Drahamanova, Valeriia O'Connor-Vilinska, Nadiia Surovtseva, Kharytia Kononenko.
Second row: Pisniachevska, Lototska, E. Loska, Ivanna Levytska, Olena Zalizniak, Olha Halahan, Tobarkar. At rear: Bezkrovna, O. Levytska.

Title page of Women's Congress program Lviv, 1934.

Village Women's Day, Lviv Women's Congress, 1934.   Courtesy Rubleva

Lviv Women's Congress, 1934.   Courtesy UNWLA

Women's Union Stanyslaviv, 1930's.

Lviv Women's Congress, 1934. Centre: Teofil Okunevsky with Mary Sheepshanks. Courtesy Rubleva.

Village women at Lviv Women's Congress, 1934.

Ukrainians. Neither group, however, reflected majority views.

Women, as individuals and as representatives of women's organizations, participated in some of the attempts at reaching a mutually satisfying agreement with the Poles. Polish women focused on building their national community and opposed Ukrainian attempts to do likewise. In 1927 one of the leading Polish feminists, Lucja Charewiczowa, published a book under a pseudonym warning Poles of the achievements of the "so-called Ukrainian" women's movement and of the danger it posed to the Polish state, the Polish population of Eastern Galicia, and Volhynia in particular. She presented a comprehensive picture of the multi-faceted work of Ukrainian women but maintained that they were motivated only by anti-Polish sentiment.[4] Charewiczowa articulated the fears of Poles who lived in areas populated by Ukrainians when she accused the Polish women of being too liberal and weak-kneed toward the minorities.

Only isolated voices were raised by Polish women against the most blatant abuses of the authorities against Ukrainians. One came from Wanda Pelczyńska, a member of parliament from Vilnius (then known as Wilno). On 10 February 1937 she defended minorities in the Sejm.

Attempts at conciliation between Poles and Ukrainians failed, and Ukrainians felt duped by each failure, further undermining Ukrainian confidence in the Polish republic. The vast majority of Ukrainian women, moreover, came into contact mainly with the most chauvinist Poles, whom they considered representative of the entire nation. It was difficult for them to develop a sophisticated view of the situation. They tended to see the world from their homes, which were threatened on the one hand by the "godless communists," and on the other by the hostile Poles.

Search for unity

Understandably, as representatives of a nation fragmented along so many different lines——geographical, political, ideological, religious and historical——Ukrainians emphasized unity. Each political group spoke from a central position; each religious group was ecumenical; each civic organization promoted joint community effort; each splinter group sought to preserve solidarity. The more diverse Ukrainian society became the more conscious it was of unity. During the inter-war years Western Ukrainians popularized the hymn "God grant us unity, for in it lies strength." A major source of pride for the Women's Union and the whole Ukrainian women's movement outside the Soviet Union was that women preserved solidarity and tactical unity that eluded Ukrainian males.

Ideally, Ukrainian women sought a common front against the Poles at the ballot box. At each electoral campaign the women said that Ukrainians should co-ordinate their efforts to prevent a split of the Ukrainian vote. The Polish government and the local administrations tried to limit effective Ukrainian participation in elections by both open and covert means. After 1927, the Women's Union always proposed that Ukrainian parties not only discuss electoral tactics, but select a single strong Ukrainian candidate in each district.

A woman in the Polish Senate

Ukrainians in Galicia boycotted the elections of 1922, which antedated the Allied sanction of Polish administration of the area. The Women's Union solidly supported the boycott. In Volhynia, formerly part of the Russian Empire, Ukrainian parties participated in the elections. Most women supported Levchanivska, who was elected to the Senate. At the swearing-in ceremony, she tried to speak in Ukrainian, but finally bowed to protocol and said the requisite "I swear" in Polish. In debates, she did not limit herself to "women's issues," but defended the interests of Ukrainians and Belorussians in general. She criticized the Polish government for allocating a bare one per cent of the budget for public welfare, while neighbouring Czechoslovakia expended more than 9 per cent. She accused the government of disregarding the needs of the minorities, maintaining that Ukrainian peasants had to rely on cultural organizations, such as Prosvita, which received no public funds, for social services. She gave reasoned and impassioned accounts of violations of human rights, police brutality, and physical and psychological terror among the minorities which made the peasants "afraid to use even those microscopic rights vouchsafed them by the law."[5] Levchanivska, however, could not become an effective politician. Her family was not rich; one of the children was sickly and had to be cared for; naturally, it was the mother who had to be near the child. She did not run for office again.

The Union becomes politicized

The brutal murder of the treasurer of the Women's Union, Olha Basarab, by the Lviv police in 1924 politicized the Union and brought it into the limelight. The deed made the seemingly innocuous work of women significant——why else would the Polish police have found Basarab a threat? Olha Levytska Basarab, we recall, had worked in the women's relief committees in Lviv, had been widowed, performed various auxiliary functions for Konovalets, and led a life not so different from that of most Ukrainian Galician women. She earned a living as an accountant, but did not consider her profession her primary goal in life. She died after vicious torture, which included pulling off her nails. On her cell wall she allegedly wrote in blood: "For the blood, the tortures, the destruction, Oh [God] return Ukraine to us." Whether the poor beaten woman had the energy to write such a statement is irrelevant——the legend came into being. Her death gave the women their own martyr who had died for their nation. The Women's Union protested the murder, in Poland and abroad. Although the Union maintained that its actions had no political implications, the circumstances of Basarab's death politicized matters. According to Sheparovych, Malytska, President of the Union at the time, was forced to resign her post under pressure from the Polish administration.

Another tragic event heightened the visibility of the Women's Union. In 1926, when Dontsova was President, Petliura, who had become a symbol of the Ukrainian Republic, was assassinated in Paris. The International Council of Women had been holding its meeting there. Olena Sheparovych, who had attended, stayed for the funeral, and was the only person there who resided in an ethnically Ukrainian land. Her presence was extremely important to the self-image of the women in the leadership of the Union, and strengthened the political role of the women's organization.

In the villages, the Union needed police permission to hold a public meeting and form a new branch. Kysilevska used the sale of chickens as an example of a political and economic problem. Poultry was a major source of income for many peasants, but by importing chickens the Polish government artificially lowered the prices. Kysilevska told an audience of women in 1926 that if they were more politicized, they could pressure the Sejm to repeal legislation on importing chickens. Then peasant women could sell their chickens at higher prices.[6]

When Ukrainians decided to participate in the elections of new representatives to the Sejm and the Senate in 1928, the Women's Union worked on two levels: it tried to assure the participation and representation of women within the Ukrainian political parties, encouraging the parties to co-operate, and it initiated a get-out-and-vote campaign.

The constitution of 1921, according to which all citizens over 21 could elect members of the Sejm, and all citizens over 30 could choose representatives to the Senate, provided for a five-year term in the Sejm. But the Sejm could also be dissolved by a two-thirds vote of its members. The Sejm was the more powerful body; the Senate merely reviewed legislation. Jointly, both houses formed the National Assembly and elected the president of the Polish Republic. Voting was by proportional representation and each locality had a polling station within six kilometres. This provision, employed to ensure the vote of conservative Polish peasants, directly benefited Ukrainians. It also made the campaigning work of the Union crucial on the village level.

Galician Ukrainian men were often reluctant to place women candidates on the voting rolls in 1927. Late in life Sheparovych recalled her arguments with Dmytro Levytsky on the matter. The women had decided that Kysilevska should run for the Senate, and Rudnytska for the Sejm. With the latter, a well-educated and effective speaker before all types of audiences, there was no opposition. Kysilevska, however, who was so effective with the peasant audiences, was an embarrassment to the older Ukrainian politicians, who were steeped in nineteenth-century gentility. The same Levytsky who actively fostered Rudnytska's political career said that in order to represent UNDO Kysilevska must do something about her frumpy appearance. Sheparovych again mediated. A daughter of a rich and progressive Ukrainian lawyer, she had received an excellent upbringing and education at home and had travelled to the major European countries as a young woman. She recognized the importance of dress and decorum when dealing with foreigners. This was especially pertinent in all Ukrainian dealings with the Poles, since the Poles had an image of Ukrainians as untamed, violent primitives. That same grandmotherly, squat, plain, asexual appearance of Kysilevska which made her popular in the villages was a drawback on the national level. Kysilevska took the admonitions about her wardrobe and grooming from Sheparovych with good grace. She proved a willing and quick learner, and her public appearances outside Galicia were as effective as in her native area. After the 1927 elections the UNDO leadership realized the value both of women candidates and of the women's vote.

In the countryside, however, there was some opposition to women's voting and running for office. For example, in the village of Hushchanky (Zbarazh district), local Polish officials persuaded Ukrainian peasants that if their wives voted, the value of the male vote would be proportionately reduced. This perverse argument arose partly because of the peasants' resentment toward the local Ukrainian teacher, Hanna Mazurenko, who forcefully promoted the rights of peasant women. The women, however, persisted in pressing their cause through the Ukrainian Radical Party. With the support of the Ukrainian intelligentsia, they not only voted in elections but also elected women to the local party organization.[7]

The participation of Ukrainian women in the elections of 1927 was significant both in numbers and in drama. Young mothers carrying babies often trudged on foot to the polls. Many waited all night for the polls to open. The participation of Ukrainian women in subsequent elections, however, was less significant, partly because the Polish administration changed districts and amended electoral laws. Another reason was that Ukrainian parties tried repeatedly to influence and control women and the women's organization.

Ukrainian political parties

There were essentially three major political configurations in Ukrainian society, and two somewhat weak ones. Emphasis here is on the Polish territories, but can be applied generally to Ukrainian population outside the Soviet Union.

In both Volhynia and Galicia, Poles tried to bolster the small pro-Polish Ukrainian parties. They were more successful in Volhynia, which had unhappy memories of Russian rule. In Galicia the openly pro-Polish party mustered few supporters. Few women were active in these groups, none of them prominently. The popularity of the extreme left fluctuated. Strikes and demonstrations initiated by the communists drew a growing following, which reflected social and national discontent more than attraction to communism.

The Communist Party of Western Ukraine (KPZU) established women's sections patterned on the Soviet model and at its second congress, held in October 1925, passed "a separate resolution about working among women."[8] Such work remained underdeveloped. The few communist women activists were not interested in women's questions. Among them the most prominent were Iryna Voloshhchak and Mariia Kikh. Olha Levytska, whose revolutionary alias was Czesława Groserowa, drafted the programme of the KPZU at its first meeting held on 29 October 1921 in one of the offices of St. George's Cathedral. Another activist, Mariia Gizhovska, a member of the executive board, left the party to lead a group which supported more direct revolutionary action. There were women among the organizers and participants of the Anti-Fascist Congress of Workers of Culture held in Lviv in 1936, but again they were not feminists and did not work strictly among women. The party, which split in 1928, was destroyed in 1938 on Stalin's orders.[9]

The old Russophile party split after the First World War. The radicals called themselves "The People's Will" and gravitated toward communism; the conservatives, backed by Russian émigrés and Polish subsidies, remained a negligible force. The women's organization, Obshchestvo Ruskykh Dam, on the other hand, showed no interest in politics.

The parties dominating the inter-war Ukrainian political scene corresponded roughly to the radical, liberal and populist-authoritarian models, with an independent, sovereign Ukraine as their goal. The first two groups agreed to co-operate with the Polish state in order to improve the economic, social, political and cultural lot of Ukrainians. The third was a clandestine organization which tried to boycott and sabotage the whole parliamentary process.

The radicals, drawing on Franko's legacy, clustered in the Ukrainian Socialist-Radical Party (USRP), which stressed agrarian reform, distribution of the large estates and social welfare. Also in the radical tradition, they subordinated the woman issue to the social one. In 1931, the party initiated the creation of the Union of Working Women, the Women's Communities, that functioned mainly among the peasants. The Women's Union, as noted, maintained a working relationship with the radical women. Generally, the Women's Community refrained from major attacks on the Union and the Union women did not criticize the radical women openly.

OUN and the Nationalist Movement

The relationship of the women and the Women's Union to the liberal UNDO and the nationalist OUN was complex. The OUN, established in 1929, sometimes claimed descent from the Ukrainian Military Organization (UVO). This claim is not entirely justified. The UVO was organized for a specific purpose and had limited aims——to continue the armed struggle against the foreign regime in Ukrainian lands. It engaged in clandestine and terrorist activity, but did not claim to become a political party. Konovalets, the head of the organization, did not seek ideological control over the membership and considered terror an unfortunate but necessary supplement to political work. Women performed various functions for the UVO and were especially effective in liaison work. It was a highly conspiratorial organization, and the assassination of Konovalets by the Bolsheviks in 1938 ensured that the full extent of its activities would never be known. Olha Basarab was involved in the organization, as was Olha Verbytska. The other women who engaged in its activities did not, it seems, play major roles.

The OUN sought to be a comprehensive ideological organization embodying the true essence of Ukrainian culture. It was a mass movement with a conspiratorial core and a terrorist section. In emphasizing the importance of organization, mobilization of the masses, and a mixture of rhetoric and action, the OUN emulated its major ideological opponents, the Bolsheviks. Like all clandestine movements, it left itself open to police infiltration and to extremely confusing permutations of agents provocateurs and double-agents. It fell victim to the inevitable fate of all such movements——splintering and internal and external violence, including murder. For many Ukrainians the whole matter is still emotionally charged. While stressing its intrinsic Ukrainian character and extolling the Ukrainian national idea, the OUN possessed elements of fascist ideology and organization, although neither was fully developed.

The OUN's views of women, equally undeveloped, were contradictory. In one of its many theses, the nationalists were ordered to treat all women honourably as comrades and potential mothers. But because the nationalists opposed liberalism and perceived radicals as crypto-communists, they viewed as anathema feminism, socialist ideals of equality of women and women's liberation.[10] While the OUN glorified the mother, the keeper of the national hearth, the bearer of children who would assure the future of the nation, it rarely elaborated on that ideal. The limitation of women's role to domesticity and acceptance of male tutelage came out very clearly in the marginal Bukovynian paper *Samostiina dumka ukrainskoi matery* (The Independent Thought of the Ukrainian Mother), which appeared in Chernivtsi in the 1930s. The function of women was to bear children; even the rearing would be done by professionals. Yet only opponents of this particular version of Ukrainian nationalism saw the irony of the nationalists' position.

Women who joined the movement disregarded the party's stand on women or on women's issues in general. They were motivated by the same dedication as the men. Nationalism in its OUN variant was largely a youth-oriented and youth-created movement. The generation coming of age a decade after the great liberation struggle felt compelled to continue the fight for Ukrainian independence. The young women underwent a process of socialization similar to that of the young men: the Polonization of schools, the abuses and police harassments, and the indignity of compulsory attendance at government-sponsored Polish patriotic celebrations. They were all aware of the shameful network of police informers in schools. They were easily angered by national discrimination, but no longer by sexual discrimination. Frequently unaware of the lengthy quest for educational benefits of the previous generation, they could see no point in women's organizations. Raised with ideals of selfless dedication, observing their Polish neighbours' patriotism, feeling acutely the humiliation of foreign rule, the young women "showed a lack of understanding, even outright hostility toward feminism."[11] In fact, they tended to see feminism as narrow feminine egotism.

The incipiently totalitarian nature of the Ukrainian nationalist movement was not readily apparent to the casual observer. On the contrary, Polish nationalist organizations, based on similar principles, had been instrumental in building modern Poland——or so the average Western Ukrainian believed. Ukrainians in Poland, especially those in Galicia, beleaguered on all sides, gravitated toward simple, clear-cut, patriotic movements. They glorified past struggles and felt ashamed of the political parties to which their parents belonged, with their compromises, failures and their inability to cope with economic crises. In the writings of Dontsov they sensed the elements of voluntaristic terrorism under the guise of dedicated nationalism. Dontsov and Mikhnovsky, both Eastern Ukrainians (the latter apparently a victim of the Cheka, the first Soviet secret police) enjoyed the same type of popularity socialist writers had had among young people before 1914. The new ideology was simple: total dedication to the nation. In it, as in the populist movement in the Russian Empire (with which the nationalist movement in Western Ukraine had many similarities), women usually played a subordinate role. They acted with the utmost dedication, whether disseminating propaganda or assassinating an official. These women considered the sexual aspect immaterial to their duties. They accepted their role as mothers and nurturers, but also joined wholeheartedly in the undertakings of the movement.

Many pragmatic feminists, raised under the sex-segregated Austrian society, developed an individual sense of worth and independence, partly strengthened by the traditional autonomy of women in pre-industrial societies. The socialization of many younger women occurred differently. First, Polish pressure toward national assimilation was much stronger than that of the Austrian monarchy. Second, the most blatant obstacles to women's equality had been removed. High-school education, youth organizations, camping trips, joint demonstrations, and ideological discussions predisposed this generation of Western Ukrainian women to peer solidarity. The latter was strengthened by the community's stress on the importance of unity, and the growing popularity of fascism in Europe. The protracted economic crisis strengthened the anti-feminist backlash. Iryna Vilde wrote poignant stories in which the young girl, pressured by the mother to study at a university and become involved in broad issues, finds an ally for her dreams of domesticity in her grandmother.

Young women who might have become the most ardent feminists became ardent nationalists instead. With the build-up of Ukrainian community organizations came clashes with the police. Frequently, they stemmed from Polish policies toward the schools. Polish students, aided by the local police, engaged in their own street demonstrations. As Rudnytska pointed out, in defence of young people, "Polish youth reacted in exactly the same manner against the decisions affecting their education made by the occupying powers as does Ukrainian youth today, but the Poles do not want to understand the noble actions of the Ukrainian youth."[12]

More and more young women became involved in clandestine organizations. The trials connected with the UVO in 1928 implicated Olha Verbytska. Young women were accused of serving as couriers for the UVO, disseminating proscribed literature, boycotting Polish patriotic functions and forming clandestine organizations. In 1929, a group of young Ukrainian women was brought to trial and charged, among other counts, with disseminating leaflets specifically addressed to Ukrainian women. Among the women were Mariia Kravtsiv, Sofiia Moisievych, Mariia Konrad, Mariia Mudryk, Anna Mryts and Zenoviia Kravtsiv. Although all were acquitted, the case further politicized the Ukrainian community. Most of the women were daughters of prominent Union activists.[13]

At first it was difficult for Western Ukrainians, both men and women, to accustom themselves to violent protest and terrorism. In one of the first attempts to rob a postman to raise funds for the UVO, both Roman Mytsyk and Stefaniia Korduba, a student at the University of Lviv and the daughter of a professor, panicked and Iaroslav Liubovych was killed by Polish police. But by the early 1930s women of the nationalist camp, many still in their teens, were involved actively in assassination attempts against various Polish officials. The assassination of Bronisław Pieracki, the interior minister, in Warsaw in June 1934, with the active participation of the young Kateryna Zarytska and Dariia Hnatkivska, epitomized the blind and selfless dedication of these young women. The assassination was condemned by Sheptytsky in strong language; UNDO informed the Polish ministry that it abhorred the action; and the political wisdom of assassinating a minister mildly favourable to Ukrainians was openly questioned. But the violence did not affect the disposition of the two young women, who continued to manifest a joyful, almost religious "love of this little piece of land which is my own" through years of Polish prison, German concentration camps and——in the case of Zarytska——a lifetime of Soviet labour camps and exile.[14]

The selfless dedication (regardless of the immediate political results), the glowing rhetoric, and the almost religious patriotism had a dramatic impact upon women's consciousness. It was strengthened by the attacks on the Women's Union and its "new woman" concept, which was caricatured as a heartless, egotistical, atheistic pervert who threatened the family and the nation. There was sporadic conflict in the 1930s. In Stryi in 1938, an anonymous article charged the entire Lviv Union leadership and Rudnytska in particular with lack of patriotism. A bitter meeting ensued, but the local Women's Union withstood the accusation.[15]

Since the 1920s, women activists had tried to contain the spread of integral nationalism among the women. On 7 January 1928, Rudnytska published a lengthy article in *Dilo* emphasizing the importance of women in the political process, both as mothers and as individuals. The Union tried to expand the youth sections precisely to offset destructive party divisions among the youth, stressing patriotism and the compatibility of motherhood with individual independence.[16] After the pacification, sporadic attempts were made to persuade women students to co-operate with the Union. In Lviv, a "Committee of students with the participation of ladies" was created to collect funds and folk items for the Chicago World Fair.[17] But the visibility and rhetoric of the nationalist camp prevailed. Some Western Ukrainian women accepted the Dontsovian ideology with great fervour as the true embodiment of the national spirit.

Yet the major reason for the spread of this mentality was the repeated failure of the tactics of conciliation with the Poles. Just as Ukrainian peasants resented the introduction of Polish or bilingual schools in Ukrainian territories, Ukrainian urban youth were angered by the Poles' failure to fulfill their promise of a Ukrainian University. Discrimination and the adverse economic situation vitiated education as a means of social mobility. On 8 October 1932, the Disarmament Committee of Women's International Organizations issued a mimeographed leaflet warning that "People's minds are hardening; there is a recrudescence of nationalist and chauvinist spirit in various countries."[18] Poland was one such country, and there was a growing, vocal and increasingly assertive Western Ukrainian minority.

UNDO

The UNDO, a coalition of moderate political parties and groups that represented the Ukrainian liberal-democratic wing, was formed in 1925. Because UNDO was a coalition rather than a new party, it was easier for the Women's Union to maintain its autonomy within it. While UNDO's relationship with the women was ambivalent, ostensibly it supported the Women's Union.

Ukrainian liberals feared that mass voting by peasant women would strengthen the conservative vote. Stepan Baran, a political activist, accused the Ukrainian women, in an article in *Dilo* on 28 July 1927, of aiding the Poles in local elections. Dontsova, the president of the Union who at that time supported legal parliamentary action, pointed out that the exact opposite had been the case: the women had doubled the size of the Ukrainian vote. In Ternopil, Baran's native town, his wife, Blanka Bachynska Baranova, founded a separate women's section of UNDO, because the local UNDO opposed women candidates for local assemblies. Moderate Ukrainian women, in turn, like their European counterparts, continued to work within the liberal camp.

The women threw themselves wholeheartedly into campaign work, canvassing and speaking on the importance of voting and of supporting Ukrainian candidates. The Union urged its members to organize meetings and rallies to promote voting.[19] It pleaded repeatedly for Ukrainian political parties to co-operate with one another:

> The National Women's Congress [the annual meeting of the Women's Union and affiliated organizations held in December 1927], convinced that only unconditional national solidarity and consolidation of all Ukrainian forces can bring us victory at the elections, calls upon all Ukrainian political parties to establish a single national voting front. It urges all Ukrainian women to help reduce party discord within the Ukrainian community, since the inter-party struggle carried on in a highly unethical manner by demagogic means threatens the nation morally.[20]

In the elections of 1927–8, women were successful on both counts: helping to organize a united front among Ukrainians and electing women. Even the Ukrainian Nationalist Youth, one of the incipient OUN groups, supported the coalition of moderate Ukrainian parties.[21] The Ukrainian women succeeded in electing women on the UNDO platform, although the other Ukrainian parties offering candidates in Volhynia did not elect any women.[22] Olena Sheparovych was elected to the executive board of UNDO at the Congress of 23 December 1928. Ivanna Blazhkevych received a similar post at the USRP meeting on 2 and 3 of February 1929.[23] In both cases, the elections were a recognition of political work of the women who were also active in the Women's Union.

After the election, Rudnytska stressed the importance of both nationalism and feminism for the development of healthy nations. She pointed out repeatedly that feminism was a constructive force in Ukrainian national life. And even though feminism brought the inherent conflict between motherhood and career into focus and contributed somewhat toward smaller families, it also helped lower infant mortality and raise the quality of life. Rudnytska feared that the success Mussolini was having in Italy would popularize his policy toward women——i.e., *faciate bambini*——and would blind Ukrainians to the real solution: better economic conditions and welfare for mothers and children. She was trying to counter the anti-feminist backlash occurring in other parts of Europe.[24]

After the elections, conservative Poles felt that the growth of Ukrainian political strength had to be stopped at all costs. The Poles saw the combination of Ukrainian community activism, political participation and economic power as a potent threat. The government was also disturbed by Ukrainian celebrations of the tenth anniversary of the Ukrainian takeover of Lviv, as well as those marking the proclamation of Ukrainian sovereignty on 22 January. Even more serious in Polish eyes were the Prosvita celebrations, which linked the village with the intelligentsia, and the expansion of Ukrainian peasant co-operatives into Volhynia. In other words, the Polish government feared most the quiet and effective Ukrainian village network.[25] The effectiveness of the Women's Union in that field, combined with Rudnytska's and Kysilevska's visibility, increased the government's fear of the Women's Union.

The economic aspect of Union work also concerned the government, particularly the decision of the annual Union meeting on 5 December 1931 to encourage the Ukrainian population to buy goods and materials produced and manufactured by Ukrainians.

In the off-year elections of 1930 the local administration used ruffians to prevent Ukrainians from electing their candidates. Official ballots had to be delivered to the polling stations on the day of the election. When Ukrainian men carrying the ballots were attacked, village women, spontaneously and unobtrusively, retrieved what ballots they could and delivered them to the polls.[26]

The OUN, meanwhile, declared the policy of accommodation with the Polish government a failure. It initiated sabotage and arson against large Polish estates. Although this was a nationalistic venture, the element of social protest should not be overlooked. The Poles retaliated with "pacification" policies, the violent pogrom against the Ukrainian population discussed earlier. Both Kysilevska and Rudnytska, as members of the Assembly and of the women's organizations, did everything possible to publicize the brutalities against Ukrainians. Both women continued to take an active part in the deliberations of the Assembly.

Such incidents bred counter-terror by the Ukrainian right: the assassination in August 1931 of Tadeusz Hołówko, a prominent politician who wrote on nationality issues, was a proponent of anti-Soviet policies and a member of the Polish administration in charge of policy toward Eastern Galicia; post-office robberies (referred to, in Bolshevik fashion, as expropriations); and the assassination of Bronislaw Pieracki, the interior minister, on 15 June 1934. Both Hołówko and Pieracki were supporters of a policy of accommodation with the Ukrainians, whose major proponents included Leon Wasilewski and Janusz Jedrzejewicz.[27]

"The OUN sabotage," according to a British historian of Polish extraction, "was increasingly resented by the large majority of the Ukrainian population, and from late 1932 the organization devoted more attention to organizing a boycott of the bilingual government school."[28] The Ukrainian clergy repeatedly condemned violence, and the attempts of Metropolitan Sheptytsky to initiate a Catholic political party or alliance were a direct result of OUN violence. UNDO branded the terrorist actions not only morally wrong, but also politically inopportune.

The Women's Union stressed women's ethical sense. Union activists argued that women carried the life-giving forces of motherhood consciously into community work, elevating the frequently tedious daily organic work to one of national significance. Yet as the policies of the Polish government became increasingly oppressive, the open, albeit frequently pointless, protests of

Ukrainian youth were becoming more difficult to condemn. While deploring violence, women activists were touched by the depth of the youths' emotional commitment.

UNDO was the major exponent of accommodation with the government. Rudnytska's visibility in the party and her effectiveness in international gatherings were due to her intelligence, political acumen, hard work and effective public presence. She was slightly hard of hearing and spoke loudly. Many men considered her abrasive and domineering. Kysilevska, twenty-three years Rudnytska's senior, was grandmotherly in appearance, avoided all feminist rhetoric and saved her wit for campaigning among peasants. Through a combination of hard work and relentless use of logic, Rudnytska threatened the male ego. In contrast Kysilevska, with her stress on motherhood, aroused little resentment.

Ukrainian-Polish Relations in the 1930s

During the mid-1930s relations between Poles and Ukrainians became even more strained. Mistrust, hatred and wariness increased as the international situation worsened. The growing power of Nazi Germany, the attraction of fascism, the subversion of socialist movements by Stalinist terror, and the ineffectiveness of international diplomacy contributed to the growing rift between the two nationalities. Within each camp, moreover, political differences became more acute.

The Women's Union tried to preserve its supra-party stand while encouraging the political involvement of its members. Its united women's front was severely strained by the opposition of the OUN to UNDO and by the growing internal dissension within both. The left and right sought to discredit the policies of UNDO, while some members of the latter tried to undermine the Women's Union. The OUN, meanwhile, accused the Women's Union of being an adjunct of UNDO. Resentment against Rudnytska on sexist, political and personal ground was intertwined with a series of attacks on the Union. Rudnytska's Jewish heritage was attacked verbally, but not in print.

The relationship of UNDO to the Union——which reflected the ambivalence of political liberalism to autonomous feminism——was severely strained in 1935, when Vasyl Mudry took over the leadership from Dmytro Levytsky. The change occurred because of a growing conviction that Levytsky was not flexible enough in his dealings with the Poles. The "normalization" phase marked, in the words of a Ukrainian proponent, "the last attempt to reach an understanding with the Poles."[29] According to Polonsky:

> The success of 'normalization' was not lasting. As so often before, it proved how
> easily liberal declarations were made in Warsaw, but it was far more difficult to

have them carried out by local officials. Moreover, as Poland's external situation became more threatening, policy toward Ukrainians...was dominated by the military...stationed in areas concerned, for whom the maintenance of 'security' was the predominant consideration.[30]

Ukrainian women became wary of Polish "good will" when the electoral regulations of July 1935 not only restructured districts to dissipate Ukrainian votes, but also gave special voting privileges to organizations of larger urban centres. The Polish women's movement had not yet penetrated the Polish countryside, while Ukrainian women activists had already shown their voting strength in the villages. In the larger cities, however, Poles were stronger.[31]

In preparing for the 1935 elections, Ukrainian women supported (in addition to Rudnytska and Sheparovych) Blanka Baranova from Ternopil, Neonila Selezinka, the co-operative specialist who ran from Zolochiv, Palahna Kvasnytsia from the village of Otynia near Stanyslaviv, and Pavlyna Markiv from Petrykiv near Ternopil. In the Senate race, they backed Kysilevska, Ivanna Paarova from Iavoriv and Stefaniia Baranovska from Stanyslaviv. But none of these women were permitted to run.

The Polish regime openly subverted the whole electoral process. As part of "normalization," the Poles had offered Ukrainians a guaranteed seat from each of the fifteen electoral districts of Eastern Galicia, along with the election of a Pole from each of them. But the government wanted to approve the candidate before the election. If the candidate was thought to be unsatisfactory, the Ukrainians could propose another one. The electoral concession was limited to Eastern Galicia. Elsewhere, Ukrainians had to face the hooligans who patrolled the polls. As part of "normalization," Horbachevsky was elected to the Senate, and Mudry became a Vice-Marshal of the Sejm.[32] Initially, it was thought that "normalization" would encompass the familiar Ukrainian desiderata: Ukrainian schools, including a university; no further introduction of Polish schools into Ukrainian districts; amnesty for political prisoners and credit for economic co-operatives in Eastern Galicia. Although Ukrainians were willing to wait for these concessions, the Poles never agreed to them even in principle.

The Ukrainian Radical and the Ukrainian Social Democratic parties rejected totally the "normalization" course, as did the Zhinocha Hromada. In distributing seats among themselves, the Ukrainian parties in UNDO offered one seat to the Women's Union. The women rallied behind Rudnytska, but the Poles rejected her candidacy. UNDO, bypassing the formal Union structure, began negotiating with individual Union members, some of whom called publicly for active support of "normalization."

The 1935 elections

UNDO's leaders approached Sheparovych and other female liberal activists to stand for election, with or without full Union backing. Since such tactics appeared dictatorial, Mudry defended the policy, arguing that the terms were the best possible and that the agreement provided the Ukrainian minority with access to an international forum which they badly needed to publicize their policies. Nevertheless, the Women's Union would not accept blatant dictates from either Poles or Ukrainian men.

Under the title "Elections without Women," Sheparovych, Anna Palii, Mariia Biliak and Mariia Mudryk, all of whom had been approached by UNDO to run, drafted a communique in which they informed the public that Ukrainian women "could not permit extraneous forces to determine who should represent Ukrainian women." UNDO was the sole party representing Ukrainians in Galicia, and not a single woman was running on its ticket. Women activists denounced male meddling in the Union, and UNDO for its alleged failure to defend the real interests of Ukrainians.

> Political equal rights——for us Ukrainian women——signify equal responsibility for all that is taking place among Ukrainians, responsibility for that which is done without us, the women, and even for that which is done against us. [For] in the final analysis, we are also responsible for our weakness, which prevents us from blocking policies we do not like.[33]

Participation in the 1935 election, in which the potential strength of the women's vote was already eroded by inter-party haggling among Ukrainian politicians and restrictive regulations, the women argued, was an exercise in futility.

The radicals and nationalists boycotted the elections and refused to negotiate with the Poles. The Women's Union, acting independently of UNDO, justified its boycott on patriotic grounds, demonstrated ill will by the Poles and discrimination against the Union by legal Ukrainian parties. Ukrainian politicians, increasingly uneasy about the influence the Union exerted on the female vote, questioned its right to speak on political issues. That touched a raw nerve. Participation in the political process and in the defence of national rights were too new to Ukrainian women to be taken for granted or to be taken away.

> What business——they say——does the Women's Union have in politics, how can...it reflect the common political thoughts and wishes of Ukrainian womanhood?
>
> Well, in addition to our by-laws, which clearly state that one of the functions of the Union is 'to represent women's rights and interests before society and the government,' we must also stress the particular role which the women's

organization plays in today's phase of the relationship between woman and society. Without doubt, the Women's Union is something more than just a women's Prosvita or the Village Farmer or the Women's Co-operative Guild. It is also a strong community of like-minded women (*svitohliadovyi zviazok*) which has fused its members into one spiritual entity (*dukhovu spilnotu*), stronger than party differences. [Its essence] lies in the shared view of the basic issues concerning the nation, the common understanding of our national interest and above all of our national honour, the same style of reacting to events, the shared views on the methods of political struggle. It is difficult to characterize the essence of this communality (*odnakovosty*), but anyone who was present at the Ukrainian Women's Congress, who attends the annual meetings of the Women's Union, will easily understand what we mean.[34]

The UNDO leadership placed the names of women on the electoral list without their approval in order to divide the women. These tactics only united the women's movement further.[35] In Iavoriv Iryna Paarova forced UNDO to withdraw her candidacy. The Union stressed that the issue involved the principle of free choice for the women's organization. An editorial in *Zhinka* on 1 December 1935, stressing solidarity on certain issues which touched women *qua* women, also pointed out that the women's organization was not a political party. The members of the Union "demonstrated great maturity." throughout the stormy 1935 elections.[36]

After Rudnytska returned to Lviv on 15 November 1935, she took over the editorial work in *Zhinka* (Sheparovych had both edited *Zhinka* and largely run the Union during Rudnytska's frequent travels to Warsaw and elsewhere). At a meeting of the Union held in Lviv on 22 November 1935, Rudnytska expounded on the political decisions taken by the Union concerning the election and "normalization." She complained publicly that *Dilo* refused to publish her rebuttal to the allegations made against her. She also pointed out that in any subsequent political compromises or negotiations on elections, women must get two seats. The Union elected Rudnytska by acclamation at the general meeting on 1 and 2 April 1936, and at a congress held on 9 and 10 October 1937.[37]

The Erosion of Unity and the Women's Union

The political role of the Women's Union continued to be debated. Rudnytska's view that "daily politicking is not in the domain of the Women's Union, nor does the Union wish to be an addendum to any one party; rather, it possesses its full organizational and ideological independence," at that time, seemed to reflect the majority view. She maintained that the Union must take a supra-party stand, while its members could take any political stance they wished.[38]

The internal cohesiveness of the Union was strained by ideological disagreements throughout 1936 and 1937 which involved Union leaders drawn primarily from female intelligentsia and did not affect rural areas. Problems arose, however, when the Village Farmer began to organize women's circles in the villages in 1936–7. The Village Farmer, as a result of "normalization," received considerably more government funds than the Union. Yet the peasant base had been one of the Union's major strengths. The down-to-earth peasant women were the pride of the Union, visible proof of a women's organization working for the general good. When Kysilevska went to work in the Village Farmer, the perception of women's solidarity was gone. On 5 October 1937, Ievhen Khraplyvy argued in *Dilo* that the Co-operative should be the sole Ukrainian organization involved in economic activity among the peasants. The Women's Union countered that it would never give up one of its oldest statutory functions. Yet the erosion of the women's power had begun. On 10 April 1939, Kysilevska herself urged the Women's Union to leave village work to the Village Farmer. At the same time, the OUN was also building up local organizations that undermined the role of the women's movement.

The Union was not popular among young people. One of the resolutions of the April 1936 congress directed training instructors to encourage young women, especially from the villages, to join the Union. But an increasing number of these women drifted either into domesticity or into the clandestine but visibly popular nationalist movement.

There was a definite connection between the nationalist movement and the attempts of the Co-operative to encompass the whole village network. Pavlykovska, involved in both the co-operative movement and the Union, reversed her priorities twenty years later. In a small book written in the United States, she stressed the important organizational work among the peasants performed by OUN members who joined the Union, and played down the preparatory work of the women in the villages that had begun a decade earlier:

> The women in the OUN performed the important tasks of communication, intelligence and concealment [of literature and arms]. In the 1930s almost all the court proceedings against the OUN included women. Women also helped political prisoners. For this purpose there existed a Committee to Aid Political Prisoners, which was not a women's organization, but the lion's share of work in it was done by women...such as Klymentyna Pankevych, A. Ryzhevska.... The enthusiasm and dedication of the underground women influenced the attitude of all Ukrainian women. They even determined the direction of the organizations some women [would later] join.
>
> Preparing [themselves] to struggle against the [Polish] occupier, some of the young women joined the existing women's organizations. Their aim was to activate the Ukrainian village, to strengthen its national consciousness and to mobilize it for active work. And the idealistic youth, from the beginning of the 1930s, gave all its enthusiasm to this task. This in large measure helped the Women's Union and other women's organizations to encompass the Ukrainian village and small towns. Thousands of young women worked as instructors in the

villages. Thanks to them the process of activization of the Ukrainian village, which was reflected in the Second World War, was achieved. They gave the Ukrainian peasant woman not only better practical knowledge, but also inculcated in her faith in the justice of their cause.[39]

Whereas the Union was concerned with the independence of individual women, the nationalists subordinated everything to "the National Cause." This "Supreme Idea" was an article of faith to be proclaimed, regardless of time, circumstance and feasibility. But the OUN was not only an organization espousing nationalism; it also reflected the people's needs and mood. OUN methods bred not only violence, but intolerance, factionalism and internecine strife. Its appropriation of patriotism threatened the fabric of the organic community institutions developed so laboriously over the course of almost a century. Yet the Women's Union, on the other hand, was a pragmatic organization based on mutual interests, consensus, practicality and moderation. The failure of accommodation with the Poles, and of co-operation with moderates within the Soviet Union, as well as popular attacks on democracy and liberalism in Western Europe rendered Union policies weak and immoral in the opinion of some Western Ukrainians.

An increasing number of Union chairpersons at the branch level gravitated toward extreme nationalism. At the congress of 9 October 1937, Olha Hasyn of Stryi, voicing the OUN position, attacked the Union for not denouncing feminism, which she argued was destructive of the nation's moral fibre. The discussion, both private and public, was stormy, but Rudnytska's scathing attack on fascism and nascent fascist movements, which sought to reduce the role of women strictly to childbearing, was met with thunderous applause. Earlier, Rudnytska prided herself on the stand taken by the Union. "With one powerful accord all the voices...proclaim two slogans: national consolidation and orientation toward our national forces."[40] At the congress, it became obvious that some women supported severe restrictions on their role. Rudnytska attributed dissension in the Union to "male intrigue which pandered to petty local ambitions worthy of Gogol's pen." Her outspoken opposition to the OUN had the support of the majority of women at the Congress (although not necessarily among women in the towns):

Ukrainian women must overcome attacks and booby-traps from some segments of their own society, namely from nationalist circles. Certainly, tactical considerations dictate that the [nationalists] try coquetry from time to time, for they understand very well that without the participation and trust of the woman-mother no new faith, no idea can root itself, and cannot be transferred to new generations. For the nationalist doctrine, the carrier of new ideas, the creative, the only determinant element in society [hromadianstvi] and in the state [derzhavi] is solely the man [muzhchyna]. According to their doctrine, the woman is to fulfill herself only through motherhood; her only sphere of activity is the family; her value is judged by the number of children she has. Nationalism reduces maternal functions solely to the biological one, taking away the mother's most honourable duty, the upbringing of children, for children under a totalitarian system are raised by the regime, upon which the woman has no influence. The Ukrainian women's movement demands that women actively participate in the life of the nation and in this we differ in our understanding of the woman's role from that of fascist doctrine.[41]

While opposing "normalization," the Union supported democracy. Repeatedly, it raised the cry that organized women must strenuously oppose the blind aping of foreign fascist dictatorships which would reduce the sphere of women's activity, as in Germany and Italy. In this respect, tolerance should have limits. The Women's Union was invited to the meeting of the International Council of Women in Zurich, at which a strong protest against the anti-feminist policies of Nazi Germany was to have been made. The Polish government blocked exit visas for Ukrainian delegates as a reprisal for the international women's organization's refusal to hold its congresses in Warsaw (the latter opposed Polish minorities policy).[42]

Charewiczowa's book on the Ukrainian women's movement, published in 1937, underlined the importance of the movement just before it became diversified.[43] Peasant women gave renewed support to the Union. The peasant woman, unaffected by modern ideology, sought rather a good life, decent conditions that could be attained most readily in one's own community, i.e., a Ukrainian state. The female intelligentsia was confronted with a gamut of world-views, many claiming to be the sole means of salvation. A few women, who were both feminists and liberals, tried to preserve a mixture of views which in the past had enabled the Union to make significant gains.[44] Before they could systematize pragmatic feminism and self-help communities, the development of modern integral nationalism either pushed these women into more conventional views or diverted them from community affairs completely.[45]

The final phase of the Union

By the end of 1936, it became evident that "normalization" would not benefit the Ukrainian community. As Polish terror against Ukrainians increased, opposition to "normalization" was voiced by the Catholic party in Stanyslaviv and by a faction within UNDO itself. Kedryn, an ardent proponent of Polish-Ukrainian understanding, summed up the final attempt at co-operation:

As Galician and Eastern Ukrainian-émigré pro-Soviet feelings were liquidated by the politics of Moscow in Ukraine and against Ukraine, in the same fashion the final attempt at an understanding with the Poles in the twenty-year period of post-Versailles Poland was liquidated by Polish national policies——[by] the

Polish government and Polish society, in the first place in those five south-eastern provinces which were inhabited by the indigenous Ukrainian population, against which the local Polish organizations, supported by all the agencies of government administration, waged a permanent war.[46]

For years, moderate Ukrainians had tried to establish a consensus among political leaders of all Ukrainian groups. At the end of 1936, informal representatives of all political groups, except the OUN, the official UNDO of Mudry, and the communists started meeting on a fairly regular basis in the offices of the Women's Union. The group, which also included journalists, called itself the "Contact Committee" (Kontaktnyi komitet), and sought support for moderate policies among Ukrainians. Late in life Rudnytska noted (with uncharacteristic sloppiness) her impressions:

> The "leaders of the nation" ran together like a flock of frightened rams. The situation was really grave: war hung in the air, abuses by the Polish administrative apparatus increased, Galicia faced the prospect of becoming either Hitler's Germany or Bolshevik Russia. And the internal relations of Ukrainians were thoroughly sick...the nationalist underground was...demoralized, riddled with Polish provocateurs....

Rudnytska considered that "the most important public act of the Contact Committee was a so-called press understanding signed in the spring of 1938 by fifteen major Ukrainian publications." Kedryn characterized the event as "a consolidation conference of the representatives of a majority of Ukrainian newspapers that appeared in Lviv, among them *Dilo, Hromadskyi holos, Nova zoria, Ukrainski visti, Zhinka*——while for some reason the nationalist *Slovo* and the publishing concern of Tyktor were absent."[47]

The Polish authorities, giving the Women's Union greater credit than Ukrainian groups were willing to do, decided to suppress the Union for hosting and actively participating in these meetings. On 5 May 1938, in a co-ordinated series of actions involving 6,000 police, the government closed the central offices of the Union, arrested all the 72 branch chairpersons and closed the 1,250 village circles in Galicia. The publication of *Zhinka* was suspended.

The Contact Committee was organized too late to be effective. The dissolution of the Union, however, was immediately challenged by the women. The Central Executive Board of the Union lodged a formal protest with the Polish ministry of internal affairs. Subsequently, on 15 October 1938, the Union and all its affiliates were reinstated. The women were jubilant:

TRUTH TRIUMPHED. NOT BY INEFFECTIVE TEARS, NOR AT THE PRICE OF HUMILITY AND SUBORDINATION, BUT ONLY BY THE FORCE OF ARGUMENTS BROUGHT IN THE APPEAL AND THEIR DIGNIFIED BEARING AND FORTITUDE HAVE THE WOMEN SAVED

THEIR UNION

announced the the newspaper *Hromadianka* (Citizen), which had immediately appeared in place of the suspended *Zhinka*. By January 1939, *Zhinka* was appearing again.

A new women's organization

The second suspension of the Union within the decade demonstrated how vulnerable it was to government interference. Events of the late 1930s had also demonstrated to women activists that the Ukrainian community did not fully support the political role they had sought to play. Ironically, it was easier to establish a political party in Poland than to accredit a community organization. Taking these three factors into consideration, the non-nationalist activists of the Union decided, within a week of the Union's suspension, to establish "an independent, separate political organization." Pragmatic feminism with political action was no longer adequate: direct political organization was required.

An appeal was drafted and signed by Sheparovych, Malytska, Rudnytska and Lidiia Metelska. A temporary executive board, reflecting the whole gamut of moderate Union activists, included Evstakhiia Tyshynska, the Catholic women's activist, Sofiia Parfanovych, the physician who had been eased out of the Temperance movement, and the writer Mariia Strutynska. Ivanna Berezhanska, Olha Holianov, Katria Holubets, Anna Kapustiev, Liuba Savoika, Olha Sukhova, and Olha Tsipanovska were also in the group. Within a month, the executive board co-opted Tonia Horokhovych, the Union activist originally from Volhynia, Mariia Bassova, Lidiia Shaviak and Oksana Dzhydzhora-Dzioba.[48]

The inaugural meeting of the group was held on 16 September 1938. Making a conscious link with previous organizations, especially the Ruthenian Women's Club, these women chose for themselves the patriotic-sounding name of the Corps of Princess Olha (Druzhyna Kniahyni Olhy). Their call was one of defiance:

> It is not for us to sit around idly, when the present critical moment demands action from all the vital forces of the Nation. It is not for us to mourn the past in hopeless sorrow when we can show our gratitude and our love to it by loyal service to the same ideas which fashioned us into one spiritual community. We must not squander our strength on other institutions when the experience of many years has demonstrated that the ideological and organizational strivings of Ukrainian women cannot fit into any general society, or existing Ukrainian political parties; that [women] must have their own frame of reference, their own independent organization. And it is not the time for us, the leading women

(*providne zhinotstvo*), to drop the rudder from our hands in this responsible moment, when danger threatens, to eliminate women from the front of national struggle at at time when the entire Ukrainian [nation] is living through an unprecedented invasion.[49]

They stressed the connection of the Corps with the Union, and its dedication to nation, family, religion and tradition. The Corps received a special blessing from Metropolitan Sheptytsky. It was supported by all the organizations and luminaries that had supported the Union.[50]

The Corps tried to allay the women's concern:

And let us not be frightened of the fact that the Corps of Princess Olha is a *political* organization, for we are living in times when for a nation with no self-government, its ancestral faith, its native tongue, its daily bread, have become politics; no one can run away from politics.[51]

The Corps was not only a political body: it reflected the prevailing trend by producing its own "ideological theses," with clear statements on all the major issues. These included the national ideal, religion, family, church, culture, education, the social order, economics, and ethics of social life. It was in its formulation of the "social order" that the most significant change occurred; while stressing freedom and responsible leadership, the word democracy was omitted. Moreover, the women "acknowledged the necessity of a strong and authoritative leadership and obedience to it."[52] The intent was patriotic, the rhetoric was nationalist, and the aim was to preserve women's rights within a rapidly changing situation.

The Corps was an organization of the intelligentsia. Peasant women did not join it, but turned instead to women's sections of the Village Farmer, Prosvita, or even physical-fitness societies. The success of the Union was evident here also: at the dissolution of the Union, peasant women moved toward other community organizations rather than toward a women's ideological society.[53]

The Corps sought specifically to widen political understanding among women and organize them for political action. In October 1938, the suspension of the Union was lifted, but the Corps remained in operation, with more political clout than the Union. It concentrated on joint actions with other political parties, such as protesting the Hungarian invasion of the briefly independent Carpathian Ukraine on 15 March 1939.[54] It also encouraged women to participate in local elections and pre-election campaigns and helped the Union politically. Despite the reinstatement of the Union, local officials often refused to release Union files, and Union members welcomed the Corps' intervention in the matter.[55] As the same women were involved in both organizations, central meetings of one followed those of the other.[56] In a letter to American-Ukrainian women, the women of the Corps stressed: "The Corps of Princess Olha and the Union of Ukrainian Women engage in mutual assistance because both have the same goal of raising the national and political consciousness of Ukrainian women and making them active participants in the life of the nation."[57] The magnitude of the impending crisis increased the need for unity: Rudnytska and Kysilevska continued to appear in the same forum.[58]

Women could not stand aside in the great struggle of the individual against the state. The International Council of Women called upon women to fight for a world order which would be based upon the same democratic principles as those of women's rights. Western Ukrainian women concurred, but also emphasized the need to concentrate on the liberation struggle of their own nation before they focused on women. Women's rights were not a matter of primary concern at the time. Austria and Czechoslovakia, with their strong women's movements, had fallen to Hitler's Germany. Poland was hardly a democracy; Romania was a highly restrictive monarchist state. The brief independent interlude of Carpathian Ukraine only made the return of Hitler's ally, Hungary, more painful. Women in France, Great Britain, and the USA were under internal pressure to return to traditional roles. Europe was poised on the verge of war. Western Ukraine was wedged between the two giants of totalitarianism: Hitler's Germany and Stalin's USSR. It was no time to take stock of the past achievements of pragmatic feminism.

17.
Ukrainian Women outside Historical Galicia

The political changes in Eastern Europe sanctioned by the Treaty of Versailles were reflected in shifted borders which at best only approximated ethnic settlement. The sovereign states that emerged after the First World War shuffled administrative districts to accommodate the political needs of the central government rather than those of the local population. The administrative restructuring of the Polish Republic in 1931, for instance, strengthened the voting power of Polish residents in the border provinces. Traditional nomenclature was changed, and historical districts broken up into smaller areas to facilitate greater local control. Thus, Eastern Galicia became the Lviv, Stanyslaviv and Ternopil provinces; and parts of historical Pidliashshia became an expanded Lublin province. In the discussion which follows the traditional Ukrainian nomenclature is used regardless of the periodic administrative changes, since it made sense to Ukrainian women, our primary subject, and helped formulate their views.

Polissia, Pidliashshia and Kholmshchyna

Volhynia, Polissia, Pidliashshia and Kholmshchyna, like Galicia, had a population that was largely Ukrainian with a sizeable Polish minority. At the end of the eighteenth century, when the old Commonwealth of Poland was being partitioned, all four areas came under the jurisdiction of the Russian Empire. Three of these territories——Polissia, Pidliashshia and Kholmshchyna——were economically backward with a poorly educated population that lacked both political and national consciousness. Polissia——swampy, desolate and picturesque——bordered on Belorussia and Poland. For the Galician Ukrainian intelligentsia, especially for young people, the area was an unexplored frontier, hitherto encountered only in literature. The distinctive garb of the "Polishchuks" added more variety to the already rich ethnological collections. In the 1920s and 30s Ukrainian girl scouts from

Galicia organized lengthy boating trips through the swampy area, stopping to meet the villagers and to camp in their barns. Sometimes the local population had to rescue the girls from attacks by Polish vigilante groups. In 1935 Kysilevska spent a few months touring the area and wrote a series of informative vignettes on this part of Ukraine, which she later published as a book. The area possessed several Prosvita circles; some, like that in Berestia, had separate women's branches.[1]

Aside from desultory efforts to propagate the Polish peasant women's organization——*Koło Kobiet Wiejskich*——in the larger villages, the Poles did not consider Polissia an area of major concern. The situation was somewhat different in Pidliashshia and Kholmschchyna, both of which the Poles considered integral parts of Poland. Here they tried to develop Polish institutions and Polish national consciousness through a mixture of force and incentive. Pidliashshia——"the area at the foot of Poland," located north-west of Galicia——as even the name indicates, was vulnerable to Polonization. Yet the limited Polish resources and the absence of local political extremism in the area gave the Poles little cause for reprisals.

Inter-ethnic relations in Kholmshchyna were more volatile. Located on low mountainous terrain between Pidliashshia and Galicia, the area had been an important and integral part of one of the major successor states of Kievan Rus'; it contained numerous towns of commercial importance in the late Middle Ages and early modern period, and these showed signs of former glory. A bitter religious legacy exacerbated national animosities. In the seventeenth and eighteenth centuries, part of the Ukrainian population of Kholmshchyna accepted the Union with Rome. In the nineteenth century, however, Russia converted the area to Orthodoxy.

In the inter-war years, when the area became part of the Polish state, some of the population reverted to Ukrainian Catholicism. At the same time, the Poles tried to persuade Ukrainians to accept Roman Catholicism, and with it, Polonization. Concurrently, the Poles limited Ukrainian cultural, religious and social organizations. Ukrainian-language schools were severely curtailed. In a concerted effort to "save the children," Galician Ukrainians, including branches of the Women's Union, arranged for boys and girls of the area to attend schools in Galicia. Some of these children lived with Galician families, while others were placed in boarding schools. Little was written about this programme because of its semi-clandestine nature, but it affected hundreds of children.

The most effective organization of Ukrainians in Kholmshchyna was Prosvita, which developed spontaneously in the towns and villages. Frequently, women established a separate women's section which had direct contact with the Women's Union in Lviv.[2] The youth organization, Plast, formally and informally (since it was often banned) organized summer programmes. Poles, in turn, sought to establish the Polish scouting organization, the *Harcerzy*, thereby replacing the Russian presence with the Polish one. The Polish peasant women's association tried unsuccessfully to establish its branches in Ukrainian villages.

Because of the time spent under Russian jurisdiction, the Ukrainian moderate left was stronger here than in Galicia. Before the Polish-Soviet agreement of Riga in 1921, a coalition of Ukrainians came to an informal agreement with the Polish moderate left groupings (the Stronnictwo Ludowe, Piast, Wyzwolenie and Lewica). The Poles agreed to the use of Ukrainian in schools and Ukrainian administration of the territories in which Ukrainians constituted the majority. They also accepted the principle of complete religious toleration and promised economic aid to Ukrainian territories. But this agreement was never implemented; the moderate Poles never exercised sufficient power to carry it out. Instead, perturbed by the rapid spread of the Prosvita movement, by 1928 the government sought to Polonize the area. When strong and vocal Ukrainian opposition rendered this effort a dismal failure, the Poles turned to another expedient——supporting the conservative "Ruthenian" minority and its attempts to organize groups to rival the dynamic Ukrainian ones. But the Ruthenians, with their dated language, references to a mythical Rus' and an equally mythical unity of Tsar and Rus', and vague political ideal did not provide a viable alternative to the simple creed of democratic nationalism.[3]

Prosvita was the umbrella under which Ukrainian women's organizations functioned in these areas. Its activity was similar to that in Galicia. Communication between Galicia and other Ukrainian-inhabited areas of Poland, restricted by the government, was never cut off completely. Consequently, Galician cultural resources and expertise helped Ukrainians in Kholmshchyna.

The Women's Union took a special interest in the Kholm organizations and encouraged the Kholm women to come to Lviv to attend various courses. The Union also encouraged its Galician members to visit Kholm formally or informally. These territories, in turn, strengthened Galician patriotism by providing a new link between Ukrainians.

Volhynia

The situation in Volhynia was different from that in Polissia, Pidliashshia and Kholmshchyna. This fertile plain between Warsaw and Kiev fed its population well. Except for Polish landlords (many of whom had lost their lands during the tsarist regime), Jewish merchants, and a sprinkling of Russian administrative personnel, the population was Ukrainian. Olena Pchilka and Lesia Ukrainka, who had lived in its cities for many years, were inspired by its peasant folklore. Many of the peasant customs dated back to pagan times. The peasant population, if not nationally conscious, was more enterprising than that of Galicia. Some had pursued the remains of a lucrative, albeit illegal, horse-trade via the northern Galician towns.[4] Others built up efficient farming, including the breeding of highly prized pigs. The tsarist administration had considered the area largely a Polish outpost, and did not readily identify its "Little-Russian seditious tendencies." It had served as a haven for Ukrainian tsarist bureaucrats, among them the father of Lesia Ukrainka. During the First World War, many Ukrainian women from Volhynia were active in the Red Cross and relief efforts. After the war, Ukrainian schools and Prosvita organizations were created in major cities. In line with the tradition of opposition to tsarist rule, women, some of whom had attended the Women's Higher Courses, became involved in politics.

Volhynia did not boycott the elections of 1922 to the Polish assembly and Senate. The moderate Volhynians preferred Polish to Russian rule, although leftist and pro-communist parties were more popular in this area than in the more conservative Galicia. Before establishing any separate women's sections, the Volhynians elected Olena Hadzinska Levchanivska to the Senate in 1922. She was active in the women's movement, participated in various international gatherings, and served her full term in the Senate.[5]

To weaken the solidarity of the Ukrainian movement, the Poles permitted the functioning of certain Ukrainian community organizations and encouraged the activities of the Ukrainian party loyal to the Poles, linked with Petro Pevny. The Volhynian Ukrainian Orthodox Church, frustrated with the Russian Orthodox Church's policy of Russification, was willing to take the extended hand of the Catholic Polish state, which was more tolerant of Volhynian Orthodox Ukrainians than of Galician Catholic Ukrainians.

Ukrainian women in Volhynia were very active in setting up private Ukrainian-language schools during the revolutionary period. Earlier, some of them had simply set up schools for children in villages not encompassed by the official government school network. Levchanivska and her brother had founded one such school, in which more than 100 pupils studied.[6] In the inter-war years, the government vacillated between policies of outright Polonization through Polish-language schools and concessions to Ukrainians. Many women went into teaching, and in the smaller villages, the school served as the centre of community life. Although the Polish government did not allow Ukrainian Galician women to teach in Galician villages, it permitted single Ukrainian women from Galicia to teach in Volhynia. These young women stimulated the interest and participation of both the pupils and their parents in Ukrainian affairs. One woman, who first went to Volhynia during the First World War, noted that the Ukrainian Revolution in 1918 awakened "the dark peasant mass, which had been so loath to show interest in anything, made it move, and made it vibrant." The inter-war period was also touched by that vibrancy.[7]

Schools, Prosvita organizations, and women's groups formed spontaneously upon the disintegration of the two empires. The Volhynian women, despite Polish protest, participated in the founding of the Women's Union in Lviv in 1921. The Galician women considered the Volhynian Women's Union part of the Women's Union as a whole, and the work of the two groups was discussed jointly.

Once again, however, the women's work became entangled in political considerations. In the 1920s, along with the network of women's groups and

Prosvita, the co-operative movement made great inroads into Volhynia. The Poles supported the conciliatory Ukrainian political parties, but increased subsidies to the Polonizing organizations. Of these, the circles of peasant women and the Polish scouts had the most direct bearing upon women. Ukrainian activists trying to co-ordinate the activities of the Women's Union and the Prosvita sections established a central Volhynian Women's Union in 1927, as it became increasingly obvious that the Women's Union in Lviv could not legally serve as a co-ordinating agency. The Poles mistrusted the Volhynian Ukrainian women as much as the Galician Women's Union, as a result of both national antagonism and sexist politics.

Between 1927 and 1938, however, under the governorship of Henryk Józewski, it seemed that the major needs of Ukrainians in Volhynia would be met. Józewski had been impressed by the sheer growth of Ukrainian organizations. Between 1918 and 1928, Prosvita had grown from 129 to 400 sections; the Native School Society from 5 to 400 schools; the Society of Peter Mohyla, which fostered self-education, from 4 to 870 circles. Józewski pursued co-operation with the Ukrainians. He sponsored the creation of "people's universities" in Mykhailivka and Rivne. These institutions, in which more men than women participated, were a combination of community colleges, trade schools and study circles. Bilingual, they fostered a spirit of co-operation between the Poles and Ukrainians who attended them. Ukrainian participants revealed pro-Polish proclivities, especially after the outbreak of the Second World War. Józewski's policies, however, were suspect to many Poles, and "he was the object of bitter attacks from the local Poles and also from the Army...which increasingly...controlled nationality policy."[8]

Whatever the motives and results of Józewski's policies for Ukrainians in Volhynia, the situation was unfavourable to organized Ukrainian women. The government periodically suspended branches of the Union, and actively fostered competing women's organizations, from the government-sponsored *Koło Kobiet Wiejskich* to marginal Ukrainian women's groups such as Zhinky Hromadskoi Pratsi (Women of Community Work), which seems to have been an adjunct of one of the minor parties. The Women's Union of Volhynia, which in the 1920s showed signs of becoming a mass organization, was reduced to less than 500 members by 1936 through repeated government harassment. It numbered eleven major branches, fifteen reading rooms and an undetermined number of peasant circles. These circles, if they could not exist legally, functioned either as Prosvita branches or as informal groups. They kept in close contact with one another and with the Union in Lviv.[9] The women's sections in Prosvita had a central organization, which was considered part of the Women's Union.

Among the most active members of the Volhynian Women's Union were Paraskeviia Bahrynivska, who headed the organization for years in Rivne; Oleksandra Pidhirska, who co-ordinated Prosvita work, was frequently its representative outside Volhynia and acted as its motivating force in Kovel; Dr. Iryna Prisnevska from Zdolbuniv and Mariia Volosevych from Kremianets.

Very active in the central Volhynian Union were Nataliia Dzivnakova, Olena Kenzhynska, Ievheniia Ovdiienko, Vasylyna Kulikova, Hanna Iazvinska, Sofiia Lozytstka-Tomkovych and Hanna Sloboda. Tonia Horokhovych, a teacher from Volhynia who worked in the central office of the Union in Lviv, was especially close to Rudnytska and provided a link for the two branches of the Union.[10]

The Volhynian Union placed great emphasis on trade courses, and Galician instructors were brought in whenever possible to help run them. The Volhynian Union also ran summer camps for children with great zeal. Like the Galician Union, the Volhynian women pursued a supra-party stand and thus came under attack by the Ukrainian intelligentsia of various political or religious predilections. The Village Farmer also sought to establish women's sections, especially in Lutsk, but ran into serious legal difficulties. The government, linking the Women's Union with mounting opposition to the Polish administration, stepped up its campaign against the Union, accusing the women of collusion in illegal actions. On 3 June 1938, the government disbanded the Volhynian Union.[11]

Bukovyna

Bukovyna, nestled in the valleys of the Carpathians, south of the Cheremosh and Prut rivers, home of two of the oldest Ukrainian women's organizations, was incorporated into the expanded state of Romania after the First World War. Ukrainians constituted a plurality of the population of Bukovyna, "the verdant land of Ukraine," but were only a small minority in Romania as a whole. The Romanians, capitalizing on successful wartime diplomacy, tried to forge a monolithic population from the various ethnic and religious groups that had settled in the area over the centuries. Unfortunately, having developed their own indigenous fascist movement, which antedated both the Italian and German variants, they relied heavily on force and intimidation in carrying out this policy.

Thus, most of the national, political, economic and educational gains that Ukrainians had wrested from the Austrian Empire were rescinded by the Romanian authorities. Ukrainians were subjected to severe Romanization. The Ukrainian intelligentsia, accustomed to opportunities for advancement in the Habsburg realm, now found itself under severe pressure. An increasing number of Ukrainians emigrated, weakening the embattled minority, which kept the cause of Bukovynian Ukrainians alive.

Ukrainian women, as much as possible, disregarded the new border and continued to view the picturesque hilly country and its dark-haired population, clad in lavishly embroidered costumes, as an integral part of the Motherland, which produced significant women writers. Kobylianska, identified more than others with the emancipation of women, remained in Bukovyna and continued writing fiction revolving around the autonomous individual. Her *Tsarivna* remained required reading for Ukrainian women with educational pretensions. Kobylianska, revered by Ukrainian women, was an honoured guest at all major women's functions in both Galicia and Bukovyna, and in all areas where Ukrainians lived.

A younger Bukovynian writer, Iryna Polotniuk, writing under the pseudonym Iryna Vilde, furthered Kobylianska's tradition. Her novels and short stories, published in Galicia, explored an ever widening vista of women's issues. Her treatment of adolescent sexual awakening was a novelty among Ukrainians. Vilde, as she was generally known, was published in the Ukrainian women's press and was active in the Women's Union.[12]

During the First World War, the Austrian government had suspended civic organizations in Bukovyna. The Zhinocha Hromada, founded in 1907 with the active help of Kobylianska, provided the initiative for the creation of the Committee of Ukrainian Women to Aid the Wounded. The Committee also organized relief efforts, set up day-care centres and in 1918 established an orphanage in Chernivtsi.

In 1920, through the persistent efforts of Zenoviia Hrushkevych, the Zhinocha Hromada was legally re-established. Bukovynian women participated in the 1921 Lviv Congress and kept up personal contacts with Galician women. Although the Romanian government severely circumscribed the Hromada's activity, the women, nevertheless, sponsored various cultural events and self-education programmes, cared for the orphanage and expanded the day-care centres. They ran a dormitory for Ukrainian women attending high school and a cafeteria for students in Chernivtsi. They helped girls and young women attend schools in Galicia. They organized courses of interest to women, such as sewing, co-operative work and accounting. They were instrumental in organizing a women's choir, directed by Halia Valylashko, and also sought to expand programmes for Ukrainian Bukovynian peasants.

Concerning other Hromada activities, Hrushkevych led protest actions against the closing of Ukrainian-language schools in 1922. Vanda Lukashevych, who headed the Hromada in 1925, was a very successful fund raiser. Olena Siretska and Mykhailyna Levytska were also among the most active members.

Olha Pavliukh-Huzar participated in the Women's Congress of National Minorities of Romania in Bucharest in 1925. It was under her chairmanship that the Hromada organized the first post-war congress of Ukrainian women in Bukovyna on 2 February 1929, in which both men and women participated. Huzar reflected the consensus of the Hromada that the major issue facing Ukrainian women was to raise the standard of living of the peasants, rather than specifically women's concerns. Huzar remained the head of the organization for many years. Bukovynian women assiduously prepared and collected materials for the Chicago International Exhibition in 1934, in which the Ukrainian women of the United States participated. In 1932, the women set up a first-aid centre in Chernivtsi headed by Stefaniia Hubko-Bezborodko, but could not expand it into a full-scale clinic because of a lack of funds and government opposition. In 1934, when the Bukovynian women participated in the Stanyslaviv Congress, the Hromada was headed by Ahlaia Fedorovych.

In the 1930s the Romanian government limited the work of the Hromada to philanthropic ventures. Information on the work of the Bukovynian women during this period is sketchy. It is known that the membership of the Hromada in Chernivtsi was about 100, but the number and size of its branches is not known.[13]

The other major Ukrainian women's organization, the Women's Society of Myrrh-bringers (founded by the Reverend Kelestyn Kostetsky in 1886), continued to exist through the inter-war years without much difficulty, but was not very active. Envisaged as a religious-philanthropic society, its emphasis was almost solely on religion.

Younger women in Chernivtsi grouped themselves in two student organizations: Chornomore (Black Sea) and the Orhanizatsiina Sektsiia Studentok (Organizational Section of Women Students). The latter was more politically aware and somewhat militant. These organizations do not appear to have survived into the 1930s.[14]

During 1931–2, the more militantly nationalist Ukrainian women organized a committee called "Culture of the Spirit," which was dedicated to Kobylianska (then still alive). It published, as a supplement to *Samostiina dumka* (Independent Thought), a journal called *Samostiina dumka ukrainskoi matery: Zhurnal osvity, tvorchosty i borotby* (Independent Thought of the Ukrainian Mother: Journal of Education, Creativity and Struggle). Its editor was Sydoniia H. Nykorôvych. The journal stressed the patriotic functions of the Ukrainian mother and the importance of women in all societies. Its writers focused on the purity of the feminine soul, the goodness of woman's heart, and the impact these qualities had on the work of "creators-geniuses and statesmen [in their striving] for good deeds." Unabashedly, an article announced: "The *leadership* of the national political life belongs to *highly idealistic men* with mature *political tact*. To the women belong the matters of culture of the heart, that is their sacred kingdom of raising children, housework and cultural and philanthropic work in the community."[15]

This was followed by Kobylianska's answer to the question of the emancipation of women. She maintained that "emancipation means the expression of energetic striving of individual freedom and rights to acquire a higher education...and the right to work in the government or private sector." She stressed that liberation must be achieved by the efforts of women themselves, and argued for military service for both men and women. Her remarks were sketchy, badly written, and, it seems, edited to suit the nationalists, so that they could use her prestige as a feminist writer to argue against feminism. They failed. Other contributors, in the second issue, especially Iliarii Karbulytsky, also argued that women, given the opportunity for work, study and self-improvement, should be equal to men.[16]

The government closed the journal before the intricacies of the discussion on the dual role of woman-mother and independent woman reached a critical stage in Bukovyna.

in Bukovyna.

Transcarpathia

In Transcarpathia, located on the western side of the Carpathian Mountains, the women's movement showed none of the cultural ambivalence that plagued this embattled outpost of Ukrainian lands, which for centuries had been subjected to Magyarizing policies. The conservative Magyarone, Rusyn and Russophile women——i.e., those residents of Transcarpathia who considered themselves Hungarians, or as belonging to a separate Rusyn nationality, or as part of the Russian people——did not develop their own women's organizations. They did not even establish women's religious or philanthropic societies. Nor were there women's monasteries in the area which would draw on the local population.

Here, as in Eastern Ukraine, the women's movement was a natural outgrowth of the democratic world-view of Ukrainian patriots. The young intelligent girl, close to the native land, emerged in local literature as the unspoiled carrier of the national and democratic ideal. Women's issues were subordinated to the central question: what do we want to be?[17]

The first women's organization in Transcarpathia was a Marian Sodality founded in 1909 in Uzhhorod. It was distinctly Ukrainian in orientation and marked the beginning of organized activity of Ukrainian women in the area.[18] Secular women's organizations were not founded until the end of the Hungarian administration.

As part of reconstruction after the First World War and owing to a vote taken in Pennsylvania among immigrants from the area, Transcarpathia became a province in the newly created Czechoslovak state. The Czechs, particularly until 1935, showed much sympathy for the Ukrainians. Eastern Ukrainian émigrés were not only permitted to settle in Czechoslovakia, but were aided in the process. The Ukrainian Free University was established in Prague in 1921, and this was followed the next year by the creation of the Ukrainian Commercial Academy in Poděbrady; both included women among the faculty and students. Ukrainian-language schools were founded. This necessitated an influx of teachers, most of them Ukrainians (but also some Russians). Among the Ukrainians, several women teachers were instrumental in building up Ukrainian community organizations. The presence of émigré Eastern Ukrainian women and the fact that they established women's organizations in Prague and Poděbrady also had an impact on the organization of women. Also of importance was the interest young Ukrainian women living in Poland expressed in the "silver land," as Transcarpathia was known poetically.[19]

The three most active women in the women's organizations here were also closely connected with the Ukrainian political movement——Iryna Voloshyn, Ielysaveta Brashchaikova-Stankova and Iryna Buryk Nevytska. The latter, as the founder and chairperson of the Ukrainian Agricultural Workers' Party, as well as a teacher and writer of children's literature, has been characterized as "the only leading female national activist in Sub-Carpathian Rus'."[20] She was instrumental in organizing a women's society in Prešov in 1922, and remained active in the women's movement.

Iryna Voloshyn organized the first secular women's society, the Zhinochyi Soiuz (Women's Union) in Uzhhorod in 1923. Initially, Ukrainian male intelligentsia resented this new organization, but gradually began to recognize its contribution to the national and the economic development of Ukrainians. Work among women in towns and villages was difficult because the local intelligentsia was frequently Russophile or communist in orientation. Nevytska complained bitterly of difficulties impeding the establishment of Ukrainian women's organizations.[21] Women, therefore, not only broke new ground in organizing themselves, but were at the same time trying to reverse centuries of policies that had stunted the national and economic growth of the population.

Branches of the Women's Union were founded, or, more frequently, women's sections of Prosvita were created. Within a few years the women developed a network of organizations engaged in what were by now routine activities: work among the peasants, day-care centres, health-care information, tips on household management, and organizing trade courses. Ukrainian opposition to women's organizations subsided, and peasant women readily joined in the work. By 1934 there were more than 250 women's circles of Prosvita connected with the Women's Union in Uzhhorod. Women felt strong enough to plan, organize and hold a women's congress, which turned into a major demonstration of Ukrainian political strength.

The congress was sponsored by three groups: the Women's Union in Uzhhorod, the women's sections of Prosvita and the Marian Sodality. It convened on 28 May 1934, the twenty-fifth anniversary of the establishment of the Marian Sodality.[22] The Ukrainian Pedagogical Society ended its own meeting before the women's congress began, and many of the male teachers participated in it.

The opening day coincided with the moveable feast of Pentecost, known to Ukrainians as the "Green Holidays." Churches and homes were decked out with freshly cut green branches and young saplings. Green——the church's colour of hope and the colour of the Holy Ghost——was featured in the vestments. The holiday enhanced the festivities of the congress. An open-air mass, held in the courtyard of the old castle in Uzhhorod, celebrated by Archbishop Oleksander Stoika and assisted by numerous clergy, was attended by throngs of people. The mood was strengthened by a march through the city, in which 2,500 women, followed by about 1,500 men, took part, many of them dressed in colourful peasant costumes and carrying blue-and-yellow Ukrainian standards, duly blessed by the archbishop at the congress. All the speakers stressed Ukrainian patriotism, the need to work for the people, and the importance of the women's contribution to raising national consciousness. Rudnytska, speaking on behalf of the Women's Union and the Ukrainian parliamentary representation, was interrupted continually by applause;

Kysilevska spoke in the name of the peasant circles and the day-care centres' society as well as the newspaper she edited. Pavlykovska, representing the economic co-operative movement, was heard with great interest. The female delegate from the Hutsul lands, Klempushova of Iaseniv; the representative of the Plast women, Boichuk; the Abbot of the Basilians, the Reverend Belyk; the Reverend Viktor Zheltvai, head of the Uzhhorod Teachers' Seminary for Women; and Member of Parliament Iuliian Revai——all were greeted with great enthusiasm.[23]

The Committee that organized the Congress also published a booklet for the occasion——*Zhinocha syla* (Woman's Power). The numerous speakers were so enthusiastic that Mrs. Stankova's report had to be shortened. The resolutions, which were carried by acclamation, were political in tone and addressed not the rights of women but those of all Ukrainians. The congress demanded more Ukrainian-language schools, the appointment of more Ukrainians to government posts, and curtailment of the anti-Ukrainian actions of some local officials and Russophile teachers. It protested the establishment of Czech-language schools in Ukrainian areas and Hungarian claims to these same areas.

The congress was both a celebration of Ukrainian womanhood and a demonstration of its strength. Shortly after the congress, a women's division of the Carpathian Sich, a paramilitary and physical-fitness society, was founded under the leadership of Tysovska. Four years later, in 1938, Czechoslovakia granted its provinces autonomy, which led to a strengthening of local community organizations. On 15 March 1939, Ukrainians in Transcarpathia proclaimed an independent Transcarpathian Ukraine. The proclamation aroused the emotional patriotism of Ukrainians thoroughout the world. Nevytska was the only woman directly involved in substantive political activity during the brief existence of the Ukrainian state led by the Reverend Avhustyn Voloshyn. The Hungarians overran the tiny state two weeks before German troops marched into Prague on 2 April 1939.[24]

The German annexation of Czech lands and the Hungarian takeover of Carpatho-Ukraine were bitter pills for Ukrainian women to swallow. Rudnytska wrote epistles to Czech women, chiding them for their lack of protest, and to German women for sitting placidly while human dignity was being trampled.[25] In the May issue of *Zhinka*, Mirna came to the defence of the Czech women, praising their loyalty and discipline. She pointed out that Czech men were more responsible for the collapse. On behalf of the Carpatho-Ukrainian movement, the Corps of St. Olha, an outgrowth of the Women's Union, dedicated an evening "to the memory of the victims of the latest events."[26]

Emigré Women's Associations

Women's organizations sprang up in all European cities with a Ukrainian émigré community, either as separate entities or as sections of community organizations. Emigré women's organizations performed two functions of great service to the Ukrainian national cause. First, the women helped initiate and arrange contacts with the outside world through women's community organizations. They also set up relief facilities for the Ukrainian community and served as a clearing-house for information about the women's movement and European politics and culture for other Ukrainians. In some cities, notably Vienna, Cracow, Poděbrady and Prague, associations of women students were formed on a more or less stable basis. These young women co-operated with women's organizations in arranging exhibits and cultural events, as well as participating in international gatherings or demonstrations.

The women tried to popularize the Ukrainian cause in the host country. In Prague, Mariia Omelchenko and Miloslava Hrdličková edited a journal, La Femme slave (1933), in which they presented the achievements of individual Slavic women and Slavic women's movements in a well-edited popular issue. However, lack of funds prevented their carrying the project beyond that year. All the émigré organizations established contacts with Canadian and American Ukrainian women, who offered them significant financial support. Some groups set up schools, dormitories, and inexpensive communal kitchens. They hosted each other's members and honoured the more prominent ones. These activities led to a communality of women with an interest in Ukrainian affairs, even though there was no formal structure for Ukrainian women's organizations outside the Soviet Union.

The centres of major émigré women's organizations were Vienna, Prague, Warsaw and, briefly, Berlin. Vienna remained a city with a distinctly international tinge. Ukrainian families had settled there, married Austrians, and their children, whose knowledge of the language was limited, still considered themselves Ukrainian. The city continued to attract university and graduate students and was almost a mandatory stop for Ukrainians travelling east or west. In the early years after the First World War, it remained an important political centre. Ievhen Petrushevych, the President-in-exile of the Western Ukrainian Republic, maintained offices there. So did Ievhen Konovalets, the highly political miltary leader of the Ukrainian Sich Riflemen and the prime force behind the clandestine Ukrainian Military Organization (UVO), composed of Ukrainian veterans of various armies. A number of influential Eastern Ukrainian leaders either lived or stayed in Vienna. Rudnytska became well acquainted with Konovalets there. Here also, the Ukrainian communist Iurii Kotsiubynsky, the son of the writer Mykhailo, convinced Nadiia Surovtseva, a promising graduate student in history at the University of Vienna and a women's activist, to serve the cause of communist Ukraine. Vienna was the focal point for co-operation between the Galician women and émigré women from Eastern Ukraine.

Ukrainian women in Vienna, who had cared for Ukrainian wounded during the war, organized themselves either in late 1920 or early 1921 as a Ukrainian Women's Community (Zhinocha Hromada). In the early years it was involved in the political activities of various Ukrainian groups, and facilitated the work of Ukrainian women on an international level. Its membership was continually supplemented by students and included daughters of Ukrainian families that settled in Vienna.[27]

The women continued some of the relief and social work of the previous years. As anti-communists, however, they found it difficult to maintain their contacts with Austrian socialist women's organizations.

During the early 1920s, Berlin became a centre of Ukrainian women's activity when Mariia Zarchy, one of the officers of the Women's Rada constituted in Kamianets, moved there. Her husband headed the Berlin UNR mission, one of many such missions being founded in the major European cities. The flurry of activity of Ukrainian women in Berlin in the early post-war years was connected with numerous international women's gatherings (see Part V). The women also carried out relief work and tracked down members of families separated during the war.

By the mid-1920s, however, the German economic crisis, personality clashes among the women (Madame Zarchy's flamboyancy did not sit well either with German women or with the staid Ukrainian women who stayed in Berlin), and the inability of the Ukrainian Women's Union (Rada) to become an authentic centre for Ukrainian women's organizations lessened the importance of Berlin as a centre for Ukrainian women. The Rada headquarters were moved to Prague.

The sizeable and influential Ukrainian émigré community in Prague and nearby Poděbrady had organized, in July 1921, a Ukrainian Civic Committee (Ukrainskyi hromadskyi komitet), which created a Section to Aid Women and Children. Its major aim, in addition to setting up day-care centres and finding foster homes, was to help Ukrainian women find gainful employment. The section relied on the work of Marharyta Ivanenkova, Valeriia Bohatska, Hanna Hryhoriieva, Valentyna Novytska and Hanna Halahan.

However, the factional strife which the Civic Committee was set up to circumvent penetrated the committee itself.[28] On the initiative of Hanna Halahan, a Ukrainian Women's Union (Zhinochyi Soiuz) was established in Prague in 1922 to co-ordinate women's work across party lines. The Union was a supra-party independent organization, although its membership overlapped with that of the Women's Section of the Civic Committee. It became part of the Czechoslovak Women's Union. Františka Plaminková, a Czech women's activist, helped Ukrainian women find outside funding. With the aid of the Nansen Committee, the women set up a cafeteria and reading room and helped find foster homes for children.[29] The women avoided the divisiveness of émigré politics, and the Women's Union was able to function until the Germans took over Czechoslovakia in 1939. Through the intervention of the Czech women's organizations, the Czech Red Cross, the Nansen Committee, the YMCA and the

Czechoslovak government allocated funds to Ukrainians which were used to set up an orphanage for Ukrainian children in Horni Černošci.[30]

In November 1921, Ukrainian women students organized a Women's Section of the Ukrainian Academic Community in Czechoslovakia, which participated actively in the work of the committee. They collected donations for Ukrainian émigrés in Poland and helped set up and run a day-care centre in Poděbrady.

When Mirna moved to Prague in 1923, the Ukrainian Women's National Council (the Rada of Kamianets-Podilsky, Berlin and Prague) moved with her. Although this Council aspired to represent all Ukrainian women outside the Soviet Union, its actual scope was minor. Without the active co-operation and support of the Women's Union in Galicia and the Ukrainian Women's Union in Czechoslovakia, the Rada would have been powerless. Mirna herself admitted as much. Nevertheless, in the absence of a stronger organization, it proved useful, and Prague was an excellent location, given the relatively tolerant nature of the government and the strength of the feminist movement in Czechoslovakia. As the same women participated in both organizations, the Rada took part in international gatherings, while the Union functioned within Czechoslovakia.[31]

With the help of Czech women, Ukrainian women became part of the Czech National Women's Council and in this way members of the Geneva-based Union Mondiale des Femmes. In the latter body, Ukrainians were particularly active in the Commission of the Spiritual Freedom of Women. Participation in the Women's International League for Peace and Freedom was also facilitated by the Czech women's association.

In 1927, in addition to the Prague Women's Union, a Women's Union was founded in Poděbrady, composed mainly of students from the Ukrainian Commercial (Hospodarcha) Academy. Its programme was a traditional combination of the feminist, national and cultural aspirations of Ukrainian women. A proposal that the Poděbrady women not co-operate with the Lviv Women's Union but rather seek out Polish women's organizations was rejected and condemned.[32] A separate Ukrainian women students' group was established in Prague by the mid-1920s, and a few years later an Association of Ukrainian Christian Women was founded in Poděbrady. Because of the religious constraints on Catholics of the time, the latter was composed of Orthodox women. During the inter-war years Ukrainian women activists in Czechoslovakia also published ten brochures and books dealing with Czechoslovakian, Ukrainian and women's topics.[33]

The support of some Czech women's organizations and of the Czech government made Ukrainian women's fund-raising in Czechoslovakia a success. The presence of Rusova and Mirna in Prague gave Ukrainian activists there prestige and involved them directly in all international undertakings. Among those most active were, in addition to Mirna, Rusova and Halahan: Mariia Sadovska, Prykhodko, Kateryna Antonovych, Stefaniia Nahirna, Shlendyk, Steshko, Eikhelman, Oleksandra Chernova and Mariia Sloniovska.[34]

The Czechs had developed a network of schools and programmes for the practical education of housewives. Ukrainians considered these quite impressive, despite the emphasis on domesticity. In her booklet on careers, Omelchenko stressed the value of each function within society and the importance of following one's inclinations and aptitudes.[35]

Admiring the Czech ideal of the thrifty, efficient and educated housewife, some male Ukrainian émigrés, especially those teaching at the Commercial Academy of Poděbrady, created a similar programme for Ukrainian female students. In 1928, they initiated what they hoped would be a series, namely, the Women's Library of the Ukrainian Bibliographic Microbe. The strange name was a continuation of an earlier publication venture linked with Serhii Efremov and the moderate Ukrainian intelligentsia at the turn of the century. The only book to appear under this aegis was Lida Pacholikova's *Lysty do Ukrainskykh zhinok* (Letters to Ukrainian Women), with an introduction by Viktor Domanytsky. Pacholikova, a Czech professional agronomist, had published most of these "letters," some of which were in Ukrainian, in periodicals. Emphasizing that the women's issue and the ideal of the new woman had not been solved, Domanytsky suggested that Ukrainian women had much to learn from the Czechs. He himself was most impressed that 65 per cent of the gross national product of Czechoslovakia passed through the hands of women. This statistical information, for which he did not cite a source, convinced him of the importance of women.

Pacholikova, who wrote regularly for Ukrainian journals such as *Nova khata*, also wrote a book in which housework was treated as a profession. She provided a cogent and useful overview of a Czech approach to the education of most Czech peasant women in practical home economics and child care. Ukrainian men, who accepted slogans of equality but avoided the kitchen, were impressed by the reassuring tone of this approach.[36]

From the 1840s onward, the Czechs developed community- and later state-run programmes and schools in which young women were taught principles of equality, but also the importance of the family. Being a mother and a housewife, Pacholikova argued, was perceived as a realistic career for the vast majority of women, especially peasants. But she also discussed some of the women's issues raised by the major Czech feminists. Ukrainian men, who rarely debated the deeper implications of feminism, found such comments revealing. But Ukrainian women, who knew the Czech system, saw the limitations of the pursuit of genuine equality. The ideal of patriotic domesticity was hardly a novel one for them, and thus Pacholikova's book made little impact upon Ukrainian women.

Warsaw was another important Ukrainian émigré centre. Ukrainian women there, predominantly émigrés from Eastern Ukraine, worked very closely with Czech Ukrainian women who set the tone of activity. Initially, the few women in Warsaw worked in conjunction with women from the Ukrainian National Republic's diplomatic mission in exile. Upon the mission's liquidation in 1921, the women established a Women's Section of the Central Ukrainian Committee in Poland. Its chairperson, Olena Lukasevych, through her husband, a physician in the diplomatic service of the UNR in Switzerland, was able to establish contact with the International Red Cross. These women were involved mainly in relief efforts among the veterans of the UNR armies and their families.[37]

In 1929, when the Ukrainian population in Warsaw had increased and settled down to civilian life, the women organized a Women's Community. The moving force behind it was the ebullient Mariia Livytska, the wife of the president-in-exile of the UNR. Livytska envisaged a Union of Ukrainian Emigré Women which, by co-ordinating contacts among various women's groups in Europe, would facilate work in the Ukrainian Women's Union, the ephemeral Rada and the international women's movement. But the Poles delayed confirmation of the statute for four years (until 1933).

It was therefore on the eve of the Stanyslaviv Congress that the Union of Ukrainian Emigré Women came into being. Its members supported the Galician women's move to establish an all-Ukrainian women's organization, which the Vseukrainskyi Soiuz Ukrainok became in 1937 once it had been ratified by the Ukrainian women and approved by the government.

The Union of Ukrainian Emigré Women became very active in the cultural sphere, and attracted an increasing number of women, including students. It organized nursing courses in Warsaw which were certified by the Polish government. It also ran supplementary Ukrainian language, literature and culture courses at which Olena Shovheniv Teliha, the poet, and Nataliia Livytska-Kholodna, the artist, taught. The women organized summer camps, aided refugees and began raising funds for the establishment of a dormitory for Ukrainian students in Warsaw. Of its smaller branches, those in Lviv and Bucharest provided congenial surroundings for women to meet (weekly in Lviv) in small groups.

The first Ukrainian women's efforts in the United States and Canada were also initially European-oriented and concerned the status of Ukrainians after the war. Olena Kysilevska's brother, Dr. Volodymyr Simenovych, organized some mass demonstrations, with the active participation of women, in Chicago and tried to edit a women's newspaper in 1918–19. The Zhinocha Hromada, founded on 4 December 1921 in New York, had "as its only aim the bringing of help to our disabled war veterans in the old country."[38] Other local women's organizations created in Canadian and U.S. cities offered help to and maintained contacts with the home country. After Kysilevska's 1929 trip to Canada and the United States, the initial number of 200 Canadian subscribers to Zhinocha dolia may have increased. Savelia Stechyshyn, a Canadian activist, and Olena Shtohryn, an American, visited Galicia and strengthened ties. The North American women generously and quickly aided victims of the severe 1927 floods in Galicia.[39]

Central women's organizations of Ukrainian-American and Ukrainian-Canadian women were established in 1925 and 1926. Hanna Chykalenko Keller, in conjunction with the ICW Congress in Washington in 1925, provided the impetus for the institutionalization of a central women's society. These organizations, while developing their own pragmatic approach to local issues, continued to meet the needs of European women and to co-operate with them. The American organization focused on trade-union issues, which were central to its largely working-class membership, and only peripherally examined political affairs. Both organizations outlasted the Galician Women's Union and the émigré women's association and are still functioning today.

18.
The All-Ukrainian Women's Union

Ukrainian history is one of partition and division of the Ukrainian state. In modern times Ukrainians' longing for unity has expressed itself in both words and dramatic gestures. Ukrainian women tried to present a united front and to establish an institution which would represent all women outside the Soviet Union. Eventually they overcame religious, political and geographic obstacles in search of this unity.

The differences between Catholic and Orthodox women did not impede the creation of a unified or consolidated women's organization because of the non-confessional nature of the women's organizations. Even the openly Catholic women's groups did not seek either to proselytize or to attack the Orthodox women, or the agnostic or atheist women of Orthodox background. Their anger was directed at the so-called free-thinking Western Ukrainian women. Yet their failure to control the Galician Women's Union increased the prestige of the latter. Of equal importance in minimizing the religious differences——which were very real in the inter-war years for many Ukrainians——was the sensitivity Eastern Ukrainian émigré women displayed to the religious sensibilities of their Western Ukrainian counterparts. They did not attack publicly or ridicule Western Ukrainian religious practices or beliefs, and even attended religious services during the general women's gatherings. The significance of this show of ecumenism or tolerance at a time when contacts between Catholics and Orthodox were either non-existent or hostile, and when Poland specifically accused the Ukrainian Catholic hierarchy of laxity in converting the Orthodox to Catholicism, should not be underestimated.

The political and geographic obstacles to joint action by Ukrainian women were much more serious. There were two political obstacles. First, the differences in political views of Ukrainian women could be as divisive as they were for the men. This was especially the case when to the radicals' latent distrust of independent women's organizations was added the open hostility of the growing nationalist camp. The women managed to contain the potential rifts. Objective political differences were caused by the political configuration in Eastern Europe. Since each statute of a women's organization had to have legal approval of the country in which the organization was established, it was difficult to create an organization that transcended political boundaries. In Poland, where Ukrainians formed the largest minority group, the government prevented the fusion of different women's organizations and restricted joint actions of Ukrainian women's groups.

Nevertheless, Ukrainian women outside the Soviet Union showed a great understanding of pluralism and tolerance in their politics. In their work within the international women's movement (discussed in Part V), they always manifested a united front. Even if disagreements arose, as in Ukrainian participation in the Women's International League of Peace and Freedom in 1937, they were effectively downplayed. The women who emerged in positions of leadership proved able to work with others and were tolerant of other views and approaches.

Actually, the most tolerant of the women were the highly politicized Eastern Ukrainian émigrés. One recalls the difficulties Ukrainians surmounted in 1918–19 merely to consider a pro-forma union of Ukrainian lands. At that time a Women's Union also existed in Lviv. Among the various organizations founded in Kiev was a Women's Union (Zhinocha Hromada), but it had little chance to develop an all-Ukrainian dimension before the fall of the Rada. After the fall of the Hetmanate, while the boundary of the Ukrainian People's Republic was shifting westward, the women sought to establish an all-Ukrainian women's centre, the Women's Council (Zhinocha Rada).[1]

> Foreseeing, during the retreat of the Ukrainian People's Republic to Kamianets-Podilskyi, the sad prospect of the scattering of Ukrainians throughout the entire European continent, Ukrainian women [who happened to] be in [Kamianets] decided to establish a women's organization patterned on the International Council of Women which could serve as a centre of organization for all women in Ukraine and which would unify all women who had already emigrated to various European cities.[2]

The Rada's first presidium reflected its all-encompassing aspirations. Sofiia Rusova, who remained in Kamianets after the UNR government left, headed the organization. The vice-presidents were Mariia Hrushevska, Konstantyna Malytska, Zinaida Mirna and Liudmyla Starytska Cherniakhivska. The first two women came from Galicia and participated in various civic functions. Hrushevska was on one of the boards of the Przemyśl Institute for Girls and had been a member of the Ruthenian Ladies' Club. The latter two were from Eastern Ukraine. Cherniakhivska was well known, and the young Mirna was becoming known for her energy and intelligence. The treasurer was the equally young and promising Western Ukrainian Milena Rudnytska. The general secretary, Mariia Zarchy, who would soon move to Berlin in conjunction with her husband's diplomatic assignment in the UNR, was replaced by the Scottish-educated Hanna Chykalenko-Keller. The recording secretaries were the Western Ukrainian, Olena Okhrymovych Zalizniak, and the Eastern Ukrainian

historian, Nadiia Surovtseva, both of whom later went to graduate school in
Vienna, but followed different political paths. (Surovtseva would return to
Soviet Ukraine, protest Stalinism, and spend most of her life in Siberian
forced-labour camps. Decades later, her experiences were recounted by
Solzhenitsyn.)

The UNR was one of the first states in Eastern Europe to ratify equal-rights
legislation for women. But the major issue facing Ukrainian women in their
central organization was the exercise of the rights of the nation rather than the
rights of women. For that reason the major functions of the Zhinocha Rada
were linked with participation in international gatherings of women, at which
the women promoted the Ukrainian cause. The Ukrainian National Women's
Council moved eventually to Berlin, and after 1924 its headquarters were in
Prague. It remained essentially an émigré organization.

Initially, the council sought to be a clearing-house for Ukrainian women's
organizations outside Ukraine. Chykalenko-Keller prepared a flexible set of
by-laws acceptable to the International Council of Women (ICW). According to
these somewhat vague by-laws, the council was composed of Ukrainian
women's groups in various parts of Europe, but its headquarters were to be in
Ukraine. "Each branch, community or syndicate will have two representatives
in the Rada, one permanent and the other alternate. A single person cannot
fulfill both functions."[3] The full autonomy of each branch was recognized, but
"to co-ordinate the work of the Rada, each section should send its reports of
activity and actions on current matters to the Executive Committee."[4]

The Women's Council sought to represent all Ukrainian women, including
the Women's Union. Keller wrote to the Union about the formal participation
of that organization in the council. The story is not too clear. The Union, which
dated its existence to 1917, although it had existed as an organization only
since 1921, ran into severe difficulties with the local Polish police, who
prevented joint action with Ukrainian women in Volhynia. It also feared that its
formal adherence to an organization based outside the Polish state might
jeopardize its chances for legal recognition and activity. Another factor,
however, was the reluctance of Galicians to merge with the Rada completely.
The Galicians had no desire to become affiliates of an émigré group. On 3
February 1924, responding to Chykalenko's letter and by-laws of the council on
behalf of the Union, Rudnytska noted that the Union was a federative
association of women's groups, that its headquarters were on Ukrainian
territory, and that formal affiliation with the council at this stage might
jeopardize its legal existence.

The émigré women, showing tolerance and understanding, did not insist
upon formal affiliation. On the international level Ukrainian women gave an
impression of unity. At all formal gatherings of women, Galicians, in turn,
made certain that Eastern Ukrainian émigré women received prominence in
Ukrainian delegations. On the whole, relations among the various Ukrainian
women's groups were cordial and without a formal structure.[5]

With the consolidation of the Versailles borders in Europe, there were growing challenges to the claim of the women's organization to represent Ukraine. Ukrainian women realized that to make an impact in women's spheres necessitated not only a single organization representing all Ukrainian women, but also women's organizations in the emigration.

Ukrainian women's groups had been formed either for relief efforts (as in Vienna), for self-help (as in New York and other parts of the United States), or to help co-ordinate aid for the old country (both in Canada and the United States). These groups functioned as separate organizations and reflected the needs of their members. Ukrainian women, trying to play an effective role in the international women's movement, found the support and participation of women from the locality in which a given congress or gathering was being held indispensable. As a matter of fact, the Congress of the ICW in Washington, D.C., in 1924 provided the impetus for the consolidation of U.S. women's groups into one organization in 1925, as well as for the Canadian Ukrainian women's organization a year later. Hanna Chykalenko-Keller, attending the congress (which the Galician women could not attend because of visa and financial difficulties), gave the final push toward the establishment of single Ukrainian women's organizations in both countries.

The ranks of the council's activists were depleted by the return to Ukraine of the Hrushevsky women, Surovtseva and others. The council's prestige suffered as a result, although it was not accused publicly of Sovietophile tendencies. Nevertheless, in the late 1920s the council was in no position to serve as a base for the union of non-Soviet women, although the need for this type of union was now even more pronounced than before. The nation itself was being more severely threatened. The attacks upon the Ukrainian family——a direct victim of the famine in the Soviet Union——certainly illustrated the need for a show of spiritual unity in geographical and political disparity. Despite the lack of an organizational centre, Ukrainian women continued to participate in various international gatherings and strengthened their ties with one another.

The women stressed the need for a viable centre for an all-Ukrainian women's organization. Meanwhile attacks upon the Women's Union in Galicia by self-styled defenders of religion, family and nation in the late 1920s and early 1930s made the Union appear progressive to various Eastern Ukrainian émigré groups. Its stress on unity, its ties with other Ukrainian women's organizations outside Galicia, and the dignity with which it conducted itself under growing pressure increased its prestige. The convocation of the Stanyslaviv Congress in 1934, attended by representatives of virtually all non-Soviet women's organizations, evoked a surge of emotion and greatly aided efforts to establish a central women's organization. The decision to create such an organization was made not by a single group of women, but by the Stanyslaviv Congress, which was by far the largest and most representative gathering of Ukrainian women outside the Soviet Union. It generated momentum and heightened the prestige of its organizers and participants, who authorized the formation of a committee to work out the details for the creation

of a World Union of Ukrainian Women (Vseukrainskyi Zhinochyi Soiuz), an
organization that was to become, in the words of its chief supporter:

> the Centre of organized Ukrainian women of the entire world, the voice for the
> interests of the Ukrainian Nation before international and foreign——particularly
> women's——organizations, and the representative of Ukrainian women to their
> own society.[6]

Olena Zalizniak, Milena Rudnytska and Mariia Strutynska were elected to
the committee and charged with the task of setting up the organizational and
legal structure of the World Union of Ukrainian Women. The committee
emphasized that it was not modelling itself on any external examples, but rather
trying to reflect the needs of Ukrainian women. It stressed that an organization
of such magnitude could not consist only of Europeans. Hanka
Romanchych-Kovalchuk, the Canadian representative in Stanyslaviv, had
expressed her support for the proposed supra-organization, but the women also
wanted the formal presence of a representative from the United States. They
conducted a detailed correspondence on the matter.[7] A decision was made to
accept the territorial principle: each area could be represented by one Ukrainian
women's organization. The major aim was to foster a feeling of unity among all
Ukrainian women. The founding members of the Union were the Women's
Union in Galicia, the Women's Union in Volhynia, the Women's Union in
Transcarpathia, the Union of Ukrainian Emigré Women in Poland, the women's
organizations in Romania, the Women's National Council (headquarters in
Prague), the Women's Union in Prague, the Women's Union in the United
States (the Ukrainian National Women's League of America), and the
Ukrainian Women's League of Canada. The president of the Women's Union
in Lviv would be ex-officio president of the All-Ukrainian Women's Union,
while the secretary would always be the representative of the Union of
Ukrainian Emigré Women. This solved the major allocation of seats between
Eastern and Western Ukrainian women.

The promulgation of the All-Ukrainian Women's Union did not take place
until 1937. In that year the Poles finally ratified the All-Ukrainian Union, and a
representative of the American-Ukrainian group, Olena Shtohryn, arrived to
convey the adherence of her organization to the Union. (The Canadians had
agreed in 1934.) The creation of the international organization for Ukrainian
women was announced immediately after the General Meeting of the Women's
Union, held in Lviv on 9 and 10 October 1937. The three hundred delegates
were triumphant.

Rudnytska permitted herself a rare moment of jubilation:

> No one can deny that the World Union of Ukrainian Women is today the only
> Ukrainian inter-territorial organization in the world, the only incarnation...of the
> idea of the sovereignty [sobornist] of the Ukrainian nation....

Even if the World Union remains only an effort, only an attempt and an idea, this very idea of all-Ukrainian unification of sisters, the very idea of contact across the oceans, the prairies, the borders and the lines of demarcation, the fusion of women's feelings, thoughts and wills for the highest ideal of the Nation deserves the strongest interest on the part of the whole community and the fullest support.[8]

To avoid renewed accusations of free-thinking, and to demonstrate their loyalty to the symbol of the modern Ukrainian nation, the women formally requested and received the blessing of Metropolitan Sheptytsky. Rusova was made honorary president for life; Rudnytska and Mirna became respectively the first chairperson and secretary. The executive board included Olena Sheparovych, Lidiia Mryts Shaviak, Dr. Iryna Prisnevska (Volhynia), Tonia Horokhovych (originally from Volhynia), Nataliia Livytska Kholodna (daughter of the president-in-exile of the UNR), Konstantyna Malytska (heading educational matters), Olena Shtohryn (USA), and Olha Tsipanovska.

The Ukrainian women considered the World Union a great achievement: they had established a Ukrainian organization that sought to represent all women. The American Ukrainian women wholeheartedly supported the Union. Recognizing the symbolic historical importance of the event, they published the letter announcing the formation of the Union, as well as its bylaws.[9]

The World Union of Ukrainian Women was founded not to establish the unity of Ukrainian women, but to manifest that unity. Again, the organization came to fulfill a deeply felt need. *Zhinka*, the newspaper of the Galician women, was to serve as the general women's newspaper. At last there existed an organized Ukrainian women's society, and a tradition of their community involvement. The Ukrainian woman had entered modernity. What the future held for her was less certain.

Part V

Ukrainian Women and International Feminism

The women's clubs of Great Britain and the United States were the first to combine forces toward the end of the nineteenth century. More formal international women's organizations developed at the turn of the century, when international organization was seen as a means of achieving peace. These women's groups were not interested primarily in asserting national rights. On the contrary, they actively sought a broader perspective than that of nationalism. Like other international organizations and groups (most of which were male-dominated) acting through a growing international network, the women met to discuss issues of common interest and to manifest their unity.

For Ukrainian women the priorities were reversed. They used the international dimension of feminism in an attempt to assert, popularize and manifest not so much their aspirations as women, but their fate as Ukrainians. The women's organizations provided yet another outlet in the perennial attempts of Ukrainians to gain wider national recognition.

For Ukrainians, the international dimension of feminism manifested itself on three interlocking levels. As a population divided among a number of sovereign states, with regional as well as ideological differences, Ukrainian women first had to overcome both internal and external obstacles before they could create a single representative organization of Ukrainian women. Since the Soviet Union did not recognize the legitimacy of women's and feminist demands, the Ukrainian SSR played no part in helping the women organize a broad feminist platform. During the turmoil that followed the First World War it was not clear which women's organization spoke in the name of Ukrainian women outside the Soviet Union. Soon, however, these women achieved a degree of national cohesion and organizational unity unequalled by the men's organizations.

In addition to the all-Ukrainian women's organization, Ukrainian women who emigrated also established organizations in their countries of settlement. The émigrés either functioned as autonomous women's groups or worked within the women's network in their adopted countries. The participation of these women in international organizations could proceed on three levels: within the Ukrainian organizations; in émigré organizations; and in the public life of the adopted countries.

Finally, Ukrainian women participated in every international women's gathering they could penetrate. Indeed, the existence of the international women's forum forced some Ukrainian women, especially hitherto uninterested women of the Eastern Ukrainian intelligentsia, to become active in the women's movement. Moreover, the patriotic aspect, popularizing the cause of Ukraine through international women's organizations, kept the men from expressing more outspoken criticisms of Ukrainian women's organizations.

Before the outbreak of the First World War, international socialism opposed the creation of separate women's groups or a separate feminist agenda, although it ardently supported women's rights. After the war, the pervasiveness of women's issues and the recognition of the potential force of women's organizations stimulated the creation of various women's groups within the

diversified   socialist   movement.   The   participation   of   Ukrainian
women——except for Kobrynska's perceptive analysis of the women's role in
that movement——did not differ from that of other women. (The rallies and
joint actions in the Austrian Empire before 1914 did not lead to the creation of
an international institutional base.)

The most active and successful initiatives of Ukrainian women in
establishing effective contacts with other women and with international
women's organizations took place in the period immediately following the First
World War. The collapse of the restrictive East European monarchies, the rise
of democratic regimes, and the enfranchisement of whole populations seemed
to herald a new era of international friendship and co-operation among people
unencumbered by governments. Women considered it an opportunity for them
not only to participate in world affairs, from which they had previously been
excluded, but also to rectify the injustices of the now defunct oppressive
regimes. They felt that the time was conducive for women to contribute to the
rebuilding of society and world order. Despite the lack of sympathy toward
their aspirations on the part of the Soviet regime, Ukrainian women outside the
USSR, sharing the mood of hope and elation, tried to make full use of the
opportunities offered by the international women's movement.

In the 1920s Ukrainian women participated with various degrees of official
recognition in the International Council of Women (ICW), in the International
Women's Suffrage Alliance (IWSA), and in the Women's International League
for Peace and Freedom. The Polish pacification-terror campaign against
Western Ukrainians in 1930–1, the escalation of Soviet terror against the
Ukrainian population, especially the famine of 1932–3 and the purges which
preceded and followed it, and the political polarization which characterized
European politics of the 1930s further shifted the focus of Ukrainian women
toward national rather than feminist concerns. Whereas in the 1920s the main
issue was the assertion of the rights of Ukrainian women, by the 1930s the
issue had become the defence of Ukraine's right to exist.

International women's organizations were more responsive to peace efforts
than to the rights of nationalities. For the average Western European and
American feminist, the latter were confining. Women entered the international
arena raising the banner of pacifism and urging the cessation of hostilities.
Meeting at The Hague during the latter half of April 1915, the Women's
International League for Peace and Freedom openly pleaded for an immediate
peace. No Ukrainians (or Russians) were present at the meeting. The Poles,
however, sent a written memorandum in which Zofia Moraczewska stressed
that Polish women could support peace only *after* Poland had gained its
national independence. Until such time the duty of the Polish women was to
fight for independence by every possible means.

Although individual Ukrainian women participated in the military actions of
the Civil War, no separate Ukrainian women's detachment was formed. Eastern
Ukrainian women, although producing a number of legendary guerrilla women
leaders, were not particularly interested in military or paramilitary action.

Peace, disarmament, and the innate evil of standing armies were causes dear to the heart of the Eastern Ukrainian intelligentsia. This predisposed Ukrainian women to seek contacts with women of anti-war views, and encouraged some European and American pacifist women to sympathize with Ukrainians.

Among the organizers of the Women's International League for Peace and Freedom were Jane Addams, Crystal Macmillan, Emily Balch, and Belgian, French, and German women. They espoused freedom for all nationalities, disarmament, international arbitration, democratic principles in foreign relations, and women's rights. The women renounced war as an instrument of policy and tried to persuade all women, regardless of political boundaries, to support a lasting peace. The League always "favoured extreme socialist movements, for instance in its idealized support of communism which it hoped would be achieved in a peaceful fashion. That orientation did not always suit Ukrainians."[1] But the League's stress on peace, freedom, self-determination, and its criticism of the Versailles Treaty's failure to guarantee the principle of national self-determination offset its "leftist tinge" in the eyes of Ukrainians.

There were two major stumbling-blocks to be overcome before Ukrainians joined the League for Peace and Freedom: the technicalities of the Ukrainian political situation and the dispersal of Ukrainian women in different European states. But, judging from Hanna Chykalenko-Keller's and Balch's correspondence, the League was willing to dismiss these factors. The pacifism of the League posed a greater problem of conscience for Ukrainian women. The League, according to its stated objectives:

> aims at binding women in every country who will not support, directly or indirectly, any war and who desire to promote the following objectives: (1) the creation of international relations of mutual co-operation and goodwill in which all wars shall be impossible; (2) the establishment of political, social and moral equality between men and women; (3) the introduction of these principles into all educational systems.[2]

Chykalenko-Keller wondered if a possible Ukrainian struggle for independence would disqualify its women from working in the international organization of women. Balch's secretary assured Keller that this was not the case, although she hoped that Ukrainians would come to realize the importance of peace. Both the leadership of the League and Ukrainians, however, realized that it was not necesary to debate these issues. The League was willing to come to an agreement enabling the participation of Ukrainian women in its work, which the Ukrainian women were willing to accept. It was important for the Ukrainian intelligentsia women to be affiliated with a progressive women's organization, since most of the Eastern Ukrainian women felt uncomfortable with the middle-class women activists from Western Europe. They participated in moderate women's organizations, but their work in the League assuaged their revolutionary conscience and made the other work more bearable.

The League was the first international organization to hold a conference after the 1914–18 war. It supported the League of Nations and stressed the duty and competence of women to help prevent the outbreak of new wars. Lidiia Drahomanova-Shishmanova, now a veteran of international congresses, lived in Switzerland at the time. She introduced Hanna Chykalenko-Keller, a graduate of British universities, to the international work of women. Through Crystal Macmillan, who had graduated from the University at Edinburgh which Chykalenko-Keller had also attended, Ukrainian women met Emily Balch, the American representative of the League, and Margaret Hoba, its Swiss secretary. Chykalenko-Keller, whose father was in Western Ukraine, and whose brothers had remained in Kiev (which in two years changed hands eleven times), realized the importance of the League for Ukraine. She re-established contact with Mariia Hrushevska, the Galician-born wife of the former President of the Central Rada, who was then in Switzerland, as well as with Liudmyla Starytska-Cherniakhivska, the writer and activist, and with the Ukrainian women's group in Galicia. By the time of the next meeting of the League, in Vienna in May 1921, Ukrainians had established their own branches of the League in Vienna, Zurich, Berne, Lviv, Przemyśl, and Tarnów, the temporary headquarters of the UNR. The Zhinocha Hromada sought to speak for the women of the Ukrainian People's Republic.

Ukrainians stressed their commitment to peace, as well as their struggle for independence:

> Members of free and independent countries may find it hard to understand the touchy national sensitivity of a nation such as Ukraine, which has been oppressed for centuries. I feel that an Irishwoman could understand us perfectly. We firmly hope that [eventually] the international spirit will get the upper hand in our country, as everywhere, and we will work for that [goal].[3]

The whole spectrum of Ukrainian women was drawn to the support of the League and through it the League of Nations. In 1920, the Ukrainian women working as a "provisional" section of the League included Mariia Dontsova, the wife of the nationalist ideologue; Valeria O'Connor-Vilinska, the writer; Oksana Lototska, an upper-class émigré; Blanka Baranova, a Galician activist; Milena Lysiak-Rudnytska, a young mathematics teacher, and Lida Khrapko-Drahomanova, an émigré. Extremely active and effective, because she was also involved in the Austrian section of the League, was Nadiia Surovtseva, a Ph.D. candidate in history at the University of Vienna, who was also the secretary of the Women's Union of the UNR. Before the Vienna Congress, representatives of Ukrainian women (Lototska, Rudnytska, Khrapko-Drahomanova and Surovtseva) met with the twenty-woman Executive Board of the League, which showed a profound understanding of the plight of Ukrainians. As Surovtseva reported:

the whole atmosphere [of the congress], all the delegates, created a most favourable impression in their discussion about Ukraine, so different from those which characterize other meetings. [These delegates] have such a broad world-view and so much good will that one instinctively has to have second thoughts about criticizing feminist organizations, and suspend the usual ironic skepticism with which women's organizations are met.[4]

To Ukrainian women, it seemed a positive sign that the requests of women from Poland, Czechoslovakia and Yugoslavia to be accepted into the League were challenged because of the expansionist actions of their respective governments.

Meanwhile, Ukrainian women in Western Ukraine organized into a unified entity. Eastern Ukrainian women, still hoping for an imminent change of government in Kiev, created small but effective women's groups in Berlin, Prague, Berne and Vienna. All these organizations, without paying too much attention to formalities, participated in many international gatherings and undertakings. Eastern Ukrainian intelligentsia women never placed much stress on organizational formalities or conventions.[5]

Chykalenko-Keller corresponded with Emily Balch and became friendly with her successor, Mary Sheepshanks. At the same time she used her connections to involve Ukrainian women in the work of other women's international organizations, as well as in women's efforts to organize and co-ordinate war-relief activities. The Chykalenko fortune was useful in these ventures. For instance, when Denmark promised to help Ukraine, Estonia and Latvia by refashioning noble estates into orphanages and hospices for children in late 1920, Chykalenko offered one of his estates for that purpose. Hanna Chykalenko-Keller spoke with Dora Taugord, the editor of the *Contemporary Woman* in Denmark, impressing upon her that, were hostilities to cease, Ukraine could not only feed its population, but also aid Latvia and Estonia. This Keller did both as an individual and in her capacity as a member of the Ukrainian Women's Council. At the same time Keller tried to impress upon Galician Ukrainians the need to work in an organization which would unite all women. Consequently, she established an Alliance for the Defence of Women for which she sought formal recognition both among Ukrainian women and in the international women's movement.

Chykalenko-Keller needed an organization of this kind to induce Ukrainians to join the International Women's Suffrage Alliance, which had been founded in 1902 and had held regular international gatherings since 1904. Its activists included American, British, New Zealand, Danish, Dutch, Icelandic and Finnish women's organizations. Keller, using her ties with Crystal Macmillan, obtained an invitation for Ukrainians to attend the Alliance's congress held in Geneva on 6–12 June 1920. In their petition to join the organization, Ukrainian women stressed the *de jure* and the *de facto* equality they had gained since 1917. The Ukrainian delegation, composed of Keller, Mariia Lozynska and Olena Savchenko, supported the congress programme, which focused on legal and economic equality of men and women, child support for out-of-wedlock progeny and abolition of prostitution. They also used the congress as a forum to popularize the cause of Ukrainian women through discussions, conversations and distribution of materials about the Ukrainian situation.[6]

Since Ukrainian women had already received the right to vote and suffrage rights were not included in the statute of any of the organizations, notably that of the Ukrainian Women's Union, which sought entry into the IWSA, Chykalenko-Keller decided to establish a special society to defend women's rights. She saw many advantages. Membership in IWSA could open up an internationally recognized forum to Ukrainian women, and would help them establish formal contacts with the League of Nations. Since Soviet Ukraine would not join this organization and Ukrainians had no other state, after 1925 Ukrainian women remained affiliated with the IWSA only through the émigré organizations.

The relationship of Ukrainian women to the oldest women's organization——the International Council of Women (ICW)——founded in 1888 in Washington, D.C., was more complex. The ICW was, in Keller's characterization, "the oldest, the most influential and most conservative of women's organizations."[7] Keller was concerned that joining the ICW might conflict with Ukrainian membership in the Women's International League for Peace and Freedom. She had to be assured by Emily Balch that relations between the two organizations were most cordial, since their goals were complementary.[8] Ukrainian intelligentsia women perceived the ICW as an organization of upper-class ladies' clubs in which democratic Ukrainians would feel out of place. The initiative for Ukrainian access to the ICW came from a colourful, ambitious, distinctive and flamboyant woman——Mariia Zarchy. Zarchy was an ardent Ukrainian patriot who retained her Jewish culture. She befriended American and British women easily, although her flamboyance evidently alienated continental women. Mrs. Zarchy, married to Serhii, a diplomat in the service of the UNR, was the general secretary of the Ukrainian Women's Union.

The International Council of Women held congresses every five years, but its committees met more frequently. Reducing national tensions was a primary goal, and it proposed to work with the League of Nations, particularly in welfare, education and reconstruction. The ICW and its national councils obtained support and recognition from both governments and international organizations such as the Red Cross. Participation in the first post-war congress of the ICW——which reflected the new democratic configuration of Europe and strengthened the efforts of women to help rehabilitate war-torn areas——transcended purely feminist concerns for Ukrainians. Even Ukrainian men who had looked contemptuously on women's organizations saw the opportunities ICW offered. Zarchy and Chykalenko-Keller received formal accreditation from the Ukrainian People's Repulic to represent Ukrainians at the ICW Congress in Oslo (Christiania) between 8 and 18 September 1920.

The ICW, much to the annoyance of its Anglo-American founders, had been plagued with issues of nationalism since 1899, when it held its first European meeting in London (the previous two had been held in Washington, D.C., in 1888 and in Chicago in 1893). As the national councils were being formed, Marianne Hainisch, the representative of the Habsburg Empire, or more precisely, of its Austrian part, argued that her country would need at least three internal councils, owing to the heterogeneity of its lands. Lady Aberdeen showed little sympathy, and noted acerbically that since Austrian women had reduced their original request for fourteen councils (the officially recognized languages of the Austrian part of the Monarchy) to three "there is hope that before long they might reduce the three to one, and then the council would be truly national."[9] But the legality of the Hungarian representative was never questioned, nor was it ever presumed that the Russians might not represent the entire Russian Empire.

The principle of representation on state and nationality levels remained unresolved, but women were willing to search for some type of equitable system. Sewall and Hainisch, for example, in Berlin in 1904——a congress to which the Kharkiv women had sent an observer——moved the creation of a committee to investigate the teaching of history in various countries, which would recommend modifications in areas that seemed to inculcate hatred of other peoples.[10] Five years later the ICW meeting in Toronto established a committee to study issues of political, national and racial representation. The political changes after the 1914–18 war further complicated the national structure of the ICW, but the unsettled situation in Eastern Europe enabled the Ukrainian delegation at Oslo to participate fully with the 350 other representatives of 26 countries at all official functions of the congress.

The Norwegian government, enjoying the first decade of its independence from Sweden, doubled the sum Norwegian women had requested as a subsidy for the congress and permitted the use of the parliament building for meetings. The King and Queen, and Michelet, the foreign minister, hosted receptions for the women. In his conversations with Keller, Michelet expressed a deep interest in the political and cultural situation in Ukraine and in the Ukrainian system of agriculture. The Swedish Ambassador to Norway, Baron Rummel, was also interested in Ukraine's grain surplus during the war. Keller and Zarchy participated in general and committee meetings, gave official reports on conditions in Ukraine, and circulated a report on the status of Ukrainian women. Parts of these reports were included in the published proceedings.[11] The report offered a grim first-hand account of the ravages of war and pestilence, and asked the Red Cross to investigate the medical and other emergency aid Ukraine needed. Scandinavian women tried to organize settlement camps and offered aid to Eastern Europe and the Soviet territories.

The work of the Ukrainian delegation to ICW was therefore quite effective. Through the women's organizations, Ukrainians reached a women's international forum even as they were losing the ears of the international community. The Berlin Section of the Ukrainian Council of Women sent a petition to the League of Nations in April 1923, requesting that it reconsider its rejection of the Ukrainian People's Republic "and in that manner help Ukraine throw off the foreign Bolshevik yoke which threatens the very existence of the Ukrainian nation."[12]

In 1921, when the congress of the International League of Women for Peace and Freedom was held in Vienna, Ukrainian women were a recognized entity. The Ukrainian Women's Community in Vienna helped make Ukrainian participation at the congress effective. It was reinforced by women working toward their Ph.D. degrees——Olena Stepaniv (she married Dashkevych in Vienna in 1920), Nadiia Surovtseva and Milena Rudnytska (who became so involved in community work that she never wrote her dissertation).

Throughout the 1920s Ukrainian women tried to maintain the momentum they had gained in the international arena. While Western Ukrainian women were holding their crucial meeting in December 1921, they also welcomed Sofiia Rusova, the activist-teacher from Ukraine who had barely escaped Soviet detention. Rusova, who had been appointed professor of pedagogy at the Ukrainian University in Kamianets-Podilskyi, proved an effective representative of Ukrainian women. Her professional experience as a teacher and writer, her political activism against the tsar, her arrests and——most importantly——her persecution under the new Soviet system, contributed to her credibility in the international forum. Her membership in the Central Rada was also a precedent for Rusova's participation in the meetings of the Interparliamentary Union. Rusova's status within the Ukrainian community, in turn, enhanced the importance of women and their role in the community. She eventually settled in Czechoslovakia and, because of its liberal policy toward minorities, had no difficulty obtaining exit visas. However, she sometimes felt uncomfortable in bourgeois West European surroundings and shared the typical *inteligent's* tendency to make fun of "ladies' organizations."

The first international women's congress in which Rusova participated was the International Congress of Women at the Hague in 1922. She even exchanged a few words with the Dutch Queen about the position of Ukrainian women. Rusova, a slight, self-effacing, emaciated woman who always dressed in black, for all her ostensible simplicity and unaffectedness, had a flair for the dramatic. Here is her account of the first public gathering of the congress:

An extremely stout Romanian, in a luxuriously pleated costume, spoke.... Ukraine followed her——an elderly, emaciated figure, all in black. Silence fell on the auditorium as she began speaking, as if a black cloud had enveloped the brightly lit earth. What is she saying? Only the naked truth about her nation, about its agony, about the courage its women are demonstrating in their struggle with all the occupying powers——Russian, Polish, Romanian. There was not much time to speak...but even that was enough. The press picked up the austere report, and the following day there was not a single woman at the congress who would not come to our delegate with expressions of sympathy.[13]

Rusova's trip was financed by Ukrainian women with contributions from women in North America.

In 1922 Ukrainian women scored another success. The Western Ukrainian Women's Union became a member of the International Co-operative Guild. Ukrainians were able to maintain their ties with this organization well into the thirties.[14]

Several meetings occurred in 1923: a congress of the International Women's Suffrage Alliance in Rome; a meeting of the League of Peace and Freedom in Dresden; an educationalists' congress in Berlin; and a meeting of the International Union for Aid to Children in Geneva. The Federation of University Women planned to hold a congress in Oslo in 1924, while the next scheduled congress of the International Council of Women was to take place in Washington in 1925. Meanwhile, smaller gatherings and rallies were held in various European cities which drew an international audience. To ensure the effective participation of Ukrainian women, Keller prepared a brochure about Ukrainians entitled *To the Women of the Civilized World*. It was published in French, German and probably English and Italian. The imprint was an innocuous "National Committee"——in order not to affiliate it with any particular organization and facilitate its use in different countries.[15] The brochure was apparently very effective. In fact, rumour had it that the author must have been a man, since no woman could have written so well.[16] An unsuccessful attempt was made at the congress in Rome to establish an umbrella organization, an "International Committee to Aid Ukrainian Women" to garner support from non-Ukrainian women. Ukrainians, nevertheless, continued to participate in the meetings of the Alliance whenever they could. They became so visible at the international gatherings that some of them even worried whether too much exposure of Ukraine's plight would trivialize it.[17]

The IWSA Congress in Rome, held from 12 to 20 May 1923, was the first major international congress of women held after the fall of the Ukrainian People's Republic and after Poland was formally entrusted to administer Galicia. It was therefore crucial for the Ukrainian women to assert their continued claims to independence and to ensure that Ukrainian women remained a viable entity in the international arena. Ukrainians planned their participation in Rome carefully. Forty-five nations were represented at the congress and the woman issue was newsworthy enough to guarantee press coverage.

The Ukrainian delegation tried to include representatives from all Ukrainian territories outside Soviet Ukraine. Olena Hadzynska Levchanivska from Volhynia had just been elected Senator to Warsaw and in this capacity she was an ideal participant at the congress. Initially she had some difficulty leaving Poland. Then, at the last minute, her child fell ill and she could not attend the congress. The Ukrainian delegation was composed of Rusova, P.Iu. Zelenivska, Nina Onatska and Mlada Lypovetska. Onatska was the wife of the Ukrainian government-in-exile's consul in Rome, Lypovetska seemed too young and was not assertive enough for Keller's taste, but Rusova could be counted upon to be forceful. Zelenivska came from the conservative segment of Ukrainian society, and it was indicative of the mood of Ukrainians that Keller, in her letter to the Vienna Ukrainian women's group, felt obliged to defend her, stressing that her political goals coincided with those of other Ukrainian women and that her tact, energy and willingness to finance her own trip to Rome would serve the Ukrainian cause well.

At the congress, Ukrainian women made contacts again with the Scandinavian women to try to assist children who had suffered during the war. More important, Rusova's impassioned fifteen-minute public address to the congress received wide coverage. Rusova stressed that despite Soviet claims, the position of many women under the Soviets had become worse rather than better. Since women were not skilled workers they often had to carry out badly paid physical labour to earn a living. The breakdown of traditional family life and the popularity of so-called free love made women and children more vulnerable to exploitation. The birth rate had declined while the death rate had soared. Education, particularly in non-Russian native languages had also suffered a setback. Despite this dismal picture, Rusova stressed the willingness of Ukrainian women to struggle for genuine liberty and equality. As an example, she reminded her audience of the long but successful struggles of Mazzini and Garibaldi.[18]

Ukrainian participation in the next congress of the League for Peace and Freedom was less dramatic. Mariia Hrushevska, Khrapko-Drahomanova and Surovtseva attended the congress in Dresden in the summer of 1923. Olena Zalizniak, who was studying in Europe, also participated. The Polish section was accepted at this congress, and Ukrainians tried to draw the League's attention to the mistreatment of Western Ukrainians by the Poles. They highlighted the example of a young high-school student, Vyshnevska, who had just been arrested in Lviv, kept in prison with prostitutes and generally harassed by the Polish police. Dontsova, who was to represent Western Ukrainian women at the congress, could not obtain a Polish exit visa to attend.[19]

Ukrainian women also worked through the League's Commission for the Study of Eastern Europe, which held many of its working meetings in Poděbrady in Czechoslovakia.[20] Ukrainians actively participated in the League until 1938. Blanka Baranova and Sofiia Rusova remained its major supporters after Surovtseva returned to Ukraine, where she was silenced and later arrested.

Like other women's organizations at the time, the League stressed disarmament and pacifism. The latter ideology was unpopular among Western Ukrainians, who were convinced that a lack of military expertise had cost Ukrainians their independence. Baranova and Rusova, nevertheless, pointed out repeatedly that Ukrainians supported peace, although the oppression of Ukrainians by their neighbours made that hope illusory. Rusova's defence of the ideals of peace, equality, international co-operation and universal disarmament did not diminish in the face of the Ukrainian situation. She remained a radical who saw the Bolsheviks as traitors to the sacred cause. She never could support co-operation with the Soviets, even in the late 1920s when the popular Soviet consul in Lviv, Iurii Lapchynsky, praised the Ukrainization policies of the Soviets and attended Ukrainian functions in Galicia. Despite growing dissatisfaction with her "leftism," the women continued to accept her. As late as the May 1924 Congress of the Women's International League for Peace and Freedom in Washington, Surovtseva and Khrapko-Drahomanova shared the forum. With slightly differing emphases, both stressed that Ukraine possessed only quasi-autonomous status and that its inhabitants, after the horrors of the wars and revolutions, supported absolute pacifism more than ever before.

An outgrowth of the work of the League (which held a congress in Prague in 1928) and Czech women activists was the establishment of the Organization of the Unity of Slavic Women (*Jednota Slovanskych Žen*) in Prague in 1927. Its aim was to foster a better understanding among Slavic women and to defend their rights. Mrs. Smólař-Čypkova invited Ukrainian women in the Czech lands to participate in the organization. Ukrainians did so willingly, but Russian émigré women in Czechoslovakia persuaded many pro-Russian Czech women to consider Ukrainians as part of the Russian group, which negated Ukrainian participation. A few years later, the Poles created a similar organization, *Wszechsłowiańskie Zjednoczenie Kobiet*, which organized a congress in Warsaw on 9 June 1931. On this occasion, the Poles refused to admit the Union of Ukrainian Women.[21] The unity of Slavic women, therefore, proved as illusory as the unity of Slavic men: the congresses of Slavic women held in Belgrade and Sofia were those of the official women's organizations of Slavic states.

The Czech feminist Františka Plaminková sought to mediate between Polish and Ukrainian women, but the obduracy of the Poles was matched by the openly anti-Polish views of Milena Rudnytska, who in 1928 was elected President of the Ukrainian Women's Union. Rudnytska's anti-Polish stand in Prague in 1928 embarrassed Ukrainian émigré women in Czechoslovakia, who considered it rude and petty. Eastern Ukrainian women émigrés in Poland had experience only with moderate Poles and knew little of the Ukrainophobia exhibited by some Galician Poles. Chykalenko and Loska were especially upset by Rudnytska and concerned about the impact her zeal had upon Mary Sheepshanks, who was playing a major role in the affairs of the League for Peace and Freedom. But Sheepshanks and the League studied the issues, and in March 1929 invited Rudnytska to speak at a conference on the political situation in Eastern Europe which was sponsored by the League in Vienna.[22] On the eve of that meeting, Mrs. Camilla Dreves visited Ukrainian institutions in Lviv as a delegate of the League. In 1934 Sheepshanks represented the League at the Congress of Ukrainian Women in Stanyslaviv.

In the mid-1920s Ukrainian women also tried to join the Federation of University Women.[23] Zalizniak initiated the establishment of the Ukrainian Society of Women with an Advanced Education in Lviv on 18 October 1924, with Olena Stepaniv-Dashkevych as its first president. It immediately petitioned for membership in the Federation, although its prospective delegate to the 1925

Brussels Congress of the Federation could not participate because the Poles would not give her an exit visa. Again, Ukrainians stressed that they had organized their Society before the Poles established theirs, and that the committee on new members, composed of British, French and Czech women, was studying their application. But again the Western Ukrainian women were refused membership in the Federation because it was based on the principle of statehood.[24]

Within the prestigious International Council of Women there was a move to return to clear-cut organizational stability and keep only organizations with a territorial base and some governmental backing as members. At the Washington congress in 1925, Russia was dropped as a member, although the chairman of the former Russian section was re-elected as an honorary vice-president of ICW. As far as Ukrainians were concerned:

Lady Aberdeen explained that according to the rules laid down early in the history of the International Council by a special committee...it was only possible to accept for affiliation National Councils in countries having a responsible government. She was afraid that under the circumstances it would not be possible to continue the affiliation of the National Council of Women of Ukrainia (sic) after the close of these Quinquennial Meetings.[25]

The Ukrainian delegation was composed of Chykalenko-Keller and Ukrainian women from the United States. They argued that Ukrainians in Western Ukraine were living "under a responsible government" and another commission was formed to look into the Ukrainian situation. Keller, meanwhile, impressed upon the Ukrainian women of the United States and Canada the need to unify their local women's clubs, which they did, forming strong and effective organizations in both countries.[26]

The Ukrainians challenged their expulsion from ICW in 1925, and at the Congress of the ICW in Vienna. In 1930, Lady Aberdeen again defended the legality of their expulsion. Rusova, pleading the cause of the dispossessed, drew on arguments of humanity and justice. The ICW, which was co-operating closely with the League of Nations and some other women's organizations, was deeply involved in disarmament programmes. In its work, it was dependent upon some Polish women and influential women of Polish extraction or with Polish connections. The Council considered this work, rather than the status of Ukrainian women in the ICW, to be of vital importance.[27] Although Ukrainians were dropped from the ICW by the end of the 1920s, they never reconciled themselves to that decision. As late as July 1938, on the eve of the ICW Congress which met in Edinburgh, Rudnytska, the president of the Ukrainian Women's Union, still considered herself part of the Board of the International Association of the Civic Rights of Women that was affiliated with the ICW. The matter was never fully resolved.[28]

The participation of Ukrainian women in the congresses of the International Women's Suffrage Association, which were held throughout the 1930s, was also unclear. Ukrainians evidently were not actually expelled from the association. Ukrainian women, however, could not attend the 1934 conference in Istanbul because none of their delegates could get Polish exit visas. In July 1939, when the last congress of IWSA was held in Copenhagen, Ukrainian women in Galicia were having difficulties preserving the integrity and legal status of their organization in Poland.

The contacts and experience gained by Ukrainian women in the women's forum were invaluable. There emerged, however, a confusing bifurcation between the Ukrainian women's movement outside the Soviet Union and feminist concerns in the 1920s and 30s. In the first decade, in the international arena, Ukrainians stressed women's concerns and rights, although feminist topics in Western Ukraine did not draw much interest. Women's interest in specifically feminist issues increased in the 1930s. Internationally, however, the work of Ukrainian women in that decade stressed the treatment of minorities in Poland, especially the "pacification," and the genocide of Ukrainians in the Soviet Union through the Great Famine of 1933. Women and women's organizations helped publicize these events. The inability or unwillingness of the West to react deepened Ukrainian misgivings about possible aid from the democratic states. This led, in turn, to increased popularity for maximalist ideologies among Ukrainians, or toward their withdrawal from active political life.

The initiative in the international field in the 1930s shifted from Ukrainian émigré women to the Western Ukrainian women's organizations. The Women's Union spoke for an indigenous population from a Western viewpoint. Their shock at Polish behaviour was genuine, and they could not understand the apparent indifference of Eastern Ukrainian émigré women to the Galicians. These, in turn, comprehending the Stalinist terror, could not understand the West's blindness to it. Both groups of women, moreover, saw the inherent danger of the growing fascist movement in Romania, Germany, Austria, Italy and, in a different guise, in Poland.

Within the Ukrainian community, the Ukrainian women pointed out that their experiences in the international forum made them better prepared for work among non-Ukrainians than some of the Ukrainian political leaders. "We Ukrainian women, who have long-standing contacts with feminist international organizations, are more familiar with the philosophy underlying these organizations than are our politicians."[29] After the elections of 1928, with Rudnytska in the Polish Sejm and Olena Kysilevska in the Senate, participation of Ukrainian women in various international gatherings was assured. That year a congress of the Interparliamentary Union was held in Berlin, and the Congress of National Minorities in Geneva.[30] Rudnytska attended both, and at the latter proposed the inclusion of women's organizations in the programme of international co-operation. Her proposal, feminist in nature, won Ukrainians more sympathizers in the women's organization.

When an international congress of IWSA was held in Berlin in 1929, Ukrainian women were represented mainly by Western Ukrainians——Olena Sheparovych, Iryna Pavlykovska, Olha Fedak, and Olha Ostrovska. The German press took an interest in Poland's discrimination against its Ukrainian minority.

The so-called Pacification marked a particularly virulent period in relations between Poles and Ukrainians. The Poles did not live up to promises made to the Council of Ambassadors to grant Eastern Galicia autonomy, nor to the codicils on the rights of the minorities. During the 1930 harvest, the OUN burned crops belonging to Polish landlords. Its action served as a pretext for a centrally organized and locally administered pogrom against the Ukrainian population in more than 1,000 villages and in scores of towns. Ukrainians were beaten and humiliated; their property and institutions destroyed. Ukrainians "who had not passed up a single international event in the 1920's and 1930's without bringing up the discriminatory policies of the Poles" documented the terror against them and tried to publicize their plight.[31] The women, relying on their international contacts, drafted and circulated petitions, and raised the question at forums. Ukrainians sought international inquiries, since the Polish Sejm and Senate were not willing to undertake an investigation.

Because of her linguistic and public-speaking skills, Rudnytska was chosen as spokesperson for the Western Ukrainian Parliamentary Union in Geneva during the 1931 meeting of the Council. She was aided by Rusova, who was impatient with the slow response of shepherding petitions, searching out persons sympathetic to Ukrainian grievances, and the slow response of international bureaucrats. Rudnytska, however, worked methodically. The Inter-Parliamentary Union created a Committee composed of representatives of Great Britain, Italy and Norway to look into charges of Polish brutality. European press coverage of the situation in Galicia was extensive, and among the petitions on behalf of Ukrainians was one by sixty-five British Members of Parliament, presented in December 1930. The British Minister of Foreign Affairs, Arthur Henderson, was one of the Committee of Three which studied the pacification. He was instrumental in inviting Rudnytska to Britain to speak to members of the House of Commons. She also met representatives of the Labour government, and was interviewed by the *Manchester Guardian*.[32]

The British were impressed by the Ukrainian arguments and a number of other petitions to the League supporting the autonomy of Galician Ukrainians flowed in. Italy, whose representative was also on the committee of the League, invited Rudnytska to Rome, where she met Mussolini. She left no account of that meeting, which apparently gained her press coverage.[33] Her criticism of Italian fascism, if anything, was even stronger after this meeting than before.

The Congress of National Minorities was held in Geneva on 29–31 August 1931, and its agenda included the events in Galicia. An effective witness for Ukrainians was Mary Sheepshanks, the secretary of the International Women's League for Peace and Freedom, whom Keller and Fedak had invited to tour "pacified" Galicia. She spoke before an influential audience at Geneva, and later testified before women's groups.[34] Her testimony was followed by that of Rusova, and supported by information on the persecution of Ukrainians. About 2,000 Ukrainians had been either arrested or placed in protective custody, while Ukrainian property destroyed by the Poles ran in the millions of *zlotys*. In the general discussion, Rudnytska was careful to stress that the Ukrainian population in Galicia constituted a majority in the area it inhabited.

The Poles, however, disregarded the chiding they received from the League of Nations' Committee in 1932 for their treatment of Ukrainians, made some desultory attempts at collaboration with Ukrainians, then in September 1934 unilaterally abrogated the minority treaties.[35] Their previous experiences with the congresses of the minorities had proved that no concrete actions would be taken against Poland, especially when Ukrainian activities were linked with the revisionist policies of Germany.

The attention of Ukrainians in 1933 focused upon the unprecedented famine in Soviet Ukraine, the new wave of purges and the show trials against Ukrainians. The projected congress of Ukrainians outside of the Soviet Union was to have attested the viability of the nation in face of such oppression. The women, preparing for their own congress of 1934, continued to push the international dimension of their activities.

At meetings in Geneva and Berne dealing with the national minorities, and at the League of Nations, Rudnytska, as the representative of Ukrainians in Poland, raised the issue of famine relief. Dr. Ewald Ammende, the secretary of the Minorities Congress in 1933, put this question on the agenda.[36] The famine, which claimed between four and seven million lives, was a result of peasant opposition to collectivization. Villages in Ukraine were stripped of food in alleged payment of taxes, and the peasants were prevented from trying to seek food elsewhere in the Union or to flee to the cities. News of the famine soon leaked out of the country, even though the event has never been admitted by the Soviet authorities.

Throughout the various stages of rapprochement between the USSR and Western countries, discussion of the crimes of Stalin, and the terror surrounding collectivization, the genocidal famine was not brought up by the Soviets. At the peak of the famine, the Soviets staged a show trial of some British nationals, limited travel to Ukraine, organized tours for such Western luminaries as G.B. Shaw and Romain Rolland, and used sympathetic Western journalists to discredit those who had reported the famine and the unprecedented destruction of families, villages, and fertile areas of Ukraine.

The Soviet regime made relief efforts impossible. Money could only be sent through the official hard-currency stores to private individuals; no food and clothing parcels were permitted. Individuals who did receive aid were in turn repressed by the Soviets for having contacts with enemies of the state. Individual peasant women in Ukraine made heroic efforts to inform the outside world of the famine and some apparently wrote letters presenting the true situation in Ukraine.

News of the famine reached Western Ukraine late in 1932, when it was just beginning. Few realized the extent of the catastrophe. Not until July 1933 was there ample documentation of the famine in the European and American press. At this time Ukrainian community organizations in Galicia established a committee to publicize the famine and organize aid to those affected. The Women's Union took part in the activities, published a brochure about the famine in different languages for women in various parts of the world, and through the International Council of Women brought the famine to the attention of the League of Nations. It was the ICW which made possible the limited discussion of the famine at the League.

In January 1933, Hitler came to power and Germany issued its first anti-Semitic legislation. The Soviet Union, badly in need of foreign credits and trading at competitive prices with the commodity it still had——wheat——blatantly but effectively denied the existence of the famine. Western Ukrainians, who had been involved with international organizations, power politics and Western media for almost fifteen years, were surprisingly realistic in their assessment of what was possible. Although little could be accomplished, Ukrainian women, faced with policies that were opposed to their ideals of peace, disarmament, international co-operation, welfare and justice, did all they could to alert the public about the famine; selflessly, they failed to perceive their own importance in the dissemination.

As a member of the Ukrainian parliamentary representation and President of the Women's Union, Rudnytska was elected a vice-president of the Relief Committee and placed in charge of foreign public relations.[37] She was one of the four members of the working committee in charge of publicizing the famine. Ukrainian immigrants in various countries tried to draw attention to the plight of Soviet Ukraine. The committees reflected the political configuration of Ukrainians and women frequently participated in them. In Berlin, for instance, there were two committees——one headed by Ielysaveta Skoropadska, the daughter of the former Hetman, the other radical-democratic in orientation.

Rudnytska raised the famine issue at the meeting of the Congress of Minorities in 1933. This time Ukrainians received the support of most Germans. Germans were interested in deflecting interest from their anti-Semitic legislation, as well as in aiding those German settlers in Russia and Ukraine who had been hit by the famine. The Congress maintained, however, that it could look at the famine only from a humanitarian, not a political point of view. Its first speaker was the representative of the Russian minority in Estonia, who spoke on the famine in "South Russia." He was followed by Rudnytska:

> I did not gloss over anything, did not modify my statements; I explained the famine in Ukraine, as well as the criminal policy of Moscow which engendered the famine, and the politics of the great powers which, to preserve good relations with the Soviet Union, close their eyes to the crimes of the Soviets in Ukraine and in this manner become co-responsible for them.

With the active lobbying of Dr. Ammende, the congress passed a resolution asking the League to investigate the famine. Press coverage of the issue was minimal.

The League, however, could not look into a famine, an internal affair of a non-member state and one with which, moreover, major members of the League wanted to trade. Fortunately for Ukrainians, the President of the League at the time was Dr. Johann L. Mowinckel of Norway, a country which had been in the forefront of aiding Eastern Europe in the famine of 1921–2. Mowinckel found a loophole in a rule that permitted the president to place before the League any matter he considered important. For that he needed an urgent petition from some established international organization. He asked Rudnytska, whom he knew through mutual friends, to provide such a petition the next day. Rudnytska described the scene:

> There was no time to write to any of the international organizations. But here again a fortunate coincidence and people of good will helped.
>
> The Committee on International Relations of the Women's Organizations [a clearing-house in which representatives of the major international organizations of women took part]...which represented millions of organized women, was meeting at the time in Geneva. At the time women's organizations enjoyed a great deal of influence in international circles, particularly in Geneva. [The Ukrainian women] for years belonged to one such organization, and maintained semi-official relations with a few others. I knew many women in the Committee——some I knew well enough to consider my good friends.[38]

Lady Margery Corbett-Ashby of the ICW invited Rudnytska to address the women. Then, with the support of the Committee, Lady Ashby personally handed the petition to President Mowinckel. The women, after all, were not trading with the Soviet Union and were not dependent upon it for a good business deal.

Armed with the women's petition Mowinckel convened a closed session of the League on the famine. There he tried to convince his colleagues that little Norway was willing to make the greatest sacrifices for famine-stricken Ukraine. He was supported by Ireland, Spain and Germany. The other countries felt that the matter was an internal one, and that it could be referred only to the International Red Cross. This Mowinckel did. He also gave an open and extensive interview to Le Matin. The French newspaper saw the interview as proof that the League recognized the reality of the famine.

For Ukrainians this was an important achievement, although it brought no relief. The Soviet Ukrainians failed or were in no position to recognize the offers of aid from the international women's movement. The Czech women's organization, through the intervention of Františka Plaminková, officially made contact with the Ukrainian Red Cross in Kharkiv in an attempt to aid famine victims. It received no reply.[39] But the international women's movement itself, which had never been united, "saw black clouds hovering over it."[40] The ideology which had given rise to the formulation of feminism as an extension of opportunity and equality, an ideology of the perfectibility of mankind, progress and belief in education, freedom and pacifism, was itself under fire from all sides. Germany, like the Soviet Union, was lost to the feminist camp. The popularity of the fascist and right radical movements further undermined the international women's movement.

Despite setbacks, the women's organizations pursued their work. Ukrainian women, while stressing their patriotism, grew more openly feminist. Rudnytska, who expressed herself bluntly about Poles and Soviet Russians, now bent over backward to keep Ukrainian women within the international feminist movement and even downplayed the opposition of Polish women to Ukrainian participation at the Istanbul IWSA congress in 1934, which made it impossible for Ukrainian women to attend. Rudnytska stressed the support Lady Corbett-Ashby continued to offer Ukrainian women, and the fact that she signed British petitions on behalf of the rights of Ukrainians in Poland. The IWSA cancelled a study conference that was to have been held in Warsaw in September 1937, partly under pressure from the British women opposing Polish authoritarianism, although the officially cited reason was the uncertain situation in Europe. The next IWSA congress, which was held in Copenhagen on 8–13 July 1939, was attended by Olena Sheparovych, Sofiia Parfanovych and Milena Rudnytska as observers.

Ukrainian participation in the International Women's League for Peace and Freedom was challenged openly by some Ukrainian women. The League was divided on its assessment of the Soviet Union, and Rusova and Olha Halahan were among the few Ukrainians willing to remain active in this organization, partly to neutralize its growing pro-Soviet wing. At a congress held in Prague from 26 to 31 July 1937, during the session on colonialism, Rusova spoke on the famine in Ukraine as an example of modern colonial policies. Half the auditorium, led by French women, challenged her; the other half applauded. Rusova and Halahan again mentioned the mistreatment of Ukrainians in the Soviet Union during the session on émigré women. They commended the Czech government on its treatment of the minorities, which contrasted so favourably with the Soviet treatment of non-Russians.

Ukrainian women gave Rusova a forum in which to defend the noble goals of the League, regardless of the sordid reality, but wondered aloud about the propriety of belonging to the radical association while the Soviets openly pursued anti-Ukrainian policies. Although the Ukrainian attitude to international radicalism was never fully debated, interest in the League waned among Ukrainians.[41] Yet, when Rusova was attacked by the Ukrainian émigré intelligentsia for her participation, women came to her defence.

Ukrainian women recognized the need for an active central Ukrainian women's organization that could be used as a base for feminist activity and as a central representative body of Ukrainian women's organizations outside the Soviet Union. The Women's Council, founded in Kamianets in 1920, which had sought to serve as a representative and co-ordinating body from Berlin, and later from Prague, was never able to speak on behalf of Western Ukrainian women. By the mid-1920s, the Council functioned as a component of the Ukrainian Women's Union. Keller's attempts in 1921–2 to establish a Society for the Defence of the Rights of Ukrainian Women failed because of technical and practical difficulties in registering a new organization in Poland (the only means of legal activity). By avoiding extreme ideologies and co-operating, the women maintained a united front throughout the 1920s and 30s. Even women who disagreed with each other——Pavlykovska with Rudnytska, and Rudnytska with Keller——worked together.

The famine further underscored the need for united action. The whole discussion about convening a congress of non-Soviet Ukrainians spurred the women to even grander celebrations of the fiftieth anniversary of Kobrynska's convocation of Ukrainian women in Galicia. A major decision of the Stanyslaviv Congress in 1934 was to create outside the Soviet Union "a Worldwide Union of Ukrainian Women...as the central organization of organized Ukrainian women of the world...which would voice the interests of the Ukrainian Nation before international and foreign agencies, primarily those of women, and [act] as the defender of Ukrainian womanhood in its own society."[42]

The Union was based on a territorial principle, and was composed of the Ukrainian Women's Union, the Volhynian Ukrainian Women's Union, the Women's Union of Bukovyna, of Transcarpathia, the organization of the political émigré women of Ukraine, and the Ukrainian Women's Leagues of the United States and Canada. In view of the oppressive political situation, only in the latter half of 1937 was the Executive Board of the Union (Holovna Rada) convened. It was composed of the President of the Western Ukrainian Women's Union and the representative of the Eastern Ukrainian emigration, who was guaranteed the position of secretary. The other positions were filled by representatives of territorial organizations of Ukrainian women in Europe and America. Keller was elected to head the committee on external relations, and Malytska that on education.

The All-Ukrainian Women's Union decided "to adhere to the International Women's League for Peace and Freedom and its national affiliates in principle," but noted that "in the existing political situation of the Ukrainian nation the work of the Ukrainian section of the League seems untimely and unrealistic."[43] Its relationship to the ICW and IWSA did not have to be discussed. Until Ukrainians had a state that recognized autonomous women's organizations, they could not formally be part of these organizations. Ukrainians, however, participated in any way they could in the work of both organizations.

The World Union of Ukrainian Women sought to defend the rights of Ukrainian women and work toward the expansion of those rights. The political situation, however, required stress upon the adjective Ukrainian rather than the noun women.

Part VI.

Soviet Ukrainian Women

The political determinant

There were qualitative differences between the conditions under which Soviet Ukrainian and other Ukrainian women found themselves. Bolshevik ideology stressed the attainment of sexual equality in all areas of productive life. Between 1919 and 1930, special women's sections were created as adjuncts to the Communist Party. Like the party, which in 1925 changed its name officially to the All-Union Communist Party of the Soviet Union, the women's sections reflected the geographical locality rather than the nationality of its members. The Ukrainian Women's Section of the Communist Party of the Soviet Union——Zhinochyi Viddil, known as *zhinvid* in the abbreviated form, was headed by Alexandra Kollontai until 1923. Mariia Levkovych headed the section until 1926, then Olga Pilatskaia took over until 1930, the year it was abolished. The *zhinviddily* were abolished on the grounds that all objective obstacles to women's equality had been removed, the women in all parts of the Soviet Union were equal with men, and that the women's issue, as such, had been resolved in the Soviet Union. The achievements of women in the first decade of Soviet rule had been, indeed, impressive.

Unlike other European governments, the Soviets had a policy of utilizing the potential of women in the work force. In the decade between the mid-20s and mid-30s, women provided a considerable part of the growing proletariat for the rapidly industrializing state, to which there was no significant immigration. In certain non-industrialized parts of the Soviet Union, women served as a "surrogate proletariat."[1]

In contrast to other governments, the Soviets used the promotion of women's rights, social and labour legislation, and other issues of direct interest to women to change society. The party leadership, not the women themselves, controlled the nature and the direction of the change. Neither the party nor the Soviet government ever had a strong representation of women in its central organs. Through the years, there were fewer than six women in the top Soviet echelons.[2]

Ironically, therefore, one of the regimes which most actively changed the status of women did so with the controlled and non-autonomous participation of women. The dichotomy resulted in ambivalent gains for women. As usual, the situation in Ukraine was further complicated by the nationality issue and Moscow's need for the land's agricultural and industrial resources.

Here, two major issues——the right of the nation and the rights of women——were at stake. Both of them are value-laden. The communists were the only Russian party to proclaim the principle of self-determination of nations in the revolutionary period. The implementation of that principle, and the recognition of Ukraine's right to genuine and full independence was, however, repeatedly contested within the party. The Brest-Litovsk peace treaty, which recognized the independence of Ukraine, was signed by Lenin's government over the resignation of Trotsky and the protests of party leaders. Outmaneuvered by the Ukrainian Central Rada in Kiev, the Bolsheviks created a rival Ukrainian government in Kharkiv in December 1917. The subsequent takeover of Ukraine by the Bolsheviks took place under the aegis of the Kharkiv government, although the vast majority of the armies involved were composed of hungry Russian masses looking for food.[3] Theoretically, the Bolshevik government in Kharkiv remained independent of Moscow until 1922, when Ukraine became a constituent republic of the new Union of Soviet Socialist Republics.

The issues are subject to interpretation, but genuine debate, and its prerequisite, a study of the unadulterated sources, is impossible. Sources on the topic, which under the best of circumstances are limited, have never been fully accessible. Many have been altered and wilfully destroyed; others have fallen prey to the ravages of time and wars. Some studies have been withdrawn from circulation. In addition, few of the major participants in the Ukrainian events have left assessments of the situation.

The interpretation of one of the underlying principles of the USSR——the right of each republic to withdraw from the Union, provided its geographical location makes such a withdrawal possible——remains unchanged. The official party line permits no leeway. It states that only reactionary enemies of the Union would even entertain the possibility of the theoretical, let alone practical, right of withdrawal. Those who last discussed this interpretation were arrested. All works published in the Soviet Union, therefore, take for granted initial and continued support of the Soviet system of government in Ukraine.[4]

Concurrently, the interpretation of the nature and limits of Lenin's commitment to the rights of the nationalities, as well as his condemnation of Russian imperialism and chauvinism, are also matters of government policy, state security or party tactics rather than scholarly analysis. It is, moreover, an article of faith that Lenin was the champion of the nationalities, that the party liberated the colonial peoples of the Russian Empire, and that they willingly joined the USSR, which happens to have expanded beyond the borders of the erstwhile Russian Empire. It is stated further that those who opposed Lenin's nationality policies were enemies of the party, and that Leninist principles of the right of nationalities have not been violated, except perhaps during the cult of the personality of Stalin.[5]

In reality, however, Ukraine has been subjected to colonial exploitation and cultural and linguistic Russification to the present day.[6] Thus, the development of feminism among Ukrainian women has been limited by forces similar to those experienced under the tsarist Empire. The consequences of an exclusive ideology and one-party rule combined with the *de facto* hegemony of Moscow have a direct bearing upon the condition of Ukrainian women in the Soviet Union.

Other aspects of women's issues also transcend the struggle for women's rights. At the heart of the matter is the point addressed by Kobrynska, the first Ukrainian feminist: to what degree can socialism, or its variant, Marxism, serve as an instrument of women's liberation and an exponent of women's aspirations without the direct input of feminist thought? Since the Soviet regime and Marxist ideology proclaimed themselves the agents of the liberation of women, and since the society that was established by an interaction of the ideology and the Party claimed to have solved the "woman's issue," the study of that "solution" is a valid undertaking, even within the confines of the ideology itself.

The extent to which socialism in its Soviet variant liberates women, and the nature of that liberation, have been the subjects of major studies. Although usually centred on the important, visible and vocal Russian population, these studies also reflect some general experiences of the women of the USSR as a whole.[7] There is an overall consensus that as an ideology of women's liberation, Marxism is effective in (1) opening up educational and occupation opportunities for women, (2) achieving legal equality for women, (3) channelling women into the work force, and (4) changing legislation that is openly discriminatory toward women. Its achievements in social legislation, in providing day-care facilities for children, in medical services, education and labour legislation——while subject to interpretation——are considerable.

It is, however, indicative of the paternalistic nature of Marxism that the issues connected with the care of the mother and child, and the definition of the attainments of women, have been formulated within male constructs. Relegating feminism to reactionary liberalism (with the attainment of socialism, liberalism *ipso facto* becomes reactionary for Marxists), Soviet Marxists have precluded the pursuit of genuine sexual equality. Since the goal of feminism——individual autonomy——is inimical to both the collectivity and economic determinism espoused by Soviet Marxism, feminism is incompatible with the ideology of the regime. Feminism, after all, is a movement which singles out a constituency, encourages the development of individual autonomy and thus, by implication, fosters individualism in society. Single-issue political movements, even if they employ egalitarian terms, seek a homogeneous society, a type of *Gleichschaltung* that is contrary to individual differences. Identification of feminism with the bourgeoisie contributes to maintaining the poor reputation that feminism had among the progressive intelligentsia before the fall of tsarism.[8]

The division of labour

Soviet Ukrainian works on Ukrainian women are few and surprisingly selective, even if the lack of "bourgeois objectivity" is taken into account. Thus, the entry on "the woman question" in the Soviet Ukrainian Encyclopedia does not even mention Olena Pchilka, although Franko and Lesia Ukrainka are mentioned briefly. Marusia Levkovych, the head of the Ukrainian Women's Section of the Party, does not merit mention, but I.E. and Mariia Vinogradov, who were relatively unimportant in the party, do. The statistical information provided about women refers to the whole of the Soviet Union, rather than Ukraine specifically.

The formulation of the basic problems of women's history is quite different from that in the West. A book entitled *Zhinky Radianskoi Ukrainy* (Women of Soviet Ukraine), a collection of articles by various authors, stress general imperial developments and contains just one brief paragraph on Kobrynska. After claiming that the first "representative International Congress of women in history met...in Paris in 1945," the study provides its readers with the following elaboration of sexual equality: "The most important issue for the women's movement remains the care for the welfare of children and youth."[9]

These views in a popular book on women's primary functions as producers and nurturers of children are accepted and repeated in scholarly works. It is, therefore, crucial to understand that for Soviet writers on women's issues the goal for women is not autonomy and self-actualization, but the degree to which women, while having children, can also pursue activities of direct benefit to society. For the Soviets, the division of labour between the sexes seems to be as sacred as it was to the European conservatives of the nineteenth century. A contemporary scholar in Ukraine writes proudly of the thousands of Ukrainian women who have qualified for various medals of mother-hero, glory of motherhood and a plain medal of honour for motherhood by having borne four to ten children:

> Because the government in the Soviet land took over a huge part of the burden of raising children, women have a chance to work, to dedicate themselves to civic work, to raise their cultural and professional level. It is most illustrative that in the USSR the greatest employment of the women's population in social production falls between the ages of 20 to 39, while in the USA it is above 35, that is, the time when the woman-mother frees herself from direct care for children.[10]

The growing stress on the Soviet family has not encouraged the Soviets to explore, even in theoretical fashion, the greater involvement of the father both in the care of children and in household management. Rather, the mother's primary responsibility for the care of children is taken for granted.

For persons who view the aspirations of women as more than a blind striving to be equal to men and who want to go beyond the limitations of the male experience, the paternalistic policies of the party toward women elicit, under the best of circumstances, at least puzzlement. That women should be equal to men because Lenin said that without that equality the revolution would fail is adequate justification for Soviet scholars. With sound Marxist logic they accept that what is good for the revolution is good for women. The scholar quoted above, who happens to be a woman and is thus apparently qualified to write on the subjects of "women and....," is eloquent on the efforts of the party not only to press for the improved quality of women's lives but to decide, with the aid of "efficiency experts" (and not of women), what type of work is best suited for women:

> To expand the sphere of professions in which women's work could be used, the party organized [in 1929 and the 1930s] in-depth studies of labour effectiveness [of women]. The results of these studies had tremendous practical and theoretical significance, illustrating the cost-efficiency [*rentabelnist*] of women's work on the condition that it is suitably located in various enterprises. The Ukrainian Institute of Work, generalizing the scientific observations on a number of Kharkiv factories, came to the conclusion that given equal conditions (qualifications, status, age of the worker) in areas which are not detrimental to the female organism, the productivity of women is equal or approximate to that of men.
>
> Special lists of professions were made and special positions in which women's work could be used were drawn up. The aim was to direct the work of women to those types of labour where it could be most effectively utilized. These lists of jobs most compatible and best suited to the female organism, with the best labour return, were approved by the Narkomat USSR, 19 May 1931.[11]

Working women

Hence, revolutionary duty, buttressed by scientific proof, urged the party to nudge women toward equality. The difference between the "new woman" of feminism and the "new Soviet Woman" is that the former follows some autonomous process, while the latter is scientific or doctrinal. The Soviet woman, moreover, is alleged to be the product of universal forces, as defined by an ideology which purports to be universal, although——especially in the area of women's concerns——it draws largely upon the Russian experience. Stress upon national developments, even if those elaborate socialist doctrines or economic theory, generally tends to be branded as bourgeois feminism. Ukrainian women are made to appear as a regional variant of the Soviet model, or——more frequently——a geographical attestation of the universal validity of that model. Little is written about women in Soviet Ukraine, and even less on the historical background, contributions and peculiarities of Ukrainian women or their organizations.

Since extensive study has been undertaken in the West on Soviet women, and it is readily available, only the peculiarities in the development of the Soviet woman in Ukraine will be highlighted here. Lacking information on the growing Ukrainian minorities in other republics of the Soviet Union, my remarks will be limited to Ukrainian women within the republic.

Just as the intelligentsia which supported the Soviet system became by definition the "working intelligentsia," a component of the working class and not of the bourgeoisie, so the women who participated in the establishment of the Soviet state became "working women," regardless of their social origin. All the achievements of Ukrainian women are considered achievements of working women. In the few studies dealing with Ukrainian women published in the Soviet Union, a specifically Ukrainian historical perspective is singularly absent. On the contrary, in line with the growing tendency to stress the similarities between Ukrainian and Russian history, differences in the position of women in Russia and Ukraine are overlooked. Continuing in the ahistorical vein of the prerevolutionary radical intelligentsia, historians refer to women's contributions to the victory of the Soviets and the growth of Soviet economy. Neither the Cossack experiences, nor the frontier settlement, nor the absence of the *mir*, nor the contact of Eastern Ukrainian women with Western women are mentioned in the discussion of Ukrainian women. Indeed, women fare badly in general historical works. The multi-volume history of the Ukrainian SSR published in Kiev pays minimal attention to women. Even the work of the special women's sections merits only six lines, and does not include the name of a single activist.[12]

Ukrainian women in the Bolshevik Party

The women's movement in Ukraine is officially considered a non-issue. The women who had been active in the party, provided they have not been liquidated or have been rehabilitated, are viewed by the party as representative of the genuine strivings of progressive women. Frequently, even the fate of these women is unknown. Ukrainian communists do not seem to have developed specific views on women. I use "seem" advisedly, for much of the work of the Ukrainian communists has not survived. Nor have Soviet Ukrainians made much use of the genuine admiration Western Ukrainians, both men and women, expressed in the 1920s at the Soviet Ukrainian achievements in sex equality and the expansion of Ukrainian educational and cultural institutions. National and sexual liberation were linked in time, and "national communism" has been identified by the party as a variant of nationalism, in its bourgeois incarnation, and not as non-Russian communism.

Discussion of the first decade of Soviet rule in Ukraine is fraught with problems. Soviet scholarship changes its interpretation of the period according to current party policy. Generally, Ukrainians outside the Soviet Union have written polemics rather than comprehensive histories of the era.[13]

Concerning Bolshevik policies in Ukraine, two salient facts should be stressed. First, the initial defeats the party suffered in Ukraine showed that it would be expedient for the party to identify itself with the Ukrainian national cause and espouse, regardless of genuine conviction, a course of Ukrainization.

Second, policies dealing with women and so-called women's issues were made in Moscow and not in Kharkiv, which until 1934 served as the Ukrainian Soviet capital. Indeed, according to a publication of the Central Section of the Working Women of the Central Committee of the Communist Party (Bolsheviks) of Ukraine, *Zhinocha volia: chytanka* (Woman's Freedom: A Reader), "large-scale activity among Ukrainian women began [only] in 1920."[14]

Zhanna Tymchenko, the author of the most comprehensive study on the role of women in the "struggle for Soviet power in Ukraine,"[15] stresses not only the inability of the many feminist organizations in Ukraine to achieve any worthwhile reforms for women under a bourgeois system, but also argues that it was important for Moscow leaders to organize and direct the correct path of socialist revolutionary struggle.

The Bolsheviks became involved in work among women in Ukraine partly to offset the popularity of the feminist Ukrainian Women's Union and its journal, *Zhinochyi visnyk* (Women's Herald). They developed mass programmes of class-consciousness raising among workers and peasants of Ukraine. They ran into severe difficulties among the peasantry, where "petit-bourgeois" parties exercised great influence.[16] Moreover, the relevance of work among women was challenged by the party itself. "Then, at the beginning of the revolution in Ukraine, it was necessary to convince even the party comrades of the necessity and importance of work among women." There seems to have been a conscious separation of work with women and work with the non-Russian nationalities. Although occasional party directives to the women's section would stress the local sensibilities of an area, that caveat generally referred to the Central Asian areas. After the Bolshevik victory, all non-party-sponsored women's organizations were considered redundant, and justified only among backward nations.[17]

The Communist Party of Ukraine (CPU), fighting off both Ukrainian communists and anti-communists, paid little attention to the women's question. In line with party policy, however, it used women to popularize the regime.

Women prominent in the Bolshevik party during the first decade of Soviet power in Ukraine were interested neither in Ukrainian nor in women's issues *per se*. Few women in the party claimed to be Ukrainian. According to an article in *Dilo* (which was well informed on Soviet affairs) on 14 March 1929, only 8 per cent of the women in the CPSU were Ukrainian, 8 per cent were Jewish, and the predominant 84 per cent were Russian; Evgeniia Bosh, a party member of long standing and an ardent supporter of Lenin, was dedicated to one party and one international Russian-speaking proletariat. Her first post in the Ukrainian government was that of minister of interior. She was not overly ambitious, showed great resilience, and remained a member of the government of Ukraine until her death in 1925.

Angelica Balabanoff, born into a rich Russified family in 1878, became a passionate adherent of Russian radicalism. She served briefly as foreign minister of Ukraine in 1919. She was one of the first women to become disillusioned with the course of the revolution and with Lenin personally, and left the country in 1921. But her memoirs are silent on the Ukrainian interlude. Alexandra Kollontai, who could have claimed Ukrainian ancestry and had been married to a Ukrainian, was the most prolific writer on women's issues, and served as Lenin's expert on that subject. She was commissar for propaganda in Ukraine in 1919, and headed the Ukrainian women's section of the party from 1920 to 1923. Her independence, personal flair and support of the so-called "workers' opposition" cost her her prominent position, although not her liberty. She chose to identify herself wholly with the Russians and to toe the official party line.

Other prominent early Bolshevik women in Ukraine were Sofiia I. Sokolovska, S.I. Hopner, N.I. Ostrovska, A.V. and O.V. Iesavi, V.M. Lapina, S.Iu. Pievtsova, D.I. Itkind and A.I. Vahranska. Detailed information is available only about Sokolovska, whose work in Chernihiv was legendary. Rather surprisingly, none of these women are even mentioned in the women's reader, *Zhinocha volia*, published in Kharkiv in 1925. That book, instead, eulogizes a number of peasant women who died in the "class struggle," or who actively assisted the Bolsheviks.

Pro-Bolshevik women's organizations were created in Moscow and transplanted to Ukrainian territories. The women's organizations that existed earlier in Ukraine were declared bourgeois and disbanded. Similarly, the new Soviet regime liquidated the popular Prosvita. It also replaced the even more widespread network of economic co-operatives, in which many women participated, with centralized economic co-operatives, evidently patterned on those in Tver and Leningrad.[18]

Among the most dramatic legislation passed by the Bolsheviks were laws dealing with women. The establishment of legal equality between the sexes abolished the power of husbands and fathers over women, and ended all discriminatory measures against them. Laws dealing with family life and children, although they are in the realm of social legislation, are generally considered in the sphere of women's rights. Marriage and divorce became secular procedures, greatly simplified and essentially available on demand. Unlike Russia, Soviet Ukraine retained the distinction between a legal marriage and common-law, non-registered marriage (the distinction was abolished in Russia in 1921).

The Bolshevik policy toward women was two-pronged. The party strove to free women from the strictures of the past and to make them a potent force in the implementation of Bolshevik power in society. It put into practice Kobrynska's suggestion that women should be used as a galvanizing force in changing society. The Bolsheviks, like the nationalists, argued that the active co-operation of women would contribute to the success of the cause: "Not limiting itself to formal equality of women, the party strives to free them from the material burdens of the antiquated household by replacing it with communal buildings, community eating halls, central laundries, and nurseries."[19]

Although the Social Democrats had refused to sanction the existence of separate women's sections of the party, the Russian communists reversed that decision and began discussing the organization of specifically women's sections by mid-November 1917. The sections were established, largely through the efforts of Kollontai, in September 1919. In the summer of the year, K.M. Samoilova joined Kollontai in industrialized Kharkiv to work "in the development of party-oriented political work among the workers." Other women, specially trained for propaganda work, formed activist groups in other cities.[20] The work was centrally organized, and instructions and correspondence were in Russian. The operation in Ukraine was small-scale, and because of its Russian character did not attract a significant following.

Women's Organizations

A. **Conferences**

A temporary form of women's organizations engineered by the party was known by the rather misleading name of conferences. They were gatherings of about 200 to 300 women selected by party activists from local women sympathetic to the party. These women, called delegates in a conscious effort to upgrade their status, were then trained to handle some issues of Bolshevik policy, and to rally party support in their constituency. Evidently, the choice of delegates (the process is often referred to as selection, sometimes as election) was not always fortuitous. Sometimes the delegates were women whose personal standing did not enable them to recruit supporters to the Bolshevik cause. In Ukraine, the tendency to rely on Russian cadres hampered women's work.

The conferences tried to kindle enthusiasm for the policies of the regime. The party pointed out that women activists should highlight the creative role of the woman-mother, the social importance of her task in raising children and her duty to sacrifice her life for the Motherland. Even in the 1920s in propaganda materials prepared for village use, motherhood and dedication were stressed. Sacrifice was the key. Often women were encouraged to take on outside employment to earn money to donate to the less fortunate or to the state.

The highlight of women's work was the convocation of conferences that gave rural women a chance to travel to the cities. There they listened to speeches by party members and discussed current topics. For the party, the main issue was not how to help women, but how to help the Bolsheviks. True, the attitude of the Soviet regime to women and the duties of the workers to the new state were mentioned, but more time was spent discussing how women could better aid the new regime. Women not only had to agitate for the party programme, but also had to gather information on the availability of food supplies. Peasant women went from house to house to ascertain where and how much food was stored, so that "the village executive committees could quickly, without errors fulfill their task in [collecting food stuffs for Russia]."[21]

Of crucial importance in the socialization of women and in raising the level of their political consciousness were courses held in conjunction with elections, party gatherings or mass rallies. The "delegates' meetings" informed women delegates of the party's views on current events and its course of action. The women were encouraged to ask questions, to familiarize themselves with the information provided, to express their enthusiasm for the policies of the regime and to transmit that enthusiasm to others. These courses, initiated in 1919 because of women's ignorance of both issues and proceedings, became in the 1920s a political school for thousands of party helpers. Run by agitators from party headquarters, the courses boosted the party programme.[22]

B. **Zhinviddily**

Yet women did not readily join the party. Moscow warned repeatedly of the "danger of the growth of petit-bourgeois influence on the broad strata of women's proletariat,"[23] which was especially true among Ukrainian women. Hence the lesson the party learned from its disastrous initial campaigns in Ukraine——the need to take the national sensibilities of Ukrainians into consideration——was carried over into the women's sector. The new *zhinviddily*, founded in Kharkiv in 1920, began by staging a non-party conference of women workers on 4–12 February. It is not known how many women participated in the conference, but 50 per cent of those present joined the party: "This marked the beginning of the women's movement aimed at attracting the huge reserve of working women to strengthen the power wrested by the October Revolution and to build up Soviet strength."[24]

The majority of women in Ukraine were most concerned about creating a better life for their families; with equitable distribution of food; with social and labour legislation; with health facilities and hygiene instruction; and with care for children. The tsarist attempt to improve work safety in factories through government inspectors was revived in plans to establish a worker-peasant inspectorate. There was, however, little effort to rationalize individual food production. The party urged those training delegates to stress the role of women as mothers, nurturers and caretakers of the young and the needy. From that it was only a step further to women's responsibility to the country, the party and the collective.

The few contemporary sources on the early efforts to recruit women to the Ukrainian party and to support its policies are remarkably frank. Often the work included arduous physical labour justified by the needs of the moment. A contemporary account of an early conference of Ukrainian women, written by a female Ukrainian communist, described the convocation of the conference. The women heard speeches of the government representative and the party on the needs of society. Then the women reportedly set up commissions to examine how they could help the government and the needy. Women workers performed the most essential tasks in setting up these agencies: they painted offices, washed the laundry, sewed and collected clothes for the army, and encouraged other women to join the work.[25]

Early accounts about Ukrainian women in the USSR stress the women's dedication to alleviating the ravages of war and hunger. Following the defeat of the Whites, the UNR and the Poles, the central Russian plains experienced a serious drought. Ukraine was called upon to aid the Volga region, and Ukrainian women, disregarding Soviet legislation which banned women from working in the mines, relieved the men to help the Volga Russians. Suspensions of regulations which were initially intended to ameliorate labour conditions for women because of extraordinary circumstances were to become a frequent characteristic of Soviet life.

The first Ukrainian Congress of Women Workers and Peasants was convened in line with Lenin's dictum that "there can be no socialist revolution if the vast majority of working women do not take a significant part in it."[26] On 3 November 1920, 1,105 women delegates met in Kharkiv and elected the congress presidium. But the party determined the agenda. S.V. Kosior, First Secretary of the CPU, called upon women to take an active part in building the Soviet state and to join the party. K.M. Samoilova, a member of the Central Committee of the Russian Party, pointed to the fusion of the progressive women and the party. At the congress, the women discussed the setting up of day-care centres, programmes to eradicate illiteracy, and measures to ensure a more equitable distribution of food supplies. They also discussed how women could increase the productivity of the factories.

C. Ukrainian *zhinviddily*

The women's sections of the Communist Party organizations were centrally co-ordinated. They were formed in conjunction with the local party group and the success of the whole programme depended upon the effectiveness of the local personnel in carrying out directives from the centre. First, the party had to train its activists; organize a practical programme of co-operative ventures, especially of dairy and poultry production; and evolve a programme of social legislation. This aspect of party activity did not take into account specifically Ukrainian conditions, but followed the directives of the centre. The Ukrainian *zhinviddily* were never very large or active. They were "a fair example of *zhenotdel* operations at a lower level," run from a two-room headquarters in Kharkiv and using, until the mid-1920s, Russian press.[27] None of the women who had been active in the pre-1914 women's organizations were welcome in the *zhinviddily*. The latter were a tool of the party, not of women.[28]

Information on the Ukrainian *zhinviddily* is incomplete and often contradictory. Stites uses the Ukrainian case as an example of the *zhenotdely*——the Russian variant of the term——functioning on a provincial level. He incorrectly overlooks Levkovych's role and considers that Kollontai ran the *zhinviddily* until 1926, and Pilatskaia afterward. Both women represented the centralizing tendencies of one wing of the Bolshevik Party; neither had close contact with the specifically Ukrainian wing or with Ukrainian communists, who, in turn, did not consider the women's issue of primary interest.

In reality, however, Kollontai had little direct control over the Ukrainian *zhinviddily* between 1924 and 1926. At this time, during the party's Ukrainization policy and the height of the influence of the so-called "national communists," women's work was co-ordinated by Marusia O. Levkovych, the head of the *zhinviddily* of the CPU Central Committee. She was a school teacher who joined the party in 1919, and was the formal and *de facto* head of the *zhinviddily* in Ukraine between August 1924 and April 1926. She was replaced by Pilatskaia, a party member since 1904 of an outspokenly Russian orientation, whose appointment signified that under Levkovych's direction the women's party organizations had been moving toward national communism. Levkovych was elected to one of the area party executive committees in 1928, helped organize the building of the Korsun hydroelectric station, was active in the first stage of collectivization, and then dropped out of sight.[29]

Soviet women activists in Ukraine complained that there was great opposition to the work of the *zhinviddily*, especially in the villages. The major problem was that the *zhinviddily* reflected the aspirations of the Muscovite centre, and not the local priorities. Frequently, Russian-speaking women were used for propaganda work in the Ukrainian villages. Another problem was that the communist women activists spouted Bolshevik rhetoric, participated in forcible grain requisitions and proposed the expropriation of even small private farms.

Ukrainian Marxist women specifically denied any possiblity of international co-operation among women. In their overview of "the women's movement in the capitalist states," there was no mention of Western Ukrainian women or their organizations, nor even of the interest evidenced by Western Ukrainian women in Soviet Ukrainian affairs.[30]

Party directives stressed the party's leading role in mobilizing the masses of peasant women, in encouraging working women to join the Communist Party and in providing leadership to other women.[31] The aims of the party and the aims of *zhenotdel* intertwined, and in one directive Kuibyshev stressed that:

> Agitation sections should co-ordinate their activity with women's sections and in their approach to the non-party masses should take into consideration the level of understanding of the female masses and their interests. No separate agitation specialists should function among the women's sections. All workers of the women's sections taking part in women's gatherings are considered part of the

general agitation section (*agitotdel*).[32]

D. Women's Publications

It quickly became apparent that the work of the *zhinviddily* in Ukraine could be more effective if some of its local publications appeared in Ukrainian. In 1921 the party began publishing a journal, *Komunarka Ukrainy* (The Communist Woman of Ukraine), which included articles in both Russian and Ukrainian and stressed the common work of Russian and Ukrainian women for the Revolution.[33] The journal openly espoused the cause of working women, attacked unemployment, argued for more public-works projects, unemployment compensation, and help from professional and party organizations for women.[34] Sometimes the journal publicized Ukrainian literature among the masses. Khvylovy's short story of a revolutionary heroine, "Kit u chobotiakh" (Puss in Boots), was published in this journal.

In line with party directives to pay close attention to the press, *Komunarka Ukrainy* began to publish exclusively in Ukrainian. Yet although it catered to Ukrainian women, it avoided specific Ukrainian issues. Rather, it followed party directives for lively local stories. Its subjects (and authors) were wives of workers, workers and peasants, and female students. It defended the family, periodically publishing stories about men abusing the liberal divorce and marriage laws, and abandoning wives and children. It published edifying stories of women working in erstwhile male professions; of their work in areas where no community organizations had existed before; their participation in local political life and economic activity. Within five years the circulation of *Komunarka Ukrainy* was about 20,000. In 1929, the journal became a weekly, expanded its coverage, encouraged women to write, and offered suggestions for further reading in Ukrainian and Russian.

But *Komunarka*, regardless of language, did not reach the vast majority of Ukrainian women, who were after all of peasant stock. A bi-monthly journal, *Selianka Ukrainy* (The Peasant Woman of Ukraine), began appearing in 1924, the same year that *Zhinocha dolia* circulated in Western Ukraine. This journal was the product of the Section of Agitation and Mass Campaigns of the Central Committee of the CPU. Within a year, however, the central section of Working and Peasant Women of the party was taking credit for the journal, which stressed such topics as the need for day-care centres, communal kitchens and medical facilities. It also carried articles on the importance of collectivization and the need to increase agricultural productivity.

None of these journals wrote about Western Ukrainian women. *Zhinocha dolia* tried to exchange publications, but the exchange was one-sided. The Kolomyia publishing house sent its journal to Ukraine regularly, but complained in October 1926 that Kharkiv had sent only three issues of *Selianka Ukrainy*.[35] Galician women published every obtainable item on Eastern Ukrainian women. On the basis of the three issues of *Selianka Ukrainy,* on 15 January 1927 *Zhinocha dolia* ran an article extolling the efforts of Soviet Ukrainian women to combat illiteracy and organize co-operatives. The 1927 almanac of *Zhinocha dolia* pointed out that Soviet Ukrainian women were the equals of men in all areas. The following year, Liudmyla Shevchenko, the granddaughter of the poet's brother, writing from Kiev, also stressed the achievements of Soviet women, but warned that the new morality, the easy divorces and abortion benefited not women but men. ''The future mother is the key to making our nation, which has recently been in decline, healthy again.''[36]

In 1925 *Zhinocha dolia* reported on the growth of the women's movement in Soviet Ukraine, on the spread of elementary education and the peasants' interest in mechanized agriculture. It also reported that a party member, Prystupa, had criticized the fact that higher schools were not yet Ukrainized, and that little money had been allocated for education. The Galician journal editorialized that the country was still subordinate to Moscow.[37] Throughout the decade the women's press in Galicia noted with pleasure the achievements of Soviet women: women constituted 25 per cent of the co-operative members of the USSR; many women headed village councils; women served as elected representatives; and the programmes organized by *zhinviddily* attracted women outside the party. The last series of statements was, interestingly, written by Mariia Bachynska Dontsova, wife of the Western Ukrainian nationalist ideologue, Dmytro Dontsov.[38] Another Western Ukrainian women's journal, *Nova khata*, highlighted the Ukrainian women's struggle with illiteracy, their economic progress and steps toward social mobility. Occasionally it published photographs of women meeting in Kharkiv (January 1927); and of the first all-Ukrainian Conference of Women Co-operative Workers (14 August 1929).[39]

By 1926, when Olga Vladimirovna Pilatskaia (1884–1937) took over the running of the Ukrainian *zhinviddily*, Ukraine claimed to have about 1.5 million women in the party organizations. About 70,000 women activists had undergone various stages of training. Pilatskaia, a dedicated communist of Russian working-class background, trudged on foot from village to village but was met with hostility. She stressed that she was working for economic and cultural progress, and the fact that she worked in Ukraine was irrelevant to her. Varvara Moirova (1890–1951), Olha Kravchenko and Mariia Levkovych, more consciously Ukrainian, apparently had an easier time organizing Ukrainian women.[40]

None of the prominent Ukrainian women activists, such as Olena Pchilka, were drawn to the work of the *zhinviddily*. Nor were special efforts made to meet the needs of the Ukrainian population. Evidently, two peasant women——Hladka and Baranova (their given names are unknown)——complained about the slow pace of Ukrainization and the difficulties in purchasing Ukrainian books.[41]

The continuation of the co-operative activities among the villages was significant for Ukrainian women in the Soviet Union. The Soviets stress that the
peasant co-operatives established after the revolution were founded by I.A.
Sammler, who died in Kharkiv on 25 June 1921. However, 1920s sources
reveal an organic connection with the popular co-operatives initiated in the
1870's and with an informal system devised by Ukrainian activists.[42]

Soviet Ukrainian women were active in the co-operative movement and
carried out the same type of practical work as Western Ukrainian women. But
little documentary information has survived on this matter. Women participated
in the movement without discussion of feminist concerns. The Soviet Ukrainian
press indicates that there was opposition to the full and equal participation of
women. The co-operatives were frequently the moving force in the
establishment of day-care centres, subsidizing cafeterias, health facilities,
training courses, hygiene instruction, literacy courses and other community
services that freed women from domestic drudgery. There was no direct
connection between the co-operative and the women's section, although at
times co-operatives cleared all the work specifically dealing with the women's
sections. The *zhinviddily* were party organizations, while the co-operatives tried
to maintain some autonomy.

Ukrainization

While women were not directly involved in the development of the policies of
Ukrainization, or "indigenization," as it is called by political scientists, it is
important to discuss this party policy to obtain an overall picture of the political
climate in Soviet Ukraine in the 1920s. These policies, first formulated by the
left wing of the Ukrainian Socialist Revolutionary Party, which supported the
Bolsheviks, sought to popularize Marxism among the indigenous population by
presenting it in a native, not a foreign, variant. Mykola Skrypnyk, an old
Bolshevik and a close friend of Lenin, embraced the idea in 1922 and the following year the policy of "rooting" Marxism and the state apparatus was
approved by the Communist Party of Ukraine, which, being urban, was
overwhelmingly Russian and Jewish. The policy remained in effect until 1933,
although its interpretation was different in Moscow and in Kharkiv. For the
supporters of the traditional unity of the so-called Russian lands, Ukrainization
was a temporary expedient to create the conditions necessary for the full-scale
integration of Ukrainian lands into the Union. But for a number of Ukrainian
communists, this policy became theoretically the only valid variant of Marxism
consonant with the real needs of the masses.[43]

Mikhail Frunze, a representative of the Russian Communist Party, formally
initiated the Ukrainization policy at the Seventh Conference of the Communist
Party (Bolshevik) of Ukraine on 7–10 April 1923. He attacked Russian
chauvinism in Ukraine and demanded that members of the party and

government apparatus learn to speak Ukrainian, respect Ukrainian culture, and encourage as many Ukrainians as possible to join their ranks. On 16 July 1923, Vlas Chubar became the first Ukrainian to chair a government executive committee, which eleven days later issued a decree on the Ukrainization of elementary schools and cultural institutions. It emphasized that the language of instruction in schools should reflect the nationality of their students and urged the publication of more textbooks in the native languages rather than in Russian. The Soviet Ukrainian government issued its most important decree on Ukrainization on 1 August 1923, when it guaranteed "a place for the Ukrainian language corresponding to the numerical superiority of the Ukrainian people in the territory of the USSR," while affirming the "equality of languages of all nationalities on Ukrainian territory."[44]

The industrialization of the USSR catalyzed the migration of Ukrainian peasants into the cities and reinforced the Ukrainization programme by creating an urban base for it. The proponents of Ukrainization within the Communist Party of Ukraine pressed for greater opportunities for the growth of Ukrainian culture in the cities.

These developments provoked great opposition from many Russian and Russified members of the Communist Party. They worried that the Ukrainian national identity, which hitherto had been intimately connected with the peasant world and its mentality, would soon undermine Russian domination of the urban areas. At the end of 1929, just as Ukrainization was beginning to achieve some of its objectives, the party turned against it. But because the Ukrainian urban base of support was growing at a rapid pace, the party could not break completely with its policy. Only the social changes introduced by collectivization, the famine of 1932–3, and the high rates of labour turnover after 1930 seriously weakened Ukrainization's urban base. After 1933, the party was able to abandon Ukrainization and purge its supporters.[45]

Return to the Homeland

Ukrainian women who remained active in Ukraine were at pains to demonstrate both their commitment to a socially progressive communist political theory and the equally progressive nature of Ukrainian nationalism. These women had never been comfortable with the feminist label. Having encountered intolerant and chauvinistic behaviour of the Russian liberals——with whom the Russian feminists most openly identified themselves——exhibited during Ukraine's liberation struggle, these women were even less likely to establish women's organizations. The Soviet regime had removed objective and subjective obstacles to women's equality. What seemed necessary in the 1920s for Ukrainian women was not so much "sexual affirmative action" as work on all levels of national and community life. It seems that many Ukrainian activists joined the co-operative movement, which was now technically Soviet. There was also a tremendous increase in the number of students.[46] The Ukrainization of schools necessitated a greater number of Ukrainian-speaking teachers. Institutions of higher learning included more women, and more of them dealt with Ukrainian subjects. A case, therefore could be made that national communism, combined with Lenin's scathing attacks upon Russian chauvinism, created the prospect of a state that would reflect some Ukrainian interests.

Although separate women's organizations did not seem warranted, participation in the creation of Soviet Ukraine seemed to many Ukrainians equally patriotic and progressive. This cause motivated a number of Western Ukrainian activists to settle in the Soviet Union, and several prominent Ukrainians returned to their homeland, having left during the war or emigrated in the 1920s.

Among the most significant families to return to Kiev was that of the former President of the Central Rada, Mykhailo Hrushevsky. Offered a position at the Academy of Sciences in Kiev, Hrushevsky, together with his Galician wife Mariia and daughter Kateryna, lived in Kiev between 1924 and 1931. Kateryna published a number of original works and helped her father with his research. The elder Hrushevska, the daughter of a Catholic priest and one of Galicia's first women teachers, had been active in the Kievan and Galician women's organizations. When she settled in Soviet Ukraine, she apparently did not join any of the new women's organizations. After Hrushevsky was transferred to Moscow in 1931, never to return to Kiev, both women sacrificed themselves for the "great man." They shared in the difficult household tasks (both had been used to servants). Kateryna was arrested after Hrushevsky's death.[47] Liudmyla Starytska-Cherniakhivska, together with her daughter Veronika, also returned to Ukraine, where for a time she was able to continue her literary activity.[48]

The return of Nadiia Surovtseva to her homeland was to have been temporary. Surovtseva, who had been secretary of the women's organization of the Ukrainian People's Republic and had argued the cause of the republic before the International Women's League of Peace and Freedom, had remained in Vienna to complete her doctorate in history. While there she learned of the failure of the armed guerrilla movement against the Bolsheviks, and probably suspected that Petliura's ranks had been infiltrated by Soviet agents. She remained actively committed to the socialist cause. Because she was a historian, some perceived links between her and Hrushevsky, but his return seems to have had little influence on her. Rather, she became disillusioned with the prospects of the UNR and with émigré life in general. Her socialist revolutionary politics drew her into the communist camp.

At the height of "national communism" she met the charismatic Iurii Kotsiubynsky (son of the writer Mykhailo Kotsiubynsky and the activist Vera Deish) mentioned in Part I). She joined the Austrian Communist Party, befriended its founder, Franz Koritschoner, and "met Klara Zetkin, Bertrand Russell and American socialist millionaires."[49] Kotsiubynsky, strengthening Surovtseva's belief in the power of the Ukrainian peasantry to adapt communism to its needs, persuaded her to work for the Soviet Ukrainian state.

He argued that Surovtseva, with her background of study in St. Petersburg, Lviv and Vienna, and as a native of the southern city of Uman, which had had a sizeable Polish minority, would be most suited to recruit émigrés from Ukraine to return to their homeland. Surovtseva agreed, but wanted to see the Ukrainian Soviet Socialist Republic first-hand. In Kharkiv she worked in the Ukrainian Radio, in the University's history department, headed by Dmytro Bahalii, and at the People's Commissariat of External Affairs.

In 1925 she was asked to testify against Kotsiubynsky, who had meanwhile, as chairman of the State Plan and deputy chairman of the Council of People's Commissars in Ukraine, been arrested and accused of harbouring "left-Trotskyite" tendencies. She refused, and was herself arrested in 1926.[50] She was charged with nationalist tendencies, and spent the next twenty-five years in forced-labour camps.

But the 1920s remained a period of Ukrainization, and several Ukrainian cultural activists moved from Polish-run territories to the new Soviet state. Theatre and music seemed to enjoy a particular flowering. The Galician Les Kurbas founded an experimental theatrical group, Berezil. His mother moved to Ukraine to take care of her son. The participation of women in this and other groups was generally limited to performing rather than creating. The same can be said for literature——women were writers, but did not formulate literary theories. That circumstance, in large measure, saved the women from ideological attacks and perhaps arrests.

Industrialization

The turn from Ukrainization to stress on the communality of Ukrainian and Russian experience, followed by the assertion of Russian hegemony, came about slowly. Initially this new policy was directed against the party membership and its most prominent cultural leaders. It was also combined with industrialization and a tightening of party control. The CPSU wanted to mobilize the entire population for a huge push toward industrialization which, with its reliance on women's labour, provided a new interpretation of women's equality. As under the tsars, but in a more organized and planned fashion, political and cultural repression of Ukrainians made the issue of women's equality appear to be a minor, or less pressing, one.

After the death of Lenin, persons prominent in the Ukrainian movement were repressed. Concomitantly, that great reservoir of traditional Ukrainian strength, the peasant *stykhiia*, the villages themselves, were caught between collectivization and pressure to join the work force in the cities, which at least assured a daily ration of bread. Whether this synchronized attack was fortuitous, an exploitation of opportunities by Stalin, or preconceived remains moot. Nevertheless, during the decade, "the entire central committee of the Ukrainian Communist Party, most of its regional and local leaders and countless others had been destroyed by the secret police acting on orders from Moscow."[51]

The destruction of the independent-minded Ukrainian communist leadership——which Moscow could carry out with impunity, since no Ukrainians outside Ukraine would defend Ukrainian communists——enabled the Russians to accomplish two goals. First, they could replace those Ukrainian communists popular among the locals with party members isolated from the Ukrainian population and therefore fully dependent on Moscow. Second, Moscow would now increase the exploitation of Ukraine and argue that those who opposed such policies were reactionary agents of foreign powers. (Some emigré leaders with a potential following in the Soviet Union were meanwhile assassinated.) The local Communist Party leadership, dependent upon Moscow, had few qualms about fulfilling Moscow's directives. Ukrainian communist women had little influence over these events.

During industrialization, the number of women in the work force increased and educational programmes available to women more than tripled. "The government exhibited paternal care over the material conditions of the women students, and allotted them special scholarships in addition to general stipends."[52] New courses were instituted to train women for skilled industrial labour. Levkovych had argued in 1929 for a more rational approach to the sugar-beet industry, and Mariia Demchenko's sugar-beet production was so legendary that illicit moonshine in Ukraine is still referred to as Cognac Demchenko. The increased involvement of women in political and trade-union work was encouraged, although most women worked in cultural and welfare committees that focused on the care of pregnant women and young mothers.[53] Affirmative-action programmes were instituted to push women into administrative positions and into regional and higher representative government.[54] But the function of the government was largely ceremonial, and no real power accrued to the women.

Women's ambitions were used to entice them to donate money and help build up Soviet armaments. Women organized groups and societies of telegraph and telephone operators, rifle groups, and other types of civil training. Propagandists highlighted women's funding of a plane for the Soviet Air Force, suitably called "Komunarka Ukrainy" (Communard-Woman of Ukraine), in 1929. Later another plane, "Woman Delegate of Ukraine," was funded, as well as a whole squadron named "8 March" after the international women's day of socialism initiated by Klara Zetkin. Subsequently, they funded a tank and a plane in honour of M.I. Ulianova, Lenin's sister. Overtime bonuses, introduced contrary to Marxist teaching, were frequently turned over by the women's labour brigades to worthy causes, such as the dirigible balloon, *Pravda*.[55] The whole programme of industrialization was aimed at the creation of an international Soviet which in effect was to become a Russian proletariat in Ukraine.

The role model for the Soviet women was the dedicated Soviet male. The pace of industrialization, the lack of machinery and the reliance on sheer physical labour both pushed women into superhuman exertion and underscored their physical weakness. In the labour-intensive economy of the Soviet Union, and particularly in the first stages of industrialization, the reliance on brute force offset many of the theoretical gains of women. Except for the shock brigades and the Stakhanovites, who continually set production records, women slid into the less lucrative, less prestigious jobs for which there was no extra pay, no incentive, and no means of rationalizing even the simplest tasks. The result was the perpetuation of women's labour in the less prestigious and hence low-paying jobs. Production quotas, volunteer overtime, and bonuses for overachievers effectively neutralized any initial ideas of equality. Hence the centrally planned economy and industrialization provided the impetus for sexual equality but failed to create a climate for its implementation and growth.

One of the major reasons for the Soviet regime's aggression against Ukraine was the latter's natural resources and industrial capacity. The party line developed by the end of the 1930s, however, stressed the selfless and friendly assistance offered by the Russians to their "little brothers." Major contortions are demanded of Soviet authors to present the story of the industrialization of the Soviet Union. The following provides a random example: "The help of the Russian nation was one of the most essential factors in the growth of the industrial output of Soviet Ukraine, although in the first stages of industrialization the [Ukrainian] republic enjoyed a relatively high level of economic development."[56]

Soviet works stress the high percentage of the allocation of the central budget for the development of industry in Ukraine, but omit to mention what percentage of the wealth making up the central budget came from Ukraine in the first place. These economic disparities had a direct bearing upon women in Ukraine, who from the 1920s were conditioned to regard the Russians, male and female, as benefactors and role models. In reality, as far as most of the women were concerned, they were neither. The discrepancy, glaring but officially suppressed, made the typical Ukrainian peasant woman and woman workers question the very feasibility of sexual-equality programmes.

According to Soviet authors, in Ukraine women in working-class families gained equality more quickly and easily than women in peasant families.[57] Both husband and wife in the cities and industrial centres had to work outside the home, since the household no longer produced goods for sale or for internal family use. Two incomes earned outside the home were necessary for survival, and dependence on external services——day care, some food preparation, housing——was essential. These changes undermined the traditional family roles, but the wife still continued to bear the primary responsibility for the household and the children. Did the women develop a sense of independence, or did they transfer their dependence to the party, state or brigade of workers? The question has not yet been studied.

The new Soviet Ukrainian woman

Without belittling the achievements of Soviet Ukrainian women in freeing themselves from patriarchal bondage and legal discrimination, the historian must look at the women's position in the socio-economic system. This involves several factors: ideology, politics, nationality conflicts and changing standards of economic progress. The situation of Ukrainian women in the Soviet Union was further complicated by the Russophilism of the party.

Despite their newly won rights and theoretical equality, women in the Soviet Union are often confronted by limitations on that equality, as well as on autonomy and the rights of the individual. Soviet Ukrainian jurists maintained that Soviet legislation had fulfilled, after two thousand years, the most noble aspirations of Roman legal thought. They argued that in Soviet Ukraine, women would be implementing the Roman aspirations: the wife is not, strictly speaking, yet a comrade for her husband, but will in the future become one. "And only Soviet law, proclaiming at the same time the woman to be independent in the economic and personal relationship, actualized at last the ancient dream of the Roman jurists and transformed that dream into concrete reality."[58]

When the husband himself——for the most part not having enjoyed or knowing independence——became a comrade, the position of the wife changed as well. Yet she was still defined in her relationship to something or someone external, not in her own terms. Just as the goal of women's emancipation in the Soviet Union was to make the woman equal to the man and not necessarily her own being, so the definition of the Soviet individual related to his/her dedication to and participation in Soviet society. The definitions of liberation and emancipation remain different in East and West.

Women did not join the work force, but the work brigade. They identified themselves with the smaller unit, functioned and received wages and bonuses through it. Frequently, the unit had a distinctive uniform in which it appeared at meetings and mass rallies. Brigades competed with each other in fulfilling the plan and setting new goals. Unlike Western competition for wages, this was technically friendly competition, not for extra overtime pay, but for bonus payments. To question the difference was to attack the regime.

The system under examination

It is impossible to ascertain what type of opposition, if any, to regimentation of women in the factories developed in Ukraine. Equally impossible is any attempt to assess nationalism in the women's work force. The effectiveness of the Ukrainization policies in such industrial centres as Kharkiv and Kryvyi Rih in the 1920s cannot be gauged. Nor is there any way of knowing whether the continuation of the "national-communist" course would have resulted in greater productivity at lesser human cost.

Some members of the Soviet Ukrainian intelligentsia and many Ukrainian peasant women——in different fashion——protested both the abuses of the regime and the subordination of women to the exigencies of the party apparatus and state economy. In Soviet scholarship, all these manifestations are attributed to reactionary nationalism and the Church. Numerous factors are overlooked.

The Church——in this case the Orthodox Church——was the least likely villain. The Orthodox Church in Ukraine had been used by the tsarist government for its own purposes. The collapse of tsarism brought with it the liberation of the Ukrainian Orthodox Church, which established an autocephalous entity despite the protests of the Russian Orthodox Church. "After the defeat of what is wrongly referred to as the civil war," wrote one urbane observer, "the church became an impenetrable spiritual fortress from whose pulpits [we] heard...forceful words of faith and inspiration. This had not been heard in the churches of Ukraine for many years."[59] The Ukrainian Autocephalous Orthodox Church immediately attracted a wide following, and a young and effective clergy. It demonstrated a surprising popularity in the urban centres, which had long been Russified. The party, which waged an open war on organized religion, was especially zealous toward Ukrainian organized churches. Repeatedly, the church was charged with collusion with enemies of the regime. The Autocephalous Church was abolished by the Communists in January 1930, and those clergy and bishops who did not join the Russian church were arrested.

Most of the Ukrainian intelligentsia, once the inevitability of Soviet rule became clear, supported the new system, which they felt was preferable to tsarism. The Western democracies still supported the old indivisible Russian Empire. But the USSR seemed to have had broken with Russia's imperialist past. The "totalitarian state" and the "cult of personality" lay in the future. Yet the political and cultural system of a single party under one-man control into which Ukraine was being drawn was heralding these developments. Pchilka, an outspoken critic of the regime, died on 4 October 1930. Her funeral was a quiet affair. Those who followed her cortège——the Hrushevskys, the Steshenkos, Mykola Sadovsky, Mykola Zerov——buried her in a silence which foreshadowed the many untimely deaths to come.

The first major trial which linked cultural activity in Soviet Ukraine to alleged clandestine schemes to topple the Soviet regime was held in Kharkiv between 9 March and 19 April 1930. It was carried live on radio. The charge was that the accused had been involved in a Union for the Liberation of Ukraine (not to be confused with a similarly named organization which had existed in Vienna during the First World War) and a Union of Ukrainian Youth (not the organization of the same name founded in Western Europe after the Second World War). Both SVU and SUM (to use the Ukrainian acronyms) were fabricated by the secret police to justify repressive actions against Ukrainian cultural and community leaders. The external forces, it was held, were hostile to the Ukrainian SSR rather than the USSR. The trial was held in the capital of Ukraine, in the grand opera house; the court and the lawyers were Ukrainian. Thus the whole case appeared to be an internal Ukrainian matter and forestalled Western interest and press coverage.

The prevailing consensus of scholarly opinion is that the charge was a fabrication of the state security organs to discredit Ukrainians and to discourage Ukrainian Jews from participating actively in the building of the Ukrainian state. Some forty persons were drawn into the case. Among them was the historian Osyp Hermaize and women of that Jewish family, especially Anna Georgievna Hermaize, who had participated actively in the work of the most pro-Ukrainian of the Kievan women's organization in the last years of the empire.[60]

The major thrust of the case was directed at Ukrainians. The defendants were accused of conspiring to overthrow the Soviet Ukrainian regime. They included a former premier, Volodymyr Chekhivsky, who had tried to reach a settlement for the UNR with the Soviets during the revolutionary years, and who had become one of the leaders of the Ukrainian Autocephalous Orthodox Church; two other high functionaries of the UNR; and six members of the Central Rada. (The President of the Central Rada, Hrushevsky, was already in Moscow.) Serhii Iefremov, a member of the Academy of Sciences, a former member of the Rada and the grand old man of Ukrainian literary criticism (he had criticized the works of Lesia Ukrainka and Olha Kobylianska for their modernism), was accused of being the lynchpin of the SVU. The student Pavlushkiv, although not his sister, was accused of spearheading the revolutionary Union of Ukrainian youth.

It was one of the first show trials in the Soviet Union, thus the extent of the terror and the ludicrousness of the accusations were not yet apparent. Nataliia Polonska-Vasylenko, the historian who lived in Ukraine at the time, maintains that the whole trial was a bewildering spectacle for Ukrainians, almost beyond comprehension. Liudmyla Starytska-Cherniakhivska, the writer, activist, and member of the moderate Socialist-Federalist Party, who had participated in many international gatherings, was the most prominent of the three women in this show trial. Polonska remembers: "It was on Maundy Thursday that [she] appeared before the court.... She did not renounce anything, and to the prosecutor's question——what does she want?——replied clearly: a free and united Ukraine."[61] Such a reply, by the way, was not contrary to the stated ideology of the party at that time, but Cherniakhivska's fate illustrated that such views went against party practice. Her husband, Oleksander Cherniakhivsky, a professor of histology at the Kiev Medical Institute, was also sentenced, while their daughter Veronika was arrested later.[62]

Starytska was among the best known of the Ukrainian intelligentsia women. She was politically active and famous for her sharp tongue. The fact that she, as well as Hrushevsky, Chekhivsky and others, had returned to Ukraine voluntarily limited the protests from abroad, since none of the émigrés would defend communist sympathizers. Yet Starytska-Cherniakhivska could be accused of numerous contacts with Ukrainians abroad, and construed as a likely candidate for a counter-revolutionary leader.

Anna Tokarivska, also a typical member of the intelligentsia, was brought to trial. Liubov Zhyhmailo Bidnova was dragged into the case because her estranged husband, Vasyl, a church historian who could not teach at a university under the tsars, had settled in Prague, where he was actively engaged in building up the Free Ukrainian University and the Ukrainian Agrarian Institute at Poděbrady. Bidnova was accused of using contacts with her husband to prepare an insurrection against the Soviets.

This case signalled a crackdown on the cultural activists in Ukraine and the tightening control of the party. The definition of an enemy of the state was continually expanded, while punishment for alleged crimes was increased. Activists of former political parties, anyone who had immigrated to Soviet Ukraine from areas outside the Russian Empire, those who had contacts or direct links with persons outside the USSR, and members of factions within the Communist Party of Ukraine were especially suspect. Relatives of enemies and "potential enemies," sisters, wives, and in-laws were routinely drawn into the dragnet. Frequently they perished without trace. The same fate awaited those who prosecuted cases, and therefore were aware of the fabricated evidence. Thus the entire family of Panas Liubchenko, the prosecuting attorney at the 1930 SVU trial, his wife and his wife's sister died in prisons of the secret police. The second wife of Skrypnyk was arrested after his suicide; the fate of their child remains unknown.[63]

The ever-widening circle of terror eroded the status Soviet Ukrainian women had gained. The visible social and political role of women made them more vulnerable to retribution. There were always others to fill the slots left vacant by arrests. The terror against the intelligentsia in Ukraine destroyed more men than women. Women who were not arrested in the Stalinist purges in the 1930s tried to find out the fate of those arrested and somehow to keep their children safe. For that reason some divorced disgraced husbands, others moved from town to town; most simply tried to survive.

Ukrainians had the dubious distinction of being the first nationality in the Soviet Union to fall victim to systematic genocide. It was masked as class warfare; its form was famine. It was most virulent in the countryside, and hit women and children as hard or even harder than men. Between four and seven million persons died as a result of the famine of 1933. The Soviets systematically denied the famine and would not permit any aid of the type organized by the Hoover Commission in 1922 to be sent. Only individuals could send hard currency to other individuals. The currency could only be redeemed at special government stores; records were kept on those with contacts abroad and later used against them. While many of Stalin's crimes were later denounced as aberrations, the Soviets' refusal to acknowledge the famine suggests that the destruction of the Ukrainian peasant base was considered crucial for the preservation of the Soviet system. None of the Soviet criticisms of Stalin mentions the 1932–33 famine.[64]

Collectivization

Food shortages plagued the Soviet state from its inception. A major reason for the Bolshevik campaigns against Ukraine had been to obtain Ukrainian wheat. In Ukraine, even during the interminable ravages of the First World War and succeeding wars, rebellions and revolutions, the peasants had food. In 1920, when the food production of the area was down by some 30 per cent, Ukraine was still able, albeit with difficulty, to export food to other republics. The defeat of the independent faction of the Ukrainian Communist Party (Borotbisty) in 1920 meant that Ukraine would support the reconstruction efforts of the entire former Russian Empire before the needs of its own population. Ukrainian peasants and workers moved into the reconstruction programme in force.[65]

A major attraction of the Bolshevik programme in Ukraine had been the promise of immediate land for the peasants. The Ukrainian peasant——fiercely individualistic and deeply attached to his land——chose to interpret the abolition of private property as a division of the large estates whose owners had either abandoned them or had been killed. Ukrainian peasants opposed collectivization, and the initial plans for collective agriculture had to be suspended.

Collectivization was renewed in 1928–9 with the initiation of the First Five-Year Plan. Stalin needed a collectivized, docile Ukraine to finance heavy industrial production. Many Ukrainian peasants not used to communal ownership and the land allocation typical of Russian villages refused to join the collective farms. They were automatically labelled middle-class peasants and full-scale propaganda warfare was initiated against them. Frequently, women were the most adamant opponents of collectivized agriculture, and flatly refused to join the collectives. A whole series of "women's revolutions" erupted. To counteract them, the party itself tried to mobilize women:

> At the time of complete collectivization the Communist Party (bolshevik) of Ukraine paid a great deal of attention to work among the peasants. On 9 June 1929, an all-Ukrainian meeting of women collective-farm members was convened...with the exhortation to foster the spread of collective farms.[66]

But despite incentives and heavy taxes levied on independent farmers, the Ukrainian peasants refused to join the collectives. Meanwhile, the purge of the old Ukrainian revolutionaries removed the last possible defenders of Ukrainian peasants within the party.

The international situation was not favourable to Ukrainians. Politics and economics worked toward the weaving of closer ties between the Western powers and the Soviets. The growing popularity of fascism and Nazism and the coming to power of Hitler in January 1933, put the USSR in a better light in Western eyes. The Soviets cultivated the West through a skillful blend of personal contacts and the sale of cheap wheat. Through an equally skillful orchestration of visits by Western figures such as the Webbs and George Bernard Shaw, and control on travel by foreign correspondents, the Soviets were able to portray themselves in a very favourable light. Suppression of Ukrainian patriots within the Communist Party, destruction of the Ukrainian intelligentsia and the depletion of the Ukrainian peasantry were denounced as slanders of reactionary and anti-Semitic Ukrainian émigrés. Nevertheless, the mass nature of the famine of 1933 could not be kept completely secret. A number of contemporary press accounts, especially those by the British journalist Malcolm Muggeridge, substantiated the few eyewitness descriptions which included those of some Ukrainian peasant women.

Collectivization and greater control of Ukraine by Moscow, combined with cultural and linguistic Russification, were intermeshed. This is how Liudmila Alekseeva, the Russian human-rights activist expelled from Moscow in 1977, later characterized the process:

> The Ukrainian peasantry stubbornly opposed collectivization. That is why, beginning in 1931, mass deportation of Ukrainian peasants to the eastern territories of the Soviet Union was instituted. In the first two months of 1931 alone, 300,000 persons were deported.
>
> The opposition was broken in 1932–3 by organizing the planned famine in the most fertile areas of Ukraine. [Moscow's] settling of accounts with the Ukrainian peasants ensured the final collectivization of farming. At the same time it undermined the potential of the Ukrainian national movement, since the basic mass of the Ukrainian population was composed precisely of peasants.[67]

The collectivization of Ukrainians served the same purpose as the terror that followed it.[68] It created a malleable, atomized population that could not effectively protest the brutalities inflicted upon it.

Terror against Ukrainian peasant women and reprisals against Ukrainian cultural activists made equality for Soviet Ukrainian women a dubious gain. Neither the 1920s nor the 1930s produced a major Ukrainian woman writer. The most promising——Zinaida Tulub, Cherniakhivska and others——were among the first to be arrested. The women who in the 1920s showed great promise as scholars were lucky if they were able to survive. Collectivization and the famine produced thousands of unsung women heroines, few of whom provided journalists and travellers with heart-rending accounts.

Peasant opposition to collectivization was portrayed by the Soviets as a class phenomenon——the rich peasants refusing to share their wealth with the poor. For the most part this was a distortion of reality. The vast majority of Ukrainian peasants deported to Siberia were not rich by any standards, nor did they exploit the poor. Statistics are not available, but accounts of the deportations abound. For instance, the family of Peter Marunchak, from the village of Umanets, near Kamianets-Podilsky, were among those exiled to Siberia in the

1930s. The mother was the daughter of a serf and the family had very little land. They had, however, supported the UNR. They were declared rich peasants in the 1920s, their taxes were continually increased, and they were held accountable for payments they could not afford. In the spring of 1930 the family was deported and all its belongings confiscated. In transport——sealed boxcars with a crack in the floor which was used as a toilet——the women and children did receive preferential treatment. They were rationed a quart of water; the men received none.[69]

In 1932 the government, under the guise of collecting back taxes, confiscated all the grain harvested by the Ukrainian peasants. Entrances to cities were blocked in an attempt to contain the peasants in the countryside. No food could be sent to the villages, and all mention of the famine, or even food shortages, was suppressed. The peasants nevertheless flocked to the railroad, many entered the cities, and some even made it to Moscow, where they went from door to door begging for food. Ukrainian cities were the first to see the effects of the famine in the streets. Western Ukrainians noted a dramatic rise in attempted escapes across the Zbruch. Moreover, the illegal "immigration" of Ukrainians to Romania, whose common border with Ukraine was not as heavily guarded as the Western one, increased markedly during 1932–3.

Ukrainian peasant women risked everything to publicize the famine. Having witnessed cannibalism and mass death, they could not believe that "Europe" was aware of the famine but was taking no action. Maurice Hindus, the American journalist who was born in Ukraine and who supported the Soviets in the 1920s, spent some time in the area around Poltava in late summer 1933, when the worst of the famine was over. In his book, *The Great Offensive*, he relates that "she [the peasant woman] thought she could come in and tell us everything that had happened. Perhaps people on the outside didn't know anything about it——visitors were so rare——and we might tell them so they would know how scandalously they had been treated——they, such hard-working folk, with no desire to be *koolacks* or to do wrong to anybody!"[70] Potential supporters of Ukrainian peasants among the communists were now isolated, both from society and within the party. Skrypnyk, under house arrest for alleged nationalist deviation, unable to humanize the party he and his friend Lenin had built up, committed suicide on 7 July 1933.

Totalitarianism

The dead were buried in mass graves, the deportations continued, and collectivization was carried out. Industrialization was accelerated through the use of shock brigades which were moved from place to place to increase norms. Workers who did not maintain the norm were fined or punished. Women entered the work force *en masse*, while continuing to perform their traditional domestic functions.

The purges——heralded in Ukraine by the suicides of Skrypnyk and Khvylovy——hit Ukraine as hard as the rest of the USSR. But after collectivization and the famine, the purges were simply another cross to bear. Stalin, a Georgian whose mother sacrificed herself for his education, whose wife committed suicide, and whose unstable daughter was raised as an isolated princess, had never shown particular interest in the position of women. They were to be good mothers, productive workers and docile citizens.

The Stalinist revolution however needed a stable family base and women who would raise children under the most adverse conditions. A new legal code made divorce difficult and abortions——which had been used as a surrogate contraceptive——illegal, except in cases where the life or health of the mother were clearly endangered. Unwritten mores reverted to more traditional women's roles and deference to men. Fecund women received their heroic motherhood titles from men who earned more money and lived better than the "heroines" did. Kobrynska's prediction of patriarchal attitudes surviving into the socialist society was proven correct. Women still had lower-paying jobs, did not rise as high in the professions as men and had less time for themselves. Lapidus sums up the position of women in the USSR in the following manner:

> Even housework, once so harshly stigmatized by Lenin, was now considered "socially useful labour," while Soviet wives were assured that achieving a comfortable homelife was a desirable goal. The ranks of the proletarian heroines were now joined by the wives of the new Soviet elite of managers and engineers, praised not for heroic feats of production but for introducing civilization into the lives of their men by planting flowers outside power stations, sewing linen, and opening fashion studios. The status and identity of a woman were no longer to be derived exclusively from her independent role in production but at least in part defined ascriptively, as functions of her performance in the roles of wife and mother.
>
> The socializing functions of the family received particular emphasis in the new orientation of the Stalin period. Marital stability was itself a condition of the proper upbringing of children. But the view of the family as a central socializing agency represented a major shift of perspective.
>
> Taken together, these aspects of Stalinism represent an effort to mobilize women intensively on behalf of a widening array of economic, social, and political objectives. Increasing demands on women were the accompaniment of expanding opportunities. Pressures toward female employment in industry, the demand on the household, and the treatment of marriage, reproduction, and socialization——all effectively broadened the definition of women's obligations to the larger community. The new image of feminine virtue incorporated wifely and maternal duties in addition to a contribution to the building of socialism.... The new Soviet heroine was to join a highly competitive participation in the economic arena with nurturing family roles of a rather traditional kind.[71]

With the stress on the "elder brother" role of the Great Russians, the Ukrainian women in effect shared the fate of their third-world sisters.

The 1930s decade was extremely difficult for the Ukrainian population. Lenin's strictures against Great Russian chauvinism were censored from the writings of the founder of the Soviet Union. Under the pretext of ridding the USSR of traitors and alleged foreign agents, Stalin unleashed a purge against all who might challenge or pose a potential challenge to his power. Ukrainians who had supported the Bolsheviks and actively opposed rival Ukrainian political forces were considered as guilty of "bourgeois nationalism" as cultural activists who had little interest in politics.

Women who had gained prominence in Ukraine, direct or accrued, in any area except the currently sanctioned line of production, were vulnerable. Olena Pchilka died, but her daughters and their husbands, active members of the Social Democratic Party, were exiled. Many lesser known activists perished in the 1930s in Siberia. The Ukrainian heroines of the 1930s——according to the official version——were those who produced the most children, milked the most cows and harvested the most sugar beets. The party laid great stress upon heavy industry, and eulogized brigades of men engaged in the noble arts of mining, welding and heavy-machine production. Women were relegated to less glamorous and less lucrative jobs.

Industrial development in Ukraine followed the pattern of the nineteenth century. Eastern Ukraine, with its rich coal deposits, was being developed, while Right-Bank Ukraine remained agricultural. Russians were brought in to replace the deported Ukrainian population and active Russification policies were pursued, especially in the industrial cities.

In 1939 the Soviet government conducted a population census, the first since 1926. (A census was held in 1937, but its returns were declared to have been falsified by "wreckers": presumably the data it revealed were too damaging to accept.) The total population of Ukraine had grown from 28,446,000 in 1926 to 31,785,000 in 1939, that is, by 12 per cent. The number of Ukrainians had increased by about 400,000, or less than 2 per cent; the Russians gained 1.5 million, an increase of 57 per cent. These figures, which were not published until 1975, confirm in the language of statistics the enormous human losses suffered by Ukrainians in the 1930s during the collectivization, famine, and mass terror.[72]

The dead as well as the living were suppressed. Major Ukrainian scholarly and literary works were removed from circulation or banned completely. Ukrainian literature and the other arts were reduced to an all-time low. The role of women, who remained *de facto* second-class citizens, in a culture which was being reduced to second-class status can be easily imagined.

The use of terms such as "Great Leader," "Father of the Nation," "elder and younger brothers" reflected the return to the mores of the older settled society. While women, except those married to high party functionaries, had to work and enjoyed *de jure* equality, *de facto* they continued to be as handicapped as women in non-socialist states. Even if one discounts the constant fear of arrest, reprisal and deportation inherent in the totalitarian system, Ukrainian women (like others in the USSR) faced the double burden of gainful employment outside the home and care of household and children. This was particularly difficult in view of the chronic shortage of the most basic items; the collectivized village did not produce all the necessary items for its own subsistence.

Yet Soviet sources stress the great changes made in the life of the Ukrainian family; the freeing of the woman from the control of the husband and of the children from parental control.

> The peasant woman reached a hitherto unattainable height in collective production. Following in the footsteps of the worker, she improved her cultural and technical level and entered male professions. Common work and common interests strengthened the family, and economic independence strengthened mutual respect among its members. The parents listened more carefully to the views of their children, and took them into consideration. Children who studied well had prospects of further advancement. With the growth of family welfare various items appeared——articles for children, books, toys, bicycles, skates, skis, chess and checkers, musical instruments, and the like.[73]

This is an official, recent scholarly analysis of the achievements of Soviet women in the 1930s. The textile industry is presented as having directly benefited women in that it provided jobs for them——in the same type of sweatshops that had led Western women to unionize.

Soviet Ukrainian works on women always stress the initiative of the party, predominantly male, and of its male leadership in raising the level of the women to that of the men. Equality is given to women——in terms defined by the men and in a manner which they consider most seemly. On a different level, it is a repetition of the old story of Eve being fashioned out of Adam's rib.

Christianity in agricultural Ukraine formally and informally penetrated the highlights in the life of the individual and the annual agricultural cycle. Folk rituals were incorporated into worship and accompanied religious ceremonies. The wedding ritual in the church was preceded and followed by family and tribal rituals that were considered part of the traditional festivities. The priest blessing the harvest, or the fruits, or, in a separate ceremony, flowers and herbs, had become a religious affair. The party increasingly (and to this day) tried to adapt the ancient ritual, stripped of its Christian overlay, to non-ecclesiastical ceremonies. In an attempt to wean the peasants away from the church but keep them working in the fields, formal harvest feasts, similar in pageantry to the priest blessing the field, were introduced by the party. Personal milestones were also marked solemnly, without benefit of clergy but using traditional artifacts to underscore the ennobling quality of socialist labour and the intermeshing of private life and community morality.

The woman issue, the use of women in productive labour outside the home, and the need to raise and socialize children led the Soviet regime into what is sometimes ambivalently referred to as societal or situational ethics. Scientific socialism, which limited itself to a broadly defined dialectical materialism, demanded of its adherents personal dedication, loyalty, decency and monogamous sexual relationships for the good of the children and society. Essentially, the Soviets wanted idealized middle-class conventionality, which in the period of the Stalinist cult of power made women particularly vulnerable.

This was especially painful for Ukrainian women, who perceived the subservient position of Ukrainians within the Union. It made the situation of the Ukrainian women even more difficult than that of the Russian women, or of the women from the smaller nationalities, who were less important in the eyes of the party than those of the larger and economically significant Ukraine.

Modernization and the more active participation of women in community life was used by the party to establish informal controls over the population. Part of the popular "Days of Harvest," initiated in 1923, were community "court" proceedings and public derision of those "who held on to reactionary forms of agriculture and believed in old wives' tales or superstitions. By the mid-1930s organized society (*hromadskist*) had a visible impact on the lives of the families."[74] In other words, party control, through a combination of terror and modernization, had increased markedly by the end of 1930s.

Soviet Ukrainian women: A balance sheet

Between 1919 and 1939 the Soviet Union enacted far-reaching legislation in an attempt to change women's way of life. Indeed, excepting Turkey, no other country of that time enacted so many changes to the status of women. The Soviets removed the formal barriers that had stood before Ukrainian women for generations, improving their legal position, and removing the hindrances to their advancement in career and educational opportunities. Yet, when one studies the major achievements of women in Ukraine, the period between 1919 and 1939 yields startling results.

On the credit side, there is a number of highly commendable achievements. The literacy rate among Ukrainians rose sharply. The number of women attending schools and extension courses also increased dramatically. The number of women employed in the labour force in positions of managerial authority, the professions, and in higher educational establishments rose in unprecedented fashion. Infant mortality and the death of women in childbirth declined sharply. Expectations for women grew, although party women gained less in Ukraine than might have been expected given the number of women who joined the party. The number of women in government positions increased, as did the availability of such positions, especially after the nationalization of industry and collectivization of agriculture.

Yet the proportion of Soviet Ukrainian women in better-paying jobs in managerial positions, and in the government and party apparatus, did not keep pace with the integration of women into the work force. Feminization of certain professions, i.e., a decline in salary and prestige in those fields to which women tend to gravitate, also became evident. Even in professions that are in large measure staffed by women, men continue to exercise positions of authority and control.

Given these relative advantages, however, Soviet Ukrainian women had singularly few individual achievements. Between 1919 and 1939 they failed to produce a major woman writer. There were few women scholars of outstanding stature and productivity. While there were a number of actresses and singers, none won world renown. Women artists who survived did not reach beyond folk art. There were no Soviet Ukrainian women political leaders. Was this lack of achievement on the part of Soviet Ukrainian women in the first twenty years of the regime a reflection on the inferiority of women? Or was the problem inherent in Ukrainians? Or was it a factor of the regime? Or of the society? Or did it reflect the normal course of events?

There were three reasons for the low profile of Ukrainian women in the Soviet Union between 1919 and 1939. Eastern Ukrainian women under the tsarist regime had chafed under political and national oppression. They failed to look beyond this oppression and analyze the specifically sexual aspects of inequality. They lacked the psychological sophistication that would have enabled them to grasp the conditioned reasons for the failure of women to live up to their potential. Success in grasping the underlying reasons for female inability to succeed in a male-dominated world is still eluding many in the United States. Thus the charge that Soviet Ukrainian women failed to grasp the reasons behind their inferior position, even when conditions of formal inequality were removed, is patently unfair.

The fairness or unfairness of the lack of higher visibility in the cultural and social performance of Soviet Ukrainian women between 1919 and 1939 is immaterial. Both reflect a reality for which part of the responsibility must be borne by Ukrainian women and a greater part by Ukrainian men, while the prime cause lay outside the control of either.

The simple reasons why the Soviet Ukrainian women of that period failed to make full use of the opportunities presented them was that the opportunities were never real. The party's totalitarian control of the population and its output, creative and productive, effectively manipulated women. The party directed the integration of women into the public sphere for its own purposes, not to respond to the needs of women. Certainly the formal conditions for equality exist in the Soviet Union. But because the party is the instrument of change, these conditions have not been met. How many of those repressed under Stalin were women?

Closely related to the exclusive control exercised by the party over Soviet society is the equally pervasive Russian control of Ukraine. All aspects of life in Soviet Ukraine, beginning with the party itself, are placed not so much within the context of the Soviet Union as within the Russian manifestation of that Union. Thus efforts to ease out the use of Ukrainian in schools——openly pushed by Khrushchev after March 1938——were rationalized as a struggle against nationalism. There is a double standard for Ukrainians and Russians. What is considered patriotic for the Russians, even when dealing with the achievements of so-called bourgeois culture, is considered not only nationalist, but subversive for Ukrainians. The treatment of Ukrainians as second-class citizens, enemies or potential enemies of the regime has had an extremely debilitating effect upon the Ukrainian intelligentsia, especially upon women.

Ukrainian women in the Soviet Union have not been given a chance to taste the fruits of equality. Ukraine bore a large part of the fighting in the world wars, was the site of the revolutionary struggles, and supported by its resources much of the industrialization of the USSR. In addition, it was hit hard by collectivization, famine and party terror. Life for Ukrainian women between 1919 and 1939 was difficult, grey and fearful. To survive, let alone bear children, was an achievement in itself. That there were Ukrainian women who continued to create new life, new forms of beauty, to preserve the folk art and folk beliefs, to maintain the very faith in life and hope, is in itself remarkable.

Leonid Pliushch, the expelled Ukrainian mathematician who spent several gruelling years in the refined torture of the Soviet psychiatric hospitals, was deeply influenced by Nadiia Surovtseva, the historian active in the women's movement during the Revolution and the 1920s. He met her after she had served her twenty-five-year sentence——decades after Kotsiubynsky had been shot, and Hrushevsky, her mentor, had died. Pliushch was impressed not only by Surovtseva's intelligence but by her ability to survive the hell of the Gulag.

> What saved Surovtseva from cracking up? The psycho-ideological basis of her courage alone could not have saved her. Ukrainian culture, for the most part, is characterized by an absence of decadence and emotional excess. In this respect Surovtseva is a true Ukrainian intellectual. Resisting the pressure of interrogations and camp guards is very difficult if one's mind is confused and one bears traces of the corruption against which one is speaking out. Surovtseva has a precise, sober mind, no evident complexes, and no repressed feelings of guilt toward other people. Yes, she made mistakes. She praised and fought for the "new Ukraine," thus helping her torturers. But she is not excessively penitent. She understands the tragedy of Ukraine and the Revolution and her own involuntary guilt.[75]

Hers was the personification of the story of Ukrainian women. Her children are spiritual, her scholarly works not produced, and her memoirs confiscated by the KGB. Yet she lived with dignity and love of the world, regardless of circumstances.

Notes

Introduction

1. *Report of the World Conference to Review and Appraise the Achievements of the United Nations Decade for Women: Equality, Development and Peace*, Nairobi, Kenya, 15 to 26 July 1985, advance mimeographed copy, Article 99, p. 113, summary of the general debate.

2. Despite the rapid growth in women's studies and the equally growing sophistication in the analysis of women's movements, which is only selectively reflected in the bibliographic essay at the end of this book, there is no theoretical study of the relationship of nationalism to feminism. Patriotic literature of various kinds generally stressed that the particular women discussed were always valuable members of their community, either by being selfless mothers or because the national group in question always treated its women with respect, recognizing their special status and contributions to the cause. The growing literature on Russian and Soviet women does not take the national aspect into account.

3. Among the many books published since this one was written is Marilyn Chapin Massey, *Feminine Soul: The Fate of an Ideal* (Boston: Beacon Press, 1985), in which she tries to fit concepts of modern feminism into the philosophical systems of the nineteenth century. What we refer to as modern ideologies, especially the variants of political salvation in which these ideologies were transplanted to Eastern Europe, were not only male constructs, but, again according to a recently published study by Linda J. Nicholson, *Gender in History: The Limits of Social Theory in the Age of the Family* (New York: Columbia University Press, 1986), reflected a particular stage of family development. The historiography of women has generally tended to be specific, not to concentrate upon long-term trends. As Anne Firor Scott wrote in her collection of essays, *Making the Invisible Woman Visible* (Urbana and Chicago: University of Illinois Press, 1984, 330), "Feminism was sometimes overt, as in the organized women's rights movement, but more often it was covert, as women built organizations of all sorts and created community institutions to carry out things they wanted to accomplish. Shut out, as they usually were, from traditional social structures...women created their own social organizations that they themselves could run." The women's organizations we are discussing in this book attempt to transcend the female world and to incorporate their activities into the whole community forum.

    The incorporation of women into history and the study of society has necessitated an expansion of the research base and of the analytical framework of historical study. Social history, the study of families, the economics of the household, a redefined study of childhood, the contribution of volunteer organizations to major social and political changes, even a redefinition of power and ideology profited and continue to profit from the deepening studies of the history of women. Indeed, in a recent article ("Gender: A Useful Category of Historical Analysis," *The American Historical Review* [December 1986]), Joan W. Scott argues that "gender is the primary field within which or by means of which power is articulated." This article recapitulates much of the current think-ing on women and builds upon it to stress, in the use of gender rather than women, the significance of placing women into a contextual framework that transcends the object/subject dichotomy. In Scott's words, "gender, then, provides a way to decode meaning and to understand the complex connections among vari-ous forms of human interaction." While true for the Western countries, a great deal more research will have to be done in the histories of other parts of the world before that statement can become truly meaningful. In fact, Scott herself, in her final summation of the need to redefine women's and men's history, simply disregards nationalism. "This new history...suggests that gender must be redefined and restructured in conjunction with a vision of political and social equality that includes not only sex but class and race." (p. 1075) For many parts of the world, that statement would be meaningful only if "race" referred, in nineteenth-century fashion, to nation as well as colour. Philosophy and religion studied beyond ca-nonical formulations are also meaningfully presented, so far, only within the American and West European context.

4. Massey writes very clearly that "The heritage of the critique of religion as ideology pervades Western liberating theory" (p. 9).

1: Historical Background

1. Writing as Pavlo Hrab, "Deshcho v spravi zhinochykh typiv," *Narod*, 1 and 15 April 1884. The quotation is from p. 108.

2. Zinaida Mirna, "Zhinochyi rukh na Velykii Ukraini do revoliutsii," *Zhinka*, 15 March 1937, 2–3; 1 April 1937, 2–3; and 1 May 1937, 6–7. Quotation from 15 March 1937, 2.

3. A.Ia. Efimenko, *Istoriia ukrainskogo naroda* (St. Petersburg, 1906), introduction. Even present-day Soviet historians complain of the paucity of works on the social history of Ukraine. A random example of this is V.I. Borysenko, *Borotba demokratychnykh syl za narodnu osvitu na Ukraini v 60–90tykh rokakh XIX st.* (Kiev, 1980). His history of village schools is an attempt to rectify the situation.

4. N.I. Kostomarov, *Ocherk domashnei zhizni i nravov velikorusskago naroda v XVI i XVII st.* (St. Petersburg, 1860) and D. Mordovtsev, *Russkiia zhenshchiny novago vremeni: biograficheskie ocherki iz russkoi istorii*, 3 vols. (St. Petersburg, 1873). On the influence of Mordovtsev, see Oleksander Lototsky, *Storinky mynuloho* (Warsaw, 1932–5), 1: 75, as well as Mordovtsev's correspondence in TsGALI, f. 320.

5. Mykhailo Hrushevsky, *Pochatky hromadianstva (genetychna sotsiologiia)* (Prague, 1921), esp. 300–16.

6. For a brief presentation of Efimenko's views, see the obituary notice on her writ-ten by Dmytro Bahalii in *Zapysky istorychno-filolohichnoho viddilu Ukrainskoi akademii nauk*, Book 1 (Kiev, 1919), 102–13.

7. Natalia Polonska-Vasylenko, *Vydatni zhinky Ukrainy* (Winnipeg, 1969) 78–9. Text in Ukrainian: *Ia beru tebe sobi za odnoho(odnu) vlasnoho(vlasnu) a pravdyvoho(–u) muzha(zhonu) pomoshchnyka(–tsiu) a sliubuiu tebe shchaslyvoho(–u) i neshchaslyvoho(–u) nihde ne opuskaty do smerty moiei abo*

tvoiei: tak mi pane Bozhe pomozhy i vsi sviatii. The later addition for the woman read: *sliubuiu tobi mylost, viru, uchtyvost i poslushenstvo malzhenskoe.*

8. For instance, Marusia Churai, the legendary author of a series of popular songs in the seventeenth century, continues to inspire contemporary Ukrainians. Lina Kostenko's *Marusia Churai: Istorychnyi roman u virshakh* (Kiev, 1979) is a best-seller. Churai's songs continue to be sung. Ihor Lisky, "Ukrainska zhinka v kozatsku dobu," *Zhinka*, 1 August 1935, 6–9, stressed the active role of all classes of Ukrainian women. The role of the upper-class women in the establishment of the Kievan Academy is highlighted in Z.I. Khyzhniak, *Kyievo-Mohylianska Akademiia* (Kiev, 1970). Poles also stressed the precariousness of life in the steppes that drew the Ukrainian women into the fray and enabled them to choose and divorce husbands at will. Parts of Dr. Antoni Rolle, *Niewiasty kresowy* (Warsaw, 1883) were reprinted that year in *Kievskaia starina*, v. 6, 268–309.

9. From a memorandum prepared for the International Women's League of Peace and Freedom, Geneva, June 1920; in the Hanna Chykalenko-Keller papers in the Archives of UVAN, uncatalogued. This is from p. 1a of a mimeographed and edited typescript, with a minor change——"charity" for the "benevolence" Keller used.

10. Mariia Livytska, *Na hrani dvokh epokh* (New York, 1972), 92.

11. I would like to thank Bohdan Krawchenko, Director of the Canadian Institute of Ukrainian Studies, for alerting me to this fact.

12. Quoted in Irena Knysh, *Try rovestnytsi* (Winnipeg, n.d.) 108; on Bashkirtsev, see Simone de Beauvoir, *The Second Sex* (New York, 1953).

13. "Znachenie matushki v prikhode," by Zhena Sviashchennika E.K. in *Kievskiia eparkhiialnyia vedomosti*, 1890, 664–6. At the turn of the century the clergy participated actively in the credit organizations aimed at ameliorating the loss of the peasants. There are amusing and anti-clerical vignettes on the life of the priests, their wives and daughters in Ukraine in Volodymyr Levenko [Leontovych], *Per pedes apostolorum: obrazky z zhyttia dukhovenstva na Ukraini* (Lviv, 1896).

14. [Oleksander Luhovy], Oleksander Vasyl Ovrutsky Shvabe, *Vyznachne zhinotstvo Ukrainy* (Toronto, 1942), 127.

15. See, for example, Tsentralnaia revizionnaia kommissia dlia revizii dvorianskikh del, in TsDIA, UkSSR (Kiev), f. 481, op. 3, spr. 8 for 1840–2.

16. G.S. Vinsky, a hot-headed soldier from the lower echelons of Ukraine's upper class, served in the Russian army under Catherine II. He was exiled to Siberia as a result of a financial scandal at the time of the final destruction of the Sich, the Cossack stronghold. In his memoirs, *Moe vremia. Zapiski* (new edition: Newtonville, Mass., 1974), he stressed the differences between Russian and Ukrainian women. He also wrote that "at this time, the Little-Russians lived only among themselves; except for Greeks and Poles, foreigners were unknown to them; they hardly had any contact even with the Great Russians" (p. 23).

17. The leading theoretician of the Decembrists, Pavel Pestel, was a typical Jacobin, enamoured of a well functioning progressive centralized state. He went so far as to advocate the expulsion and extermination of the Jews. He did not co-operate with the Poles, and did not recognize Ukrainian claims to regional autonomy.

18. Vasyl Shchurat, "Osnovy Shevchenkovykh zviazkiv z poliakamy," *Vybrani pratsi* (Kiev, 1963), 242–350.

19. As late as 1919, the wife of a liberal Russian politician asked the Ukrainian

political leader and historian Dmytro Doroshenko to recite some Ukrainian poems she had known in her youth. Dmytro Doroshenko, *Moi spomyny pro nedavnie-mynule (1914–1920)* (Munich, 1969), 484.

20. Pavlo Zaitsev, *Zhyttia Tarasa Shevchenka* (Paris, 1955), 98–9.

21. N.V. Chekhova, "Marko Vovchok," *Soiuz Zhenshchin*, no. 2 (August-September 1907): 13, and continuation no. 1 (January 1908): 11–12 and no. 2 (February 1908): 14–17.

22. The Ukase proscribed the publication of works in Ukrainian, except for a very few in a literary-ethnographic genre, and those only in Russian orthography. Its instigator, the otherwise liberal minister of education, Count Uvarov, proclaimed loudly: "There never was, there is not now, nor will there ever be a Ukraine."

23. She was married to Panteleimon Kulish, a prominent conservative, and came from an activist Ukrainian family from Chernihiv. A branch of the family became completely Russified. One of them, the Russian children's writer, Nadezhda Alexandrovna Belozerskaia, nevertheless kept up contacts with the old home, wrote fondly of Little Russia, as the Russians called Ukraine, and was friendly with Ukrainian families, especially the Berenshtams. She corresponded with Mordovtsev and named her son Taras. Some of the letters to her were written in Ukrainian. TsGAII, f. 58, op. 1.

24. She was the daughter of a teacher in one of the private women's schools in Kiev who was exiled for his liberal political views. She married the only son of Olena Pchilka, and it was Pchilka who encouraged her writing and got her early poetry published in Galicia. See Pchilka's letter to Omelian Ohonovsky of 29 March 1889, in TsDIA, UkSSR (Lviv), Kolektsiia Naukovoho Tovarystva im. Shevchenka, Pysma Ohonovskomu, f. 309, op. 1, spr. 2385, 63. The unpublished memoirs of Sudovshchyk-Kosach, entitled "Khaos," were written in Russian and apparently were never completed. The original is in the Archive of the Museum of Lesia Ukrainka in Kiev.

25. In a letter to Mykhailo Drahomanov, her uncle, she took the West Ukrainian feminist Nataliia Kobrynska to task: "She suggested topics such as 'The Ukrainian woman and her role in the national renaissance.' I don't even know how to go about handling it." Letter of April or May 1893, in Olha Kosach-Kryvyniuk, *Lesia Ukrainka. Khronolohiia zhyttia i tvorchosty* (New York, 1970), 197. See also "Novye perspektivy i starye temy," reprinted in *Zibrannia tvoriv*, v. 7, 76–99. Pavlo Horiansky, "Zhadka pro Lesiu Ukrainku, *Zhyttia i revoliutsiia*," no. 2 (1926): 98–102, recalled both how quickly Lesia sewed and how well she spoke at a student meeting in the fall of 1898 in Dorpat (present-day Tallin) to a group headed by Fedir Matushevsky.

26. Answering a questionnaire of Omelian Ohonovsky in 1892, in TsDIA, UkSSR (Lviv), Kolektsiia NTSh, Korespondentsiia Ohonovskoho z Pchilkoiu, f. 390, spr. 2585, 74 and the following unnumbered page. There was no love lost between Pchilka and Vovchok. Pchilka in private called her a "pushy *katsapka*" and questioned the authenticity of her writings. *Katsap* (a word of uncertain origin) was the derisive Ukrainian name for Russians. The Russians, in turn, called the Ukrainians *khokhly,* from the word for forelock.

27. In her *Avtobiohrafiia* (Kharkiv, 1931), 9.

28. Typed autobiography in Hanna Chykalenko-Keller papers in the UVAN Archives, not catalogued.

29. Sofiia Rusova, "Spomyny pro pershyi teatralnyi hurtok v Kyivi,"

Literaturno-naukovyi vistnyk LXXX, book IV–VI (April-June 1918): 104–7; Nataliia Doroshenko [Savchenko], "Deshcho pro ukrainsku dramatychnu shkolu: Uryvok z spomyniv pro nedavne mynule," *Ridnyi krai*, no. 7 (1912): 15–20. On the Ukrainian theatre in general, see Instytut mystetstva, folkloru i etnohrafii im. M.T. Rylskoho, *Ukrainskyi dramatychnyi teatr*, 2 vols (Kiev, 1959–67); O. Kazymyrov, *Ukrainskyi amatorskyi teatr (dozhovtnevyi period)* (Kiev, 1965); and Dmytro Antonovych, *Trysta rokiv ukrainskoho teatru 1619–1919* (Prague, 1925).

30. Article reporting on the event of 15 January 1908 in *Russkie vedomosti*, 17 January 1908.

31. Lototsky, *Storinky mynuloho,* 2: 213.

32. *Russkie vedomosti*, 17 January 1908.

33. TsDIA, UkSSR (Kiev), f. 102, op. 100, ed. khr. 32g3, 1908: Po Kievskoi gubernii, demonstratsii, mitingi i massovye besporiadki; 26.

34. Report dated 18 November 1908, ibid., 39. See also *Ridnyi krai*, no. 15 (1908): 11.

35. If one considers that the threatened minorities are the groups most likely to band together, then the preponderance of Polish, Jewish and, to a lesser degree, Russian community organizations at the turn of the century, especially in the provinces of Kiev and Volhynia, can be understood. For a full list see *Ves iugo-zapadnyi krai; spravochnaia i adresnaia kniga po Kievskoi, Podolskoi i Volynskoi guberniiam* (Kiev, 1913). This is not to say that Ukrainians did not need more community organizations; many of them were simply not conscious of that immediate need.

2: Women and Education

1. M.K. Chaly, *Vospominaniia* (Kiev, 1890–95), 1: 85, originally published in *Kievskaia starina.*

2. *O zhenskikh uchilishchakh: Svod zamechanii na VII glavu proekta ustava obshcheobrazovatelnykh uchebnykh zavedenii ministerstva narodnogo prosveshcheniia*, compiled by Mikhail O. Kosinsky and V.V. Wessel ([St. Petersburg], 1864). The general history of the establishment of higher schools for women in the Russian Empire is covered in E.O. Likhacheva, *Materialy dlia istorii zhenskogo obrazovaniia v Rossii*, 2 vols. (St. Petersburg, 1899–1901), see also Sophie Satina, *Obrazovanie zhenshchin v dorevoliutsionnoi Rossii* (New York, 1966) and Richard Stites, *The Women's Liberation Movement in Russia* (Princeton, 1978); on Kharkiv, see I.P. Lazarevich, *Deiatelnost zhenshchin* (Kharkiv, 1883). Elementary schools, including schools for girls, are discussed in V.I. Borysenko, *Borotba demokratychnykh syl za narodnu osvitu na Ukraini v 60–90–tykh rokakh XIX st.*

3. Livytska, 66.

4. Catherine II founded the Smolny Institute for upper-class Russian women. On women's schools in Ukraine, see Oleksander Konysky, "Zhinocha osvita na Ukraini," *Zoria*, 12 February 1884; E.O. Likhacheva, *Materialy*, 251; *Ukrainska Radianska Entsyklopediia*, 5: 83.

5. Koroleva, born on 3 March 1888 of a Spanish mother who died at childbirth, had

a most unconventional childhood. She spent the first five years of her life in Ukraine. Her father, of mixed Spanish and Ukrainian-Lithuanian-Polish heritage, a member of the French Academy of Sciences, travelled widely in search of exotic insects. He refused to see the child until she was about twelve years old, and Noel-Natalena, as the girl was called to reflect the Eastern and Western heritage, was raised in Spain, France and Italy by various members of the family in a number of convent schools. When her father married a descendant of the Czech family von Los (a number of whom had been executed by the Habsburgs in 1620) and settled in Kiev, he sent for his daughter, brought her baby playmate from Volhynia to rekindle the Ukrainian ties, stressed her family's tradition of service to the people among whom they lived and the ideal of *noblesse oblige*. After the First World War, she married Vasyl Koroliv-Stary, who talked her into writing in Ukrainian and doctored her biography to make it appear that she was Ukrainian by origin, because he felt that Ukrainians would not otherwise accept her as a writer. She wrote a number of religious-historical novels in Ukrainian, although her first works, encouraged by Anatole France, a friend of her father's, had been in French. See Natalena Koroleva, *Bez korinnia* (Cleveland, 1968), 3rd ed. See also Livytska's memoirs.

6. The two major sources on the Kievan Higher Courses for Women are a booklet of thirty-five pages published in Kiev by the University Press in 1884 entitled *Istoricheskaia zapiska i otchet o kievskikh vysshykh zhenskikh kursakh za pervoe chetyrekhletie 1878–1882* in TsDIA, UkSSR (Kiev), f. 707, op. 151, spr. 30; and a series of documents and correspondence about the courses dated from 12 September 1878 to 16 June 1879, ibid., f. 442, op. 828, od. zb. 146. M.N. Chertkov, an official in the office of the Governor-General in Kiev, in a letter to A.E. Timashev on 25 September 1878, singled out Gogotska as being prominent in a whole group of persons "who at best are of doubtful reliability" (*blagonadezhnost*), TsDIA, UkSSR (Kiev), f. 442, op. 828, od. zb. 146, 17. Gogotska had tried unsuccessfully in 1875 to help G.G. Tsvetkovsky become editor of *Kievskii telegraf* and director of a college-preparatory school, the Halahan Collegium. The appointments were blocked by the police, who argued that not only were Tsvetkovsky's views suspect, but the whole college was one "where overt Ukrainophile tendencies are dominant," TsGIA, USSR (Moscow), f. 102, Delo Politsii, Osoboe Otdelenie 554, 1889–96, 16. Tsvetkovsky and his family lived in St. Petersburg and the police there sent attestations of the entire family's loyalty, including the three children's (all three students——Mariia, Georgii and Konstantyn), ibid., 21–2 .

The Halahan Collegium was founded by Hryhorii and Kateryna Halahan in 1869 in memory of their son Pavlo. It produced a number of leading male Ukrainian patriots. See Hlib Lazarevsky, "Ta ne bude luchshe: Spohady emigranta pro stari panski sadyby v Ukraini," *Hromadianka*, 1 November 1938, 3–4. Lazarevsky stressed the philanthropic and educational work of the old families in Ukraine, among them the Tarnovskys and the Dunin-Borkovskys. The Imperial government closed the school in 1916.

7. Lists of both female and male students of the university, which included information on the social origin and financial aid, were kept by the police, TsDIA, f. 442, op. 831, 121–35 for the year 1881; see also ibid., op. 836, od. zb. 53, 3–10; and 379. Among the students expelled from the capitals was Apolinariia Andreevna Khorostianska, ibid., op. 835, od. zb. 121, 3.

8. According to Professor N.N. Shiller of Kiev University in a letter of October 1885 to the Governor-General of Kiev requesting permission to hold a fund-raising musical; TsDIA, f. 442, op. 835, spr. 173, 9–11.

9. *Ridnyi krai*, no. 5 (8 February 1908): 2. Ukrainians at the 1908 convention of the supporters of the All-Imperial Initiative Group for People's Universities raised a proposal on the right of all citizens to a higher education in their native language. One chairman (Syromiatnikov) resigned in protest; another (Dril) refused to put it to a vote; and the whole convention disintegrated; *Ridnyi krai*, no. 2 (1908): 4.

10. Chykalenko, unpublished memoirs, vol. 2, notes, unnumbered pages at the end. UVAN Archives, Chykalenko file.

11. Polonska-Vasylenko, *Vydatni zhinky*, 130; I have been unable to locate the Berlo memoirs. Kovalevska was not involved in the Ukrainian movement.

12. Not only was Ukrainian not recognized, but the Shevchenko Scientific Society had not been invited. *Istoriia Naukovoho Tovarystva im. Shevchenka: Z nahody 75-richchia ioho zasnuvannia 1873–1948* (New York, 1949), 29.

13. See Livytska, *Na hrani, passim* and the various works of Drahomanov for the most graphic examples.

14. See especially Lototsky, 2: 75, 101–16, and 192–6. Halyn, 66 and 88 paints a slightly darker picture.

15. *Entsyklopediia Ukrainoznavstva*, 2: 690; Stites, 166. According to *EU*, in 1897, 13.7 per cent of women aged nine to forty-nine were literate in Ukraine; 39.1 per cent of the men in that age bracket could read; while 20.5 per cent of men over fifty were considered literate, only 6.5 per cent of the females could read. Stites's statistics are for 1905, but there was no significant change in the eight years: 13.7 per cent of the women in the empire were literate, compared to 32.6 per cent of the men.

16. Strunina, "Pervye voskresnye shkoly v Kieve," *Kievskaia Starina*, book 5 (1898): 287–307. We must keep in mind, however, that in certain areas of Ukraine, notably in the west, the *zemstva* had not been established for fear of sedition. The Polish uprising of 1863 and the unrest which had preceded it certainly played a role.

17. See, for example, Iu.Ia. Iatsevich, *Nachalnoe narodnoe obrazovanie v Poltavskoi gubernii* (Poltava, 1894), 43. In 1867, a nobleman from the southern provinces of the empire complained of the shallow and boring life for both sexes, and as a solution suggested greater involvement in the elementary education of the peasants. He also noted that the reforms of the clergy, especially the fact that the parish would no longer be mandated to the family of the deceased priest, would force the daughters of the clergy to seek gainful employment. See the pseudonymous K-in, in *Zhenskii vestnik*, vol. 8 (1867): 49–54, in the column: "Vnutrennoe obozrenie: nechto o zhenshchinakh: zhenskie obshchestva v provintsii, voskresnye shkoly." A fictionalized account of Ukrainian clergy life is given in Ivan Nechui-Levytsky, *Cherez kladku*. A critical view is provided by Volodymyr N. Leontovych writing as Volodymyr Levenko, *Per Pedes Apostolorum: Obrazky z zhyttia dukhovenstva na Ukraini*.

18. The writer Nadiia Kybalchych provided sensitive portraits of the difficulties facing women teachers in the villages, including subtle harassment and open sexual abuse. She also derided young women who went into teaching out of sheer boredom. See "Zasudzheni," a short story in *Bahattia*, an almanac edited by Ivan Lypa in Odessa in 1905.

19. Nadiia Kybalchych wrote a series of short stories, drawn from real life, about guilt-stricken Russian women teaching in Ukrainian villages and attracted to the language of the children. A good example of the genre is her "Pavlo Podosenko," in *Svitlo* (May 1911). In the same issue of the magazine, M.M. Rubakin, known for his bibliophile and pedagogical activity, published an article as a reply to the question: "How can one create a scientific literature for the Ukrainian people?" Rubakin worked closely with Kh.D. Alchevska, the Sunday-school activist. On the language aspect and peasant unwillingness to send children to primary schools, see Iatsevich, 9, 21 and 95.

20. The report of Sadovsky on the Third Duma in *Ukrainskaia zhizn*, no. 5 (1912): 17–27. D.D. [perhaps the historian Dmytro Doroshenko] argued, at a student meeting in Kiev in 1906, that Ukrainians had been robbed of their own education and of their history, *Nova hromada* (October 1906): 121–9. See also Khrystia Alchevska, "Ridni dumy i diisnist," *Meta*, no. 7 (1 April 1908): 2–3; no. 8 (15 June 1908): 6–7; and no. 11/12 (15 August): 11.

21. There is a fuller discussion in M.I. Mukhyn, *Pedahohichni pohliady i osvitnia diialnist Kh. D. Alchevskoi*, (Kiev, 1979), esp. 59–60.

22. Ibid., 58. Mukhyn does not identify the society.

23. Khrystyna Danylivna Alchevska (1843–1920) grew up in Kursk in a family headed by an old-fashioned dictatorial father. Her mother died early, and the girl educated herself secretly, wept over the poetry of Shevchenko, wrote admiring letters to Herzen, and published her first poems in Bulgarin's conservative *Severnaia pchela*. These poems caught the eye of Oleksa Alchevsky, who married Khrystyna after a two-year courtship by correspondence, brought her to Kharkiv and, until his suicide over business affairs, provided her with a stable financial base, which enabled her to pursue educational work among the poor. When in 1863 it became clear that they could have Sunday Schools in Russian or none at all (Alchevska had been teaching in Ukrainian), she chose the schools. The best available study is that of M.I. Mukhyn; see also Maria Derkach, "Khrystyna Danylivna i Khrystia Oleksiivna Alchevski," *Zhinka*, 1 March 1938: 3–4 and Kh.D. Alchevskaia, *Peredumannoe i perezhitoe. Dnevniki, Pisma, vospominaniia* (Moscow, 1912).

24. *Exposition Universelle Internationale de 1889. Actes du Congrès International des Oeuvres et Institutions Féminines* (Paris, 1890), 301–7; *International Council of Women* (Berlin, 1904), 98, report of the Russian feminist Anna Filosofova.

25. One need only recall the role of Karazin in the establishment of the University of Kharkiv in 1805. For a discussion of schools in Kharkiv, see Lazarevich. Alchevska's school had an average staff of fifty women teachers, about 3,000 students and an operating capital of 12,000 rubles.

26. TsDIA, UkSSR (Kiev), f. 2052, op. 1, spr. 96, correspondence of Kh.D. Alchevska. The letter on the school to be named in honour of Shevchenko is dated 6 February 1908. The younger Alchevska, Khrystia, argued that the school should be named in hounour of Kvitka, one of Kharkiv's leading families and a name less likely to perturb the government. On a typical programme of courses in the school, see the letter of Khrystia Alchevska to Nikolai Fedorovich Sumtsov, a professor at Kharkiv University, TsDIA, f. 2052, op. 1, spr. 97.

27. For instance, by 1910 the young Khrystia Alchevska was directing to Sumtsov young people seeking advice on how best to counteract the removal of books from community libraries, TsDIA, UkSSR (Kiev), f. 2052, op. 1, spr. 103. Police

accounts of conditions in the Ukrainian provinces illustrate the involvement of Ukrainian activists in enlightenment activity.

3: Ukrainian Women in Political Life

1. A good brief introduction to the subject is I.L. Rudnytsky, "The Role of the Ukraine in Modern History," *Slavic Review* 22 (June 1963): 199–216.

2. Jurij Borys, "Political Parties in the Ukraine," in *The Ukraine, 1917–21: A Study in Revolution*, ed. T. Hunczak (Cambridge, Mass., 1977) 129–30. For an incisive discussion of the emergence of pro-independence ideology see Ivan L. Rudnytsky, "The Fourth Universal and Its Ideological Antecedents," ibid., 186–219.

3. In response to a letter of Mykhailo Pavlyk, a Galician activist who tried to persuade the ailing writer to give up the risks involved in politics and save her energies for writing. In Lesia Ukrainka, *Korespondentsiia*, 10: 145.

4. The actual reason was more sordid. Apparently, Volodymyr Antonovych's second wife did not fit into the group, and to avoid unpleasantness the *hromada* limited itself to men; Chykalenko, *Spomyny* (New York, 1955), 93. A wealth of information can be found in the unpublished memoirs of Ievhen Chykalenko in the UVAN archives, "Spohady, Shchodennyk, Lystuvannia," divided into the periods 1861–81, 1882–5 and a diary covering events up to 1919.

5. Drahomanov, *Lystuvannia Kyivskoi staroi hromady z Drahomanovym 1870–1895*, (Warsaw, 1937), 1: 189.

6. Recent Soviet scholars, among them O.R. Mazurkevych and T.M. Riznychenko, have attributed the proclamation to Alchevska. For a fuller discussion, see M.I. Mukhyn, *Pedahohichni pohliady i prosvitnia diialnist Kh. D. Alchevskoi.*

7. Mirna, in *Zhinka*, 1 April 1937, 2, was impressed that "the women did not produce traitors. There were no Tikhomirovs, no Goldenbergs, no Azef." Tikhomirov, a leader of the terrorist wing of the populists, became a conservative in 1886; Goldenberg, who plotted to assassinate Alexander II, became a police agent; Azef was a notorious double agent.

8. Kovalevsky remained under surveillance and was hounded out of various jobs. The police attended his funeral and noted who was there. TsGIA, USSR (Moscow), f. 102, ed. 1536, D 1883. Nadiia S. Smirnytska (1852–89), a populist from Kiev, was among those who took poison with Mariia Vinogradova.

   Among the most active populists in Ukraine were Olha Rozumovska Zhelnovska, who belonged to a populist circle in Odessa in the 1870s; Varvara Iliashenko (1855–?) and Ahata Ishchenko (1858–?), peasants from Poltava, joined the revolutionary activities of their employers. Sofiia Prysetska Bohomolets (1856–92) died after an unsuccessful attempt at escape from prison.

   The Ukrainian intelligentsia continued to favour the populists. The Social Revolutionary Party, the last populist incarnation, which was founded in 1903, eventually split into national factions. Ukrainian was used regularly in propaganda materials of the Social Revolutionaries. For instance, in 1908, in a raid on Olha D. Kseshynska, who had close contacts with the peasants in the Chernihiv area, of the 23 confiscated brochures, eleven were in Ukrainian. TsDIA, UkSSR (Kiev), f. 274, op. 4, od. zb. 301, 40.

9. *Nasha meta*, 7 November 1919, 4–5.

10. M. Drahomanov, *Lysty do Ivana Franka* (Lviv, 1908), 107–8, 115, and 434–5.

11. To Ohonovsky, in TsDIA, UkSSR (Lviv), Kolektsiia NTSh, f. 390, op. 1, 74.

12. The decision to draft such a petition was taken on 19 December 1904 at the celebration honouring the novelist Ivan Nechui-Levytsky. TsGIA, USSR (Moscow), D.P. VIII, no. 2, ch. 21, 63–4.

13. Sofiia Rusova, *Nashi vyznachni zhinky* (Kolomyia, 1934), 40.

14. *Ridnyi krai*, no. 4 (1912): 4.

15. Ibid., no. 25 (1909): 9–12; no. 15 (1912): 6.

16. Editorial in *Ridnyi krai*, no. 25 (1909): 2.

17. *Voiuiuchoho ukrainstva*, was the phrase used in *Literaturno-naukovyi vistnyk*, no. 5 (1931): 452, as quoted in Rusova, *Nashi vyznachni zhinky*, 41.

18. Livytska, *Na hrani dvokh epokh*, is very critical of Mikhnovsky.

19. Report of the police, in TsGIA, USSR (Moscow), f. 102, O.O. Delo Departmenta Politsii, no. 438, 1899, 4.

20. Rusov, "Kak ia stal chlenom Gromady," *Ukrainskaia zhizn*, no. 10 (1913): 40–9.

21. TsGIA, USSR (Moscow) f. 102, No. 438, 2.

22. There is a brief discussion by Sadovsky in *Ukrainskaia zhizn*, no. 7–8 (1912): 28.

23. Serhii Efremov, "Na sviati Kotliarevskoho (zhadka samovydtsia)" in *Pryvit Ivanovy Frankovy v soroklitie ioho pysmenskoi pratsi 1874–1914* (Lviv, 1916), 169–76, states that it was not Andriievska who spoke first but the writer Kotsiubynsky, since Andriievska did not trust herself. Efremov that year criticized Kobylianska and Lesia Ukrainka, charging them with modernism and lack of community involvement. It seems that his memory might have been coloured by sexism.

24. On Kseshynska, see TsDIA, UkSSR (Kiev), f. 274, op. 4, od. zb. 301, 40; the date is 1908. On Lyss and Cherkesova, the date is 1903; materials in Tsentralnyi gosudarstvenni arkhiv oktiabrskoi revoliutsii, Moscow, f. 102, op. 141, ed. khr. D 7852, 28–9 and 32.

    A police circular dated 14 November 1910, referring especially to material published in Galicia and warning about the possibility of such propaganda emerging throughout the empire, TsDIA, UkSSR (Kiev), f. 385, op. 2, od. zb. 1, part I, Zhandarmskoe Upravlenie Odessy, 13 January 1902 to 24 November 1916. See esp. 146–50. Virtually all the local police reports mention literature in Ukrainian; for instance, f. 274, op. 1, od. zb. 35, no. 507; f. 1335, op. 1, od. zb. 3 1535, esp. 46; f. 274, op. 1, od. zb. 3624, 161; 301, op. 1, spr. 3206, 25–6.

25. "Khaos, spohady, 1901–1905," 1–139.

26. *Na hrani dvokh epokh*, 175; see also Boshyk, 432.

27. For example, *Kotsiubynsky iak hromadskyi diiach* (Kiev, 1986), 15, using as evidence Okhrana information found in TsDIA, UkSSR (Kiev), f. 274, no. 1215, 54. See also TsDIA, UkSSR (Kiev), f. 274, op. 4, od. zb. 301 and TsGIA, USSR (Moscow), f. 102, D.P. VII, no. 8468 (25 August 1906–29 January 1913: po nabliudeniiu za formalnym doznaniem o deiatelnosti Kievskoi revoliutsionnoi organizatsii Spilka).

28. A police report on Spilka, in TsGIA, USSR (Moscow), f. 102, D.P. VII No. 8468, 121.

29. TsGIA Moscow, f. 102, D.P. VII No. 8468, 3. The police, as well as Lenin, used the latinized form Galitsiia when referring to Galicia (Halychyna). Lenin signed the party programme of Mykhailo Levytsky to the Second Comintern Congress,

29 July 1920; "Privet galitsiiskim komunistam.... V. Ulianov," quoted with pride in the official Soviet publications, including a picture book on the area of Lviv. See *Lvivshchyna* (Kiev, 1974), 8.

30. Osyp Hermaize, "Do biohrafii B.D. Hrinchenka," *Zhyttia i revoliutsiia*, no. 4 (1926): 78–80. The paper was published by Ie.Kh. Chykalenko and Volodymyr N. Leontovych. V.F. Durdukovsky, Orest I. Levytsky, N.V. Lysenko, M.I. Pavlovsky and S.A. Iefremov were among the other collaborators.

31. Later, the police followed the activities of women and Ukrainians. For example, in Katerynoslav "the SD...together with organized groups of women plan to set aside 10 February as the day of the women workers, demanding equality, participation in the political process and an improvement in the working conditions." From a police report of 30 January 1913, TsDIA, UkSSR f. 1597, op. 1, od. zb. 384, 5. The women's issue was used to politicize the population. In one proclamation of the Kievan SD, dated 23 February 1914, the backwardness of the women workers ingrained in them is considered to be the major obstacle facing women; in TsDIA, UkSSR (Kiev), f. 274, op. 43 B, No. 339, 2 and 10.

32. The daily life of Ukrainian activists had its ups and downs. In early February 1907, a period of reaction, the poet Oleksander Oles wrote a letter to Alchevska in which he despaired of his own writing and of the fate of Ukraine. Rather than argue with him, she sent him a recent article of M.F. Sumtsov in *Iuzhnyi krai* on Ukrainian literary developments as proof that Oles's pessimism was unfounded; TsDIA, UkSSR (Kiev), f. 2052, op. 1, od. zb. 93.

33. Pchilka in *Ridnyi krai*, no 25 (1911): 1–2.

34. For example, in Kharkiv in 1911, TsGIA, USSR (Moscow), f. 102, 00 242 20 h 88 B/1912, 227, and TsGAOR, f. 102, op. 141, ed.khr. D 7852 (1903), 41.

35. TsGIA, USSR (Moscow), f. 102, 5 46/ 1915, 2–4.

36. Among the pertinent articles of Efimenko on these matters are "Natsionalnost po g. V. Solovevu," *Nedelia*, no. 36 (1888); "Po povodu ukrainofilstva," *Nedelia*, no. 25 (1881); "Ukrainskie elementy v tvorchestve Gogolia," *Vestnik Evropy*, (July 1902); "Maloruskii iazyk v narodnoi shkole," *Slovo*, no. 1 (1881).

37. *Zasiv*, 9 December 1911, 619; TsGIA, USSR (Moscow), f. 102, O.O. 59–88 B 1911, 143–4.

38. Even before the outbreak of hostilities, the Russian government strengthened its vigilance against Ukrainians by patrolling the borders more closely and keeping the merchants who did business with the Austrians under surveillance. For examples of typical circulars see TsDIA, UkSSR (Kiev), f. 275, po. 1, od. zb. 3B, No. 2243, 180–2. Monitoring of Ukrainian newspapers was stepped up; for instance, a secret directive dated 28 January 1914 specifically called attention to the need to screen all Ukrainian newspapers carefully for possible sedition, ibid., f. 385, op. 1, od. zb. 3B, 208.

39. Common theft grew, both in the villages and in the cities. To cite a few random examples from Ukrainian territories: a letter of M.A. Ienia in Chernihiv to N.A. Belozerska, dated 22 July 1907, noted that the peasants refused to talk to strangers and had begun locking their doors, TsGALI, Moscow, f. 58, op. 1, ed. khr. 34, 1–2. Whole areas were terrorized by robber bands; that Serhii N. Baha was one of the better known leaders, TsGIA, USSR (Moscow), f. 102 0.0. 242 20 h 88 1B, 1912, 85, 133, 157. Peasants were willing to operate as hired killers, ibid., 0.0. 20 88 B, 1911, 128–9. In Kharkiv, students were helping peasants organize for armed demonstrations. The police singled out Maistrenko and Reznichenko, TsGIA,

USSR (Moscow), f. 102, 0.0. 20 88 B, 1911, 156–9 (no first names given).

40. Zinaida Mirna, in *Zhinka* (1 May 1937): 6.

4: Women's Organizations in Ukraine

1. According to Mirna, in *Zhinka* (15 March 1937): 2–3, who based her account on the memoirs of Mariia Berenshtam-Kistiakovska, which I have not been able to locate. Also TsDIA, f. 442, od. zb. 53, 3–10.

2. She was Natalia Kyrylivna Shcherban; Lototsky, 2: 93; among the women active in the circle were Olha Kosach, Lesia Ukrainka's sister; Olena Koroleva, related to the writer; and Vira (Popova) Matushevska, who would become active in the Ukrainian movement.

3. See, for example, TsGIA, USSR (Moscow), f. 102, O.O. 20–88 B 1911, 155; ibid., O.O. 59–88 B 1911, 132 and TsDIA, f. 1597, 1–19.

4. Hanna Radych and Liudmyla Strutynska-Sadovska were elected in 1915 to the Holovna Studentska Rada in St. Petersburg: Lototsky, 2: 116.

5. Among its activists in the 1890s were women from the Dondukov-Korsakovsky, Florinsky, Kotliarevsky, and Gagarin families. For a full discussion, see Nikolai Kolmakov, *Ocherk deiatelnosti Kievskogo slovianskogo blagotvoritelnogo obshchestva* (Kiev, 1894).

6. TsDIA, f. 442, op. 636, od. zb. 647, ch. VII, 524–30. The initiative came from Countess Adelaide K. Plater, who was also active in the Society of Mutual Aid for Working Women. She was supported by Sofiia F. Rutkovska, Nadezda Il. Dovnar-Zapolska, Lidiia Zagorskaia and Evgeniia K. Havryk. See also op. 625, spr. 273, 1–9. The Kiev police were more suspicious than the police in Russia proper. For example, Tsvetkovska, whose husband was not cleared by the Kiev police for work in the Halahan school despite loyal and efficient service in St. Petersburg and a good police report, continued to follow the work of the society.

7. The society is mentioned by Mirna in her article in *Zhinka*, 15 March 1937, 2–3. Information is also found in TsDIA, UkSSR (Kiev), f. 442, op. 837, od. zb. 3, 14 and ibid., op. 643, spr. 48. Its Russian name, under which it was registered, was *Obshchestvo dnevnykh priiutov dlia detei rabochego klassa v Kieve.*

8. TsDIA, UkSSR (Kiev), f. 442, op. 659, spr. 204, 1–10.

9. *Obshchestvo Vzaimnogo vspomozheniia trudiashchikhsia zhenshchin*; TsGIA, USSR (Moscow), f. 516, ed. khr. 5, 33; *Soiuz Zhenshchin*, no. 3 (October 1907): 14, and interview with Liubov Drazhevska, 18 September 1980 in New York. Her mother had been active in the Association.

10. Mariia Tkachenko Livytska, *Na hrani dvokh epokh*, 115–18. Hanna Chykalenko Keller (daughter of Ievhen Chykalenko), "Kyivska zhinocha hromada v pershykh rokakh XX stolittia," *Zhinka*, 15 February 1939, 2–3.

11. TsGIA, USSR (Moscow), f. 102, O.O. 9–34 B 1908, 86–7, 178; also ibid., O.O. 59–88 B 1911, 95. Quotation from *Soiuz Zhenshchin*, no. 5–6 (1908): 27.

12. *Zhenskoe delo*, 15 September 1916.

13. Information on the Branch in *Ves Iugo-zapadnyi krai* (Kiev, 1913), 284; annual reports of the branch were published as separate booklets; the letter from the police in TsDIA, UkSSR (Kiev), f. 442, op. 643, spr. 48, 149. Rozaliia Isakovna

Margolin was the mother of Arnold, the lawyer who became an active supporter of the Ukrainian cause after he noted the common sense of the Ukrainians in the trial of Mendel Beilis. Beilis, a Kiev Jew, was acquitted in the celebrated trial of a charge of ritual murder of a Christian. Information on the family corroborated by Arnold's daughter, Liubov Margolena Hansen, in Washington in October 1982.

14. *Otchet za 1912 god*, 15, in TsDIA, f. 442, op. 643, spr. 48. In addition to Shatz and Margolina, Elizaveta M. Sholtz and Olga Rabinovich were active in the board.

15. Letter of 23 November 1905 to her sister and brother-in-law, in *Khronolohiia*, 761.

16. The unpublished manuscript "Khaos: spohady, 1901–1905," 82, in the Lesia Ukrainka Museum.

17. A brief introduction to the Prosvita movement is available in Volodymyr Doroshenko, *Prosvita: ii zasnuvannia i pratsia* (Prosvita: its establishment and activities) (Philadelphia: Moloda Prosvita, 1959). Doroshenko suggests that the first Prosvita was established in Katerynoslav on 8 October 1905. The police records, which otherwise reflect Doroshenko's story, seem to point to an earlier date. Doroshenko was a participant in some of the events about which he writes. See also Stepan Persky, *Populiarna istoriia tovarystva Prosvita* (Lviv, 1932).

18. Henryk A. Falkenbork, in the all-Russian Society for People's Universities, developed this line of reasoning, TsGIA, USSR (Moscow), f. 102, D.O. op. 236(II), ed. khr. 194, No. 2, 1906, 25.

19. TsGIA, USSR (Moscow), f. 102, D.O. op. 236/II, ed. khr. 194, ch. 2, 1906, 12.

20. Ibid., f. 102, op. 13, ed. khr. 163 m 15 L 5/1912, 1–4.

21. The Novocherkasy Polytechnic students organized a clandestine affiliate of Prosvita in 1912, TsGIA, USSR (Moscow), f. 102, op. 13, ed. khr. 163 m 15 L 5/1912. Professor Ioannikii A. Malinovsky of Tomsk University, with the active support of Hryhorii N. Sydorenko and other senior railroad engineers, organized a Prosvita, ibid., f. 102, op. 9, ed. 331, 1908, 1.

The possible connection with the Galician Prosvita perturbed the police. There were those who seriously believed that the Eastern and Western Ukrainians might be preparing for a joint revolution. When a Prosvita congress was held in Lviv in 1909, the police shadowed the young student Viktor Prykhodko, who had travelled from Kamianets to Lviv, ibid., f. 102, op. 10, ed. khr. 216/1909. There were also student arrests in Poltava in conjunction with this; Solovey, *Rozhrom Poltavy, passim.*

22. The police also noted that the Society for the Propagation of Intermediate Education in Kiev had a Ukrainian, Naumenko, on its board of directors, TsGIA, USSR (Moscow), f. 102, D.O. op. 236/II, ed. khr. 194, No. 2, 1906, 15–18. Nor did they fail to remark that the proclivity of Ukrainians to join the societies for the spread of education made those societies suspect.

23. The petition is on permanent exhibit in the Lesia Ukrainka Museum, Kiev.

24. Ibid., f. 102, D.O. op. 236/II, ed. khr. 194, ch. H 1906, 32–4, file dated 1906–9.

25. The police infiltrated the successor Prosvita, according to an article in *Zasiv*, no. 2 (11 March 1911): 19. Information on the Chernihiv Prosvita in *Kotsiubynsky iak hromadskyi diiach*, 21–114, largely on the basis of the Chernihiv Oblast Archives, f. 336, No. 918, as well as materials in TsGIA, USSR (Moscow), f. 102, DO 37 h 59, 1908.

26. *Nova hromada*, no. 12 (December 1906): 151.

27. *Zasiv*, no. 39, 25 November 1911, 605.

28. TsDIA, UkSSR (Kiev), f. 274, op. 4, od. zb. 301, 493 and ff., dated 18 July 1911.

29. *Ridnyi krai*, no. 1 (1908): 15–16; *Zasiv*, 16 August 1911, 443, 445–6.

30. *Ridnyi krai*, no. 4 (1908): 13.

31. Olena Pchilka, "Zhinochyi zizd," *Ridnyi krai*, no. 39 (1908): 2.

32. It was chaired by Professor Vladimir Ia. Zhelezov, while Ivan A. Novikov, the secretary of the Kiev Agrarian Union, was the secretary. The meeting demanded freedom of the press and of assembly, abolition of martial law, curtailment of the powers of the police, termination of the war with Japan, and amnesty for political prisoners. TsGIA, USSR (Moscow), f. 102, ed. khr. 99–47, 1905, 1–2.

33. Ibid., f. 516, ed. khr. 12, 11–17; *Soiuz zhenshchin*, (October 1907): 14; TsGIA, USSR (Moscow), f. 102, O.O. 59–88 B 1911, 140 and O.O. 242 H 20 88 B 1912, 161–2. Among the women active in the the group was Liudmila Gabel, whose father was an émigré from Austria, ibid., O.O. 59–88 B 1911, 141.

34. Ibid., f. 516, ed. khr. 8; *Soiuz zhenshchin*, February 1908; ibid., f. 512, ed. khr. 99–47, 1905, 30. They published some of their minutes and were thinking in November 1905 of publishing a collection of historical documents on the women's movement in Russia; ibid., f. 516, ed. khr. 14, 201–2.

35. Ibid., f. 516, ed. khr. 28, 28, for both quotations.

36. Ibid., f. 516, ed. khr. 12, 2.

37. Ibid., f. 516, ed. khr. 5, 37 for the quotation. Chekhova, the president of the Union, received many letters from non-Russian women demanding national autonomy.

38. Ibid., f. 516, ed. khr. 5, p 71. Shakhmatova complained that the Constitutional Democratic Party would give the vote "to all the Samoeds, Chukhchi, Tungus and Iakuts, but deny it to women." Ibid., ed. khr. 1, 50.

39. The wife of the governor of Kamianets-Podilskyi, Dunin-Borkovska, organized a society that was loosely affiliated with the Union, *Soiuz zhenshchin*, no. 3 (October 1907): 14; also TsGIA, USSR (Moscow), f. 516, ed. khr. 7.

40. Quoted in a news item on the women in *Nova hromada: Literaturno-naukovyi misiachnyk*, no. 1 (1906): 131–2; see also TsGIA, USSR (Moscow), f. 516, ed. khr. 5, 66.

41. Complete English translations of the four universals are available in Hunczak, ed., *The Ukraine, 1917–1921*, 382–95.

42. The few persons writing informative sketches on the history of the Ukrainian women's movements had limited access even to published sources. Hence, Pchilka is sometimes credited with having established a central Ukrainian women's organization which "issued a manifesto demanding autonomy for Ukraine." Iryna Pavlykovska, *Na hromadskyi shliakh: Z nahody 70-littia ukrainskoho zhinochoho rukhu* (Philadelphia, 1956), 72.

43. See especially the discussion in *Ridnyi krai*, no. 8 (1909): 8–9; and no. 9 (1909): 12–13.

44. Ibid., 13.

45. "Do ukrainskoho zhinotstva," ibid., no. 9, (1908): 1–2.

46. Ibid., no. 39 (1908): 2.

47. Ibid., no. 43 (1909): 11; report of the Congress in *Soiuz zhenshchin*, no. 12 (December 1908): 12. I have been unable to locate Pchilka's paper. A likely repository is the Pchilka papers at the Institute of Literature, UkSSR Academy of Sciences in Kiev.

48. TsGIA, USSR (Moscow), f. 516, ed. khr. 5, 37; see also *Lesia Ukrainka, Khronolohiia*, especially 767.
49. Letter of the younger Khrystia Alchevska to Sumtsov, sometime in 1910, in TsDIA, UkSSR (Kiev), f. 2052, op. 1, spr. 103. In the native village of Taras Shevchenko in a library named in his honour there were few Ukrainian books, but the anti-Ukrainian diatribes of the reactionary Prince Meshchersky published in Kiev were on standing order. See the review article "Otchet o deiatelnost Kievskogo obshchestva gramotnosti," *Nova hromada* (March 1906): 140.
50. There is a particularly strong article on the subject in *Ridnyi krai*, no. 25 (1909): 9–12.
51. Report in *Ridnyi krai*, no. 2 (1908): 4; see also the editorial "Spodivani narodni universytety ukrainski," ibid., no. 5 (1908): 2.
52. The Kiev City administration had among its officers Vera V. Ivanova, in the army division; Lidiia S. Lisovska in the insurance branch; Ludmila Al. Skorniakova and Vera D. Mikulina in health. Mariia I. Ilinska served as an accountant in the Orphans' Court; *Ves Iugo-Zapadnyi kray*, (1913), 234.
53. Liudmyla Starytska Cherniakhivska and Sofiia Rusova were on the Committee for the Collection of Funds for the Memorial of Taras Shevchenko. Ibid., 231–2.
54. *Zasiv*, 4 March 1911, 5.

5: Priests, Wives and Daughters

1. Detailed information on economic and community relations between the parsonage and the peasants, based on a study of two Galician districts with a preponderantly Ukrainian village population, is to be found in Józef Półćwiartek, *Z badań nad rolą gospodarczo-społeczną plebanii na wsi pańszczyźnianej ziemi przemyskiej i sanockiej w XVI–XIX wieku* (Rzeszów, 1974).
2. Nykolai Laszkevych and Zeno [sic] M. Malkovych, Lviv, 5 December 1861 to the Przemyśl diocesan office; WAP, AGKB, Syg. 9497.
3. There is only one serious work of fiction, by an Eastern Ukrainian writer, namely, Hnat Khotkevych's *Kaminna dusha*, which imputes infidelity to a Uniate priest's wife and impotence to the priest because of a mother-fixation.
4. In the lands which had accepted the Union but which fell, upon the partitions of Poland, to the Russian Empire, and in which Russia forcibly introduced Orthodoxy, the women more readily joined secret religious societies for the preservation of Catholicism. See material on the area around Kholm, in AGAD, Warsaw, especially dealing with the Societies of Devotion to the Heart of Jesus, to which some Ukrainian women belonged.
5. WAP, AGKB, Syg. 4608, 546–9; the initial salary of the priest was about 200 złoty. There were between 300 and 900 parishioners in the villages to which he moved.
6. In the early versions of the statutes for the institutes, the founders counted on continuing donations for the widows from the landlords (*didychi, patrony i koliatory*). See statute of the Institute of Widows and Orphans, article 6 (1843). A fund for Widows and Orphans was created in Lviv in 1823, and a series of drafts of the organization's statutes (in German, Latin and Ukrainian) was discussed and

studied between that time and 1843, when the final draft was approved. For a discussion of the initial difficulties, see the introduction to the published brochure of the Lviv Statute of 10 January 1884 in WAP, AGKB, Syg. 9339, 295–311. The unpublished working drafts of the statutes, of the various dioceses, in the same file, demonstrate the gradual initiation of the clergy into public activity. Later, when new dioceses were established in Hungarian territories of the empire, the clergy showed the same reluctance. See the letters of the Reverend Varfolomei Shaich of Priashiv to the Przemyśl diocese, WAP, AGKB, Syg. 9339, 330–6.

7. Brochure in WAP, AGKB, Syg. 9339, 1. Similar plea in an earlier text in WAP, AGKB, Syg. 9338, pages unnumbered.

8. WAP, AGKB, Syg. 9339, 145–52.

9. Bishop Lev Chekhovych, Dr. Teofil Khaluzhansky, Mieczysław Ripperschild and Rev. Dr. Teofil Kormosh were members of the Committee.

   The institutes remained under the direct patronage of the bishop, and were administered by priests elected for that purpose by the general meeting, which was held annually and lasted two days. The general membership was intimately involved in reimbursement of funds, investments and all revisions of statutes and by-laws. The discussions at the meetings provided a forum for innovative and ambitious clerics. WAP, AGKB, Syg. 4793, 195–7 and ibid., Syg. 9339, 160–2. Rev. Vasyl Sologub, for instance, bitterly criticized the Przemyśl institute for poor fiscal management, for failing to encourage trade and small business among Ukrainians and for not encouraging more Ukrainian young people to study. He argued that the priest should be the real modernizer in the village, WAP, AGKB, Syg. 9338, 336.

10. In WAP, Syg. 9339, Lviv Statute, edition of 1884, paragraphs 29 and 38. A simi-lar resolution was proposed by the otherwise extremely conservative Reverend Alexander Zubrytsky in Przemyśl, Syg. 3993, 436; it was incorporated into the 1894 Przemyśl Statute, ibid., 465.

11. Józef Kobylański, *Polacy i Rusini. Słowo z okazii wyborów* (Lviv, 1883), 3.

12. Persky, *Populiarna Istoriia tovarystva Prosvita*, 140. See also *Pershyi vinok* (Lviv, 1887), 95 and 100. A theatre group functioning between 1873 and 1877 was headed by Teofiliia Romanovych. Osterman later helped establish the women's organization in Stanyslaviv.

13. The conservatives set up a rival society, named in honour of Mykhailo Kachkovsky, a prominent Ukrainian judge. Despite the aid they received from the Russians and Austrians, those societies were not popular.

14. "Z lystiv Iustyny V*," *Zoria*, no. 1880, 166; see also Ol-ch [sic], "Z istorii rukhu ukrainskoho zhinotsva v Halychyni," *Meta*, no. 1 (1 March 1908): 6. I have not been able to establish the identity of the authors.

15. The quotation is taken from a review of a brochure published in 1904 marking the silver anniversary of the Obshchestvo Ruskykh Dam in "Z rukhu halytskykh zhinok," *Meta*, no. 2 (15 March 1908): 4–5. The date of the founding of the society is given as 14 December 1878 in a note prepared in the 1920s requesting the Polish government's permission to renew the activities of the society, Oblasnyi DIA, Lviv, f. 300, spr. 5, 4. See also "Z lystiv Iustyny V*," *Zoria*, no. 14/15 (1880): 206; as well as Kobrynska's article in *Pershyi vinok* (Lviv 1887), 95. Severyna Kabarovska, in a series of articles on the beginnings of the Ukrainian women's movement in Galicia, written in 1919 and published in *Nasha meta*, dated the founding of the Society to 1876. She probably had in mind the

informal sisterhood. Also see "Zahalni sbory [sic] ruskykh dam," *Dilo*, 10 (20) December 1880: 2.

16. The young writer Konstantyna Malytska became a recipient of the bounty of the ladies, as did a number of other young women who became teachers and were subsequently very active in the women's movement. Among these were Ivanna Vytkovytska, Anna Levytska, Olena Zhelykhovska, Ievfrozyna Velychko and others. In 1888 the leadership of the society reflected its conservative leanings. It was chaired by Iustyna Nychai, the secretary was Pavlyna Leontovych and on its executive board were Falyna Syvuliak, Anna Vintsykovska, Ievheniia Lepka, Sofiia Makar, Klavdiia Aleksevych, Anna Heisyk, Teofiliia Rudzynska, Savyna Ianovska and Ievhenia Paievetska. Most of the women were wives, or otherwise related to conservative Ukrainian clerics. *Dilo* 13 (25) December (1888).

17. "Obshchestvo ruskykh dam. Nepoklykani pokrovyteli. Desorganizatsiia," *Pravda* 12 (1878): 781–5; quotation from 781.

18. *Pershyi vinok*, 62; the struggle for the Society is reflected in the bibliographic entry in Ivan S. Levytsky, *Halytsko-ruskaia bybliohrafiia* (Lviv, 1888), 2: 33, no. 2047, which notes the publication in 1879 of the *Statut Zhinochoho patriotychnoho t-va Halychyny*.

19. *Zoria*, no. 14/15, 207, by Iustyna V*.

6: *Women's Education and Society's Aspirations*

1. Jan Hulewicz, *Sprawa wyzszego wykształcenia kobiet w Polsce w wieku XIX* (Cracow, 1939), 112. This is the most exhaustive study of Polish education for women; Hulewicz does not discuss Ukrainians. Probably the fullest first-hand accounts of education for Ukrainian girls can be found in the journal *Uchytel* (Teacher), published in Lviv from 1869 to 1874. Especially interesting are a series of articles on the upbringing and education of women which appeared between July and October 1870.

2. The school system perpetuated social inequality. Grammar schools were either the three-year "trivial" dead-end schools or the four-year ones which prepared pupils for trade, commercial or academic high schools. See the comments on the second-rate status of Ukrainian schools in a speech by Teofil Okunevsky to the Austrian parliament on 4 March 1899, published by the Lviv Stavropygian Society under the title *Iak dbaie Ts. K. Rada Shkolna kraeva o rusku narodnu shkolu*; see also Bogusława Czajecka, "Przygotowanie kobiet do pracy zawodowej na tle ruchu feministycznego w Galicji" (Ph.D. dissertation, Jagiellonian University, 1977), 110–13 and 471–80; Zygmunt Dulczewski, *Walka o szkole na wsi galicyjskiej w świetle stenogramów Sejmu krajowego 1861–1914* (Warsaw, n.d.).

3. Text in *Dilo*, 3 (15) (1887): 1.

4. Ukrainian priests, who were required by law to teach religion in the schools, ran into particularly bitter conflict with Polish teachers, who were not only nationalists but also at times anti-religious. Two examples, from May and August 1910, will suffice. Maria Fedurko, a teacher at the village school in Hladyshevo, threw the holy pictures that a visiting Ukrainian bishop had given the children

into the fire, commenting on how nicely the Ukrainian pictures burned. The school board exonerated the teacher of the serious charge of blasphemy, and transferred her to a Polish-speaking village. In another Ukrainian village, another Polish teachers, Maria Pliczek, disparaged Catholicism in general, but she was only transferred to a different village. Ukrainian teachers, however, often lost their jobs for less open criticism of religion. Czajecka, 481: "it was no secret that Polish teacher, Maria Pliczek, disparaged Catholicism in general, but she was only transferred to a different village. Ukrainian teachers, however, often lost (Warsaw, 1958), 1: 298.

5. Trembitska, 6–7; Kysilevska, "Uryvky zi spomyniv——roky 1878–1888," *Zhinochyi svit* (Toronto), (May 1976): 15–16; Czajecka, 121–9, and Uliana Kravchenko, *Spohady uchytelky* (Kolomyia, 1936).

6. Deputy Sodomora, in 1910, specifically argued that the trade school for women established at Petrychy had a low attendance because the women could not understand Polish.

7. Czechs, like Ukrainians, had for the most part lost their upper class, either in the bloodbath which followed the battle of the White Mountain in 1620, or in the cultural Germanization that accompanied the growth of Austrian nobility. The Poles, who lost their political independence only in 1795 and kept their nobility, did not stress the importance of folk art in the same fashion as Ukrainians and Czechs.

8. Czajecka, 235.

9. She went to Freudethal in Eastern Silesia during the winter of 1899–1900; letters from the period in TsDIA, UkSSR (Lviv), f. 663, op. 1, spr. 248.

10. For example, *Dilo*, 16 July 1903, 1, ran an article entitled "How does one set up peasant dormitories?" The unpublished memoirs of Trembitska are located in the uncatalogued archives of *Nashe zhyttia* in New York.

11. The dormitories are discussed more fully in an appendix to this chapter. For information on the allocation of funds of the Ladies Society, see *Dilo*, passim, 1888. Also see *Halychanyn*, 17 (13) November 1906, for a call to collect funds for a dormitory for conservatives.

12. AAN, Rada Główna Opiekuńcza, Syg. 537, Liga Kobiet; *Dilo*, 9 (21) April 1892, 2, reported that the Reverend O. Kobrynsky called for the creation of a civic committee to speed up the building of the Bilous dormitory. Bilous, the editor of *Ruska rada*, carried on a lengthy correspondence with František Rehoř, in *Památník národního písemnictví*, Rehoř papers, Syg. 1-B/37 30 M 60.

13. *Dilo*, 26 July (7 August) 1890, 1, stated that priests and teachers should encourage peasant boys to think in terms of a teaching career.

14. Unpublished memoirs of Kravchenko in Kravchenko Archives.

15. Kravchenko, unpublished memoirs on the Seminar; Katria (Banach) Hrynevych, "Spomyny," in *Almanakh ukrainskoho studentskoho zhyttia v Krakovi* (n.p., 1931), 20. The Galician School Board, in the person of Count Los, feared in 1899 that once new seminaries for women were established, women teachers would outnumber men (Czajecka, 317). The feminization occurred in the inter-war years. The Polish Pedagogical Congress in Lviv in November 1909 would not let the women participate in the proceedings, although it supported the demands placed through the Związek Równouprawniena Kobiet; Czajecka, 529. On the position of the teachers, see Dulczewski, 146–7.

16. The Society was reorganized as Ridna Shkola in 1912; Lev Iasinchuk, *50 lit*

Ridnoi Shkoly, 1881–1931 (Lviv, 1931).

17. Najdus, 2: 415; in September 1905 the Society had 695 members. Within a year its membership had grown to 1,273. There is no information on the division between the sexes. In July 1909, for instance, the Society requested the Przemyśl diocese to forward 800 questionnaires about schools in the whole district, WAP, AGKB, Syg. 5134, under 21 July 1909.

18. *Sprawozdanie dyrekcji Seminaryum Nauczycielskiego Zenskiego w Przemyślu z 1897 r.*, 45.

19. When she resigned, Katria Hrynevych became the editor: women and children were the natural combination. The fullest discussion is in Iasinchuk, although his presentation slights the role of women.

20. Hulewicz, 248; "Petycja kobiet do Sejmu," *Przedświt* (Lviv), no. 10 (1893).

21. Ukrainians wanted a Ukrainian seminary in Kolomyia; they received finally, a bilingual seminary in Berezhany; see Czajecka, 319, 320, 479. It was not until 1891 that the Lviv seminary became fully bilingual. Bohachevsky's speech on education in *Dilo*, 13 (26) September, 1902.

22. *Zhinocha dolia*, 1 April 1926, 6.

23. Czajecka, esp. 471; one Ukrainian priest even opposed rudimentary education for peasant women because it would entail unnecessary interference in the sacred family life of the peasants.

24. The Polish Lviv Gymnasium for girls (Słowacki) was founded in 1902 by the Lviv University faculty for their daughters. It had a high academic level and, according to the unpublished memoirs of Sheparovych, "was composed 90 per cent of gifted and ambitious daughters of Lviv's Jewish elite who competed among themselves." In the first year it had five Ukrainian students: Milena Rudnytska, Klymentyna Kulchytska, Stefa Korytovska (Chorpita), Mariia Zaiachkivska (Tomashevska) and Nataliia Turkevych. Sofiia Halechko, who in 1915 would join the Ukrainian military ranks, was also a student in that class, but did not openly admit to being Ukrainian at that time.

25. From *XXVII Sprawozdanie dyrekcyi c.k. Gimnazijum w Jarosławiu, 1911*, Ministry regulations dated 27 February 1910, L. 503555 and 1 V. 1910, L. 11999.

26. *Zjednoczenie, pismo poświęcone idei zespolenia Zydów z narodem polskim*, no. 2–3 (1905): 50; Najdus, 188; Pachucka, 89–93; Walewska, 68.

27. *Vydavnytstvo Moloda Ukraina*, no. 4, "Zvit z diialnosty tovarstva Ukrainskyi studentskyi soiuz u Lvovi za chas vid. 1 XI 1911 do 30 X 1912" (Lviv, 1912).

28. Olena Stepaniv, *Na peredodni velykykh podii* (Lviv, 1930), 6.

29. *Dilo* 2 (14) July 1899; see also *Solomiia Krushelnytska, spohady, materialy, lystuvannia*, 2 vols. (Kiev, 1978), especially 1: 341–3.

30. The seminary had no Ukrainian teachers; the teaching of that language as required by law was most primitive, and the girls spoke better German than Ukrainian. Moreover, women who refused to take the certification examination in Ukrainian even for religion, because they found that language too difficult, readily received teaching positions in distinctly Ukrainian villages. *Dilo* 8 (20) March 1880, 2; 2 (4) April 1880, 2 on the Benedictines. See also Kliavdia I. Aleksovych, "Shkola Divocha v Peremyshli," *Uchytel* 12 (24) March 1870, 38.

31. *VI Zvit dyrektsii litseia ruskoho Instytuta dlia Divchat v Peremyshli z pravamy derzhavnykh shkil za rik 1908/9*, 3–4. Also WAP, Przemyśl, Ukraiński Instytut dlia Dziewczat, Syg. 4, especially Ivan Matkovsky, *Ruskyi Instytut dlia Divchat v Peremyshli, ieho povstanie, rozvii i teperishnyi ustrii, na pidstavi aktiv, protokoliv*

i vlasnykh spomyniv (Przemyśl, 1897) for a convenient overview. See also WAP, AGKB, Instytut Wdów i Sierot, Syg. 4793, 199–201.

32. Until 1897, Ruthenian rather than Ukrainian was used in the name. The change had to be certified again in 1922, and repeated in 1937 to satisfy the Polish authorities. WAP, IUD, Syg. 8, which contains titles and materials pertaining to the ownership.

33. Professor Lev Chekhovych was empowered by the Board on 30 March 1901 to study the possibilities of opening a private seminary affiliated with the Institute, WAP, IUD, Syg. 5, Knyha protokoliv, meeting of 30 March 1901, point 3.

34. "Non-Ruthenian" spirit used at the general meeting of 20 June 1899; the problems with parents are discussed in Matkivsky, 37.

35. Whole argument with Mrs. Nesterovych (I could not establish her first name) in WAP, IUD, Knyha zasidan, Syg. 5, meetings of 20 October and 26 November 1900. She was the wife of a conservative Ukrainian priest.

36. Reverends Berunets, Sovitenko and Volodymyr Rymiavets; WAP, IUD, Syg. 5, Knyha zasidan, 29 March 1902. Among the most outspoken critics of modernizing Ukrainianism were the four Cherliunchakevyches, Dr. Cyril, Dr. Iosyf, Severyn and Tadei, as well as the Reverend Mykhailo Zubrytsky.

37. The Reverend Rymiavets of Lishkovato, who was threatened with a libel suit by the Society, owed it 557 kronen and 57 groschen as of 5 December 1902.

38. WAP, IUD, Syg. 5, Knyha Zasidan, 10 November 1903, 3 December 1903, and 29 January 1904.

39. IUD, Knyha zasidan, meetings of 30 March and 6 June 1901.

40. *Dilo*, 20 January 1892.

41. For instance, the social breakdown of the 233 girls who studied at the Institute in 1908–9 and whose age ranged from ten to twenty, was: daughters of priests——161; of lawyers——10; or physicians——6; of bureaucrats——26; of grammar-school teachers——11; of the gentry——2; of townsmen——4; of low-level government employees [*sic*]——3; of peasants——10. The figures and categories are taken from the report in WAP, IUD, Syg. 10.

42. Zvit Litseia, IUD, Syg. 10, 1909, 14.

43. Matkivsky, 79.

44. Ibid., 57.

45. Zvit litseia z 1909 roku, IUD, Syg. 10, 40.

46. Nesterovych, 137.

47. See the brief history of the Gymnasium by Petro Isaiv and Anna Kobrynska, "Narys istorii himnazii sester vasyliianok u Lvovi," in Vasyl Lev et al., eds., *Propamiatna knyha Himnazii Sester Vasyliianok u Lvovi* (New York, 1980). Other articles in this source are also useful.

48. "Ispyt v Lvivskim ruskim instytuti Divochim SS. Vasyliianok," *Zoria*, 15 August 1885, 175–6. The Basilian School, also called the Institute, although run by Basilian nuns, had been founded by Metropolitan Sylvestr Sembratovych in 1884 for the education of Ukrainian girls in a patriotic and religious fashion. See also Czajecka, 482.

7: Kobrynska's Feminist Socialism

1. This point has not been raised in the few works on Kobrynska. An obituary notice on Engels, in Kobrynska's *Nasha dolia*, (Lviv, 1896), 3: 116–17, serves as an introduction to some polemics on the woman issue and provides the most direct acknowledgement of Engels's influence. A convenient introduction to Kobrynska's assessment of the role of the women's movement in society is a brief speech she delivered in 1898 at a jubilee celebration of the rebirth of Ukrainian literature in Galicia; in *Dilo*, no. 238 (1898), reprinted in I.O. Denysiuk and K.A. Kril, ed., *Nataliia Kobrynska, Vybrani tvory* (Kiev, 1980), 325–8. This source is cited hereafter as *Kobrynska* (1980).

2. There is some doubt as to the exact year of birth. Omelian Ohonovsky, *Istoriia literatury ruskoi* (Lviv, 1893), 3: 1265–4, basing himself on an autobiographical sketch by Kobrynska, gives the date of birth as 1855. That date, according to Kobrynska, *Vybrani tvory*, ed. O.N. Moroz (Kiev, 1958), is also carved on her gravestone. An earlier edition of Kobrynska's works, *Vybrani opovidannia* (Lviv, 1954), dates her birth at 1851. Irena Knysh, *Smoloskyp v temriavi: Nataliia Kobrynska i ukrainskyi zhinochyi rukh* (Winnipeg, 1957), 10, maintains that the error was made by Ohonovsky. Both dates cause minor problems. If Kobrynska was born in 1855, then her parents who had been married in 1848 had either been childless for seven years or their children had died. The former is unusual; the latter possibility is not mentioned. On the other hand, if 1851 is the correct date of Kobrynska's birth, then her marriage at the age of twenty in 1871 is somewhat late for the times.

3. Latter episode recounted by Olha Oleksandra Duchyminska, "Moi spomyny pro Nataliiu Kobrynsku," *Zhinocha dolia*, 15 June–1 July 1934, 3–4. The account of the Badeni episode is taken from Ozarkevych's memoirs. There is a fuller discussion in Irena Knysh, 147–8.

4. The existence of Kobrynska's autobiography, "Ia ,i zhinoche pytannia" (The Woman Question and I), is mentioned in an introductory note by Iryna Velychko, a younger relative of Kobrynska, to a letter of Ivan Franko which was published in *Zakhidnia Ukraina* (Kharkiv), no. 5 (May 1930): 43–4; hence O.N. Moroz, ed., 15, errs when he cites this as a source for the autobiography itself.

5. "Avtobiohrafiia," in *Kobrynska* (1980), 318. This published document is different from the version mentioned previously.

6. "Iak uzhe do Franka pysala-m [*sic*], shcho dohlupalam sia do moikh idei sama, bez pomochi muzhchyn, svoiim vlasnym zhyttiam i vlasnym dosvidom." Letter to Pavlyk, published in *Kobrynska* (1980), 402. There is a note of exasperation in her letters to Pavlyk and Franko for their failure to stress her own development.

It did not occur to Kobrynska that women were considered lower in status than men until, at the age of twelve or thirteen, she came across some Polish polemics on the alleged inferiority of women. She had interpreted some men's superior attitude toward women as a lack of social graces on their part. Now there appeared to be an argument for an innate difference in the status of the sexes. Among the persons with whom the earnest adolescent discussed her views was a Polish gentry woman who owned most of the land in the villages where her father was the pastor. This woman acquainted Kobrynska with the popular writings of Klementyna Tańska-Hoffmanowa (1798–1845). Kobrynska was "eccentrically religious, and who knows, had I not latched onto positivist and anti-religious literature, I might have ended up a religious fanatic." "Avtobiohrafiia," 317. Hoffmanowa saw women as wives, daughters and mothers, but argued that to be able to fulfill these roles they must be educated. She stressed the importance of native history and literature, and criticized flighty French fashions. Kobrynska accepted the latter argument and turned to the serious pursuit of learning.

7. The Ozarkevych home, though not unique within the Galician context, was certainly exceptional. Most similar clerical families were not as vibrant, not as open to new ideas, and certainly not as supportive of women as Kobrynska's immediate milieu. A childhood friend of Kobrynska also stressed the importance of Kobrynsky in Nataliia's development. "She grew up at the turn of the last century in a depressing, morally terrorized atmosphere, in the darkness of the vanishing horizon, surrounded by bowed foreheads of slaves. She was brought up according to the tenets of the old, patriarchal system to be educated enough to marry well and to become a good chatelaine. And she would have been wasted in the mass of the then primitive womanfolk...had not fate given her a friend for life." *Pershomu bortsevy za prava zhinky* (Lviv, 1921), 9, a brochure published by Soiuz Ukrainok in honour of Kobrynska.

8. "Avtobiohrafiia," 318.

9. Ibid., 319. See also Mykhailo Vozniak, "Shliakhom do pershoho vinka," in the literary supplement to *Novyi chas* (Lviv, 1937), from Kobrynska's letter to Mykhailo Pavlyk, quoted in Knysh, 18. This generation was not given to the confessional autobiographical writing like the following generation of radicals who rediscovered religion in their middle age (such as Volodymyr Okhrymovych, *Chomu ia navernuvsia: Pryliudne vyznannia viry* (Lviv, 1920), or Osyp Nazaruk's various works.

10. "Avtobiohrafiia," 319. See also Duchyminska, "Moi spomyny pro Nataliiu Kobrynsku," *Zhinocha dolia* (July, 1934): 3–7. Despite a thirty-year difference in age, Duchyminska became an intimate friend of Kobrynska in the last years of the latter's life. Kobrynska confided to her both the decision not to have children and the constant remorse she felt at not having had children. It was a decision that Kobrynska regretted, especially in her old age.

11. While Kobrynsky lay dying, another tragedy unfolded within the families close to him. One of the women Franko loved passionately was Olha Roshkevych, the daughter of a priest in the vicinity of Kobrynska's home town. Not only did Franko plan to marry her, but, more importantly to him, he was grooming her to become the first woman writer in Galicia. He encouraged both Olha and her sister Mykhailyna to translate, to collect folk materials, and to write fiction. Franko's socialism ruined his career, and after his arrest, Olha's family persuaded her to marry Kobrynska's younger brother Volodymyr, a candidate for the priesthood. Volodymyr also had a sweetheart, an orphan from a neighbouring priest, but she was too poor for him to be able to marry her. Olha and Volodymyr apparently agreed on a marriage of mutual convenience, in line with their own progressive views. They would be free to love whomever they chose and would not consummate their marriage.

A few passages in the corespondence between Olha and Franko suggest that their relationship was not platonic. Some letters that Franko wrote Olha after she had visited him clandestinely in Lviv hint that they may have been lovers before her marriage to Kobrynsky. In the prevailing ethos of the progressives that would have sealed the bond of true marriage, regardless of public marriage vows. Her marriage to Kobrynsky was a way out of an impasse, and Olha must have been rather surprised that Franko (for all his free thinking) rejected the idea of a marriage of convenience as undignified and unworthy of a true male (*muzhchyna*). On Franko and Roshkevych, see Knysh, *Kobrynska*, esp. 9–36; Franko, *Tvory, passim*, and Roman Horak, "Kartky z pershoi liubovi," *Zhovten*, no. 8 (August 1979): 126–43. Horak argues that Olha rejected Franko in order not to impede his literary work.

Madame Shumynska, in the twilight of her days, mused about the expectations of modern youth, their stress on love and independence, useless things that did not exist in her days. "For a Piece of Bread" was patterned somewhat on the tragic loves of her brother and Olha Roshkevych, Franko's sweetheart. Beautiful Halia, realizing that she is unable to raise the necessary dowry to marry the man she loves (but who in turn cannot support her) dooms herself to unhappiness. Seeing no way out, she marries a decent man whom she does not love. She realizes that if the social situation had been different——had she been able to work to support herself and her man until he became established in his profession——her sacrifice would not have been necessary. She arrives at this decision coolly, rationally, almost without rancour. Women cried when they read the story; they could identify themselves with the romantic heroine who could not afford to be heroic. "For a Piece of Bread" first appeared in *Zoria* in 1884; "The Spirit of the Times" in *Pershyi vinok* in 1887.

12. "Moi spomyny pro Nataliiu Kobrynsku," *Zhinocha dolia*, (15 June–1 July 1934): 4. Duchyminska continued: "I must admit that I felt awkard, since I knew much less about the feminist movement than about literature, and for the first time I was embarrassed by [my lack of familiarity with feminism.]"

13. Quotation from *Nasha dolia* (1896), 3: 142. The clearest presentation of Kobrynska's views can be found in "Zhinocha sprava v Halychyni," *Nasha dolia* (1893) 1: 1–35; see also *Nasha dolia*, 3: 7, 17; and 2: 3, footnote on Polish women.

14. See her "Iak to buvalo" in *Zhinocha dolia*, 15 June–1 July 1934 (nos. 12–13): 11–12. A list of members of the Society, formally called Tovarystvo Ruskykh Zhenshchyn, copied from the original membership roll, can be found in this issue of *Zhinocha dolia*, 12–13.

15. *Statut tovarystva Ruskykh zhenshchyn v Stanyslavovi potverdzhennyi resheniiem ts.k. Namisnytstva z 12 padolysta 1884* (Lviv, 1884), quoted in Levytsky, 2, no. 65232.

16. "Pro pervisnu tsil Tovarystva ruskykh zhinok v Stanyslavovi, zaviazanoho v 1884 r.," *Pershyi vinok*, 451–61.

17. *Pershyi vinok*, 461. Polish women at the time were stressing the national, rather than the international element in learning for women. Defence of national rights formed the basis for the Polish women's organization founded in Galicia two years after the Stanyslaviv meeting; see Wawrzykowska-Wierciochowa, 243. The *Zrzeszenie kól kobiecych na Litwie, Rusi, Kolońjach w Rosyi,* another women's organization for the Poles within the Russian Empire, had as its first aim: "The attainment of strength, through common organization, to defend national rights and the women's movement." Uniwersytet Jagiellonski, Bibljoteka, Dział Rękopisów, MS 7990.

18. *Pershyi vinok*, 458.

19. Ibid., 461.

20. Kobrynska tried to alleviate these women's fear of modernity and to draw them into the camp of the modernists by demonstrating how much women could gain from changes in society and government. She argued that a single income was becoming inadequate for the survival of a middle-class family, that change was inevitable, and that it was wiser to understand the changes than to be confronted by their consequences. Privately, she wrote to Franko that "the Galician women support the contemporary literary trend and belong to the most radical party in the land." But she also knew that these conscious women were very few. Quoted in Nataliia Kobrynska, *Vybrani tvory*, ed. O.N. Moroz, from Instytut literatury, AN UkSSR, Arkhiv Franka, fond 214, letter 705.

21. *Dilo*, 13 December 1884, 1. Excerpts of her speech can also be found in Ohonovsky, *Istoriia literatury ruskoi*, 3: 1275–6.

22. "Nove zerkalo," *Dilo*, 13 December 1884.

23. Criticism of Ukrainian Galician women had become so common in describing the first stages of the women's movement that it lost all sense of proportion. Getting ninety-five women together in Stanyslaviv to initiate the organization of a women's society was a considerable achievement. For instance, the first public political rally of Ukrainians in Lviv was held in 1880, the second only two years later. The first editor of the newspaper that would become the most influential Ukrainian Galician daily, *Dilo*, offered to edit it free of charge until the subscriptions reached three hundred. Ievhen Olesnytsky, *Storinky z moho zhyttia* (Vol. 1) (Lviv, 1935), 1: 153.

24. A handwritten account of the proceedings of this trial can be found in Przemyśl, Archiwum Wojewódzkie, Syg. 9687.

25. Quoted in Knysh, 79.

26. See the letter of Lesia Ukrainka to Pavlyk, asking him not to publish a story by Kobylianska intended for the "Second Wreath," in *Olha Kobylianska v krytytsi ta spohadakh* (Kiev, 1963), 30.

27. Franko described himself as editor of *Pershyi vinok* in *Narys istorii ukrainsko-ruskoi literatury do 1890 roku* (Lviv, 1910), 252; also quoted in Knysh, 133. This is repeated by Soviet authors, N.O. Tomashuk, *Olha Kobylianska: Zhyttia i tvorchist* (Kiev, 1969), 18. This book is based upon archival material, including a number of letters of Kobrynska to Franko. In one of these letters, Kobrynska rejects a story sent by Kobylianska to *Pershyi vinok*, and Franko rejects another. This would point to co-editorship at best; Tomashuk sees in Franko, however, "the actual editor of the almanac."

28. Advertisements were run in *Nasha dolia*.

29. Two symptomatic passages will suffice. In reviewing the first volume of *Nasha dolia* in *Narod* (1 February 1894), Pavlyk wrote: "We raise these issues so that [Kobrynska] might once and for all admit her mistakes and, getting rid of them, be better able to work for true progress amid our womanhood." In 1904, writing an introduction to an edition of Kobrynska's letters, Pavlyk admonished her: "now that Kobrynska has moved from Bolekhiv to Lviv she could have dedicated herself wholeheartedly to uplifting her unfortunate sisters." *Perepyska M. Drahomanova z N. Kobrynskoiu, 1893–1895* (Lviv, 1905), 15. Drahomanov was not very supportive of Kobrynska. Certainly, presenting the situation of women in the Russian Empire in a rosy light did not endear Kobrynska's publications to Drahomanov.

30. The situation became serious enough in 1895 for the Austrian Reichsrat to deliberate on the need for the education of women and to quote the statistic that 11 per cent of marriageable women in the empire were not married for lack of men. The economic condition of these women was critical. Fuller discussion in Bogusława Czajecka, "Przygotowanie kobiet do pracy zawodowej na tle ruchu feministycznego w Galiciji," 49. Writing in *Pershyi vinok*, Kobrynska saw the growth of petty thievery and of prostitution as one aspect of the problem. There is a discussion of the Austrian superfluous women in English in Katherine Anthony, *Feminism in Germany* (New York, 1915).

31. *Nasha dolia*, 1 (1893): 10–14; 30–31.

32. Ibid., 2 (1895): 4–5.

33. Ibid., 15–16.

34. Ibid., 16–17.

35. See "Zhinocha sprava v Halychyni," *Nasha dolia*, 1: 1–35; see also 2: 7–17.

36. Ibid., 2: 16.

37. Ibid., 10.

38. Kobrynska was right. By 1900, 12 per cent of the work force in Galicia was made up of women. See Walentyna Najdus, *Szkice z historii Galicji* (Warsaw, 1958), 1: 188.

39. *Nasha dolia*, 2: 94.

40. Her speech was reprinted as a booklet by *Dilo* in 1901; the copy she sent Vilma Sokolová has a note that the statute was approved by the governor on 19 September 1900. Even so, Kobrynska's role in the day-care movement was belittled. Franko suggested she copied the idea from the Czechs. She objected; *Nasha dolia*, 3: 129. The Ukrainian teachers' organization considered itself the author of the day-care scheme, dating it much later than Kobrynska's initial discussion; see Lev Iasinchuk, *50 lit Ridnoi Shkoly 1881–1931* (Lviv, 1931). I could locate only the heavily censored second edition; the first one was confiscated.

41. *Nasha dolia*, 1: 18; 3: 7, 17.

42. Ibid., 2: 98–9.

43. Kobrynska, Popovych and Kravchenko contributed materials to a Polish almanac published to raise money for the famine-stricken, *Dla głodnych*. *Dilo*, in its review of 28 May (9 June) 1890, reprinted the poems of Popovych and Kravchenko with the comment that the authors should model themselves more on Pchilka. Kobrynska, who wrote a review of Marja Schlegel's *Na przebój* (Into Battle) (Cracow, 1889), was criticized for Polonisms in her language. In a letter of 17 January 1900, Iaroshynska commented to Kobylianska that she was glad Hrushevsky had praised Kobrynska elsewhere at the time, because she needed praise to encourage her to write; TsDIA, UkSSR (Lviv), f. 663, op. 1, spr. 248, 139.

44. Hankevych had the Academic Brotherhood (Akademichne Bratstvo) publish *Pro zhinochu nevoliu v istorychnim rozvoiu* (On Women's Slavery in its Historical Development), but the whole edition was confiscated. It was published again, unchanged, in Toronto in 1918 under the auspices of the Robitnycha Knyharnia i Vydavnycha Spilka. Hankevych, stressing economic determinism, ended with an ingenious biological theory. Since the liberation of women was inevitably built into economic progress, its realization was only a matter of time. Progress demands equality of women with the more highly developed men. Hence

Hankevych argued that the physical differences between men and women were the result of unhealthy, exploitative economic development. The working-class woman, who was not pampered by unnatural civilization, was, according to Hankevych, already more like a man than the middle-class woman. But the middle-class woman was being forced down the social scale and would end up working in order that she might attain equality with the male. Hankevych was lucky to have the brochure confiscated; his influence on radical young women in Galicia would have diminished had his views been more widely known.

45. Letter to Iaroshynska in *Kobrynska* (1980), 407; Iaroshynska's correspondence was originally prepared for publication by Pavlyk from materials given him by her father in 1906, two years after her untimely death. There does not seem to be any material antedating 1899. See TsDIA, UkSSR (Lviv), f. 663, op. 1, spr. 248;
46. *Nasha dolia*, 3: 63–7 and 17–30.
47. See the review of Nietzsche in *Nasha dolia* 1: 69.
48. Irena Knysh began her work on Kobrynska as part of a projected history of Ukrainian women, which was never completed. Although she serialized her book in the Canadian-Ukrainian press, she had to publish it in 1957 at her own expense.

8: Widening Circles of Community Involvement

1. WAP, AGKB, Syg. 9492 has a particularly rich collection of such letters.
2. Letter to Kobylianska, in *Kobrynska* (1980), 404; Kobrynska's article on the petition and its follow-up is to be found in *Dilo*, 28 May–9 June 1890, along with the full text of the petition.
3. Any constitutional state was considered much more advanced than the Russian Empire, which then had no constitution, but did have higher education for women.
4. *Nasha dolia*, 1 (1893): 8.
5. The most comprehensive discussion of this topic is to be found in John-Paul Himka, "Young Radicals and Independent Statehood: The Idea of a Ukrainian Nation-State, 1890–1895," *Slavic Review* (Summer 1982): 219–51.
6. Anna and her sister Kateryna Pavlyk Dovbenchuk had begun talking about socialism to the peasants of the mountain villages. The Pavlyk women were arrested on a number of occasions. Anna showed both oratorical skill and knowledge of the Austrian penal code in conducting her own defence. For example, she reported that in Kolomyia on 12 February 1886, "All I said [to the peasants] was that I wanted all people to be well off in the world. Even if at such a moment I did say that we must strive toward equalization of wealth between the rich and the poor, such a statement could in no way be understood in any other fashion than as a justification of well-being for all." But she reached only a limited number of people and would not have been so well known had Drahomanov not written about her extensively. Court transcript in TsDIA, UkSSR (Lviv), f. 663, op. 1, od. zb. 125, 284–8.
7. "Spomyny z prohul'ky do Prahy," *Zoria* (1891), 438–9; 455–6; see also *Dilo*, 27 July (8 August) 1891, 1–3.
8. The manuscript of the article she wrote in Ukrainian for Sokolova is in *Pámatník*

Národního Písemnictví, Sokolova-Seidlová fund, letter of 21 September 1891 in *Kobrynska* (1980), 406–7.

9. The petition was finally studied in the Reichstag Petition Commission at the end of November of that year. In referring the petition to the government, the commission recommended a positive course of action. The Polish press reports simply called it the petition of the Galician women, without recognizing the initiative of Ukrainian women.

10. *Nasha dolia*, 1 (1893): 7.

11. Hermina Shukhevych was one of its initiators. In an interview in *Zhinka*, on 1 March 1935, 2, she insisted that 1892 was the founding date, but referred to preliminary meetings. *Nasha dolia*, 2 (1895): 85, noted 1893 as the date of the first general meeting and provided information on other women's organizations.

12. Dariia Shukhevych in a letter of 1 April 1893 to Řehoř wrote that Ukrainians would use Czech and British women as their models.

13. The other speakers in the first year were Professor Ivan Verkhratsky, who spoke on mushrooms, a staple in the Ukrainian diet; Ivan Franko, on a Polish legend about Shevchenko; and Professor Volodymyr Shukhevych on the mating instinct in insects. His talk was entitled "The Efforts of Insects on Behalf of Their Progeny." *Nasha dolia*, 2 (1895): 86.

14. Ibid., 2: 85.

15. Letter of Trud to NTSh, 29 October 1902, in NTSh Archives, TsDIA, UkSSR (Lviv), f. 309, op. 1, spr. 285, sviazka (*sic*) 13, 1–2.

16. *Nasha dolia*, 3 (1896): 131.

17. LNV 17 (1897): 48–9. Hrushevsky took the standard position that the Galician women's movement was not well developed because of the low level of industrialization. Since daughters of clergy married easily, Hrushevsky maintained there really was no economic pressure for higher education. He rated Kobrynska's work highly against this dismal background.

18. Letter from P. Dutkevych and O. Tomashivska to NTSh, 18 October 1903, in NTSh Archives, TsDIA, UkSSR (Lviv), f. 309, op. 1, spr. 285, sviazka 13, 1–2.

19. On the last point, see Najdus, 1: 256.

20. The text of the appeal is in *Moloda Ukraina: Chasopys ukrainskoi molodizhi*, no. 4 (1901): 141–3.

21. Olena Berezhnytska-Budzova, "Kruzhok ukrainskykh divchat," *Nova khata*, no. 5 (1939): 2.

22. Report in *Moloda Ukraina* (April 1901): 140.

23. Severyna Kabarivska "Shliakh do organizatsii," *Nasha meta*, 23 November 1919, 3.

24. TsDIA, UkSSR (Lviv), f. 309, op. 1, spr. 285, sviazka 13, 4–5; "Pered zahalnymy zboramy kruzhka Ukrainok u Lvovi," *Meta*, no. 3, 1 April 1908, 1–2.

25. Mariia Biletska (1864–1938), a teacher and editor, and Olimpiia Kurivets Luchakovska, were very adept at setting up this type of emergency aid.

26. *Moloda Ukraina* (April 1901): 141.

27. "Vidozva: Tovaryshky i sestry," ibid., 141–3.

28. Emphasis in the original.

29. The peasant and women workers took a significant part in the agrarian strikes of 1901 and in the rallies for the vote. Ol-ch, "Z istorii rukhu ukrainskykh zhinok v Halychyni," *Meta*, no. 1 (March 1908): 6.

30. Konstantyna Malytska, *Pro zhinochyi rukh: referat, Vydavnytstvo kruzhka divchat*

(Lviv, 1904), 3.

31. Ibid., 40. The other speakers were Natalka Budzynovska, Severyna Danylevych and Dariia Shukhevych; Mariia Biletska and Olena Berezhnytska were the chairpersons. See O. Berezhnytska-Budzova, final segment of "Kruzhok ukrainskykh divchat," *Nova khata*, no. 7–8 (1939): 7.

32. Quoted by Lozynsky, "Pershi kroky: Z pryvodu zboriv ukrainskoho zhinotstva dnia 12 liutoho 1904 roku u Lvovi," *LNV* 24 (1904): 173. Text by Katria Lozenko.

33. Olena Budzova, in *Nova khata*, no. 7–8 (1939): 6.

34. Letter to Stefaniia (Levytska) Fedorovych dated 28 January 1904, in TsDIA, UkSSR (Lviv), f. 663, op. 1, spr. 248.

35. Letter of Iaroshynska to Fedorovych, 4 March 1904, in TsDIA, UkSSR (Lviv), f. 663, op. 1, spr. 248; Olena Berezhnytska-Budzova in *Nova khata*, no. 6 (1939): 3, noted that "as in any organization, we had our 'opposition,' which was even very valuable; it was frequently represented by Stefa Levytska (Fedorovych) and Severyna Danylevych."

Correspondence of Iaroshynska and Malytska, in which the former encouraged Malytska to stay on, in TsDIA, UkSSR (Lviv), f. 663, op. 1, spr. 248, 67–76. Katria Hrynevych, a Ukrainian raised in Cracow, who was beginning to write fiction in Ukrainian, became the editor of the magazine for children, *Dzvinok*.

36. "Zhinka i Svoboda," *Dilo*, no. 49 (1906), also reprinted in *Kobrynska* (1980), 372–6.

37. Ibid.

38. The editors wrote:

> The aim of the paper is to awaken...women to broader social life and to encourage them to organize as conscious citizens.
>
> Much remains to be done on that score. We need energy and strong will both from society as a whole, which understands the present subservient position of women, and from women themselves. [The last] consideration merits first place.
>
> Work toward the liberation of women is cultural work and will benefit [the whole community]. *Meta*'s goal is to raise the consciousness of our womanhood, drawing it into public life, so that women can and dare raise their voices in universal human affairs.
>
> And that is why *Meta* will closely monitor the development of the women's movements in other countries so that they can serve as models for us. Furthermore, we will discuss the latest developments in scientific, literary and political life.
>
> The extent to which *Meta* will be able to live up to its tasks depends upon the financial and moral support of Ukrainian women.

"Nashi zavdannia," *Meta*, 1 March 1908, 1,; also Malytska in *Almanakh Zhinochoi doli* (1927), 5.

39. "Z sviatyni Temidy. Vrazhinnia z rozpravy," *Meta*, 15 July 1908, 3.

40. *Nadzvychainyi dodatok do zhinochoho chasopysu Meta.*

41. Severyna Kabarovska, "Shliakh orhaniizatsii ukrainskoho zhinotstva (Korotenkyi ohliad orhanizatsiinykh ioho zmahan)," *Nasha meta*, 23 November 1919, 1–3; 30 November 1919, 3–4; and 14 December 1919, 3–6 for the fullest account. Among the participants, in addition to the Lviv women, were women from Stryi,

Przemyśl, Kalush, Sambir, Vynnyky, Iavoriv, Bolekhiv, Kolomyia, Berezhany, Ternopil and Bohorodchany.

42. A reading room in Lviv, *Czytelnia dla Kobiet*, was patronized by Ukrainian and Jewish women, and served as a clearing-house for the preparation of the deputation to Badeni. Czajecka, 752–4.

43. The full archival holdings are in AAN, Warsaw, Liga Kobiet Polskich.

44. There are numerous examples of clergy fostering the growth of an aware laity in WAP, Przemyśl, AGKB, Syg. 5136, *passim*. On the Pichl book, see Syg. 4768, 109–11.

45. *Promova Natali Kobrynskoi na zahalnykh zborakh Ruskoi Okhronky*, 5.

46. Statutes in rough and in final copy of this society are in WAP, Przemyśl, AGKB, Syg. 4846; printed version in Syg. 5132.

47. Julia Głąb, wife of a factory welder, was a Ukrainian who married a Pole but did not change her rite. Her husband's brother, an ardent Roman Catholic theology student, forged her signature and petitioned for a change of rite in her name. The Ukrainian priest, describing the case, and investigating the forgery, mentioned that he organized a women's society as a means of keeping the young women in his church, WAP, Przemyśl, AGKP, Syg. 4846, 372–4. Change of rite was restricted by Vatican regulations from encroachments by the Roman Catholic Church. Even within the Catholic Church, change of rite necessitated formal procedure and petitions.

48. WAP, Przemyśl, AGKB, Syg. 4845, letter of 24 July 1897, referring to Franko's visit of 8 January of that same year.

49. Women were more likely to join votive organizations, such as the Society for the Veneration of the Sacred Heart of Jesus, which spread through the formerly Catholic territories of the Ukrainian lands under the Russian Empire, AGAD, Warsaw, esp. Syg. 709, 1487.

50. Shakh, 1: 159–60.

51. *Dilo*, 25 April 1912, and 16 September 1912; the committee was composed of Halshka (*sic*) Huvareva, Varvara Litynska, Mariia Luzhnytska, Leontiia Studynska and Emiliia Tsehelska. All were women with close family ties to high church officials in Lviv.

52. *Rusalka: zhenskii almanakh* (New York, 1922), esp. 56.

53. Information from the notes of Oksana Duchyminska in archive of the Ukrainian National Women's League of America, New York, uncatalogued. On Kosmowska, see Zofia Mazurowa, ed., *Wspomnienia o Irenie Kosmowskiej* (Warsaw, 1974). Three years earlier, at the first congress of Ukrainian Galician and Bukovynian Businessmen (12 February 1906), there had been no women; Volodymyr Nestorovych, *Ukrainski kuptsi i promyslovtsi v Zakhidnii Ukraini* (Toronto, 1977), 16–18.

54. In 1924 she was elected to the governing board of the Central Ukrainian Economic Co-operative, Maslosoiuz. Later, a Lviv company, Dnister, refused to hire her, even though she did very well during a three-month trial session, lest she distract the thirty male employees. *Zhinka*, 15 February 1937, 4.

55. Kost Levytsky, *Istoriia politychnoi dumky halytskkykh Ukraintsiv* (Lviv, 1927), 2: 634. Emphasis in the original.

56. Olena Stepaniv, *Naperedodni velykykh podii* (Lviv, 1930), 16–24; also see an unsigned article by Milena Rudnytska "Dvadtsiatypiatylittia svitovoi viiny," in the last issue of *Zhinka*, dated only August 1939, 1; and Malytska's obituary article

on Biletska in *Zhinka*, 1 February 1938, 2–3.

57. In 1907 women in the Austrian Empire were dealt a double blow. The electoral reform of 1907 perpetuated the disenfranchisement of women. Many radical women had expected Austria to be among the first states to introduce woman suffrage; Czajecka, 748–50. Maria Dulebianka, a Polish socialist from Lviv, tried to challenge the legality of the system by running for deputy, but her candidacy was rejected on technical grounds. She ran as an independent, and was supported by Jewish and Ukrainian women as well as by Polish feminists.

Developments within international social democracy, moreover, led some women to question socialist support of women. A conference of women socialists, meeting on the eve of the socialist conference at Stuttgart in 1907, came out firmly for women's rights and equality of women in all areas, including suffrage. But the Social Democrats decided not to support the so-called limited women's right, and not to co-operate with feminist organizations.

The criticism of the women's organizations levied by the socialists made the work of the women's organizations in Western Ukraine easier. The women activists were no longer easily stigmatized as socialists. Stressing local activities and local initiative they began organizing peasant groups. Young girls, as they graduated from schools in towns in which there had been a women's society, often helped in the creation of some women's or community group in the villages or smaller towns to which they returned. Women were also being drawn into political work among the peasants.

The Ladies' Club in Lviv expanded its outreach programmes. With the young women's help, it established an extremely effective organization for the care of domestic servants. This society eventually co-operated with similar groups in other cities, and stimulated the formation of regional affiliates; TsDIA, UkSSR (Lviv), f. 309, op. 1, spr. 285, sviazka 13; NTSh, Lysty zhinochykh organizatsii, especially a letter of the Society of Domestic Servants dated 10 October 1905, signed by Mariia Biletska and Olha Hnatiuk.

58. The Appeal was signed by Mariia Biletska, Ievheniia Verhanovska, Olha Hamorak, Olena Zalizniak, Olimpiia Luchakivska, Konstantyna Malytska, Olena Stepaniv and Ievheniia Iasenytska. It was published in *Vidhuky: Organ Ukrainskoi Molodi*, no. 2 (February 1913): 1–2. Konstantyna Malytska, "U richnytsiu velykykh zmahan," *Nova khata*, 1 November 1935, quoted a more poetical version of the resolution:

> Although European diplomats raised the white flag of peace upon the political horizon, we continue to hear the battle-cry. A nation such as ours, which is struggling for the right to live and to develop, must always stand guard, for it does not know the hour or the day when the thunder will roar. But not every cloud pours hail, not every lightning flash is fatal. There are clouds which bring a rain beneficial to the harvest of the well-tended fields; there is lightning which pierces through the gloom to clear the atmosphere. We await such a momentous lightning which will light our own way, which will lead us to our own goal.

The women drafted two appeals, and in later accounts of the event the two are often presented as one.

59. I. Vykhor, "Na strichu velykym podiiam," *Vidhuky*, no. 1 (February 1913): 4–5. According to Stepaniv, *Na peredodni*, 24, Fedortsiv was Vykhor.

The women established an Organizational Committee. It published a small booklet on *Zhinka v davnii ukraini* (Woman in Ancient Ukraine), in which the active role of women was stressed. The issue of women in the army was clear to those women: equality in service and in struggle; review in *Vidhuky*, no. 2 (February 1913): 19–20, signed S.N.

9: Olha Kobylianska in Literature: Feminism as the Road to Autonomy

1. Ivan S. Levytsky, *Halytsko-ruskaia bybliografiia*, 2, Dopolnenie, #3416.
2. In a letter full of light-hearted remarks to the Reverend Leshchynsky of Komancha, written on 11 (23) December 1855 by his friend from the seminary identified only as Pavel, we find some of his wife's verses, "for she is good at it." WAP, Przemyśl, AGKB, Syg. 9492. This matter-of-fact remark suggests that the wife's poetry writing was not an unusual practice among women. Bukovynian women were most familiar with German, through which they were introduced to Western European classics and to German patriotic literature, which in turn led them to write in Ukrainian. Both Olha Kobylianska and Ievheniia Iaroshynska began writing in German before they became major Ukrainian authors.
3. She took copious notes and wrote a series of autobiographical works. The gaps in the story are as eloquent as the inclusions. It is sufficient to mention *Spohady uchytelky* (Kolomyia, 1936), *Zamist avtobiografii* (Kolomyia, 1934), and *Moi tsvity* (Kolomyia, 1933).
4. Pre-publication criticism of *Spohady uchytelky* by Iryna Vilde, written in 1933, can be found in the Kravchenko Archive.
5. She did not give up the notion of writing in German completely, and in 1900 considered it as a means of earning money; unpublished correspondence of Ievheniia Iaroshynska to Kobrynska, esp. letter of 25 December 1900 in TsDIA, UkSSR (Lviv), 663, op. 1, spr. 248.
6. According to *Kobrynska* (1980), 434, twenty letters of Kobrynska to Kobylianska remain; of these, two dealing with the petition are published in the above source.
7. Unpublished letter of Kobylianska to Iaroshynska, 2 October 1894, in TsDIA, UkSSR (Lviv), Iaroshynska papers, 91; similar sentiments in her letter to Pavlyk, 27 October 1894, in Kobylianska, 5: 266–8.
8. Letter to Pavlyk, asking him to print a news article about the society in *Narod*, Kobylianska, 5: 266–8; see also her letter to Makovei, dated 4 April 1897, 294–6.

    The Western Ukrainian intelligentsia had to assert its identity continuously, but operated within a political framework which, within limits, was based on compromise. Hence its members did not need to lock themselves into consistent ideologies, but at the same time they wanted to appear firm and committed. The result was a stress on symbols. Orthography was a case in point. The Narodovtsi——the broad camp of democrats, liberals and socialists——were all committed to the cause of the people. They insisted on using the Ukrainian vernacular, the language spoken by the peasants on both parts of the Zbruch. They wanted to do away completely with the stilted, pompous and arcane mixture of Ukrainian and Church Slavonic which passed for the written language——*iazychiie*, the archaic "tongue"——and replace it with the living *mova* (language) of the people. The conservatives latched onto the *iazychiie*, and were especially forceful in defending the useless "hard sign" that followed certain consonants. As a group they were frequently referred to as the "hards." Their opponents, who wanted to do away with a series of orthographical consonants, were known as "softs." The battle seemed to be about orthography, but in reality it was a struggle between progress and social and intellectual traditionalism.

9. For a time the young women paraded their anti-clericalism and intellectual posturing; see an article in *Meta* by M.T., "Zhinotstvo na Bukovyni," 1 April 1908, 4–5, which denigrates the work of the earlier generation of women. The young women supported the protest of the progressive youth against "Hryts z Hadynkovets," as Bishop Hryhorii Khomyshyn, known for his opposition to socialism, was derisively called, when he visited Chernivtsi in 1908. See *Meta*, 15 August 1908, 2–4.

10. Stefanyk, like the other democrats, exhibited the inverse snobbery of his peasant origins. In a letter to Wacław Moraczewski, the husband of Sofiia Okunevska, he made derisive comments about Krushelnytska's social origin; see Krushelnytska, 1: 377. After meeting the singer, however, he wrote to Kobylianska in friendly fashion about Krushelnytska's democratic ways, trying to talk Kobylianska into coming to a concert despite the fact that it would be attended by the whole "high society of the clergy," ibid., 379.

11. S. Dovhal, "Olha Kobylianska v Prazi," *Nova Ukraina* (April-June 1928): 70–78; quotation from 74.

   Professor Stepan Smal-Stotsky, the dean of Ukrainian Bukovynian literary scholars, argued that Kobylianska was far from the cries of fashionable "emancipation" and that she stressed the ideal of motherhood and the role of wife as the highest achievements of a woman. No one challenged such tactless twisting of Kobylianska's views; *Ol'ha Kobylianska, Almanakh u pamiatku ii soroklitnoi pysmennytskoi diialnosty 1887–1927*, (Chernivtsi, 1928), 278. Smal-Stotsky corresponded with Kobylianska specifically to prepare a biographical sketch about her for this edition.

12. Kobylianska, "Avtobiografiia," in *Svit*, 25 April 1928, 4–6.

13. Kobylianska, *Deshcho pro ideiu zhinochoho rukhu* (originally a talk at the Women's Society on 14 October 1894, published by Pavlyk), (Kolomyia, 1894), 10.

14. Shapoval, "Znaiomstvo z Olhoiu Kobylianskoiu (Uryvky spomyniv)," *Nova Ukraina* (October-November 1927): 83–93.

15. Domesticity, especially the women's handicrafts which were the staple of all German-inspired education for women, was ridiculed. Rather, domestic work was presented as essential. If performed willingly and rationally, it was rewarding and pleasantly strenuous. The heroine had no children and was very happy.

10: Sisters across the Zbruch

1. *Vydatni zhinky Ukrainy*, 110 and 143.
2. Information on the Russophiles is scarce. The Okhrana reported on 5 May 1914

on the growth of influence of Austrian Ukrainian patriotism and complained of its popularity among the peasants, TsDIA, UkSSR (Kiev), f. 301, op. 1, spr. 3204, 25–6, 49; spr. 3207, 24. Levytska, *Na hrani*, 99, describes her surprise at meeting two young ladies from the Dudykevych family in Odessa whose language and views she found incomprehensible. *Nova Ukraina*, 1 July 1922, 18–21, reported how a Dudykevych, presumably Bohdan, organized working women. Paraskeva [*sic*] Mala and Konstantsiia Lukasevych are singled out. The Dudykevyches were stalwart Russophiles, and Bohdan became a major communist leader in twentieth-century Galicia. Volodymyr Antonovych, in a letter to Drahomanov dated 8 September 1885, *Korrespondentsiia Drahomanova*, 28, maintains that during that year Moscow channelled one half-million rubles to support the Galician Russophiles.

3. Unsigned article, "Stanovyshche Rusi suprotiv Liadskomoskovskoi borby," in *Meta* (Lviv), no. 1 (September 1863): 71.

4. Fedir Vovk, "De-shcho y z moikh avstro-ruskykh spomynok," in *Pryvit Ivanovy Frankovy*, 157, described a stormy conversation between his wife and Kornylo Sushkevych, a rich and prominent lawyer.

5. Pchilka had met Ostap Terletsky earlier. See her *Opovidannia z avtobiohrafiieiu*, ed. T. Cherkasky (Kharkiv, 1926), 22; also Knysh, *Try rovesnytsi*, 72; and the unpublished memoirs of Olena Fedak Sheparovych, in the possession of her daughter, Olha Kuzmovych. The same trip is mentioned by Chykalenko, in his unpublished "Spomyny," UVAN Archives, vol. 2, 122, entry for 28 May 1912, which mentions that a special dinner was held at which Pchilka was present.

6. Quoted in Knysh, *Try rovesnytsi*, 141.

7. We are at a distinct disadvantage in discussing the genesis of *Pershyi vinok* because of our inability to gain access to the unpublished materials of Kobrynska and Pchilka. However, most of Franko's legacy, as well as many memoirs about him, have been made available. Hence we have an incomplete and, it would seem, a rather one-sided view of the matter. This probably could be rectified were Kobrynska's unpublished memoirs, "Ia i zhinoche pytannia," available. Dr. Iryna Velychko, Kobrynska's niece, in a very brief article in 1929, wrote that "an untapped source for the description of this matter is the extensive correspondence of Nataliia Kobrynska with Olena Pchilka, Hanna Barvinok, Klymentyna Popovych-Boiarska and others, most especially her interesting correspondence between 1884 and 1906 with Ivan Franko." At the time of writing, this source remains unavailable to Western researchers. Iryna Velychko, "Do genezy vydannia pershoho zhinochoho Almanakha 'Pershyi Vinok,'" *Almanakh Zhinochoi doli* (1929), 34–7; quotation from 35.

   Kobrynska, like the intelligentsia generally, placed great stock in literature and the power of the press. But, according to Velychko, she was also persuaded "by the positivism of Buckle, who supported the idea that each initiative should originate within the circle of those whose primary interest [it sought to serve]." Ibid., 36.

8. Letter of Kobrynska to Franko, undated, quoted in Velychko, "Do genezy," 36.

9. Letter of Kobrynska to Franko, 5 September 1885, in *Kobrynska* (1980), 391–2. The letter was written three days after the executive board meeting.

10. Ibid., 392. In view of Franko's later claim that he was the actual editor of the almanac, his failure even to let Kobrynska know that he was in her home town when she returned from a crucial meeting of the Society, which would fund the

undertaking, was strange behaviour indeed. The fact that Franko was a supporter of the women's movement and, in the words of the persons who edited the few published letters of Kobrynska, "was her friend and mentor (*druh i nastavnyk*)," was illustrative of the underlying superiority with which the Ukrainian radicals treated women; ibid., 430; in the introduction, 16, Ivan O. Denysiuk and Kateryna A. Kril refer to Franko as Kobrynska's teacher and comrade.

11. Letter of 8 March 1887, ibid., 398.

12. Quotation from a letter to Ohonovsky, written sometime in 1892, in Ohonovsky's unpublished correspondence, TsDIA, UkSSR (Lviv), f. 109, Korespondentsiia, 74. Velychko noted that Pchilka made the orthography issue a condition of her participation, *Almanakh Zhinochoi doli* (1929), 37.

Pchilka showed great independence and initiative, handled personal tragedy and crises with amazing fortitude, and did not necessarily discuss the feminist concerns she undertook. In her autobiography, dictated in mid-1920s, she gave only factual information on *Pershyi vinok*. She stressed the originality of a publication limited to women but linking Ukrainian women who were otherwise separated by political borders. She was also emphatic that Franko had played only an advisory role, and that Kobrynska and she were the real editors of the almanac. She recalled that Franko talked them out of publishing an early short story by Kobylianska, and that she, Pchilka, paid half of the publication costs. "It seems——I continue to recollect——that the title of the collection was my idea, in a letter to Kobrynska." That was correct; Kobrynska wanted to call the almanac simply *Zhinochyi almanakh,* but Kobrynska, the positivist always in control of her emotions, gave in to the expansive, extroverted and domineering Pchilka. Pchilka's sensibilities waxed poetic. The more exotic title *Lada*, the pagan godess, had been pre-empted in the 1850s by Shukhevych in his journal for ladies, so Pchilka settled for *Pershyi vinok*. Pchilka, *Opovidannia z avtobiohrafiieiu*, 33.

13. A pun on the Russophiles' insistence upon the use of the old hard sign following some consonants. From a letter Konysky wrote in Kiev, 28 November (O.S.) 1884 to Ohonovsky, in TsDIA, UkSSR (Lviv), f. 309, op. 1, spr. 2385, 13–15.

14. *Kobrynska* (1980), 394.

15. 29 March 1889, in TsDIA, UkSSR (Lviv), 309, op. 1, spr. 2385, 63–4.

16. "The look of the book did not interest me. I did not like the title *Pershyi vinok*, did not understand the word almanac, and had not heard about a women's movement...," this woman reminisced in *Nova khata*, no. 14 (1937): 6. Sydora Navrotska-Paliiv, who was nineteen at the time, recalled that the older generation made fun of Kobrynska, "the women's rabbi," ibid., article entitled "50 lit tomu."

17. Velychko, in *Almanakh Zhinochoi doli* (1929), 37.

18. Symptomatically, Franko, in an article on *Pershyi vinok* in which he claimed to have been its editor and credited Kobrynska and Pchilka only with initiating and paying for the project, noted that marriage cut off the writing of many women. About his own wife he wrote: "I consider my wife a Galician woman; although she comes from Ukraine [she gave to the *Wreath*] her only article, "Carpathian Boiky and Their Family Life," which was based partly on her own observations and partly on written and oral materials delivered by Reverend Ivan Kuziv." His wife showed little interest in writing. Franko's article was reprinted in part in *Iuvileinyi almanakh Zhinochoi hromady* [1921–1931] (New York, [1931]).

19. There are many references to these plans. For instance, Lesia Ukrainka asked Pavlyk not to publish a short story by Kobylianska because "we want it for the

Second Wreath...so don't put it in *Narod* (People)." *Olha Kobylianska v krytytsi ta spohadakh* (Kiev, 1963), 30; see also N.O. Tomashuk, *Olha Kobylianska: Zhyttia i tvorchist* (Kiev, 1969), *passim*.

20. *Lysty do Ivana Franka i inshykh* (Lviv, 1908), 108.

21. Correspondence in WAP, Wroclaw, Ossolineum, Syg. 14779 II; published in L.B. Swiderski, ed., *Eliza Orzeszkowa, Listy II: do literatów i ludzi nauki* (Warsaw, 1938), 253–80. Oleg Sztul edited the Franko segment. Among others, Orzeszkowa, in a letter dated 20 March 1886, complained that she "cancelled her subscription to *Dilo* because Russian censorship cut out whole articles from the newspaper and covered whole columns of it with black grease, leaving nothing to read in it." Borys Hrinchenko noted ruefully that he had not seen some of his books in print, since Russian censorship would not allow them into the Russian Empire. See Hrinchenko's letter to František Rehoř, in Prague, Státní Literární Archív Památníků Národního Písemnictví B/38 30 M 60, dated 6 December 1894.

22. For instance, in a letter of 28 November 1888, she showed the necessary deference: "You are an exceptionally hard working person. My God! I'm not of the lazy sort, but I can see that my work will never yield similar results. Probably my feminine upbringing warped me forever." *Kobrynska* (1980), 403.

23. "In Galicia the main ground for radical work——peasants——already exists, while we in Ukraine must first of all build up an intelligentsia, return to the nation her "brain" and then, together with our neighbours, acquire those rights which Galicia gained a long time ago...." Originally in an article published in *Zhyttie i slovo*, a journal published by Olha Franko in Lviv and edited by Ivan in 1894–7. In *Zibrannia tvoriv* (Kiev, 1977), 8: 23.

24. Letter to Drahomanov written in April or early May 1893, in *Khronolohiia*, 197.

25. One of the first letters she wrote to Kobylianska, 17–18 May 1891; ibid., 484.

26. For example, Lesia Ukrainka's sister, Olha Kryvyniuk, described a series of lectures by a Dr. Talberg on hygiene for women, in Kiev, and how funny it was to see women struggling to put on their coats alone. This was in winter 1895. Ibid., 310.

27. See the brief account in V.I. Kalynovych, *Politychni protsesy I. Franka ta ioho tovaryshiv* (Lviv, 1967); see also "Vypysky z sudovykh aktiv u spravi Pavlyka Mykhaila i Anny," in TsDIA, UkSSR (Lviv), f. 663, op. 1, od. zb. 125, 15–22, where the Austrian policeman, writing in Polish, noted that Konysky had spent time in the area of the Galician oilfields, allegedly escaping the Russians and harbouring pro-Uniate sentiments. Reverend I. Okunevsky, because he had sent his carriage for the Konyskys, also fell under police suspicion. See also Mykhailyna Roshkevych, "Pro Olhu Kobyliansku," in *Olha Kobylianska v krytytsi ta spohadakh* (Kiev, 1963), 352.

28. October 1911, 11.

29. George Y. Boshyk, "The Rise of Ukrainian Political Parties in Russia, 1900–1907: With Special Reference to Social Democracy" (Ph.D. thesis, University of Oxford, 1981), 218, even maintains that the centre of RUP activity shifted to Lviv.

30. "Sprava ukrainskykh katedr: nashi naukovi potreby," *Literaturno-naukovyi vistnyk* (January 1907): 213–20; quotation, 218.

31. Dmytro Doroshenko, *Moi spomyny pro davnie mynule*. The most graphic description is on p. 52.

11: The National-Liberation Struggle

1. "Snytsia: voiennyi narys," in *Snytsia: noveli i narysy* (Chernivtsi, 1922). Few women, even those whose exceptional military heroism was undisputed, wrote of their experience. On the contrary, they seemed to downplay their activities and even to question the appropriateness of writing about their accomplishments. Life itself was so difficult during the prolonged hostilities that one educated middle-class woman pointed out that if it were not for the women providing the basic necessities of food and shelter, if it were not for their ability to develop survival skills, life would not have gone on. See for instance Dariia Dzerovych's unpublished memoirs, 42–50; and a first-hand account of the situation in Ukraine by a woman who travelled throughout the Ukrainian territories, Nataliia Romanovych Tkachenko, "V kraini horia i ruiny (podorozhni vrazhinnia)," *LNV* 66, no. 2–3 (August-September 1917): 295–331; 67, no. 4 (October 1917), 135–51; 68, no. 5–6 (November-December 1917), 254–83. See also *International Council of Women. Report on the Quinquennial Meeting, 6th, 1914–1920 Christiania* (1920), 410: "Ukraine, especially its Western part, has been for the last six years a huge battlefield."

2. This is an important but rarely confronted issue which goes beyond the scope of the present work, although it also had a great impact upon women. The most striking example of this tendency is the gradualness with which the Ukrainian People's Republic proclaimed its independence, through four universals. A similar tendency is evident in the futile assurances of goodwill which Vynnychenko sought from the Bolsheviks. Repeated examples of this national moderation and deference to the Russians can be found in the journal *Ukrainskaia zhizn*, which Petliura, who came to be identified with Ukrainian nationalism, edited before the First World War.

    For their part, the Russians, with very few exceptions (which include women), showed either outright hostility or a monumental blind spot to the legitimate claims of Ukrainians. Even persons considered friendly to the Ukrainian cause misunderstood it. Tuhan-Baranovsky, the liberal economist who identified himself somewhat with Ukrainians, wrote in January 1914, in response to a poll taken by *Ukrainskaia zhizn*: "I think that if there were no Galicia, we could await the gradual assimilation of the Ukrainian nation to Russia.... I ascribe the prime importance in the Ukrainian [national] renaissance to the establishment of a Ukrainian centre outside the territories of Russia." *Ukrainskaia zhizn*, no. 1 (1914): 15–16. Only a person ignorant of recent historical events in Ukraine could have made such a statement.

3. Yet Russian women did not show much interest in discovering related Slavs. While the Russians, as a result of the war, discovered "the piece of Russian land, Galicia," and manifested that interest by publishing a number of books and brochures about it in 1915, Russian women did not show much interest in Galician women.

4. Olena Pchilka in *Ridnyi krai*, no. 1 (1915): 1. Among those closed were *Rada*, the only Ukrainian daily, and *Maiak*; the ones suspended were *Ukrainska khata* (which was influenced by Kobylianska), *Dniprovi khvyli* in Katerynoslav, and *Vistnyk znannia* in Poltava.

5. TsDIA, UkSSR (Kiev), f. 301, op. 1, spr. 3206, 25–6, dated 5 May 1914, three

months before the outbreak of the war. By August, the informers and the police hinted about contacts of Ukrainian and Polish peasants of the Russian Empire "with foreigners," ibid., 49; see also ibid., spr. 3207, 27, for a report of February 1913 mentioning the work of tsarist agents in Galicia.

6. Ibid., f. 274, op. 1, od.zb. 3264. (*Perepiska s kievskoi guberniei i nachalstvom shtaba Kievskogo voennogo okruga o politicheskoi proverke lits rabotaiushchikh v gospitaliakh i sanitarnykh chastiakh.*)

7. Ibid., f. 274, op. 1, od 3 B No. 3624, 310 for examples of the detailed police screening of the women working in the hospitals.

8. *Ridnyi krai*, no. 2 (1915): 2.

9. *Ukrainskaia zhizn*, no. 5–6 (1915): 110.

10. Malytska, "Na khvyliakh svitovoi viiny," originally in *Dilo* (1937), reprinted in *Vykhovnytsia pokolin*, 58–81, ruefully noted that the sumptuous aid the German exiles received in Siberia illustrated the benefits of belonging to a strong, unified nation. See also Doroshenko, *Moi spomyny pro nedavnie mynule*, 44–6. Solovei, *Rozhrom Poltavy*, 202, recounts the tragic story of Ivan Pryima, the headmaster of a secondary school in Przemyśl, and Mykhailo Petrytsky, a member of the Viennese Reichstag, who were brought to the Russian Empire during the war, stayed on, and were shot by the Bolsheviks in Kharkiv in 1921.

11. For a discussion of the area around Kholm, and the impact it had upon the more central Ukrainian territories, see the October 1915 report of the Komitet Centralny Obywatelski Królewstwa Polskiego, Archiwum Akt Nowych, Warsaw, Syg. 37. The memoir literature attesting to these developments is too rich to be mentioned here.

12. The Jews, as an embattled minority, had set up numerous self-help associations in various Ukrainian cities and towns. But in the major cities, especially in Kiev, after 1905 and after 1917–18, co-operation of liberal Jews and democratic Ukrainians increased. Nevertheless, more Jews sided with the revolutionary Russians who disregarded the nationality question. The Poles, with their growing aspirations to resurrect the Commonwealth, disregarded Ukrainians completely. For reaction among women, see Halina Nowacka, "Ruch niepodległościowy w Kijowie," *Służba ojczyźnie*, 345–50.

13. TsGIA, USSR (Moscow), f. 102, 5 ch 46 B/ 1915, 360; 378–9; 326–7, 476 and 128; also ibid., op. 16, ed. khr. 104, pr. 1915, 146–7.

14. Ibid., 52.

15. By emphasizing revolutionary activities, one sometimes overlooks the persistence of the needs of daily existence and the preoccupation with minutiae by the governments. Thus, in the same police file in which the activities of Evgeniia Bosh, Lenin's collaborator in Vinnytsia and the area around Odessa are chronicled, we come across the unsung saga of the noblewoman Mariia Mykhailivna Pluzhanska, who on the momentous date of 9 November 1917 filed a complaint that on 29 October her home had been hit by two shells, one of which made a dent in the back wall and damaged the front door, while the other broke windows and damaged the roof. "I humbly ask that specialists be sent," she wrote, "to view and assess the damage, so that after the war I may be reimbursed." This was duly done: the damage was assessed at 174 rubles; TsDIA, UkSSR (Kiev), f. 419, op. 1, spr. 7047a, 143–9.

16. Nataliia Romanovych-Tkachenko, "Iz dniv voli," *LNV* 67, no. 1 (July 1917): 121–41. Tkachenko perished in 1937. Olena Pchilka's assessment of the

revolution is not available and her role in it remains strangely passive or silent.

17. Mirna, "Ukrainky v Tsentralnii radi," *Almanakh Zhinochoi doli* (1929), 14; Solovei has similar stories about Poltava in *Rozhrom Poltavy, passim*.

18. Khrystiuk, 1: 96 and 2: 20–1, on texts of the national-minority legislation and the convocation, in September 1917, of the Congress of Nationalities.

19. In Petrograd, as St. Petersburg was renamed during the war, the first regiment to join the workers was a Volhynian one.

    It would be instructive to study the incidence of revolutionary change-over within the military units which had a high proportion of non-Russians. Twenty-three per cent of the imperial forces were composed of Ukrainians, according to A.H. Tkachuk, "Krakh sprob Tsentralnoi Rady vykorystaty ukrainizovani viiskovi formuvannia v 1917 r.," *Ukrainskyi istorychnyi zhurnal*, no. 11 (1967): 8.

20. Lysaveta Zhuk, "Ukrainske Zhinoche Kolo," *Hromadianka* (November 1946): 5–6.

21. *Borotba, Organ tsentralnoho komitetu Ukrainskoi partii sotsialistiv revoliutsioneriv*, 31 December 1917, 24. Even small conservative Ukrainian groups stressed the importance of the active involvement of women. For instance, I. Volotynovsky published a newspaper in Kiev with a large banner headline, "Praise be to God, forever let Him be praised," in which he stressed the need for women's battalions to defend "not only Ukraine...but her neighbour, Russia, to save it from want and destruction." *Svitova zirnytsia*, no. 7 (1917–8): 2; and no. 2 (1917): 10.

22. Olimpiia Pashchenko, reminiscing about her election to the Teachers' Congress and the Constitutent Assembly, in *Nova khata*, no. 8 (1937). See also the unpublished letter of Mariia Hrushevska to Hanna Chykalenko Keller, 15 May 1920, in Keller Archive, UVAN, New York, uncatalogued.

23. The secretary of the Executive Council was Olha Ivanivna Chubuk. She kept the minutes after the Bolshevik takeover, and moved back to her native Poltava. In the fall of 1920 she was one of the many Ukrainians arrested and executed. The fate of the minutes is not known. Solovei, *Rozhrom Poltavy*, 173. Iu.I. Tereshchenko, *Politychna borotba na vyborakh do miskykh dum Ukrainy* (Kiev, 1974), 9, mentions that some materials of the "bourgeois-nationalist Central Rada" are located in the Tsentralnyi derzhavnyi arkhiv Zhovtnevoi revoliutsii in Kiev, fond 1115. Some of the published materials of the Rada appear occasionally in *Ukrainskyi istoryk* (New York). Information on the first meeting of the Rada on 8 April in *Visty [sic] z Ukrainskoi Tsentralnoi Rady u Kyivi*, no. 4 (April 1917), reprinted in *Ukrainskyi istoryk*, no. 1–4 (69–72) (1981): 180–91. On women in the Central Rada, see Zinaida Mirna, "Zhinky v Ukrainskii Tsentralnii Radi," *Almanakh Zhinochoi doli* (1929), 12–19 and her "Pratsia zhinotstva v Tsentralnii radi," *Zhinka*, 15 May 1937, 2. Khrystiuk, 1: 16, notes that Mrs. Skrypnyk represented the student groups in the Rada. Olha Oleksandrivna Hrushevska represented the left wing of the All-Imperial SR Trudovik faction; letter of Maria Hrushevska to Chykalenko-Keller, 15 May 1920, in the Keller fund in the UVAN Archives, uncatalogued.

24. The Treasury was headed by the prominent liberal economist, Tuhan-Baranovsky, who still viewed the interests of Ukraine within an imperial context. Of the women in the Rada, Cherniakhivska was the most vocal proponent of outright independence, according to a Galician ex-prisoner-of-war who worked as a clerk

in the Central Executive Rada; interview with Oleksander Zhorliakevych in Przemyśl, 22 April 1977, later confirmed by a letter dated 10 June 1978. On Radzymovska, see Ivan Rozhin, *Valentyna Radzymovska: Korotkyi narys zhyttia ta naukovoi i hromadskoi ii diialnosty* (Winnipeg, 1969).

25. As it was later characterized by a Rada member, Ievhen Chykalenko, in "Spomyny 1919," 68, unpublished manuscript in the UVAN archives.

26. For instance, see an article in *Dilo* (Lviv), 21 November 1918, "Polozhennia Ukrainskoi Narodnoi Respublyky v Kyevi."

27. Nationality issues cut across the entire fabric of life. A specific example can illustrate the difficulties of pigeonholing even families. The Vynogradov family was a little known case in point. Oleksandra Oleksiivna Vynohradova, an ardent Social Revolutionary and Petliura's first fianceé——she broke the engagement because of Petliura's Marxist social-democratic views, which she could not reconcile with her populist politics——was also an ardent Ukrainophile (she married a Prosvita activist, a man of Jewish origin, Kopeliovych). Her sisters Halia (a sculptor) and Varia (a pianist) refused to speak Ukrainian, although they knew it well. Oleksander Zhorliakevych, letter of 10 June 1978, 3–4. He was also very bitter about the failure of Jews to support Ukrainians, and the Jewish attacks on Petliura (whom Zhorliakevych did not support personally). Oleksandra Oleksiivna had told him that Petliura slapped the face of anyone who used the pejorative *zhid* in Russian (p. 3).

28. Text of the legislation in Khrystiuk, 2: 175; *narodna* refers to both nation and people; the legislation of the Rada would sway toward the second interpretation, but because the Bolsheviks popularized the term "people's," many Ukrainians in the West tend to translate *narodna* as national.

29. Polonska-Vasylenko, *Istoriia Ukrainy*, 544; also Czajecka, 817.

30. The boundaries of Ukraine were essentially ethnic and thus satisfied Wilson's Fourteen Points. Because of their continued recognition of the non-existent Russian Empire, the Allies nevertheless refused to grant recognition to Ukraine or to consider the boundaries agreed upon in the Brest-Litovsk treaty.

31. At the time of writing, Skoropadsky's memoirs were being prepared for publication by the East European Research Fund in Philadelphia. Pavlo Skoropadsky was a descendant of the eighteenth-century Ukrainian Hetman. On his mother's side he came from the Myklashevsky family, which produced prominent Cossack gentry, cultural activists and later liberal military men in the Russian Empire. Starodub, the city where Pavlo Skoropadsky attended secondary school, had been the seat of one of the Myklashevskys who had collected much of the material that served as the basis of the *Istoriia Rusov* (the influential anonymous eighteenth-century history of the Cossack period). The Myklashevskys had been early supporters of the emancipation of serfs and the founders of a productive chain of textile mills. Skoropadsky married Oleksandra Durnovo (the daughter of General Petr Durnovo, of the well known conservative family) in 1897. Her mother, however, had come from the originally Ukrainian Cossack family of the Kochubeis, who had been among those who warned Peter I of the anti-Russian campaign Mazepa had been planning in 1709. Mrs. Skoropadsky bore six children and was not active in women's organizations.

32. Quoted in Polonska-Vasylenko, *Istoriia*, 492.

33. See, for example, an article written by Mykola Liubynsky, one of the Ukrainian negotiators at Brest-Litovsk, "Iak pryishly nimtsi," *LNV* 72, no. 12, (December

1918): 202–15 (published in Kiev). He singled out Anastasiia Bitsenko, a member of the Soviet Russian delegation, for completely denying the right of any Ukrainian political party to a separate programme and doubting if anyone in Ukraine even read Ukrainian books. Trotsky, the major Soviet negotiator, walked out of the peace talks, and refused to admit the justice of any of the Ukrainian claims.

34. Naturally, women were prominent in tending to the sick, but they also participated actively in attempts to establish a Ukrainian university in Kamianets-Podilskyi. Of particular significance in this respect was the work of the chairperson of the organizing committee for the university; see Olimpiia Pashchenko, *op. cit.*; Mirna, "Zhinochyi rukh na Velykii Ukrainy," *Zhinka*, 1 April 1937, 2–3. The Kamianets-Podilskyi University was an attempt to continue the existence of the Kiev Ukrainian University. On the latter, see Oleksander Hrushevsky, "Ukrainskyi narodnyi universytet," *LNV* 68, no. 5–6, (November-December 1917): 320–5.

35. Chykalenko, "Spomyny 1919," 138.

36. Examples such as these have fed the imagination of Ukrainians outside the USSR in later years. See for instance Vasyl Zadoianny, "Zhinky heroini ukrainskoi vyzvolnoi borotby," *Dorohovkaz: Orhan voiatskoii dumky i chynu* (Toronto), no. 4 (January 1965): 2–8; also Luhovy, *passim*, and Iryna Shmigelska Klymkevych's account of her service in a Cossack detachment headed by a man calling himself Honta, in *Kalendar Chervonoi kalyny* (1925), 97–9.

37. See George Luckyj's translation of Mykola Khvylovy, *Stories from the Ukraine* (New York, 1960); Halyna Zhurba's "V pereleti rokiv," *Nova Ukraina* (September 1928): 58–78.

   The historian Oleksandra Efimenko died a victim of marauding bands, which Soviet sources say were nationalist and others maintain were communist. Nadiia M. Kybalchych (born 1857), who wrote under the pseudonym Natalka Poltavka, committed suicide in December 1918, unable to bear the deprivations.

38. Blanka Baranova, "Ukrainske zhinotstvo i nashi vyzvolni zmahannia," *Novyi chas*, 1 November 1937, giving 13 August as the date of the first meeting. An article on a branch of the Ukrainian women's organization in Berne in *Nasha meta*, 5 October 1919, dates it 3 August.

39. "Uchast predstavnytsi zhinok v pershii derzhavnii naradi," *Nasha meta*, 9 November 1919, 1, unsigned.

40. Ibid., 16 November 1919, 5. This is certainly not one of the better examples of Petliura's rhetoric, but then it was not the time for polished works.

41. "The Sanitary Conditions in Ukraine," submitted by Mme. Serge Zarchy, General Secretary of the Ukrainian National Council of Women in International Council of Women, *Report of Quinquennial meeting, 6th, 1914–1920, Christiania* (1920), 419, quoting a report of Major Lederrey, member of the International Red Cross Society, painted a grim picture:

> In October 1919, 30 per cent of the Ukrainian army were victims of exanthematic fever, and 60 per cent of typhus recurrens. Moreover, the civilian population were in the same unfortunate sanitary circumstances as the army. For instance, in the Province of Podolia, which numbers 4 million inhabitants, 60,000 were attacked by exanthematic fever and 80,000 by typhus recurrens.

The statistics speak for themselves. But the number of victims instead of decreasing becomes larger every day. Besides the above-named diseases there have been also many cases of enteric fever and cholera with a very high percentage of deaths (56 per cent), and even a few cases of Asiatic plague have been recorded lately....

In Galicia too, the epidemics are spreading very rapidly.

The quotation in the text is from ibid., 420.

42. The petition read:

Dear Sisters: For two years the Ukrainian nation has been struggling with its enemies for the right to exist, for an independent sovereign Ukraine, but enemy powers do not want to give us that right and have carried on a lengthy bloody struggle. In vain!

Our entire Ukrainian people, as one person, recognized the independence of Ukraine; all Ukrainian women have come to the defence of the native hearth against our old enemies. No one can conquer this force.

But in these continual national battles our sons, husbands and fathers are dying on the field of honour and from these battles awful illnesses are being spread in our land, and we do not have the means with which to save our wounded and our sick——they are dying without medical help, for it is forbidden to transport medicines and bandages.

We are not asking for help.

Our state is rich in bread, we have the means to pay for everything, we are turning to you, sisters, only with the request that you raise your voice before your governments and demand the rescinding of the ban on exporting to Ukraine medicines and bandages.

You, women and mothers draped in eternal sorrow at the loss of husbands and sons who died in the defence of their fatherland, take this matter to your hearts.

You lucky ones whose husbands and sons returned home and are working now on the reconstruction of their native States——to you we entrust the lives of our people.

What international covenant sanctioned this inhuman atrocity which forces a people 40 million strong to die without medical help?

Women of the entire world! The Ukrainian women turn to your hearts and your consciences!

Text in *Nasha meta*, 2 November 1919, 1. The original proclamation was dated 7 October 1919.

43. Unpublished personal memoirs of Sheparovych, and *Nasha meta*, 9 November 1919, 8.

44. Ibid., 2 November 1919, 19, and 16 November 1919, 1–2, as well as Chykalenko, unpublished "Spomyny," entry dated 10 November 1919, 179.

45. I.Kv., "Stanovyshche zhinky v bolshevytskii Rossii," *Nasha meta*, 14 December 1919, 6–7.

46. Quotation from Stepaniv, *Na peredodni*, 35. Stepaniv, with the help of Katria Putsula Lototska, was able to recall that in addition to the two of them, the other women members were: Mariia Bachynska-Dontsova, Olha Levytska-Basarab,

Pavlyna Mykhailyshyn, Mariia Petruniak, Mariia Gizhovska-Krilyk; Sofiia Khudiak-Lypkova, Mariia Terletska, Anna Lentsiuk-Tsar, Nataliia Rykhvytska, Emiliia Kushnir, Anna Kushnir-Pletnyk, Ianka Konyk, Mariia Khmyr-Kozak, Sofiia Khmyr-Levytska, Sofiia Navrotska-Trach, Stefaniia Pashkevych, Savyna Sydorovych, Handzia Dmyterko, Ivanna Murska, Anna Levytska, and five women whose first names I have not been able to establish: Oprysko, Vaniv-Voloshchak, and the three Oryshkevych sisters.

Stepaniv was taken prisoner by the Russians, exiled to Siberia, and apparently exchanged for the communist activist Bochkareva. When she returned to Lviv she joined the Western Ukrainian military forces. After the war, she completed her Ph.D. in Vienna, married a fellow officer, Roman Dashkevych, and taught geography in the high schools of Lviv. The marriage was unsuccessful and the couple separated. Stepaniv was again exiled to Siberia when the Bolsheviks took Lviv in 1944. She returned home in the late fifties, and died in 1963. Halechko, who had been Stepaniv's classmate in the gymnasium, was taciturn, withdrawn and, according to Sheparovych's unpublished memoirs, did not even admit to being Ukrainian. Her joining the Ukrainian contingent of the army came as a surprise to all.

"Uchast zhinotstva u Vyzvolnykh Zmahanniakh 1918–1920 rr.," *Novyi shliakh*, 14 March 1981; quotation from 13.

"We did not ask our parents," Devosser continued in a letter written in April 1981; "they were in the provinces. The girls were raised at home in a patriotic spirit, so it is no wonder that at the first call to come to the defence of the Fatherland everything was ready." Letter in possession of author. Devosser went to Ķiev; she sharply criticized the female commander of the unit, Mariia Kryva; see also *Litopys Chervonoi kalyny*, no. 4 (1930): 19–20.

The Jewish woman was Khaia Keisler from Rohatyn. See *Zvit upravy gimnaziinykh kursiv z ukrainskoiu vykladovoiu movoiu u Vidni 1914/15*. The fullest accounts of the Women's Committee are in the memoirs of Dzerowycz and Trembicka, and in S. Kabarovska, "Pro povstannia i diialnist Ukrainskoho zhinochoho komitetu pomochy dlia ranenykh u Vidni——i pro podibni iomu," *Almanakh Zhinochoi doli* (1930), 63–71.

They were defended by Stepan Baran; three men also involved, *Dilo*, 20 June 1938, 3.

Sheparovych was involved in the coup through her husband. Instead of encouraging women's participation, Western Ukrainians tended to be critical of women during times of crisis. Even Handzia Dmyterko-Ratych, not given to complaining, wrote bitterly that "the critical comments on the inferiority of women...hurt the women in the army." See her "Z zbroieiu v rukakh," in *Ukrainske zhinotsvo Ditroitu* (1955), 243.

"Boiove zvidomlennia z 7 padolysta 1918," *Dilo*, 3 November 1918, 1.

Marja Herbutowna, "Młodziez akademicka we Lwowie, .1916–1918," *Służba ojczyźnie*, 9–14. Polish women in turn complained that the clergy and some men stymied the activities of the women; Sofia Moraczewska, "Liga Kobiet Galicji i Sląska," ibid., 145–50. In addition to their regular organizations, the Polish women organized a "League for Military Alert," first in Russian Poland in 1913, and the following year in Galicia and Silesia. During the war, the Rada Główna Opiekuńcza, a semi-official agency co-ordinating aid to Poles, had women's sections which played a vital role, although distinctly subordinate to the men.

Materials on RGO, arranged by activities in particular localities, are located in the AAN, Warsaw. The parts most relevant to Ukrainians are in RGO, Syg. 901, 771, 767, 755, 759, 826, 900, 1279, 1308, 539, 536, 736–745. All the radical Polish women actively sided with the Poles against Ukrainians, men or women.

54. *Nasha meta*, 26 February 1919, 4; also see Sofiia Oleksiv-Fedorchak, "Z lystopadovykh spomyniv," 2 and 32; Olena Sheparovych, "Lystopadovi spohady," *Zhinka*, 1 November 1936, 2–3, as well as her "V desiatylittia," *Almanakh Zhinochoi doli* (1930), 48–53, and "Ukrainskyi chervonyi khrest u Lvovi," *Visti kombatanta*, no. 3 (1961): 25–32. *Dilo* naturally covered the events extensively, without gilding them.

55. F. Bekesevych-Matskiv, "Z viddali 55 rokiv," *Svitlo* (Toronto) (November 1974): 390–1, describing the situation in Ternopil.

56. MLR, "Chy treba nam okremykh zhinochykh organizatsii," *Nasha meta*, 7 August 1919, 2. The author was Milena Rudnytska, who came to play a prominent role in the Western Ukrainian women's movement.

57. From the Polish side the delegates were Maria Dulebianka, also a socialist activist, Marja Opeńska and Dzieduszycka; see *Nasha meta*, 15 February 1919, and 1 March 1919, 2–3; no. 6, 9 March 1919, 2–3; as well as Sofiia Oleskiv-Fedorchak, "Z lystopadovykh spomyniv," ibid., 2 and 32; and 1919, *Visti kombatanta*, no. 3 (1961): 29–30.

58. "Rana, shcho beznastanno kervavyt," *Nasha meta*, 14 December 1919, 2–3, for a graphic description of Pykulychi camp.

59. Shakh, 2: 151.

60. On Oleskiv, see *Nasha meta*, 28 September 1919, 17; on Przemyśl, ibid., no. 1, 1919. On the arrests in Lviv in 1919, there are a few brief articles in *Nova khata* (November 1928).

61. A protest meeting was held in Lviv on 24 November 1919; see the account in *Nasha meta*, 30 November 1919, 1. A suggestion to write down the oral history of the times was made by Slava Ia., "Dopys z provintsii," *Nasha meta*, 23 November 1919, 5. There does not seem to have been a comprehensive follow-up, although the women did make an effort at interviewing some peasants.

62. The article first appeared in *Ukrainskyi prapor* and then was reprinted in *Nasha meta*, 23 November 1919, 3–5 and 30 November 1919, 5–6. At the time, she was signing her name Milena Rudnytska-Lysiak. The title of the article was "Lvivske zhinotstvo pidchas padolystovoho perevorotu." Although she mentioned it in her later article on UHA women, Rudyntska upgraded the importance of the kitchen work in the later account. The quotation is from *Nasha meta*, 30 November 1919, 6.

63. According to K. Malytska, "Pro znachinnia vlasnoi presy dlia zhinotstva i iak vona v nas rozvyvalasia," *Almanakh Zhinochoi doli* (1927), 6, the major reason the majority of women failed to support this newspaper was that it was funded by the socialists.

As befits a future leader of Western Ukrainian women, Rudnytska considered the women themselves guilty for failing to press their representation. M. Rudnytska, "Chomu ukrainski zhinky ne maiut predstavnytstva v Natsionalnii Radi," *Nasha meta*, 1 February 1919: "Who is guilty in this? The opposition of the males who lead the country or perhaps the indolence of the women? I am afraid that it is the latter."

Ukrainian women in Lviv, despite later patriotic writing, were perturbed by the cavalier attitude of Ukrainian men. *Dilo*, on 19 November 1918, published the following note, which was only signed by "A Lviv Ukrainian Woman." *Dilo* did not comment on the text, which was prepared for presentation to the government of the Ukrainian Republic. It printed the note in its entirety:

> From the circles of women we have received the following comments: The temporary basic law on state independence [*derzhavna samostiinist*] of the Western Ukrainian People's Republic provides that the Constituent Assembly and all government representative agencies of the Republic will be based upon a universal, equal, direct, secret and proportional electoral law without regard to sex. That means that the Ukrainian woman will achieve her rights in our People's [*narodnia*] Republic.

> If this is the case, then justice for the Ukrainian woman would demand that she be given representation in the present temporary legislative body of the Republic, in the Ukrainian National Council [*Ukrainska Natsionalna Rada*]. I think that the council, which enacted the above provisional law about the suffrage rights of women, cannot and will not have any reservations about women participating in it now. This can be done without difficulty. The Ukrainian women can gain representation in the council in much the same fashion as eminent citizens were co-opted into it last week.

> In this matter I turn first and foremost to the Ukrainian women of the city of Lviv. Let them first come to an understanding among themselves and then present their case to the presidium of the counci with the demand for representation and determine their candidates [*oznachyt kandydatok*], and the council will certainly fulfill this demand.

> Finally, one more item: we are building a Peoples' Republic in our land. Let our womanhood delegate to the council individuals who by their own proven convictions give full assurances [*zaporuka*] that they will truly uphold and defend the national-republican ideas [*narodno respublykanski ideii*].

64. *Nasha meta*, 9 November 1919, 1.
65. Editorial, ibid., 24 August 1919, after the journal had been suspended for a time.
66. One is reminded of Kobrynska's quip about the widows of the clergy being the true proletariat of Galicia. Now the women, especially Teodora Bezpalko, made the claim very consistently. See Bezpalko's "Zhinka i vyborche pravo," *Nasha meta*, 5 October 1919, 5 and 12 October 1919, 5; and D.S., "Respublyka," ibid., 1 February 1919, 1–2.
67. Rudnytska, "Trahichnyi konflikt zhinky iak matery," in *Nasha meta*, fuller discussion below.
68. O.H., ibid., 25 February 1919, 1–2. Most likely that author was Olena Kysilevska.

12: Organizing the Union

1. The women of the extreme left in Galicia broke away to join the Communist Party of Western Ukraine, which was destroyed by Stalin in 1938. The die-hard

old Russophile Ladies' Society, boosted by Russian émigrés, became a miniscule anachronism running a dormitory in Lviv. This society is discussed Chapter 13.

2. At the 1917 Congress in Lviv, Ievheniia Makarushka was elected president; the secretary, Stefaniia Savytska Salamanchuk, was soon replaced by Iryna Studynska-Tysovska; see *Almanakh Zhinochoi doli* (1927), 127; see Kabarovska's article in *Nasha meta*, 30 November 1919, and [Milena Lysiak-Rudnytska] "Chy treba nam okremykh zhinochykh organizatsii?," ibid., 7 August 1919. For a discussion of membership statistics, see note 9 below.

    The executive board of the Barvinok Circle, which decided on 19 October 1921 to go ahead with the planning of the Congress, consisted of Mariia Voloshyn, O. Korenets, K. Malytska, Sofiia Oleskiv (who had published in *Nasha meta*), M. Rudnytska, O. Sheparovych and Stefaniia Shypailo.

3. Sheparovych and Rudnytska remained very close, united by a common sense of patriotic duty. In a letter of encouragement in the 1950s, Rudnytska tried to convince her dejected colleague: "Just as a black man cannot shed his skin, so we will remain Ukrainian...and must work in that community;" Rudnytska file, UVAN archive, uncatalogued.

4. On the Congress, see "V desiatlittia vseukrainskoho zhinochoho ziizdu," *Almanakh Zhinochoi doli* (1930), 150–3; Rudnytska, "Piatnadtsiatlittia odnoho zizdu," *Zhinka*, 1 January 1937, 1, and ibid., 15 January 1937, 1; see also the anonymous "Iuvilei Soiuzu Ukrainok v Rivnomu," *Nova khata*, no. 9 (1937). An announcement of the congress was published in *Svoboda* (Jersey City), 13 December 1921. Rudnytska based her article on notes that she later lost.

5. "Chy treba nam okremykh zhinochykh organizatsii?," *Nasha meta*, 7 August 1919, 3.

6. News item in *Svoboda* (Jersey City), 14 January 1922.

7. Text in M. Lozynsky, "Polska politsiia u Lvovi rozihnala Vseukrainskyi zhinochyi zizd," *Svoboda*, 19 January 1922.

8. The resolutions have not been published, and the minutes of the meetings do not seem to exist. Rudnytska mentioned them in an article written in 1937. The quotation is from a letter she wrote to Chykalenko-Keller, 3 February 1924, in Keller file, UVAN Archives, uncatalogued. Also an article in *Svoboda*, 17 March 1922.

9. The population of inter-war Poland was about 30 million; roughly 15 per cent were Ukrainians, who constituted for the most part the native population of the eastern part of the country. Ukrainians were mainly farmers, only 1.1 per cent were of the so-called intelligentsia. The petty bourgeoisie and the merchants had very few Ukrainians. About 80 per cent of the merchants in the eastern part of Poland were Jewish; throughout Poland, more than half the merchants were representative of national minorities. For an analysis of demographic data, see Marian Marek Drozdowski, *Społeczeństwo, Państwo, Politycy II Rzeczypospolitej* (Cracow, 1972). On the political background, see Mirosława Papierzyńska-Turek, *Sprawa ukraińska w Drugiej Rzeczypospolitej, 1922–1926* (Cracow, 1979); Antony Polonsky, *Politics in Independent Poland 1921–1939: The Crisis of Constitutional Government* (Oxford, 1972); Stephan Horak, *Poland and Her National Minorities* (New York, 1961); and Ivan Kedryn, *Zhyttia, podii, liudy: Spomyny i komentari* (New York, 1976).

    Reliable statistics on the Union are not available and the information is not consistent. According to *Sprawozdanie z zycia mniejszości narodowych*, no. 1

(1936): 35, as of 29 March 1936, the membership of the organization was 50,000, an increase of 11,000 from the previous year. The Union's report for 1936 mentioned that it had 67 branches, 1,101 circles and 45,000 members. In a letter from the Ukrainian Women's Union to the Ukrainian Women's League of America in April 1937 (exact date not given, the letter is in the uncatalogued archives of the Ukrainian Women's League in New York), 75 branches are mentioned, and 1,150 peasant circles, with a total of 50,000 members. That is also the number given by Konstantyna Malytska, "Pislia rozviazannia Soiuzu Ukrainok," *Zhinochyi svit* (June 1938). Lucja Charewiczowa, the Polish feminist and patriotic activist, writing under the pseudonym C. Mikułowska, *"Ukraiński" ruch kobiecy* (Lviv, 1937), 11, quoted the number 39,199 as having been officially announced by the Union itself in 1936. Milena Rudnytska, "Ideolohichni pozytsii i zavdannia matirnoho Soiuzu Ukrainok," *Informatsiinyi lystok MSU* (New York, 1951) gave the membership as 100,000.

According to M. Feliński [R. Różycki], *Ukraińcy w Polsce odrodzonej* (Warsaw, 1931), Prosvita in 1928 had 84 branches and 2,916 reading rooms. Among the other major Ukrainian organizations in which women were active were Silskyi Hospodar (Village Farmer), the Association of Day-Care Centres, the Temperance Union, Marian Sodalities, women's sections in political parties and some philanthropic societies. The Union was the most numerous and the most ef-fective; most women accepted it as their representative on the international arena. The Poles blocked the establishment of a united Ukrainian women's organization for all Ukrainians in the Polish territories; letter of Milena Rudnytska to Hanna Chykalenko-Keller, 15 July 1923, in the Ukrainian Academy of Arts and Sciences in the US (New York), Chykalenko-Keller Archive, uncatalogued.

According to *Amerykanskyi prosvitianyn* (Lviv: Prosvita, 1925) "there is no shortage of women in the organization. They are mostly young women, which is understandable, since they do not have as many duties as the married ones. More frequently, however, Prosvita sponsored sewing and home economics courses. The peasant woman is emerging from her narrow confines. Villages whose resources are meagre established unions [of villages] to fund courses and maintain a reading room." The same source also notes the existence of 760 amateur theatrical groups in Eastern Galicia and 263 choirs, while there were only 10 Ukrainian orchestras in 1925. See pp. 3–6; the quotation is from p. 5.

10. Zinaida Mirna, a Ukrainian activist originally from the Kuban, noted the unusually large number of women peasants actively involved in the women's movement. She considered the solidarity between the classes in Galicia of singular importance; Mirna, "Vrazhennia z Ukrainskoho zhinochoho kongresu v Stanyslavovi," *Zhinocha dolia*, no. 15–16 (1934): 3–4. *Ukrainska Zahalna Entsyklopediia: Knyha znannia v 3-okh tomakh* (Lviv, 1932), ed. Ivan Rakovsky, 3: 169, in identifying the Women's Union, characterized its aim as follows: "to organize Ukrainian women, especially the peasants...for the raising of their cultural and economic level and for the full utilization of all their potential rights in society and in the state."

11. Polonsky, *Politics in Independent Poland*, 22, estimates that 20 per cent of the coal mines, 99 per cent of the basalt mines, 60 per cent of the chemical industry, 20 per cent of oil refineries and 30 per cent of the metal industry were in government hands. Railways, merchant marine, posts and telegraphs and telephones were about 95 per cent government-owned. All commercial aviation

and all armaments were also in the hands of the government.

12. Ukrainian merchants supported Ukrainian cultural and community ventures, while the co-operative was frequently their chief support.

Some statistical data on the Central Co-operative Association and its finances are available in Ivan Martiuk, *Tsentrosoiuz* (n.p., 1973); see also Volodymyr Nestorovych, *Ukrainski kuptsi i promyslovtsi v Zakhidnii Ukraini* (Toronto 1977). Mikułowska, citing no sources, gives the number of co-operatives in 1930 as 3,377 with a membership of 443,000; in 1933 she stated that 57,601 of these were women. The co-operative movement began in Galicia in the 1860s, but the central association was created only in 1883 (Narodna torhivlia——a retail co-operative), and the co-ordinating agency (Kraievyi soiuz reviziinyi——Territorial Audit Union) in 1903. After the First World War the name was changed to Reviziinyi soiuz ukrainskykh kooperatyv——Audit Union of Ukrainian Co-operatives. In 1932 it had a capital of 45 million złoty, and donated 120,000 złoty of the profits to Ukrainian cultural and welfare organizations. See also Ivanna Blazhkevych, "V chyikh rukakh rozvii nashoi kooperatsii," *Zhinocha dolia*, 1 February 1931, 19–24 (3–18 confiscated); Uliana Starosolska, "Zhinka i kooperatsiia," *Nova khata*, no. 14, 1937, as well as the articles of Neonila Selezinka, Kharytia Kononenko and Kysilevska in *Nova khata, passim*.

By 1934, the Audit Union had more than half a million members and 20 million złoty. But only 13 to 15 per cent of the members were women, *Zhinocha dolia*, 1 March 1934, 7–8. The decline in capital was due to restrictive Polish policies.

13. Ivan Martiuk, *Tsentrosoiuz*, 30. Martiuk errs somewhat; the Village Farmer moved toward organizing women *en masse* only in 1936. The Village Farmer, founded in 1899, while technically not a co-operative but an association, aimed at disseminating rational farming techniques among the peasants, encouraging both involvement in the co-operative movement and *ad hoc* co-operative ventures.

14. Text of instruction in *Zhinocha dolia*, 1 May 1934.

The Ukrainian women participated in a meeting of the International Women's Co-operative Guild in 1922 when it was headed by Emma Freudlich of Vienna, who was the only woman member of the Economic Committee of the League of Nations. Ukrainian participation was most compromising for Polish groups, which had not yet organized themselves nationally, according to Anna Szelagowska, *Międzynarodowe organizacje kobiece* (Warsaw, 1934). Economic concerns had also gone hand in hand with the pre-war organization of women. Women's co-operatives, self-help associations and trade-training courses continued to grow steadily after the founding of the first women's co-operative, Trud (Labour), in Lviv in 1902. Without engaging in theoretical analyses of the relationship between feminism and the principles of economic co-operation, the Ukrainian women plunged into co-operative ventures as a matter of necessity.

15. One of the few village women to complain repeatedly of opposition from men was Hanna Mazurenko of the Women's Union in Hushanky. Yet the work of the circle prospered, and her own husband, Konstantyn, offered the women active support. *Zhinocha dolia*, 15 June 1928, 6. Mrs. L. Burachynsky, in an undated letter I received in July 1981, also recalled sporadic opposition from men; short-lived opposition to a women's organization in the village of Kidach is documented in *Zhinocha dolia*, 1 January 1927, 2. Here is a random example of the initial lack of consistency in the terminology used: in the village of

Hrabkivtsi, as late as March 1927, the wife of the local pastor, Reverend Loshny, initiated the formation of a Women's Group (Hurtok) which was affiliated with the Co-operative and was also a part of the Union, ibid., 15 November 1927, 5.

16. Kolomyia was the site of the meeting, ibid., February 1926, 3.

17. Kysilevska had wanted to be a singer, an accepted escape-route from constricting Galician life. Her mother had insisted on having girls receive the same education as boys. Solomiia Krushelnytska, like Kysilevska, also the daughter of a priest, had proved that it was possible to convert a voice with hard work into an international career. But Kysilevska's father had died; she lost her voice as a result of a respiratory illness, and became a teacher.

18. *Zhinocha dolia*, September 1926. Also see letter of Olena Sheparovych to Kysilevska, ibid., November 1925, 3; there is an obituary notice on Iuliian Kysilevsky in ibid., 15 March 1929, 11.

19. *Zhinka*, September 1935, 1.

20. "Metodyka pratsi u silskykh kruzhkakh Soiuzu Ukrainok," *Zhinka*, 1 December 1936, 5.

21. By William Simens, the Volodymyr Simenovych, M.D. who was Kysilevska's brother, quotation from *Zhinocha dolia*, October 1925, 6.

22. Editorial in *Zhinocha dolia*, October 1926, 3.

23. Ibid., December 1926, 3.

24. Neonila Selezinka, an activist in both the Women's Union and the co-operative movement, pointed out that the peasant women understood the importance of the co-operative movement better than the intelligentsia women, ibid., January 1926, 4.

25. Ibid., August-September 1927, 6.

26. Ibid., September 1925, 5–6.

27. The text of the instruction is in ibid., 1 May 1934, 2. Among the duties of this person was also the popularization of the Ukrainian press, especially *Zhinocha dolia, Zhinocha volia, Nova khata* and *Hopodarsko-kooperatyvnyi chasopys*.

28. See, for instance, an article by Stefa H. in *Zhinocha dolia*, December 1927, 2–3, urging the women of the towns to "drop your backwardness and harmful distaste for the intelligentsia, and enter the ranks of the Women's Union. Get yourself a good speaker, who would duly defend your rights in the organization, and do not shy away from any work." See also the uncatalogued correspondence of Odarka Skochdpol with Uliana Kravchenko, in the Kravchenko archive. In Stusiv, for example, the Women's Circle disintegrated after the wife of the pastor, Reverend Karpinsky, moved out. It was rejuvenated through the efforts of the indefatigable teacher, Olha Bohachevska, ibid., 1 March 1928, 3.

29. See article on the annual meeting of the Union on 27–8 December 1928 in *Dilo* of 4 January 1929, 4; also letter from George Perfecky, 5 February 1983, to the author.

30. Since the Catholic Church, which had official status in the Habsburg Monarchy, did not recognize divorces, neither did the Austrian codex. Poland kept the legal systems of the former partitioning powers for more than a decade, so that areas previously under Russian rule provided for divorce, while those under Austrian law did not.

31. For example, at the annual meeting of 27–8 December 1928 the following branches, circles and federated associations were represented: Berezhany, Halych, Horodok, Dolyna, Kolomyia, Klepariv, Kalush, Zboriv, Zolochiv, Zhovkva,

Iavoriv, Kopychyntsi, Sokal, Skole, Stryi, Synevidsko Vyzhnie, Staryi Sambir, Stanyslaviv, Przemyśl, Pidhaitsi, Radekhiv and Rohatyn. Greetings were sent from branches of the Union in Chortkiv and Horodenka as well as from the Zhinocha Hromada in Chernivtsi (Olha Huzar); *Zhinocha dolia*, 1 January 1929, 2; also *Dilo*, 4 January 1929, 4.

32. The best available introduction to the primary-school issue is Stanisław Mauersberg, *Szkolnictwo powszechne dla mniejszości narodowych w Polsce w latach 1918–1939* (Wrocław, 1968); discussion of the "Materiańska mowa" [*sic*] is on 11. See also Mieczysław Iwanicki, *Oświata i szkolnictwo ukraińskie w Polsce, 1918–1939* (Siedlce, 1975) for statistical information on Ukrainian-language schools.

33. Mauersberg, 59; by 1939 the number of public schools with Ukrainian as the language of instruction had declined from 3,600 to 450; ibid., 103, quoting the Ukrainian deputy Dmytro Velykanovych.

34. Mauersberg, 90; also *Zvidomleniia z diialnosty Ukrainskoho pedahohichnoho t-va, 1 IX. 1922 do 31 VIII. 1923* (n.p., 1923); Drozdowski, 70; also Akademiia Nauk Ukrainskoi RSR: Instytut Suspilnykh Nauk, *Sotsialni peretvorennia u radianskomu seli: na prykladi zakhidnykh oblastei Ukrainskoi RSR* (Kiev, 1976).

35. Severyna Paryllie, OSBM, "30 littia vazhnoi nashoi stanytsi," *Zhinka* (August 1936), editorial, 1–2. Mother Paryllie was a frequent contributor to the women's press. She was Jewish and survived the Second World War in hiding, while one of her nieces, who had also become a Catholic, refused to hide. Mother Severyna died in the early 1950s in Western Ukraine in a private home after the Soviets had disbanded the monasteries.

36. The best documentation is to be found in the materials on the Ukrainskyi Instytut dlia divchat, Przemyśl, WAP, UID, especially Syg. 7 and 17. According to the latter, in 1921, of the 192 students, 12 were funded by the Union, and 15 were orphans under the care of the Union. The Union was also instrumental in getting other community organizations to sponsor needy women students, including émigrés from Eastern Ukraine. See also "V iakomu napriami rozbuduvaty divoche shkilnytstvo," *Zhinka*, 15 March 1937, 6.

37. *Zhinocha dolia, Almanakh* (1928), 77. In 1935 the Union asked the Ukrainian Institute for Girls in Przemyśl to take over the supervision of the sewing courses it had run, WAP, UID, Syg. 9, 14 May 1935, 308. Also Rusova, "Chy potribna zhinkam osvita," *Hromadianka*, 15 December 1938, 7; *Zhinka* constantly encouraged women to study and prepare for various professions.

38. *Dilo*, 5 May 1929, 11. Among the courses taught were languages, history, geography, civics, economics, accounting, fashion design, interior design, drawing, chemistry, home economics, hygiene, stenography, typing and marketing. Some sewing and physical education were also included.

39. The tension between the orders was generally caused by property disputes; the convent house at Zhuravnytsi was contested by Basilian nuns, Josephite nuns and Sisters Servant alike; information in the correspondence of Bishop Kotsylovsky to Bishop Lakota, in WAP, Przemyśl, AGKB, Syg. 9484.

40. Letter of a participant, Ievheniia Verbytska, to the author, dated Toronto, 6 June 1981. Fuller discussion of the issue is to be found in the author's "The Ukrainian University in Galicia, a Pervasive Issue," *Harvard Ukrainian Studies* 5, no. 4 (December 1981): 497–545. Drozdowski, 22, notes that in the 1920s the gentry children in grammar schools constituted a bare 0.2 per cent of the entire

population, while the same group accounted for 3.3 per cent of first-year university students. Of the 2,020 students in Lviv entering institutions of higher learning, only 340 were of the Greek-Catholic rite. Only 420 of the total were women, of whom very few were Ukrainians. See L. Horbacheva, "Chy nam ne potribno inteligentsii," *Zhinka*, 15 October 1935, 2.

41. The most open discussion of the conflict between the two organizations was held at the general meeting of the Association on 27 March 1927 in Lviv. Information on the Society is to be found in a letter by Olena Zalizniak to Chykalenko-Keller, dated 15 June 1923, in the UVAN archives, and in Lvivskyi oblasnyi derzhavnyi arkhiv, "Ukrainskoe tovarystvo zhenshchin s vysshym obrazovaniem vo Lvove (*sic*)," f. 119, op. 1, spr. 1, 1 October 1924—3 May 1928. Minutes of the Association are preserved there. Fuller discussion is provided at the end of the chapter.

42. Few émigré women from the Eastern Ukrainian territories who were prominent in the women's movement answered the siren call of the homeland. Foremost among them were the Hrushevsky women who returned in 1924, and Nadiia Surovtseva. [See Part VI for their subsequent fate.] Some Galician women, also motivated by the ostensible opportunity for patriotic work in the motherland which, in slightly changed circumstances, could have been theirs, were also lured to the Ukrainian SSR. The largest group left in 1925. Most eventually perished in the purges. Western Ukrainians, for their part, also relegated them to obscurity, along with the national communists. But the wife of Ivan Krushelnytsky, the pianist Olena Levytska, did not emigrate with her husband and in-laws, although she let them take her daughter. When the family perished in the purges, she led one of the few successful fights to get the child back. Burachynska, letter, 14 August 1981.

43. Rudnytska, [unsigned article, but authorship confirmed by her son], "Borotba z bolshevyzmom," *Zhinka*, 1 September 1936, 2–3.

44. See the account in *Zhinocha dolia*, January 1929, 2; minutes and more detailed information are not available.

45. The following resolutions were passed at the meeting: "The Congress 1. stressed the importance of the elections for Ukrainians in their struggle with the Poles; 2. called for a united front against the Poles with a direct plea to all the parties to co-operate. The Congress enjoins all Ukrainian women to use their power to minimize party squabbles in Ukrainian society in view of the moral harm which threatens the Ukrainian nation because of party struggles in the pre-vote stages carried on by unethical, extremely demagogic means. 3. called on all parties to support the needs of women, to make certain that an adequate number of women appear on their lists, and that they choose only those women who enjoy the support of the masses or of women. Therefore, the Congress demands that political parties consider only those women candidates of whom the central women's organization, the Union, approves, and 4. expressed support for the actions of the Women's Union to date in the defence of Ukrainian women's interests and entrusted it to continue the matter." Text in *Zhinocha dolia*, January 1928, 2.

46. Nataliia Iurchyshyn and Valia Tanasevych worked in Tsentrosoiuz; Nadia Petryk at Silskyi Hospodar. Full account in *Dilo*, 24 February 1929, 5.

47. Full text, ibid., 21 March 1929, 1.

48. Speech at the Sejm, 22 March, report ibid., 24 March 1929, 1.

49. *Dilo*, defending the Union, commented on an article in *Proletarska pravda* which had gleefully discussed the suspension of the "ladies' society" that the author

obviously was ignorant of what he was writing about. "Bilshovytskyi nekrolog dlia SU," ibid., 9 April 1929, 1–2. Coverage of women's activities declined markedly once the suspension affair ended. The text of document lifting suspension is in *Zhinocha dolia*, 1 June 1929, 2.

13: Toward a Democratic Union

1. *Zhinocha dolia*, 1 January 1926, 18; 1 October 1925, advertising section. Olha Melnyk complained: "It is difficult for me to combat Polish and Jewish competition, all the more so since I am the only Ukrainian working in the field and must learn through practice. Nevertheless, the outlook for the future is bright," ibid., November 1925, 14. The German wife of Dr. Orest Deskaliuk realized that she could do a good business selling Ukrainian folk artifacts. She established the *Ukrainische Volkskundliche Werkstatt* in Vienna but could not find a Ukrainian woman "with commercial savvy and energy" to help her in the venture. Mrs. Deskaliuk, who came from an old merchant family in Hamburg, opened a branch of her shop in Berlin and built up contacts with the USA. "It became fashionable in Germany and America to wear what was called 'Ukrainian blouses,' and her business prospered," ibid., 1 April 1929, 4.
2. Ibid., 12 April 1931.
3. *Nova khata*, no. 1, 1928; the congress was held on 14 December 1927, *Zhinocha dolia*, 1 January 1928, 1–2; Mikułowska, 22–5.
4. *Istoriia Lvova*, 170; Shakh, 1: 137; and Mariia Krushelnytska, "Potreba orhanizatsii sluh po mistakh," *Zhinocha dolia*, 1 January 1929, 15.
5. Letter of Franka Stakhova in uncatalogued archives of the Ukrainian National Women's League of America; Polonsky, 315 and 371–3. In feeble attempts to defend their actions, the Poles dredged up a high-school student, Wiktor Iwanchów, as he signed himself, who admitted to burning harvested wheat at a farm in Sushyn to ingratiate himself with his Ukrainian classmates. This type of evidence dredged up by the special government commission provoked laughter even in the Sejm. Sejm minutes, 18 December 1932. There is a full discussion of the pacification in two collections of documentary sources: Emil Revyuk, comp., *Polish Atrocities in Ukraine* (New York, 1931) and *Na vichnu hanbu Polshchi, tverdyni varvarstva v Evropi* (Prague, 1931).
6. This is the text of the resolution:

   In order to be able to carry out a planned action in defence of women teachers and women employed in private Ukrainian offices, the General Meeting has decided to establish within the executive board (*Holovnyi vydil*) a separate committee (*referat*) for the defence of the professional interests of women....

   The General Meeting of the Union of Ukrainian Women condemns vehemently the decision of the Presidium of the Central Executive Board of Ridna Shkola which reduces by 25 per cent the salaries of married female teachers....

   The General Meeting of the Union of the Ukrainian Women vehemently condemns the position taken by the professional organization of the teachers of Ridna Shkola, which did not defend their colleagues, but instead supported the decision of the Presidium of Ridna Shkola to reduce the salaries of married women teachers.

Text in *Nova khata*, no. 1 (1932): 13.

7. *Zhinochyi svit* (August-September 1933): 18.
8. A number of her letters to Kravchenko are preserved in the Kravchenko archive.
9. Text in *Zhinocha dolia*, 1 April 1934, 2.
10. Some of the directives were published in *Zhinocha dolia* in the first months of 1934. Gurgula signed directive no. 10, ibid., 15 January 1934, 2. Her work was highly valued by the archeologist Iaroslav Pasternak, director of the Museum; see TsDIA, UkSSR (Lviv), f. 3c309, op. 1, spr. 4, NTSh, 36.
11. A first-hand account of this momentous congress, which left a lasting impact on its participants, is given in a letter Olia Abrahamovska wrote to her sister Stefaniia. Stefaniia, who had emigrated to the United States and supported her family in Galicia, insisted that her sister use some of the money to attend the congress. Despite protests that the money would be better spent on the house, or on food, or to pay for travel for seasonal work in Belgium, Olia attended the congress and was deeply moved by it. The quotation is from her letter dated 9 August 1934, in the uncatalogued archives of the Ukrainian Women's League in New York.
12. The role of the Ukrainian Catholic Church in the life of the Ukrainian community became even more visible in independent Poland than it had been under Austrian rule. In Austria, even in the face of the local Polish administrator, the priest dealt with the Austrian government in the registration of births, deaths and marriages. After 1919 or, *de jure*, 1923, the priest as part of his sacerdotal functions had to deal with the Polish administration. There were immediate clashes on the use of language and the renovation of churches. WAP Przemyśl, AGKB, Syg. 4768 and 4769 *passim*.
13. *Zhinocha dolia*, 15 July 1934, 6; also *Iuvileina knyha SUA, 1925–40*, 215.
14. The full text of the resolutions is in *Zhinocha dolia*, 1 and 15 August 1934, 15–17, and 1 September 1934, 14–15, as well as in *Zhinochyi svit* (July-September 1934): 4–6, and the following issue, which was not available to me. Also in the separate booklet *Rezoliutsii Ukrainskoho zhinochoho kongresu (Stanyslaviv, 23–27 chervnia 1934)* (Lviv, n.d. [1934]).
15. A share in the co-operative cost 40 złoty. The first executive board included Olha Tsipanovska, Ievheniia Makarushka and Nataliia Doroshenko, the first two veterans of the women's movement, the last an émigré (before 1914) from Ukraine. The auditors were Iryna Luneva, Ivanna Levytska, Evheniia Khraplyva and Iryna Shokh, all from Lviv. The executive board was composed of Rudnytska, Olena Sheparovych, O. Kmitsykevych, M. Koltuniuk, and O. Popovych. *Zhinocha dolia*, 15 November 1934, 3.

A number of Ukrainian newspapers had either supplements for women (*Novyi chas* in Lviv, published by Ivan Tyktor; *Ridnyi krai* and *Chas* from Chernivtsi; *Ukrainskyi holos* in Winnipeg) or carried articles of interest to women (*Hromadianskyi holos, Ukrainskyi holos* in Przemyśl, *Podilskyi holos* in Ternopil, *Svoboda* in Jersey City). But that did not reflect the women's view nor did it encourage women to write.

Selianka Ukrainy began appearing in Kharkiv in January 1925, but Western Ukrainian women could not establish regular contact with that journal. In June of the same year the glossy monthly *Nova khata* appeared "for educated women, with aspirations to be a modern women's journal." A chic journal whose purpose was to make Ukrainian women more sophisticated, it introduced new styles and furnishings. Lidiia Burachynska, "Pro zavdannia zhinochoi presy," *Zhinocha dolia*, 1 January 1933, 4. The circulation of *Nova khata* was slightly over 2,000. Feliński, 118–19.

16. Copy in possession of author.

17. There are detailed descriptions in *Zhinocha dolia*, 1 October 1935, 15, of a Stryi festivity; ibid., 15 October 1935, 14–15, of one in Rohatyn; and *passim* throughout the journal.

18. Ina Brusna, "V hostyni v selianok," *Zhinka*, 15 September 1936, 3.

19. "Zahalnyi zizd," Ibid., 1 April 1935, 2–4; *Zhinocha dolia*, 1 March 1935, 2; and ibid., 15 May 1935, 3.

20. *Zhinka*, 1 April 1935, 1.

21. Ibid., November 1937, 13, quoting the resolution of the 1937 Congress. From 15 September 1936 to 1 May 1937, 1010 new circles of Soiuz Ukrainok were established, ibid., 1 May 1937, 13.

Appendix

22. Lvivskyi oblasnyi derzhavnyi arkhiv, f. 300, op. 1, spr. 3, 35–41.

23. Ibid., 42.

24. For instance, in 1930, the deficit of the 14 June event was 185 złoty. The women agreed to donate 10 złoty each for the purpose, ibid., 43.

25. The women hoped to inherit 500 złoty after the death of Petronela Biretska Reshetylo in 1934 if her son could not be located, ibid., spr. 4, 5–13.

26. In 1926 the debt totalled 13,488 złoty, spr. 1, 4, leading the women to ask for regular subsidies from the government. Dormitory residents were charged on a sliding scale: some paid 100 złoty a month for room and board, others paid less, and some did not pay at all, ibid., 25 and 26. In 1928–9 the dormitory received: 16,730.40 złoty in tuition; a grant of 1,072.99 złoty from Narodnyi dim; 1,000 złoty from the city government; 2,000 złoty from the ministry of welfare; 30.00 złoty from special government funds, and 3,465.78 złoty from various unspecified sources. See spr. 1, 12. In 1925 it had also received 1,000 złoty from the ministry of education and religion.

27. Report of the general meeting of the Society, 13 December 1930, ibid., spr. 1, 48–9.

28. Spr. 6, quotation from 17. Regulations on behaviour in the dormitory.

29. A typed article in files of the Society in Lvivskyi oblasnyi derzhavnyi arkhiv, f. 119, op. 1, spr. 6, 1–13. Minutes of the general meetings and of the executive board, as well as a few letters and press clippings, make up the first five articles of the holdings.

30. Minutes of the general meeting of 27 March 1927, ibid., spr. 3, 26.

31. Ibid., 31.

14: Feminism: The Road to Autonomy

1. See the editorial in *Hromadianka*, 15 December 1938, defending the journals published by Olena Kysilevska. See also Mariia Strutynska, "Materynstvo u feministychnomu svitohliadi," *Almanakh Zhinochoi doli* (1930): 22–7.
2. Olena Fedak Sheparovych, "Modernyi feminism i ukrainska zhinka," ibid. (1928), 23. Sheparovych used Gertrude Bäumer as an example of the priorities involved: nation, party, women.
3. M. Bachynska-Dontsova, "Na bizhuchi temy zhinochoho rukhu," ibid. (1928), 87–90; quotations from 90. Dontsova retreated from public life and died a virtual recluse in New York in the 1950s.
4. Sheparovych, ibid. (1928), 23.
5. All quotations from *Zhinka*, 15 February 1935, 1.
6. A. Dychkovska, "Do statti 'Kilka sliv pid rozvahu nashomu zhinotstvu,'" *Zhinocha dolia*, 15 February 1929, 6.
7. *Zhinka*, 1 January 1935, 3.
8. Kysilevska, "Zatrata vidvichnoi zhinochosty," *Almanakh Zhinochoi doli* (1928): 38–41.
9. Quotation from Mariia Krushelnytska, "Nova zhinka," ibid. (1929): 29–31; see also Zinaida Mirna, "Feminizm v muzhchyn," *Zhinka*, 15 March 1938, 4, and *Nova khata*, no. 2 (1930): 5.
10. Ibid., no. 2 (1937): 6–7.
11. As late as 1953, in a review of a novel written by Mariia Strutynska (under the pseudonym M. Marska), *Buria nad Lvovom* (set in the 1930s), published in the Philadelphia Ukrainian Catholic newspaper *Shliakh* (no. 39, 1953), the reviewer wrote with impunity that the book reflected "the dualistic ideology of women of the type of Lviv's Women's Union or, rather, its leadership. We have here divorces, and free love among the already married, and a hint of abortion and love without fear...and a declaration about Ukraine, and a slightly critical tone toward 'the nationalism of the OUN' and a lack of understanding of the purity of customs...." Aparently the issue was a hornet's nest even then, for none of the other Ukrainian American newspapers would publish a criticism of the review. Letter of Anhela Talanova, a member of the Union of twenty years' standing, written to Rudnytska, 27 February 1953; Rudnytska Archives, UVAN, uncatalogued.
12. For instance, articles by Dr. Roman Mohylnytsky from Volhynia in *Zhinocha volia*, the supplement for the peasant women to *Zhinocha dolia*, in 1934. The situation in Galicia was not much different.
13. For instance, D. Polotniuk (Vilde's real name was Dariia Polotniuk), "Osobysta moral," *Zhinocha dolia*, 15 July 1934, 7–8. See also the review of current literature on women's education by another writer, Mariia Strutynska, in *Almanakh Zhinochoi doli* (1928): 45–8.
14. *Zhinocha dolia*, 1 October 1925, 16 on the *Zhinochyi Trud* in Kosiv and a letter of Lidiia Burachynska dated 3 October 1982 to the author.
15. Minutes in *Zhinka*, 1 April 1935, 3.
16. *Nova khata*, no. 1 (1932): 13.
17. *Zhinka*, 15 May 1935, 2.
18. Rudnytska, *Ukrainska diisnist i zavdannia zhinky,* (Lviv, 1934), 22. Originally a

speech at the Stanyslaviv Congress of Women held in 1934.

19. "Silsko-hospodarska orhanizatsiia zhinotstva," *Zhinocha dolia*, 15 May 1935, 13.
20. "Feminizm i kriza demokratii," ibid., 1 July 1934, 15.
21. "Na shliakhu rozbudovy osobystosty," *Zhinka*, 15 January 1935, lead articles.
22. Ibid., 1 January 1935.
23. Ibid.

15: Challenges to the Union

1. Thus, *Peremyski Eparkhiialni Visti*, 3 October 1919, 51, reminded priests that the regulation of 20 October 1917 on the use of Ukrainian as an official language was still obligatory. By law, priests registered births, marriages and deaths, and these functions pitted them against the government. Bishop Hryhorii Khomyshyn of Stanyslaviv reminded his priests in January 1927 (*Vistnyk Stanyslavivskoi Eparkhii*, 9) that they need only fulfill the stipulations of the Concordat, article VIII, that contracted them to say public mass at the request of secular authorities. Later, when the education debate flared up, Khomyshyn sent a letter of practical advice to his clergy (*VSE* (July 1930): 55–63) in which he pointed out that the Grabski Law of 9 April 1926 on the use of Polish in schools was null and void, because it directly contradicted the Law of 31 July 1924 and the regulation of the Council of Ministers of 24 October 1924, both of which assured education in the native language. A recent laudatory account of Khomyshyn is given by Petro Melnychuk, *Vladyka Hryhorii Khomyshyn* (Rome, 1979).

2. The number of Ukrainian nuns in inter-war Poland remained small. Complete statistics are not available. According to *Sprawozdanie Mniejszości Narodowych*, vol. 4 (1934): 114, there were 1,605 nuns in 121 convents. The greatest number belonged to the Sisters Servant: 460 nuns in 78 houses. The Basilians had 255 in 12 houses; Studite nuns numbered 97 in 4 houses; Josephite sisters 80 in 9 houses; Myronosnytsi counted 65 in 3 houses. Three orders cared for the sick——Holy Family with 48 nuns in 8 houses, the Order of St. Josaphat had 40 nuns in 5 communities; and St. Vincent de Paul 16 nuns in two houses.

3. This picked up momentum in the 1930s. One of the nuns involved in the entire Ukrainian educational system mused that her order, the Sisters Servant, "Ukrainized the village"; interview with Reverend Mother Amaliia (Chaban), Warsaw, 20 January 1976. Various specific cases of setting up nursery schools in WAP, AGKB, for instance in Hrebenne in 1934, Syg. 4769, 421–7. This particular case is interesting because the Polish nobleman (originally of Ukrainian origin) Paweł Fryderyk Sapieha donated property and promised food supplies for the children. See Przemyśl, Archiwum Diecezjalny ob. g.-k. w Przemyślu, Ordynariat, Sprawy zakonnic, Syg. 453, on the years 1891–1913, and ibid., AGKB, Syg. 4769. Ambrosii Androkhovych's article on the dowry of a Basilian nun in 1775, on the basis of materials he found in the Lviv Stavropygian library, was published in *Nova khata*, no. 20 (1926), and reflected the interest in the subject.

4. The AGKB offers repeated examples of the difficult life of priests, especially those caring for extended families. Suggestions were made that new priests pledge

not to take on extra financial responsibilities at least for the first few years after consecration, Syg. 4433, dated 1923. Other worries were that economically hard-pressed priests charged high fees of their parishioners: the Reverend Ievhen Kulchytsky of Lypivka was accused of charging high fees, Syg. 4430, 225–30, while the aged Reverend Savyn Kmytsykevych expected high fees for performing marriage ceremonies in March 1937, Syg. 4188.

5. Reverend Orsky, writing in *Peremyski Arkhyeparkhiialni visti*, (August 1930): 132.

6. As phrased by Orsky in "Katolytska aktsiia a tserkovni tovarystva," in ibid. (June 1934) 89.

7. *Sprawozdanie z zycia mniejszości narodowych...za IV kwartał 1930* (1931), 42. Mariia Ianovych was a member of the organizational committee convened in Lviv to work out a programme for a Ukrainian Catholic National Party on 24 November 1930, *Sprawozdanie...za II i III kwartał, 1930*, 46.

8. Khomyshyn vehemently condemned "all acts of sabotage and all subversive organizations"; text of the March 1931 letter in *Chas*, 25 March; see the discussion in Polonsky, 373.

9. Dzerovych bypassed the bishops and at one point reported directly to the Papal Nuncio. The Stanyslaviv Eparchy withdrew some of its financial support from Catholic Action, and Dzerovych openly complained about failure of parish priests to subscribe to all Catholic Action publications. Report of Dzerovych dated 31 January 1939, in WAP, Przemyśl, AGKB, Syg. 9483, 94–102.

10. See, for instance, an unsigned article, a paraphrase of the meditations of A. Kuliesho, "Zhinka v parokhii v nynishnykh chasakh," *Meta*, 12 August 1936, and Iaroslava Isaiv, "Perezhytky feminizmu," ibid., 28 February 1937.

11. This committee was illustrative of the public role the church wanted to play. It was headed by Bishop Ivan Buchko and included clerics in its membership.

12. *Sprawozdanie...za IV kwartał 1931* (Warsaw, 1932), 128.

13. The sodalities had originally been founded by the Jesuits to promote devotion among men, but by the nineteenth century had become women's organizations. See O. Orsky, "Katolytska aktsiia a tserkovni tovarystva" *Peremyski eparkhiialni visti* (June 1934): 75–88, and a letter of Sodality youth to the Ukrainian bishops, in WAP, Przemyśl, AGKB, Syg. 9585, 167, dated 7 September 1927. Retreats among youth for both sexes grew in popularity: a closed retreat for the youth of Przemyśl in 1935 attracted 9 participants, while in 1936 the number was 240, Syg. 5265, dated 6 May 1936; also *Zhinocha dolia*, 1 December 1934, 2. Also UZEK, 2: 634 (Lviv, 1932), as well as Mariia Tomashivska, "Ukrainska katolytska aktsiia zhinok," *Materiialy studiinykh dniv Federatsii tovarystv ukrainskykh studentiv katolykiv Obnova, II, Apostolstvo myr+an* (Louvain, 1957, mimeographed), 51–7. The Apostleship of Prayer, a Catholic attempt to offset secularization and Protestantism, found more supporters among women than among men. In the words of a diocesan report of Przemyśl in 1934: "men view it not with hostility, but certainly with reserve." WAP, AGKB. Syg. 4768, 400. Feminization also overtook the Societies of Good Death, which were to prepare one for the inevitable demise.

14. For instance, the creation of the Ukrainian Catholic Alliance in 1931 was welcomed by the editors of *Sprawozdanie...za 1 kwartał 1931*, 131.

15. *Zhinocha dolia*, 1 June 1939, reported on Marian celebrations held on 14 May in Iavoriv, Stryi, and other towns; there is information on the 1938 celebrations in

WAP, Przemyśl, AGKB, Syg. 4770, reports from October; also sygs. 5267 *passim*. *Zhinocha volia*, 15 May 1933, reported that more than 100,000 persons participated in the "Youth for Christ" festivities.

16. WAP, AGKB, Syg. 4768, 407, reports of 1934 complaining of growth of extreme nationalism. Also letter of Burachynska, dated July 1981, to the author.

17. Mirna, "Za etyku politychnoi borotby," *Zhinka*, 1 January 1935, 3; Rudnytska, "Sofii Rusovii v den ii 80-littia," *Zhinka,* 1 March 1936, 9.

18. Rudnytska, like all public figures, knew Metropolitan Sheptytsky, attended all public religious functions, and had been baptized in the Ukrainian Catholic faith of her father rather than following the Jewish religion of her mother. At the time she was considered a free thinker and was separated from her husband.

19. The lecture and discussion were first published in Nazaruk's *Nova zoria* and later as the book *Zhinka i suspilnist: Referat vyholoshenyi na zasidanni Generalnoho instytutu Katolytskoii aktsii u Lvovi dnia 13 kvitnia 1934 roku* (Lviv, 1934).

20. An unpublished brief memoir Rudnytska wrote for her son, Ivan L. Rudnytsky, when he was preparing the correspondence between Nazaruk and Lypynsky for publication. In Rudnytska's personal files.

21. P. 19 of the book version.

22. Book version, 37–8.

23. Ibid., 45–6 for both quotations.

24. Trying to rectify Ianovych's tactical error, the Women's Section of Catholic Action, the Marian Sodality of Women Students, the Catholic Domestics' Society (Buduchnist), the Lviv Co-operative Dolia (formerly Widows and Orphans of Priests), the Marian Sodality and an Association of Ukrainian Girls of St. Joseph (about which I have been unable to find more information) reminded the Women's Union, in a letter published in *Zhinocha dolia*, 15 April-1 May 1935, 7–9, that an attempt to introduce "Christian principles" into the Statute had been made by some women in February and March 1935. See also the minutes of the meeting, *Zhinka*, 1 April 1935, 3.

25. Text of protest of Przemyśl women in *Zhinka*, 1 March 1936, 7; see also "Panove, zalyshit nas v spokoiu," ibid., 4, as well as "Zla volia chy khora uiava," ibid., 15 February 1936, 2. Kysilevska, as usual, argued from a practical premise that the Women's Union, like other major community organizations such as Prosvita and Ridna Shkola, was based upon broad principles, and its statute should not be tampered with, especially at a time when the work of the Union was both important and difficult. *Zhinocha dolia*, no. 8–9 (15 April-1 May 1935): 8–9.

26. *Zhinka*, 1 April 1937, 2; report of the work of Parfanovych published that year as a brochure under the title *Vidrozhennia*. Two years later she published a useful little book on women's anatomy, health and hygiene, *Higiiena zhinky*.

27. *Nova khata* (November 1928): 2, obituary article bemoaning the absence of activist women at her funeral.

28. She seems to have developed her views on these issues in the year that Piłsudski staged his coup against the Polish Republic. Most of the relevant articles by Blazhkevych were published in *Zhinocha dolia* in 1927; see especially the August, November and December issues for 1927.

29. Blazhkevych, "Spohady pro Olhu Kobyliansku," in *Olha Kobylianska*, 438–44; also *Zhinocha dolia*, February 1926 and February 1927, as well as *Hromadskyi holos*, no. 41 (1927).

30. Letter of Franka Nakonechna Stakhova to author, dated 10 November 1980; also

letter of Lidiia Burachynska, dated 4 July 1981; as well as Pavlykovska, *Na hromadskyi shliakh*, 49.

31. For example, *Zhinochyi holos*, no. 76 (November 1937): 7, reported that allegedly students at the University of Warsaw had been told to sit in rows determined by nationality——Poles, Jews, etc. Jews and Ukrainians protested and were supported by the more liberal Poles.

32. *Statut Soiuzu ukrainskykh pratsiuiuchykh zhinok "Zhinocha Hromada"* (Lviv, 1935), 3–4, from which the quotation is taken.

33. Letter of November 1980. Her son has her files, but she feels that it is still too soon to open them.

34. For instance, see *Zhinochyi holos*, 5 February 1938 and *Zhinka*, 1 March 1938, 9. Even the émigré Socialist-Revolutionary Party criticized the Women's Union by imputing to women reactionary religious humility. The women, who, according to Konstantyna Malytska, had never been plagued by religious dissension between Catholics and Orthodox, resented this allegation. In the first issue of *Zhinka* for 1935, Mirna did not mince words in answering her close compatriots, drawing on the expertise of intelligentsia polemics. Malytska, "My v osvitlenni polky," *Nova khata*, no. 11 (1937): 2; Mirna, "Za etyku politychnoi borotby," *Zhinka*, 1 January 1935, 3.

35. Among the women active in the co-operative movement were also Olha Duchyminska Myhul, who remained in the Union, V. Dzerovych-Sobolta and R. Doberchak, whose relations with the Union became strained. *EU*, 8: 2830–2; letter of Burachynska, 4 July 1982.

36. Volodymyr Nesterovych, *Ukrainski kuptsi i promyslovtsi v Zakhidnii Ukraini, 1920–1945* (Toronto, 1977), 192–6, complains that the women insisted that Ukrainian merchants display signs in Ukrainian, which would certainly have antagonized Polish customers. Melaniia Nyzhankivska pointed out in *Zhinocha dolia*, 1 April 1934, 7, that the Union placed undue stress upon the co-operatives and overlooked the private economic sector.

37. In addition to Rudnytska, the members of the Board of the Union included Lukiia Bobeliak, Lida Horbacheva, Iryna Gurgula (she worked in the National Museum), Liubov Zakharko, Olena Kashtaniuk, Kysilevska, Dr. Stefaniia Korenets, Myroslava Mryts, Oleksandra Nestor, Nataliia Rubel, Mariia Fedusevych Piasetska, Olha Tsipanovska, Olena Sheparovych, and Dr. Vira Iatskevych Kos. Its alternate members were Oksana Dzhydzhora-Dzoba, Liuba Saiko, Bohdanna Tatukh, Stefaniia Fedorcha, and Lidiia Shaviak. The Auditing Commission included Iryna Luneva, Karolyna Liubomyrska, Zenoviia Maikovska, Olha Paliiv, and Olena Lukasevych; report in *Zhinka*, 1 May 1936, 5. The earlier quotation is also from this source.

38. Full text in *Zhinka*, 1 May 1936.

39. May 1939, 2; Kysilevska made her suggestion in the 16 April 1939 issue of *Dilo*. See also Rudnytska's report to the 1937 general meeting of the Union, in *Zhinka*, 1 November 1937.

16: Women as a Political Force

1. Burachynska, in a letter of 14 August 1981, stressed the opposition of the OUN women to feminism; she expanded upon the topic in a series of interviews and in a letter of 3 October 1982.

2. Rudnytska, "Dvadtsiatypiatyrichchia patsyfikatsii," *Svoboda*, 27 September 1955.

3. Phrase used by Rudnytska, minutes of the Sejm, 26 February 1932.

4. Mikułowska, *"Ukraiński" ruch kobiecy* (Lviv, 1937); she was especially perturbed by the attraction Ukrainianism had exercised in the Antonovych family, on Viacheslav Lypynsky, the conservative thinker and political activist, and on the then young writer Halina Dąbrowska, who continues to write under the pseudonym Zhurba. Charewiczowa also stressed that Milena Rudnytska was partly of Jewish descent, implying that the difficulties the Union was experiencing might have this at their root and that Rudnytska probably would not continue as President.

5. From the debates of the Sejm held on 18 April 1925; another memorable debate in which she took part was on 28 July 1924. The swearing-in ceremony was held on 28 November 1922.

6. O. Halychanka, "O rivni prava," *Zhinocha dolia*, October 1926, 2–3. This was one of Kysilevska's pseudonyms.

7. "Peremoha kotsiuby nad lopatoiu," ibid., November 1926, 6 and 15.

8. Ievhen M. Halushko, *Narysy istorii ideolohichnoi ta orhanizatsiinoi diialnosti KPZU v 1919–1928 rr.* (Lviv, 1965), 95. Halushko, who stresses the achievements of the KPZU, based his research mainly on Polish police reports, which saw communist infiltration in all Ukrainian activities.

9. "Tykh dniv ne zmerkne slava," *Vilna Ukraina* (Lviv), 11 April 1961, and "Pamiat hortaie storinky istorii," ibid., 3 October 1964.

10. Texts of programmes in Petro Mirchuk, *Narys istorii Orhanizatsii Ukrainskykh Natsionalistiv*, vol. 1, 1920–1939 (Munich, 1968), 92–101.

11. Rudnytska, "Vidnoshennia molodi do zhinochoho rukhu," *Zhinka*, 15 February 1935, lead article.

12. Meeting of the Sejm, 29 May 1928, discussing the refusal of Ukrainian high-school students of Stanyslaviv to participate in the celebrations of the Constitution of 3 May. *Dilo*, on 11 April 1929, reported on riots of Polish students in Lviv against the minorities, in which Jewish and Ukrainian students' homes were destroyed.

13. *Dilo* naturally gave extensive coverage to the case, see especially issues of 20 to 26 April 1929. Also Mirchuk, 27. Near Ternopil the elderly Olha Bohachevska, who could no longer teach because she refused to take the oath of loyalty, was fined for allegedly dissuading the children of the village of Soroka, Skalat district, from participating in government celebrations, *Dilo*, 19 April 1929, 4.

14. The phrase used by Hnatkivska, displaying unusual emotion, some forty years after the assassination, in a conversation with the author in April 1980. In prison, she married the young Mykola Lebed, who had given the bomb to the assassin. The bomb did not explode and a gun was used. *Zhinocha dolia* and *Zhinka* reported the trial, as did the entire Ukrainian press. The defendants refused to testify in Polish, and did not speak at all. Other women involved, directly or indirectly, were Iryna Khomiak (Kravtsiv), Mariia Chorna, Olena Chaikivska, Vira Svientsitska, Mariia Kosiv, and Anna Chemerynska. The last two had escaped Poland before the trial.

15. *Novyi chas* (Lviv), 3 and 15 December 1938; "Proty anarkhii," *Zhinka*, 1 January 1939, 1–2; letter of Rudnytska to Sheparovych discussing the émigré situation among Ukrainian women: "remember the last meeting of the Union in Stryi?," Rudnytska correspondence, UVAN archive, uncatalogued. The nationalist women in Stryi were headed by Melaniia Kravtsiv. Letter of Lidiia Burachynska, 3 October 1982.

16. Olena Sheparovych, "Ukrainska studentka," *Smoloskyp: Zhurnal natsionalistychnoi molodi* (January 1928): 7–10.

17. Zynoviia Kravtsiv, "V odnii aktualnii spravi," *Studentskyi shliakh* (November-December 1932): 263–5.

18. ICW, Library of Congress Manuscript Division, ICW files, ms. 3403, Box 4, flyer dated 8 October 1932.

19. The Union issued a circular urging political participation in the voting, *Zhinocha dolia*, 15 May 1927; see also issues of 15 November and December 1927.

    Dontsova singled out the area of Toporiv, where, according to a story in *Dilo*, 97 per cent of all the registered women had voted. More than 100 of them, some with children, waited at the polls from morning till night for a chance to vote. Dontsova was angry that *Słowo Polskie* of 22 July 1927 had accused the Women's Union of training political agitators, while the communist *Svitlo* referred to the Union as bourgeois. See "Vybory i zhinotstvo," *Zhinocha dolia*, 15 August 1927, 2.

20. Text in *Dilo*, 7 January 1928, 5.

21. The call to support UNDO, which appeared in the 21 January 1928 issue of *Dilo*, was signed by Bohdan Kravtsiv, Osyp Bodnarovych and Mykhailo Demkovych-Dobriansky.

22. The Ukrainian Socialist Party, the Ukrainian Labour Party (Partiia pratsi), and both the right and left wings of the Alliance of Peasants and Workers (Silsko-Robitnychyi Soiuz) were involved in Volhynia. The Jewish parties in Poland did not elect any women. Relatively few Polish women were elected to either of the two houses. The latter fact was duly commented upon by Kysilevska, now elected to the Senate, in *Zhinocha dolia*, 15 March 1928, 2–3.

23. *Sprawozdanie...za styczeń, luty i marzec, 1929*, 40 and 42.

24. See especially her "Natsionalizm i feminizm," *Dilo*, 9 May 1929, 1.

25. See *Sprawozdanie...za listopad-grudzień, 1928*, 24–6 and 42–3.

26. "Vybory bez zhinok," an article on the participation of women in elections in Poland, probably written by Rudnytska and Sheparovych, was to have been published in *Zhinka* in August 1935, but was confiscated. Copy in Rudnytska files.

27. *Bunt młodych, Polityka*, and *Biuletyn Polsko-Ukraiński*, the last founded in Warsaw in 1933, were important publications in this matter. For a biased but detailed account of court proceedings against the OUN, see Roman Jurys and Tadeusz Szafar, *Pitaval polityczny, 1918–1939* (Warsaw, 1971).

28. Polonsky, 374. *Sprawozdanie...za III kwartał, 1931* (Warsaw, 1931), 110, 130–1. *Sprawozdanie...za IV kwartał, 1931* (Warsaw, 1932), 3–5 even congratulated itself on the minorities' recognition of the necessity to accommodate to the Polish regime. The government even argued that UNDO's stress on the autonomy rights granted to Ukrainians by the Allies in the March 1923 resolution of the Council of the Ambassadors weakened the Western Ukrainians' claim to independence.

29. Kedryn (Rudnytsky), *Zhyttia*, 252.

30. Polonsky, 459–60.

31. The provision stated that in electoral districts of more than 75,000 people, women's organizations could vote in the local electoral colleges. "Vyborcha ordynatsiia do soimu i ukrainske zhinotstvo," *Zhinka*, 1–15 July 1935, 3.

32. Kedryn, 253–4.

33. The article and the communiqué were to have appeared in *Zhinka*, 15–16 August 1935, but were confiscated by government censors. The text is taken from Rudnytska's personal file.

34. As an afterthought, this passage continued: "The women's organization can be compared in a way to the role the veterans' organization plays in contemporary affairs, since it also does not have any pretentions to be a political party, yet it expresses its views on matters of overall national importance and there are occasions on which it shows greater solidarity than the political parties." Ibid.

35. "Holosy presy," *Zhinka*, 1 September 1935, 2. Living in Galicia, which operated under the Austrian codex that did not permit divorce, Rudnytska was merely separated from her husband. When he moved to Warsaw, he filed for divorce and she did not contest it. During the male backlash, this personal aspect of Rudnytska's life was cited as proof of the immorality of the women's movement. Rudnytska's personal conduct remained exemplary. She did not remarry, although her former husband did. She also took her former husband's candidacy to the Sejm in the 1938 elections with good grace.

36. *Zhinka*, 1 December 1935, 4. Rudnytska and Anna Palii formally objected to an article in *Ukrainski visti* alleging that the Union was undergoing a crisis because some of its leaders had been expelled from UNDO. The Union, the two women reminded its audience, had never been an affiliate of UNDO, and UNDO's action toward its members did not necessarily have a direct bearing upon the Union.

37. Kedryn, 255. Although his support of his sister was never as ardent as she would have wished, Kedryn nevertheless stressed her popularity.

38. *Zhinka*, May 1939, 2; see also the August 1939 issue, 8–9, on relations with the co-operative. Iryna Hladka complained that there were not enough women in leading positions in the co-operative movement.

39. Pavlykovska, 54.

40. "Normalizatsiia na tsenzuri," *Zhinka*, no. 15–16 (August 1937), 2; report to Congress, ibid., no. 21–22 (November 1937), 3.

41. "Dopovid na zahalnomu zizdi SU," ibid., résumé, with some parts quoted. The above is a direct quotation. See also the unsigned article, "Shukaite muzhchyny," ibid., no. 11–12 (June 1937).

42. Ibid., 1 March 1937, 4; the editorial on Zurich was heavily censored; the clearest anti-totalitarian statement of the Union is that in ibid., 15 September 1937, "Konsolidatsiia, totalizm, zhinotstvo."

43. Mikułowska, *"Ukraiński" ruch kobiecy* (Lviv, 1937); review in *Nova khata*, no. 11 (1937). The Ukrainian women found the Polish women's attacks——which stressed Ukrainian achievements——quite flattering. *Nova khata* exploited Charewiczowa's criticism of Rudnytska's "mixed blood" and separated marital status to the latter's advantage.

44. For instance, see the account of what turned out to be the last meeting of the chairpersons of the Union, held in Lviv on 23 December 1938, in *Zhinka*, 1 January 1939, 12–13.

45. The Ukrainian Catholic Church was having similar problems with the intelligentsia, and in 1937 the controversial Bishop Khomyshyn forbade the

clergy in his diocese to belong to lay organizations. Ukrainian community activists protested immediately, not only because the ban went against the tradition of Ukrainian community life, but also because the Polish clergy were most active on the community level. Collective letter of Ukrainian activists to Khomyshyn, 24 February 1938, in WAP, Przemyśl, AGKB, Syg. 9492, 42–8.

46. Kedryn, 271; he also provides a full discussion of the results of normalization from the Ukrainian vantage point.

47. Rudnytska quotations from the Nazaruk note in her private files; Kedryn, 269.

48. *Hromadianka*, 1 October 1938.

49. Ibid., "Mortuos plango, vivos voco."

50. Among them were: Rusova, Kravchenko, Mirna, Chykalenko, Soiuz Ukrainok Ameryky (Ukrainian Women's League of America), as well as an Orhanizatsiia Ukrainok Natsionalistok pry Ukrainskii Natsionalnii Kolonii v Mandzu-Di-Ho, headed by Korda-Fedorova.

51. *Hromadianka*, 1 October 1938, 1.

52. Ibid., 2. The programme of the Corps was drafted into the ideological theses of the Corps of Princess Olha. Among these ideas were: National-Political Ideal, the Role of Women in the Actualization of the National Ideal, Religion and Church, Family, Spiritual Culture, Education, Principles of Social Order, *Hospodarstvo* (homemaking/national economy), and Ethics of Social Life.

53. Based on the report of Mariia Bassova, ibid., 11.

54. Editorial, ibid., 1 November 1938; for a copy of a letter on the work of and relation between the Corps and the Union, see "from the Corps to the Ukrainian Women's Alliance," undated in the uncatalogued files of the UNWLA. The protest against the Magyar action of March 1939 is to be found in Kedryn, 287–8.

55. *Hromadianka*, 15 November 1938, 6.

56. The first national conference of the Corps was held a day after the national conference of the branch chairs of the Union on 24 December 1938; *Zhinka*, 1 January 1939, 13.

57. See the UNWLA Archives letter mentioned in note 54 above.

58. *Zhinka*, 1 January 1939, 13.

17: Ukrainian Women outside Historical Galicia

1. *Iuvileivna knyha SUA*, 214; *Zhinocha dolia* serialized Kysilevska's articles in 1935 as they appeared, and they were published in the lavishly illustrated volume, *Po ridnomy kraiu: Polissia* (Kolomyia, 1936).

2. *Zhinocha dolia*, 1 March 1928, especially the correspondence on p. 15.

3. *Nashe zhyttia* (Kholm), especially 1 January 1920, 8 August 1928 and 8 January 1929.

4. Some of the buildings along the so-called Sokal border (the major Galician town bordering Volhynia lent its name to this border, which legally did not exist in the inter-war years) were specially equipped with multi-storey cellars for hiding horses; during the Second World War Jews and others hid in these cellars with varying degrees of success.

5. A Reverend Oleksander Hadzinsky, in the Podillia region, was under *Okhrana*

surveillance early in the century for preaching in Ukrainian, TsDIA, UkSSR (Kiev), f. 301, op. 1, spr. 3201, 25. I could not ascertain whether he was Levchanivska's father. She was born in 1881, attended the St. Petersburg Higher Courses, and participated in the Ukrainian Hromada. She perished in 1943 in Kazakhstan, where the Soviets deported her. Sofiia Ivanchuk, "V imia velykoi idei," *Ukrainskyi holos*, 18 April 1955, 11. Ivanchuk also reports that many Volhynian women activists were shot by the Soviets in 1943; among them were Dr. Hanna Roshchynska of Kremianets, Liuba Lebedivska, and Olha Nestorovska, along with her husband and their sons, aged seven and seventeen.

6. See the article on Levchanivska in *Nova khata*, no. 1 (1926); a snippet of her memoirs is in ibid., no. 15–16 (1936).

7. Tsetsyliia Volianska-Gardetska, "Volynski vchytelky," ibid., no. 24 (1936).

8. Polonsky, 461; see also the wealth of information on the whole issue in the various rich sources on the internal history of the republic in the AAN Warsaw. First-hand information on the Polish Scouting movement is found in WAP, Wrocław, Ossolineum, Sygs. 15029, 15036.

9. Lidiia Burachynska, "Zhinochi orhanizatsii na Volhyni," *Nova khata*, no. 15–16 (1936): 3, also "Iuvilei Soiuzu Ukrainok v Rivnomu," ibid., no. 12 (1937); "Zhinochyi rukh na Volhyniai," *Zhinka*, 1 February 1937, 5, and an untitled note, ibid., 15 April 1937, 3; also report in *Zhinocha dolia*, 1 and 15 January (1935); as well as *Iuvileina knyha SUA, 1925–1940*, 214.

10. Interviews in Toronto on 14–15 March 1982 with Ms. Horokhovych.

11. Oleksandra Pidhirska had been bitterly attacked by *Volynska nedilia*, 23 December 1934, mainly for her political independence; see also *Zhinocha dolia*, 1 February 1935, 9; on the dissolution of the Volhynian Women's Union, see *Hromadianka*, 15 November 1938, 6, which complained that the reaction to this dissolution in the Galician press was minor. Discussion of the work of the Volhynian Union is provided in *Zhinka*, July 1937, 13.

12. Among her major works are *Bie vosma, Metelyky na shpylkakh*, and, after the Second World War, *Sestry Richynski*.

13. The fullest available account is by Stefaniia Khortyk, "Zhinocha hromada v Chernivtsiakh," *Nova khata*, no. 15–16 (1935); some additional information is in ibid., no. 2 (1932): 14. A report on the 1929 congress is in *Zhinocha dolia*, 15 March 1929, 6.

14. *Iuvileina knyha SUA, 1925–1940*, 214; *Almanakh Zhinochoi doli* (1929), 85–6.

15. *Samostiina dumka ukrainskoi matery*, no. 1, (1931): 6.

16. "Emantsypatsiia ukrainskoi zhinky," ibid., no. 2 (1931): 5–6.

17. Paul Robert Magosci, *The Shaping of a National Identity: Subcarpathian Rus', 1848–1948* (Cambridge, Mass., 1978), 147.

18. *Zhinocha dolia*, 1 July 1934, 18.

19. Grade schools in Ukrainian villages were taught in Ukrainian, with Czech introduced only in the fifth grade; Kysilevska, "Z moikh mandrivok," ibid., 1 June 1934, 5–6; Magosci, 170, 226–7.

20. Magosci, 315. Her husband had spent a few years in the U.S. as a pastor.

21. Iryna Nevytska, "Zhinochyi rukh na Pidkarpatti," *Zhinka*, 1 March 1935, 3; there is an article on Carpathian women by Chykalenko-Keller in *Zhinocha dolia*, 1 May 1934, 9–10.

22. According to *Iuvileina knyha SUA, 1926–1940*, 214, Nevytska headed the women's sections of Prosvita, with headquarters in Uzhhorod; Iryna Voloshyn,

the Women's Union in that city, and Brashchaikova-Stankova a major branch of the Union in Khust; the fullest first-hand account of the congress is by Olena Kysilevska "Z moikh mandrivok: Zhinochyi kongres na Pidkarpatti," *Zhinocha dolia*, 15 June–1 July 1934, 18–19. Neither Rudnytska nor Pavlykovska, one representing the Galician Women's Union, the other Narodne Mystetsvo, seems to have recorded her impressions of the event, although both mentioned it very favourably in other contexts. This congress preceded the Stanyslaviv congress, convened on 23 June, by almost a month.

23. The only negative note came, uncharacteristically, from a local police official, a Russophile, who objected to the speakers' use of *Pidkarpatska Ukraina* (Subcarpathian Ukraine) and *pidkarpatska ukrainska zhinka* (Subcarpathian Ukrainian woman). He prevented Revai from finishing his speech, but did not carry out his threat to suspend the meeting.

24. "Zhinky v derzhavnomu budivnytstvi Karpatskoi Ukrainy," *Zhinka*, 15 January 1939, 2; Magocsi, 237–46.

25. *Zhinka*, editorial, 1 April 1939; see also the 15 March 1935 story.

26. Ibid., 1 May 1939, 14. There had been a discussion of the subject by the women, but no details are available.

27. The Viennese Ukrainian Women's Community sent greetings to the convention of the Ukrainian Women's League in 1932, signed by the president, Natalka Gros (*sic*), and the secretary, Myroslava Hrekh: UNWLA Archives, New York, uncatalogued. The only information on the founding of the Community is an unpublished note Rudnytska wrote on Nazaruk. He was the only man present at the meeting which established this group. The meeting was held in one of Petrushevych's offices; Rudnytska wrote the draft of the by-laws.

28. The Civic Committee liquidated itself in 1925 mainly because of personality clashes in which only males were involved; a Union of Ukrainian Organizations in Czechoslovakia was established in the following year. It seems to have been an umbrella organization. *Nova Ukraina*, no. 8–10 (1925): 150–3 and no. 3–4 (1926): 149–50.

29. Most of these women's husbands were actively involved in Ukrainian political life, which they also criticized as divisive and destructive. They founded the Civic Committee "to preserve the physical and cultural existence of Ukrainian émigrés, because the official representatives are too busy with inter-party strife." From a mimeographed report, "Try roky pratsi Hromadskoho komitetu v ChSR, 7 lypnia 1921 do 7 lypnia 1924." The report also refers to Rusova as head of the Women's Section, which she could have become only in 1922, since she did not leave Kamianets until late in 1921. Also in *Nova Ukraina*, no. 16–18 (1922): 87–8. On Plaminkova's support for Ukrainians, see Mariia Omelchenko, ed., *Frantishka Plaminkova: z nahody 60. iuvileiu* (Prague, 1935), as well as articles in *Zhinocha dolia*, 15 May 1928, 7, and *Zhinka*, 1 February 1935.

30. *Nova Ukraina*, no. 8–9 (1926): 83–5.

31. Mirna complained:

> The weak position of the UNR in international circles is naturally not conducive to the development of the Rada's work. [Poor] material émigré circumstances also do not generate energy to work, while émigré psychology destroys the attempts and aspirations of the Rada to unify all émigré women's organizations. Women either drop out, change their relations with the Rada, or finally, for personal reasons, do not wish to

support a unified émigré women's centre.

The Women's Rada itself, however, considers it its duty to hold firmly to its organization, to preserve at least a small centre which at a suitable time may become the nucleus around which Ukrainian women could organize. Maintaining without a break relations with international women's organizations, this centre in time could provide an opportunity to continue and develop these connections, and not [have to] initiate them anew each time.

Mirna, "Ukrainska natsional'na zhinocha rada," *Almanakh Zhinochoi doli* (1928), 194–7; quotation from 197. See also a letter from Rusova to Ukrainian Canadian women, quoted in Kohuska, 20–2; as well as "Ukrainska zhinocha natsionalna rada v Prazi," *Nova khata*, no. 11 (1935).

32. *Nova Ukraina*, no. 12 (1927): 74. The initiators were Halyna Stadnyk, Tamara Petrova, and Misses Stakhiv and Vynohradnyk.

33. They were published under the aegis of Chesko-Ukrainska knyha and consisted of the following: M. Omelchenkova, *Česko-Ukrajinské styky*, 40 pp.; Karel Havlichek-Borovsky, *Vybir poezii*, trans. I. Franko, 190 pp., 130 ill.; Omelchenko, Hr., *Prvni tři redakce "Křtu sv. Vladimira" Karla Havlíčka Borovského*, 19 pp.; T.G. Masaryk, *Iak pratsiuvaty,* trans. H. Omelchenko, 128 pp.; M. (*sic*) Omelchenkova, *Vybir fakhu*, 45 pp.; M. Omelchenkova, *T.G. Masaryk*, 428 pp., 75 ill.; Symon Narizhny, *Iaroslav Gol* (1931), 47 pp.; H. Omelchenko, *Jan Pravoslav Kovbek i ioho ukrainski sympatii*, 24 pp. and Edvard Benesh, 152 pp.; M. Omelchenko ed., *Frantishka Plaminkova* (1935).

34. "Ukrainskyi zhinochyi soiuz v Prazi," *Nova khata*, no. 10 (1932): 7; Kateryna Antonovych, *Z moikh spomyniv* (Winnipeg, 1965–73), no. 23–7, especially no. 27, 225–37. I have been unable to establish the first names of some of these women.

35. Omelchenko, *Vybir fakhu*, 17.

36. The book was mimeographed, and only 100 copies appeared. The other proposed discussions on the organizational forms of the women's movement and the scope of women's activity did not appear. The women themselves had already tackled those issues in practice.

37. As late as 1923, in a letter to the Berlin Women's Union dated 5 September, Lukasevych complained that there were only five Ukrainian women in Warsaw and no prospects of a separate women's organization; Chykalenko-Keller collection, UVAN archive, uncatalogued. On the later work of the Warsaw Ukrainian women, see Olena Montsibovych, "Pratsia Soiuzu v Varshavi," *Ukrainska dumka* (London), 27 May 1976; Mariia Livytska's lively memoirs, *Na hrani dvokh epokh* (New York, 1976), unfortunately break off at 1920. Brief mention of the Women's Section in Warsaw is made in *Nova Ukraina*, no. 16–18, (1922), to the effect that it received 646 Czech crowns from the Ukrainian Civic Committee in Prague.

38. Unsigned, handwritten ms. in the uncatalogued files of the Ukrainian Women's League of America, New York. According to this source, during the 1920s the New York Ukrainian women sent out about 12,000 dollars. Among the recipients were organizations of men and women, veterans and non-veterans alike. They included the Community Homes for Disabled Veterans in Lviv, Kalush, Sčepórno (Poland), and Vienna. Money was also sent for use on behalf of political

prisoners, presumably in Poland. The Co-operative in Ternopil, the Girls' School in Przemyśl (without specifying which one), Prosvita headquarters, Ridna Shkola, the Shevchenko Scientific Society, and the Ukrainian Orphanage in Lviv were among the recipients.

39. *Iuvileina knyha SUA, 1925–1940*, 14; see also the correspondence of the American Ukrainian Women's League with the Women's Union in Lviv in the SUA archives; Kohuska, 529 and Kysilevska, *Za more, ale do svoikh: spomyny* (Kolomyia, 1930). Savelia Stechyshyn, "Zhinochyi rukh v Kanadi," *Almanakh Zhinochoi doli*, 46–53.

18: The All-Ukrainian Women's Union

1. The Zhinocha Rada was but another reincarnation of the Zhinocha Hromada of the Ukrainian People's Republic (also called Rada). The Eastern Ukrainian women did not set much store by the names of organizations, and argued that the Women's Rada had been founded in 1917, the date of the founding of the Hromada.

2. Z. Mirna, "Ukrainska natsionalna zhinocha rada," *Almanakh Zhinochoi doli* (1928), 194. At the time, neither the U.S. nor Canada occurred to the women meeting in Kamianets as possible sites of Ukrainian community life.

3. The text is in the Chykalenko-Keller holdings, UVAN Archive, uncatalogued; typed draft on legal-size paper, probably 1921–2.

4. The phrase that followed was baffling, either an oversight or an example of the cavalier attitude toward organizational structure that was characteristic of the Eastern Ukrainian intelligentsia: "the executive committee, after studying the reports, will present them to the constituent meeting." They probably meant an annual, or general meeting.

5. From Rudnytska's hand-written letter to Chykalenko in the Chykalenko file, UVAN.

6. [Rudnytska], "Vsesvitnyi soiuz Ukrainok," *Zhinka*, November 1937, 1.

7. The archives of the SUA are incomplete, and some of the correspondence with the Lviv centre exists not in the original but in hand-transcribed copies. See also *Zhinka*, 1 April 1935, 2, on the meeting of 28 March 1935; ibid., November 1937, 15 and *Nova khata*, no. 21–2 (1937): 3.

8. *Zhinka*, 15 November 1937; the article is not signed, but her authorship was established through her files and corroborated by her son. *Nova khata*, 15 October 1937, 3. *Iuvileina knyha soiuza Ukrainok Ameryky (sic) (1925–40)*, 59–64.

9. Ibid., 59–60; statute, 60–4.

Ukrainian Women and International Feminism

1. Unpublished ms. of either an article or the beginning of memoirs of Hanna Chykalenko-Keller, in the Keller archive, UVAN, New York, undated; the archive itself is unpaginated.

2. From the letterhead of the League.

3. Quoted by Chykalenko-Keller in her note on the League, in the UVAN archives; see also her article "Spohad pro chuzhynku, shcho stanula nam u pryhodi," about Crystal Macmillan, in *Zhinka*, 1 February 1939, 8–9; on the Ukrainian Women's Community in Berne, see *Nasha meta* (Lviv), 5 October 1919, 1. Keller was depressed at the time, since she felt she had to divorce her husband "because as a result of political conditions our views and thoughts have developed along different paths," unpublished letter to her father, written on 9 December 1919, in the Keller archive in UVAN.

4. Nadiia Surovtseva, "III Internatsionalnyi kongres Zhinochoi ligy myru i svobody i ukrainske zhinotstvo," *Svoboda* (Jersey City, N.J.), 8 August 1921, as transcribed by Myroslava Lutsiv-Dragan for the Rudnytska project on the history of the Ukrainian women's movement, in Rudnytska Archives, UVAN, unpaginated. A subsequent article on the congress in that newspaper, signed by a *radianyn* (from the Kievan newspaper appearing before the 1914 *Rada*, not from the Ukrainian word for Soviet), stresses that the participation of Ukrainian women was justified not only their international successes, but also by the pacifism espoused by the League, which most suited the calling of women——motherhood. See "Zhinocha internatsionaliia," *Svoboda*, 25 August 1921 (vid spetsialnoho korespondenta *Svobody*).

5. Accordingly, specific accounts of actions of the Women's Council, as well as its nomenclature, vary somewhat. The council, an outgrowth of Kiev women's organizations, was established in Kamianets-Podilskyi in 1919, and later its headquarters moved to Prague. One of its effective branches, which sometimes acted as the council, functioned in Berlin; Z. Mirna, "Ukrainska natsionalna zhinocha rada," *Almanakh Zhinochoi doli* (1928), 194–7; Kharytia Kononenko, "Ukrainska zhinocha natsionalna rada: na marginesi prypynennia diialnosty," *Nova khata*, no. 13–14 (1939). See also various letters and memoranda in the Keller archive.

6. Chykalenko-Keller archive; Rusova's letter of authorization signed by Marie Zarchy, Conseil national des femmes ukrainiennes, comité provisoire, and by secretary Antoni Krawtschenko, dated 1 June 1920. Rusova was still in Ukraine and could not attend. See also articles in *Vpered* (Lviv), 3 July 1920; *America* (Philadelphia), 8 August 1920 and *Svoboda* (Jersey City), 3 April 1920; and a letter of Crystal Macmillan to Chykalenko dated 3 April 1920, thanking her for the interest Ukrainian women had shown in the work of the IWSA and noting that "You in Ukrainia have, I believe, even voted for your constitutional assembly." Dorota Melenevsky visited Macmillan on behalf of Ukrainians. Also of interest is Keller's letter of 19 June 1920 to Soiuz Ukrainok, in the Keller collection.

7. Quotation from a typewritten report by Keller in the UVAN files (report on legal size paper, five pages, undated.)

8. Letter of Emily Balch to Keller, 12 October 1920, in Keller papers.

9. *ICW, Meeting in Boston* (1909), 5–6, on the discussion of the London meeting.

10. Ibid., 202. A joint commission of French and German historians did just that in the textbooks of both countries only after the *Second* World War.

11. *ICW. Report on Quinquennial Meeting, 6th, 1914–1920, Christiania* (1920), 358–60, 419–21, 457. See also Keller's typed report to the UNR, in Keller archive.

12. Copy in Keller archive, signed by Mirna, L. Halyn, Iuliia Vilenska, Olha

Levytska, Iryna Simovych, O. Porsh, E. Sokovych, Keller and Iryna Loska. The Ukrainian women were following the lead of Lady Aberdeen of ICW and the IWSA, which sent a memorandum to the League on the participation of women, at a meeting with President Wilson on 10 April 1919; *Women in a Changing World: The Dynamic Story of the ICW since 1888* (London, 1966), no author, appendix 7, 344–5.

13. Rusova, "Z Vidnia do Hagy (Vrazhinnia na Vsesvitnyi zhinochyi kongres), *Nova Ukraina*, 15 June 1922, 25–7; 1 July 1922, 14–18.

14. In 1922 it was headed by Emma Freudlich, the only woman member of the Economic Committee of the League of Nations. Freudlich was a Viennese and knew the East European situation. Among the fourteen members of the League, there were no Polish organizations, a fact which Poles noted with genuine concern. See Anna Szelagowska, *Międzynarodowe organizacje kobiece* (n.p., 1934). Ukrainians remained active in the guild, and Zalizniak, as director of Women's Co-operative *Trud*, participated in a congress in Paris as late as 2–3 September 1937.

15. See Keller's letter of 8 June 1923, in Keller archive, probably to Rudnytska.

16. Olena (Okhrymovych) Zalizniak to Keller, 15 June 1923, Keller archive. The Polish delegation to the Rome Congress requested the banning of the brochure.

17. Zalizniak assured Keller that she had met two American women activists who did not know the location of Ukraine, so Zalizniak argued that the brochure about Ukrainian women should be made more widely available. Keller archive.

18. My account is based mostly on accounts and correspondence in the Keller archive. Ukrainians were slightly offended by the British women, who, in a manner that seemed high-handed, had sent the money collected in Australia and New Zealand for the relief of the famine in Ukraine to a "South Russian" committee.

19. Malytska went so far as to write, in a letter to Keller on 14 July 1923, "There is lawlessness here that hardly ever existed in tsarist Russia," Keller archive, letter written on Soiuz Ukrainok stationery.

20. Balch's *Our Slavic Fellow Citizens* had appeared in Philadelphia in 1910.

21. Instead, the Poles, with political animosity between the two nationalities heightened by the pacification campaign, would admit only Mrs. Bohuslavska, whose constituency was an outgrowth of the political party of Petro Pevny, the Volhynian who based his career on the support of the Poles. See Mirna, "Obiednannia slovianskykh zhinok," *Zhinka*, 1 June 1936, 9–10.

22. *Dilo*, 27 March 1929.

23. Letter to Keller, 15 June 1923, in Keller archive.

24. "Ukrainskoe tovarytstvo zhenshchin s vysshym obrazovaniem vo Lvove [*sic*]" in the files of the Lvivskyi oblasnyi derzhavnyi arkhiv, f. 119, op. 1, spr. 2, "Zvit z zahalnykh zboriv...17 October 1925." The last available minutes in this file are dated 6 May 1928. An editorial in *Nova khata*, no. 12 (1936), however, states that the Society existed until 1934, when it was suspended by the Polish authorities. From the minutes of the Society between 1925 and 1928, it seems the membership never exceeded twenty, and the women, although active, faced an impossible task in overcoming the resistance of the Ukrainian community to this type of an "elitist" organization. In 1926 the International Federation of University Women informed Ukrainians that they could not be members because they did not represent a country, according to minutes of 14 November 1926. Fuller discussion in

Chapter 12, Appendix II.

25. ICW, *Report on the Meeting in Washington, 1925*, 113.

26. The Poles affiliated with ICW in 1924, with Senator Józefa Szebeko serving as the first President of the National Council of Women of Poland; the Czech women had had a separate organization since 1901 (headed by Plaminkóva). In 1924 they formally became part of the ICW as Czechoslovak women; the Hungarians had been a separate entity since 1904, so there was a precedent for keeping Ukrainians. The Ukrainian American and Canadian women, whose monetary support funded much of the travel involved in the participation of Ukrainians in international meetings, were apparently ready to fund the travel of a number of Galician women to Washington, but there was a mix-up in communications.

27. ICW, Library of Congress, ms 3403, Box 2 "Women's International Organizations on Peace and Disarmament Commissions."

28. "Zhinochyi rukh na chuzhyni," *Hromadianka*, 1 October 1938, 15.

29. Rudnytska, "Dva kongresy," *Nasha khata*, no. 11 (1928): 6; *Dilo*, 26 June 1928, 2, and 29 June 1929, 2; *Zhinocha dolia*, 1 November 1928, 3.

30. The Congress of the Organized National Groups in the Countries of Europe was a semi-formal organization of European minorities that represented about 30 million people living in states which belonged to the League of Nations. The congresses of minorities were convened in Geneva on the eve of the September sessions of the League of Nations. Western Ukrainians joined this organization, which Rudnytska characterized in 1928 as "not being an international organization of a high order...but nevertheless it provided a forum for us." See "Borotba za pravdu pro velykyi holod," *Svoboda*, 16 July to 9 August 1958.

31. Rudnytska, "Fragmenty z ukrainskoi zakordonnoi aktsii," *Svoboda*, 11 April 1956.

32. Ibid.; see also Andrzej Chojnowski, *Koncepcje polityki narodowościowej rządów polskich w latach 1921–1939* (Wroclaw, 1979); *Sprawozdanie z spraw mniejszości narodowych...III kw. 1931.*

33. Rudnytska's letter to Volodymyr Tarnopolsky, 19 September 1954, in Rudnytska files in UVAN archives, uncatalogued. Rudnytska came to know the Norwegian, Rolf Andvord, well. He was helpful in expediting petitions on behalf of famine-stricken Ukraine to the League of Nations.

34. "Die Internationale Frauenliga für Friede und Freiheit und die Minderheitenfrage——Milena Rudnicka, ukrainische Abgeordnete im Polnischen Seim," *Schweizer Frauenblatt*, 6 November 193Ր. Also "Kongres Mniejszosci narodowych w Genewie" in *Sprawozdanie...III kw. 1931.*

35. The fullest available discussion in English is in Polonsky, esp. 371–3.

36. Ammende, who was close to Cardinal Theodor Innitzer of Vienna, became the secretary of the Vienna Committee to Aid Starving Ukraine organized by Innitzer; letter of Mirna of 28 January 1934 to Ukrainian Women's League in the United States, Archive of the UNWLA, uncatalogued.

37. Letter of Rudnytska of 16 January 1934: "Our Union is not directly involved in aid to starving Ukraine...the relationship of the Women's Union and the Committee to Save Ukraine (Komitet riatunku Ukrainy) is strengthened by the fact that I am the first vice-president of...the committee and its public relations officer in charge of foreign relations (*referentka zakordonnoi propagandy*)." Archive of UWLA, New York, uncatalogued. Ukrainian women in the U.S.

organized a committee to aid Ukraine in January 1934; the sculptor Archipenko donated a statue for its fund-raising campaign; Liubov Margolina Hansen, the daughter of Arnold Margolin, a Jewish member of the UNR government, was active in this committee. The Catholic Church, especially Metropolitan Sheptytsky of Lviv and the Austrian cardinal Innitzer, organized relief efforts for Ukrainians before the lay organizations did. Innitzer was aided by Evald Ammende. The Ukrainian Catholic Church was the first organization to carry out fund-raising activities——in the USA, Bishop Constantine Bohachevsky ordered a campaign to raise funds by the end of 1933, letter to UWLA, 6 February 1934, in UWLA archives New York. The Prague Ukrainian Women's Society co-operated with the Ukrainian-American organization. The fullest account of Ukrainian relief and information effort is in Rudnytska, "Borotba za pravdu pro Velykyi Holod," *Svoboda*, nos. 134–152, 16 July to 9 August 1958.

38. Both quotations from the above article. For reasons which have to do with post-Second World War organizations of Ukrainian women and which are not dealt with here, Rudnytska stressed that it was the Lviv Ukrainian Women's Union which enjoyed these contacts.

39. Mirna, "Plaminkova i ukrainske zhinotstvo na emigratsii," in Omelchenko, ed., *Plaminkova*, 26–31.

40. *Zhinka*, 15 April 1935.

41. Rusova "Harni idei i diisnist," *Zhinka*, July 1937, 2–3; see also *Zhinka*, 15 September 1937, 5; and October 1937, 2, as well as *Holos*, 29 August 1937.

42. *Zhinka*, November 1937.

43. Ibid.

VI: Ukrainian Women in the Soviet Union

1. The point is most forcefully argued by Gregory Massell, *The Surrogate Proletariat: Moslem Women and Revolutionary Strategies in Soviet Central Asia, 1919–1929* (Princeton, 1974).

2. Richard Stites, *The Women's Liberation Movement in Russia,* 326.

3. The best studies of the Ukrainian Revolution are: Pavlo Khrystiuk, *Zamitky i materiialy do istorii Ukrainskoi revoliutsii, 1917–1920 rr.* (Vienna, 1921–2), 4 vols.; Volodymyr Vynnychenko, *Vidrodzhennia natsii,* 3 vols. (Vienna, 1920); Serhii Mazlakh and Vasyl Shakhrai, *On the Current Situation in the Ukraine* (Ann Arbor, 1970); V. Shakhrai (V. Skorovstánsky), *Revoliutsiia na Ukraini* (Saratov, 1919); Isaak Mazepa, *Ukraina v ohni i buri revoliutsii 1917–1921,* 3 vols. (Prague, 1941; 2d ed. Neu-Ulm, 1950–52); Arthur E. Adams, *Bolsheviks in the Ukraine: The Second Campaign, 1918–1919* (New Haven, 1963); Jurij Borys, *The Sovietization of Ukraine, 1917–1923: The Communist Doctrine and Practice of National Self-Determination,* 2d. rev. ed. (Edmonton, 1980); John S. Reshetar, Jr., *The Ukrainian Revolution, 1917–1920: A Study in Nationalism* (Princeton, 1952); Oleh S. Pidhainy, *The Formation of the Ukrainian Republic* (Toronto and New York, 1966); Taras Hunczak, ed., *The Ukraine, 1917–1921: A Study in Revolution* (Cambridge, Mass., 1977); Dmytro Doroshenko, *History of Ukraine, 1917–1923* (Winnipeg and Detroit, 1977); Oleh S. Fedyshyn, *Germany's Drive to*

the East and the Ukrainian Revolution, 1917–1918 (New Brunswick, N.J., 1971); Richard Pipes, *The Formation of the Soviet Union: Communism and Nationalism, 1917–1923*, 2d rev. ed. (Cambridge, Mass., 1964); Frantishek Silnitsky, *Natsionalnaia politika KPSS v period s 1917 po 1922 god* (Munich, 1978). Mariia Levkovych wrote a 91-page booklet, *Zhinka v revoliutsiinii borotbi ta hromadskii viini na Ukraini*, published in the mid-1920s in Kharkiv. I have not been able to locate it.

4. See "Part One: The Jurists' Case," in Michael Browne, ed., *Ferment in the Ukraine* (New York, 1971), 31–93.

5. The best study of the Soviet interpretation of their nationalities policies is Lowell Tillett, *The Great Friendship: Soviet Historians on the Non-Russian Nationalities* (Chapel Hill, 1969).

6. The best studies of twentieth-century Ukraine as a colony of Russia remain: Mykhailo Volobuiev, "Do problemy ukrainskoi ekonomiky," *Bilshovyk Ukrainy*, no. 2 and 3 (1928), reprinted in *Dokumenty ukrainskoho komunizmu* (New York, 1962), 132–230; and Ivan Dzyuba, *Internationalism or Russification?* (London, 1968).

7. The major works in English on Soviet and East European women are: Barbara W. Jancar, *Women Under Communism* (Baltimore, 1978); Richard Stites, *The Women's Liberation Movement in Russia*; Joni Lovenduski and Jill Hills, eds., *The Politics of the Second Electorate: Women and Public Participation in Britain, USA, Canada, Australia, France, Spain, West Germany, Italy, Sweden, Finland, Eastern Europe, USSR, Japan* (London and Boston, 1981); Xenia Gasiorowska, *Women in Soviet Fiction, 1917–1964* (Madison, 1968); Donald R. Brown, ed., *The Role and Status of Women in the Soviet Union* (New York, 1968); Norton T. Dodge, *Women in the Soviet Economy: Their Role in Economic, Scientific, and Technical Development* (Baltimore, 1977); Alena Heitlinger, *Women and State Socialism: Sex Inequality in the Soviet Union and Czechoslovakia* (London, 1979); Tova Yedlin, ed., *Women in Eastern Europe and the Soviet Union* (New York, 1980); Alastair McAuley, *Women's Work and Wages in the Soviet Union* (London and Boston, 1981); Gail Warshofsky Lapidus, Dorothy Atkinson and Alexander Dallin, eds., *Women in Russia* (Stanford, 1977); Gail Warshofsky Lapidus, *Women in Soviet Society: Equality, Development, and Social Change* (Berkley and Los Angeles, 1978); *idem*, ed., *Women, Work, and Family in the Soviet Union* (Armonk, N.Y., 1982); Jenny Brine, Maureen Perrie, and Andrew Sutton, eds., *Home, School and Leisure in the Soviet Union* (London and Boston, 1980); Michael Paul Sacks, *Women's Work in Soviet Russia: Continuity in the Midst of Change* (New York, 1976); and *idem*, *Work and Equality in Soviet Society: The Division of Labor by Age, Gender, and Nationality* (Urbana, 1982); Alfred G. Meyer and Sharon L. Wolchik, eds., *Women, State and Party in Eastern Europe* (Durham, 1985); and Jerry F. Hough, "The Impact of Participation: Women and the Women's Issue in Soviet Policy Debates," in Hough, ed., *The Soviet Union and Social Science Theory* (Cambridge, Mass., 1977).

8. The formulation of the legal rights of women includes a concern for the childbearing function of women. The equal-rights provision of the 1936 Constitution, in effect until 1977, read:

> The woman in the Soviet Union is endowed with equal rights to those of the man in all branches of economic, state, cultural and community-political life. The opportunity of utilizing these rights is

guaranteed by giving the woman equal rights with the man in the right to work, payment of wages, rest, social security and public education, by the government's defence of the interests of the mother and child, by giving pregnant women paid leaves, a wide network of birthing houses, nurseries, and child care centers.

Translated from a Ukrainian version of the 1936 constitution, article 122. The original Ukrainian word for "endowed" is *nadaietsia,* which connotes granting from above.

9. *Zhinky Radianskoi Ukrainy, aktyvni budivnyky komunistychnoho suspilstva* (Kiev, 1971), 169.

10. Liudmyla Vitruk, *Zhinky-trudivnytsi v period sotsialistychnoii industrializatsii* (Kiev, 1973), 116.

11. Ibid., 23, basing herself on G.N. Serebrennikov, *Zhenskii trud v SSSR* (Moscow, 1934).

12. *Istoriia Ukrainskoi RSR*, 6: 387–30, 150, and 174.

13. Works on Soviet historiography: Cyril E. Black, ed., *Rewriting Russian History: Soviet Interpretations of Russia's Past*, 2d rev. ed. (New York, 1962); Konstantin Shteppa, *Russian Historians and the Soviet State* (New Brunswick, N.J., 1962); John Keep, ed., *Contemporary History in the Soviet Mirror* (New York, 1964); Lowell Tillet, *The Great Friendship: Soviet Historians on the Non-Russian Nationalities* (Chapel Hill, 1969); Nancy Whittier Heer, *Politics and History in the Soviet Union* (Cambridge, Mass., 1971); Anatole G. Mazour, *The Writing of History in the Soviet Union* (Stanford, 1971); and Ivan Myhul, "Politics and History in the Soviet Ukraine: A Study of Soviet Ukrainian Historiography" (unpublished Ph.D. dissertation, Columbia University, 1973).

14. K. Filatova, "Revoliutsiinyi rukh robitnyts i selianok Ukrainy," in *Zhinocha volia: chytanka* (Kharkiv, 1925), 23. Filatova was one of the major activists in the all-Union Bolshevik programme to integrate women into party life.

15. Zh.P. Tymchenko, *Trudiashchi zhinky v borotbi za vladu rad' na Ukraini 1917–1920* (Kiev, 1966), and her "Uchast zhinok-robitnyts Kieva u revoliutsiinii borotbi (berezen 1917–sichen 1918)," *Ukrainskyi istorychnyi zhurnal*, no. 1 (1982): 57–65.

16. *Trudiashchi zhinky v borotbi za vladu*, 19–20.

17. Quotation from Marusia Levkovych, "Vstup: zamist peredmovy," *Zhinocha volia: chytanka*, 1. Similar sentiments pepper the documents in the Smolensk archive; see esp. file 423, instruction to Women's Oblast Section, 1922.

18. *Istoriia Ukrainskoi RSR*, 6: 151; Petrograd was renamed Leningrad in 1924.

19. Quoted in Tymchenko, *Trudiashchi zhinky*, 94.

20. Ibid., 95.

21. *Zhinocha volia* (Kharkiv), 26.

22. Vitruk, *Zhinky-trudivnytsi*, 104.

23. From a circular dated 1922, signed by the secretary of the Russian Central Committee of the Russian Communist Party, V. Kuibyshev, and the vice-chairman of the central *Zhenotdel*, V.A. Moirova, to all oblast and gubernia committees of the Russian Communist Party, in Smolensk archive, folder 428, 87. Eventually Kuibyshev became a key party functionary in Ukraine.

24. Quotation from N.V. Astakhova and E.N. Tsellarius, *Tovarishch Olga* (Moscow, 1969), 127; Tymchenko, 97.

25. *Zhinocha volia* (Kharkiv), 25–35.

26. V.I. Lenin, *Tvory*, vol. 29, 157, quoted in Tymchenko, 126. See also *Zhinocha volia*, 26; of the delegates 366 were peasants, 707 workers, and 32 members of the intelligentsia, Tymchenko, 127.

27. Quotation from Stites, 338; see also *URE*, 2: 1625; Tsellarius, 124.

28. Interviews with Liubov Drazhevska about Kharkiv, held in New York, October 1980.

29. On Levkovych, see Vitruk, 81 and 102; Levkovych is mentioned in vol. 4 of *URE*, published in 1979, as having been active, along with Pilatskaia and Samoilova, in the women's sections. She did not merit a separate entry.

30. *Zhinocha volia*, 31–40; Tymchenko, 122 on the particularly difficult conditions in organizing women in the villages.

31. The Russian term used is *shefstvo nad krestiankami,* for instance in the typed series of directives on work among peasants in the Smolensk archive, file 247, 35. Similar directives occur in reports on the work of the central *Zhenotdel*.

32. Circular dated 8 May 1922, in Smolensk archive, file 208, 2.

33. The orthography of the journal, as was frequent in such publications at the time, was inconsistent. For instance, the July-October (no. 7–8) issue of *Komunarka Ukrainy* for 1921 was subtitled *Organ tsientralnogo otdela rabotnitsy sielianok Kommunisticheskoi partii (bolshevikov) Ukrainy* [*sic*]. At this time an attempt was made to reflect the speech patterns of the workers in the areas around Kharkiv, and these used their own mixture of Russian and Ukrainian. Among the contributors were M.O. Skrypnyk, Lenin's right-hand man in Ukraine at the time, Inessa Armand, one of Lenin's closest female friends, and others.

34. V. Gorlovsky, "Bezrabotnitsa na Ukrainy i mery borby s neiu," *Komunarka Ukrainy*, no. 1 (1923): 19–21.

35. *Zhinocha dolia*, 1 October 1936, 7.

36. *Zhinocha dolia: Almanakh* (1927), 130; Shevchenko's article, "Rodynnyi ta hromadskyi stan zhinky v Ukraini," ibid. (1928), 80–93; quotation on 83.

37. *Zhinocha dolia* (November 1925); *Dilo* of 14 March 1929 carried an extensive feature on women in the Soviet Union.

38. *Zhinocha dolia*, 15 March 1926, 5.

39. *Nova khata*, no. 3 (1927), no. 5 (1929), and no. 8 (1929). The last piece of information was all the more telling, since the Ukrainian Galician co-operative had sent its observers to a related general co-operative meeting in Soviet Ukraine, and none of the Galician women had been included.

40. Astakhova and Tsellarius, 95, 122–3; *URE*, 2: 1625.

41. *Zhinocha dolia*, 1 January 1926, 15. The tsarist police archives note that Nykolai Dmytrovych Hladky of Kharkiv belonged to the Ukrainian faction of the Social Democratic Party in 1906, TsDIA, f. 1335, op. 1, od.zb. 3 B 1535.

42. A general discussion of the co-operative from the Soviet viewpoint is found in *Istoriia Ukrainskoi RSR*, 6: 71–5.

43. Volodymyr Kubijovyč, ed., *Ukraine: A Concise Encyclopaedia* (Toronto, 1963–71), 1: 810–11, provides a brief discussion.

44. "Pro zakhody zabezpechennia rivnopravnosti mov i pro dopomohu rozvytkovi ukrainskoi movy," in *Kulturne budivnytstvo v Ukrainskii RSR* (Kiev, 1959), 242–7.

45. Iwan Majstrenko, *Borotbism: A Chapter in The History of Ukrainian Communism* (New York, 1954), 218.

46. The number of students in all educational establishments increased from 1,961,800 in 1924 to 5,564,600 in 1936. *Sotsialistychna Ukraina: Statystychnyi zbirnyk* (Kiev, 1937), 133.

47. O. Stepanyshyna, "Ostanni roky zhyttia Mykhaila Hrushevskoho," *Ukrainskyi istoryk*, 1–4 (69–72) (1981): 174–9. Hrushevsky died in 1934, at the age of 68, in Kyslovodsk from complications arising from the lancing of a simple carbuncle. He had been arrested earlier, and although freed through the personal intervention of Stalin himself, continued to be hounded by the police and prevented from returning to Kiev. Foul play was generally presumed in his death. Kateryna's areas of expertise were ethnicity, folklore, *dumas*, and ancient magic rituals used in housekeeping.

48. *Claudius Appius, Hetman Doroshenko.* For a listing of Starytska's works published in the USSR, see Heinrich E. Shulz, Paul K. Urban, and Andrew I. Lebed, eds., *Who was Who in the USSR: A Bibliographic Directory Containing 5,015 Biographies of Prominent Soviet Historical Personalities* (Metuchen, N.J., 1972).

49. Leonid Plyushch, *History's Carnival: A Dissident's Autobiography*, ed. and trans. Marco Carynnyk (New York, 1977), 158. Kotsiubynsky led one of the detachments that captured Kiev from the Directory in 1919, *Istoriia Ukrainskoi RSR*, 5: 245.

50. On Polish women's organizations in Uman, see *Iugo-zapadnyi krai*, 607; on Surovtseva's positions, *EU* VIII, 3105; also Pliushch, 159, and 247.

51. Szporluk, *Ukraine*, 78.

52. Vitruk, 61. Former working women and poor peasants received twice the fellowship stipend of other women; Krupskaia's sixtieth birthday was marked by instituting a special fellowship in her honour. Between 1925 and 1933 the number of women students in Ukraine increased from 8,000 to 33,000.

53. Ibid., 91.

54. Ibid., 73, 79.

55. Ibid., 98–9; also *Istoriia Ukrainskoi RSR*, 6: 396–7.

56. Ibid., 203.

57. Ibid., 392.

58. V. Boshko, "Stanovyshche zhinky za radianskym pravom," *Zhyttia i revoliutsiia*, no. 3 (1925): 72. The claim of fulfilling Roman law is all the more surprising in view of the lack of Roman legal tradition in the area.

59. Oleksander Semenenko, *Kharkiv, Kharkiv* (New York, 1976), 29. The autocephaly of the Ukrainian Orthodox Church (i.e., its independence from the government and the Moscow patriarchate) was proclaimed under the Ukrainian People's Republic on 1 January 1919. Metropolitan Vasyl Lypkivsky also formally announced the independence of the Ukrainian church from the Cathedral of St. Sophia in Kiev on 23 October 1921.

60. TsDIA, UkSSR (Kiev), f. 442, op. 643, spr. 48, 169.

61. *Vydatni zhinky Ukrainy*, 150. Hirniak maintained that it was the daughter, Rona (Veronica), who was arrested in the SVU process, because for a time she had been married to a German officer. Liudmyla Starytska persuaded the secret police to arrest her in place of Rona. They did let the daughter go, but arrested her again a few months later. Iosyp Hirniak, *Spomyny*, ed. Bohdan Boychuk (New York, 1982), 330.

62. Rona, as the young woman was known, went mad under questioning, and

Starytska, returning from exile, was unable to find her, although she searched through most of Siberia. The last time Starytska was seen alive was in Kiev, on the eve of the German retreat in 1943. Mariia Turkalo, "Velyka Hromadianka," *Svoboda*, 11 March 1953. Turkalo was present at the trial and saw Veronica being arrested later. The most reliable information on SVU is the brief article by Yaroslav Bilinsky in *EU*, 8: 3005–6.

63. See, for instance, Semenenko, *Kharkiv, Kharkiv*, 161 on Liubchenko's wife; he also mentions Skrypnyk's first wife, Mariia Mykolaivna, who was Lenin's secretary in 1917–18, 121. On Skrypnyk, see Ivan Koshelivets, *Mykola Skrypnyk*, (Munich, 1972).

64. Works on the famine in English include: Dana J. Dalrymple, "The Soviet Famine of 1932–34," *Soviet Studies* 15, no. 3 (1964): 250–84 and 16, no. 3 (1965): 471–4; James E. Mace, "The Man-Made Famine of 1933 in Soviet Ukraine: What Happened and Why," *Almanakh Ukrainskoho Narodnoho Soiuzu 1983* (Jersey City and New York, 1983), 12–43; Roman Serbyn and Bohdan Krawchenko, eds., *Famine in Ukraine: 1932–1933* (Edmonton, 1986). Most comprehensive is Robert Conquest, *Harvest of Sorrow* (New York, 1986).

65. *Istoriia Ukrainskoi RSR*, 5: 251.

66. Ibid., 6: 215.

67. "V chomu vyiavliaetsia rusyfikatsiia Ukrainy?" *Suchasnist* (Munich), March 1982, 78.

68. The best descriptions and analyses of the purges include: Zbigniew Brzezinski, *The Permanent Purge——Politics in Soviet Totalitarianism* (Cambridge, Mass., 1956); Barrington Moore, *Terror and Progress USSR: Some Sources of Change and Stability in the Soviet Dictatorship* (Cambridge, Mass., 1954); Robert Conquest, *The Great Terror: Stalin's Purge of the Thirties*, rev. ed. (Harmondsworth, 1971); Roy Medvedev, *Let History Judge* (New York, 1971); and Aleksandr Solzhenitsyn, *The Gulag Archipelago*, 3 vols. (New York, 1974–9).

69. In the 1950s Rudnytska was compiling personal depositions of peasants who survived the ordeal. This is the story of Petro Marunchak, then living in London; Rudnytska file in UVAN archive, uncatalogued.

70. Maurice Hindus, *The Great Offensive* (New York, 1933), 126–7. Hindus then whitewashed the story by having the peasants organize a successful rescue effort in face of inefficient bureaucracy.

71. Schlesinger, for instance, reported on the press campaigns which identified the joys of motherhood with the benefits of Soviet power. He quoted a typical comment: "A woman without children merits our pity, for she does not know the full joy of life. Our Soviet women, full-bodied citizens of the freest country in the world, have been given the bliss of motherhood." *The Family in the USSR* (London, 1949), 254; cited in Gail Warshofsky Lapidus, *Women in Soviet Society: Equality, Development and Social Change* (Berkeley and Los Angeles, 1978), quotation in text from 112–13.

72. Szporluk, *Ukraine*, 79.

73. *Istoriia Ukrainskoi RSR*, 6: 393.

74. Ibid., 6: 393, 395.

75. Plyushch, *History's Carnival*, 159.

Bibliography

Introduction

Only materials of direct relevance to the study of women's movements in Ukraine and of Ukrainian women's movements have been included in this bibliography. Its *main* purpose is to suggest avenues for research into the history of Ukrainian women. I have not included here the large and growing literature in general social, women's and family history that is indispensable for even marginal study of Ukrainian women but which is readily accessible. Instead, I have stressed sources in Ukrainian history. To facilitate further research I have also, rather unconventionally, included materials from Kiev and Lviv to which I have not been unable to gain access to but which are of *a priori* significance to the topic. More conventionally I have included only materials I have found directly relevant to the presentation of the topic. All materials, even those remotely connected with Ukrainian matters, relate to Ukrainian women and to women in Ukraine; I have included the ones I found most useful. Through the years I have profited from the insights of numerous scholars, the work of many researchers, and from my own research in topics not directly related to women's movements. I have sought to make the list comprehensive; it certainly can never be complete. The relations of Polish and Ukrainian women are discussed briefly in M. Bohachevsky-Chomiak, "Socialism and Feminism: the First Stages of Women's Organizations in the Eastern Part of the Austrian Empire," in Tova Yedlin, ed. *Women in Eastern Europe*, 44–64; and in "Feminizm, socjalizm i nacjonalizm: Polacy i Ukraińcy," in *Suchasnist*, Summer 1985, 178–86; Russian and Ukrainian women in "Ukrainian and Russian Women: Conflict and Cooperation," in Peter Potichnyj, Marc Raeff, Jaroslaw Pelenski, and Gleb N. Zekulin, eds., *Ukraine and Russia in their Historical Encounter* (forthcoming); and on Jewish women in "Jewish and Ukrainian Women: A Double Minority," in Howard Aster and Peter J. Potichnyj, eds. *Jewish-Ukrainian Relations in Historical Perspective* (forthcoming, Edmonton).

Introductory histories of Ukraine, especially those which take into consideration social and economic developments, offer some, but not much, factual information on the life of women. Mykhailo Hrushevsky's classic *Istoriia Ukrainy-Rusy* (reprinted in New York by Knyhospilka in 10 vols., 1954–8) offers a dated yet solid presentation. The eight-volume Soviet *Istoriia Ukrainskoi Radianskoi Sotsialistychnoi Respubliky* (Kiev, 1977–9), in its openly biased manner, offers a wealth of information, especially on the early stages of Ukrainian history and prehistory. Omeljan Pritsak's *The Origin of Rus'* (Cambridge, Mass.: Harvard Ukrainian Research Institute, 1981, projected 6 volumes), while offering extremely original interpretations, is based upon written sources in which women play a very limited role.

Of the shorter works on Ukrainian history, Nataliia Polonska-Vasylenko's two-volume *Istoriia Ukrainy* stresses the contributions of women to a greater degree than the many other introductory works. The following are useful:

Standard Reference Tools

Entsyklopediia ukrainoznavstva. ed. Volodymyr Kubijovyč and Zenon Kuzelia (v. 1 only). 2 vols. Munich and New York: Shevchenko Scientific Society, 1949 (v. 1, pts. 1–3); Paris and New York: Shevchenko Scientific Society, 1955 ff. (v. 2, pts. 1 ff.)

Istoriia ukrainskoho viiska. 2d ed. Winnipeg: Ivan Tyktor, 1953.

Istoriia Ukrainskoi RSR. 8 vols. Kiev: Naukova dumka, 1977–9.

Lawrynenko, Jurij. *Ukrainian Communism and Soviet Russian Policy Toward the Ukraine: An Annotated Bibliography, 1917–1953.* Munich: Research Program on the USSR, 1953.

Levytskii, Ivan E. *Halytsko-ruskaia bybliohrafiia XIX st. z uvzhliadneniem ruskikh yzdanii, poiavyvshykhsia v Uhorshchyni y Bukovyni 1801–1886.* 2 vols. Lviv, 1888–95.

_____. *Ukrainska bibliografiia Avstro–Uhorshchyny za roky 1887–1900.* 3 vols. Lviv, 1900–11.

Mashotas, V.V. *Komunistychna Partiia Zakhidnoi Ukrainy.* Lviv, 1969.

Polonska-Vasylenko, Nataliia. *Istoriia Ukrainy.* 2 vols. Munich: Ukrainian Free University, 1976.

Ukraine, A Concise Encyclopaedia. ed. Volodymyr Kubijovyč. 2 vols. Toronto: University of Toronto Press, 1963–71.

Ukrainska Radianska Entsyklopediia (Kiev: 1959–65). 17 vols. ed. Mykola Bazhan et al. The second edition, begun in 1977, was completed in 12 volumes in 1985.

Ukrainska zahalna entsyklopediia: knyha znannia v 3-okh tomakh. Lviv, 1932.

Women in the Soviet Union: Statistical Returns. Moscow: Progress Publishers, 1970.

Zhenshchina i deti v SSSR: Statisticheskii sbornik. Moscow: Statistika, 1969.

Zhenshchiny v SSSR: Statisticheskie materialy. Moscow: Statistika, 1970.

Zhenshchiny v SSSR: Statisticheskii sbornik. Moscow: Statistika, 1975.

Zhinka sotsialistychnoi Ukrainy: statystychnyi dovidnyk. comp. M.M. Filipov et. al. Kiev: Narodne hospodarstvo i oblik, 1937.

These publications contain, in varying degrees, information on the women's movement and individual women. Exceptional women, especially women writers, merited special studies. I have included only those which have some direct bearing upon the organized activity of women. There are no comprehensive studies of organized Ukrainian women. Instead, there are accounts, more or less laudatory, of the lives of exceptional women whose achievement was measured by the proclivities of the authors or cursory descriptions of women's organizational activities. The latter were often written by participants, who sometimes tended to be defensive, but rarely placed their subjects within broader contexts. Generally, these articles and booklets were written for special occasions and reflected the festive mood that inspired them. Little or no attempt was made to integrate the presentation of women's activities into the life of the community. Distance from the events described sometimes led me to place a given work into the category of secondary rather than primary sources. The bibliography that follows lists some of the most useful works on the Ukrainian women's movement.

General Works

Chyz, Martha. *Woman and Child in the Modern System of Slavery——USSR*. Translated from Ukrainian by Olha Prychodko. Toronto: SUZERO and New York: DOBRUS, 1962.

Iuvileina Knyha Soiuza Ukrainok Ameryky 1925–1940. New York, 1941.
Has some information on Ukrainian women in Ukraine.

Knysh, Irena. *Smoloskyp u temriavi: Nataliia Kobrynska i ukrainskyi zhinochyi rukh*. Introduction by Olena Kysilevska. Winnipeg, 1957.
A detailed study based upon available published material.

Luhovy, Oleksander (Oleksander Vasyl Ovrutsky Shvabe). *Vyznachne zhinotstvo Ukrainy*. Toronto: Author, 1942.
Exuberant if not always accurate account of Ukrainian women of major historical significance.

Ministerstwo Spraw Wewnętrznych. Wydział Narodowościowy (tylko do uzytku słuzbowego). *Sprawozdanie z zycia Mniejszości Narodowych*. Warsaw, 1928–31.
Official publication, with varied format and limited circulation, contains information and detailed articles on the situation of the nationalities.

Pavlykovska, Iryna. *Na hromadskyi shliakh: Z nahody 70-littia ukrainskoho zhinochoho rukhu*. Philadelphia: Svitova Federatsiia Ukrainskykh Zhinochykh Orhanizatsii, 1956.
Preface by Olena Zalizniak. Incomplete and with some factual errors, but illustrative of the modern Ukrainian women's movement; interesting photographs.

Polonska-Vasylenko, Nataliia. *Vydatni zhinky Ukrainy*. Winnipeg: Ukrainian Women's Association of Canada, Natalia Kobrynska Foundation, 1969. Introduction by Oleksander Ohloblyn; Preface by Natalia Levenets-Kohuska.
A historical account of the lives and achievements of exceptional Ukrainian women, generally stressing politics and

culture, and concentrating on the period before the nineteenth
century, although it also includes some women of the
nineteenth and twentieth centuries.

Rusova, Sofiia. *Nashi vyznachni zhinky.* 1st ed. Kolomyia: Zhinocha dolia,
1934; 2d ed. Winnipeg: Ukrainian Women's Association of
Canada, 1945.
Especially valuable for the personal recollections which
Rusova uses to illustrate her story.

Sprawozdanie stenograficzne Sejmu Rzeczypospolitej, 1922–39.

Sprawozdanie stenograficzne Senatu Rzeczypospolitej, 1922–39.
Both contain full parliamentary proceedings in which several
Ukrainian women participated.

Svitovyi Kongres Ukrainskoho Zhinotstva, November 12–13, 1948,
Philadelphia.
Unnumbered pages, some illustrations, mainly on the
founding of this organization, but also brief articles by Mariia
Strutynska, Dariia Rebet and Lidiia Burachynska on women's
organizations in Galicia, women in the liberation struggle and
the economic work of women, respectively.

*Ukrainian Woman of Detroit. Jubilee Book in Commemoration of 70th
Anniversary of Ukrainian Feminist Movement and 35th
Anniversary of Social Activities of Ukrainian Women of
Detroit, Michigan.* Detroit: United Ukrainian Women's
Organizations, 1955. Edited by Lydia Burachynska.
Also has articles of interest to the student of the Ukrainian
women's movement in Ukraine. Texts in Ukrainian.

"Ukrainskyi Zhinochyi Soiuz v Avstrii" in *Ukrainka u vilnomu sviti: Zbirnyk
vydanyi u 75-littia zhinochoho rukhu i 10-littia Svitovoi
Federatsii Ukrainskykh Zhinochykh Orhanizatsii z nahody
Svitovoho Kongresu Ukrainskoho Zhinotstva u Niu Iorku,
24–27 chervnia 1959 r.*
Most articles deal with émigré women's organizations
founded in the 1950s.

Vyznachni zhinky Ukrainy (Seriia persha), Liubov Drazhevska, "Olena Pchilka:
Zirka ukrainskoho vidrodzhennia"; N. Danylenko,
"Starytskykh-Cherniakhivskykh-Steshenkiv zahublenyi rid."
n.p.: Obiednannia Ukrainskykh Zhinok na Emihratsii, 1956.
Danylenko was a friend of Liudmyla Starytska
Cherniakivska, and Drazhevska also knew some of the
persons about whom she writes.

*Woman of Ukraine: Her Part on the Scene of History, in Literature, Arts and
Struggle for Freedom.* Philadelphia: Ukrainian National
Women's League of America, 1955. Contributors: Lydia [sic]
Burachynska, Olena Chekhivska, Olimpia Dobrovolska, Petro
Mehyk, Stephania Nahirna, Halyna Selehen, Alexandra

Sulima, Olena Trofimovska, Prof. Dr. Natalie Polonska Vasylenko.

> A 48-page brochure in English with illustrations and statistical tables.

Zalizniak, Olena. "Pochatky ukrainskoho zhinochoho rukhu," in *Sribnyi Vinok: Iuvileinyi zbirnyk Soiuzu Ukrainok Ameryky.* Philadelphia, 1950.

> A 14-page article in an unpaginated volume. The rest of the book contains mainly photos and materials on the Ukrainian National Women's League of America.

Certain publications which are not readily classifiable at times included materials of interest to the historian of women's movements. Various *Almanacs* and *Collections* published on special occasions contain information about women. The following are especially useful:

Almanakh ukrainskoho studentskoho zhyttia v Krakovi, 1931.

Almanakh Zhinocha dolia. Kolomyia, 1927, 1928, 1929, 1930.

Amerykanskyi Prosvitianyn. Lviv: Prosvita, 1925.

> Has information on community organizations in Western Ukraine.

Iliustrovanyi kaliendar tovarystva Prosvita. Lviv, various years.

> Lists Ukrainian merchants and professionals; annual.

Istorychnyi almanakh Chervonoi Kalyny. Lviv, 1921–39.

> Annual; memoirs mainly on the struggle for independence, including some by women.

Kobrynska, Nataliia, ed. *Nasha Dolia.* vol. 1, Stryi, 1893; vol. 2, Lviv, 1895; vol. 3, Lviv, 1896.

Kobrynska, Nataliia and Olena Pchilka, eds. *Pershyi vinok: Zhinochyi Almanakh.* Lviv, 1887. Repr. New York: Ukrainian National Women's League of America, 1984.

Pamiatkova knyzhka Soiuza Vyzvolennia Ukrainy. Vienna, 1917.

> Overview articles by Andrii Zhuk, Volodymyr Doroshenko and others.

Rusalka, Zhenskii Almanakh, New York: V.M. Brode, 1922.

> Some works of Lesia Ukrainka, printed in the old orthography, are included in this collection.

Shevchenko Scientific Society, Ukrainian Archives, vol. XXII. *Propamiatna knyha Himnazii Sester Vasyliianok u Lvovi.* Editorial Staff: Wasyl Lew, Anna Kobrynska, Dora Rak, Stefania Bernardyn, Lidia Diachenko, Olha Dziadiw. New York, 1980.

> Collection of short memoirs, a brief historical sketch and photographs.

Studentskyi visnyk. Prague, no. 2, 1926 (fourth year of publication).

Zhinocha volia: Chytanka [peredmova Marusia Levkovych]. Kharkiv: Chervonyi shliakh, n.d. [1925].

Reports of schools, both annual and those published for special occasions, in addition to factual information, included articles and memoirs of some use in the study of women. Sometimes lists of students include information on their social origin. Most useful are:

Vydavnytstvo Moloda Ukraina, no. 4. *Zvit z diialnosty tovarystva Ukrainskyi studentskyi soiuz u Lvovi za chas vid I. XI. 1911 do 30. X. 1912.* Lviv, 1912.

Zvidomlennia z diialnosty Ukrainskoho pedahohichnoho tovarystva, 1922–23.

Zvit Dyrektsii Litseia Ruskoho Instytutu dlia Divchat [v Peremyshli] za 1910 do 1917 (14 vols).

Zvit Dyrektsii pryvatnoi gimnazii SS. Vasyliianok u Lvovi. Lviv, from 1906 through 1913, 8 volumes and also published annually in the inter-war period.

Zvit upravi gimnaziialno-naukovykh kursiv v Vidni, 1915.

Zvit Upravy Pryvatnoi Zhinochoi gimnazii "Ukrainskoho instytuta dlia Divchat" v Peremyshli z pravamy derzhavnykh shkil. Published intermittently in the inter-war period.

Journals and Newspapers

Journals and newspapers edited by and for women constitute a major source on their history. The following are the most significant ones. Much of the material included in them is episodical. I have, moreover, singled out in separate entries those articles which are of particular importance to the history of women. They are included in the primary sources.

Meta: Organ ukrainskykh postupovykh liudei (vydaie i vidvichaie Dariia Starosolska), Lviv, 1908.

Moloda Ukraina: Chasopys dlia ditei starshoho i menshoho viku (dodatok do *Ridnoho Kraiu*), vydaie i ukladaie Olena Pchilka, no. 1, January 1914.

Nasha meta: Chasopys dlia robitnoho zhinotstva, Lviv, 1. February 1919–14. December 1919.

Nashe zhyttia (January 1944 to present), Philadelphia, New York. Carries both memoir materials and brief articles on the history of Ukrainian women. Edited between 1944 and 1946 by Claudia Olesnytsky; 1946–50 by Olena Lototska; then 1950 to 1972 by Lidiia Burachynska, and since May 1972 by Uliana Starosolska-Liubovych.

Nova khata, Lviv, 1925–39. Edited first by Mariia Derkach, then by Lidiia Burachynska. Monthly to 1934, then bi-monthly.

Samostiina dumka ukrainskoi matery: Zhurnal osvity, tvorchosty i borotby, edited by Sydoniia Hnida Nykorovych, Chernivtsi, 1931. I was able to locate only two issues. Nykorovych was a co–editor of *Samostiina dumka* (1931–4) and *Khliborobska pravda* (1935–8), both published in Chernivtsi.

Selianka Ukrainy, Kharkiv, 1924–31. Iliustrovanyi dvotyzhnevyk. Orhan tsentralnoho viddilu robitnyts i selianok KP(b)U. In 1929 the official guide to Kharkiv, *Ves Kharkiv*, characterized this as "A bi-weekly community-political (*hromadsko-politychnyi*) and literary-scholarly women's journal. The organ of the Central Bureau of Women Workers and Peasants of the Central Committee of the Communist Party (bolsheviks) of Ukraine."

Svit molodi, 1934–9. 1934–6 as addendum to *Zhinocha dolia*; 1936 separate publication. Monthly for young women, ed. Iryna Vilde.

Zhinka, vol. 1–5, 1 January 1935 - August 1939; 1938 nos. 1–6 called *Hromadianka*; ed. Olena Sheparovych and Milena Rudnytska; bi-monthly.

Zhinocha dolia, Kolomyia; ed. Olena Kysilevska, 1924–39. Bi-monthly.

Zhinoche dilo, bezplatnyi dodatok do *Dila*, Lviv 21.VI.1912 vesna, 31.XII.1912 zyma, ed. Volodymyr Bachynsky.

Zhinochyi holos, Lviv, 1931–9; chasopys ukrainskykh pratsiuiuchykh zhinok, ed. Franka Stakhova.

Zhinochyi svit, zhurnal dlia ukrainskoho zhinotstva v Amerytsi, Pittsburgh–Detroit, 1933–7, ed. Mariia Bek; orhan SUA 1933–4.

Other Ukrainian newspapers and journals which have the greatest amount of information about women or the most directly relevant materials are:

Dilo, major Western Ukrainian newspaper; 1883–7 (3x week), 1888–1939 (daily).

La Femme Slave, Prague, 1933, edited by Mariia Omelchenko and Miloslava Hrdličková, August 1933–4.

Hromadskyi holos, published by the Ukrainian Radical Party and from 1926 by the Ukrainian Socialist-Radical Party; from 1892–1906 monthly (with interruptions), 1906–09 bi–monthly, 1910–37 weekly.

Komunarka Ukrainy, Orhan tsentralnoho otdela robitnyts ta selianok Tsentralnoho Komitetu Kommunistychnoi partii (bolshevykov) Ukrainy, Kharkiv, 1921-?. Characterized by *Ves Kharkiv* as "illustrated mass journal for women workers and peasants."

Literaturno–naukovyi vistnyk, Lviv, monthly 1898–1906; 1907–14 and 1917–19, Kiev; 1922–32, Lviv. Rich in historical and literary comments.

Meta, ed. Ksenofont Klymkevych, Lviv, Stavropihiia, September 1863-January 1864 monthly; March-November 1865 bi-monthly.

Meta, Lviv, 1931–9, ed. V. Kuzmovych; weekly of Ukrainian Catholic Alliance.

Narod, 1890–5, Lviv and Kolomyia; bi-weekly journal of the Ruthenian-Ukrainian Radical Party.

Nova hromada, Kiev, 1906.

Nova hromada, dvotyzhnevyi zahalno-kooperatyvnyi, literaturno-mystetskyi ta ekonomichno-naukovyi selianskyi zhurnal. Vydaie Vseukrainska Mizhkooperatyvna Rada *Vukorada*, Kiev and Kharkiv, 1923.

Nova Ukraina, Prague, 1922–8. Populist journal founded by Mykyta Shapoval.

Nova zoria, Lviv, 1926–28 weekly, 1928–39 bi-weekly. Edited from 1928 by Osyp Nazaruk. Organ of the Ukrainian National Catholic Party from 1930.

Peremyski eparkhiialni vidomosti, 1889–1939; up to 1914 *Vistnyk peremyskoii eparkhii*.

Pravda, Lviv, 1867–79; 1888–96. Bi-monthly and monthly at various times; published articles on women and by a few anonymous women.

Ridna shkola, Lviv, 1932–9, bi-weekly.

Svitlo, Ukrainskyi pedagogichnyi zhurnal, Kiev, 1910–14, monthly.

Ukrainska khata, Kiev, 1909–14.

Vidhuky, Organ ukrainskoi molodi, Lviv, 1913.

Vistnyk stanyslavivskoi eparkhii, January 1927 - July 1934.

Zasiv, Ukrainska tyzhneva narodnia iliustrovana gazeta, Kiev, 1911.

Zhinochyi visnyk, newspaper published in Kiev in 1917 by the organization of Ukrainian women in the Ukrainian People's Republic, which called itself both Ukrainskyi zhinochyi soiuz and Ukrainska zhinocha spilka, both meaning Ukrainian Women's Alliance or Union. I have been unable to see an issue, but the journal's existence is attested even by Soviet scholars, for example Zhanna Tymchenko.

Zoria, pysmo literaturno-naukove dlia ruskykh rodyn, Lviv, from 1880–4, then 1884–97; ed. Omelian Partytsky, bi-monthly.

Also useful are some non-Ukrainian journals, especially:

Dwutygodnik dla spraw wychowania i pracy kobiet, Lviv, 1895–7, ed. Paulina Kuczalska-Reinschmidt.

Zhenskii vestnik: Ezhemesiachnyi obschestvenno–nauchno–literaturnyi zhurnal posviashchennyi zhenskomu voprosu, St. Petersburg, 1904–1917. Both this journal and the following one discuss some of the problems Ukrainian women shared with Russian women, but give very little information about Ukrainian women.

Zhenskoe delo, ezhenedelnyi illiustrirovannyi zhurnal, Moscow, 1910–16.

Less useful are:

Gospodyni polskiej, Przemyśl, 1918. Short-lived Polish women's newspaper in
     a city with an active Ukrainian community.

Promień, pismo póswięcone sprawam młodziezy szkolnej; Lviv, 1901–2.

Przewódnik Oświatowy TSL, organ Towarzystwa Szkoły Ludowej poświęcony
          sprawam oświaty pozaszkolnej i narodowego wychowania
          ludu polskiego.

Archival Sources

Czechoslovakia

In Prague, the Státní Literární Archív Památníků Národního Písemnictví
has a number of unpublished letters of Nataliia Kobrynska, Hermina
Shukhevych and other Ukrainian activists in the František Rehoř file. The
Karolinum Library has rare Ukrainian women's publications and periodicals.

Poland

Extremely rich materials on the daily and community life of Ukrainian
women exist in the holdings of the Wojewódzkie Archiwum Państwowe in
Przemyśl, long a Ukrainian city (Peremyshl). As one would expect, information
on women is scattered throughout the archive, which is organized along topical
and chronological lines and is still being catalogued. There is a typed
Inwentarz, prepared by Wanda Kaput, to most of the catalogued holdings.

The Archive of the Diocese of the Ukrainian Catholic Church in Przemyśl
(Archiwum Grecko-Katolickiego Biskupstwa) has very detailed files of the
Institute of Widows and Orphans, which include a rich collection of letters,
reports and petitions as well as minutes of meetings. They are mostly
hand-written in Ukrainian, and many of them are extremely frank. There are
also rich materials on community and parish organizations from which information on women's organizations, especially before the First World War, can be
gleaned. Files on the teaching of religion, mandatory in all schools, are relevant
to women, since there were many women teachers, all of whom were licensed
to teach religion after 1911. Diocesan permission was necessary to hold
open-air masses, say two masses on the same day, arrange for processions, etc.
Reports from regional deaneries highlight community life. There are also some

parish lists on the basis of which demographic studies could be made. Although the parish lists are limited to territories now in Poland which had Ukrainian Catholic parishes before 1946, they are illustrative of conditions prevailing in the Catholic areas of Ukraine.

The holdings on the Ukrainian Institute for Girls (Ukrainskyi instytut dlia divchat) are complete and contain all the handwritten minutes of the civic committee which supervised and ran the institute. Detailed information on fund-raising, construction and technical maintainance of the Institute is available, as well as programs of study and various functions held there. Less complete, but nevertheless significant, information is available on other schools, including the gymnasium in Przemyśl and the nearby teachers' seminary.

The archives of the Diocesan Consistory (Kapitula GKB) contain additional correspondence and reports dealing with a number of women's issues, as well as a separate file on nuns (although material about female religious is also scattered throughout the archive). There is extensive material on Catholic Action, as well as diocesan publications.

Useful also is Zbiór szczoliowy zespołów akt szkolnych w Przemyślu, Syg. 4 "Prywatna jednoroczna zeńska szkoła krawiecko-bieliźniarska z ukraińską mową nauczania Filii Związku Ukrainek w Przemyślu" (1937) and Syg. 5 "Prywatny Ukraiński Kurs Seminaryjny w Przemyślu". A number of occasional publications dealing with schools and festivities, not available elsewhere, are scattered among the holdings of the archive.

The City Library is also a good source not so much for rare books as for occasional publications which contain reports on the doings of women. Most of the books are not fully catalogued and therefore still difficult to find, but the cataloguing is going on.

Other archival collections in Poland yield materials tangentially related to women's movements in Ukraine. Biblioteka Zakładu Narodowego im. Ossolińskich, Dział Rękopisów, the regional archive in Wrocław, Ossolineum, has new material on Polish scouting (*Harcerstwo*) in Galicia and Volhynia which is of marginal interest, as it describes the difficulties of organizing Polish women in Lviv, Rivne, etc. The most useful holdings are:

Bruchalska, Marja, "Cuda Boze nad mieszkańcami i dziecmi Lwowa 1918," pp. 48–71.

Bruchnalska, Marya, "Materiały dotyczące udziału kobiet polskich w powstaniu styczniowym."

_____. "Wykaz kobiet więzionych i zsyłanych na Sybir i w głąb Rosji."

Grzymatowski, Stanisław. "Działalność młodziezy akademickiej w ruchu harcerskim w Kijowie 1912–1918." Warsaw, I 1965.

"Materiały do zarysu historii Lwowskiej Chorągi Harcerek."

Opieńska-Blauth, Janina, "Polskie Harcerki w pierwszym dziesięcioleciu 1911–1921."

Skirmunttowna, Jadwiga, "Dwadzieścia pięć lat wspomnień o Marii Rodziewiczownie." Bibl. Zakładu Narodowego im. Ossolińskich, Dział Rękopisów, Syg. 14052 I, II. Wrocław.

"Związek Harcerstwa Polskiego na Wołyniu Chorągiew Zenska i Męska 1918–1939," Tom I, Część 1 & 2. Warsaw, 1978.

The repositories of Leon Wasilewski and Maria Feldmanowa contain only occasional references to individual women.

Uniwersytet Jagielloński, in Cracow, Biblioteka, Dział rękopisów, has unpublished materials on Polish women's organizations in Ukraine. Of particular interest is MS 7990, the program of Zrzeszenie kół kobiecych na Litwie, Rusi, Koloniach w Rosji.

In Warsaw itself, Archiwum Akt Nowych has interesting material on some Ukrainian territories in the First World War in the Rada Główna Opiekuńcza. The files of the Liga Kobiet Polskich, an auxiliary of the Piłsudski camp active on Ukrainian territory (1915–33), are located in this archive.

Archiwum Akt Dawnych, in the files of the Russian Tsarist Law Court, (Prokurator Varshavskoi Sudebnoi Palaty), has material on Ukrainian peasant women of Volhynia and Kholm.

The precise whereabouts of Uliana Kravchenko's private archive, with which the author worked in Warsaw, are not now known. In addition to Kravchenko's works, it contains correspondence with women's and community leaders.

RSFSR (Moscow)

In Moscow, material directly relevant to the subject is housed in the Tsentralnyi gosudarstvennyi istoricheskii arkhiv. In f. 102, Departament Politsii, the files on Sofiia Rusova, Mykola Kovalevsky, Volodymyr Antonovych, Prosvita and the Spilka are of direct importance. File 516, Soiuz ravnopraviia zhenshchin, disclosed new information on both Ukrainian and Russian women. The Tsentralnyi gosudarstvennyi arkhiv literatury i iskusstva has materials of Danylo Mordovtsev (f. 320) and a very small file on Mykhailo Drahomanov (f. 1065). These are of lesser importance.

Ukraine

Tsentralnyi derzhavnyi istorychnyi arkhiv, Kiev
The reports of the *Okhrana*, the tsarist secret police, filed geographically and chronologically, cover Ukrainian territories. Information on women and on Ukrainian organizations is scattered throughout police files from Kiev, Poltava, Katerynoslav, Odessa, Volhynia, Podillia, Kharkiv. Most useful are f. 442, op. 659 spr. 204; op. 823 od.zb. 171; op. 639 spr. 48; op. 644 od.zb. 50; op. 625 spr. 273; op. 636 od.zb. 647 ch. VII, all having to do with police matters.

Files on the Kiev Women's Higher Courses that include material on the so-called Ukrainophiles are: f.442, op. 828, 835 through 856, f. 707, op. 151, spr. 30, which contains a 35-page booklet on the courses published in 1884 and various handwritten reports on the courses and the individuals connected with them.

Papers of the Ukrainian Sunday School activist in Kharkiv, Khrystyna D. Alchevska, have been moved here as fond 2052. They contain rich correspondence with Professor M.F. Sumtsov, the poet Oleksander Oles, and others. There are a number of letters to and from Alchevska's daughter, the poet Khrystia.

Police and government files on "granting permission to philanthropic societies to hold fund-raising events" contain a wealth of information on community organizations, national and social relations, small schools and relief activities. Also included are published reports of organizational activities, which were printed in very limited editions.

Tsentralnyi derzhavnyi istorychnyi arkhiv, Lviv
f. 663, op.1, od.zb. 125. Vypysy z sudovykh aktiv u spravi Pavlyka Mykhaila i Anny i inshykh.
Oblasnyi derzhavnyi arkhiv, Lviv:
        This repository contains invaluable information on the community organizations of Western Ukraine, and the bulk of the holdings of the library and archive of the Shevchenko Scientific Society. Of its rich collections I found the following most useful to the topic:
f. 119. Lvivskyi oblasnyi derzhavnyi arkhiv. Ukrainske tovarystvo zhinok z vyshchoiu osvitoiu u Lvovi.
f. 300. Lvivskyi oblasnyi derzhavnyi arkhiv. Obshchestvo Russkikh Dam.
f. 3c309. Naukove Tovarystvo im. T.H. Shevchenka. Uprava, Perepyska riznykh osib.
f. 3c309 op. 1 zviazka 11, od. kh. 238. Naukove Tovarystvo im. T.H. Shevchenka, Uprava, Lysty Kobylianskoi i dovirenykh osib v spravakh vydannia tvoriv.
f. 309 op. 1 spr. 285 zviazka 13. Lysty zhinochykh hromadskykh i hospodarskykh organizatsii v spravi udilennia im materiialnoi pomochi, ukomplektuvannia bibliotek knyzhkamy i t.d. 1902–05.
f. 663 op. 1 spr. 248. Mykhailo Pavlyk. Lystuvannia Evhenii Iaroshynskoi z Olhoiu Kobylianskoiu i inshymy, 1881–1906 (materiialy pryhotovleni ii batkom v 1906).
f. 309 op. 1 spr. 2385. Naukove Tovarystvo im. T.H. Shevchenka, Lviv. Kolektsiia. Lysty do Ohonovskoho Emeliana vid korespondentiv z prizvyshchamy O-P; 1884–92.

Although I have not been able to gain access to *Instytut literatury Akademii nauk Ukrainskoi RSR, Kiev* or to *Biblioteka Akademii Nauk, Lviv*, in the interests of facilitating further research I am including information on the materials located there.

Instytut literatury Akademii nauk Ukrainskoi RSR in Kiev has the unpublished materials of: Nataliia Kobrynska (f. 13), Uliana Kravchenko (f. 132), Olena Pchilka (f. 28), Lesia Ukrainka (f. 2), Ivan Franko (f. 3), and Osyp Makovei (f. 59).

The library in the Lviv Manuscript Division is also the repository of rich archival holdings, among them those of M.S. Vozniak, as well as correspondence of various women writers.

USA and Canada

Archives of Columbia University, Butler Library, New York.

Nothing specifically on Ukrainian women, but the many nostalgic memoirs and letters of Russian women who called Ukraine their home illustrate one of the problems that faced Ukrainian women.

Library of Congress, Washington, D.C. Manuscript Division. Holdings on the International Council of Women.

The *National Archives* in Washington, D.C., house the most complete copy of the documents of the Smolensk Party archive captured during World War II. Some of this material is of tangential interest to persons writing about Soviet Ukrainian women.

Archive of the Ukrainian Academy of Arts and Sciences (Ukrainska vilna akademiia nauk) in New York contains the following repositories:
Chykalenko, Ievhen. "Shchodennyk, 1907–1917," and "Spomyny, 1919–1930."
> Parts have been typed, some of the diary entries are unnumbered, and there is a handwritten epilogue.

Chykalenko-Keller, Hanna.
> Material primarily on the period 1919–30, particularly rich on the relations of Ukrainian women with international feminist organizations. There are also parts of unfinished memoirs and an autobiographical sketch, as well as some correspondence.

Hrynevych, Katria.
> Contains both published and unpublished materials.

Rudnytska, Milena.
> Includes episodic material on the history of the Ukrainian women's movement that Rudnytska and others were

preparing for publication in the 1950s. No comprehensive work emerged from the project.

Archive of the Ukrainian National Women's League of America, Central Office in New York.

Correspondence with Ukrainian women's organizations and women activists in Europe, some of it dealing with attempts to help alleviate the 1933 famine.

Kimpinska-Patsiuk, Aleksandra, from the Sokal region in northern Galicia, emigrated to Canada, left a small collection of food recipes annotated with descriptions of the daily life of peasant households.

Trembitska, Kateryna. "Moi pershi lita pratsi i vrazhinnia iak uchytelka na seli i v misti vid roku 1900," 34 handwritten pages, and a number of brief accounts of her contemporaries.

Various occasional publications which frequently contain brief documentary materials on European Ukrainian women are located here. There is no index.

Archives of Nashe zhyttia

The journal of the Ukrainian National Women's League of America, whose editorial office was transferred from Philadelphia to New York in 1973. The archive contains correspondence, unpublished memoirs and photographs, as well as occasional publications and commemorative programs. The materials are not catalogued or organized.

Public Archives of Canada, Ottawa

The Kateryna Antonovych Collection (MG 31, H50; Finding Aid No. 15157). For a description of this collection see Canadian Institute of Ukrainian Studies, University of Alberta, Occasional Research Report No. 13 (1985), *The Kateryna Antonovych Collection*, prepared by Dennis Sowtis and Myron Momryk.

The Olena Kysilewska Collection (MG 31, H42; Finding Aid No 1516). For a description of this collection see Canadian Institute of Ukrainian Studies, University of Alberta, Occasional Research Report No. 12 (1985), *The Olena Kysilewska Collection*, prepared by Dennis Sowtis and Myron Momryk.

Interviews

Burachynska, Lidiia. Series of interviews and correspondence, 1978–1983.

Drazhevska, Liubov. Series of interviews in 1980–82 in New York.

Horokhovych, Antonina (Tonia). Interviews 14 and 15 March 1982, in Toronto.

Nementowska, Julia (Nusia), daughter of Uliana Kravchenko. Series of interviews conducted in Przemyśl in March and May-June 1977 and October 1981.

Zhorliakevych, Oleksander. Interviews in Przemyśl in March and May-June 1977.

Private Collections

Unpublished personal memoirs of Rostyslava Nychay Bohachevsky, in the possession of the author.

Letters of a number of Ukrainian women activists written in reply to queries by the author. Especially significant are those by Lidiia Burachynska, who edited *Nova khata* and *Nashe zhyttia*.

Daria Dzerowycz, née Witoszyńska, "Erinnerungen." Manuscript for the family finished on Christmas, 1974, with an additional 19 pp. on the life of Ukrainians in Vienna, written in October 1977.

The East European Research Institute in Philadelphia, Pennsylvania, houses the papers of Viacheslav Lypynsky, which are being catalogued and prepared for publication. Included in its holdings is correspondence, especially among émigrés of the 1920s, that deals with the women's movement.

Some private papers of Milena Rudnytska in the archive of her late son, Ivan L. Rudnytsky, at the University of Alberta.

Unpublished personal memoirs of Olena Fedak Sheparovych, in the possession of Olha Kuzmovych.

Published Primary Sources

Alchevska, Khrystyna. Remarks at the *Exposition Universelle Internationale de 1889*, Actes du Congrès International des Oeuvres et Institutions Féminines. Paris, 1890.

_____. *Peredumannoe i perezhitoe. Dnevniki, pisma, vospominaniia*. Moscow: 1912.

_____. "Pismo," in *Ukrainskaia zhizn*, no. 4, 1912, 85–90.

Andrukhovych, Konstantyn K. *Z zhytia rusyniv v Amerytsi: spomyny z r. 1889–1892*. Kolomyia, 1904.

Antonovych, Kateryna. *Z moikh spomyniv*. Ukrainian Free Academy of Sciences Series: UVAN Chronicle, Winnipeg, 1965–73, nos. 23–7.

Bahalii, Dmytro. Obituary of A. Iefimenko. In *Zapysky Istorychno-Filolohichnoho viddilu Ukrainskoi akademii nauk,* 1: 102–13. Kiev, 1919.

Baranova, Blanka. "Ukrainske zhinotstvo i nashi vyzvolni zmahannia." *Novyi chas,* 1 November 1937.

Barvinok, Hanna (O.M. Kulish). *Opovidannia z narodnykh ust.* Kiev, 1902.

Bekesevych-Matskiv, F. "Z viddali 55 rokiv." *Svitlo* (Toronto) (November 1974): 390–91.

Berenshtam, Vladimir. V.G. *Korolenko kak obshchestvennyi deiatel i v domashnem krugu.* Moscow, 1922.

Berenshtam-Kistiakovska, Mariia. "Ukrainski hurtky v Kyivi druhoi polovyny 1880-ykh ta pochatku 1890-ykh rokiv." *Za sto lit,* bk. 3 (1928): 206–25.

Berezhnytska-Budzova, Olena. "Kruzhok ukrainskykh divchat." *Nova khata,* no. 5 (1939).

The Black Deeds of the Kremlin: A White Book. ed. S.O. Pidhainyi et al. 2 vols. Toronto, 1953.

Bobrzyński, Michał. *Z moich pamiętników.* ed. Adam Galos. Wrocław, 1957.

Bogdanowicz, Marian. *Wspomnienia.* 2 vols. Cracow, 1958.

Bogoliubov, A.A. *Zhenskii Russko-Slavianskii Soiuz.* St. Petersburg, 1899.

Borodchak, K. "Zhinka v borotbi za vyzvolennia zakhidnoi Ukrainy." *Ukrainski robitnychi visti,* 14 March 1931.

Borovikovskii, A. "Iz ukrainskikh motivov. Stikhotvorenie." *Zhenskii vestnik* (St. Petersburg), vol. VII (1867): 83–4.

Bosh, Evgeniia. *God borby: Borba za vlast na Ukraine s aprelia 1917 goda do nemetskoi okupatsii.* Moscow, 1925.

Boshko, Volodymyr. "Navkolo novoho shliubnoho kodeksu." *Zhyttia i revoliutsiia,* no. 2 (1926): 100–13.

Boshyk, George Y. "The Rise of Ukrainian Political Parties in Russia, 1900–1907: With Special Reference to Social Democracy." D. Phil. Thesis, University of Oxford, 1981.

Bujak-Boguska, Sylwia. *Na straży praw kobiety. Pamiętnik Klubu Politycznego Kobiet Postępowych 1919–1930.* Warsaw, 1930.

Bujwidowa, Kazimiera. *O postępowym i niepostępowym ruchu kobiecym w Galicji.* Lviv, 1913.

_____. *U źródeł kwestii kobjecej.* Warsaw, 1910.

Chahovets, Vsevolod. *Mariia Zankovetska.* Kiev: Mystetstvo, 1949.

Chalyi, Mikhail Kornilevich. *Vospominaniia.* Kiev, 1890–95.

[Charewiczowa, Lucja] Mikułowska, C. *"Ukraiński" ruch kobiecy.* Lviv, 1937.

Chekhova, E.N. "Vospominaniia o zhenshchinakh-professorakh." In Valk et al., *Sanktpeterburgskie vysshie (Bestuzhevskie) kursy,* 176–87.

Chekhova, N.V. "Marko Vovchok." *Soiuz Zhenshchin,* no. 2 (August-September 1907): 13, continuation in no. 1 (January 1908): 11–12 and no. 2 (February 1908): 14–17.

Chernetskii, Kirill E. *Gigiena liubvi.* Kiev, 1885.

Chernetsky, Antin. *Spomyny z moho zhyttia*. London: Nashe slovo, 1964.

Chivonibar, A. *Bosiaki, zhenshchiny, deti*. Odessa, 1904.

Chykalenko, Hanna. "Feminizm i kriza demokratii." *Zhinocha dolia*, nos. 12–13 (1934): 14–17.

_____. "Materiialy do biohrafii Evhena Chykalenka." *Literaturno–naukovyi vistnyk*, no. 6 (1930): 510–23.

Chykalenko, Ievhen. *Spohady, 1861–1907*. New York, 1955.

Congress of Women, Chicago, 1893. ed. Mary Kavanaugh Oldham Eagle. Chicago: W.B. Conkey, 1894.

Czajecka, Bogusława. "Przygotowanie kobiet do pracy zawodowej na tle ruchu feministycznego w Galicji." Ph.D. dissertation, Jagiellonian University, 1977.

Daszyńska-Golińska, Zofja. *Kwestia kobieca a małżeństwo*. Warsaw, 1925.

_____. *Prawo wyborcze kobiet*. Warsaw: Związek Polskich Stowarzyszeń Kobiecych w Warszawie, 1918.

_____. *Przełom w socjalizmie*. Lviv, 1900.

Davis, Menie Muriel Dowie. *A Girl in the Carpathians*. 3d ed. London, 1891.

Devosser, Stefaniia Vitoshynska. "Uchast zhinotstva u vyzvolnykh zmahanniakh 1918–1920 rr." *Novyi shliakh* (Toronto), 14 March 1981, 13.

Dmyterko-Ratych, Hanna. "Iz zbroieiu v rukakh." In *Ukrainian Woman of Detroit: Jubilee Book in Commemoration of 70th Anniversary of Ukrainian Feminist Movement and 35th Anniversary of Social Activities of Ukrainian Women of Detroit, Michigan*, 241–43. Detroit: United Ukrainian Women's Organizations, 1955.

Docheri Oktiabria: rabotnitsy i selianki Ukrainy v dni Velikoi Proletarskoi Revoliutsii 1917–1922. Kharkiv, 1922.

Domanytskyi, Vasyl. *Pro Halychynu ta zhyttia halytskych ukraintsiv*. Kiev: Prosvita, 1909.

Dontsova, Mariia Bachynska. "Na bizhuchi temy zhinochoho rukhu." *Almanakh Zhinochoi doli*. Kolomyia, 1928.

"Dopys iz Tsishchanivskoho." *Dilo*, no. 46 (1880).

Doroshenko, Dmytro. *Moi spomyny pro davnie–mynule, 1901–1914*. Winnipeg, 1949.

_____. "Politychnyi rozvytok naddniprianskoi Ukrainy: vstup do istorii ukrainskoi natsionalnoi revoliutsii 1917–1920," 50–66. *Kalendar Dnipro*. Lviv, 1935.

_____. *Z istorii ukrainskoi politychnoi dumky za chasiv svitovoi viiny*. Prague, 1936.

Doroshenko, Volodymyr. "Katria Hrynevych." *Literaturno–naukovyi visnyk* (Regensburg) (May 1948): 115–20.

_____. *Ohnyshche ukrainskoi nauky: Naukove tovarystvo imeny T. Shevchenka. Z nahody 75-richchia ioho zasnuvannia*. New York, 1951.

_____. "Zhinky v RUP." *Nashe zhyttia*, no. 4 (April 1950): 12–13.

Dovnar-Zapolskii, M.V., and A.I. Iaroshevich, eds. *Ves Iugo-Zapadnyi krai: spravochnaia i adresnaia kniga po Kievskoi, Podolskoi i Volynskoi guberniiam.* Kiev, 1913.

Drahomanov, Mykhailo. *Arkhiv Mykhaila Drahomanova, Tom I: Lystuvannia Kyivskoi Staroi Hromady z M. Drahomanovym (1870–1895 r.r.)* Pratsi Ukrainskoho Naukovoho Instytutu, Tom XXXVII. Warsaw, 1937.

_____. *Avstro–Ruski spomyny, 1867–1877.* Lviv, 1889–92.

_____. *Lysty do Ivana Franka i inshykh, 1887–1895.* Lviv: Ukrainsko-Ruska vydavnycha spilka, 1908.

Duchyminska, Olha. "Moi spomyny pro Nataliiu Kobrynsku." *Zhinocha dolia*, 15 June/1 July 1934: 3–7.

_____. *N. Kobrynska iak feministka.* Kolomyia, 1934.

Dudkevych, Valeriia. *Holubyi khrest.* Lviv, 1938.

Dudykevych, Bohdan. "V borbe za shchastia naroda." *Stalinskoe plemia*, 11 June 1953.

Duszyna, Bronisława. *Kobieta w ruchu spółdzielczym.* Warsaw, 1939.

Efimenko, Aleksandra. *Istoriia ukrainskogo naroda.* Volume in series: Istoriia Evropy po epokham i stranam v srednie veka i novoe vremia, ed. N.I. Kareev and I.V. Luchitskii. St. Petersburg: Brockhaus-Efron, 1906.

_____. *Iuzhnaia Rus: ocherki, issledovaniia i zametki.* 2 vols. St. Petersburg: Obshchestvo im. T.G. Shevchenko dlia vspomoshchestvovaniia nuzhdaiushchimsia urozhentsam Iuzhnoi Rossii, uchashchimsia v vysshykh uchebnykh zavedeniiakh Sanktpeterburga, 1905.

Efimenko, Oleksandara (*sic*). *Istoriia ukrainskoho naroda.* 2d ed. Kharkiv: Derzhavne vydavnytstvo Ukrainy, 1922.

Engels, Fridrikh. *Pochatok rodyny, pryvatnoi vlasnosty i derzhavy, na pidstavi doslidiv L.H. Morgana.* Lviv: Ukrainsko-ruska vydavnycha spilka, 1899. Reprint, New York: Ukrainska federatsiia amerykanskoi sotsiialistychnoi partii, 1919.

Fedak-Sheparovych, Olena. "Ukrainska studentka." *Smoloskypy* (Lviv), January 1928: 7–10.

Feliński, M. [Rajmund Rózycki]. *Ukraińcy w Polsce odrodzonej.* Warsaw, 1931.

"Fond vdovycho-syrotynskyi i taiemnycha movchaznist." *Pravda* (Lviv), no. 10 (1878).

Franko, Ivan. "Do istorii sotsiialistychnoho rukhu." *Literaturno–naukovyi vistnyk* 25 (1904): 134–52.

_____. *Narys istorii ukrainsko-ruskoi literatury do 1890 roku.* Lviv, 1890.

_____. Review article on *Nasha Dolia*, I, 1893. In *Tvory* 16: 191–3.

_____. *Tvory.* 20 vols. Kiev: Derzhlitvydav, 1950–56.

_____. *Zhinocha nevolia v ruskykh pisniakh narodnykh.* Lviv: Zoria, 1883.

Głos kobiet w kwestii kobiecej. Cracow, 1903.

Goldelman, Solomon. *Juden-Bauern in der Ukraine.* Munich, 1973.

Halychyn, Stephania, ed. *500 Ukrainian Martyred Women.* New York, 1956.

Hankevych, Mykola. *Pro zhinochu nevoliu v istorychnim rozvoiu.* Toronto, 1918.

Hirniak, Iosyp. *Spomyny.* ed. Bohdan Boychuk. New York: Suchasnist, 1982.

Horiansky, Pavlo. "Zhadka pro Lesiu Ukrainku." *Zhyttia i revoliutsiia,* no. 2 (1926): 98–102.

Horokhovych, Tonia. "Pamiati Busi." *Svoboda,* 27 August 1955.

Hrab [Hrabovskyi], Pavlo. "Deshcho v spravi zhinochykh typiv." *Narod,* 1 and 15 April 1884.

Hrinchenko, Borys. *Iakoi nam treba shkoly.* Kiev, 1906.

_____. *Narodni vchyteli i ukrainska shkola.* Kiev: Hromadska dumka, 1906.

_____. *Tiazhkym shliakhom.* Kiev, 1907.

Hrinchenko, Mariia (née Dolenko). *Pro derzhavnyi lad u vsiakykh narodiv.* Lviv, 1905.

Hrushevska, Kateryna, ed. *Pervisne hromadianstvo,* 1926–9. Six issues published under the aegis of Vseukrainska Akademiia Nauk.

Hrushevsky, Mykhailo. *Pochatky hromadianstva (Genetychna sotsiologiia).* Prague: Ukrainskyi sotsiologichnyi instytut, 1921.

_____. "Retsenziia na *Nashu doliu,*" *Zapysky Naukovoho Tovarystva im. Shevchenka* 17 (1897): 48–9.

_____. "Retsenziia *Tsarivny.*" *Literaturno–naukovyi vistnyk* 1 (1898): 174–80.

Hrynevych, Katria. *Shelomy v sontsi.* Lviv, n.d. Dedicated to Konstantyna Malytska.

_____. "Spomyny," *Almanakh ukrainskoho studentskoho zhyttia v Krakovi.* Lviv, 1931.

Humenna, Dokiia. *Dity chumatskoho shliakhu.* 4 vols. n.p., 1948–51.

_____. *Kurkulska villia.* n.p., 1946.

Iadryntsov, N. "Zhenshchina na Sibire v XIV i XVII st.: istoricheskii ocherk." *Zhenskii vestnik* (St. Petersburg), vol. 8 (1867): 103–23.

Ianovska, Liubov. "Mii roman." *Literaturno–naukovyi vistnyk,* October 1917: 99–113; November–December 1917: 213–51.

Iaroshynska, Ievheniia. *Zapovit. Zbirka opovidan dlia ditei.* Lviv: Ruske tovarystvo pedagogichne, 1907.

Iasinchuk, Lev. *50 lit Ridnoi shkoly 1881–1931.* Lviv, 1931.

Iatsevich, Iu.V. *Nachalnoe obrazovanie v Poltavskoi gubernii.* Poltava: Poltavskaia Gubernskaia zemskaia uprava, 1894.

Ichenhaeuser, Eliza. *Bilder vom Internationalen Frauenkongress, 1904.* Berlin: A. Scherl, 1904.

_____. *Der gegenwärtige Stand der Frauenfrage in allen Kulturstaaten.* Leipzig, 1894.

Iefremov, Serhii. "Na sviati Kotliarevskoho (zhadka samovydtsia)." In *Pryvit Ivanovy Frankovy v soroklitie ioho pysmenskoi pratsi 1874–1914,* Lviv, 1916, 169–76.

The International Council of Women, 1899–1904. Report of Transactions of Executive and Council. ed. May Wright Sewall. Boston, 1909.

_____. *Report of Transactions of the Fourth Quinquennial Meeting held at Toronto, Canada, June 1909.* ed. the Countess of Aberdeen, President ICW. London: Constable, 1910.

_____. *Report on the Quinquennial Meeting. Vienna, 1930.* Ed. the Marchioness of Aberdeen and Temair, President of ICW. Neighley: Rydel Press, 1931.

Iustyna, V. "Z lystiv." *Zoria*, no. 12 (1880): 14–15.

Iuvilei 30–litnoi diialnosty Mykhaila Pavlyka, 1874–1904. Lviv, 1905.

Ivan Franko v spohadakh suchasnykiv. Lviv, 1956.

Ivanchuk, Sofiia. "V imia velykoi idei (v pamiat moim zemliakam)." *Ukrainskyi holos,* 18 April 1955: 11.

Jahołkowska-Koszutska, Ludwika. *Herezje w ruchu kobiecym.* Warsaw, 1907.

Jelinek, Edvard. *Polske pani a divky.* Prague, 1884.

Kabarovska, Severyna. "Shliakh organizatsii ukrainskoho zhinotstva (korotenkyi ohliad organizatsiinykh ioho zmahan)." *Nasha meta* (Lviv), no. 22 (23 November 1919): 1–3; no. 23 (30 November 1919): 3–4; no. 24 (14 December 1919): 3–6.

Kedryn, Ivan. *Zhyttia, podii, liudy: spomyny i komentari.* New York: Chervona kalyna, 1976.

Khrystiuk, Pavlo. *Zamitky i materiialy do istorii ukrainskoi revoliutsii 1917–1920.* 4 vols. Vienna, 1921–2. Reprint, New York, 1969.

Kikh, Mariia. "Pamiat hortaie storinky." *Vilna Ukraina,* (Lviv), 3 October 1964.

_____. "Tykh dniv ne zmovkne slava." *Vilna Ukraina* (Lviv), 2 April 1961.

Klushynska, Dora. *Chomu zhinky zhadaiut politychnykh prav.* New York: Holos pravdy, 1918.

Kobrynska, Nataliia. "Nitsheanski motyvy." *Dilo,* 20 June 1907: 1–2; 21 June 1907: 1–2.

_____. "Slovo na iuvylei 25-littia literaturnoi diialnosty Ivana Franka." *Literaturno–naukovyi vistnyk* 1 (April 1898): 122–4.

_____. "Spomyny z prohulky do Prahy." *Zoria* (1891): 438–9, 455–6.

_____. *Vybrani opovidannia.* Lviv, 1954.

_____. *Vybrani tvory.* ed. I.O. Denysiuk and K.A. Kril. Kiev: Dnipro, 1980.

_____. *Vybrani tvory.* ed. O. Moroz. Kiev, 1958.

_____. "Zhinka i svoboda." *Dilo,* 13 March 1906: 1–2.

Kobylianska, Olha. "Avtobiohrafiia." In *Almanakh u soroklittia diialnosty.* Chernivtsi, 1928.

_____. *Deshcho pro ideiu zhinochoho ruchu.* Kolomyia, 1894.

_____. "Emantsypatsiia ukrainskoi zhinky." *Samostiina dumka ukrainskoi matery,* no. 2 (1931): 5–6.

_____. *Snytsia: noveli i narysy.* Chernivtsi, 1922.

_____. *Tvory.* Kiev, 1983.

Kobylianska, Olha. *Almanakh u pamiatku ii soroklitnoi pysmennytskoi diialnosty 1887–1927.* Ed. Lev Kohut. Chernivtsi, 1928.

"Kobylianska, Olha: Z nahody 35-littia tvorchosty." *Nova Ukraina,* no. 1 (30 March 1922): 29–31.

Kobyliansky, Josef. *Polacy i Rusini: Słowo z okazyi wyborów.* Lviv, 1883.

Kohuska, Natalka L. *Chvert stolittia na hromadskii nyvi 1926–1951: Istoriia Soiuzu Ukrainok Kanady.* Winnipeg: Ukrainian Women's Association of Canada, 1952.

Kolmakov, Nikolai. *Ocherk deiatelnosti Kievskogo slovianskogo blagotvoritelnogo obshchestva.* [Kiev], 1894.

Konyskyi, O. Ia. "Galichina i rusiny [*sic*] iz dorozhnikh zametok i nabliudenii." *Vestnik Evropy* 5 (September 1886): 111–39.

_____. "Zhenshchyny profesory na universyteti v Bolonii." *Zoria,* nos. 20–23 (1883).

_____. "Zhinocha osvita na Ukraini." *Zoria,* no. 3–4, 13 and 15 February 1884.

Korenets, Olha. "Nataliia Kobrynska, hromadianska diiachka i pysmennytsia," *Literaturno–naukovyi vistnyk,* no. 6 (1930): 523–32.

Korinets [*sic*], Olha. "Obrazky." *Literaturno-naukovyi vistnyk* (February 1910): 323–9.

Koroleva, Natalena. *Bez korinnia: zhyttiepys suchasnytsi.* 3d enlarged ed. Cleveland, 1968.

Kos, Mykhailo. *Pro polovi spravy.* 3d ed. Lviv, 1912.

Kosach-Kryvyniuk, Olha. *Lesia Ukrainka. Khronolohiia zhyttia i tvorchosty.* New York: Ukrainian Academy of Arts and Sciences, 1970.

Kosinskii, Mikhail. *O zhenskikh uchilishchakh.* ed. with Nikolai Vessel. [St. Petersburg], 1864.

Kovalenko, Olena, "Z narodom——proty vorohiv." *Radianskyi Lviv,* March 1948: 54–8.

Kovalevskaia, Sofia Vasilevna (Korvin-Krukovskaia), *Vospominaniia detstva.* Moscow, 1960.

Kravchenko, Uliana. *Dlia nei——vse.* Kolomyia, 1931.

_____. *Moi tsvity.* Kolomyia, 1933.

_____. *Na vyzvolnomu shliakhu. Kartyny.* Kolomyia, 1930.

_____. *Prima vera.* Jubilee edition, Kolomyia, 1925 (first ed. Lviv, 1885).

_____. *Spohady uchytelky.* Kolomyia, 1936.

_____. *Tvory: povne vydannia u 100-richchia zhinochoho rukhu.* Toronto, 1975.

_____. *V zhytti ie shchos.* Kolomyia, 1929.

_____. *Zamist avtobiografii.* Kolomyia, 1934.

Kravtsiv, Zynoviia. "V odnii aktualnii spravi." *Studentskyi shliakh* (Lviv), November–December 1932: 263–5.

Kyianky. Kiev, 1963.

Kysilevska, Olena. *Po ridnomu kraiu. Polissia.* Kolomyia, 1936.

———. "Uryvky zi spomyniv——roky 1878–1888: pershi pochatky hromadianskoi sluzhby." *Zhinochyi svit* (Toronto), May 1976: 15–16.

———. "Za more ale do svoikh (spomyny)." In Kohuska, Natalka L., *Chvert storichchia...*, 529–38.

Lakota, Hryhorii. *Podruzhne pravo v novim kodeksi tserkovnim*. Zhovkva: Pechatnia OO. Vasyliian, n.d.

Lazarevich, I. P. *Deiatelnost zhenshchin*. Kharkiv, 1883.

Lazarevsky, Hlib. "Ta ne bude luchshe: spohady emigranta pro stari panski sadyby v Ukraini." *Hromadianka*, 1 November 1938: 3–4.

Levenko, Volodymyr [Leontovych, Volodymyr]. *Per pedes Apostolorum: obrazky z zhytia [sic] dukhovenstva na Ukraini*. Lviv, 1896.

Levytsky, Ivan Nechui. *Nad Chornym morem*. Leipzig: Ukrainska nakladnia, n.d. [1889].

Levytsky, Kost. *Istoriia politychnoi dumky halytskykh ukraintsiv 1848–1919*. 2 vols. Lviv, 1926–7.

———. *Pro prava ruskoi movy*. Lviv: Prosvita, 1896.

———. *Ukrainski polityky: sylvety nashykh davnikh posliv i politychnykh diiachiv*. 2 vols. Lviv, 1936–7.

Levytsky, Orest. "Hanna Montovt." *Literaturno-naukovyi vistnyk*, 1910, *passim*.

Levytsky, Vasyl. *Istoriia vykhovannia i navchannia: pidruchnyk dlia shkilnoho ta zahalnoho vzhytku*. Lviv: Nova ukrainska shkola, 1925.

Likhacheva, Elena. *Materialy dlia istorii zhenskago obrazovaniia*. St. Petersburg, 1899–1901.

Livytska, Mariia. *Na hrani dvokh epokh*. New York, 1972. 1899–1901.

Lototsky, Oleksander. *Storinky mynuloho*. 4 vols. Warsaw, 1932–5.

Lozynsky, Iosyp. *Ruskoje wesile w Peremyszly*. Przemyśl, 1835.

Lozynsky, Mykhailo. "Deiaki religiini obriady ta zvychai z pohliadu higiieny tila i dukha." *Literaturno-naukovyi vistnyk* 27 (July 1904): 19–38.

———. "Dva internatsionalni robitnytski kongresy, Shtutgart i Amsterdam." *Literaturno-naukova biblioteka* 40, 10 October 1907: 95–107; 11 October 1907: 292–304.

———. "Klerykalizm i vilnodumnist." *Literaturno–naukovyi vistnyk*, February 1910: 306–23.

———. "Pershi kroky: z pryvodu zboriv ukrainskoho zhinotstva." *Literaturno-naukovyi vistnyk* 25 (1904): 173.

———. "Polska politsiia u Lvovi rozihnala vseukrainskyi zhinochyi zizd." *Svoboda*, 19 January 1922.

———. "Z Avstryiskoi Ukrainy." *Literaturno-naukovyi vistnyk* 33 (January 1906): 167–88.

Lutsiv, Luka. "Divchyna v okopakh." *Kalendar Chervonoi Kalyny* (1925).

Lutsky, Ostap, ed. *Za krasoiu: Almanakh v chest Olhy Kobylianskoi*. Chernivtsi, 1905.

Lysenko, Ivan, and Kyrylo Myloslavsky, ed. *Ivan Alchevsky: spohady, materialy, lystuvannia.* Kiev, 1980.

M.M. *Kotsiubynskyi iak hromadskyi diiach: dokumenty, materialy, publikatsii.* Kiev: Naukova dumka, 1968.

Makarushka, Ostap. Review of *Nasha Dolia. Zoria,* 15 July 1895, 278–9.

Makovei, Osyp. "Pro natsyonalnu svidomist rusynok i narodni stroi." *Zoria,* 15 January 1895, 38–40.

_____. "Z zhyttia i pysmenstva: emantsypatsiia nashoho zhinotstva." *Literaturno–naukovyi vistnyk* 1 (April 1898): 98–106.

Makukh, Ivan. *Na narodnii sluzhbi.* Munich, 1958.

Malytska, Konstantyna. "Pani Doktor: Pamiati Kharyti Kononenko." *Hromadianka,* no. 2 (November 1946): 7–9.

_____. "Pislia rozviazannia Soiuzu ukrainok." *Zhinochyi svit,* June 1938.

_____. *Pro zhinochyi rukh: referat.* Lviv: Vydavnytstvo kruzhka divchat, 1904.

_____. "Pro znachennia vlasnoi presy i iak vona v nas rozvyvalasia." *Almanakh Zhinocha dolia.* Kolomyia, 1926.

Mandryka, Hanna. *Vybrane.* Ed. Stefaniia Bubniuk and Teodora Havrysh. Winnipeg, 1962.

Margolin, Arnold. *The Jews of Eastern Europe.* New York, 1926.

"Mariia Hrinchenkova, posmertna zhadka." In Vseukrainska Akademiia Nauk, *Zapysky Istorychno-Filolohichnoho viddilu,* bk. 21–2 (1929): xxxv–xxxviii.

Markevich, Nikolai [Mykola Markovych]. *Obychai, poveriia, kukhnia i napitki malorossiian. Izvlecheno iz nyneshniago narodnogo byta.* Kiev, 1860.

Matkovskyi, Ivan. *Ruskyi Instytut dlia divchat v Peremyshli, ieho povstanie, rozvii, i teperishnyi ustrii na pidstavi aktiv, protokoliv i vlasnykh spomyniv.* Przemyśl, 1897.

Mazurowa, Zofia, ed. *Wspomnienia o Irenie Kosmowskiej.* Warsaw, 1974.

Ministerstvo Kultury Ukrainskoi RSR. *Nataliia Kobrynska: Bibliohrafichnyi pokazhchyk.* ed. O.N. Moroz; comp. P. H. Babiak. Lviv: Lvivska derzhavna naukova biblioteka, 1967.

Mirchuk, Petro. *Narys istorii Orhanizatsii Ukrainskykh Natsionalistiv.* Vol. 1: 1920–1939. Munich, 1968.

Mirna, Zinaida. "Ukrainska Natsionalna Zhinocha Rada." *Almanakh Zhinocha dolia* (1928): 194–7.

_____. "Zhinochyi rukh na Velykii Ukraini do revoliutsii." *Zhinka,* no. 4 (1937).

Mirza-Avakiiants, Nataliia. *Selianski rozrukhy na Ukraini 1905–7.* Kharkiv, 1925.

Montsibovych, Olena. "Pratsia Soiuzu v Varshavi." *Ukrainska dumka* (London), 27 May 1976.

Mordovtsev, Daniil. *Russkiia zhenshchiny novago vremeni: biograficheskie ocherki iz russkoi istorii.* 3 vols. St. Petersburg, 1874.

Nazaruk, Osyp. *Hreko-katolytska tservka i ukrainska liberalna inteligentsiia.* Lviv, 1929.

_____. *Rik na Velykii Ukraini.* Vienna: Ukrainskyi prapor, 1920.

_____. *Zhinka i suspilnist: referat vyholoshenyi na zasidanni Generalnoho instytutu Katolytskoii aktsii u Lvovi dnia 13 kvitnia 1934 roku.* Lviv, 1934.

_____. and Olena Okhrymovych. "Khronika rukhu ukrainskoi akademichnoi molodizhy u Lvovi." *Sich: Almanakh v pamiat 40-kh rokovyn osnovania tovarystva Sich u Vidni,* 387–435. ed. Zenon Kuzelia and Mykola Chaikivsky. Lviv, 1908.

Nestorovych, Volodymyr T. *Ukrainski kuptsi i promyslovtsi v Zakhidnii Ukraini.* Toronto: Kliub ukrainskykh profesionalistiv i pidpryiemtsiv, 1977.

Nevytska, Iryna. "Zhinochyi rukh na Pidkarpatti." *Zhinka,* 1 March 1935, 3.

Ohonovsky, Omelian. *Istoriia literatury ruskoi.* 4 vols. Lviv, 1893.

Okhrymovych, Volodymyr. *Chomu ia navernuvsia: pryliudne vyznannia viry.* Lviv, 1920.

Okunevsky, Iaroslav. *Lysty z chuzhyny.* Chernivtsi, 1898.

Okunevsky, Teofil. *Iak dbaie Rada shkolna kraieva o rusku narodnu shkolu: promova v Soimi, 4. III. 1899.* Lviv, 1899.

Olesnytsky, Evhen. *Storinky z moho zhyttia.* 2 vols. Lviv, 1935.

Olha Kobylianska v krytytsi ta spohadakh. Kiev, 1963.

Omelčenková, Marie. *Česko-ukrajinské styky.* Prague: Česko-ukrajinska knihovne, 1928.

Omelchenko, Mariia. *Vybir fakhu.* Prague, 1925.

_____. ed. *Frantishka Plaminkova, z nahody 60-litnioho iuvileiu.* Prague: Chesko-ukrainska knyha, 1935.

Orlov, Georgii, comp. *Zhenskie podvigi.* Moscow, 1899.

Orzeszkowa, Eliza. *Kilka słów o kobietach.* Lviv, 1873.

_____. *List do kobiet niemieckich.* 1900.

Ozarkevych, Evhen. *Neduhy poshestni: poradnyk higiienichno-likarskyi.* Lviv: Naukove tovarystvo im. Shevchenka, 1911.

O zhenskikh uchilishchakh. Svod zamechanii na VII glavu proekta ustava obshcheobrazovatelnykh uchebnykh zavedenii Ministerstva Narodnogo Prosveshcheniia. Ed. Mikhail Osipovich Kosinskii and Nikolai Vessel. St. Petersburg, 1864.

Pacholikova, Lida. *Lysty do ukrainskykh zhinok.* Poděbrady: Zhinocha Knyhozbirnia Ukrainskoho Bibliografichnoho Mikroba, no. 1. Bratislava, 1928.

Pachucka, Romana. *Pamiętniki (1886–1914).* ed. Jan Hulewicz. Wrocław, 1958.

Paryllie, Severyna, OSBM. "30–littia vazhnoi nashoi stanytsi." *Zhinka,* August 1936: 1–2.

Paszkowska, Marja. *Zycie i Praca.* ed. Leon Wasilewski. Warsaw, 1929.

Pavlyk, M. "Deshcho pro rukh rusynok." *Narod,* 1 and 15 July 1894, 218–19.

_____. ed. *Perepyska M. Drahomanova z N. Kobrynskoiu, 1893–95.* Lviv, 1905.

_____. "Pershi stupni ukrainskoho zhinotstva." *Narod,* 15 February 1890, 42–50.

_____. Review of *Zhinocha dolia,* vol. I. *Narod,* no. 3, 1 February 1894, 46–9.

_____. "Shche izza T–va ruskykh zhinok na Bukovyni." *Narod,* 1 November 1895, 331–3.

Pchilka, Olena [O. Kosach]. *Opovidannia z avtobiohrafiieiu.* Kharkiv: Rukh, n.d.

Pelensky, Ie. Iu. "Suchasne ukrainske seredne i vysoke shkilnytstvo v Halychyni i na Volyni," in *25-littia T-va Uchytelska Hromada.* Lviv, 1935.

Pergamin, N.N. *Polovaia zhizn i analiz sredstv sposobstvuiushchikh zachatiiu.* Kiev, 1890.

Pershomu ukrainskomu bortsevi za prava zhinky. Lviv: Soiuz Ukrainok, 1921.

Petrazycka-Tomicka, Jadwiga. *W zyciu i w literaturze.* Lviv, 1916.

_____. *Związek równouprawnienia kobiet we Lwowie. Przyczynek do historji równouprawnienia kobiet w Polsce.* Cracow, 1931.

Półćwiartek, Józef. *Z badań nad rolą gospodarczą-społeczną plebanii na wsi pańszczyźnianej ziemi Przemyskiej i Sanockiej w XVI-XIX wieku.* Rzeszów: Wyzsa szkoła pedagogiczna, 1974.

Polinovskii, M.B. *Pisma devushek.* 2d ed. Odessa, 1898.

Popovych, Bohdan. *Pid ukrainskym nebom.* New York, 1972.

Potocka, Anna Stanisławowa, z Rymanowa, z Działyńskich ostatna. *Mój pamiętnik.* Cracow, 1927.

"Pro ruske zhinotstvo. Lysty halychanky." *Pravda* (1879): 36.

Prystai, Oleksii. *Z Truskavtsia u svit khmaroderiv: spomyny z mynuloho i suchasnoho.* 4 vols. Lviv, 1933–7.

Pryvit Ivanovy Frankovy v soroklitie ioho pysmenskoi pratsi 1874–1914. Lviv, 1916.

Rezoliutsii Ukrainskoho Zhinochoho Kongresu, Stanyslaviv, 23–27 chervnia 1934. Lviv, 1934.

Rolle, A. *Niewiasty kresowe.* Warsaw, 1883.

[Rolle], Antonii I. "Ukrainskiia zhenshchiny (perevod s polskogo)." *Kievskaia starina* 6 (1883): 268–309.

Rolle, I. "Zhinky pry chyhyrynskim dvori v druhii polovyni XVII viku." *Zoria* (1896): 11–33; 54–116, 293–315; 418–35; 436–79.

Romanovych–Tkachenko, Nataliia. "Iz dniv voli." *Literaturno–naukovyi vistnyk* (July 1917): 121–41.

_____. "V kraini horia i ruiny (podorozhni vrazhinnia)." *Literaturno–naukovyi vistnyk,* August–September 1917: 295–331; October 1917: 135–51; November–December 1917: 254–83.

Romanowiczowna, Zofja. *Cienie: kilka oderwanych kart z mojego zycia.* Lviv, 1930.

_____. *Tadeusz Romanowicz.* Lviv, 1934.

Romanowska, M. *Jak zyje, pracuje, i walczy kobieta pracująca w Polsce.* Warsaw, 1928.

Rudchenko, U., ed. *Narodnyia iuzhnorusskiia skazki.* Kiev, 1869.

Rudnytska, Milena. "Borotba za pravdu pro velykyi holod." *Svoboda,* 16 July–9 August 1958.

———. "Dvadtsiatypiatyrichchia patsyfikatsii." *Svoboda,* 27 September 1955.

———. "Fragmenty z ukrainskoi zakordonnoi aktsii." *Svoboda,* 11 April 1956.

———. "Hromadska pratsia ukrainskoho zhinotstva na Ukraini mizh dvoma svitovymy viinamy." *Ukrainskyi holos,* 1 August 1954: 11.

———. "Natsionalizm i feminizm." *Dilo,* 9 May 1929.

———. "Rolia zhinotstva u vyzvolnii borotbi UHA." In *Ukrainska Halytska Armiia (Materiialy do istorii).* Winnipeg: Dmytro Mykytiuk, 1958.

———. *Ukrainska diisnist i zavdannia zhinky.* Lviv, 1934.

Rusova, Sofiia. "Spomyny pro pershyi teatralnyi hurtok v Kyivi." *Literaturno–naukovyi vistnyk,* April–June 1918, 104–7.

Satina, Sophie. *Obrazovanie zhenshchin v dorevoliutsionnoi Rossii.* New York, 1966.

Schmitz, Laurenz. *Polovaia zhizn cheloveka i vospitanie rebenka.* Odessa, 1892.

Selezinka, Neoniliia. "Rolia zhinky v kooperatsii." *Zhinocha dolia,* no. 15–16 (1934): 10–11; no. 17: 10–11; no. 18: 8–9.

Semenenko, Oleksander. *Kharkiv, Kharkiv.* New York: Suchasnist, 1976.

Serotsinskii, K. *Zhenshchine pobeditelnitse.* Odessa, 1879.

Severova, N.B. *Krest Materinstva.* St. Petersburg, 1904.

Shakh, Stepan. *Lviv——misto moiei molodosty.* 3 vols. Munich: Khrystyianskyi holos, 1955–6.

Shapoval, Mykyta. "Doba khatianstva." *Ukrainska Khata,* 35–6. New York, 1955.

———. "Znaiomstvo z Olhoiu Kobylianskoiu (uryvky spomyniv)." *Nova Ukraina,* no. 10–11 (1927): 83–93.

Shats, Sabina. Obituary. *Nasha pravda,* nos. 3–8 (1928): 331.

Shchurat, Vasyl. *Vybrani pratsi z istorii literatury.* Kiev: Akademiia nauk Ukrainskoi RSR, 1963.

Sheparovych, Olena Fedak. "Lystopadovi spohady." *Zhinka,* 1 November 1936: 2–3.

———. "Modernyi feminizm i ukrainska zhinka," *Almanakh Zhinochoi doli* (1929): 23–7.

———. "Ukrainska studentka." *Smoloskyp* (Lviv), January 1928: 7–10.

———. "Ukrainskyi Chervonyi Khrest u Lvovi, 1918–1919," *Visti Kombatanta,* no. 3 (1961).

———. "V desiatylittia." *Almanakh Zhinochoi doli* (1930): 48–53.

"Shkoly hospodarstva dlia selianskykh divchat," *Shkolna chasopys* (Lviv), no. 8, 1880.

Shmigelska-Klymkevycheva, Iryna. "Z moikh spomyniv." *Kalendar Chervonoi kalyny*, 1925.

Simovych, Vasyl, ed. *Lystuvannia Lesi Ukrainky z I. Makoveiem, iz dodatkom lystiv Oleny Pchilky ta vlasnykh spomyniv pro pobut Lesi Ukrainky v Chernivtsiakh*. Lviv: Khortytsia, 1938.

Skrypnyk, Mykola. *Statti i promovy z natsionalnoho pytannia*. Ed. Ivan Koshelivets. Munich: Suchasnist, 1974.

Solomiia Krushelnytska: spohady, materialy, lystuvannia. 2 vols. ed. Mykhailo Holovashchenko. Kiev, 1978–9.

Solovei, Dmytro. *Holhota Ukrainy*. Winnipeg, 1953.

_____. *Rozhrom Poltavy: spohady z chasiv vyzvolnykh zmahan ukrainskoho narodu 1914–1921*. Winnipeg: Trident Press, 1974.

Sowiński, Jan. *O uczonych Polkach*. Krzemieniec, 1821.

Statut T-va Russkykh zhenshchyn v Stanyslavovi potverdzhennyi risheniam ts. k. namisnytstva z 12 padolysta 1884, ch. 65232. Lviv, 1884.

Statut Zhinochoho patriotychnoho T-va Halychyny 1879. Lviv, 1879.

Stepaniv, Olena. "Moi spomyny z shkilnykh lit." *Ridna shkola*, no. 13–14, 1933.

_____. *Na peredodni velykykh podii: vlasni perezhyvannia i dumky, 1912–1914*. Lviv, 1930.

Strunina, L. "Pervye voskresnye shkoly v Kieve." *Kievskaia starina* 5 (1898): 287–307.

Strutynska, Mariia [V. Marska]. *Daleke zblyzka*. Winnipeg, 1975.

_____. "Zhinky Revoliutsii." *Literaturnyi-naukovyi dodatok Novoho chasu*, no. 3, 1937.

Studynsky, Kyrylo. "Zustrich Olhy Kosachevoi z Melitonom Buchynskym 1872." *Nasha kultura*, no. 10 (October 1936): 731–8.

Surovtsova, Nadiia. "III internatsionalnyi Kongres Zhinochoi Ligy Myru i Svobody i ukrainske zhinotstvo." *Svoboda*, 8 August 1921.

Svetla, Karolina. *Z nashykh boiv i zmahan: opovidanie*. Lviv, 1912.

Swiderski, L.B., ed. *Eliza Orzeszkowa, Listy II: do literatów i ludzi nauki*. Warsaw, 1938.

Szelegowska, Anna. *Międzynarodowe organizacje kobiece*. n.p., 1934.

Szeptycka, Zofia z Fredrów. *Wspomnienie z lat ubiegłych*. Wrocław, 1967.

Trylovskyi, Kyrylo. "Nataliia Kobrynska i ii naiblyshchi." *Zhinka*, June 1937.

Tsehelska, Olena. *Hanuska ide do mista*. Lviv: Dilo, 1938.

Turkalo, Mariia. "Velyka hromadianka." *Svoboda*, 11 March 1953.

Ukrainka, Lesia. "Novye perspektivy i starye temy." In *Pro literaturu: poezii, statti, krytychni ohliady, lysty*, 133–55. ed. O.K. Babyshkin. Kiev, 1955.

_____. *Tvory*. 10 vols. Kiev, 1965.

_____. *Ukrainski baptisty i ikh chasopys. Besida za 1894 rik*. Lviv: I. Franko, n.d. [1894]

_____. *Zibrannia tvoriv*. Vol. 8: *Literaturno-krytychni ta publitsystychni statti*. Kiev, 1977.

Ukrainskyi Hromadskyi Komitet v Chekhoslovatskii respublitsi. *Ukrainska hospodarska akademiia v Ch.S.R.* Prague, 1923.

Utochkin, V. *Grekhi molodosti.* Odessa, 1896.

Velychko, Iryna. "Do Frankovykh dniv." *Zakhidnia Ukraina,* no. 5 (May 1930): 43–4.

Vengzhyn, Mykola [Taras Virnyi]. *Z zhytia gimnazystiv.* Przemyśl, 1907.

Vinskii, G.S. *Moe vremia: zapiski.* ed. P.E. Shchegolev. St. Petersburg: Izdatelstvo Ognia, n.d. Reprint, Newtonville, Mass.: Oriental Research Partners, 1974.

Volevachivna, Marusia. "Spomyny selianky." *Literaturno–naukovyi vistnyk,* February 1907, 208–11.

Vovchok, Marko [Mariia Vilinska-Markovych]. *Marusia* (Toronto, 1971). Translation from Paris 1878 edition by I.H. Sydorenko.

_____. *Tvory.* 6 vols. (Kiev 1956).

Vse-Ukrainska Akademiia Nauk, Komisiia Zakhidnoi Ukrainy. Materiialy dlia kulturnoi i hromadskoi istorii Zakhidnoi Ukrainy, vol. 1. *Lystuvannia I. Franka i M. Drahomanova.* Kiev, 1928.

Vykhovnytsia pokolin: Konstantyna Malytska, hromadska diiachka, pedahoh i pysmennytsia. Toronto: Nakladom Svitovoi federatsii zhinochykh orhanizatsii, 1965.

Vynnychenko, Volodymyr. "Zina." *Literaturno–naukovyi vistnyk,* September 1909, 385–97.

Wasilewski, L., M. Halyn, S. Stempovski, A. Topchybashy-Tabuis, *Spohady.* Warsaw, 1932.

Zhena Sviashchennika E.K. "Znachenie matushki v prikhode," *Kievskiia eparkhiialnyia vedomosti* (1890): 664–6.

Zvychaina, Olena. *Ohlianuvshys nazad.* Munich, 1954.

Secondary Sources

Akademiia Nauk URSR, Instytut mystetstvoznavstva, folkloru ta etnohrafii. *Ukrainskyi dramatychnyi teatr.* Kiev, vol. 1, 1967; vol. II, 1959.

Akademiia Nauk URSR, Instytut suspilnykh nauk. *Sotsialni peretvorennia u radianskomu seli: na prykladi zakhidnykh oblastei Ukrainskoi RSR.* Kiev: Naukova dumka, 1976.

Amfiteatrov, Aleksandr Valentinovich, *Zhenshchina v obshchestvennykh dvizheniiakh Rossii.* Geneva, 1905. First published under the title: *Die Frau in den gesellschaftlichen Kreisen Russlands.*

Antonovych, D. *Trysta rokiv ukrainskoho teatru, 1616–1919.* Prague, 1925.

Astakhova, Nataliia V. and E.N. Tsellarius. *Tovarishch Olga.* Moscow, 1969.

Atkinson, Dorothy, Alexander Dallin and Gail Warshofsky Lapidus, eds. *Women in Russia.* Stanford, 1977.

Bachynsky, Iuliian. *Vzaimni vidnosyny sotsiial-demokratychnykh partii ukrainskoi i polskoi v skhidnii Halychyni* (vidbytka z *Nashoho holosu*). Lviv, 1910.

Balcerek, Marian. *Rozwój opieki nad dzieckiem w Polsce w latach 1918–1939.* Warsaw, 1978.

Bass, I.I. *Ivan Franko: biohrafiia.* Kiev, 1966.

Bebel, August. *Die Frau in der Vergangenheit, Gegenwart und Zukunft.* 6th ed. Zurich, 1887.

_____. *Die Frau und der Sozialismus.* 1879. An English translation from the 33rd German edition of 1904 by Daniel de Leon, reprinted in New York by Schocken Books, 1971 as *Woman Under Socialism*.

Biletsky, Leonid. *Try sylvetky: Marko Vovchok, Olha Kobylianska, Lesia Ukrainka.* Winnipeg: Ukrainian Women's Association of Canada, 1951.

Bilshai, Vera Lvovna. *Reshenie zhenskogo voprosa v SSSR.* Moscow: Gosudarstvennoe izdatelstvo politicheskoi literatury, 1959.

Bohachevsky-Chomiak, Martha, "Feminism in Action: The Ukrainian Women's Union between the World Wars." *Women's Studies International* (Supplement to Women's Studies Quarterly). no. 2 (July 1982): 20–24.

_____. "Feminism in Ukrainian History." *Journal of Ukrainian Studies*, no. 12 (Spring 1982): 16–30.

_____. "Natalia Kobrynska: A Formulator of Feminism," in Andrei S. Markovits and Frank E. Sysyn, eds. *Nationbuilding and the Politics of Nationalism: Essays on Austrian Galicia*, 196–219. Cambridge, Mass.: Harvard Ukrainian Research Institute, 1982.

_____. "Socialism and Feminism: The First Stages of Women's Organizations in the Eastern Part of the Austrian Empire," in Tova Yedlin, ed. *Women in Eastern Europe and the Soviet Union*, 44–64. New York: Praeger, 1980.

_____. "Ukrainian Feminism in Interwar Poland," in Sharon L. Wolchik and Alfred G. Meyer, eds., *Women, State, and Party in Eastern Europe*, 82–97 and 381–3. Durham: Duke University Press, 1985.

Borysenko, V.I. *Borotba demokratychnykh syl za narodnu osvitu na Ukraini v 60–90-kh rokakh XIX st.* Kiev: Naukova dumka, 1980.

Boulding, Elise. *The Underside of History: A View of Women Through Time.* Boulder: Westview Press, 1976.

Braun, Lily von Gizycki. *Die Frauenfrage, ihre geschichtliche Entwicklung und wirtschaftliche Seite.* Leipzig, 1901.

_____. *Die Stellung der Frau in der Gegenwart.* Berlin, 1895.

Brown, Donald, ed. *The Role and Status of Women in the Soviet Union.* New York, 1968.

Bussey, Gertrude, and Margaret Tims. *Women's International League for*

Peace and Freedom, 1915–1965. London: Allen and Unwin, 1965.

Buszko, Józef. *Sejmowa reforma wyborcza w Galicji 1905–1914.* Warsaw: Państwowe Wydawnictwo Naukowe, 1956.

_____. *Zum Wandel der Gesellschaftsstruktur in Galizien und in der Bukowina.* Vienna: Verlag der Österreichischen Akademie der Wissenschaften, 1978.

Charewiczowa, Lucja. *Kobieta w dawnej Polsce: do okresu rozbiorów.* Lviv: Pánstwowe Wydawnictwo Książek Szkolnych, 1938.

Charov, Antin. *Peremozhnyi shliakh Zhovtnia.* Kharkiv, 1932.

Cherikover, I. *Antisemitizm i pogromy na Ukraine 1917–18.* Berlin: Ostjüdisches Historisches Archiv, 1923.

Chlebowczyk, Józef. *Procesy narodowotwórcze we wschodniej Europie środkowej w dobie kapitalizmu.* Warsaw, 1975.

Chojnowski, Andrzej. *Koncepcje polityki narodowościowej rządów polskich w latach 1921–1939.* Wrocław: Ossolineum, 1979.

Clements, Barbara Evans. *Bolshevik Feminist: The Life of Aleksandra Kollontai.* Bloomington: Indiana University Press, 1979.

Conze, Werner, ed. *Sozialgeschichte der Familie in der Neuzeit Europas.* Stuttgart: Ernst Klett, 1976.

Dodge, Norton. *Women in the Soviet Economy.* Baltimore: The Johns Hopkins University Press, 1966.

Doroshenko–Savchenko, Nataliia. "Zhinochyi rukh na Naddniprianshchyni," *Svoboda,* 29–31 December 1954.

Drozdowski, Marian Marek. *Społeczeństwo, Państwo, Politycy II Rzeczypospolitej: Szkice i Polemiki.* Cracow: Wydawnictwo Literackie, 1972.

Dubrovsky, V. *Selianski rukhy na Ukraini pislia 1861 r.* Kharkiv, 1928.

Dulczewski, Zygmunt. *Walka o szkole na wsi galicyjskiej w swietle stenogramów Sejmu Krajowego 1861–1914.* Warsaw: Ludowa Spółdzielnia Wydawnicza, n.d.

Dunin-Wasowicz, Krzysztof. *Czasopismiennictwo ludowe w Galicji.* Wrocław, 1952.

_____. "Publicystyka Iwana Franki w prasie ruchu ludowego w Galicji." *Kwartalnik Instytutu Polsko–Radzieckiego,* no. 1–2 (1955).

_____. *Ruch ludowy w Galicji do l wojny światowej i jego powiązanie z ruchem socjalistychnym.* (Pierwsza konferencja metodologiczna historyków polskich), t. II. Warsaw, 1953.

Frauenbewegung, Frauenerziehung und Frauenarbeit in Osterreich. Vienna, 1930.

Geiger, H. Kent. *The Family in Soviet Russia.* Cambridge, Mass.: Harvard University Press, 1968.

Haidalemivskyi, P. *Ukrainski politychni partii: ikh rozvytok i prohramy.* [Vienna]: Nakladom Ukrainskoi Viiskovoi misii, 1919.

Halushko, Ievhen Maksymovych. *Narysy istorii, ideolohichnoi ta orhanizatsiinoi diialnosty KPZU v 1919–1928.* Lviv: Vydavnytstvo Lvivskoho universytetu, 1965.

Heitlinger, Alena. *Women and State Socialism: Sex Inequality in the Soviet Union and Czechoslovakia.* London: Macmillan, 1979.

Hermaize, Osyp. "Do biohrafii B.D. Hrinchenka," *Zhyttia i revoliutsiia,* no. 4 (1926): 78–80.

_____. *Narysy z istorii revoliutsiinoho rukhu na Ukraini.* Kiev, 1926.

Himka, John–Paul. *Socialism in Galicia: The Emergence of Polish Social Democracy and Ukrainian Radicalism (1860–1890).* Cambridge, Mass.: Harvard Ukrainian Research Institute, 1983.

Holzer, Jerzy. *Mozaika polityczna Drugiej Rzeczypospolitej.* Warsaw, 1974.

Horak, Roman. "Karty z pershoi liubovy." *Zhovten,* no. 8 (1979): 126–43.

_____. "Zhinka iaka ishla poruch." *Zhovten,* no. 11 (1980): 110–26.

Hornowa, Elzbieta. *Ukraiński obóz postępowy i jego współpraca z polską lewicą społeczną w Galicji 1876–1895.* Wrocław, 1968.

Hoshko, Iu.H. *Hromadskyi pobut robitnykiv Zakhidnoi Ukrainy.* Kiev: Naukova dumka, 1967.

Hough, Jerry F. "The Impact of Participation: Women and the Women's Issue in Soviet Policy Debates." In *The Soviet Union and Social Science Theory,* Cambridge, Mass.: Harvard University Press, 1977.

Hulewicz, Jan, *Sprawa wyższego wykształcenia kobiet w Polsce w wieku XIX.* Cracow, 1939.

_____. *Udział Galicji w walce o szkole polskie 1899–1914.* Warsaw, 1934.

_____. *Walka kobiet polskich o dostęp na uniwersytety.* Warsaw, 1936.

Hunczak, Taras, ed. *The Ukraine, 1917–1921: A Study in Revolution.* Cambridge, Mass.: Harvard Ukrainian Research Institute, 1977.

Hurzhii, I.O. *Narodzhennia robitnychoho klasu Ukrainy (kinets XVIII-persha polovyna XIX st.).* Kiev, 1958.

Ievheniia Iaroshynska: bibliohrafichnyi pokazhchyk. ed. M.P. Humeniuk; comp. V.H. Holubets. Lviv, 1969.

Istoriia derzhavy i prava Ukrainskoi RSR 1917–1967. vol. I, 1917–1937; vol. 2, 1937–1967. Kiev, 1967.

Iwanicki, Mieczysław. *Oświata i szkolnictwo ukraińskie w Polsce w latach 1918–1939.* Siedlce: Wyzsza szkoła pedagogiczna, 1975.

Jancar, Barbara Wolfe. *Woman under Communism.* Baltimore: Johns Hopkins University Press, 1978.

Kachkan, V.A. "Mykhailo Pavlyk——zbyrach i doslidnyk folkloru." *Ukrainske literaturnoznavstvo,* no. 18 (1973): 91–5.

Kalynovych, V.I. *Politychni protsesy Ivana Franka ta ioho tovaryshiv.* Lviv, 1967.

Kaplan, Marion A. *The Jewish Feminist Movement in Germany: The Campaigns of the Jüdischer Frauenbund, 1904–1938.*

Westport, Connecticut: Greenwood Press, 1978.

Kazymyra, O. *Ukrainskyi amatorskyi teatr (Dozhovtnevyi period).* Kiev: Mystetstvo, 1965.

Kelly, Rita Mae, and Mary Boutillier. *The Making of Political Women: A Study of Socialization and Role Conflict.* Chicago: Nelson-Hall, 1978.

Khmil, I.V. *Trudiashche selianstvo Ukrainy v borotbi za vladu rad.* Kiev, 1977.

Klemensiewiczowa (Sikorska), Jadwiga. *Przebojem ku wiedzy: Wspomnienia jednej z pierwszych studentek krakowskich z XIX wieku.* Wrocław: Ossolineum, 1961.

Knysh, Irena. *Ivan Franko ta rivnopravnist zhinky: u 100-richchia z dnia narodyn.* Winnipeg, 1956.

_____. *Smoloskyp v temriavi: Nataliia Kobrynska i ukrainskyi zhinochyi rukh.* Winnipeg, 1957.

_____. *Try rovesnytsi 1860–1960. Do storichchia narodyn Uliany Kravchenko, Marii Bashkirtsev, Marii Zankovetskoii.* Winnipeg, 1961.

_____. *Zhinka vchora i siohodni.* Winnipeg, 1959.

Knysh, Zynovii. *Na povni vitryla: Ukrainska viiskova organizatsiia v 1924–1926 rokakh.* Toronto, 1970.

Kobersky, Karlo. *Ukrainske narodnytstvo po obokh bokakh Zbrucha.* Lviv and Kolomyia: Hromada, 1924.

Kompaniiets, I.I. *Revoliutsiinyi rukh v Halychyni, Bukovyni ta Zakarpatskii Ukraini pid vplyvom idei Velykoho Zhovtnia.* Kiev: Akademiia nauk URSR, Instytut istorii, 1957.

Koshelivets, Ivan. *Mykola Skrypnyk.* Munich: Suchasnist, 1972.

Kozak, Stefan, and Marian Jakóbec, ed. *Z dziejów stosunków literackich polsko-ukraińskich.* Wrocław, 1974.

Kóźniewski, Kazimierz. *Ognie i ogniska: drogi i przemiany harcerstwa polskiego.* Warsaw, 1961.

Kravets, Mykola M. *Narysy robitnychoho rukhu v Zakhidnii Ukraini v 1921–1938 rr.* Kiev, 1959.

_____. *Selianstvo skhidnoi Halychyny i pivnichnoi Bukovyny u druhii polovyni XIX st.* Lviv, 1964.

Kravets, Olena Mykhailivna. *Simeinyi pobut i zvychai ukrainskoho narodu.* Kiev: Naukova dumka, 1966.

Kuvenkova, Oleksandra Fedorivna. *Hromadskyi pobut ukrainskoho selianstva: istoryko-etnohrafichnyi narys.* Kiev: Naukova dumka, 1966.

_____. , O.M. Kravets, T.D. Hirnyk, V.T. Zinych. *Sviata ta obriady Radianskoi Ukrainy.* Kiev, 1971.

Kyshakevych, Tatiana. "University Education in Ukraine." Ph.D. dissertation, University of Pittsburgh, 1976.

Lapidus, Gail Warshofsky. *Women in Soviet Society*: Berkeley, University of California Press, 1978.

Lavrinenko, Iurii. "Ukrainska sotsiial–demokratiia (Hrupa USD) i ii lider, Lesia

Ukrainka." *Suchasnist*, nos. 5, 6, 7–8 (May–August 1971): 68–86; 56–71; 132–50.

Leshchenko, M.N. *Klasova borotba v ukrainskomu seli v epokhu domonopolistychnoho kapitalizmu (60–90-i roky XIX st.)*. Kiev: Naukova dumka, 1970.

Losky, Ihor. "Ukrainska zhinka v kozatsku dobu." *Zhinka*, September 1935: 6–8.

Lypa, Ivan, ed. *Bahattia: ukrainskyi almanakh*. Odessa, 1905.

Madison, Bernice. *Social Welfare in the Soviet Union*. Stanford, 1968.

Magocsi, Paul Robert. *The Shaping of a National Identity: Subcarpathian Rus, 1848–1948*. Cambridge, Mass.: Harvard Ukrainian Research Institute, 1978.

Maianets, Levko. "Pro shliub na Rusy-Ukraini v XVI-XVII vv." *Zoria*, 1 July 1885: 149–52; 15 July 1885, 169–71; 15 August 1885, 183–5; 1 September 1885, 198–200; 15 September 1885, 209–11.

Mandel, William. *Soviet Women*. New York, 1975.

Martiuk, Ivan. *Tsentrosoiuz*. n.p., 1973.

Massell, Gregory. *The Surrogate Proletariat*. Princeton, 1974.

Matthews, Mervyn. *Class and Society in Soviet Russia*. London: Allen Lane The Penguin Press, 1972.

Matveev, G.K. *Istoriia semeino-brachnogo zakonodatelstva Ukrainskoi SSR*. Kiev, 1960.

Mauersberg, Stanisław. *Szkolnictwo powszechne dla mniejszości narodowych w Polsce w latach 1918–1939*. Wrocław: Pracownia Ustroju i Organizacji Oświaty Polskiej Akademii Nauk, 1968.

Melnyk, Ievheniia. *Prava radianskoi zhinky-trudivnytsi i materi*. Kiev: Naukova dumka, 1971.

Moraczewska, Zofja. *Związek Pracy Obywatelskiej Kobiet*. 2d ed. Warsaw, 1933.

Mukhyn, M.I. *Pedahohichni pohliady i osvitnia diialnist Kh.D. Alchevskoi*. Kiev: Vyshcha shkola, 1979.

Najdus, Walentyna. "Klasowe związki zawodowe w Galicji," *Przegląd Historyczny*, no. 2, 1960.

_____. *Szkice z historii Galicji*. vol 1. Warsaw, 1958.

Neidle, Cecyle S. *America's Immigrant Women*. Boston: Twayne Publishers, G.K. Hall, 1975.

Nieuwazny, Florian. "Olena Pchilka——popularyzatorka literatury polskiej na Ukrainie." In Stefan Kozak and Marian Jakóbec, eds., *Z dziejów stosunków literackich polsko-ukrainskich*. Wrocław, 1974.

Omelchenko, Mariia. "Sotsiialna opika nad molodiu v Chekhoslovachyni," *Literaturno-naukovyi vistnyk*, April 1925.

_____. *Vybir fakhu*. Prague, 1925.

Paczkowski, Andrzej. *Prasa polska w latach 1918–1939*. Warsaw, 1980.

Papierzyńska–Turek, Mirosława. *Sprawa ukraińska w Drugiej Rzeczypospolitej*

1922–1926. Cracow, 1979.

Persky, Stepan, *Populiarna istoriia tovarystva Prosvita.* Lviv, 1932.

Piotrowski, Jerzy. *Praca zawodowa kobiety a rodzina.* Warsaw: Instytut gospodarstwa społezcnego, 1963.

Półćwiartek, Józef, *Z badań nad rolą gospodarczo-społeczną plebanii na wsi pańszczyźnianej ziemi przemyskiej i sanockiej w XVI-XIX wieku.* Rzeszów: Wyzsza szkoła pedagogiczna, 1974.

Polonsky, Antony. *Politics in Independent Poland, 1921–1929: The Crisis of Constitutional Government.* Oxford, 1972.

Próchnik, Adam. *Kobieta w polskim ruchu socjalistycznym.* Warsaw, 1948.

Radziejowski, Janusz. *Komunistyczna partia Zachodniej Ukrainy, 1919–1929.* Cracow, 1976.

Ransel, David L., ed. *The Family in Imperial Russia: New Lines of Historical Research.* Urbana: University of Illinois Press, 1978.

Rosaldo, Michelle Zimbalist, and Louise Lamphere. *Woman, Culture and Society.* Stanford, 1974.

Rozhin, Ivan. *Valentyna Radzymovska: Korotkyi narys zhyttia ta naukovoi i hromadskoi ii diialnosty.* Winnipeg: Ukrainian Free Academy of Sciences, 1969.

Serczyk, W.A. "Akademiczna Hromada w Krakowie." In C. Bobińska, ed., *Studia z dziejów młodziezy Uniwersytetu Krakowskiego.* Cracow, 1964.

Slabchenko, Mykola. *Materiialy do ekonomichno–sotsiialnoi istorii Ukrainy XIX st.* 2 vols. Odessa, 1925–7.

Słuzba ojczyźnie: Wspomnienia, Miesięcznik walk o niepodległość, 1915–1918. Ed. M. Rychterowna. Warsaw, 1929.

Solchanyk, Roman. "The Foundation of the Communist Movement in Eastern Galicia, 1919–1921." *Slavic Review,* 30, no. 4 (December 1971): 774–94.

Státní Knihovna Ceskoslovenské Socialistické Republiky (Slovanská knihovna), Ústav Jazyků a Literatur. Ceskoslovenské Akademie Věd. *Sto Padesát Let Cesko–ukrajinských literárních styků 1814–1964, Vědecko-Bibliografický Sborník.* Prague, 1968.

Stites, Richard. *The Women's Liberation Movement in Russia: Feminism, Nihilism and Bolshevism 1860–1930.* Princeton, 1978.

Suvorin, A.S. *Khokhly i khokhlushki.* St. Petersburg, 1907.

Tabiś, Jan. *Polacy na uniwersytecie kijowskim 1834–1863.* Cracow: Wydawnictwo Literackie, 1974.

Tereshchenko, Iu.I. *Politychna borotba na vyborakh do miskykh dum Ukrainy v period pidhotovky Zhovtnevoi revoliutsii.* Kiev, 1974.

Tomashuk, N.O. *Olha Kobylianska: zhyttia i tvorchist.* Kiev, 1969.

Tymchenko, Zhanna P. *Trudiashchi zhinky v borotbi za vladu rad na Ukraini 1917–1920.* Kiev, 1969.

_____. "Uchast zhinok–robitnyts Kyieva u revoliutsiinii borotbi (berezen

1917–sichen 1918)." *Ukrainskyi istorychnyi zhurnal*, no. 1 (January 1982): 57–65.

Tyshchuk, B.I. *Halytska Sotsialistychna Radianska Respublika 1920*. Lviv: Vydavnytsvo Lvivskoho universitetu, 1970.

Valikonite, I. "Litovskii statut——odin iz vazhneishykh istochnikov istorii polozheniia zhenshchin v velikom Kniazhestve Litovskom." In E. Gudavicius et al., *1529 Metu Pirmasis Lietuvos Statutas*, 38–46. Vilnius, 1982.

Valk, S.N., N.G. Sladkevich, V.I. Smirnov and M.L. Tronskaia, ed. *Sankt–peterburgskie vysshie zhenskie kursy (bestuzhevskie) 1878–1918: Sbornik statei*. Leningrad, 1965; 2d ed. 1973.

Vasileva, E.K. *Semia i ee funktsiia; demografo-statisticheskii analiz*. Moscow: Statistika, 1975.

Vaskovych, Hryhor. *Shkilnytsvo v Ukraini 1905–1920*. Munich: Ukrainskyi vilnyi universytet, 1969.

Vincenz, Stanisław. *Na wysokiej połoninie: obrazy, dumy i gawędy z wierchowiny huculskiej*. Warsaw, 1980.

Vitruk, Liudmyla D. *Zhinky-trudivnytsi v period sotsialistychnoi industrializatsii*. Kiev: Naukova dumka, 1973.

Voloshchenko, A.K. *Narysy z istorii suspilno-politychnoho rukhu ta Ukraini v 70-kh ta pochatku 80-kh rokiv XIX st*. Kiev: Naukova dumka, 1974.

Vosberg, Fritz. *Die polnische Frauenbewegung*. Lissa, 1912.

Vovk, Mykhailo. "Zhinky zakhidnoi Ukrainy v revoliutsiinomu rusi." *Radianskyi Lviv*, no. 3 (March 1948): 51–3.

Vozniak, M. "Khto sprychynyv areshtuvannia Franka i tovaryshiv 1877?" *Zhyttia i znannia*, May 1936: 134–6.

———. "Ostanni znosyny P. Kulisha z halychanamy (z dodatkom ioho lystuvannia z Pavlykom)." *Zapysky Naukovoho Tovarystva im. Shevchenka* 148 (1928): 165–240.

———. "Shliakhom do Pershoho vinka," *Novyi chas*, February-April 1937.

———. *Z zhyttia i tvorchosti Ivana Franka*. Kiev, 1955.

Vytanovych, Illia. *Istoriia ukrainskoho kooperatyvnoho rukhu*. New York: Tovarystvo ukrainskykh kooperatyv, 1964.

Walewska, Cecylja. *W walce o równe prawa*. Warsaw, 1930.

Wawrzykowska-Wierciochowa, Dionizja. "Cezaryna Wanda Wojnarowska." *Z Pola Walki*, no. 3 (1963): 180–208.

———. *Od prządki do astronautki*. Warsaw, 1963.

———. "Rosyjskie przyjaciółki narodu polskiego w latach 1860–ch." *Kwartalnik Instytutu Polsko–Radzieckiego*, no. 3–4 (16/17) (1956): 116–56.

———. "Stan badań nad dziejami kobiety polskiej." *Kultura i społeczeństwo* 7, no. 1 (1963): 97–110.

———. *Wysłouchowa*. Warsaw, 1976.

———. *Z dziejów kobiety wiejskiej: szkice historyczne 1861–1945*. Warsaw, 1961.

Wierna Służba: Wspomnienia Uczestniczek Walk o Niepodległość 1910–1905. Ed. H. Piłsudska, M. Rychterówna, W. Petezyńska, M. Dąbrowska. Warsaw, 1927.

Wisłocki, Juliusz. *Prawa głosowania kobiet.* Warsaw, 1932.

Women in a Changing World: The Dynamic Story of the International Council of Women since 1888. London: Routledge and Kegan Paul, 1966.

Z istorii chekhoslovatsko-ukrainskykh zviazkiv. Bratislava, 1959.

"Z Peremyshlia." *Dilo,* no. 19, 1880.

Zadoianny, Vasyl. "Zhinky–heroini ukrainskoi vyzvolnoi borotby 1917–21 rokiv." *Dorohovkaz* (Toronto) (January–February 1965): 2–8.

Zadvorny, Anatolii M. *Radianska simia: ii suchasne i maibutnie. Pro rol simi v umovakh sotsialistychnoho suspilstva ta ii dalshyi rozvytok.* Kiev: Vydavnytstvo politychnoi literatury Ukrainy, 1975.

Zahul, D., V. Atamaniuk, and S. Semko, eds. *Zakhidnia Ukraina: Literaturno-hromadskyi zbirnyk.* Kiev, 1927.

Zaitsev, Pavlo. *Zhyttia Tarasa Shevchenka.* Paris, 1955.

Zaleska, Zofia. *Czasopisma kobiece w Polsce (Materiały do historji czasopism roków 1818–1937).* Warsaw, 1938.

Zeberek, Gerhard. *Początki ruchu socjaldemokratycznego w Kijowie w latach 1889–1903.* Cracow: Wydawnictwo Literackie, 1981.

Zhinky Radianskoi Ukrainy——Aktyvni budivnyky komunistychnoho suspilstva. ed. M.M. Pidtychenko et al. Kiev: Vydavnytstvo politychnoi literatury Ukrainy, 1971.

Zhuchenko, Mariia. "Ukrainske zhyttia v Kyivi na svitanku voli." *Literaturno–naukovyi vistnyk,* July 1917, 150–54.

Zhuk, Elysaveta. "Ukrainske zhinoche kolo," *Hromadianka,* no. 2 (November 1946): 5–6.

Zhurba, Halyna [Dombrovska-Nyvynska]. "Rik 1917: spomyny." *Kalendar Prosvity 1937.* Lviv, 1936.

Zhyvotko, Oleksandra. "Teoniia z Fedevykh Sokolovska Kabarivska, 1889–1952." *Svoboda,* 15 August 1952.

Zosenko, Oleksa. *Marko Vovchok: zhyttia, tvorchist, mistse v istorii literatury.* Kiev: Akademiia Nauk URSR, 1964.

Index